In the Sign of the Golden Wheel

THE COMPLETE WORKS OF SANGHARAKSHITA include all his previously published work, as well as talks, seminars, and writings published here for the first time. The collection represents the definitive edition of his life's work as Buddhist writer and teacher. For further details, including the contents of each volume, please turn to the 'Guide' on pp.659–67.

FOUNDATION

1 A Survey of Buddhism / The Buddha's Noble Eightfold Path
2 The Three Jewels I
3 The Three Jewels II
4 The Bodhisattva Ideal
5 The Purpose and Practice of Buddhist Meditation
6 The Essential Sangharakshita

INDIA

7 Crossing the Stream: India Writings I
8 Beating the Dharma Drum: India Writings II
9 Dr Ambedkar and the Revival of Buddhism I
10 Dr Ambedkar and the Revival of Buddhism II

THE WEST

11 A New Buddhist Movement I
12 A New Buddhist Movement II
13 Eastern and Western Traditions

COMMENTARY

MEMOIRS

POETRY AND THE ARTS

COMPLETE WORKS **22** **MEMOIRS**

Sangharakshita

In the Sign of the Golden Wheel

EDITED BY KALYANAPRABHA

Windhorse Publications
17e Sturton Street
Cambridge
CB1 2SN
UK

info@windhorsepublications.com
www.windhorsepublications.com

Cover design by Dhammarati
Cover images: Front: Sangharakshita with Yogi Chen, Kalimpong, 1967. Courtesy of Clear Vision Trust. Back flap: Sangharakshita and the Dalai Lama, Everton Villa, May 1957. Courtesy of Clear Vision Trust.

Photograph of standing Buddha by courtesy of Padmajaya. The photograph of Allen Ginsberg in Calcutta was taken by Peter Orlovsky and is reproduced by kind permission of the Allen Ginsberg Estate. All other photographs are from the Clear Vision archive, Manchester, UK.

Typesetting and layout by Ruth Rudd
Printed by Bell & Bain Ltd, Glasgow

British Library Cataloguing in Publication Data:
A catalogue record for this book is available from the British Library.

ISBN 978-1-911407-38-6 (hardback)
ISBN 978-1-911407-39-3 (paperback)

CONTENTS

LIST OF ILLUSTRATIONS

PRECIOUS TEACHERS

WITH ALLEN GINSBERG IN KALIMPONG

North-eastern Himalayan Region, 1950s

Sangharakshita's Kalimpong

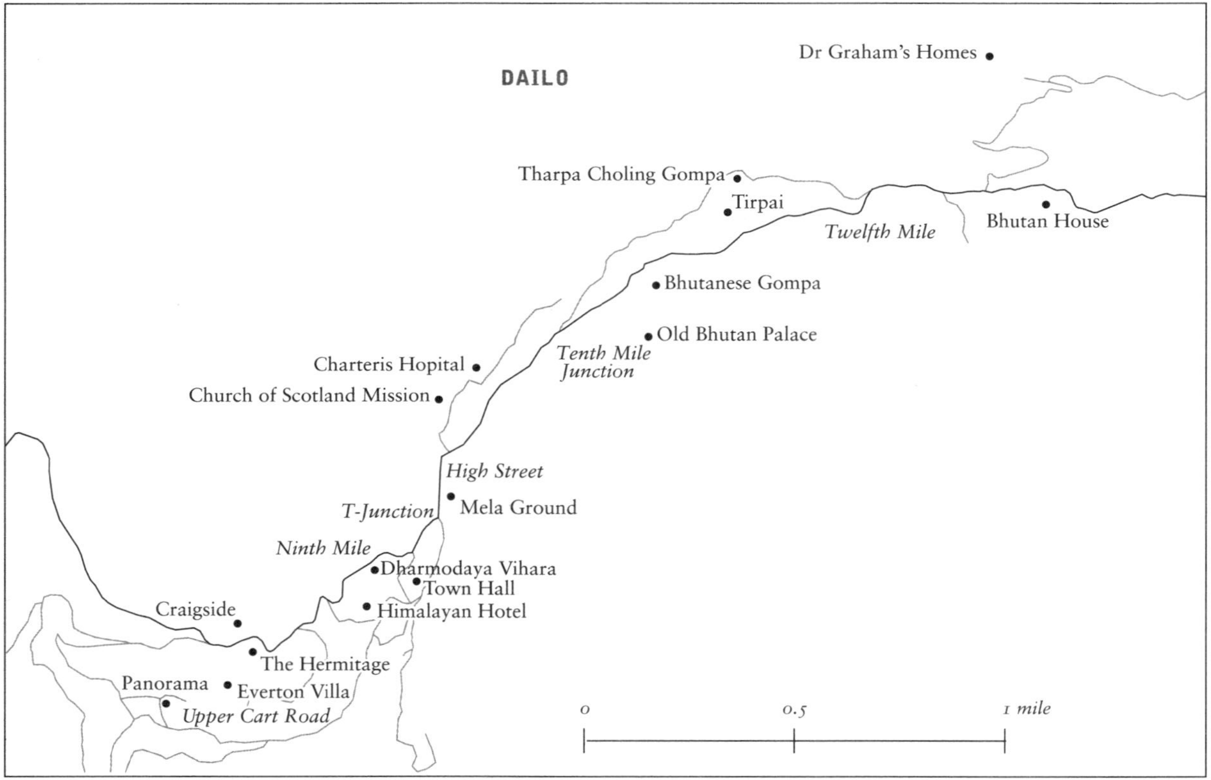

This map is based on descriptions in the text, information from the internet, and some 'best guesses'. Readers with any further information are requested to contact the publisher so that the map can be updated for any future edition. The Triyana Vardhana Vihara was located on the edge of Kalimpong, to the south-west.

FOREWORD

'Life's memories are not life's histories, but the original work of an artist.' These words from the Bengali poet Rabindranath Tagore form the epigraph introducing *In the Sign of the Golden Wheel*, the first of the two memoirs included in this volume – but they apply also to the second, *Precious Teachers*, and even to the short essay with which the volume concludes, *With Allen Ginsberg in Kalimpong*.

What is meant by 'the original work of an artist'? What is art? Sangharakshita has given expression to his understanding of what art truly is in an essay, *The Religion of Art*. It is, he writes, 'the organization of sensuous impressions into pleasurable formal relations that express the artist's sensibility and communicate to his audience a sense of values that can transform their lives'.[1] 'Formal relations' could refer to the way an author deals with his material: the organization of the memoirs into chapters, for instance. But what is the author's sensibility? What are the values he communicates? And can they transform my life or yours? I hope this foreword goes some way to addressing these questions.

In the Sign of the Golden Wheel was written forty years after the events it describes. Nevertheless, Sangharakshita takes us back with ease into the world in which he lived from May 1953 to May 1957. As to what characterizes those years, the middle period of the fourteen years when the eastern-Himalayan town of Kalimpong was his base, the memoir's title gives us a clue. These years were lived 'in the sign of' the golden wheel or perhaps one could say, at the service of the golden wheel, the eight-spoked golden wheel of the Dharma, the *dharmacakra* which the Buddha set rolling two and a half thousand years ago – which perhaps explains why this memoir begins and ends with the festival of *vaiśākha pūrṇimā*, the celebration of the Buddha's Enlightenment, that moment in human history when the Dharma first broke through into human consciousness.

But how is the author to convey to us, his readers, the experiences that were his when those experiences span such broad dimensions? Sangharakshita is well aware of the problem and in Chapter 19 he quotes the Victorian art critic, John Ruskin. In writing about a life, Ruskin says, it is

> impossible to trace it steadily through successive years. Some forces are failing while others strengthen, and most act irregularly.... For all clearness of exposition, it is necessary to follow first one, then another, without confusing notices of what is happening in other directions.[2]

Sangharakshita does manage something of the impossible and there is a chronological progression that can be discerned through the book. At the same time each chapter, with its evocative title – 'The Scent of Gardenias', 'Proof-Reading at 110°F', 'The Unacceptable Face of Communism', 'The Presence in the Corner' – shines a light on a different aspect of his experience or tries to communicate something new. He once wrote of there being four kinds of disciple: those who are like patients, those who are like friends, those who are like sons, and those who are like lovers.[3] Perhaps one could say there are four kinds of readers: those who are looking for the medicine of the Dharma, that is to say for teachings; those who, like friends, wish to know Sangharakshita more deeply as a man; those who want to be shown the way to live, as a son might look to a father; and those who are open to, even seeking out, the most esoteric of encounters. Perhaps you are looking for a little of each of these – and each is to be found in these pages.

Sometimes the teachings are quite direct – in the summary of a lecture on the mantra *oṃ maṇi padme hūṃ*, for example. Sometimes they are a little more hidden. 'Brickbats – and a Bouquet' is the title of one chapter and we see Sangharakshita facing the blasts of the worldly winds of praise and blame, showing us, reminding us, how one may live as a Buddhist with the worldly winds that are inherent to *saṃsāra*. There are chapters in which he shares his inner life, including his meditation practice, which he kept up daily but did not always find easy: he still had to deal with wandering thoughts and negative emotions, and even periods of complete dryness. At other times his meditation practice was a source of tremendous inspiration and extracts from his diary describe some of the visions and insights that arose.

'Reflect on everything that happens to you,' he is reported as having said years later to one of his disciples. His reflections on his own experience are illuminating, perhaps none more so than the implications of discovering, as he does on a visit to Sarnath in 1956, that his *bhikkhu* ordination, which had meant so much to him, was technically invalid.[4] His capacity to reflect is supported by an ability both to analyse and to synthesize. On a number of occasions we find him teasing out and exposing the machinations of those who might be considered 'enemies' and who certainly caused him considerable trouble, not least when he became editor of the *Maha Bodhi* journal in 1954. There were those on the editorial board who were not at all keen on the appointment and put obstacles in his way. He was accused by one reader of being a Mahāyānist with 'vetulyan', i.e. heretical, ideas! He was not deterred. The monthly journal was an effective vehicle for the communication of the Dharma to a wide audience; through the *Maha Bodhi* the golden wheel's radiance might shine afar. Under his editorship it became the leading English-language Buddhist journal with contributors including Edward Conze, Lama Govinda, and other foremost Buddhist writers and scholars of the time. Through his editorials (collected together in *Beating the Drum, Complete Works*, vol. 8) he was able to inspire, challenge, encourage, and in general to express views on a wide range of topics. He was always concerned to establish right view, an essential basis for Buddhist life, both in his written work and in his lectures. The memoir records striking examples of intellectual battles against the intransigent views of Brahmins, universalists, and others who sought to undermine the basic tenets of the Buddha's teaching.

There are two aspects to the Dharma: doctrine and method, right view and right practice. Sangharakshita's life was concerned to embody both to the highest degree. That the Dharma is something not only to be understood and reflected upon but to be practised in relation to every aspect of daily life is evident on almost every page, from his description of his very modest diet to his distaste for handling money. But perhaps the greatest challenge of Dharma practice comes in relation to other people. Throughout the book we are introduced to the wide range of people with whom Sangharakshita made friends and we see his sympathy – and occasional disappointment or exasperation – with them. His vivid recollection of so many whom he encountered bears testimony to the degree to which he was, and is, able to 'see' people: their strengths and weaknesses, their eccentricities, and their spiritual aspirations – if they had any. Through the memoir we meet people of many different nationalities and backgrounds, ordinary townsfolk, rich and poor, politicians, a Maharaja, monks and nuns, saints and scholars, Buddhist, Hindu – or neither. For instance, there is cheerful Padam Bahadur, one of the cook-bearers who worked for him for a while, and who 'at times struck me as being a Nepalese version of Sam Weller, Mr Pickwick's quick-witted Cockney servant'; or Dr Irene Hudson, a Canadian Buddhist-cum-Theosophist, 'eccentric and opinionated' but 'of a generous disposition'.

Sangharakshita seems to have been a natural teacher and educator and during his years in Kalimpong he taught many people. Aniruddha, the angry monk who had formerly thrown him out of the Dharmodaya Vihara, came to him for English lessons. There was Meera, the pretty, teenaged sister of Sachin, who, 'though she seemed to enjoy her lessons with me', was 'not very bright'. But it was with his friend Sachin that the greatest pleasure was to be found. 'When we studied poetry together, we were both sometimes left ... in a mood bordering on the ecstatic.'

Of the personalities who had the most influence on his life during these years – though in very different ways – four figures stand out. German-born Lama Govinda was a kindred spirit who himself understood, and perhaps helped Sangharakshita understand, the inner bond between religion and art in their truest sense. In his introduction to Sangharakshita's collection of poetic aphorisms, *The Veil of Stars,* written during these years, Govinda quotes the great German poet and philosopher Novalis: 'Poets and Priests were one in the beginning', thus giving recognition to these two vital aspects of Sangharakshita's own life and being.

Dr Mehta of Bombay was from a Parsi background and had once been naturopathic physician to Gandhi. He now saw himself as a kind of prophet receiving guidance directly from God. Sangharakshita and he developed a kind of friendship and in early 1956 our author spent some weeks with him and others at his Nature Cure Clinic in Poona where the two men exchanged on many topics including meditation and the God-given guidance. This gave Sangharakshita the incentive to take his own practice of meditation further and to look for the Buddhist equivalent to spiritual guidance that comes from beyond the ego.

Dhardo Rimpoche, the Tibetan lama who in time he came to revere as a living bodhisattva, was both friend and teacher. Their connection begins in this memoir and features again in *Precious Teachers*.

The man who had perhaps the most decisive influence on Sangharakshita as regards the future was Dr B. R. Ambedkar, architect of India's Constitution and first Law Minister under Nehru. Ambedkar had tried with utmost energy to reform the lot of the masses of Indians regarded by caste Hindus as 'untouchable' (as he was himself). Another drumbeat through this memoir is the approaching decision to convert to Buddhism which Ambedkar came to see as the only means for real emancipation from 'the hell of caste' for himself and his followers – a matter he discusses with Sangharakshita in 1955. A year later he leads half a million people in the greatest mass conversion seen by the world. Then comes one of those strange and inexplicable 'coincidences': Sangharakshita's presence in Nagpur at the time of Dr Ambedkar's tragic death seven weeks later in December 1956. It is one of the key events in the whole story.

There are a number of deaths recounted in the chapters of *In the Sign of the Golden Wheel*, from that of Miss Barclay's cat (who is buried with due Buddhist rites) to the mysterious, even sinister death of Raja Sonam Topgay Dorji, the Bhutanese ambassador. No doubt due to his life as a monk, it is with death and the ending of life rather than with birth that Sangharakshita comes into contact – though we see him giving support to two young friends when an unplanned pregnancy occurs.

Teaching the Dharma through talks and lectures was one of his foremost activities and the one that seems to have given him the deepest fulfilment. As his first memoir explains, he discovered when giving his first lecture, aged twenty-one, that

> ideas ... wove themselves Persian carpet-wise into intricate patterns, and these patterns dipped themselves in colourful words, without the slightest difficulty.[5]

He took the opportunity of giving talks wherever he could: in Kalimpong and Darjeeling, in Gangtok, at Tagore's University at Shantiniketan, in Calcutta, and Assam, Bombay, and elsewhere.... He was a popular speaker and drew audiences of sometimes thousands of people – speaking now to students, now to the poorest communities. One set of lectures are of especial note. They took place in the summer of 1954, at the Indian Institute of Culture in Bangalore at the invitation of theosophists B. P. and Madame Wadia. Sangharakshita vividly recalls his experience in giving the lectures. He writes:

> By the time I gave the last lecture [whose theme was the bodhisattva ideal] I had a very large – and appreciative – audience ... as I spoke, and they listened, time almost stood still, and it was as though we were transported to another world.

It was these four lectures which, over the following two years, he wrote up and expanded and which were published in the Buddha Jayanti year, 1956–7, as *A Survey of Buddhism*.

The Buddha Jayanti was celebrated all over the Eastern world, marking the 2,500th year of the Buddha's *parinirvāṇa*. We feel its approach through the pages of *In the Sign of the Golden Wheel*. It is as if all the tremendous effort to 'work for the good of Buddhism' that had gone into the previous six or seven years since arriving in Kalimpong now bore fruit. It was for Sangharakshita an *annus mirabilis*. In addition to the *Survey*, which attracted highly favourable reviews,

> I had visited the principal Buddhist holy places in the company of Dhardo Rimpoche, I had met the Dalai Lama, I had forged a special link with the newly-converted followers of Dr Ambedkar, I had received Tantric initiation from Chattrul Rimpoche, and I had been enabled to establish in Kalimpong a vihara that would serve both as my personal headquarters and as a centre of living Buddhism.

And so he leaves us with the image of himself as a tiny cell in the multi-dimensional body of the sangha, the Buddhist spiritual community.

On the wall above my shrine hangs an unusual image. In the centre is the Buddha, seated on a lotus from which emanate lotuses in the four directions on each of which sit a number of figures or on one a pile of precious Dharma texts. This is the Triratna Refuge Tree, also known as the Tree of Refuge and Respect. On the lotus nearest to me I see Sangharakshita, my own teacher, surrounded by eight figures: to his right and left I can make out a Chinese and an Indian, and above him sit six Tibetans. These eight are the precious teachers who feature in the second memoir included in this volume of the *Complete Works*: the Indian Jagdish Kashyap, the Chinese Yogi Chen, and the six Tibetans: Chattrul Sangye Dorje, Kachu Rimpoche, Dhardo Rimpoche, Jamyang Khyentse Chökyi Lodrö Rimpoche, Dudjom Rimpoche, and Dilgo Khyentse Rimpoche.

Precious Teachers was published nine years after *In the Sign of the Golden Wheel*. It covers the last period in Kalimpong, 1957–1964, and was dictated in 2006 to Nityabandhu, a Polish friend who was then living with Sangharakshita at 'Madhyamaloka' in Birmingham, UK, for Sangharakshita had become partially sighted. It was the last memoir to be written, although chronologically it comes fourth in the series of five. It bears many of the characteristics of the previous memoir, which I have already noted, so here I want to highlight just some of its outstanding features.

In the *Garava Sutta* the Buddha makes clear how imperative it is to live revering that which is greater than oneself.[6] Sangharakshita, it seems, has a natural tendency to venerate; it is a crucial aspect of his sensibility. In *Precious Teachers* he gives expression to the reverence and gratitude he feels towards his eight teachers, to each of whom we are introduced in a separate chapter (with the exception of Jagdish Kashyap who appears only briefly in the first chapter, having made his main appearance in the first memoir, as well as more briefly in the second). As he often does when introducing us to the people he came to know, the author is able to give quite a vivid impression with a few well chosen words. For instance, he describes his first impression of Dudjom Rimpoche:

> [a] comparatively small figure [in a] dark blue *bokku*, standing hatless in the bright sunshine … absolutely still … I had the distinct impression that … his mind, also, was absolutely still, as though the various winds that usually agitate the surface of our consciousness had in his case ceased to blow and he was at peace, in the deepest sense of the phrase, with himself and with the world.

The way he comes to know his teachers is different in each case. Dhardo Rimpoche is at first more of a friend. In 1956 they tour the Buddhist holy places at the invitation of the Government of India, and later they find themselves discussing how to deal with the troublesome French nun. But in October 1962 Dhardo Rimpoche becomes his teacher and preceptor when he gives Sangharakshita the bodhisattva ordination with its sixty-four bodhisattva vows.[7]

Along with his friend Khantipālo, Sangharakshita spent many hours at the hermitage of the Chinese hermit Yogi Chen, listening to what amounted to an extended talk, given over four months, on the topic of meditation, as well as a fourfold account of the hermit's biography – outward, inward, secret, and most secret.

From his six Tibetan teachers he received what are known variously as empowerments, *abhiṣekas*, *wongkurs*, or initiations. These are of great note in the first place because they created an indissoluble spiritual connection between Sangharakshita and his Tibetan teachers, connections that have stayed with him, and no doubt supported him, ever since. Secondly, these initiations would become the source of practices precious to Triratna Order members: *sādhanas* or visualization practices given at ordination. The initiations that Sangharakshita received from his Tibetan teachers include those of Green Tārā (from Chattrul Sangye Dorje); Amitābha and Kurukullā (from Dilgo Khyentse Rimpoche); Mañjughoṣa, Avalokiteśvara, Vajrapāṇi, and Tārā (from Jamyang Khyentse Rimpoche); Padmasambhava and Amitāyus (from Kachu Rimpoche); the Medicine Buddha and White Tārā (from Dhardo Rimpoche); and Vajrasattva (from Dudjom Rimpoche). What the real meaning is, and what the real experience of so-called 'empowerment' or initiation, is a matter to which Sangharakshita gives serious attention in Chapter 11.

But although the book's title points us to the outstanding feature of this memoir, readers should not suppose that Sangharakshita spent all his time with his teachers, nor, therefore, that he would only write about them in recalling the years 1957–1964. Far from it. During those years he had his own vihara, the Triyana Vardhana Vihara, where, among other things, as he tells, us, he even turned part-time farmer. As ever, he came into contact with many different people and writes about them; among the most memorable are Ani-la, the intransigent French nun; Marie-Elise, the Kazini of Chakhung whose arrival in

Kalimpong as a new bride is not without its complications; and Jivaka, the world's first female to male transsexual, all of whom have part of a chapter or more devoted to their story. Other themes, too, are present: writing, both poetry and prose; and politics. In 1962 the dream of '*Hindi-Cheeni bhai-bhai*' (Indians and Chinese are brothers) withered and China invaded the north-eastern frontier, not far from Kalimpong. It is with this as background, when things were all astir in Kalimpong, that Sangharakshita received the letter that would change the whole course of his life, and in fact the course of Buddhism in the West. He received an invitation from the English Sangha Trust to come and spend some time in London. He left for England in the summer of 1964 for what he imagined would be a four to six month visit. This trip, his friends assured him, 'was sure to be a success'. With these words this memoir concludes.

But not this volume. There is one more short text that belongs to this period, written for a book of tributes to the Beat poet and activist, Allen Ginsberg.[8] *With Allen Ginsberg in Kalimpong* recounts how the 'slouching, dirty, dishevelled, hirsute' American poet appeared one day in June 1962 at Sangharakshita's vihara, how the two were soon engaged in conversation, and how Sangharakshita (who had not heard of the poet before) was introduced to two volumes of Ginsberg's poetry, *Howl* and *Kaddish*. Allen Ginsberg was keen to meet the Chinese Yogi Mr Chen for he had a very particular question which he wished to put to him. What that question was and its effect on the Chinese hermit you will discover in the final pages of this volume.

To know a life is to come to know the man, and reading these memoirs is a means to encounter, to come to know, Sangharakshita. Rich though they are, they do not – cannot – do full justice to one who is, at his own admission, a rather complex personality. Interested readers may wish to turn to other writings that come from this period: the *Maha Bodhi* editorials, his letters to his friend, Dinoo Dubash, and especially the many poems which communicate aspects of experience, and a sensibility, that only poetry can.[9] In allowing ourselves to be influenced by the life and being and consciousness of one who deeply goes for Refuge to the Three Jewels, as the traditional idiom has it, we may find indeed that we, and our lives, are transformed.

Kalyanaprabha
Great Malvern
22 August 2018

In the Sign of the Golden Wheel

Life's memories are not life's histories,
but the original work of an artist.[10]

Rabindranath Tagore, 1861–1941

I

THE SCENT OF GARDENIAS

One morning in early May, my devotions being over, I closed the summer-house door behind me and made my way back to The Hermitage by the path that ran between the ornamental trees. On passing the gardenia bush I noticed among the glossy evergreen leaves two white double flowers. They were the first gardenias of the year. Having plucked them I bore them indoors and placed them in a jar in the centre of my table, whence they diffused their rich scent through the room as I had my tea and toast, taught first a Nepalese and then a Tibetan student, and finally continued working on my new article 'The Religion of Art'.[11] I was glad the gardenias had begun to appear. Vaiśākha Pūrṇimā, the full-moon day of the month Vaiśākha, corresponding to April–May in the Western calendar, was little more than two weeks away, and flowers would be needed for the decoration of the shrine.

Vaiśākha Pūrṇimā was the most important festival in the Buddhist year. It was the anniversary of the day on which the wandering, freelance ascetic Gautama had attained supreme, perfect Enlightenment and become the Buddha or Enlightened One. According to late Sinhalese traditions it was also the anniversary of his birth thirty-five years earlier and his *parinirvāṇa* or final passing away forty-five years later, so that throughout Buddhist South-east Asia, as well as in modern India, Vaiśākha Pūrṇimā was known as the 'thrice-sacred' festival. It would be the fourth time I had celebrated it in Kalimpong since my arrival in the little Himalayan township in 1950, and the first time I had celebrated

Standing Buddha from Lama Govinda

it at The Hermitage since the Young Men's Buddhist Association (India) had become the Kalimpong branch of the Maha Bodhi Society with me, the Association's founder, as *bhikṣu*-in-charge, and I wanted this year's celebrations to attract as many people as possible and to be an inspiration to Buddhist and Hindu alike. I therefore booked the Town Hall for a public meeting on the first Sunday after the Vaiśākha Pūrṇimā, started preparing The Hermitage for the specifically religious observances of the thrice-sacred day itself, and sent out hundreds of printed invitations and programmes. I also wrote to the Sub-Divisional Officer asking him to give the pupils in government schools a holiday on Vaiśākha Pūrṇimā, and to Monsignor and Mother Superior with a similar request in respect of Buddhist pupils attending the Catholic Mission schools.

Our full-moon day meetings were usually held in the summer-house, where the place of honour was occupied by the wooden image of the standing Buddha given me by Lama Govinda,[12] but as the place was rather small I decided that the biggest room in The Hermitage should be turned into a temporary shrine. This room normally functioned as the games room, where our younger members played ping-pong, and since it had not seen paint for a good many years and looked decidedly shabby I asked our Nepalese landlady to get it painted. She agreed, but did nothing, and in the end I bought a couple of tins of white paint and did the job myself. At least, I did most of it myself. Joe did the rest the following day, which was Vaiśākha Pūrṇimā eve, while Miss Rao stitched curtains[13] and other members and friends decorated the place with greenery (I was not in favour of the usual paper flags), as well as decorating in a similar manner the bamboo arch that I had caused Man Bahadur[14] to erect at the front gate and for which I had made a 'welcome' sign from red cloth and cotton wool.

At this point there was a catastrophe. After going home for lunch, Joe had returned to help me finish setting up the temporary shrine, which was already resplendent with electric-blue hangings, rows of brass offering bowls, and (borrowed) silver butter-lamps. Intending to do something to our alabaster Buddha-image, he set it down on the edge of the ping-pong table, which was being used as a worktable. Unable to bear the weight of the heavy image, the top of the table at once see-sawed violently, precipitating the image onto the floor and breaking off its head. Everyone was horrified, especially our Tibetan and Nepalese members, for whom the breaking of a Buddha-image was inauspicious in the extreme and bound to bring bad luck, and strange looks were cast at the wretched *upāsaka*, who stood petrified with confusion and chagrin. One who could be responsible for something as inauspicious as the breaking of a Buddha-image must be highly inauspicious himself, the looks seemed to say, and it was obvious that the incident had served to confirm the impression, which I knew some of our members had formed, that there was something uncanny about the elderly Canadian Buddhist who wore colourful American clothes that were several sizes too big for him, who waggled his bottom when he walked, and who accosted young men in a way they found acutely embarrassing. After the celebrations Joe stuck the head of the Buddha-image on with glue, but unfortunately he failed to get the upper and lower portions of the neck quite flush, and since the glue was of the super-adhesive variety the mistake could not be rectified. The alabaster image, given me a year or two previously by a devout Burmese couple, was therefore relegated to one side of the shrine, a position it retained when the latter was moved back to the summer-house. Visitors rarely noticed the dark ring round its neck, but it was some years before those who had been present forgot how Joe had broken a Buddha-image, and some years before the aura of inauspiciousness that came to surround the eccentric Canadian *upāsaka* was entirely dispelled.

At the time of its occurrence, the catastrophe cast a damper on our preparations for the thrice-sacred festival, and it was not until the following day that spirits were fully recovered. After an early morning puja in the summer-house, held for the benefit of our more regular members and friends, we gave the first wave of visitors tea and started putting the finishing touches to the decorations. In the case of the temporary shrine, this mainly consisted in arranging flowers in the various vases we had managed to collect, as well as in scattering them, Indian style, on and around the image table. Many more double white flowers having appeared among the glossy evergreen leaves of our gardenia bush, I had, besides other flowers, plenty of velvet-petalled, richly scented gardenias at my disposal. While I was trying to place them where they would show to the greatest advantage, a little girl brought me a bunch of gardenias from her mother. In the course of the morning more bunches of gardenias arrived, as well as two or three small basketfuls of the same exotic flower, until I had far more of them than were needed for the vases and image table. Yet still the gardenias continued to come. The gardens of Kalimpong seemed to be raining gardenias upon us, the deluge culminating in the arrival of a perfectly enormous basketful sent down from 'Krishnalok' by Princess Irene of Greece.[15] Gardenias lay in fragrant white heaps on the floor. There must have been thousands of them. I therefore began sticking them into the greenery with which the temporary shrine had been covered, so that eventually the room was practically lined with gardenias. Those left over I stuck in the greenery surrounding the entrance, the windows, and the veranda posts – stuck them, indeed, in every nook and cranny. By the time I had finished the place was a veritable paradise of gardenias, and the rich scent of gardenias filled the air.

That night the former games room was packed, and the silver butter-lamps cast a warm glow over eager, expectant faces and colourful national costumes, as well as over the solid walls of gardenias on either side. The meeting should have begun at six o'clock, but the Governor of West Bengal, who happened to be staying in Kalimpong and whom I had invited through the SDO, did not turn up until more than an hour later. Dr Mookerji was a retired college professor whose appointment to the governorship had taken everybody by surprise, but who with his simple, unassuming ways had soon won for himself a place in people's affections. He was also a Christian (not a convert, but a member of an 'old' Anglican family), and I was concerned lest he should not know that shoes had to be removed before entering the shrine, and dropped a hint to that effect. But I need not have worried. Dr Mookerji knew very well what to do, and in fact sat through the puja and through my own sermon on the significance of Vaiśākha Pūrṇimā, as well as through the musical items that followed, with as great an appearance of devotion as any of the older Buddhists or Hindus present. After he had left there was more music, and it was with the sound of the sitar, and of youthful voices raised in praise of the Buddha, that the meeting eventually came to an end.

I had originally intended to dismantle the temporary shrine the next day, but in such numbers did people continue to come in order to worship that I decided to leave it as it was for the time being. In any case, though Vaiśākha Pūrṇimā itself was over, the year's celebrations were far from being concluded. The public meeting in the Town Hall was still to come, and organizations that were also celebrating *Buddha Jayanti*, as the thrice-sacred festival was generally known in India, had invited me to address them. One of these was the Maitri Sangha, the Bengali cultural organization where I had already given a number of lectures and where I had a small following of educated Bengalis sympathetic to Buddhism. On the present occasion, however, I was not the only speaker, there being three others on the platform with me: Bhadant Anand Kausalyayan, the elderly Punjabi monk who took me on long walks whenever he was in Kalimpong; Swami Gangeshwarananda, the incumbent of the local Ramakrishna Mission ashram; and Dr George Roerich, the Tibetologist.

I was more than a little surprised that Gangeshwarananda had been invited to speak, since he was very unpopular in Kalimpong on account of his evil temper and was known to be hostile to Buddhism. I could only assume that the organizers had invited him because he was the religious representative of the Bengali Hindu community, so to speak, and because they were confident he would observe the proprieties. But if such was their confidence, it proved to have been misplaced. When it was his turn to speak the swami launched into a virulent attack on Buddhism, an attack which ended with his exclaiming, in tones of the utmost contempt, 'But what sort of religion can you expect from someone who died from over-indulgence in pork!' The little audience was deeply shocked. I said nothing at the time, but after the meeting I protested to the secretary of the Sangha, as did several other people. I also called on the president of the Sangha on my way back to The Hermitage and protested to him too. Genial Dr Boral was quick to promise that such an incident would not occur again. A few days later I heard that Mrs Charu Mitter, the influential Bengali lady whom some called the Queen of Kalimpong, was extremely displeased with the swami's behaviour and that, like Dr Boral, she intended there should be no repetition of the incident.[16]

Whether prompted by Gangeshwarananda's attack on Buddhism, or for some other reason, the morning after the Maitri Sangha meeting I started writing a satirical sketch on Brahmanism entitled 'How Buddhism Disappeared from India'. Bhadant Anand, to whom I read extracts, thoroughly enjoyed this little *jeu d'esprit*, but though I finished it a couple of weeks later the work was far too scathing to be publishable in India and I never gave it a final revision.

The lectures at the Maitri Sangha were all in English, but at our public meeting in the Town Hall (which in fact preceded the Maitri Sangha meeting by a week) the lectures were in four or five languages. The reason for the diversity was that the population of Kalimpong was a polyglot one, and I wanted everybody to be able to hear the Dharma in his mother tongue or, at least, in a language with which he was familiar. This policy – or rather principle – of mine was well known in the town and our Vaiśākha Pūrṇimā public meeting was therefore attended by people from all sections of the community, whether Buddhists or Hindus, hill people or plainsmen. Though the lectures were in so many languages, there was no disharmony between them in point of content, much less still any disharmony between one speaker and another, and when after the three-hour programme my helpers and I took down the decorations we could congratulate ourselves on a truly successful meeting. The day before there had, however, been a little disharmony between one of the speakers and Joe. The speaker in question was Miss Barclay, an elderly Englishwoman of generous disposition but uncertain temper who had arrived in Kalimpong earlier in the year and was now one of The Hermitage's most frequent visitors. The scene of the disharmony was my room. Joe had come to discuss the next day's public meeting with me, and Miss Barclay was furious with him for taking up my time, as she saw it, when she wanted to talk with me herself. Her outburst astonished the poor Canadian *upāsaka*, who was accustomed to being at the originating rather than at the receiving end of such displays of temperament, and I had to intervene to restore the peace between these two Western followers of the Dharma. (Miss Barclay had recently become a Buddhist, much to the annoyance of the local missionaries.) Later I explained to Joe that it was by no means unusual for Miss Barclay to fly into a tantrum and that he should not take it too seriously.

The good people of Kalimpong had hardly finished celebrating Buddha Jayanti when there came news of an event that for many days intermitted all other topics of conversation. Everest was conquered. Edmund Hillary and Tenzing Norgay had succeeded in reaching the top of the highest mountain in the world, where hitherto no human foot had trod. The Nepalese, in particular, were wildly excited, for Tenzing Norgay was a Sherpa, and inasmuch as the Sherpas were Nepalese by nationality, even if not by ethnic origin (they were in fact of Tibetan stock), his achievement could be regarded as demonstrating, in the eyes of the whole world, the superiority of the Nepalese people in at least one field. They might not have produced an internationally renowned writer or scientist, or even an internationally renowned politician, but they had produced Tenzing Norgay, the conqueror of Everest. So proud were the Nepalese of their hero, and to such an extent did they identify with him, that they were impatient of any reminder that Tenzing Norgay was technically an Indian citizen and that he had not stood on the summit of Everest alone. Among younger Nepalese the name of Edmund Hillary was hardly ever mentioned, while that of Sir John Hunt, the leader of the expedition, was not mentioned at all. Listening to them, one could easily have thought that Sherpa Tenzing, as he was generally called, had reached the top of Mount Everest by his own unaided efforts.

I myself felt little or no excitement when, on the morning of Tuesday 2 June, Miss Barclay brought the news that Everest had been conquered. Though I could appreciate the courage and determination that had made such an achievement possible, the idea that a mountain, or any other part of nature, was something to be 'conquered', was foreign to my whole way of thinking and feeling. Mountains were alive. Indeed there were mountains, Everest itself being one, which could be said to have personality, in the sense of having the power to attract people and influence them. A mountain of this kind was a sacred mountain, and the proper attitude towards it was one of reverence and worship. In the words of a modern pilgrim to Mount Kailas, the most sacred of all the mountains in the Himalayan system:

> This worshipful or religious attitude is not impressed by scientific facts, like figures of altitude, which are foremost in the mind of modern man. Nor is it motivated by the urge to 'conquer' the mountain. Instead of conquering it, the religious-minded man prefers to be conquered by the mountain. He opens his soul to its spirit and allows it to take possession of him, because only he who is *inspired* or 'possessed' by the divine spirit can partake of its nature. While the modern man is driven by ambition and the glorification of his own ego to climb an outstanding mountain and to be the first on top of it, the devotee is more interested in his spiritual uplift than in the physical feat of climbing. To him the mountain is a divine symbol, and as little as he would put his foot upon a sacred image, so little would he dare to put his foot on the summit of a sacred mountain.[17]

Lama Govinda's sentiments were very much my own, and I was therefore unable to share the jubilation of our Nepalese members and friends that Everest had been conquered and that a man of their own blood had been the first to stand on the untrodden snows of its summit.

But Tuesday 2 June, the day on which I received the news of the conquest of Everest, was also Coronation Day. Later it was rumoured that the news of Hillary and Tenzing's achievement had been deliberately held back in order that its release on that day might be a present, as it were, to the new monarch, Elizabeth II, on the occasion of her coronation. Be that as it may, I was as little excited by the Coronation as I was by the news of the conquest of Everest. Nine years had passed since my departure from England, and I had no thought of returning. Moreover, I was a monk, and since that be-rainbowed August morning six years ago when I had gone forth 'from home into the life of homelessness'[18] it had been my conviction that one who had renounced the world had no exclusive mundane loyalties, whether national or racial. Though known in Kalimpong as 'the English monk' I did not really think of myself as such. Language and literature apart, my links with the country of my birth were tenuous, being more or less limited to the occasional exchange of letters with English Buddhists. It was therefore hardly surprising that I should not have been excited by the Coronation or that I should have given it no more thought than did my Nepalese and Tibetan friends. The only people who were at all excited by it were the handful of elderly British residents who had stayed on after Independence and, of course, the occupants of that stronghold of Scottish Presbyterianism, Dr Graham's Homes, where 500-odd children of mixed parentage were brought up as Christians and taught to think of the United Kingdom as 'home' and where, not surprisingly, the film of the Coronation was soon being shown. I did not see the film. Not only was I not interested in seeing it, but monks were not supposed to see films and in any case I knew that I was *persona non grata* at the Homes. Miss Barclay saw it, however, and afterwards gave me an account of the feudal pomp and ecclesiastical circumstance by which the coronation ceremony had been surrounded. She also lent me her copy of the *Daily Mirror* Coronation number.

Of only one picture of the coronation do I retain even a faint recollection – a picture of the Queen, newly crowned and sceptred, sitting in the Coronation Chair and looking strangely young for so great a responsibility. More vivid is my recollection of another picture, which I may actually have seen not in the *Daily Mirror* Coronation number but in an earlier issue of the same popular newspaper. This was a picture of three women in deep mourning standing together, heavily veiled, in attitudes expressive of sorrow, shock, and resignation. Below was the caption 'Three Queens – One Grief'. The occasion was the funeral of King George VI, and the three queens were Queen Mary, Queen Elizabeth the Queen Mother, and Queen Elizabeth II, one of whom had just lost a son, one a husband, and one a father. There was a quality of timeless, archetypal tragedy about this triple image that I found deeply moving. It was as though the three Fates or three Norns were mourning doomed humanity.[19] I had seen Queen Mary during the War, walking over Westminster Bridge accompanied by a single lady-in-waiting. Then too she was in mourning, the Duke of Kent, her youngest son, having been killed recently in a flying accident. Years earlier I had seen the future Queen Elizabeth II, then Princess Elizabeth. Riding with my father on the top of a red double-decker London bus, when I was six or seven years old, I had found myself looking down over the wall of a West End mansion. In the garden two little girls were playing, one slightly bigger than the other. 'Look,' said my father, as the bus moved on, 'there are the two little princesses, Elizabeth and Margaret Rose.'

But these were only memories. Not long after Vaiśākha I had a visitor who came straight from the Britain of the second Elizabethan Age, as it was hoped the new reign would prove to be, and who provided me with a more direct and tangible link with my native land. The visitor was a very small, very upright, very severe-looking woman in traditional Tibetan dress, complete with rainbow-apron. She was Dawa's mother. Dawa Tsering Bhutia was one of our oldest and most faithful members. Though in government service, he was secretary of our little branch of the Maha Bodhi Society, as he had been of its predecessor the Young Men's Buddhist Association (India) in his student days. Reliable and conscientious to a fault, he was at the same time inclined to be anxious, and it was with considerable trepidation that he brought his formidable little mother to see me. Had her Dawa been behaving himself while she was away, she wanted to know, or had he been wasting his time hanging round the bazaar and getting into bad company? She hoped he had not been drinking, or smoking, or chewing tobacco, since otherwise she would have to give him a good thrashing. Fortunately I was able to reassure her on all these points, and her rigid features relaxed a little. What I would have said had she also hoped that her son was keeping clear of women I do not know. My young friend was desperately in love with a Nepalese girl whom he wanted to marry and was terrified lest his mother should find out, since she had often declared that under no circumstances would she allow him to marry anyone but a Tibetan. During his mother's visit

Dawa was very much on tenterhooks, in case I should inadvertently let slip something about him that he did not want her to know; but luckily this did not happen, and mother and son were able to leave The Hermitage apparently reassured, in her case, and relieved, in his.

The strait-laced, strong-minded little Tibetan woman made quite an impression on me. Our conversation was carried on mainly in English, a smattering of which she had picked up from the family for whom she worked as an ayah in England and to whose service she would soon be returning. But although her very limited English was decidedly of the fractured variety, with occasional lapses into Nepali, she spoke it not only with the utmost aplomb but with an upper-class accent and intonation that would have done credit to a duchess. Listening to her, I could at times have fancied that I was in a drawing room in the Home Counties rather than amid the foothills of the Eastern Himalayas. The link with my native land with which she provided me, at least for half an hour, was a direct and tangible one indeed.

Not that Dawa's mother was my only visitor during this period, that is, my only visitor from outside Kalimpong (visitors from the town itself came every day, at all hours). There were visitors from Poland and America, France and Germany. The French visitor was Miss Delannoy, the short, untidy Sorbonne alumna who had spent a couple of weeks in Kalimpong earlier in the year and who even then had seemed to be more interested in Buddhism than in the subjects she was supposed to be studying.[20] Having made a trip to Nepal, she was in fact now staying in Ghoom, and shortly after her arrival in Kalimpong took the Three Refuges and Five Precepts from me. She was, I noticed, more balanced than she had been at the time of her previous visit. The German visitors were Dr and Mrs Liebenthal. Frail and evidently poor, the gentle old couple had not come direct from Germany, which they had left in the thirties. They had come from China via Shantiniketan, at whose Cheena Bhavan Dr Liebenthal was now teaching.[21] A Sinologist of international repute, he had translated the Chinese version of the *Sūtra of the Lord of Healing* into English and on his second visit to The Hermitage he presented me with a copy of this work, by which he clearly set great store.[22] My most interesting visitor, however, was not from Poland or America, France or Germany. He was from Japan.

Dr Kajiyama arrived at The Hermitage two days after Vaiśākha Pūrṇimā, when the temporary shrine was as yet undismantled and the scent of gardenias still filled the air. He arrived at the end of our evening puja, and after showing him his room (he was an expected guest rather than a casual visitor) I accompanied Miss Barclay and Miss Delannoy to the bazaar, both those ladies having attended the puja. While I was out the young Japanese scholar must have sat and meditated in the deserted shrine-room, between the walls of gardenias, for he afterwards told me that even in the Zen monasteries of his native Japan he had not experienced so peaceful an atmosphere. During the month he stayed with me he gave not the slightest trouble. He was an ideal guest. Slim and self-effacing, he flitted about like a shadow, being particularly careful not to disturb or interrupt me when I was busy. One afternoon I took him and Anand-ji (as Bhadant Anand was generally called) to see Dr Roerich,[23] and the veteran Tibetologist was glad to have news of the Pāli Institute at Nalanda, where Dr Kajiyama was studying and teaching and whence he had travelled up to Kalimpong to escape the burning heat of the plains. The Institute had been started two years earlier by my teacher Bhikkhu Jagdish Kashyap, and though the ever-sceptical Anand-ji had doubted of its success it was now doing well and had attracted some distinguished scholars. Halfway through his stay Dr Kajiyama spent a few days in Darjeeling, which was 8,000 feet above sea level to Kalimpong's 4,000. It was as though Kalimpong was not cool enough for him, and probably the misty, pine-clad slopes of the Queen of the Hill Stations were more reminiscent of Japan than were the maize-planted terraces of her more tropical younger sister. However that might have been, Dr Kajiyama must have thought of his native land quite a lot, for we talked about Japan, and discussed Japanese Buddhism, on more than one occasion. In particular we discussed Aśvaghoṣa's *Awakening of Faith in the Mahāyāna*.

I had come across this seminal work, in Suzuki's translation, during my wandering days in South India. I had found it in the library of a Hindu ashram where I was staying, and so great an impression did it make on me that I at once copied the entire text into my notebook.[24] That notebook I still had with me and I still reflected, from time to time, on the teachings of the profound and cryptic little work, which according to some modern scholars was an original Chinese composition, but which had in any case exerted a strong influence on practically all the major schools of Far Eastern Buddhism. I was particularly struck by the concept – or rather image – of 'perfuming', distant reflections of which even found their way into my poetry. In Early Buddhism *saṃsāra* and *nirvāṇa* were mutually exclusive realities, which left unresolved the question of how they were related. According to Aśvaghoṣa, or whoever wrote under that name, the relation between them is one of mutual perfuming. Clothes have no scent in themselves, but if they are permeated with perfumes then they come to have a scent. Similarly, the pure state of Suchness (Aśvaghoṣa's term for the Absolute) is without defilement, but upon its being 'perfumed' by ignorance there appear on it the marks of defilement. In a corresponding manner, the defiled state of ignorance is devoid of any purifying influence, but upon its being 'perfumed' by Suchness it comes to have such an influence. Indispensable though the help of Buddhas, bodhisattvas, and spiritual friends may also be, a man is able to renounce *saṃsāra* and realize *nirvāṇa* primarily because his deluded mind is permeated by the perfume of Suchness – a perfume far surpassing the scent of gardenias.

2

TEA GARDENS, TAMANGS, AND A TALKING CALF

Longview was one of the biggest tea estates in the Darjeeling District, but I had heard of its existence only recently, when I received a visit from its new, South Indian manager. R. A. Padmanathan was a reader of the *Aryan Path*, to which I was a regular contributor; the *Aryan Path* was printed and published in Bangalore by the Indian Institute of Culture, and the director of the Institute was Padmanathan's cousin. On learning from this cousin that the Buddhist monk whose name appeared so frequently in the pages of the Institute's journal lived in Kalimpong, thus being virtually his next-door neighbour, Padmanathan lost no time in coming to see me. The visit was followed by an exchange of letters between us, an exchange which culminated, towards the end of June, in his inviting me to Longview and my accepting the invitation. Though I had been living in the District for over three years I had as yet had no more than a glimpse of the world-famous tea gardens, and the idea of spending a few days in one of them appealed to me.

I did not go to Longview alone. Sachin accompanied me.[25] He was one of my oldest pupils, having attended the evening tutorial classes which, shortly after the establishment of the now defunct YMBA,[26] I had started for the benefit of those of our members who were fearful of not passing their school or college examinations. After an unsuccessful attempt at a science degree in Darjeeling (his father had wanted him to be a doctor) he was back in Kalimpong, attending the Scottish Universities Mission (Arts) College, and now came to me for tuition in Logic and English Literature. Logic we both found interesting, at times even fascinating, but English Literature – especially English poetry – was sheer, unadulterated delight. Besides going through the Calcutta University's IA Prose and Poetry Selections page by page and line by line, I dictated paraphrases of the poems to him, the ability to reproduce 'in your own words' the meaning of Wordsworth's 'Immortality Ode' or Shelley's 'To the West Wind'[27] being, apparently, highly prized by the examiners. Not that we confined ourselves to the Selections. Sachin's love of literature was hardly less than my own, and we often wandered, in the course of these tutorials, far beyond the limits of what was academically prescribed. Love of literature constituted, indeed, a strong bond between us. It had been a major factor in the development of our friendship, which now that Sachin was back in Kalimpong was flourishing more vigorously than ever. Rarely did a day pass without our seeing each other, either at The Hermitage or at the bungalow in the Scottish Mission compound where he lived and where, if he happened to be out, I sometimes talked with his father, who was a doctor in the Mission hospital. When Padmanathan invited me to Longview it was therefore natural that I should tell Sachin, natural that he should want to accompany me, natural that I should be willing for him to do so, and natural, finally, that we should decide to extend the scope of our excursion and return to Kalimpong via Kurseong and Darjeeling.

The evening before our departure I learned that Gyan Jyoti's jeep would be going down to Siliguri in the morning. Gyan Jyoti was the prominent Newar Buddhist merchant who had invited Kashyap-ji (as my teacher was generally known) to Kalimpong and who, since Kashyap-ji had taken me there with him and then left me to 'work for the good of Buddhism', was indirectly responsible for my presence in the town.[28] Though we did not often meet, he was always ready to oblige me, and thus it was that I travelled to Siliguri in the front seat of his jeep, while Sachin followed by bus. Within half an hour of our leaving The Hermitage we had crossed Teesta Bridge, 3,000 feet below Kalimpong, and were speeding along the muddy potholed track that wound between the foothills to the plains. The rainy season was well advanced, and I saw that the Teesta had risen dramatically and that its waters were no longer jade green or turquoise in colour but a dull ochre

Sachin and Sangharakshita

laced with soapsuddy yellow. There had already been a few landslides, but the road had been cleared, and the other occupants of the jeep and I were beginning to congratulate ourselves on an uneventful journey when, only a few miles from the plains, we suddenly found our passage blocked by three enormous boulders. These had to be dynamited out of the way before we could proceed, with the result that it took five hours instead of the expected three to reach the would-be-industrial shanty town that was Siliguri, where the Longview jeep was waiting. Half an hour later, having been swallowed by the rolling green acres of the tea gardens, which extended up into the first range of foothills, Sachin and I were being deposited at the entrance to the manager's bungalow and welcomed by Padmanathan.

According to the dictionary a bungalow was a one-storey house, but the building in which we now found ourselves, and where we were soon partaking of a late lunch with our host, was more like a country mansion than the modest suburban dwelling that, in England at least, the Hindi-derived term had come to designate. The table at which we sat could have accommodated twenty people, while the enormous dresser that stood against one wall and the massive sideboard that stood against another held, respectively, dinner services, and glassware and silverware, that must have been shipped from England decades ago. Obviously in the spacious days of the Raj the manager of a Darjeeling tea estate had lived in considerable splendour, waited on by a horde of servants, and entertaining lavishly. In this respect, at least, Padmanathan was far from emulating his imperial predecessors. He lived very simply, making use of only a few of the twenty-odd lofty rooms, keeping only a handful of servants, and doing little or no entertaining. Though clad, as no doubt his predecessors had been clad, in khaki shorts and open-necked shirt, he did not really give the impression of being the manager of an important tea estate. With his serious expression, and mild manners, he gave the impression, rather, of being a college professor or not very successful lawyer.

Lunch was not only late but lengthy, Padmanathan having a lot to say to me, and after the meal Sachin and I barely had a chance to try out the bungalow's ping-pong table before it was time for afternoon tea and a visit to the temple. When he took over, Padmanathan explained, there was not a single place of worship in the whole estate. He had therefore built the labourers a temple, and from the way he showed this to us it was clear he was quite proud of the little whitewashed structure on the edge of the labour force's assembly ground. It was open-fronted, and divided into two compartments, each with its own bell. One compartment contained images of Radha and Krishna, both standing; the other, a sedent image of the Buddha. Having shown us the temple Padmanathan took us to see first the tea gardens, with their thousands of rows of flat-topped bushes, and then the various offices. Though our host drove us round for quite a while, we were far from seeing the whole estate which, he informed us, comprised 1,500 acres and had a labour force of 3,000. Most of the labourers were Tamangs, which meant they were Buddhists, but according to Padmanathan they were totally ignorant of Buddhism and had, in fact, no interest in religion. The rest of the labourers were either Thapas or other Nepalese Hindus or – though there were very few of these – Nepalese Christian converts.

By the time we returned to the bungalow Sachin and I had seen and heard so much that was new to us that we felt quite tired, and were content simply to sit on the veranda without speaking. Situated on a ridge as it was, the bungalow commanded a breathtakingly extensive view of the plains, and as darkness fell – the 'embalmèd darkness'[29] of the tropics – we could see the lights of Siliguri twinkling in the distance. How was it, I wondered, that a place that looked so sordid by day could contrive to present so magical an appearance at night! But I did not wonder for long. The air was cold, my mosquito-curtained bed was inviting, and we had to be up at 5 o'clock in order to accompany Padmanathan to the assembly ground and see the labour force being given its orders for the day.

If I had expected to see dawn break, next morning, on 3,000 heads, then I was disappointed. Only four or five hundred men, women, and children actually turned up, many of them carrying the traditional *tokri* or cone-shaped wicker basket. They were, I had to admit, an unattractive lot. Though sturdily built, they were for the most part squat, bandy-legged, low-browed, and broad-featured, with expressions that ranged from the dull and apathetic to the coarse and brutal, so that one had to remind oneself that these were human beings and, as such, one's brothers and sisters – even one's brother and sister Buddhists. When the force had assembled, and it was obvious no more labourers would be turning up that day, Padmanathan made his way to the temple, stepped inside the first compartment, rang the bell, put on his spectacles, and read out two verses from the *Bhagavad Gītā*. He then stepped into the second compartment, rang the bell there too, read out two verses from the *Dhammapada*, took off his spectacles, and rejoined the little band of assistants and overseers with whom he had been talking. The assembled labourers took no interest in these proceedings. 'Burra Saheb's job is to run the estate,' their sullen looks seemed to say, if they said anything at all. 'Religion is the job of Brahmins and lamas.' For Padmanathan had engaged a Nepalese Brahmin to officiate in the Hindu half of the temple and a Tamang lama to officiate in the Buddhist half, and the two functionaries were in obsequious attendance upon him as he performed his own supernumerary ministrations. These ministrations over, he was free to give the labour force, or as much of it as had turned up, its orders for the day, which he did through the medium of the overseers, his own Nepali being insufficient for that purpose. The overseers then led off their respective contingents to various parts of the estate, while Padmanathan took Sachin and me to his office for breakfast.

After breakfast our host showed us more of the estate, this time initiating us into the mysteries of the tea-producing process, from the picking of the 'two leaves and a bud'[30] with which the process began to the dispatching of the big, fragrant wooden chests with which it concluded. Picking was usually done by women, Padmanathan explained, as we looked out over one of the gardens, where scores of pairs of female hands were working with incredible rapidity, right hand and left hand alternately tossing the young shoots and leaves back over the picker's shoulder into her *tokri*. Women were in any case more reliable than men, he continued; because they had children to feed they worked regularly, whereas the men worked only when they needed liquor money and were often drunk for days on end. The bushes on which the shoots and leaves grew were, I noticed, all no more than breast high, for though the tea plant was really a tree, belonging to the same family as the camellia, in cultivation its growth was restricted for the convenience of the picker. It was no doubt for the same reason that the tops of the bushes were kept perfectly flat. Planted out as they were at regular intervals, in long straight rows, the neat little bushes gave the hillside something of the appearance of a Dutch formal garden of clipped yew.

Each time a picker filled her *tokri* she took it to the overseer, who weighed it and entered the weight against her name in a little book. At the end of the day the weights were added up and she would be paid according to the total. Thus the faster she worked the greater would be the number of times she filled her *tokri*, and the greater the number of times she filled her *tokri* the more she would be paid. In this way an active young woman could earn what by local standards was a good wage.

From the gardens the freshly-picked shoots and leaves were transported to a factory, where they went through the remaining stages of the tea-producing process, all of which Padmanathan showed us. The unfortunate herb was spread on trays, rolled, fermented, baked, and tortured in a variety of other ways, before being sifted into grades and packed ready for dispatch to Calcutta. For the whole time we were inside the factory I was not only conscious of the extreme humidity; I was also conscious of a pervasive, overpowering odour – the odour of tea. It was an odour reminiscent, not of the delicate aroma wafted from the four o'clock incarnation of 'the cup that cheers but does not inebriate',[31] but rather of the stench emanating from yesterday's used tea-leaves. I was therefore not sorry when, our initiation into the mysteries of tea-production being complete, Sachin and I eventually emerged with Padmanathan into the comparative coolness of the air outside and were taken back to the bungalow, where my host and I at once plunged into a serious discussion – a discussion that lasted until lunchtime and was continued in the evening.

The fact of the matter was that I was deeply concerned about the Tamang labourers, who after all comprised by far the greater part of the Longview labour force. They were Buddhists, in the sense that they had been born into 'Buddhist' families. More precisely, they were Nyingma Buddhists, that is, followers of Padmasambhava, the Precious Guru, one of the two co-founders of the Tibetan Buddhist tradition. Yet according to Padmanathan they were totally ignorant of Buddhism and had no interest in religion. Something had to be done, and done quickly, since otherwise they might cease in the course of another generation to be Buddhists even in name. The idea that eventually occurred to me, as Padmanathan and I talked, and which I at once communicated to him, was that he should establish a branch of the Maha Bodhi Society at Longview, a branch that would be responsible for spreading the basic teachings of Buddhism among the labour force and which I myself would visit regularly. Within a few years the Tamangs would be completely changed; they would be Buddhists in fact as well as in name and true followers of the Precious Guru. Though Padmanathan did not mislike the idea of there being a branch of the Maha Bodhi Society at Longview, he was far from sharing my confidence that it could be a means of changing the Tamangs. I had seen for myself, he commented ruefully, how little interest the labourers took in what went on inside the temple. It had been a great disappointment to him. At least some of them, he had thought, would get into the habit of going to the temple to pray, whether to the Buddha or to Radha-Krishna (it didn't really matter to whom), and to offer the lama or the Brahmin a few annas. But none of them ever did. A few of the Hindu office staff sometimes went to the temple, but the Tamang and other labourers gave it a wide berth. The nearest the latter ever got to it was when they came to the assembly ground to be given their orders for the day, and even then they took no more notice of the temple than if it had been an ordinary building. It was as though they did not appreciate what he had done for them.... Later on, Sachin having joined us, Padmanathan returned to the theme. Not only had he built the labourers a temple. He had also provided them with a free dispensary; but they steadfastly refused to avail themselves of its services, preferring to rely instead on old wives' remedies of their own when they fell sick or were injured. It was the same in the case of the shop he had opened for their benefit. This too they refused to patronize, even though they could buy provisions there at wholesale prices. He couldn't understand them. They seemed not to respond to kindness. Why, when asked which of his various predecessors they had liked best they invariably mentioned the name of Mr —, a British manager who abused them and swore at them, who was very free with his fists, and who was not above laying into them with a whip. Sometimes he thought, our host added, that if they had a voice in the matter the labourers of Longview would vote to bring back Mr —, whip and all.

Next day I had another serious discussion, this time with the Deputy Commissioner, Sri Dutt-Majumdar, whom I had already met once or twice. He arrived a couple of hours before lunch, having come to confer with Padmanathan on a problem that had lately arisen and with which he was having to deal: the problem of the infiltration of some of the tea estates by Communist agitators. The Communist Party – or parties – was not illegal in India: those were in any case the heady days of Indo-Chinese friendship, when according to the popular slogan the peoples of India and China were brothers, friends, mates;[32] but agitation in the tea estates could lead to strikes, strikes to loss of production, and loss of production to loss of foreign exchange, tea being one of India's most valuable exports. As Deputy Commissioner, Dutt-Majumdar was therefore concerned with the matter. Infiltration by Communists was also of concern, it seemed, to the good Fathers of North Point, the famous Catholic college on the outskirts of Darjeeling. One of their number had recently called on him at his office, so Dutt-Majumdar informed me, to report that the English Buddhist monk who lived in Kalimpong was, in fact, a Communist spy, and to suggest that in the interest of national security he should be expelled from the District. 'I know very well why he reported you,' Dutt-Majumdar smilingly assured me. 'You have nothing to worry about.'

I too knew why the Jesuit Father had reported me. Indeed, I thought I knew the reason for his action better than Dutt-Majumdar himself did. It was not merely that, in accordance with my teacher's behest, I was working in Kalimpong for the good of Buddhism, thus diminishing the influence of the missionaries, Catholic and Protestant alike, in what they were accustomed to regard as their very own territory. A few months earlier I had sent to the Calcutta English-language dailies a letter exposing a particularly odious method of obtaining conversions to Christianity that had come to my notice in Kalimpong, and the publication of this letter had aroused the wrath of the missionary fraternity throughout north-eastern India and made me even more notorious among them than I was already. The method in question was that of 'conversion through pregnancy', as I termed it. A Christian girl would be encouraged to associate with a non-Christian boy who, when she became pregnant, would be pressurized by the Mission authorities first into agreeing to marry her, then into agreeing to marry her in church, and finally, since only Christians could be married in church, into agreeing to become a Christian. Sometimes the pressure included threats of physical violence. All this I explained to Dutt-Majumdar, who was naturally interested, the more especially since the boys whose cases I mentioned came from communities entitled to official protection from exploitation by outside agencies.[33] He therefore asked me to let him have the facts in writing, at the same time promising to take action in the matter.

When Sachin and I took leave of Padmanathan that afternoon I was well content with the success of our visit, and had much to think about as the Longview jeep zigzagged up the succession of hairpin bends that led to Kurseong. In Kurseong we spent an hour or two at the TB Sanatorium visiting Lachuman, an old pupil of mine who was now a patient there, then caught the bus to Darjeeling. On my previous visits to Darjeeling I had been the guest of a hospitable Punjabi shopkeeper, but he was out of station (as the phrase went) and I decided to stay at the Gandhamadan Vihara instead. Situated on the sheer hillside below the main road into Darjeeling, the Gandhamadan Vihara was the religious and cultural centre of the town's two or three dozen Barua families, the Baruas being Theravādin Buddhists from East Bengal. It comprised a small shrine-cum-lecture hall, a row of guest rooms, and a one-room wooden *kuti* for the use of the resident *bhikṣu*. At that time there was no resident *bhikṣu*, nor had there been one, I gathered, for several years. There was, however, an orange-robed guest, in the person of the same Burmese *mahāthera* or 'Great Elder' who had once visited me in Kalimpong and whom I had put up for the night. With him I therefore renewed acquaintance, having breakfast with him next morning and accompanying him to the house of Kali Kinker Barua, the secretary of the local Bengal Buddhist Association, for a *bhojana*-

dāna or ceremonial food-offering. I also renewed acquaintance, during that and the following day, with two leading members of the Tamang Buddhist Association, besides spending time with personal friends and visiting the town's English bookshops with Sachin, who was staying with his maternal grandmother.

The two members of the Tamang Buddhist Association were brisk, dapper little P. T. Lama and his big, pan-chewing brother Inspector T. Moktan. The latter, who was in the West Bengal police, was the more religious-minded of the two, and always came to see me when his duties took him to Kalimpong. A widower with two small daughters, he had decided, most uncharacteristically for a Nepalese, not to remarry. Though the two brothers were looking for me, and I was looking for them, we did not meet until we happened to bump into each other in the bazaar. They at once took me to the Tamang Gompa, as the pagoda-style Nyingma temple was called, and showed me the new *maṇi* chamber they were constructing there. A *maṇi* was a prayer-wheel or, more accurately, a prayer-cylinder, and a *maṇi* chamber was a chamber containing, not a prayer-cylinder such as was twirled by old-fashioned Tibetans as they took their evening stroll, but a giant version of the same devotional aid, a version which in this case would stand eight or ten feet high and occupy practically the entire chamber. They were constructing the *maṇi* chamber in memory of their mother, the brothers explained; it was nearly completed, as I could see, and they would like me to speak at the opening ceremony. I at once accepted the invitation. The principal object of worship in the Tamang Gompa was the enormous sedent image of Padmasambhava that had given me, three years ago, so overwhelming an impression of the spiritual reality of the Precious Guru, and I was happy to renew my connection with the place.[34] I also accepted the invitation because I knew that even educated Buddhists like P. T. Lama and Inspector T. Moktan knew very little about Buddhism, and I was glad, while remaining personally not keen on prayer-cylinders, to have the opportunity of explaining the meaning of an ancient Buddhist tradition.

A few weeks later, therefore, I was back in Darjeeling and back at the Gandhamadan Vihara. This time Sachin did not accompany me. He was more than willing to do so, but according to the Hindu calendar both the days for which I would be away were inauspicious and his mother did not want him to be away from home then. On arriving in Darjeeling

I again renewed acquaintance with the Burmese Maha Thera, then spent the remainder of the day seeing people, visiting bookshops, and executing various small commissions for Sachin and Miss Barclay. The day concluded with a three-cornered philosophical discussion between me and two Bengali Hindu friends – a discussion which lasted until the stroke of midnight. Next morning, after an early *bhojana-dāna* at the home of Kali Kinker Barua, I made my way down the hillside to the Tamang Gompa, my host escorting me. The opening of the new *maṇi* chamber was a very public occasion, with the Deputy Commissioner, Sri Dutt-Majumdar, presiding, and my own lecture as the principal item on the programme.

I had decided to speak on the meaning of the mantra *oṃ maṇi padme hūṃ hrīḥ*, this being the mantra embossed on the great copper cylinder that stood awaiting the push that would give it its first ponderous revolution on its axis. A good part of my lecture was devoted to explaining the significance of the Jewel (*maṇi*) and the Lotus (*padma*), which were, I said, universal symbols, being found, in different forms, all over the world. In the words of the summary I afterwards wrote of the lecture:

> The lotus grows in water, and water always represents life. Philosophically speaking, life is what we call *saṃsāra*, the repeated process of birth and death. Life and birth are closely connected, and for this reason the Lotus stands for the *garbha*, the feminine principle, as well. It also represents the heart, and the emotions, since these are both associated with the feminine principle.
>
> The jewel, on the other hand, symbolizes light. Light represents knowledge. The source of light is the sun, the heat of which fecundates the earth. The *maṇi* or jewel therefore represents the active generating power, the masculine principle. Since reason is supposed to predominate in man, it also stands for reason, intellect and spiritual understanding.

In explaining the significance of these two symbols I was careful to insist that whereas a concept had only one meaning a symbol suggested innumerable meanings, so that the significance of a symbol could never be exhausted intellectually. It was therefore possible to interpret the words *maṇi padme*, literally 'jewel lotus', in a number of ways.

They could signify the presence of a spiritual reality behind the veil of appearances, or the fact that every man and woman possessed the potentiality for Enlightenment, or the desirability of harmonizing the rational and emotional sides of our personality. Thus the meaning of *maṇi padme* was not abstract and philosophical but concrete and practical, and might be summarized as follows:

> All our thinking is in terms of pairs of opposites. We think of the true and false, right and wrong, etc. The jewel and the lotus represent the ultimate duality of existence. In China these two principles are called yang and yin; in India they are sometimes called Purusha and Prakriti, Shiva and Shakti. When we say that the jewel is in the lotus, we are reminding ourselves that things are not really separate from each other, and that our dualistic way of looking at things is a delusion. When we realize, by spiritual practice, that duality is only the creation of our own minds, we become enlightened.

The references to Purusha and Prakriti, and Shiva and Shakti, were for the benefit of the Hindu members of the audience, the opening of the new *maṇi* chamber being not only a very public occasion but something of an interfaith one as well. It was not that I really believed in the possibility of establishing an exact correspondence between Buddhist and Hindu symbols.

Besides explaining the meaning of the mantra I sought to account for the effect produced by its repetition. Words were sounds, and sounds consisted of vibrations. Every word we uttered not only conveyed a meaning but set up certain vibrations, which could be either harmonious or discordant. It was these vibrations, and not the rational content of the words, which influenced us most deeply, and it was possible for us to be influenced in this way because we, too, were made up of vibrations. Not only our physical bodies, but our minds as well, were vibrating at a certain rate. Everything in the universe vibrated. Buddhism and science agreed that nothing in the world was solid, but that everything was in a state of perpetual oscillation. At this point I referred to an American scientist's success in measuring the power of mantra vibrations numerically by means of radiation (particularly radiesthesia). The highest rate at which a mantra could vibrate, according to this authority, was 250,000 times a second. Several mantras vibrated at this rate, the mantra *oṃ maṇi padme hūṃ* being among them. This information, which I had gleaned from the writings of the Tantric scholar Dr Benoytosh Bhattacharya, was music to the ears of my Tamang Buddhist friends, as was the information, gleaned from the same source, that the revolution of a *maṇi*-cylinder released beneficial cosmic forces in favour of the person revolving it. When I sent a copy of the printed summary of my lecture to Lama Govinda, however, he responded with a flat rejection of the idea that the emotional and spiritual effect of a mantra had anything to do with its vibrational value as measured by a scientific device. Mechanistic interpretations of this kind, he roundly declared, were rank materialism, and as such quite inconsistent with the principles of true Buddhism. In deference to his superior understanding of the subject I therefore never reprinted the little article in which I had summarized my lecture at the opening of the Tamang Gompa's new *maṇi* chamber, but years later, particularly after becoming acquainted with Pythagoreanism, I sometimes wondered, *pace* Lama Govinda, whether there might not be a correlation, even a correlation expressible in mathematical terms, between the numerical frequencies and ratios that obtained in the outside world and human emotions, and whether the one might not, conceivably, have an effect on the other.[35]

The new *maṇi* chamber having been opened and the massive cylinder given its initial push, I returned to the Gandhamadan Vihara and spent the next few hours absorbed in one of the books I had bought the previous day. It was T. S. Eliot's *The Use of Poetry and the Use of Criticism*. In my lecture I had spoken of the desirability of harmonizing the rational and emotional sides of our personality. There were certainly sides of my own personality that needed to be harmonized and integrated, though these were not so much the rational and the emotional as the religious and the aesthetic. Sometimes the two overlapped, even coincided, but more often they remained separate and distinct, even mutually antagonistic. This meant that usually they tended to alternate, sometimes even within the space of a single day, with now one now the other predominating, whether in respect of my inner preoccupations or my outward activities.[36] On the day of the opening ceremony this was certainly the case. Having given a lecture on the meaning of a Buddhist mantra in the morning, and spent the afternoon absorbed in English literary criticism, in the evening I attended the full-moon day puja in the Vihara's shrine-cum-lecture hall, administering the five precepts to the assembled Baruas and delivering my first sermon in Hindi.

On returning to Kalimpong next day I found the town in an uproar. At least the Hindu part of it was in an uproar. A butcher had been about to cut the throat of a calf when the innocent creature opened its mouth and said, apparently in good Nepali, 'Have mercy. Don't kill me. I am Holy Mother Cow.' News of the miracle spread like wildfire. Pious Hindus flocked from all parts of the town to have *darshan* of the calf, to prostrate themselves before it, and to implore its blessing. Neck profusely garlanded with marigolds, and forehead smeared with vermilion, it was taken in procession through the bazaar amid scenes of tremendous enthusiasm. Whenever it stopped for a moment, people pressed forward to dip their fingers in the precious deposit and apply it to their foreheads, cow-dung being endued, for orthodox Hindus, with all kinds of purificatory properties. Money was also collected on behalf of the now deified calf, and at the end of an hour the fortunate quadruped was the richer by 35,000 rupees. The principal contributors were the saffron-turbaned Marwari merchants, who occupied a prominent position in the town's economy and who were known as much for their strict Hindu orthodoxy as for their business acumen. A piece of land was being purchased for the calf, I was told, and a shed-cum-temple erected where it would be able to live out its days in peace. As for the butcher who had been the witness of the miracle, he had forsworn his sanguinary trade and become a vegetarian, and was going to spend the rest of his life in the calf's service as its priest and personal attendant.

The majority of our members, especially the younger ones, did not believe the calf had actually spoken, least of all that it had claimed to be Holy Mother Cow in person. There was general agreement, though, that something strange must have happened in the butcher's shed. Perhaps the butcher experienced a sudden revulsion as he lifted his knife against the innocent creature, a revulsion so strong that he *thought* he heard the calf speaking and begging him to spare its life. A few of our members rejected even this rationalistic explanation. The whole thing was a deliberate hoax, they declared. There had been no talking calf, no repentant butcher. The story had been fabricated by the local branch of the All-India Cow Protection Society; they had fabricated it in order to whip up support for their flagging anti-cowslaughter campaign, and Hindu popular sentiment, always volatile, had done the rest. To me it was obvious the cow-protectionists had been involved, if only to the extent of taking advantage of a rumour favourable to their cause, and I was pleased some of our members had seen through their machinations. A few weeks earlier I had started a new series of weekly lectures at The Hermitage. One lecture was entitled 'How to Develop Discrimination', and it had led to some lively discussion. In Kalimpong, as elsewhere, one had to learn to discriminate between religion and superstition, between individual devotion and collective hysteria, and the knowledge that some of my closer associates were beginning to do this was very heartening.

3
DEATHS AND ENTRANCES

Less than a hundred years earlier, Kalimpong had been part of Bhutan, just as Darjeeling had been part of Sikkim, the Raj having nibbled at the corners of both kingdoms. None the less there were very few Bhutanese living in the town, though with their striped *chubas* (knee-length in the case of the men), cropped hair, and bare feet those that did live there made a particularly colourful contribution to the ethnic and cultural diversity of the place. What they lacked in numbers they more than made up in weight, at least where the Buddhist community was concerned, Kalimpong's leading Buddhist family being Bhutanese. This family was the Dorji family. The head of the family, Raja Sonam Topgay Dorji, lived in princely style at Bhutan House, which was situated three miles up the road from me, on the other side of town. Though his official designation was that of Trade Agent to the Government of Bhutan, he functioned as both prime minister and foreign minister of his undeveloped country, as well as being its *de facto* ambassador to India. Moreover, he controlled trade between Bhutan and India by the simple expedient of keeping as much of it as possible in his own hands, with the result that besides being the most powerful man in Bhutan, next to the king, he was extremely wealthy. Indeed, the Dorji family was reputed to be wealthier than the royal family. But powerful and wealthy though he now was, Raja Dorji's origins were distinctly plebeian. His father, who was the son of a syce, had rendered important services to the British and been suitably rewarded, while Sonam Topgay himself, following in his father's footsteps, had been made a titular raja, had married a Sikkimese princess, had become Trade Agent to the Government of Bhutan, and had built Bhutan House.

During my first months in Kalimpong I visited Bhutan House more than once, and met both Raja and Rani Dorji, as well as meeting their eldest son and their two daughters, one of whom was to become queen of Bhutan. While Topgay Raja, as he was generally known, mingled freely with the citizenry of Kalimpong and was a popular figure in the lower bazaar, his wife, who was the sister of the Maharaja of Sikkim, held herself icily aloof and was far from popular. Her unpopularity was due less to her aloofness, which in any case was expected from a member of the aristocracy, than to her extreme tightfistedness and the utter ruthlessness with which she distrained upon debtors and evicted tenants the minute they were in arrears. She was in fact a formidable personage, and few people dared cross her path. Unfortunately, I had been obliged to cross it when, some three years earlier, she was the chairman and I the general secretary of the Sacred Relics Reception Committee (the relics in question were those of Śāriputra and Maudgalyāyana, the Buddha's chief disciples, which were then touring India after being returned by the Victoria and Albert Museum). For purely personal reasons Rani Dorji was determined that the relics of the two *arhants* should not be lodged at the Tharpa Choling Gompa, the biggest and most important Buddhist monastery in Kalimpong, and there exposed for the veneration of the public, whereas I was no less determined that they should be lodged there and succeeded, eventually, in winning the support of the other members of the committee.[37] Since then Rani Dorji had refused to have anything to do with me, with the YMBA (she had attended a lecture or two in its very early days) or, more recently, with the Kalimpong branch of the Maha Bodhi Society.[38]

One morning towards the end of September, however, a few days after we had celebrated the birth anniversary of Anagarika Dharmapala, the founder of the Maha Bodhi Society,[39] Gyan Jyoti came with an invitation to lunch at Bhutan House. As I already knew, Raja Dorji was dead. He had died two nights ago, a condolence meeting had been held at the Town Hall, and I had myself written to Jigme Dorji, the late Raja's eldest son, expressing my sympathy for him and the rest of the family. Anand-ji was also invited, Gyan Jyoti informed me, as was the Venerable Mahanama, the latter being a cousin of Gyan Jyoti's who had recently arrived in Kalimpong and who, though a monk, cherished aspirations to stardom in the world of films. Four days later I accordingly walked half a mile up the road to the Dharmodaya Vihara, the English-style family house which was the religious and cultural centre of the local Newar Buddhists, where Anand-ji and Mahanam-ji were staying and where I had myself spent the first ten months of my life in Kalimpong.[40] From there the three of us were driven to Bhutan House, passing beneath the enormous *vajra* or thunderbolt-sceptre that lay across the top of the front gate and gave the whole place, I always thought, a sinister and threatening look. Rani Dorji and her children were waiting on the veranda to receive us. Though black was not the traditional Buddhist colour of mourning, they all wore black *chubas*, knee-length in the case of Jigme and his brothers, which served to accentuate the pallor of their countenances. Not surprisingly, they looked not only grief-stricken but deeply shocked. Raja Dorji had died, it seemed, rather unexpectedly. According to Gyan Jyoti it was unclear what he had died from, how long he had been ill, or even if he had been ill at all, and rumour was already rife in the bazaar. Grief and shock were however mingled, in the family's looks, with a third expression which I found it more difficult to identify but which was almost one of horror. What could this mean? But I had no time to speculate. After they had silently saluted us and we had silently responded to their salutations, the stricken family conducted Anand-ji, Mahanam-ji, and me first to the dining room for the ceremonial food-offering and then upstairs to Raja Dorji's room for the more specifically religious part of the proceedings.

The body was laid out on a richly decorated bed in the middle of the room with its head, only the top of which was visible, towards the glass-fronted shrine on the right. Silver butter-lamps were burning and the resinous fragrance of Tibetan incense filled the air. On the far side of the body, facing us, were a large framed photograph of Raja Dorji and masses of flowers. On this side were three chairs, and on these my brother monks and I were invited to take our seats while Rani Dorji, Jigme, Tashi, Kesang, and the two younger sons, who were barely out of their teens, together with the servants of the house, all stood behind us. Anand-ji being very much my senior in ordination, I had naturally assumed that he would be giving the funeral sermon; but to my surprise he asked me, in an undertone, to give it instead. According to monastic convention a request from a senior to a junior monk had the force of a command, and for the next twenty-five or thirty minutes I therefore spoke, as the custom was, of the merits of the deceased, of the shortness of human life, of the inevitability of death, and of the necessity for practising the Dharma while there was still time and while one was still possessed of health, strength, and mental energy. Though I had not really known Raja Dorji, having met him only once, and though my contact with his wife had ended unfortunately, I spoke with considerable feeling, as I could sense that Rani Dorji and her children stood at one of those junctures in human life where only the Dharma is of any avail, and I wanted them to realize this. Perhaps they did realize it, to an extent, for I felt a relaxation in the atmosphere behind me, as if my words had helped lighten the load of grief, shock, and something akin to horror, by which they were oppressed. When I had finished speaking Anand-ji softly started up the *paritta-gāthās* or 'verses of protection', in the chanting of which Mahanam-ji and I joined, after which he 'transferred merits' to the deceased Raja by pouring water into a bowl to the accompaniment of the appropriate formulas. Rani Dorji, Jigme, and the rest of the family, then offered each of us a robe and, one by one, prostrated themselves before us three times in the Tibetan fashion.

A funeral sermon often makes quite a deep impression on its auditors at the time, but the impression rarely lasts. In Rani Dorje's case, however, the words I had spoken over her dead husband's body seemed to have had an effect that was more than usually durable. At any rate, after the ceremony at Bhutan House her attitude towards me underwent a slight but definite modification. No longer refusing to have anything to do with the young monk who had dared cross her path, she now came to see me occasionally, each time bringing with her a small offering (sometimes it was a *very* small offering). For a person of Rani Dorji's rigid and unforgiving disposition this represented a change of heart indeed, and though the general opinion in Kalimpong was that Rani Dorji was not capable of a change of heart, but only of a change of tactics (some opined she did not have a heart at all), as representing a change of heart I for one was willing to regard it. Not that she modified her attitude towards me immediately. It was a year or more before the modification was sufficiently marked for me to be sure I was not imagining things and that there actually had been a change of heart on her part. Meanwhile, it did not occur to me to speculate on the possible effects of my sermon. In the days following the ceremony at Bhutan House two other questions occupied my mind. What was the reason for the expression of near horror I had seen on the faces of the Dorji family, and that continued to haunt me, and why had Anand-ji asked me to give the funeral sermon instead of giving it himself?

An answer to the first question was not long in coming. The rumours that had circulated in the bazaar since Raja Dorji's death condensed into a single rumour, that rumour hardened into a general belief, and the belief, in its turn, into an accepted fact. Raja Dorji had not died a natural death. He had been killed by means of black magic. If such was the case, or if Rani Dorji and her children believed it to be the case, then it explained the expression, unidentifiable but almost one of horror, that I had seen mingled, in the latter's faces, with the grief and shock. Black magic was practised throughout the Himalayan region, and Nepalese Hindu *jakris* or witch doctors and Bhutanese Dukpa Kagyu lamas alike were popularly credited with fearsome powers. (Mme Blavatsky's 'dread Dad-Dugpa clan'[41] may well have been not the product of her fertile imagination, as sometimes alleged, but of her contact with Bhutanese lamas of the Dukpa Kagyu school.) Moreover, the Dorji family was not without enemies, both inside and outside Bhutan, and it was entirely feasible that someone who was unable or unwilling to attack it openly should have decided to have recourse to a weapon traditionally employed by the weak against the strong. If they believed that this was what had happened, and that Raja Dorji had indeed been killed by means of black magic, the Rani and her children would have had a sense of dark, destructive forces having been unleashed against them by they knew not whom. They would have felt that hovering above Bhutan House there was a black cloud, lightning from which had already struck down the head of the family and might at any moment strike down one or more of them.

The question of why Anand-ji had asked me to give the funeral sermon took longer to answer. Certainly he had not asked me to give it because of any incapacity on his own part; as I well knew, he was an accomplished speaker, in both Hindi and English, not to mention Sinhalese and his native Punjabi. Neither had he asked me, I felt sure, because I needed practice in the art of speaking, since he was aware I had quite enough of that anyway. Why then had he asked me, especially when his relegating the central role in an important religious ceremony to the juniormost monk present could have been seen as constituting a slight to the rich and powerful family at whose invitation that ceremony was being performed? Anand-ji must certainly have had a reason for so obvious a departure from protocol. Since he was very much my senior it would hardly have been in accordance with monastic etiquette for me to ask him point blank what that reason was, and though he was in the habit of taking me for long walks whenever he was in Kalimpong (he had been semi-resident in the town since early spring), and though he was friendly and communicative, I felt I did not yet know him well enough to be able to dispense with etiquette to that extent. But if I did not know him very well, I knew quite a lot about him. I knew about his studies at a monastic college in Ceylon, about his two years in the West, about his association with Kashyap-ji (with whom and Rahul Sankrityayana he had formed a famous trio), about his work as a translator of Pāli canonical texts and modern English novels, about his high-level involvement with the movement for the propagation of Hindi, the national language, and about his Communist sympathies. Anand-ji's was in fact a many-sided personality, and if I did not know him very well it was partly because it was difficult to tell which of his numerous activities and interests were more expressive of the 'real' Anand-ji or even whether there existed, behind them, a 'real' Anand-ji at all. Not surprisingly, different people saw him in different ways. The German pilgrim Hans-Ulrich Rieker, who had met him two or three years earlier in 'the great monastery of the Buddhist monks', as he terms the Maha Bodhi Society's Calcutta headquarters, describes him as having 'the glance of a wise and mature man' and as being 'adverse to trivialities', as well as being quiet and amiable and possessed of a fundamental conscientiousness.[42] (Mahanam-ji, whom he also met, is described, under the name of Kaccana, as attaching considerable importance to an elegant appearance and as leaving a trail of cheap perfume behind him wherever he went.) What struck me about Anand-ji, in the course of our long walks along the less frequented roads of Kalimpong, was his communicativeness (up to a point), his highly rationalistic approach to Buddhism, his ready wit, his proneness to mockery, and his profound cynicism. I also noticed that he had, in common with other cynics, a streak of sentimentality in his make-up, the beneficiaries of this weakness being his various young protégés. One of these had already spent a few weeks in Kalimpong with his patron, and at Anand-ji's request I had taken him to Darjeeling and had him admitted to the Government College, the principal of which happened to be a friend of mine. Two or three months later, and only a few days before the death of Raja Dorji, another of these protégés turned up, and it was from this young man that I eventually discovered why Anand-ji had asked me to give the funeral sermon instead of giving it himself.

Dinesh was small and slightly built, with dark brown skin, thick, wavy black hair, close-set brown eyes, a rather prominent nose, and a big, sensual mouth. Since the Newar monks at the Dharmodaya Vihara did not take kindly to the idea of their again having to accommodate one of Anand-ji's non-monastic protégés, my elder brother in the Sangha asked me if I would mind putting Dinesh up at The Hermitage for a while. I did not mind, especially as Dr Kajiyama had left and I now had no one staying with me except my diminutive young cook-bearer Man Bahadur. I already knew a little about Dinesh. Apparently he had once worked for Anand-ji, had gone to teach Hindi in a remote part of rural Assam, and had there got into serious trouble about which he had written to Anand-ji and on account of which, I recollected, Anand-ji had been extremely worried. What the trouble was he soon told me. He had fallen in love with one of his pupils, and she with him, and they had entered into a liaison. Unfortunately for them, the people of the village where he was teaching were Tais, and moral standards were extremely strict, with the result that when the liaison was discovered the girl's brothers tried to kill him and he had to flee for his life. He did not even have time to say goodbye to his beautiful Mynah-bird, as he called her, Mynah being the girl's actual name, and had spent several days and nights hiding in the jungle before being able to make his way back to civilization, Kalimpong, and Anand-ji.

The episode had given him a nasty shock. At one stroke he had lost his job, his mistress, and very nearly his life. But he was of cheerful disposition, and naturally resilient, and though he shed tears when he told me his story, and continued to shed them whenever he thought of his beautiful Mynah-bird, not many weeks had passed before the tears were mingled with laughter at his own foolishness and eventually they ceased altogether. When Anand-ji was in Kalimpong, and he was often away attending the meetings of a wide variety of progressive organizations down in the plains, Dinesh usually spent much of the day at the Dharmodaya Vihara helping him. Otherwise he stayed at The Hermitage, where he passed his time either reading or playing ping-pong with our younger

Dinesh (right) and friends outside The Hermitage

members, with several of whom, Sachin especially, he was soon on terms of friendship. When he had been with me for a month, and it had begun to look as though his stay was going to be prolonged indefinitely, it occurred to me that since he was, after all, a Hindi teacher, I might as well take advantage of his presence to improve my knowledge of that language. I had already made a start by practising my colloquial Hindi on him (he preferred practising his English on me), but I now wanted to study literary Hindi. The best way of doing this, we agreed, was for me to read a Hindi text with him and then translate it into English by myself, consulting him (and Bhargava's *Hindi–English Dictionary*) only when necessary. What better text could there be for me to read and translate than one of Anand-ji's writings? Eventually we chose his well-known *Bhikshu ke Patra* or 'Letters of a Buddhist Monk', a collection of essays on a variety of topics in epistolary form. This henceforth we read, and I translated, every morning straight after breakfast. From time to time Dinesh also read to me from a celebrated anthology of Urdu couplet poetry, reading first the Urdu originals and then the subjoined Hindi translations. Some of the couplets were so appealing that it was not long before I had learned them by heart. Many were, of course, on the subject of love (*ishq*). Anand-ji's 'Letters' proved to be less appealing. Mildly ironic in tone, it dealt with topics of general interest from the standpoint of a dilute rationalism only faintly tinged with Buddhism. The work was *patla*, Dinesh and I agreed; it was 'thin and weak', and after I had translated five essays we stopped reading it. If Anand-ji wanted to be known as the Voltaire of India, as he once told me he did, then *Bhikshu ke Patra* was not going to win him that particular laurel.

Since both Dinesh and I saw quite a lot of Anand-ji when he was in Kalimpong, and since we were reading one of his books together, it was only natural that his patron and my elder brother in the Sangha should be the subject of conversation between us. Dinesh had known Anand-ji for several years, and had a number of stories to tell about him, not all of them very creditable to the latter in his monastic capacity. One of his stories related to an incident that had taken place not long before he went to teach Hindi in Assam, and in which he himself had also been involved. Anand-ji had attended a meeting of the Association for the Advancement of the National Language at Indore with him and two other workers, and the four of them were travelling back to Wardha by the night train from Mhow. A few stations after Mhow the train suddenly stopped and was unable to proceed further. Investigation revealed that owing to a serious mistake by the pointsman the engine had run into the siding. What was more, beyond the heap of sand there was a drop of about two hundred feet, so that had the engine not been stopped by the sand the whole train would have plunged to the river below. The incident had given Anand-ji quite a fright, Dinesh told me. He was morbidly afraid of death, and did not like to talk about it or to hear it mentioned. He was even reluctant to attend funerals, which as a monk he was sometimes obliged to do.

Here, then, was the explanation of why Anand-ji had asked me to give the funeral sermon at Bhutan House instead of giving it himself. He had asked me to give it because in a sermon of this kind it was impossible to avoid speaking about death and death was a subject that made him feel extremely uneasy. Either because Dinesh told Anand-ji that he had related to me the story of their narrow escape from a watery grave, or because I myself happened to mention the incident when we were out walking, one day the subject of the fear of death came up between us, and Anand-ji told me about two similar incidents in which he had been involved. More than twenty years earlier, when he was studying in Ceylon, a train coming from behind had almost overtaken him as he was walking along the railway line one evening. Had he not leapt down onto the footpath at the last minute he would certainly have been killed. Four or five years later he made his first journey by air, flying from Bangkok to Rangoon. On its onward flight the plane on which he had travelled was struck by lightning and blew up in mid-air. These two incidents had given him a morbid fear of death, a fear which the third incident had served to exacerbate. Since my rationalistic friend seemed relieved to be able to talk about them, I suggested he should write an article describing the three occasions on which, as he believed, he had been 'about to enter the domain of Death'. This he eventually did, after a few reminders. Entitled 'On the Verge of Death', the article was published in the *Maha Bodhi*,[43] the Maha Bodhi Society's Journal of International Buddhist Brotherhood, of whose editorial board I had in the meantime become a member.

While it was natural that Anand-ji should be the subject of conversation between Dinesh and me, and natural that Dinesh should regale me with stories about his patron, it was even more natural that the young Hindi teacher should tell me about himself. He was an Untouchable, or rather, untouchability having been officially outlawed, an ex-Untouchable. A native of the then Madhya Pradesh,[44] he had been born into a very poor family (Untouchables were poor almost by definition), had received only a limited amount of education, had worked for Anand-ji when the latter was general secretary of the Association for the Advancement of the National Language, and had become a qualified teacher of Hindi. At one stage he had spent a couple of years in Bombay, that deceitful Mecca of the rural poor, making his living as an itinerant massage boy and in any other way that offered. It was as a result of hearing, in the course of that autumn, about Dinesh's experiences that I wrote the poem 'The Bodhisattva's Reply', with its vignettes of the prostitute and the massage boy, the exploited, robotic factory workers, and the despised early morning scavengers from the outcaste village.[45] The story of Dinesh's life had, in fact, moved me deeply, and given me a better understanding of the plight of India's ex-Untouchables who, despite legislation, were still being treated with inhuman cruelty by their caste Hindu compatriots and co-religionists. Three years later that understanding, for all its limitations, was to stand me in good stead when I came in contact with the newly converted ex-Untouchable Buddhists of Bombay and Nagpur and started working among them.

The fact that Dinesh spent much of the day at the Dharmodaya Vihara when Anand-ji was in Kalimpong, while Anand-ji himself often called at The Hermitage to take me for a walk and a talk, made for closer relations not just between Anand-ji and me but also between the two Buddhist establishments. Usually I did not go to the Dharmodaya Vihara. Before Anand-ji's appearance on the scene I had not set foot in the place for two years. My ten-month stay there had ended unpleasantly. Taking advantage of my absence in Sarnath, where I had gone to receive the higher ordination, the angry-looking Newar monk who had recently arrived from Kathmandu shut down YMBA activities at the Vihara, telling our members that the place did not belong to them and that they were not wanted there. *I* would be allowed to stay, he told me on my return, but I would have to pay him a hundred rupees a month for my room. This I could not do, and he therefore proceeded to act in such a manner as to force me out.[46] Thus I had painful memories of my last days at the Dharmodaya Vihara, and not wishing to revive them usually did not go there. By the time Anand-ji started making the place his headquarters, however, these memories had lost much of their sting, and I could revisit the scene of my tribulations with comparative equanimity. Relations between the Dharmodaya Vihara and The Hermitage were therefore closer now. One result of this development was that I was asked to speak at the Vihara's Vaiśākha celebrations, which were held the day after our own. Another was more surprising. Three months after the celebrations Aniruddha, the angry-looking Newar monk who had ousted me from the Dharmodaya Vihara, turned up at The Hermitage one morning and asked me to teach him English. If he did not quite remember how badly he had treated me, he must at least have had a vague recollection of his wanting a hundred rupees a month from me for my room, for he immediately added that his companion Mr Bhumiveda, who was staying with him at the Vihara and also wanted to study with me, would be paying tuition fees for them both.

For the next two months I taught the dour, choleric Newar monk and the plump, jolly, gold-toothed Thai layman almost daily, Aniruddha being the more painstaking of the two and Bhumiveda the brighter. At the end of that period Aniruddha had to discontinue his studies with me, as his presence was required in Lumbini. Bhumiveda continued to come. Not only did he continue to come. He asked me if in addition to teaching him English I would teach him Indian Philosophy, with the result that our lessons in English grammar and composition were from then on interspersed with discussions on Sankhya, Yoga, and the rest of the six (Hindu) classical systems. Bhumiveda was not interested in Buddhist philosophy. He was not even interested in Buddhism, though he had been born into a Buddhist family and treated Buddhist monks with all the deference that a well-brought-up Thai layman was expected to treat them with. Aniruddha had introduced him to me as a retired publicity officer, but as I got to know him better – and he was more communicative now that he came without Aniruddha – it transpired that he had been much more than that. He had in fact had quite a colourful career. Among other things he had been a surveyor, the superintendent of a jail, and the governor of a province. In this last capacity he had taken part in a *coup d'état*. He was one of those who had held a revolver to the head of the (unelected) prime minister and forced him to resign. (It was difficult to imagine Bhumiveda holding a revolver to anyone's head, but this is what he told me.) After the *coup d'état* he quarrelled with the prime minister's successor, whom he had helped to seize power, and was compelled to flee the country.

It was a familiar story. All over Buddhist South-east Asia politicians and others (not excluding monks) who were in trouble at home came to India on pilgrimage and lay low there until things had blown over and it was safe or politic to return. Doing the rounds of the holy places and making ceremonial food-offerings to the monks (if one was not a monk oneself) had the double advantage of earning merit and saving face. If one wished to promote a reputation for piety one might even 'take the robe' for a few weeks, not eating after midday or handling gold and silver, and undergoing other hardships. Bhumiveda had certainly not taken the robe, but since he was officially on pilgrimage he may have dropped in at a holy place or two. He had met Aniruddha in Calcutta, at the Maha Bodhi Society's headquarters, Aniruddha had invited him up to Kalimpong, and now here he was, paying much more than a hundred rupees a month for a room at the Dharmodaya Vihara, studying English and Indian Philosophy with me, and having a very good time. He was something of a hedonist. Calling on him at his room one morning, Dinesh and I found him sitting on the floor in his *lungi* surrounded by a dozen or more Thai gourmet dishes he had prepared and looking for all the world like a lay version of the Laughing Buddha.[47] Not that Kalimpong was able to satisfy all his fleshly wants. He had, I gathered, asked two or three of our younger members to show him where the town's brothels were, offering to pay for them too, and had been astonished by their embarrassment and astonished to learn that prostitution was virtually unknown in Kalimpong, at least among the Nepalese. What was wrong with the young men of the place, he wanted to know, and where on earth did they go in the evening?

If Bhumiveda wanted to study Indian Philosophy but not Buddhism or Buddhist philosophy, Bill Small wanted to study Buddhism but not Indian Philosophy. The latter was a tall, well built, fresh-faced young American from Shantiniketan who had arrived in Kalimpong at about the same time as Dinesh and was staying with Miss Barclay. He had not been with that lady for more than a month before the uncertainty, and withal the violence, of her temper became too much for him to bear. I therefore agreed to put him up at The Hermitage. This infuriated Miss Barclay, who in any case had been annoyed that I should go on teaching Bill after she had quarrelled with him. But I did not worry, as I was used to her ways and knew she would soon come round. Bill, for his part, now went in such terror of her that whenever she came to see me, which she quite frequently did, he kept well out of the way until she had gone. When he had been with me for less than a week, and I had given him a few more tutorials (he was writing a thesis on Buddhism for his MA) I received a visit from Father Eberhardt, who, not finding Bill at home, asked me to send him down to St Augustine's Priory as soon as possible. It was *very* urgent.

The following day Bill returned from the Priory white-faced and trembling. He would have to leave Kalimpong the next day. He had been very foolish. In his letters to his parents in America he had been highly critical of Pandit Nehru and of the policies of the Indian government. Now they had found out, and if he did not leave immediately, of his own accord, he would be ordered to leave and might not even be allowed to remain in India and finish his course at Shantiniketan. 'Get out right away, Bill!' Father Eberhardt had urged him. 'It's your *only* chance! They're *after* you!' The next day, therefore, the fresh-faced young American was gone. A couple of weeks later I told Joe what had happened. The lines of suspicion on the eccentric Canadian *upāsaka*'s gaunt features deepened. 'But how did Father Eberhardt know what was in Bill's letters?' he demanded after a pause. I had to admit I had not thought of that. Not long afterwards I heard that Joe had been seen paying one of his visits to Chandralok, the Central Intelligence Bureau's new regional headquarters, and sure enough, next time I saw him he had something to report. Father Eberhardt had an informant inside Chandralok, where, of course, all letters to and from foreign residents in Kalimpong were opened and read. The informant was a Catholic convert who whenever he visited the Priory, as he naturally did from time to time, passed on information to Father Eberhardt. *That* was how Father Eberhardt knew what was in Bill's letters. But why, I wondered, had the good father used his knowledge to scare Bill into leaving Kalimpong? Joe smiled superiorly. Bill was a Catholic by birth; he had visited the Priory a few times, and Father Eberhardt obviously feared that by studying Buddhism with me he was imperilling his immortal soul. There was never any question of his being ordered to leave Kalimpong on account of the foolish things he had written to his parents. The authorities were not as sensitive as all *that*. But this did not mean they were totally devoid of sensitivity. For one thing, they did not like foreign missionaries obtaining information through converts who worked for the Central Intelligence Bureau, and Father Eberhardt had been ordered to leave Kalimpong forthwith. As for the informant, *he* had disappeared.

What with Aniruddha and Bhumiveda, and Bill and the intellectual Narendra (who studied Western philosophy with me after Bill had left), besides two young Newar traders and a monk official from Tibet House, not to mention Sachin, during the latter part of the year I did quite a lot of teaching. I could have done much more. People of all ages and backgrounds would turn up at The Hermitage wanting me to take them on as pupils. Usually I had to refuse, either because they looked too dull to learn, or because we had no common language, or because I suspected them of thinking that if they studied English with an Englishman (it was English most of them wanted to study) they would acquire the language automatically, without having to make an effort themselves. One of those I refused was the round-faced young Newar nun from Kusinagar who had arrived in Kalimpong with Mahanam-ji and was staying with Gyan Jyoti and his family. Perhaps it was fortunate that I refused her. A month later she became very ill, and was found to be pregnant – not by Mahanam-ji, apparently, but by someone much higher up in the monastic hierarchy.

In between tutorials I wrote articles and poems, visited friends, and gave lectures and sermons, including funeral sermons. Funeral sermons in the plural not the singular, for towards the end of November there was another death and another funeral – not, indeed, of a personage as distinguished as Raja Dorji, but of someone who, to one person at least, was no less dear than Raja Dorji had been to his family. This was Miss Barclay's sixteen-year-old cat, whom she had brought with her from England. She had warned me the previous day that he was dying and that she would be bringing the body to The Hermitage for cremation. Now he was dead, and here was Miss Barclay coming up the path followed by Ang Tsering, the capable, cheerful Sherpa who had once worked for me and whom I had been sorry to lose.[48] Ang Tsering bore a wooden box and in the box was the body of Miss Barclay's cat. We cremated it at the bottom of the garden, the whole business taking about two hours, since there was not much wood and the body burned very slowly. As the flames leapt up I chanted some Pāli verses and spoke a few words about the deceased cat and about death and impermanence. Afterwards Miss Barclay went and did some shopping, returning from the bazaar an hour or two later to have lunch with Dinesh and me. She was less distressed by the death of her pet than I had expected. Perhaps she had been worried she might die before he did, and that after her death he would not be treated kindly or looked after properly. If that was the case, his dying in Kalimpong and being cremated with full Buddhist honours may well have come as a relief to her.

A few days after the death and cremation of Miss Barclay's cat I paid another visit to Darjeeling, once more staying at the Gandhamadan Vihara. The Burmese Maha Thera was no longer there, but the resident monk's *kuti* was not tenantless, being occupied (at least until my arrival) by a saffron-robed, though not shaven-headed, Miss Delannoy, now the *anagārika* Dharmarakshita. I had last seen the anxious-looking, rather exigent Frenchwoman two or three months earlier when, having been ordained in Calcutta by a Bengali monk, she had spent a few days in Kalimpong and I had given her letters of introduction to the Burmese Maha Thera, Kali Kinker Barua, and P. T. Lama. Now she was comfortably installed at the Gandhamadan Vihara, was studying Madhyamaka philosophy and Tibetan, and had already made a number of friends whom she wanted me to meet. Most of these friends were Hindus, and since like most Hindus they were convinced that the Buddha had *not* denied the existence of God and that Buddhism was in no way different from Hinduism, being in fact a part of it, meeting them involved me in more than one lengthy and rather inconclusive discussion. I also met a few of my own Hindu friends, one of whom was full of a Tantric yogi who had recently spent three weeks in the town, living at the cremation ground and using for his *asan* or seat the embalmed body of an eight-year-old girl. The main reason for my being in Darjeeling was to address a meeting organized by the Tamang Buddhist Association, and this I did on the day following my arrival, speaking on 'The Problem of Ahiṃsā' to an audience of more than a hundred people. The *anagārika* also spoke, describing how she had become a Buddhist after seeing an image of the Buddha in the Khmer gallery of the Musée Guimet.[49]

Darjeeling was not to be the last place I visited that year, nor the remotest. Early in December, when the poinsettia or 'Christmas red' was lifting its scarlet crowns by the wayside, Sachin and I left for Calcutta. With us went Bill, who had come up to Kalimpong for a couple of days to collect the colourful bamboo-and-thread 'spirit traps', each of them four feet in diameter, that he had ordered from a Nyingma lama before his hasty departure from the town at the end of October. Sachin and I had been planning to visit Calcutta for some time. I had work with the Maha Bodhi Society, while he had friends and relatives to see. We would be 'out of station' for five or six weeks, and on the way to Calcutta would be calling at Shantiniketan.

4
THE ABODE OF PEACE

The overnight journey from Siliguri to Manihari Ghat was not an enjoyable experience, especially if one's compartment happened to be crowded, as ours certainly was; but there was at least one compensation: the sight of the sun rising above the river as one crossed by paddle steamer from the northern to the southern bank of the Ganges to catch the connecting train a few miles downstream.

Sachin, Bill, and I had left Siliguri the previous evening, after making arrangements for the dispatch of the boxes containing Bill's 'spirit traps'. Dinesh saw us off. I felt a little uneasy at leaving him at The Hermitage with no companion save Man Bahadur, who in any case could not be relied on to spend much time at his place of work, since my young ex-Untouchable friend sometimes became depressed when he thought of the plight of his family in the plains and since, moreover, his Nepalese contemporaries did not always show him much consideration, one of them having in fact once struck him a blow that reduced him to tears. I therefore assured him that I would write to him regularly, and asked him to write to me. The inter-class compartment into which my two companions and I had managed to insert ourselves being so crowded, there was no question of our lying down for the night, at least not on the hard wooden seating, and Sachin and I therefore sat up throughout the journey while Bill, either more resourceful or less concerned about appearances, climbed up onto the luggage rack and stretched out there.

Though I had not had more than two hours' sleep, I felt not at all tired the following morning when, on our arrival at Manihari Ghat, we descended from the train and ploughed our way in semi-darkness through half a mile of soft, loose sand to the ferry, our red-shirted coolies preceding us with our luggage. As we embarked, the sun lifted his burning brow above the horizon and within minutes, as it seemed, there was a silver disc shining through the mist and lighting up the vast expanse of the river with a dull, leaden gleam. Half an hour later, when we were in midstream and out of sight of land, the silver disc, breaking free of the mist and the banks of low cloud, turned to a disc of burnished gold that glittered down at us from above the twin funnels of the ferry out of a sky immaculately blue. So brightly did it eventually glitter that it was no longer possible to look at it, and I turned away to gaze out over the waters of the Ganges, now jewel-bespangled, and to listen to the sound of the giant paddle-wheels churning their way through the turbid water. With four or five hundred other souls I was suspended between two mighty elements, those of water and air, a third element, fire, being represented by the sun that shone so fiercely upon us.

Hardly had we reached Sakaligali Ghat, after spending two hours on the ferry, than our ears were assaulted by a continuous hollow drumming sound so loud that it almost drowned the cries of passengers disembarking. The sound came from beneath our feet; it came from the lower deck of the ferry – came from the madly pounding feet of the hundreds of red-shirted figures who, as soon as the vessel came alongside, stampeded on board, swarmed up the stairways, and rushed to stake a claim to the luggage of the first, second, and inter-class passengers (third class passengers generally carried their own luggage), it being understood that the first coolie to lay hands on one's bundles and boxes had the right to be engaged to carry them. I did not always respect this convention, usually preferring to ignore the younger, more active coolies in favour of their older colleagues, who though slower were more reliable, and on this occasion too probably followed my rule. Be that as it may, we were soon off the ferry and into the train, which proved to be less crowded than the one in which we had spent the first part of our journey, so that we were able to watch the unfolding panorama of the Bengal countryside, with its lotus ponds, mud huts, and groves of coconut palms, from a position of comparative comfort. On our arrival at Bolpur, we took a broken-down old taxi to Shantiniketan, where Sachin and I were soon installed in the guest house.

Shantiniketan means 'the Abode of Peace', and situated as it was in the heart of rural (West) Bengal the place certainly deserved the name. I had first heard that name in 1945 when, still in the army and stationed in Calcutta, I had been in the habit of spending as much of my off-duty time as I could at the Ramakrishna Mission Institute of Culture, where it was possible to meet some of the most distinguished members of the city's Bengali intelligentsia. When, having heard the name of the place two or three times, I enquired of my friend Kantaraj, the diminutive Ramakrishna Order swami who worked at the Institute, what sort of place Shantiniketan was, he mischievously replied that it was an educational institution where they turned boys into girls and girls into boys, meaning by this that the school's 'artistic' atmosphere had the effect of rendering the male students effeminate and the female ones mannish. During the next few years I continued to hear the name of Shantiniketan, the Abode of Peace, usually in connection with the fine arts or in a way that suggested it was a kind of Bengali counterpart to the British arts and crafts movement. Since my arrival in Kalimpong I had heard it more often than ever, mainly due to the presence in the town, during the summer months, of Pratima Devi, the niece and daughter-in-law of Rabindranath Tagore, the founder of Shantiniketan, who since the latter's death in 1941 had been mainly responsible for keeping alive the flame of his vision for the place and with whom I became quite well acquainted, she being prior to my removal to The Hermitage virtually my next-door neighbour.[50] 'Oh you *must* visit Shantiniketan!' she had insisted, as though Shantiniketan was the very Mecca not only of Bengali but of world culture. My friends Lama Govinda and Li Gotami[51] had sung the same siren song (they had come to know each other when he was a professor there and she a student), and it seemed I had no alternative but to visit the place sooner or later. Hence, my work with the Maha Bodhi Society calling for another visit to Calcutta, I had decided that this time I would spend a few days at Shantiniketan *en route*.

Started by Tagore at the turn of the century as an experimental school with five pupils and five teachers, Shantiniketan had developed into 'a centre of Indian culture, a seminary of Eastern studies, and a meeting place for the East and the West',[52] though without altogether losing its rural character and without growing too big for it to be possible for everybody to know everybody else. Visva-Bharati, or 'Universal India', as the great Bengali poet had called his miniature world university, included an art school and a music school, a technical institute and a handicrafts department, as well as a school of Sinology, all of which I visited in the course of the next few days and in all of which I met interesting people, both Indian and non-Indian. The first person I met after my arrival, however, apart from some young Bengali friends of Bill's, was Mme Combastet, the elderly, *soignée* Frenchwoman to whom I had given English lessons in Kalimpong earlier in the year. Other Western women might go around in saris and *shalwa-kameez*, but Mme Combastet stuck firmly to her Parisian fashions and looked, indeed, much more ready for a walk down the Champs-Elysées than for a stroll in rural Bengal. Despite her sartorial intransigence she was, it seemed, a popular, even an influential figure around the place, perhaps not least because she was in the habit (as I had noticed in Kalimpong) of assuring her Bengali friends that just as the French were the aristocrats of the West so the Bengalis were the aristocrats of the East. At any rate, she was influential enough to be able to suggest that before leaving Shantiniketan I should give a lecture. I should give it at Cheena Bhavan, as the school of Sinology was called – which on the penultimate day of my visit I did. Not surprisingly, I chose for my subject 'Buddhism and Art'.

Pratima Devi being then in residence at Uttarayan, the house in which Tagore himself had lived, I naturally lost no time in calling on her. The sweet, dignified old lady was delighted to see me in her beloved Shantiniketan, and as usual treated me with great kindness and consideration. Though it was as a poet and novelist that he was known to the world, having been awarded the Nobel Prize in Literature in 1913, towards the end of his long life Tagore had produced a series of extraordinary paintings and drawings; some of these were on display at Uttarayan, and when we had talked for a while Pratima Devi showed them to me, after which she took me for a stroll round the house's beautiful gardens. I also called on Dr and Mrs Liebenthal, who were then staying at Uttarayan, as well as on Professor and Mrs North, whom I had already met in Kalimpong, Professor North having in fact given a talk at The Hermitage on 'English Literature'. There were also visits to Cheena Bhavan, where I met Shantibhikshu Shastri and his wife, and

Professor Tan Yun-Shan. The first was a Buddhist, a scholar in Sanskrit and Tibetan, and a former *bhikkhu*. Not only was he a former *bhikkhu*. He was married to a former nun, and at the conclusion of our initial meeting he and Sujata invited me to have lunch with them a couple of days later. Both were very glad to see me and relieved to be able to talk about themselves without restraint. As I well knew, within the reformist Theravādin community to which they technically belonged (he was a caste Hindu convert, she a Newar by birth) the position of a former *bhikkhu* or a former nun was a difficult one, and if the former *bhikkhu* and the former nun happened to be married to each other their position was doubly and trebly difficult. Shantibhikshu, who was very much the older of the two, was obviously not yet quite comfortable in his new role. Despite his layman's white shirt and dhoti, his manner was still very much that of the bachelor scholar, even of the scholar-monk. Sujata, on the other hand, had adjusted perfectly to the change, and was evidently overjoyed to be married. With her bobbed hair, short Western-style frock, and heavy make-up, she not only exuded satisfaction but was led to remark, in the course of our discussion, that there were others who were thinking of taking the step she and Shantibhikshu had taken. From what I knew of some of the younger Newar nuns I could well believe this to be the case, though I doubted if many of them would be able to find a former *bhikkhu* as highly qualified as Shantibhikshu and in as good a position to support them, therefore, as he was to support her. In India and Nepal, as in Sri Lanka, a former *bhikkhu* was unlikely to be as well off financially as a *bhikkhu*. Consequently few *bhikkhus* disrobed, even when they no longer had – if they had ever had – a real vocation for the monastic life.

Professor Tan Yun-Shan wore the traditional black dress of the Chinese scholar, complete with black skullcap. He had been at Cheena Bhavan since its earliest days, having in fact been responsible for starting the school and being, even now, the moving spirit behind the place. He had started it with the support of General Chiang Kai-shek and his Kuomintang government. With the defeat of Chiang and the Nationalist forces by the Communists in 1949, and the former's withdrawal to Taiwan, Professor Tan had lost that support, and the nature of Cheena Bhavan's position in relation to the government of the People's Republic, the armies of which had recently invaded Buddhist Tibet, was unclear. Indeed, like that of many overseas Chinese, Professor Tan's own position was unclear, not to say ambiguous, it being rumoured that the new regime in Peking wanted to replace Chiang Kai-shek's protégé with a nominee of their own. Naturally nothing was said of all this in the course of our meeting. Professor Tan showed me the Bhavan's collection of Chinese books, the centrepiece of which, at least in my eyes, was the Taishō edition of the Chinese Tripiṭaka, the one hundred thick, closely printed red volumes of which were said to contain more than 1,600 separate Buddhist texts, both canonical and extra-canonical. The following day I had tea with him, and he showed me his house and garden, which he evidently had tried to make as much like the traditional Chinese scholar's house and garden as Indian conditions permitted. Professor Tan had, it seemed, put down roots in the land of his adoption, and it was not going to be easy for China's new masters to dislodge him.

But interesting as I found the scholars of Shantiniketan, including some whose names I have forgotten, I found the artists and poets more interesting still. They were quite a mixed bunch. There was the famous sculptor Ramkinkar, a stocky, grizzled figure in rumpled Western-style shirt and trousers whom I met at Kala Bhavan, the school of art, and with whom I talked at some length. Like many educated Bengalis, he was interested in Buddhism, at least to the extent that Buddhism was part of Indian culture, and I had already seen the figure of the meditating Buddha that he had created in the Kala Bhavan grounds. Considerably larger than life, its rough, 'unfinished' surface texture reminded me of that of some of Epstein's later work, especially his portrait busts. Ashok Raha, with whom I also talked at some length, was by vocation a Bengali poet and by profession a teacher of English literature. We talked mainly about Shelley, for whom he expressed great admiration. His admiration did not surprise me. I knew that most Indian aficionados of English poetry favoured the Romantics, Shelley in particular, and that the youthful Tagore himself had been hailed by his fellow Bengalis as the Bengali Shelley. While I certainly did not regard Shelley as the greatest of English poets, as some Indians did, I too admired and loved him, and my conversation with Ashok Raha, bringing back as it did memories of my ecstatic adolescent reading and rereading of *Adonais*, *Prometheus Unbound*, and *Epipsychidion*, had the effect of reviving my interest in the poet and making me resolve that as soon as I reached Calcutta I would buy his poems and read them all again. Meanwhile,

Ashok-da lent me his own copy of the Oxford edition of the complete poetical works, which he recommended as the best available, containing as it did Mary Shelley's notes and prefaces, so that late that night, while Sachin was out with Bill and his young friends, I had the satisfaction of renewing my acquaintance with the poet in the appropriately romantic surroundings of Shantiniketan.[53]

Though at Shantiniketan, as elsewhere, Indian aficionados of English poetry tended to favour the Romantics, the Victorians were by no means neglected. Collecting Sachin from a meeting one afternoon, after fulfilling a couple of engagements of my own, I found some of Browning's poems being recited extremely well,[54] with great feeling, without any of the mimetics which Bengalis seemed to think appropriate when reciting – or rather declaiming – poetry in their own language. Whether or not twentieth-century English poetry was neglected at Shantiniketan I did not stay long enough to find out. But I did meet a twentieth-century English – or rather a twentieth-century American – poet in the course of my visit. This was John Berry, who not surprisingly was a friend of Bill's and whom Bill, in fact, took me to see. The twentieth-century poet lived in a very un-twentieth-century mud hut, and with him, too, I had a long talk. He did not show me any of his poetry, but before Bill and I left he sang for our benefit, to the guitar, two songs that may have been of his own composition.

Besides artists and poets, during the five or six days Sachin and I spent in the Abode of Peace I also met, as though for good measure, a popular novelist. This was Annada Shankar Ray, a sophisticated figure in a dark Western-style suit who occupied, as it seemed, some kind of official position and who was the author of a number of satirical novels in Bengali. He was married, not surprisingly, to a Western woman, an American who, again not surprisingly, was a translator of Bengali fiction and poetry. The name of Leela Ray was in fact almost as well known as that of her husband, and the pair were the centre, in Shantiniketan at least, of a cosmopolitan literary circle consisting mainly of anglicized Bengalis and European and American expatriates, some of whom had, like themselves, married across the racial and cultural divide. Thus it was only natural that on the eve of my departure Leela Ray, who knew me as a contributor to the *Aryan Path* and other magazines, should give a tea party for me, a tea party at which I saw both people whom I had met already and people whom I had not met. It was on this occasion,

I think, that Kshitish Roy, the translator of some of Tagore's poetry, whom I had not met before, invited me to contribute to the *Visva-Bharati Quarterly*, of which he was editor.

All too soon our visit to Shantiniketan was over, and after a hasty lunch Sachin and I were bowling along the road to Bolpur in cycle rickshaws to catch the Calcutta Mail, the very train from which we had descended less than a week earlier. Bill came with us to the station to see us off. Despite my having so many other people to see, the fresh-faced young American and I had managed to spend a fair amount of time together, discussing, among other things, Professor Burtt's comments on his thesis, which was now complete. He also took the opportunity of sharing some of his worries with me. One of these related to an incident which had taken place some weeks earlier and caused him considerable distress. Like most Westerners in Shantiniketan, he slept under a mosquito net. One night the mosquitoes were particularly numerous and persistent, and seeing how grievously his young servant, who slept on the floor of the same room, was being tormented by them, he democratically invited the boy to join him under the mosquito net, which the boy very thankfully did. Next morning a Bengali woman, happening to pass by, saw through the window a slim brown form emerging from beneath the mosquito net and from Bill's bed, with the result that within hours the news that the American student was sleeping with his young servant had spread through the campus. He had *not* slept with the boy, Bill assured me, almost with tears in his eyes, not in the sense that anything had actually *happened* between them, and I had no difficulty believing him. None the less, it was obvious that Bill had a decided liking for teenage boys and spent a good deal of time in their company, his particular favourite being Alok, a golden-skinned eighteen-year-old Adonis who seemed to be as fond of Bill as Bill was attached to him. Bill's greatest fear, now that his thesis was completed and he was due to return to America, was that something might happen to prevent Alok joining him in New York, as they had planned he should, there to finish his education. If *that* happened, he told me, as we sat side by side in the rickshaw on our way to Bolpur (Sachin was in another rickshaw with the bulk of our luggage) he did not know what he would do. He was *very* fond of Alok.... Whether he actually confessed to being in love with the young Bengali I do not remember, but after a long pause he sighed wearily and said, half to himself, 'I guess I must be homosexual.'

I did not know what to reply, if reply indeed was needed. The truth was that I knew little more about homosexuality than what I had gleaned, ten or twelve years ago, from the pages of Havelock Ellis's *The Psychology of Sex*,[55] and in any case doubted, *pace* Freud, whether a strong emotional attraction to a member of one's own sex necessarily meant that one was sexually oriented in the same direction. Moreover, this was the first time that anyone had told me, in so many words, even that he 'must be' homosexual, and my silence was due as much to embarrassment as ignorance.

It was therefore in silence that Bill and I covered the rest of the distance to Bolpur, where we found Ashok-da waiting at the station and where, a few minutes later, Sachin and I said our goodbyes and boarded the train. On the first stage of our 300-mile rail journey, that from Siliguri to Manihari Ghat, I had passed the time talking to a friend of Sachin's who happened to get into the same compartment. Now, on the last stage of that journey, the time was shortened by a long conversation with a ticket-inspector who was interested in Buddhism, so that when, three and a half hours after our departure from Bolpur, the train clanked its way through the sordid northern suburbs of Calcutta and into Sealdah Station, I was surprised to see that we were already there. The station was not a pretty sight. Encamped along the broad platforms, between the iron pillars, the stacks of wooden crates, and the refreshment kiosks, as well as outside in the station forecourt, were thousands, perhaps tens of thousands, of refugees from the former East Bengal, all living in conditions of the utmost wretchedness and degradation.[56] Some of the earlier arrivals had contrived to build shelters out of gunny bags, flattened kerosene tins, and bits of cardboard, and from most of these, of which there must have been hundreds in the forecourt, there fluttered the red flag of Communism, Communist Party cadres having done more to relieve the sufferings of the refugees, apparently, than had the Congress state government, and being in fact very active among them. With the help of the young men from the Maha Bodhi Society office who had been sent to meet us, we pushed through the throng of passengers, both arriving and departing, hawkers, refugees, and beggars, and ten minutes later were being deposited outside the pink sandstone façade of the Sri Dharmarajika Vihara[57] and the taxi driver was doing his best to overcharge me. As I usually did on such occasions, I left the tall, formidable *durwan* or gatekeeper to settle with him on my behalf and, followed by Sachin, made my way down the side of the Vihara to the three-storey building that was the Society's headquarters. Here we were greeted by Devapriya Valisinha, the general secretary of the Society, and others who were known to me, both monks and laymen, assigned our quarters (my old room on the second floor), and served very strong tea in cups of very thick white china. We then went out, on foot – out into the hustle and bustle that was Calcutta at five o'clock in the afternoon or, indeed, at almost any hour of the day or night.

After the sightseeing and socializing of Shantiniketan I would have been content to spend the evening quietly, perhaps with a book, but Sachin, who had not been to Calcutta before, was eager to see the bright lights of the big city. For him, as for so many young hillmen, Calcutta represented freedom, represented opportunity, represented excitement – represented, in short, Life with a capital L, and apart from New York (a distant, impossible dream) there was no place on earth that he, like them, was more desirous of seeing. Moreover, he was anxious to meet his relatives and since some of them lived in central Calcutta, a part of the city with which I was reasonably familiar, he wanted me to accompany him and help him locate the place. Having drunk our tea, out into the evening air we therefore went, cutting across College Square, with its crumbling statues of bygone dignitaries, into College Street, and going along College Street, past the butchers' stalls and the sweetmeat shops, as far as Wellington Square, famous venue of political meetings, where, turning right, we pursued our course down Dharamtala Street to the Esplanade and Chowringhee, all the while taking good care, whenever we were forced off the crowded pavement, to avoid the single-decker double tramcars that, every few minutes, came clanging and swaying along, all full and all with scores of passengers hanging on outside.

From Chowringhee we did not have very far to go to Hindustan Building, a solidly built, rather gloomy pile situated in the midst of dingy side streets. Sachin's relatives, who comprised two separate households occupying adjacent flats on the second floor, were delighted to see him and made me, too, very welcome. There were quite a lot of them, especially in the form of aunts and female cousins, besides several small children. In the course of the next few weeks I accompanied Sachin to Hindustan Buildings a number of times, and got to know the occupants of one flat quite well. Some of them, indeed, visited us at the Maha Bodhi Society, and one, an unmarried school teacher who was always referred to, even within the family, as Miss Singh, as though she was a school teacher even at home, became seriously interested in Buddhism and attended my lectures. During this first visit, however, they naturally were a little shy of me, Hari-didi bringing tea to me in the front room while Sachin was being entertained in the rooms behind. On our way back to the Maha Bodhi Society, two hours later, my companion and I looked into the bookshops in Dharamtala Street, these being still open, as were most shops. Not only were the shops open, the streets were full of people and there was plenty of noise. Even after I had gone to bed the roar of traffic, punctuated by the sound of human voices raised in anger or supplication, could still be heard, and it was a long time before I was able to sleep. If Shantiniketan was the Abode of Peace, I reflected as I lay there, surely Calcutta was the City of Dreadful Noise.

But Calcutta was not only the City of Dreadful Noise. It was also the city of palaces, most of them now in ruins, and the city of (mainly political) processions, of which there were said to be more than 300 a year. It was the city of Kali and Saraswati,[58] of Clive and Siraj ud-Daulah,[59] of William Carey and Warren Hastings,[60] of Thackeray and Macaulay,[61] of Sri Ramakrishna and Swami Vivekananda,[62] of the Tagores and the Mullicks.[63] It was the city of Governor-Generals and Viceroys, of museums and learned societies, of the Victoria Memorial and the Ochterlony Monument,[64] of the Hindu Mahasabha and the Muslim League,[65] of students and workers. For me, of course, Calcutta was the city of Anagarika Dharmapala and the Maha Bodhi Society, with the Sri Dharmarajika Vihara and the headquarters building constituting, in my eyes, a tiny island of Buddhism in the midst of the vast ocean of Hinduism, an ocean in which there were only two or three other islands, each one tinier than that whereon I was encamped. Literally, and even, to an extent, metaphorically, my life in Calcutta centred on the Society. Attractive and interesting though the city might be, the Society was my base, and it was from this base that I went out and to which I returned.

5
AMONG THE UNIVERSALISTS

My connection with the Maha Bodhi Society went back to the early months of 1947, when shortly after discharging myself from the army I stayed for a month or more at the headquarters building and helped with office work. The sun was setting on the Raj. Lord Mountbatten had just succeeded Lord Wavell as Viceroy, and the date for the handover of power to an independent India – and an independent Pakistan – was soon to be advanced to midnight of 14 August. During the war years the Society had kept a low profile, mainly on account of its pre-war links with Japan, but even though hostilities had now ceased the shabby, neglected headquarters building showed little sign of renewed religious activity. The Sinhalese *bhikkhu*-in-charge, who insisted on being styled His Holiness the High Priest, spent more time dabbling in municipal politics than in spreading the Dharma, so that eventually, disgusted with the worldly, unspiritual atmosphere of the place, I left Calcutta in the hope of finding less arid pastures elsewhere. Not surprisingly, I left with a decidedly negative impression of the Maha Bodhi Society.[66]

This impression was reinforced two years later at Sarnath, the site of the Buddha's 'first sermon', when having spent the intervening period as a freelance wandering ascetic I asked the *bhikkhus* who ran the Society's centre there for ordination as a novice monk. My request was not only turned down with flimsy excuses that were no better than lies. I was treated with suspicion and hostility and made to feel that anyone who went barefoot and refrained from handling money, as I then did, must be out of his mind.[67] None the less, a year and a half later those same *bhikkhus* were happily participating in my higher ordination,[68] while I myself was staying, on my way to Sarnath from Kalimpong, as well as on the way back, at the Calcutta headquarters building. The fact was that the Maha Bodhi Society was effectively the only Buddhist organization in India, so that if one was in any way concerned with the revival of Buddhism in the land of its birth one could hardly avoid being involved with it. Moreover, Devapriya Valisinha, the general secretary of the Society, had recently returned to Calcutta from Ceylon, where he had spent the war years, and with his arrival on the scene the Society had begun to emerge from its state of suspended animation. Soon he and I were in correspondence, and I had not only organized the reception given by the Buddhists of Kalimpong to the Sacred Relics of Śāriputra and Maudgalyāyana, which Valisinha had recovered from the Victoria and Albert Museum, but had been invited to join the delegations accompanying the relics to Sikkim and Nepal.[69] Finally, Valisinha had asked me to write a biographical sketch of Anagarika Dharmapala, the founder of the Maha Bodhi Society, for inclusion in the Diamond Jubilee Souvenir that he was planning to bring out, and during the autumn of the previous year I had spent several weeks with him in Calcutta for this purpose.

The writing of the biographical sketch brought about a change in my connection with the Society – indeed in my attitude towards it. Before writing the sketch I knew little more about Dharmapala than that he was a Sinhalese, that he had sought to wrest the Maha Bodhi Temple at Bodh Gaya, the site of the Buddha's Enlightenment, from Hindu ownership and control, and that besides reviving Sarnath as a centre of Buddhist pilgrimage he had succeeded in awakening interest in Buddhism among a section of the English-educated intelligentsia, especially in Calcutta. But as I went through his diaries, and read the articles he had written for early issues of the *Maha Bodhi* journal, I came to realize that Dharmapala was not just an organizer and activist, as I hitherto had supposed, but also a yogi and ascetic with an intense inner life. I came to realize, too, that the Maha Bodhi Society I had encountered in 1947, and even later, bore little resemblance to the Maha Bodhi Society that had existed in Dharmapala's time and that could, with Valisinha's arrival on the scene, conceivably exist again. Moreover, I had observed, in the course of my two months at the headquarters building (the longest period I had yet spent there) that a covert and unacknowledged struggle for control of the Society was going on between Valisinha and his supporters on the one hand, and on the other Jinaratana, the High Priest, and the opportunist elements he had introduced into the Society, and even into its governing body, during Valisinha's prolonged absence in Ceylon. As Dharmapala's personal disciple and recognized successor, as well as general secretary for life, Valisinha was probably in the stronger position, but Jinaratana's resourcefulness and cunning were not to be underestimated. I therefore decided to throw my weight, such as it was, into the balance on the side of the *real* Maha Bodhi Society and give Valisinha whatever help and support I could.

The result was that on my return to Kalimpong the Young Men's Buddhist Association (India), which I had founded in 1950, became the Kalimpong branch of the Maha Bodhi Society, with me as *bhikṣu*-in-charge, while the following autumn Valisinha wrote inviting me to move down to Calcutta and relieve him of the burden of editing the *Maha Bodhi* journal. I was willing to relieve him of his burden. I was not willing to move down to Calcutta. Further correspondence ensued. In the end it was agreed that I should edit the monthly from Kalimpong, but that I should come down to Calcutta and bring out my first two numbers from there. This would enable Valisinha to hand over to me properly, besides enabling us to work out the logistics of producing a magazine that was being edited in a place 300 miles away from the place where it was printed, published, and distributed. Thus it was that I came to be visiting Calcutta again, this time with Sachin, and again staying at the headquarters building, in the same corner room in which, a year earlier, I had written my biographical sketch.

My companion and I were not long in settling into a sort of routine. We had breakfast together, sometimes at a restaurant – the Society's standard breakfast of tea and two slices of toast being not always sufficiently substantial if one had been fasting since noon the previous day, as I at least had been – after which I saw Sachin onto a bus or tram and returned to the headquarters building. In the evening, if he was back in time from whichever of his relatives he had been visiting that day, we went out for a stroll, lingering over the second-hand bookstalls and finishing up, more often than not, in a restaurant where he could have a non-vegetarian meal and I a cup of very indifferent coffee. During the day I read, wrote letters, and worked on the proposals for the improvement of the *Maha Bodhi* journal which, at Valisinha's suggestion, I had started drafting. Some days there was a puja or other religious ceremony to attend in the temple, as it was called, which occupied the first floor of the Sri Dharmarajika Vihara and was connected with the corresponding floor of the headquarters building by a little covered bridge. When I wanted a change from reading and writing I talked to the other occupants of the building, especially to my brother monks, most of whom I met in any case at our ante-meridian lunch, which in accordance with (Theravādin) custom we took separately from the laity.

Dhammaratana and Soratha, who both came from Ceylon, were already known to me, as was the Bengali monk Silabhadra. Dhammaratana's dark face always wore an apologetic smile. Quiet and studious by nature, and as sluggish in movement as he was slow of speech, he was a member of the editorial board of the *Maha Bodhi* journal and sometimes helped with proof-reading. Though he had been a monk for twenty or more years, he was still technically a novice, and for reasons I never succeeded in fathoming steadfastly refused to take the higher ordination that would make him a *bhikkhu*. Soratha, who was much better known to me, was a very different kind of person. Bright-eyed and bustling, and so small that he was known as the Little Monk, he was as talkative as Dhammaratana was taciturn, a great reader of Sinhalese newspapers, and a science student at one of the local colleges. 'Does an amoeba have karma?' he had asked me, the first time we met, to which I replied, 'Does an amoeba have consciousness (*cetanā*)?' and such exchanges had since become customary between us. I enjoyed his company more than I did that of the other monks, the more especially as he was a mine of information about Ceylon and Sinhalese Buddhism. Silabhadra, whom I knew only slightly, had taken the robe late in life after a career at the bar. Even now there was, I sometimes thought, more of the lawyer about him than the *bhikkhu*.

A monk I had not met before was Aniruddha, only son of wealthy, string-pulling Mrs Moonasinghe (a lady whose ambition it was to paint the Maha Bodhi Temple at Bodh Gaya bright yellow), and great-nephew of Anagarika Dharmapala. Though it was rumoured that he was being groomed to succeed Valisinha as general secretary, the tall, almost hulking young man showed no sign of harbouring any such aspirations or even of taking much interest in the affairs of the Society.

Quiet and unassuming, he showed greater interest in making friends not just with me but also with Sachin, and more than once accompanied us to Hindustan Building, where he soon was so much at home with Sachin's aunts and female cousins that I started wondering if he was not better suited to family life than to monastic life. Perhaps it was a case of the mother seeking to realize her spiritual, or at least her socio-religious, ambitions through the son.

The only brother monk to whom I did *not* talk when I wanted a change from reading and writing, though I had known him longer than I had known anyone else in the building, was Jinaratana, the High Priest. Nor did he go out of his way to talk to me. The reappearance, as a member of the monastic order, of the same young Englishman who had been the witness of some of his unmonklike, not to say un-Buddhist, behaviour back in 1947,[70] had given him a nasty jolt, and though I was careful not to allude to the past, and though in the course of my previous visit much of the awkwardness between us had been dispelled, he was still not quite at ease with me. He may even have remembered telling me, on more than one occasion, 'You'll see. Within two years I shall be general secretary of the Society.' Whether he remembered or not, he was still only one of the two joint secretaries (the other was *bhikkhu*-in-charge of the society's Sarnath centre) and no nearer to the general secretaryship than he had been six years earlier. If anything, he was further from it than ever. Contrary to his expectations, Valisinha had returned; he had returned and stayed, and during the twelve months that had elapsed since my last visit Dharmapala's conscientious, hard-working disciple and successor, besides strengthening his position relative to that of the aspiring High Priest, had contrived to bring about certain changes in the Society – changes that went some way towards making it a more truly Buddhist organization. The biggest change was one whose significance was largely symbolic. As I was already aware, six months earlier the Society had acquired a new president. What was more, the new president was a Buddhist.

That a Buddhist society should have a Buddhist president might seem nothing out of the ordinary. Surely it was axiomatic that such a society – especially one that had been founded expressly to revive Buddhism in India, and whose journal had for masthead the Buddha's exhortation to his disciples to go forth and preach the Dharma – would no more have a non-Buddhist for president than a Christian religious body would have a non-Christian at the helm of its affairs or a Muslim religious body a non-Muslim. In the case of the Maha Bodhi Society it was apparently *not* axiomatic. The three previous presidents of the Society, whose tenures between them covered a period of nearly forty years, had all been Bengali Brahmins, the third being in fact the son of the first. Some Buddhists and sympathizers with Buddhism outside the Society were surprised, even outraged, by such a state of affairs. 'Why does your Maha Bodhi Society have a Bengali Brahmin for its president?' the ex-Untouchable leader Dr Ambedkar had demanded, belligerently, in the course of our first meeting only a year earlier.[71] Himself an ex-Untouchable, Bhimrao Ramji Ambedkar had spent a lifetime fighting to liberate his people from the social, economic, and religious disabilities imposed upon them by the caste Hindus, particularly the Brahmins, and to him it was incredible that an organization dedicated to spreading the teachings of the Compassionate One should have a Brahmin for its president. Adding insult to injury, from his point of view, was the fact that the Society's Bengali Brahmin president, Syama Prasad Mookerjee, was also president of the Bharatiya Jana Sangh, a right-wing Hindu political party, and an old political opponent of his. I had therefore hastened to assure him that it was not *my* Maha Bodhi Society. Though happy to help the Society in whatever way I could (I had just written my biographical sketch of Anagarika Dharmapala), I did not actually belong to it, mainly on account of its having a Brahmin for president and because its governing body was dominated by caste Hindus who had no real interest in Buddhism. Moreover, some of the Buddhist members of the Society were as dissatisfied with the present state of affairs as he was and both they and I hoped that before long we would have an opportunity of doing something about it.

The opportunity had come sooner than I, or Ambedkar, or anyone else could have expected. In May Syama Prasad Mookerjee, who was opposed to the Congress government's policy in Jammu and Kashmir, entered the state without a permit, was arrested and held in custody, fell ill a month later, and died the day after being admitted to hospital. This dramatic development left the Maha Bodhi Society in need of a new president. There were two candidates. One was the Maharaj Kumar, or Crown Prince, of Sikkim, who was a Mahāyāna Buddhist. The other was Dr Sarvepalli Radhakrishnan, Vice-President of India and historian of Indian philosophy, who was a Telegu Brahmin from Andhra.

Canvassing was vigorous, with the Buddhist members of the governing body tending to support the Maharaj Kumar's candidature, while their Hindu colleagues tended to support that of Dr Radhakrishnan – partly because he was a Hindu, admittedly a very scholarly one, and partly on account of his occupying high political office. Valisinha was determined that the Maharaj Kumar should be elected, and to this end had recourse to a tactic which, though perfectly constitutional, had not been tried before and which no one would, in fact, have credited the normally shy, retiring little general secretary with possessing either the imagination to devise or the boldness to execute. The tactic was based on the fact that the *bhikkhus* working for and supported by the Society, of whom there were hardly more than a dozen in the whole of India, were *ipso facto* members of the governing body. Normally they did not attend its meetings. They did not attend them because they could not afford to do so on the pittance they received from the Society, and because the governing body, or rather its Hindu-dominated rump, the members of which all lived in Calcutta, refused to pay their travelling expenses. What Valisinha did was write to the *bhikkhus* urging them to attend the crucial meeting at which the new president was to be elected, and undertaking to meet their travelling expenses out of his own pocket (the exercise had cost him two thousand rupees, he told me with a rueful smile, and he would not be able to repeat it). Figures in varying shades of yellow and orange were therefore able to descend on Calcutta from Sarnath, Bombay, Delhi, Madras, and elsewhere, to attend the crucial meeting, and to vote for the Maharaj Kumar, with the result that – Buddhists being for once in the majority – the Society now had a president who was a Buddhist. The only yellow-robed figure not to vote for the Maharaj Kumar was Jinaratana.

Accustomed as they were to having things their own way, the Hindu members of the governing body, save for two or three non-Bengalis who were friends and supporters of Valisinha's, were shocked and dismayed by their failure to secure the election of Dr Radhakrishnan. They had been as determined to secure his election as Valisinha had been to secure that of the Maharaj Kumar. Such was their determination that, on getting wind of the little general secretary's tactics, they had not scrupled to spread scurrilous stories about the Maharaj Kumar in order to undermine support for his candidature. Alarmed, Valisinha had written to me asking if the stories were true, as Kalimpong was next door to Sikkim and I might be supposed to have my ear to the ground, and I had replied that to the best of my knowledge they were not. Support for the Maharaj Kumar's candidature thus remained firm, and to the shock and dismay of the Hindu members of the governing body he was elected. So shocked and dismayed had they been, that after the meeting they had rounded on the victorious Buddhists (so Valisinha told me) and accused them of narrow-mindedness, bigotry, and sectarianism in wanting to have a Buddhist as president of the Society.

Their reaction did not surprise me. Hindus were universalists. For them all religions were one, all paths led to the same goal, so that it was a matter of comparative indifference whether the head of a Buddhist organization happened to be a Buddhist or a Hindu. Indeed, as Hindus possessed, innately, a far deeper knowledge of Buddhism, or of any other religion, than its own professed adherents, it was actually better that a Buddhist organization should be headed by a Hindu than by a Buddhist. 'But Buddhism is in our *blood*,' Hindu friends would insist when I attempted to correct their misunderstandings of Buddhist doctrine, meaning that they had the ability to understand Buddhism without the necessity of actual study, simply by virtue of the fact that they had been born and brought up in India.

I was not a universalist. I did not believe that all religions were one, or that all paths led to the same goal, and I had therefore been heartily glad, six months earlier, to hear that it was the Maharaj Kumar of Sikkim, and not Dr Radhakrishnan, who had been elected president of the Maha Bodhi Society. Not that I had anything against his Bengali Brahmin predecessors. All three were very distinguished men. One was an educationist, another the chief justice of Bengal, while the third, the Maharaj Kumar's immediate predecessor, was an educationist-cum-politician. But although they may have been prudent managers of the Society's finances, and have imparted to it a degree of acceptability among the Bengali intelligentsia, the fact that they were not themselves Buddhists meant that they were incapable of providing the spiritual leadership a Buddhist organization needed if it was to fulfil its function and be an effective vehicle for the dissemination of the Buddha's teaching. To what extent the Maharaj Kumar would be able to fulfil this function remained to be seen, but in the headquarters building, at least, a new spirit was already astir, and I felt happier to be living and working there than I had done the previous year. The only person in the building untouched by the new spirit was Jinaratana. He continued to lurk in the shadows, so to speak, ready to strike down any friend or supporter of Valisinha who was foolish enough to give him the opportunity. (Eventually one did.) Though conscious of his dark, brooding presence at the edge of the bright space that had opened within the Society, I did not allow myself to be disturbed, and every day relieved Valisinha of a little more of the burden of editing the *Maha Bodhi* journal.

I had relieved him of the greater part of it when my daily routine – and Sachin's – received an unwelcome interruption. Sachin was taken ill. At first it seemed to be nothing more serious than an attack of malaria, probably caught in Shantiniketan. Dr Soft, the Society's honorary physician, a septuagenarian Punjabi in the coarse white homespun of the orthodox Gandhian, whom I immediately called in, prescribed Comoquin tablets, as well as rest and liquid diet, and told me there was nothing to worry about. Three days later, however, Sachin's temperature having in the meantime fluctuated dramatically, his pulse was so low that Dr Soft started suspecting it might be either influenza or typhoid and changed the prescription accordingly. He also warned me that the patient had to be kept absolutely quiet. This was easier said than done. Not that Sachin himself was any problem. Like Good Deeds in the medieval morality play, he was 'sore bound' – not by his sins, indeed, but by sickness – and 'could not stir'.[72] The problem was the various female cousins who sat on his bed talking to him for so long – sometimes for three or four hours at a stretch – that he was quite worn out. As they were relatives, I did not like to ask them to leave (they were quite impervious to hints), especially as I had not told Sachin how serious his condition might be and did not want him to know. Altogether it was a worrying time. All I could do for the sufferer, apart from taking his temperature and giving him his medicine every two hours, and soup at similar intervals, was to make him as comfortable as I could and keep Dr Soft informed about developments by telephone. In between I wrote letters and read proofs, leaving Sachin's bedside only to shop for him and, one evening, to give a lecture in the Society's lecture hall downstairs. This was the first of the weekly lectures Valisinha had asked me to give, and whether by accident or design the date of the lecture was 24 December, Christmas Eve, and my topic 'Buddhism and God'.

After more than a week in bed Sachin started to recover. He had not had typhoid, though he may have had influenza, and when his temperature and pulse had been normal for three days running I judged him well enough to get up and go for a stroll in College Square. Here we sat on a bench for half an hour, at the foot of a pedestal that had lost its statue, enjoying the winter sunshine and doing our best to ignore the unrestrained curiosity of the Bengali passers-by, some of whom stopped dead in their tracks in order to take a better look at us. A few days later, Dr Soft having pronounced him out of danger, my companion was again spending the greater part of his time visiting relatives, while I continued easing myself, as I thought, into the editorial chair of the *Maha Bodhi* journal. I was no stranger to the pages of that publication. Articles, book reviews, and poems of mine had been appearing in the Society's 'Journal of International Buddhist Brotherhood', as it styled itself, for the last few years, and since July I had been contributing a monthly column entitled 'In the Light of the Dhamma' under the pseudonym of Himavantavasi. Himavantavasi, the 'Dweller in the Snowy Mountains' (the name had been found for me by Anand-ji), was a Buddhist hermit living in the Himalayas. He had no direct contact with the outside world, but reports of what was going on there, especially in the Buddhist part of it, somehow reached his ears from time to time and 'In the Light of the Dhamma' represented his reactions to what he heard.[73]

It was the first time I had written under a pseudonym, and from a literary point of view, at least, the experience was an interesting one. Though the views to which I gave expression were very much my own, the manner in which I gave expression to them was not, in the sense that it was not quite the manner in which I would have expressed them had I been writing under my own name. 'Himavantavasi' was not so much a pseudonym as a mask. The mask represented a character, a character whom I had imagined but who was so real to me that whenever I sat down to write my column I became Himavantavasi. The mysterious 'Dweller in the Snowy Mountains' was an extension of my own personality, through whom I could say things in a way in which I could not otherwise have said them and through whom, therefore, I could experience myself in a way that I could not otherwise have done. Himavantavasi enabled me to be myself more fully.

Not that I wanted to 'be myself' in the subjective, individualistic sense of that phrase. What I wanted was to give expression to my views, views which I hoped were genuinely Buddhist, and to give expression to them in as many different ways as possible. I therefore intended to go on writing my column even as editor of the *Maha Bodhi* journal. Indeed, as I settled myself more firmly into the editorial chair, in the last days of the old year and the first days of the new, I was planning to give Himavantavasi a stablemate. I was preparing to don another mask, the first-person-plural-using mask of 'the Editor', and to write each month one or more editorials. Through this mask, too, I would give expression to my views, but I would give expression to them not in the naive manner of the 'Dweller in the Snowy Mountains' but in the weightier, more authoritative manner appropriate to the official organ of a society that was, after all, both the leading Buddhist organization in India and the best known Buddhist organization in the world. Hitherto there had been no editorials in the *Maha Bodhi* journal. Yet there were numerous issues to which it ought to be drawing the attention of Buddhists both inside and outside India. Was not the ancient Buddhist site of Nagarjunakonda, in the newly created Andhra state, about to be totally submerged under a government irrigation scheme, despite the protests of historians and archaeologists? And had not Dr B. C. Roy, the chief minister, categorically refused to declare Vaiśākha Pūrṇimā a public holiday in West Bengal, even though the Union authorities had recently declared it a central government holiday?[74]

Hardly had my editorials on these issues been sent to the press, however, than I met with a serious disappointment. I would not be occupying the editorial chair of the *Maha Bodhi* journal after all. In fact there was no editorial chair for anyone to occupy. Instead there was an editorial settee into which seven or eight persons, myself included, were to be squeezed. There was to be an *editorial board*. In theory there was already an editorial board, and it was precisely because the other members of the board invariably left all the work to him that Valisinha wanted me to relieve him of the burden of editing the Society's journal. None the less, when the little general secretary proposed, at the governing body's first monthly meeting of the year, that I should be formally appointed editor, his proposal met with fierce opposition from the Hindu members, and it was with the greatest difficulty that, aided by two or three friends and supporters, he had got them to agree even to my being a member of the newly constituted editorial board.

The reason for this opposition on the part of the Hindu members of the governing body was not far to seek. I was critical of certain aspects of Hinduism, particularly the caste system, and made no attempt to conceal my views. This had led to their dubbing me anti-Hindu. *They* were of course universalists, in whose eyes to be critical in any way of other religions, with the possible exception of Islam, was to be intolerant, and intolerance was the unforgivable sin. That I was anti-Hindu was a fact that had been confirmed for them, a few months earlier, by a review I wrote of a new translation of Tulsidas's *Rāmacaritamānasa* – a review Valisinha had published in the *Maha Bodhi* journal. The sixteenth-century Tulsidas, the 'Servant of the (Sacred) Basil', was a great poet; his retelling of the story of the hero-king Rama, one of the *avatāras* of the god Vishnu, was a classic of Hindi literature, and the bible of the Hindi-speaking people of (Hindu) northern India. But Tulsidas was also an orthodox Brahmin. His perfervidly devotional apostrophes to Vishnu-Rama were mingled with repeated references to Brahmins as the *bhūdevas* or 'earthly divinities'. A Brahmin was to be worshipped, even though he possessed all the vices, whereas a Shudra, however virtuous, was to be despised.[75] Though conceding that the poem undoubtedly contained passages of great artistic merit, I therefore described the work as a whole as 'sadly marred by sectarian bias, devotional extravagance carried almost to the point of frenzy, and social orthodoxy in its more repulsive form'. This description did nothing to endear me to the Hindu members of the governing body at the time and was now partly responsible for the fierceness of their opposition to Valisinha's proposal.

Though disappointed that I was not, after all, to occupy the editorial chair of the Society's journal, I was not discouraged. As Valisinha pointed out, my position was no worse than his had been. I was a member of the editorial board, the other board members (himself excepted) would take little or no interest in the actual production of the magazine, though they might criticize it afterwards, and I would be left to do all the work. I was quite ready to do all the work, even though I would now be doing it not as editor but only as one member of an editorial team whose existence was confined to the front inside cover of the *Maha Bodhi* journal.[76] My only real worry was that the governing body might try to restrict my editorial freedom. Some of them, I knew, wanted to make sure I did not send articles direct to the press from Kalimpong, without them being seen and approved by one of themselves. But I was willing to take an optimistic view of the situation, and therefore continued to absorb myself more and more deeply in the work of implementing my plans for the improvement of the magazine.

I was not so deeply absorbed in the work, however, as to have no time for anything else. For pilgrims coming from the Buddhist countries of South-east Asia, Calcutta was the gateway to Bodh Gaya and the other holy places of northern India. The headquarters building was therefore a busy place, especially during the winter months, and it was inevitable that I should sometimes meet people. Among the people I met was U Thein Maung, the chief justice of Burma and a leading Buddhist of that country, to whom the Society subsequently gave a public reception. Devapriya-ji – as Valisinha was generally called by his friends and colleagues – also took me with him whenever he went to meet distinguished Buddhists who were passing through Calcutta but not staying at the headquarters building. In this way I met Jigme Dorji, whom I had last seen standing white-faced and horror-stricken beside his father's body, and the Maharani of Sikkim. The Maharani was, of course, the mother of the Maharaj Kumar of Sikkim, the Society's president. I had not met her before, but I had heard quite a lot about her, mainly from my old friend and supporter Marco Pallis, who was never tired of singing her praises as the most beautiful, intelligent, and vivacious woman one could possibly hope to meet, in Sikkim or anywhere else. That must have been some years ago. Now the Maharani was a stout, elderly woman of considerable charm but with only the remains of beauty. Her story was, I knew, a sad one. The mother of five children by the Maharaja, she had formed a connection with an incarnate lama from Tibet and, as a result, had given birth to a daughter, now nearly grown up. This had led to her banishment to a palace outside Gangtok, where she lived in seclusion, taking no part in public life. Though she was separated from the Maharaja, they were not divorced (he was said to be still quite fond of her), and she retained the title of Maharani. Was it my imagination, or did I not detect a hint of melancholy in her expression? She received us very graciously, but declined to visit the Society, probably on account of the equivocal nature of her position.

Dr Irene Bastow Hudson, MD, could never have been beautiful, and 'charm' and 'grace' were not the first words that sprang to mind in connection with her. Intellectual rather than intelligent, and despite her seventy-odd years possessed of demoniacal energy, she was a Canadian Buddhist-cum-Theosophist who had arrived in Kalimpong the previous summer with a letter of introduction from an old friend of mine in England. Though eccentric and opinionated, she was of a generous disposition (Joe, who had known her by reputation in Canada, maintained that she tried to buy people), and after her return to Canada had sent me two very welcome parcels of English classics (Spenser, Addison, Burns, and others), some volumes being school prizes she had won towards the end of the previous century. She also agreed to finance the publication of a collection of my poems, the final proofs of which had already reached me from the Bombay publishing house that was bringing it out. Now she was back in Calcutta, and staying at the Grand Hotel, where I very soon had the opportunity of thanking her for her generosity. She had more or less decided to settle in Kalimpong, she told me over a cup of tea, and would go there as soon as her luggage had been cleared. Meanwhile, there was a lot she could do in Calcutta. For one thing, she could visit the headquarters of the Maha Bodhi Society. This she accordingly did the following afternoon, staying on for my weekly lecture, on 'Practical Buddhism for the Layman', and attending the *paritrāṇa* or 'protection' ceremony that Aniruddha and I conducted in the temple afterwards.

Not that the elderly Canadian Buddhist-cum-Theosophist was the only Western visitor to the headquarters building that winter. Quite soon after my arrival I received visits from Dr Weintrob, a devotee of Anandamayi Ma who had spent three weeks at The Hermitage the previous year, and Mr Dameki, a Pole whom Anagarika Dharmarakshita (Miss Delannoy) had put in touch with me. How Dr Weintrob came to be staying at The Hermitage is something of a mystery. Probably he was simply escaping from the heat of the plains. Whatever the reason may have been, so intense was his devotion to the Bengali woman mystic that although he had intended to stay much longer in Kalimpong he announced, after only three weeks, that he was unable to bear the pain of separation from her and was returning to Benares forthwith. He was still in Benares, living at Anandamayi's ashram, and visiting Calcutta for a few days had heard that I was in the city. From the way he spoke it was clear that he was as devoted to Anandamayi as ever and, in fact, quite besotted with her. I could not but be reminded of my own contact with the 'Blissful Mother', more than five years earlier, when I had been shocked and disgusted by the scenes of hysterical devotion that were sometimes enacted in her presence.[77] Mr Dameki, as I had gathered from the *anagārika's* letter, was not a devotee but an intellectual, and we had a long conversation on Buddhism, yoga, and similar topics. The Society's most distinguished Western visitors during this period, however, were Professor and Mrs Franklin Edgerton, whom I showed round the temple with Devapriya-ji and Dr Soft. Professor Edgerton was the author of the newly published *Grammar and Dictionary of Buddhist Hybrid Sanskrit* and had recently delivered a series of lectures on 'Buddhist Hybrid Sanskrit Language and Literature' in Benares.

Among the people whom I met at the headquarters building, or who came to see me, was one who was neither a Buddhist pilgrim nor a Western visitor. This was Phani Bhusan Sanyal. I had met him at the Ramakrishna Mission Institute of Culture in 1945, when I was in the army and he a graduate student, and had sometimes accompanied him on his weekly visits to the shrine of Sri Ramakrishna's saintly consort, popularly known as the Holy Mother, to whom he was greatly devoted.[78] Now I was a Buddhist monk and he a professor of Economics at a nearby Anglican missionary college and still unmarried. We had re-established contact shortly after my ordination as a *bhikkhu*, and he came to see me whenever I was in Calcutta, usually bearing a gift in the form of two or three slender green sticks of tuberose, of whose fragrance he knew I was particularly fond. A textbook example of an ectomorph, and light-skinned even for a Bengali Brahmin, he invariably came dressed in a white shirt and dhoti (with, in winter, a dark *chadder* or shawl, elegantly draped) and wearing on his feet the black patent leather pumps of the *babu* or gentleman. In the course of my present visit to the city of Anagarika Dharmapala and the Maha Bodhi Society (as Calcutta was to me) or of Sri Ramakrishna and Swami Vivekananda (as it was to him) he came to see me not once but several times, the first time bearing not only sticks of tuberose but a copy of the Penguin selection of the prose of T. S. Eliot. If I happened to be free (Phani's visits were always unannounced) we went out book-hunting together, he being as great a lover of the printed page as I was and Calcutta being, for both of us, the city of bookshops. Among the bookshops to which he had introduced me, two or three years earlier, there was one that specialized – rather surprisingly, it being located in the depths of a department store – in Continental literature, and here I now bought translations of Baudelaire, Rimbaud, and Rilke.

Phani had also introduced me, two or three years earlier, to his widowed father, a retired judge of the Calcutta high court, taking me to meet him at what I assumed was the family's ancestral home. Conversation turned to the Ramakrishna Mission Institute of Culture, and to its secretary, Swami Nityaswarupananda. 'The fellow's no better than your Jinaratana,' observed the old man, who seemed to be as well acquainted with the affairs of the Maha Bodhi Society as he was with those of the Ramakrishna Mission. 'Has a car and a chauffeur and lady friends. Don't know what the Mission is coming to nowadays. Swamis are supposed to be *monks*.' These *obita dicta* were not very welcome to my spiritually-minded friend, who would much rather have talked about the *real* Ramakrishna Mission of Swami Vivekananda and the other direct disciples of Sri Ramakrishna than about its degenerate descendant, but out of respect for his father he remained silent. For my part, I was not surprised by the retired judge's remarks, though I had not realized that knowledge of Jinaratana's misdeeds was so widespread. In some respects Calcutta was a small place.

My connection with the Ramakrishna Mission went back a long way. It went back further than my connection with the Maha Bodhi Society. It went back, in fact, to the day when, as a nineteen-year-old soldier newly arrived in Colombo, I made my way along a road lined with flame-of-the-forest trees and knocked, not without apprehension, on the door of the local Ramakrishna ashram. The two swamis I met there were men of learning and spirituality and from them I imbibed, in the course of the seven months I spent in Ceylon, something of the spirit of Indian culture and something of their own enthusiasm for the spiritual life.[79] So deep was the impression made on me by the two swamis, and by the literature I read under their guidance, that I kept up my connection with the Mission in Calcutta and Singapore, to which I was subsequently posted, as well as after my return to Calcutta. Indeed, on leaving the army at the beginning of 1947 I took refuge in the Ramakrishna Mission Institute of Culture, then located in Wellington Square, where I had met Phani more than a year earlier. Swami Nityaswarupananda wanted me to help edit the new edition of the Institute's three-volume *Cultural Heritage of India*, but after a month there was no sign of the work actually starting and I therefore left for Jinaratana and the Maha Bodhi Society.

I left with my faith in the Ramakrishna Mission considerably diminished. The Institute having been given a block of flats in Russa Road for its new premises, and the tenants having refused to move out before they had found alternative accommodation, Nityaswarupananda had ordered the novice in charge of the eviction proceedings to hire a gang of hooligans and drive the recalcitrant parties out by force, citing in justification of these brutal measures the *Bhagavad Gītā's* teaching of *niṣkāma karmayoga* or the yoga of disinterested action. The *Bhagavad Gītā* was one of the texts I had studied in Colombo. I had studied it with the commentary of Śaṅkara, the great non-dualist philosopher. The fact that its teaching was capable of being understood in such a way as to justify violence cast a new, lurid light not only on the Ramakrishna Mission but, also, on the nature of Hinduism;[80] and though, in the course of my two years as a freelance wandering ascetic, I sometimes stayed at Ramakrishna ashrams, and indeed was made welcome there, my connection with the Mission gradually ceased to have any real meaning for me. Moreover, as my understanding of Buddhism deepened, and with it my experience of spiritual life, I came to realize that, in the words Anagarika Dharmapala wrote at the top of every page of his diary, 'The only refuge for him who aspires to true perfection is the Buddha alone.'

On one of my first visits to Calcutta after my ordination as a *bhikkhu*, however, I decided that I ought to acquaint the swamis I had known with the change in my condition, if only for old time's sake. Though some of them, I knew, had entertained hopes that I would become a swami and work for the Ramakrishna Mission, they at least would be pleased that I had renounced the world like themselves, albeit as a Buddhist monk. After all, they were universalists. They were universalists *par excellence*, Sri Ramakrishna having demonstrated the oneness of all religions by personally practising Hinduism, Islam, and Christianity in turn and discovering they led to the same goal. To see Nityaswarupananda, now installed in the Institute's new premises, I accordingly went. With me went Phani who, on our re-establishing contact, had warmly congratulated me on the step I had taken, at the same time gently reproaching me for my insistence that Buddhism was a separate religion from Hinduism. No congratulations were forthcoming from Nityaswarupananda. On seeing my yellow robe his face darkened. 'Why have you become a *Buddhist* monk?' he demanded, contemptuously. 'Hinduism is a great ocean, Buddhism only a tiny stream.' While all religions were one, some religions, it seemed, were more one than others.

Since then my contact with the Ramakrishna Mission had been limited to hearing its Kalimpong representative launch a virulent attack on Buddhism at a Buddha Jayanti meeting, and I had not expected to have any further dealings either with Nityaswarupananda or the Institute. This was not to be the case. When I had been three weeks in Calcutta, and was still seeing my first issue of the *Maha Bodhi* journal through the press, I received a telephone call from Irene Ray, an Englishwoman who was married to a Bengali doctor and whom I had met in Kalimpong two or three years earlier.[81] Irene was not only a devotee of the Ramakrishna Mission; she organized the Institute of Culture's weekly lectures, and edited its monthly Bulletin, and now she was telephoning to invite me to deliver next week's lecture. I accepted the invitation, and it was agreed I should speak on 'The Meaning of Buddhism and the Value of Art', a subject that had preoccupied me for some time, especially since my Shantiniketan lecture, and on which I had been doing some research in the Society's library. A few days later, therefore, I again met Nityaswarupananda, who appeared to have reconciled himself to seeing me in a yellow robe, and I delivered my lecture in the Institute's very modern auditorium to an audience of about 200 people – considerably more than came to my lectures in the Society's old-fashioned and rather shabby hall.

The following day I was again at the Institute, this time attending a recital of devotional music by the famous Dilip Kumar Roy, a disciple of Sri Aurobindo. To my surprise I met Swami Siddhatmananda. He was one of the two swamis I had known in Colombo, and we had not seen each other for nearly ten years. Unlike Nityaswarupananda, he showed no sign of displeasure at my having become a Buddhist monk, and greeted me warmly. He was in Calcutta for an operation, he explained – for hydrocele. Afterwards my friend Kantaraj, who still worked at the Institute, was at pains to disabuse me of any wrong notions I might have as to the nature of the complaint. Hydrocele, he solemnly assured me, was an accumulation of semen in the testicles due to prolonged observance of strict chastity, and the purpose of the operation the swami would be undergoing was to drain off the accumulation.

My lecture on 'The Meaning of Buddhism and the Value of Art' having been greatly appreciated, Irene asked me to write it out in article form for publication in her Bulletin, which I gladly did.[82] A speech I made shortly before my departure from Calcutta met with a much less favourable reception, and no one asked me to write it out for them. Speaking as the representative of Buddhism at the International

Congress of the World Fellowship of Faiths, held in the Senate Hall of Calcutta University, the pillared neo-classical façade of which confronted the Ajanta-style façade of the Sri Dharmarajika Vihara from the other side of College Square, I emphasized that Buddhism rejected the idea of God and exhorted man to rely for deliverance on his own efforts. This emphasis of mine so upset His Holiness the Shankaracharya of Puri (not the amiable old gentleman with whom I was already acquainted but his much more orthodox rival), who was presiding over the session, that he spent a good part of his presidential address attempting to prove that Buddhists, even though they professed not to believe in God, really did believe in him, and that atheists and theists were bound for the same goal. For so long did he go on that people began leaving the hall in droves, and in the end, when he had been speaking for more than two hours, one of the organizers stepped up to the dais and removed the microphone. Far from being disconcerted by this high-handed treatment, His Holiness looked round the virtually empty hall with an air of triumph, as though he had succeeded in routing all opposition.

Subsequently I wrote for the *Maha Bodhi* journal an editorial in which I protested against the attempt being made in some quarters to force Buddhism into a doctrinal framework repugnant to it. 'It is time Buddhists stopped allowing people of other religions to tell them what they "really" believe,' I declared.[83] My comments referred not only to the Shankaracharya of Puri but to one of the speakers at the Sadharan Brahma Samaj's Fraternity of Faiths meeting, held a few days before the Parliament of Religions, which I also attended as representative of Buddhism. According to this speaker all religions believed in the Fatherhood of God and the Brotherhood of Man, and apart from the former belief the latter was unthinkable – a position I was obliged to controvert in my own address, declaring that though Buddhism denied the very existence of God its followers had exemplified the spirit of Brotherhood more fully than the adherents of other religions. In Calcutta I had indeed fallen among universalists.

But I was not to be among the universalists much longer. By the end of the third week of January Devapriya-ji and I had finalized our arrangements for the editing of the Society's journal over the next few months, that is, until my next visit to Calcutta; and after Sachin had spent a few more days visiting his relatives, and I had paid a few more visits to bookshops, my companion and I were again pushing our way through the throngs of people surrounding Sealdah Station – this time in the reverse direction. Devapriya-ji and one of the *bhikkhus* came to see us off, as did Miss Singh and other relatives of Sachin's and a number of friends. We left Calcutta with rather more luggage than we had brought. Both of us had presents for friends in Kalimpong, while I had some two dozen books that I had either been given or had bought, among them the Oxford edition of Shelley's complete poetical works. Above all, we had with us a very large and heavy box Anagarika Dharmarakshita had asked me to bring up to Kalimpong for her and which gave us a good deal of trouble on the way.

6

ASSAM IDYLL

The first thing I heard on arriving at The Hermitage was that Miss Barclay had died that morning. As it was then three o'clock (we had reached Kalimpong later than expected owing to engine trouble on the way up from Siliguri) I went straight to the Manjula cottage, in the upper half of which Miss Barclay had established herself a few months earlier. What could have happened? Had Miss Barclay had a heart attack (in view of her violent temper this was not unlikely)? Or committed suicide? Or been murdered? So unexpected was the news of the elderly Englishwoman's death that speculations as to its possible cause preoccupied me to the exclusion, for the time being, of much in the way of an emotional reaction to the event.

Even when I was inside the four walls of the Manjula cottage, and standing in what had been Miss Barclay's sitting room, it was some time before I was able to find out much about what had happened. The police were there, in the form of a Bengali sub-inspector and a Nepali sergeant, and the Maha Bodhi Society, as represented by Dawa, Joe, and Dinesh. There was also Mrs Perry, the proprietress of the Himalayan Hotel, and an Englishman whom I did not recognize but who appeared to be with Mrs Perry. On my way upstairs I had heard voices raised in heated argument and now, as I entered the room, all eyes were turned on me and several voices in unison demanded, 'Was Miss Barclay a Buddhist?' 'Why, yes,' I replied, as I sought to regain my breath, 'She was.' Dawa looked round the room in triumph, and could not forbear exclaiming, 'I told you so!' Mrs Perry managed to look both crestfallen and incredulous. At this point the Bengali sub-inspector interposed. 'Can you *prove* Miss Barclay was a Buddhist?' he asked. Again all eyes were turned on me, and I could almost hear the sudden intake of breath. Joe was clearly sceptical, and even Dawa looked a little anxious. Mrs Perry's face lit up with renewed hope, as did that of the unknown Englishman. 'Yes,' I replied composedly, 'I can.' The fact was that Miss Barclay had joined the Young Men's Buddhist Association (India), as the Kalimpong branch of the Maha Bodhi Society then was, as an associate member, and in completing the membership application form, which she of course signed, had described herself as Buddhist by religion. 'That settles it, then,' said the sub-inspector briskly. 'Produce your proof at the *thana* and you can collect the body from the mortuary tomorrow morning.'

This was my first intimation that Miss Barclay's body was not still on the premises, as from the presence of so many people I had assumed. Indeed, from the circumstance that there were clearly two parties in the room, one Buddhist and one Christian, and that they appeared to have been vigorously disputing possession of Miss Barclay's body, one could almost have fancied that the body was lying there on the floor between them and that they had been fighting for it as literally as the Greeks and Trojans had fought for the body of Patroclus beneath the walls of Troy.[84] But though Miss Barclay's body was not on the premises her belongings still were, and for these, when they had been packed in boxes and the boxes sealed, I had to give the police a receipt. While this work was in progress Mrs Perry left, taking with her the unknown Englishman, though not before she had introduced him to me and it had transpired that he was Dr David Snellgrove of the School of Oriental and African Studies in London, that he was a Tibetologist, and that he was staying at the Himalayan Hotel.

On our way back to The Hermitage Dawa and Dinesh told me what they knew of the circumstances of Miss Barclay's death, some of which I had already learned from the police. Apparently she had risen quite early, perhaps while it was still dark, had made her way down the outside staircase to the toilet, had missed her footing, had fallen, and in falling had struck her head against one of the cement pillars that supported the cottage's projecting upper storey. Her servant Ang Tsering, the Sherpa who had once worked for me, had found her body lying in the drain beside the veranda when he came in for work from the bazaar and had at once retraced his steps and informed the police. Within hours the news of the Englishwoman's death was all over Kalimpong. As soon as he heard it Dawa had hastened along to The Hermitage in the expectation, as he now told me, of my being back from my travels and either there or at the Manjula cottage. On learning from Man Bahadur that I was not yet back, and having waited for an hour, he decided to go to the Manjula cottage himself to find out what was happening. By the time he arrived Miss Barclay's body had been removed, and Mrs Perry was claiming the right to take charge of her former guest's effects. She was also claiming the right to take possession of Miss Barclay's body after the autopsy. Miss Barclay had been a Christian, she told the police, and as a Christian herself she intended to make sure that Miss Barclay's body was given a proper Christian burial. Dawa naturally denied that Miss Barclay had been a Christian. Everybody knew she was a Buddhist, he declared, and the disciple of Venerable Sangharakshita. Mrs Perry countered by saying that having an interest in Buddhism was one thing, actually being a Buddhist quite another: Miss Barclay had only had an *interest* in Buddhism. This annoyed Dawa considerably, and the argument became quite heated. With the arrival of Joe and Dinesh it became more heated still, with Mrs Perry, vigorously supported by Dr Snellgrove (as he turned out to be), claiming Miss Barclay's body on behalf of the Christians, and Dawa, supported rather less vigorously by Joe and Dinesh, claiming it on behalf of the Buddhists. The police did not know what to think. It was at this point that I had arrived.

While the three of us were talking Sachin turned up with two other young Nepalis, one a cousin and one a friend. Not having got down when our car dropped me at the gate of The Hermitage, he had learned of Miss Barclay's death only after reaching home. Now he had come wanting to know if he could be of assistance. He and I having discussed the sad news, all six of us walked the mile or so up the road to Sachin's house, which was situated above the road, in the Scottish Mission compound. Here I met his father, Dr Ravi Singh, who besides being the popular 'Nepali doctor' of the Mission hospital was the local police surgeon. He had already performed the autopsy on Miss Barclay, he told me, in his usual friendly and cheerful manner. There was a slight bruise on the forehead, and there was no doubt that the poor lady had died of concussion, probably as the result of the fall. *Jyeo*, the body was in the dead house (as the tin shack that served as the hospital mortuary was called), and *jyeo, jyeo*, we could collect it in the morning, as the police had said.

At ten o'clock next morning, therefore, Miss Barclay's body was brought to The Hermitage in the back of a jeep. It was brought in a plain wooden coffin, the work of a carpenter in the bazaar who had stayed up half the night to have it ready in time. With the coffin came five lamas, as Tibetan monks were called, incorrectly, in Kalimpong, at least by non-Tibetophones. Dawa had brought them to see me soon after breakfast, and I had already discussed with them the arrangements for the funeral. Miss Barclay having been a student of Tibetan, it seemed appropriate that she should be sent on her way with at least minimal Tibetan Buddhist rites, especially as these were more colourful than anything I could manage on my own. Thus it was that five stalwart, red-robed figures were now manhandling the heavy coffin through the door and into the games room, where it was carefully lowered onto the ping-pong table, the trestles of which creaked beneath the weight. This having been done, they squatted in a row on the floor of the adjacent library and reading room, drew their texts and their *dorjes* and bells from the capacious bosoms of their robes, and started up a deep-throated, monotonous chant that, punctuated by the tinkling of bells and the occasional resounding clash of cymbals, continued for the next couple of hours. While this was going on people who had known Miss Barclay came with wreaths, bunches of flowers, and *khatas*[85] to pay their last respects. Besides our own members there were Dr Roerich and Mrs Perry and, I was glad to see, several Church of Scotland missionaries, whom I made a point of welcoming and asking to come in, this being the first time any of them had visited The Hermitage and they were clearly unsure what they might encounter.

When the lamas had finished chanting and been served with three cups (or rather bowls) of tea in the traditional manner, the lid of the coffin was removed and Sachin, Dawa, Dinesh, and I gathered round to take our last look at Miss Barclay. Apart from a faint bruise on her right temple she looked as she usually did, though her features were set in what I thought was a rather stern expression. Before closing the lid I went into the sitting room, where Mrs Perry and the missionaries were having tea (Dr Roerich had already left), and asked if anyone would like to come and take a last look at Miss Barclay. A shudder passed visibly through the group. 'Oh no!' quavered several voices, in tones of horror. 'Oh no thank you!' As our young members had not hesitated to look, and indeed were still crowded round the coffin for that purpose, this reluctance on the part of the missionaries was rather surprising. The lid of the coffin was therefore closed, the coffin itself loaded onto the jeep, and accompanied by me and the five lamas and as many of our members as could squeeze into the vehicle, and escorted by others walking behind, the Honourable Helena Beatrix Barclay set out on the last journey of her nine-and-fifty years.

It was a journey that soon became a triumphal progress. As we drove, almost at walking pace, through the High Street, pedestrians moved respectfully to one side and tradesmen came to the doors of their shops, many of them with flower garlands and *khatas* that they proceeded to place either on the bonnet of the jeep or on the projecting end of the coffin. How pleased Miss Barclay would have been, I thought, to know how popular she was! Our destination was the Tibetan cremation ground up at Tirpai, a thousand or more feet above the bazaar. I had been there before, on my way to the Tharpa Choling Gompa, and had enjoyed the cool air, the vibrant stillness of the place, and the uninterrupted view of the snows. There could hardly have been a more magnificent setting for a cremation. What I had not realized at the time was that men and women were cremated separately, on two different spots, and in different ways. Men were cremated lying on a kind of iron bedstead, whereas women were cremated standing within a stupa-like structure, and it was therefore a few yards from the latter that our jeep eventually came to a halt.

What followed was not very pleasant. Having unloaded the coffin from the jeep, the lamas removed the lid, lifted out Miss Barclay's body, and proceeded to strip it, a clothed body being, as I knew, more difficult to burn. All this took place behind an improvised screen of white cloth, but as the screen was only breast high and I was standing on a slight elevation of the ground I could see everything that was being done, as could some of our young members, who in fact were peering round the edges of the screen. The lamas then hauled the startlingly white body up to the top of the stupa-like structure and lowered it inside. Or rather, they tried to lower it. Either because Miss Barclay was too stout or the funnel too narrow the body refused to go right in. Again and again the lamas lifted it and lowered it, but all to no avail. This was the most dreadful part of the proceedings. As the red-robed figures struggled with the body in the hot sun Miss Barclay's head lolled from side to side, and her long flaxen hair, which she had worn in neat braids round her head, cascaded over her shoulders and bosom. 'They're desecrating the temple of the Holy Ghost!' screamed a voice I recognized as being that of Mrs Bullock. 'I *told* you not to come!' shrieked Joe in reply. The Bullocks, as they were popularly known, were a missionary couple from China with whom Joe had recently become acquainted and who had persuaded him, against his better judgement, to take them with him to witness the cremation. Eventually, when they had lifted and lowered for ten or fifteen minutes, one of the lamas crawled inside the stupa-shaped structure and pulled on Miss Barclay's legs from below, the idea being to have the corpse straddle the iron bar traversing the middle section of the structure. His efforts proved successful, and Miss Barclay's head having disappeared from view the other lamas clambered down, willing hands thrust logs of wood in the four apertures at the structure's base, and at last all was ready for me, as chief mourner, to light the funeral pyre.

Soon clouds of smoke were billowing from the funnel of the kiln, as the stupa-shaped structure seemed to have become, and tongues of flame were darting forth. The lamas, seating themselves on the ground, again took out their texts and their *dorjes* and bells and embarked on another two-hour session of chanting, bell-ringing, and cymbal-clashing. By the time they finished the body had been reduced to ashes, and all that remained for those of us who were still there was to have a last cup of tea in Miss Barclay's memory and go home. My hand having been burned when I lit the funeral pyre, I stopped by at Sachin's house and had it dressed, after which Sachin and Dinesh accompanied me back to The Hermitage. Our talk, naturally, was of our departed friend. It was strange, mused Sachin at one point, that Miss Barclay should have died only two months after her beloved sixteen-year-old cat, who had travelled out from England with her in his own basket and occupied his own fully paid-up seat on the aeroplane.

But although Miss Barclay was no longer with us in the flesh the boxes in which her belongings had been sealed were still solidly present. What was more, they were still at the Manjula cottage. The morning after the funeral, therefore, I hired a jeep and with the help of Sachin, Dawa, and a few of our other members, as well as that of the faithful Ang Tsering, brought them down to The Hermitage and stored them in a back room. When Sachin came to see me the following day, shortly after lunch, he found me not my usual cheerful self, and under his concerned questioning I was eventually obliged to admit that I had been feeling depressed ever since the previous morning, when we had all gone up to Miss Barclay's old quarters and removed her belongings. What exactly it was that made me feel depressed I could not say. It was not simply the fact of Miss Barclay's being dead, though her death had saddened me, especially in view of the way it had happened. The feeling was definitely connected with the sight of the boxes, and of the things the police had thought it not worth the trouble of sealing up and which I had sorted out. It was as though Miss Barclay's belongings had been orphaned. More than that. It was as though they had been abandoned, and having now no common owner or protector, and therefore no purpose in common, could only separate and go their different ways. Part of the 'garden' on the upper floor of the Manjula cottage as they had been, with the disappearance of the Lady of the garden (albeit a less young and amiable one than Shelley's),[86] they were sharers in the general dissolution of the place. They presented a picture of desolation. They evoked images of 'bare ruined choirs',[87] both arboreal and monastic – images of towns reduced to rubble and cities where not one stone had been left standing upon another. It was this, or something like this, that lay at the back of my depression.

Whatever the explanation, the mood did not last, if only because there were many other matters to which I had to give my attention. There were letters to be written, including an urgent one to a *bhikkhu* in Assam about my forthcoming tour there, material for the February issue of the *Maha Bodhi* journal to be edited and sent to Calcutta, and the enquiries of casual visitors to be dealt with. In any case, so far as Miss Barclay herself was concerned there was, I reflected, no real cause for depression on my part. Unfortunate though her death may have been, she had died a Buddhist. Not that her conversion to Buddhism had been merely formal (though I had received her into the Buddhist community in the traditional manner), as conversions of Hindus and Buddhists to missionary Christianity were apt to be in Kalimpong. She had become a Buddhist because she was convinced of the truth of the Buddha's teaching, and I had little doubt that it was owing to her contact with the Dharma that the last four or five months of her presence amongst us were the happiest period of what had been, by her own account, a life of singular unhappiness. The fact was a source of considerable satisfaction to me, as was the fact that I had borne with her outbursts of temper, her tantrums, and her angry tirades (of all of which I was the recipient, not the object), even though I was more than once sorely tempted to relieve myself of so burdensome a friendship by discouraging the exigent Englishwoman's almost daily visits to The Hermitage. I was heartily glad, moreover, that I was able to *prove* that Miss Barclay was a Buddhist and that we had been able, therefore, to give her a (Tibetan) Buddhist funeral – a funeral which had demonstrated her popularity with the local people and which on the whole had been, as our members and friends agreed, a great success.

The only person who did *not* think that Miss Barclay's funeral had been a success was Joe. When the Canadian *upāsaka* came to see me a few days later he was in a bitterly critical mood. We had done everything we should not have done, and nothing we should have done. Worst of all, we had not consulted *him* about the arrangements. The funeral had been a complete and utter failure. Knowing that in his eyes nothing done without the benefit of his advice could be well done, and that he was in any case of a hypercritical nature, I did not take much notice of his tirade, and having regaled me, as he thought, with an account of how Mrs Bullock had flown to the telephone to tell her missionary friends all about the horrors of Buddhist funerals, he therefore soon turned from savaging our funeral arrangements to savaging Dinesh. It had been a great mistake on my part, he declared with some vehemence, to leave the young ex-Untouchable to look after The Hermitage while I was in Calcutta. Though thanks to his own efforts (and Dawa's, he should in justice have added) the full-moon day celebrations and other activities had continued, it had not been with any help from Dinesh. Why, he had not even bothered to keep the place clean. All he had done was spend my money. He had been grossly extravagant, and it was surprising that I wanted to have anything more to do with such a feckless, unreliable, dishonest creature.

As I listened to Joe's outburst I thought of the fable of the Fox and the Grapes[88] and smiled to myself. I knew more about what had been going on in my absence than he appeared to realize. Anand-ji had spent a few days in Calcutta during my sojourn there, both on his way to Nagpur from Kalimpong and on his way back to Kalimpong from Nagpur, and after his arrival from Nagpur had shown me a letter he had received from Dinesh. Anagarika Dharmarakshita having arrived unexpectedly from Darjeeling and taken it for granted that in my absence she was free to occupy The Hermitage for a few days, he had gone to stay with Joe, thinking it hardly proper for him to be living under the same roof as a nun, or rather, for a nun to be living under the same roof as him. Out of the frying pan into the fire! Joe had attempted to rape him, and he had been obliged to take refuge in the Dharmodaya Vihara, even though protégés of Anand-ji's were not particularly welcome there. These revelations did not surprise me, my elder brother in the Sangha having already informed me, on his arrival from Kalimpong, that Joe had proposed to Dinesh that he should come and live with him, making the proposal in such a way, as Anand-ji delicately put it, as to lower himself in Dinesh's eyes. They did not surprise Sachin either, when he learned about them. He had a revelation of his own to make. Joe had once tried to persuade Dawa to spend the night with him, he told me. This I had not known before, and I could well imagine the embarrassment the rather strait-laced young Tibetan would have felt when the full significance of the elderly *upāsaka*'s proposal dawned on him. Dinesh was far too streetwise to be embarrassed even by an attempted rape, but the experience had none the less upset him, as he himself admitted to me on the night of my return to Kalimpong. I had therefore arranged for him to spend a week in Wardha with his family by way of consolation.

Naturally I did not let on to Joe that I knew what had really been going on at The Hermitage – and elsewhere – in my absence, though I may have protested against the notion that Dinesh had been extravagant. As I knew only too well, he had not had the means of being extravagant, least of all at my expense. The truth was that I was going through a period of financial stringency, and the Kalimpong branch of the Maha Bodhi Society with me. This was due mainly to the fact that during the previous six-month period my only fee-paying student had been Mr Bhumiveda, and even his contributions had ceased when I went to Calcutta. What was to be done? One possibility was that we organize film shows in the Town Hall for the benefit of the branch's funds, which would at least have the effect of lessening the drain on my own resources. It was a possibility I had already explored in Calcutta, the famous film actor Raj Kapoor, whom I had met in Bombay two years earlier,[89] having given me a letter of introduction to his distributors there and having agreed to our showing two of his films without payment of the usual charges. On my return to Kalimpong I therefore discussed the matter thoroughly with Dawa and the secretary of the Town Club, which was responsible for the letting of the Town Hall, and it was settled between us that the film shows would be held in the first week of April. Despite the desperate state of our finances it was not possible for us to hold them earlier, as I would be leaving for Assam in two weeks' time and we would need a full month for our preparations.

The next two weeks were very busy ones for me. Though Miss Barclay's funeral was over, there were letters to be written about her affairs, including a long one to Mrs Mitter, the owner of the Manjula cottage, who lived in Calcutta. There was also a memorial service to be arranged. This was held in the summer-house shrine at the end of the garden, and took the form of my chanting the *Maṅgala, Ratana*, and *Karaṇīyamettā Suttas* and delivering a sermon on 'The Recollection of Death' to our assembled members and friends. Nor was I yet finished with Miss Barclay's boxes. Their contents had to be listed *in detail*, so I was informed one afternoon by two members of the West Bengal police, one of them the same sub-inspector who had asked me if I could prove Miss Barclay was a Buddhist. They and I, together with Sachin, who had been having lunch with me, therefore spent the next four hours listing Miss Barclay's belongings separately, from the largest to the smallest, after which they were repacked in the boxes and the boxes again sealed, this time with my own seal and the official seal of the West Bengal police. A few days later Anagarika Dharmarakshita arrived from Gangtok, the capital of Sikkim, having spent the last month visiting the tiny Himalayan principality, and pitched her little tent on one of the terraces above The Hermitage. She was on her way back to Darjeeling, and stayed for only a few days, in the course of which we discussed the state of Buddhism in Sikkim and she showed me her books (the books that had made the large box I had brought up from Calcutta for her so heavy) and read aloud to me some extracts from Racine, thus giving me my first experience of the great French poet's sonorous alexandrines.[90] After her departure I wrote up the Notes and News section of the February issue of the *Maha Bodhi* journal (a task that naturally had to be left until the last minute), typed it, and sent it to Calcutta. This done, I was free to leave for Assam, and soon was once again dropping with dizzying rapidity down a succession of hairpin bends to Teesta Bridge and the plains.

With me in the car was Sachin's friend Hasta Bahadur Lama. Being unable to accompany me himself as he was attending college, and not wanting me to travel alone as I had been suffering from malaria and was not yet fully recovered, Sachin had arranged for the young Tamang to accompany me on this occasion. Though one of our members since the days of the Young Men's Buddhist Association (India), only in recent weeks had Hasta been much seen at The Hermitage, usually turning up there with Sachin, who had recently struck up a friendship with him. Some freak of heredity had distinguished him from the generality of Tamangs, certainly from the squat, bandy-legged specimens of the tribe I had seen at Longview. Relatively tall, and slim but well built, he was possessed of a copper-coloured skin, hair that was brown rather than black, a somewhat retroussé nose, and eyes that were, as the emperor Akbar's were said to have been, 'vibrant as the sea in sunshine'. Joe, who was apt to accost Hasta with cries of 'Oh you gorgeous creature!', much to the young man's embarrassment, professed to be quite overpowered by these eyes (or perhaps he actually was). By disposition Hasta was reserved and self-contained, with a distinct preference for sports rather than study, and though I did not know him very well I was glad of his company, the more especially as my illness had left me feeling rather depleted. Unfortunately the train, which we boarded at Siliguri, was so overcrowded that we could not find seats and eventually, when the time came to retire, had to spread our bedding on some boxes in the corridor. Unable to sleep, I passed an uncomfortable night, in the course of which I developed a slight temperature. In the morning we managed to get some breakfast in the dining car and at 10.30 reached Amingaon, where we had to detrain and cross the Brahmaputra.

I had crossed the Ganges on a number of occasions, but this was the first time I had crossed the Brahmaputra, and though we were probably crossing it at a point where it was comparatively narrow it seemed even broader than the Ganges, the Padma arm of which its main stream, the Jamuna, eventually joined. It was also the first time I had visited Assam, and I had to admit that I knew little more about this most north-easterly state of the Indian Union than that it was big and 'backward' (i.e. economically undeveloped), that it was thinly populated, with a high proportion of tribal people, many of whom had been converted to Christianity, that much of it was still covered with jungle, and that it produced tea and the famous straw-coloured tussore silk, shawls of which were hawked from door to door in cities all over India. I did, however, know that once it had been a centre of Buddhism, especially of Tantric Buddhism, and that even now it was a centre of Tantric Hinduism. At Kamakhya, in western Assam, there was a famous Kali temple, which marked the spot where the goddess's pudenda had fallen when she was dismembered by her wrathful consort Shiva.[91] My old friend Buddharakshita had been there as a boy.[92] The temple was situated at the top of a small hill, he told me, and pilgrims were given *prasad* not in the form of consecrated food, as was the custom elsewhere, but in the form of a piece of white cloth with red stains on it – the goddess's menstrual rag. During our wandering days he had in fact been eager that we should visit the place together. But if Tantric Hinduism had survived in Assam, Tantric Buddhism had not. Buddhism had not survived there in any form. Though there were said to be forty or fifty thousand Buddhists in the state, the majority of them were comparatively recent immigrants of Thai or Bengali stock who were followers of Theravādin Buddhism in its Thai form in the case of the Tais (as they were called, apparently to distinguish them from the Thais of Thailand) and in its Burmese form in the case of the Bengalis. It was in order to establish personal contact with these isolated Buddhists that I was visiting Assam, many of them having come to know of me through *Stepping-Stones*, our monthly journal of Himalayan religion, culture, and education, which thanks to the vigorous colportage of a brother disciple of mine had circulated widely in the state during the twenty months of its existence.[93]

The crossing of the Brahmaputra having taken little more than twenty minutes, we disembarked at Pandu to find our connection waiting at the platform and were able to secure seats without much difficulty. Securing food was another matter. There was nothing to be had at the tiny rural stations along the way, and it was only on our arrival at Lumding Junction in the evening that Hasta, at least, was able to eat. I then slept for a couple of hours, having been too tired during the day and perhaps too out of sorts to pay much attention to the scenes through which we were passing. Some time after midnight we reached Mariyani, where Venerable Dharmawansa and a novice, together with four or five lay supporters, were waiting to meet us. Buddharakshita and I had known the young monk when we were ourselves still laymen, the three of us having lived together for a few weeks at the Maha Bodhi

Orphanage in Calcutta during the 1947 Hindu-Muslim riots,[94] and I had met him once or twice since receiving my higher ordination. It was he who had made arrangements for my tour, and sent me my travelling expenses, and it was he who now whisked Hasta and me away by jeep to the little town of Jorhat and to the Jorhat Buddha Vihara, which we reached about an hour later. The Vihara had been built by a small group of, mainly, Bengali Buddhists, and with some of these I talked for a while before going to bed at three o'clock, having been travelling for more than thirty-six hours and having had only two hours' sleep.

In the morning I felt unwell, but it was Magha Pūrṇimā, the February–March full-moon day, people were already turning up at the Vihara, and as soon as I had forced down a morsel of breakfast I was obliged to devote myself to them. At 10.30, by which time the place was full, I inaugurated the day's celebrations by hoisting the five-coloured flag and giving a speech on its significance. The five colours represented the six colours of the Buddha's halo, I explained, the sixth colour, which was indescribable, being represented by the five colours in combination. As for the colours of the halo themselves, *they* represented the five principal elements of the Buddha's physical body in their refined, transmuted form. The Buddha's attainment of Enlightenment had changed the watery content of his body into blue light, his bones into white light, his blood into crimson light, his flesh into orange light, and his marrow into yellow light, while his body as a whole had been changed into a light of a colour for which there was no earthly name. The gross had been changed into the subtle, matter into pure radiance. Thus the Buddhist flag was a symbol of the transformation of un-Enlightened into Enlightened humanity – a transformation that could be brought about by following the Path taught by the Buddha. Though it had been designed, in its present form, by Col. Olcott, the co-founder of the Theosophical Society, the World Fellowship of Buddhists had recently adopted the five-coloured flag as the international Buddhist flag, so that it now was not only a symbol of the transformation of the individual Buddhist but a symbol, also, of the unity of all followers of the Buddha, and I was therefore glad to have had the privilege of hoisting it on the present occasion.

Hardly had I finished speaking than there arrived from a nearby temple a ragged little procession of monks, novices, and men and women devotees escorting a stupa-shaped reliquary containing, so I was told, bone relics of the Buddha. The reliquary, which was evidently of local workmanship, was adorned with large imitation cabochons of red and green glass, and borne by the oldest of the monks, who proceeded to deposit it on the image table in the Vihara's shrine-room where, its lid having been removed, the relics inside were exposed to view and a short puja conducted of which they were the focal point. The sight of the procession and the reliquary, but especially of the reliquary, with its gaudy imitation cabochons, affected me strangely. It was as though I was witnessing the arrival not of a concrete, visible reminder of the Master's life and teaching, as Buddha-relics were supposed to be, so much as that of the local fetish or ju-ju. The Bengali Buddhist laity were, it seemed, little better than fetish-worshippers, and their religion was in effect a species of fetishism, with the monks as the custodians of the fetish. Theravādin Buddhism had degenerated in their hands from a universal into an ethnic religion, or at least into a religion that incorporated a strong ethnic element. Not that I was in principle opposed to a universal religion like Buddhism incorporating an element of this kind. It was a question of proportion, and the sight of the procession and the reliquary had given me the impression that the pious supporters of the Jorhat Buddha Vihara and of the neighbouring temple had not got the proportion right. The impression did not, however, prevent me from joining in the puja – which I quite enjoyed – along with the other monks. After the puja came the *bhojana-dāna* or ceremonial food-offering. About a hundred people came forward, one by one, to drop a few spoonfuls of rice or curry into my bowl (as the custom was, I was carrying this with me), but I was unable to eat anything solid and took only a little soup and some fruit.

In the afternoon the Vihara was the scene of a well attended public meeting. Held under the presidency of a member of the State Assembly, it started at two o'clock and did not finish until a good three hours later. The principal item on the programme was my own speech which, the requirements of health coinciding with the dictates of tradition, I delivered sitting down. It was Magha Pūrṇimā, I reminded my audience. We were commemorating the day on which 1,250 monks of varying spiritual attainments spontaneously came together in order to pay their respects to the Buddha. On that occasion the Buddha uttered what was probably the best known verse in the entire Pāli canon. 'Cease to do evil,' he declared. 'Learn to do good. Purify the mind. *This* is the teaching of the Enlightened Ones.'[95] Ceasing to do evil corresponded to the practice of ethics, the first stage of the path leading to Nirvāṇa. Learning to do good corresponded to the development of mental concentration, the second stage, while purifying the mind – purifying it of the stain of spiritual ignorance, the greatest of all stains – corresponded to the development of wisdom, the third and final stage. Having explained each stage in some detail, I turned to the question of Buddhist education,[96] pointing out that it was the duty of Buddhist parents to bring up their children in the knowledge and practice of the Dharma. In conclusion, I congratulated the Buddhists of Jorhat on the fact that, though few in number, they had succeeded in building a vihara and appealed for the establishment of a Buddhist college of the traditional type. As usual, I spoke vigorously and with feeling, with the result that I started running a temperature and after the meeting had to lie down. None the less I continued to have visitors. Most of them were English-educated Hindus who, while sympathetic to the Buddha's teaching as they understood it, had no interest in the rather ethnic Buddhism of their Bengali Buddhist neighbours and who normally would not have set foot inside the Vihara. Naturally they had a lot of questions to ask the English monk (for as such Dharmawansa had been careful to advertise me), and it was several hours before I was free. By this time I had developed a severe headache and my temperature had risen. After taking some tomato juice and fruit I therefore retired for the night and took no further part in the celebrations, which continued until quite late and concluded with the ordination of two teenage boys as novices.

While I was dealing with the questions of my English-educated visitors Hasta was being subjected to a friendly interrogation by some of the more curious of the Vihara's lay supporters. Was he a Buddhist, they wanted to know. Yes, he was a Buddhist. Was he a follower of the Theravāda? No, he was not a follower of the Theravāda. What was he, then? He was a follower of the Mahāyāna. The Mahāyāna! What was that? But Hasta had reached the limits of his knowledge, and had to admit, as he told me afterwards, that he did not know what the Mahāyāna was and that they would have to ask me. Though the lay supporters may well have attributed the young Tamang's replies to modesty rather than to ignorance, there was no doubt that Hasta was woefully ill-informed about his own religion, and I could not but hope that having been made aware of this he would in future be more regular in his attendance at The Hermitage where, if I did not have much to say about the Mahāyāna, I certainly had a lot to say about the fundamental principles of the Dharma and about the application of those principles to one's daily life.

Though the Jorhat Buddha Vihara had been built mainly by Bengali Buddhists, it was in fact the Tais who made up the greater part of the Buddhist population of Assam. They apparently had migrated from Thailand several generations – even several centuries – ago, and unlike their Bengali co-religionists, who were more urbanized, lived in isolated villages of their own and engaged in agriculture. There were two of these Tai villages only fifteen miles from Jorhat, Dharmawansa informed me, and he had arranged for me to visit them. Accompanied by Dharmawansa himself, as well as by Hasta and several of the Vihara's lay supporters, including the young man who had translated my speeches the previous day and whose services would again be required, I accordingly set out by station-wagon to meet the Tai Buddhists and observe their way of life. I did not set out until some time after lunch, the doctor having warned me that there was congestion at the back of the lungs and that if I did not take rest pneumonia might develop.

On my arrival at Balijan, the first of the two villages, I was given an extremely cordial reception by the monks, novices, and lay people of the place and conducted to the vihara, the steeply pitched roof of which was reminiscent of Thai rather than Indian architecture. Here I talked, and discoursed on the Dharma, for about three hours uninterruptedly, for such was the atmosphere of devotion by which I was surrounded, and so great was the evident eagerness for religious instruction on everyone's part, that despite my continuing temperature I had no alternative but to rise to the occasion and give of my best. From Balijan our little party, escorted by the villagers and by boys carrying five-coloured Buddhist flags, proceeded on foot to Nasyam, the second of the two villages, where we were to spend the night. Here too I was kept busy talking and discoursing on the Dharma (the Tais seemed to have an insatiable appetite for sermons), and it was past midnight when I got to bed. I did not get to bed, however, before having some unexpected visitors. I was lying down, but still discoursing, when word was brought me that three sahibs had arrived at the vihara and were asking to see me. The three sahibs turned out to be Swale Ryan, the ex-army man who had helped me found the Young Men's Buddhist Association,[97] and two planters from the tea estate nearby where he was now working. He had heard I was in the neighbourhood, he announced in his usual hail-fellow-well-met fashion, and had dropped in to say hello. As it was late, the visitors did not stay long. He would send a jeep for me the day after next, Swale promised before they left, as he wanted to show me round the estate. Only when I was on my own, and free to go to bed at last, did I realize that despite the exertions of the day I was not feeling tired. On the contrary, I felt quite buoyant.

The following morning, by special request of the villagers, I gave a talk on the differences between Buddhism and Christianity. Buddhism was a non-theistic religion, I explained, whereas Christianity was theistic. Buddhists meditated, whereas Christians prayed. The Buddhist monk was a teacher and exemplar, whereas the Christian priest was an intermediary between God and man. In Buddhism one gained Enlightenment by means of one's personal efforts, whereas in Christianity one was saved through the merits of a redeemer. Buddhism emphasized wisdom and compassion, whereas Christianity emphasized faith. For Buddhists the Buddha was an Enlightened human being, whereas for Christians Christ was the incarnate son of God. These simple antitheses depicted the differences between the two religions much too starkly, of course, but they had to be depicted starkly if they were to be made clear to the villagers, who apparently had been troubled by the preaching of the missionaries; and in any case I had only an hour or two in which to comply with their request and make, moreover, a definite impression on their minds. When the talk had been given, and the Refuges and Precepts administered, I and the rest of the party left for Jorhat, this time travelling not by station-wagon but by bullock cart. Though the sleek white bullocks stepped out with a will, so that the unsprung wooden vehicle, with its iron-bound wooden wheels, bumped and rattled its way along the deeply rutted track at a reasonable speed, it took us more than an hour to reach the road where we were to catch the bus. Either because we had been misinformed about the time of its arrival, or because it was behind schedule, the bus did not turn up for nearly three hours. As we were waiting, two Sinhalese Buddhists who were working as mechanics in a nearby tea estate came and spoke to me, while an aged Brahmin, on learning than I was a Buddhist, did his best to convince me that the Buddha was the ninth incarnation of the god Vishnu.

Back at the Jorhat Buddha Vihara, which we reached at about three o'clock, I found that I again had a temperature and therefore lay down. The rest of the day passed quietly. I had a lengthy discussion on Buddhism with a friend of my translator, and talked with Dharmawansa, and that was about all. Like the translator himself, the friend belonged to a community that had migrated from Thailand long before the Tais but which unlike the Tais had in the course of centuries become more or less completely Hinduized. As for Dharmawansa, though hailing from Bihar he belonged, as far as I knew, to the Bengali Buddhist community. At the time when Buddharakshita and I lived with him he was invariably quiet and composed, walking with a grave, dignified gait, his eyes modestly downcast, and was so meek as not to resent the thrashing Buddharakshita once gave him. In fact he became meeker than ever. He was still quiet and composed, and still walked with a grave, dignified gait, but now that he was older, and moreover incumbent of the Jorhat Buddha Vihara, he was, I thought, not quite so meek as before. At any rate, he was quietly assertive in his dealings with the Vihara's lay supporters and besides having organized my tour was at pains to take me wherever there was something worth seeing and wherever he thought my presence might do some good. Thus it was that, the morning after our return from Nasyam, he took me to see the Jorhat Technical Training Institute, where we were shown round by the foreman and where I gave a short address to the students. The jeep not turning up to take me to the tea estate as Swale had promised, the rest of that day, too, passed quietly. As it happened, this was just as well. I had a high temperature, and pains in the head, all the afternoon and evening, and went to bed early.

The community to which my translator and his friend belonged was not the only immigrant community to have been Hinduized. As I discovered the next morning, when Dharmawansa and I, together with Hasta and two novices, were given a ceremonial food-offering at the house of a lay supporter of the Vihara, the Bengali Buddhists of Assam had been Hinduized too, though to a much lesser degree and probably even before they entered the region. When I had given the family the Refuges and Precepts, and they had ceremonially offered food, our host, a Mr Barua, indicated that before Dharmawansa and the others fell to I should offer a portion of the food to the images in the domestic shrine behind my head. There were two images, one of the Buddha, the other of Lakshmi, the Hindu goddess of wealth. Without saying anything, I put the image of Lakshmi carefully to one side, and made the offerings to the image of the Buddha only. Probably Mr Barua was not surprised by my action. He must have known that the monks of his religion never worshipped the Hindu gods and goddesses, though the laity sometimes did, even if they were not supposed to. This was the first time I had seen a Hindu deity installed beside the Buddha in a Bengali Buddhist domestic shrine, and it was not to be the last. Hinduism being so very much the dominant religion in India, it was not easy for the Buddhist laity to withstand the constant pressure to Hinduize, and I could readily understand how, in the absence of a monastic order, those whose Buddhism consisted in little more than making offerings to the monks were in the long run bound to succumb to that pressure altogether.[98]

Having returned to the Vihara from the Barua house, I made ready to leave Jorhat on the next stage of my tour. Catching the bus from Jorhat to Mariyani Junction, Hasta and I, accompanied by Dharmawansa and my translator, caught the train from Mariyani Junction to the village of Dishenpani. It was extremely hot, and the train rather crowded, so that by the time we reached our destination two hours later, at about three o'clock in the afternoon, Dharmawansa and my translator were hardly less exhausted than were the two visitors from Kalimpong. At the station our little party was met by some lay supporters and taken by car to Dishenpani Vihara, where we were welcomed by Venerable Nandawansa, the incumbent, and others, and where I talked for a while with a group of high school students. I was not feeling at all well, however. Besides having a high temperature, I felt weak in all my limbs, and after taking a dose of medicine went straight to bed. Fortunately I woke feeling somewhat better, and after eating a little breakfast gave a sermon for the benefit of the assembled lay supporters and administered the Refuges and Precepts. We then left Dishenpani for Chalapathar.

The two villages being both situated on the banks of the Brahmaputra, we made the journey by country boat. This was the most idyllic part of my whole tour. Although it was already quite hot, there was a coolness coming from the river, which together with the breeze created by the vessel's motion made the trip an extremely pleasant one. As we approached the village we were met by boys with gongs, and before long were being welcomed ashore by the assembled populace and escorted to the vihara amidst scenes of great enthusiasm. The name of the Tai village of Chalapathar was already familiar to me. It was the village where Dinesh had taught, where he had entered into a liaison with one of his pupils, and where he had been in danger of losing his life at the hands of the girl's brothers when the relationship was discovered. On our way to the vihara, which was situated about a mile from the river, I therefore looked about me with interest. It was as though we were in Thailand rather than India. Not only were the simple thatched houses raised on stilts. In both complexion and cast of feature the villagers were distinctly Mongoloid, while their costume was characteristic of South-east Asia rather than of the Indian subcontinent, the men being uniformly clad in white shirts and sarongs and the women and girls, no less uniformly, in tight-fitting white blouses and black sarongs. All looked healthy and happy, and I was conscious of the presence of a brighter, cleaner atmosphere than that which usually prevailed in the country's Hindu villages, sunk as the latter so often were in apathy and gloom. It was also noticeable that the inhabitants of Chalapathar, lively and expressive though they were, at the same time comported themselves in a disciplined and orderly fashion, so that it was not difficult for me to believe that their moral standards were indeed strict, as Dinesh had discovered to his cost. At the vihara I naturally had to deliver a sermon and administer the Refuges and Precepts, after which there came the usual ceremonial food-offering. Out of complaisance to our hosts I tried to eat, but could manage no more than a little soup and half a slice of toast. Indeed, my temperature having shot up I was obliged to lie down for a while, rising only to hear a group of evidently well-trained children recite devotional verses not just in Pāli but also in Sanskrit.

Our departure from Chalapathar was even more spectacular than our arrival. At least mine was so. Not wanting me to exert myself unnecessarily, the villagers made a seat for me in the village woodcart, and with the women pulling in front and the girls pushing behind I was conveyed in triumph as far as the railway line. Why the men did not lend a hand was not clear. Perhaps the woodcart was female property. Or perhaps the women and girls were simply more devotionally inclined and more eager to 'make merit'. Be that as it may, they pulled and pushed with a will, to the accompaniment of a good deal of laughter. It was, in fact, a very jolly occasion, with the men shouting encouragement and the women and girls chattering among themselves like so many magpies. Looking down at the happy faces surrounding the cart, and at the array of dazzling white blouses and shiny-black sarongs, I thought I had rarely beheld a more charming sight. Was Dinesh's Mynah-bird, as he called her, one of the merry throng, or had she been married off to prevent her getting into further mischief and gone to live in another village? Whichever may have been the case, it was more than likely that she was already beginning to forget her erstwhile lover, even as he had already begun to forget her. At the railway line I dismounted from the cart, the villagers paid their last respects to the two yellow robes, and our little party – still four in number – started walking along the track in single file to Safarai Station. Here we caught the train to Tinsukhia Junction, which we reached two or three hours later, at about 7.30 in the evening, after a quite comfortable journey. From Tinsukhia Junction it took us only an hour to get to Digboi, where we were met by a Bengali lay supporter, another Mr Barua, and where, having been driven to this gentleman's residence, I spent several hours in discussion with him and other lay supporters before finally retiring for the night.

Digboi was to be the farthest point of my tour. I had originally intended to go as far as Sadiya, which was only a hundred or so miles from the easternmost extremity of India, where it bordered on both Burma and China, but though my temperature was normal I was still not eating, and moreover had developed a troublesome cough, and mindful of the warning I had been given by the doctor in Jorhat I therefore decided to go no further and, in fact, to return to Kalimpong forthwith. I did not leave Digboi without seeing something of the little town, which was an important centre of the Indian oil industry and expanding rapidly. The following morning, after breakfast, a friend of my translator's came and took us for a drive round the oilfields, where the derricks towered black against a smoke-obscured sky and the smell of oil filled the air. Indeed, the whole town was grimy with oil. It was as though a black blight had fallen upon the green face of the earth and was spreading in all directions. If this was what economic development meant then I, for one, preferred that Assam should remain 'backward'. In the afternoon, having administered the Refuges and Precepts to our host and his family, I talked with some of the lay supporters who had come to pay their respects to me and my brother monk. There were only a few Buddhists in the town, they told me, most of them being from Chittagong in East Bengal, which now that it was part of (East)

Pakistan was not the healthiest place in the world for a follower of the Enlightened One to be.

The train arriving nearly two hours late, our little party did not leave Digboi until eight o'clock that night. At Tinsukhia Junction, where we had to change, we managed to secure seats, and after sleeping, on and off, for a few hours, finally woke at four o'clock to find we had reached Mariyani. Here Dharmawansa and my translator got down, leaving Hasta and me to continue our journey without them. In the course of the day the compartment gradually became very crowded, so that I was not sorry when, at about five o'clock in the afternoon, we reached Pandu and had to detrain in order to cross the Brahmaputra. At Amingaon, on the other side, we secured seats only with difficulty, and for the whole of the rest of the journey the train was crowded to an uncomfortable degree. When night fell, Hasta climbed onto the luggage rack and slept there, while I curled up on the seat below. At half-past seven we reached Siliguri, and less than an hour later, having breakfasted in the station restaurant, we were seated in the Land-Rover and heading for the hills.

On our arrival at The Hermitage, soon after midday, I took a little stew, and having rested and read some *Spectator* essays[99] went to see Sachin, who was overjoyed that I was back and gave me a bottle of cough mixture. Next day I was well enough to take a proper (rice) meal, my first for nearly two weeks, and started going through my mail, putting together the March issue of the *Maha Bodhi* journal, and writing letters. Almost the first letter I wrote was to Venerable Dharmawansa, thanks to whom I had been able to make my tour. I was glad to have seen something of Assam, and to have made personal contact with the Buddhists of the state. In particular, I was glad to have had an opportunity of visiting the Tai Buddhist villages, and observing the way of life of the people there. Despite my poor health the tour had been, on the whole, quite idyllic, and my only real regret, as I looked back, was that I had not been able to stay longer or go further.

7
SELLING TICKETS – AND THANGKAS

Gold might or might not be deserving of the opprobrious epithets heaped on it by moralizing poets, and money might or might not be the root of all evil, but abstention from handling gold and silver was certainly one of the precepts taken by the *śrāmaṇera* or novice monk at the time of his ordination. I had been ordained as a *śrāmaṇera* at Kusinara in May 1949, and on my arrival in Kalimpong nearly a year later was still observing the precept strictly, not touching money in any form, even though I knew that the majority of *śrāmaṇeras* and *bhikṣus* honoured the precept more in the breach than the observance. For my first six months in the town I continued to observe the precept, relying on my alms bowl for food and on the generosity of friends and lay supporters for whatever else I needed. At the end of this period I found myself in a quandary. I had either personally to accept some money that had been collected for my support during the rainy season, when it would be difficult for me to go out on my morning almsround, or risk exposing the well-meaning person who had collected it to the charge of retaining it for his own benefit. In the end I decided, most reluctantly, to accept it, and allowed the grubby currency notes and tarnished coins to be counted into my hand. Subsequently I found myself having to raise funds for the Young Men's Buddhist Association (India), as I still had to do for the Kalimpong branch of the Maha Bodhi Society, and in this way came to be more involved with money than I had been for many years.

According to a celebrated Mahāyāna treatise, the possession of gold and silver allowed a monk to be more useful to others and to help them.[100] Very likely it did, but I was inclined to regard the argument as a rationalization and to wish that I, for one, could have helped people through my Buddhist work *without* the necessity of handling gold and silver, or rather, of having anything to do with money. One of the circumstances that had made my Assam tour so idyllic was the fact that, our tickets for the journey once purchased, I could simply forget about money. Whether I was with the Bengali Buddhists or the Tai Buddhists, food, clothing, shelter, and medicine (the four basic necessities for which the monk was dependent on the lay community) were all provided, and for the time being, at least, I needed nothing more. It was like being on the open road, as I had been during my years as a wandering ascetic, when equipped with my bowl and my robe as a bird with its two wings (the traditional simile) I was free to fly whithersoever I wished.

Now the idyll was over. I was back at The Hermitage, and into my role as *bhikṣu*-in-charge of the Kalimpong branch of the Maha Bodhi Society. My wings were again folded, and like Baudelaire's albatross (I had read the French poet a lot during the past few months) I had been obliged to exchange freedom for captivity. According to Baudelaire, the Poet was in the same predicament as the albatross. Exiled on the ground, he was unable to walk because of his great wings.[101] The Monk, or at any rate the Mystic, was also in that predicament, I thought, for at times circumstances forced him, too, to let his wings drag at his sides, as it were, or at least to fold them. But regardless of whether or not *my* wings were folded, or whether I even possessed wings at all, I had to walk as best I could. There was a lot to be done now that I was back in Kalimpong. Not only was there mail to be opened, an issue of the *Maha Bodhi* journal to be put together, and letters to be written (to say nothing of a regular meditation practice to be kept up). There were also visitors to be seen, Sachin to be helped in his studies, the branch's monthly accounts to be made up, and copies of some of my more recent poems to be dispatched to the editor of *The Illustrated Weekly of India*.[102] Most pressing of all, there were arrangements for the holding of the film shows to be finalized – the film shows which would, I hoped, place the finances of the Kalimpong branch of the Maha Bodhi Society on a more secure footing and lessen the drain on my own resources.

At the time of Raj Kapoor's agreeing that we could show two of his films without payment of the usual charges I was going through a period of financial stringency, and the Kalimpong branch with me. Since my return from Calcutta the stringency had increased, the expenses of Miss Barclay's funeral having swallowed up whatever money I had, and though I could expect to be reimbursed from her estate, this was going to take a long time (in the end it took a year), and meanwhile I had to continue subsidizing the branch's activities and supporting myself and my few dependants. By the time I left for Assam the state of my own, and the branch's, finances was indeed desperate, and two weeks later it was more desperate still. Within days of my being back in Kalimpong I was confronted by the fact that I had, literally, no money, and no prospect of having any until the arrival of the next instalment of the grant which, on the recommendation of my teacher Kashyap-ji, I was receiving from a wealthy Hindu philanthropist.[103] News that the English Buddhist monk was in financial difficulties was not long in getting around, and even reached Darjeeling. Anagarika Dharmarakshita sent me a cheque for a hundred rupees by way of a loan, at the same time taking it upon herself to advise me regarding the kind of life I ought, as a Buddhist monk, to be leading. 'Those who give help cannot refrain from offering advice,' I confided to my diary. Next day I wrote to her returning the cheque, explaining that to accept a loan would only render my position more difficult later on. I also made it clear that I wanted no advice on spiritual matters. Later in the week, when I was still without any money, Sachin turned up one morning with thirty rupees he had borrowed for me from his father. Touched by his thoughtfulness, for I had said nothing to him about my difficulties, I accepted the loan – partly because it was a small one and therefore easily repayable, and partly because it came unaccompanied by any advice.

Before my departure for Assam it had been settled that our film shows would be held in the first week of April. The cruellest month[104] – in India cruellest because hottest – was now almost upon us, and after talking with Dawa, the secretary, I therefore called a committee meeting in order to assign responsibility for such matters as the printing of tickets and the putting up of posters. In the course of discussion it transpired that we would need to borrow or hire a ciné projector. Sachin volunteered the information that a friend of a friend of ours in Darjeeling owned one, or had access to one, and two days later, therefore, only a fortnight after my return from Assam, I found myself once more seated in a Land-Rover and once more dropping down a succession of hairpin bends to Teesta Bridge and, this time, not the plains but an even longer succession of even more acute hairpin bends *up* to ever-misty Ghoom, 8,000 feet above sea level, and thence along the ridge and down a few hundred feet to the Queen of the Hill Stations. As we approached the town I saw on the hillside the pink and white and red of the beautiful flowering trees, at this time of year at their best.

The friend to whom Sachin had alluded was Omiya, the popular Bengali proprietor of a small watch-repair shop on Mackenzie Road. *His* friend was Tilak Prasad, a Nepalese who taught at one of the local colleges and whom I already knew slightly. Both young men were Hindus by birth, English-educated, and quite Westernized in their outlook, but whereas Omiya, who was the elder of the two, was still very much a bachelor, Tilak was already married and the father of a child. Contrary to my expectation, Omiya was not in his shop when I called there after breakfast the following morning (normally he was to be found nowhere else during business hours), but eventually I tracked him down and arranged to meet him and Tilak Prasad at the latter's place that afternoon. Yes, he had access to a ciné-projector, Tilak was able to assure me a few hours later, over a cup of tea. The college had one, and he was confident of being able to borrow it for us. It would take him a little while, however, to arrange matters with the principal. I therefore decided to stay in Darjeeling three more days. This would enable me to see a few people, as well as to make quite sure that Tilak was, in fact, able to borrow the ciné projector for us and that I would not have to look for one elsewhere.

One of the people I wanted to see was Dr Hudson, who had decided, in the end, to settle in Darjeeling rather than Kalimpong, at least for the time being, and whom I found comfortably installed in a pleasant bungalow with a cook-bearer and an ayah. She seemed pleased to see me, perhaps because she was in need of someone to talk to (her servants understood her English, apparently, no better than she did their Nepali). At any rate, she talked uninterruptedly for six hours, mostly about Buddhism and Theosophy, and I was able to get away only after promising to have tea with her the following day. Tea with her at four o'clock the following day I accordingly had, trying not to intervene when miscommunication between the irate mistress, with her two words of Hindi, and the puzzled servants, with their broken English, became too acute. This time Dr Hudson held forth on the subject of radiaesthesia, about which she seemed to know a good deal, and soon had me performing, in this connection, various experiments with her crystal pendulum – experiments which I found quite interesting. We also discussed meditation. Before eventually allowing me to depart she insisted on giving me a viaticum in the form of a (homoeopathic) dose of arsenic, the pendulum having indicated a deficiency of that substance.

From crystal pendulum to diamond sceptre – the 'diamond sceptre of the lamas', as it was sometimes called – was perhaps only a short step, at least from the Jungian point of view. Short step or not, early next morning I was making my way to Aloobari Gompa (Aloobari, or 'Potato Field', was a small settlement too far from Darjeeling to be called a suburb and too near to be called a village), where one might reasonably expect to find the acknowledged symbol of the Vajrayāna, and even of Tibetan Buddhism itself, very much in evidence. On my arrival at the *gompa*, which was a temple rather than a monastery, I was welcomed by the head lama and his assistant, as well as by Dorje Bhutia, an English-educated young man of the locality who, as his surname indicated, was a 'Darjeeling-born' Tibetan. Situated on the quiet hillside, away from any habitations, the unpretentious, whitewashed building was a peaceful place. It was also very well maintained, even though the locality was not, to all appearances, a prosperous one. What was more, the *lhakhang* or 'house of divinities', as the Tibetans called it, besides being richly decorated was dominated by a giant sedent image of Padmasambhava. Though not so big as the one in the Tamang Gompa, in the heart of the bazaar, the sight of which had affected me so profoundly four years earlier, it was no less impressive. The light that came through the doorway revealed the same 'diamond sceptre' and skull cup, the one held in his right hand, the other cradled in his left, the same red cloak, the same trident-tipped staff resting in the crook of his arm, the same 'lotus hat' with the vulture feather, the same moustached face, the same 'wrathful smile'.

As it happened, I had received that very week a review copy of *The Tibetan Book of the Great Liberation*, the beautifully illustrated fourth volume in Dr Y. W. Evans-Wentz's famous Oxford Tibetan Series, and in fact had brought it with me to Darjeeling so that I could go on reading it. Among other riches, the volume contained 'An Epitome of the Life and Teachings of Tibet's Great *Guru* Padma-Sambhava', based on excerpts rendered into English by the late Sardar Bahadur Laden La, Darjeeling's most famous son, assisted by Lama Sonam Senge. Though the mysterious and inspiring figure of Guru Rimpoche – the Precious Guru – was imprinted so vividly on my consciousness, during the four years that had elapsed since my experience in the Tamang Gompa I had been able to find out no more about the facts of his life than was already known to me from scholarly histories of Buddhism. With biographical fact in the ordinary sense, however, the Laden La/Evans-Wentz 'Epitome' was little concerned. Its eighty-odd pages were replete with marvels and miracles, some of them quite bizarre. As I subsequently observed when reviewing the volume as a whole for the *Aryan Path*:[105]

> While the present Epitome is of very great anthropological interest, one cannot help regretting that it was not possible for the first comprehensive account in English of the great Guru's career to have presented him in a more balanced and, we think, in a truer way as a thinker and saint rather than as a 'Culture Hero' and thaumaturgist. Though the text translated in the next section [i.e. the 'Yoga of Knowing the Mind'] does enable us to gain a more complete picture of his personality, those who have been fascinated by the spiritual authenticity of the *Life of Milarepa* [an earlier volume in the Oxford Tibetan Series] will, we are afraid, be deeply disappointed by the Epitome of Padma-Sambhava's Biography.

After all, various books were ascribed to the great Guru, and from these Lama Govinda, at least, had got a vastly different impression of him, an impression, namely, that he was – as my good friend had recently written to me, in words I took the liberty of quoting in my review – 'a very sane and profound thinker, a great saint, and a powerful personality, who impressed the people around him so deeply that in their urge to convey his greatness to posterity, they had to take resort to the superhuman and to the miraculous.' I was also critical of Evans-Wentz's tendency, in some of his elaborate annotations, to assimilate Buddhist to Hindu teachings, as well as of Carl Gustav Jung's identification, in the 'Psychological Commentary' that constituted the Foreword to the volume, of the One Mind of the 'Yoga of Knowing the Mind' with the Unconscious of modern psychology. None the less, I was grateful for *The Tibetan Book of the Great Liberation*, and read it with avidity. If it failed to enlighten me as to the historical biography of Padmasambhava, it certainly made me better acquainted with his *symbolical* biography, and more vividly aware of Padmasambhava the myth, as distinct from Padmasambhava the man. So well had I become acquainted, by the time of my visit to the Aloobari Gompa, with the symbolical biography of the great Guru, that I was able to explain to the two lamas and Dorje Bhutia the significance of episodes of which they had not even heard. Dorje Bhutia, in particular, was greatly excited by these explanations, and on my happening to mention the source of my information insisted on coming to see me that same day in order to inspect for himself the wonderful book in which the secrets of his religion were revealed. At four o'clock in the afternoon, therefore, as arranged, the young Darjeeling-born Tibetan arrived on my doorstep, and I had the satisfaction of showing him my copy of *The Tibetan Book of the Great Liberation* and allowing him to go through its pages.

I was staying, as nowadays was my custom when visiting Darjeeling, at the Gandhamadan Vihara, the Bengali Buddhist centre on the steep hillside below Chota Khagjhora, a rather insalubrious locality on the main road into town. There was still no resident *bhikṣu*, nor any likelihood of there being one, the monks of the Bengali Buddhist Association, of which the Vihara was a branch, not being very keen, by all accounts, on living in a place as cold as Darjeeling could be and ministering to its tiny Theravādin community. But if there was no resident *bhikṣu* there was at least a resident nun, in the person of Anagarika Dharmarakshita, who was occupying not, indeed, the wooden *kuti* reserved for members of the monastic order, but one of the row of pukka guest rooms immediately adjacent. On my arrival at Chota Khagjhora from Kalimpong she was not at home, but we met that evening, after I had been out and about all day, and though the hour was late, and I was tired, she insisted on telling me all about her latest troubles and difficulties. I listened without saying very much, for though not unsympathetic I knew the aggrieved *anagārika* well enough, by this time, to be aware that she had a tendency to compound her difficulties, such as they were, by her own tactless and aggressive behaviour. This tendency was well illustrated by an unpleasant incident which occurred that very evening. While we were talking (or rather, while she was talking and I listening), an elderly Bengali Buddhist who was a permanent occupant of one of the guest rooms came back from work the worse for drink and proceeded to create a disturbance. Out rushed the *anagārika*, her face scarlet, and quivering with indignation, and upbraided the offender severely, reminding him that the place was a vihara and that he should behave accordingly. The elderly Bengali was not disposed to take this lying down, and retaliated with a torrent of coarse abuse. No doubt he should not have been drinking, nor have created a disturbance in what was supposedly a monastery, but the *anagārika* should have known better than to scold a man while he was under the influence of alcohol and better, moreover, than to scold him so harshly.

The *anagārika* was far from seeing matters in this light, and when, the following afternoon, we visited a leading lay supporter of the Vihara, a Dr Barua, in order to discuss Buddhist activities in the area, she complained bitterly to him and his wife about the way in which the drunken Bengali had spoken to her. As she saw it, she had simply acted to protect the sanctity of the Vihara and been insulted for her pains. If the Bengali Buddhists of Darjeeling had any regard at all for their religion, or for those who *did* observe its precepts, they would not allow one of the guest rooms at their religious centre to be polluted by the presence of a drunkard but would throw him out immediately! Excessive though the *anagārika*'s reaction the previous evening may have been she did, of course, have a point. As I had noticed on my previous visits, two or three of the guest rooms were occupied, permanently as it seemed, by some rather disreputable-looking Bengalis, presumably Buddhists, who took no part in the religious activities of the place, minimal as these were, and who appeared to have turned their corner of the premises into what was virtually a drinking and gambling den. Two days later, therefore, when Kali Kinker Barua, the secretary of the Vihara, gave me a ceremonial food-offering at his house, as he always did at least once whenever I was in Darjeeling, I raised the matter with him. The situation down at Chota Khagjhora was not very satisfactory, he admitted. But what was he do? He could hardly ask the occupants of the guest rooms to leave. The rent they paid was the Vihara's only regular source of income. There was no *dāna* worth mentioning. There was no *dāna* because there were no activities, and there were no activities because there was no resident *bhikṣu*. To all this there was little I could say, especially as I knew that Kali Kumar was a devout (Theravādin) Buddhist who had the interests of the Vihara very much at heart. Like the Kalimpong branch of the Maha Bodhi Society, the Darjeeling branch of the Bengal Buddhist Association suffered from lack of adequate financial support. Kali Kumar had solved the problem by letting some of the guest rooms, albeit to the wrong sort of people. I was trying to solve it, at least temporarily, by holding benefit film shows. We were both in the same boat.

What with having tea with Dr Hudson, visiting the Aloobari Gompa, and spending time with the *anagārika* and my Bengali Buddhist hosts, besides seeing various other people I knew, my additional days in Darjeeling were fully occupied. Omiya and Tilak I met several times after our initial coalescence, and eventually Tilak was able to inform me that he had arranged matters with the principal and that Omiya would be bringing the ciné projector to Kalimpong in good time for our first performance. I was now free to leave Darjeeling, which I did straight after breakfast the following morning. I was not able to bid the Queen of the Hill Stations farewell, however, without having been obliged to hear more about the *anagārika*'s troubles and difficulties. Her recital of these had in fact culminated, the day before, in her telling me that she felt depressed and homesick and shedding a few tears. But deliverance was at hand. Scarcely had she finished wiping her eyes and blowing her nose than there descended on the Vihara, enquiring for her, a French married couple. They were theosophists, it transpired. Like Dr Hudson, the husband seemed to know a lot about radiaesthesia, and he in fact soon offered to 'give some energy' to me as my vibrations were weak. Radiaesthesia seemed to be catching on in the West, I reflected, at least in theosophical circles. The arrival of her two compatriots was a tonic to the *anagārika*, and before the visit was over she had arranged to take them to Ghoom the following morning – the morning of my departure – and show them the famous Ghoom monastery. I was therefore able to leave her in a state of excitement as extreme as that of her previous depression. My own feeling, as I left Darjeeling behind me, was predominantly one of relief. Now that I had succeeded in borrowing a ciné projector there was no reason why the selling of tickets, and other preparations for the film shows, should not go ahead. Apart from our having to pick up two police constables and their prisoner, an unkempt Nyingma lama, the journey passed without incident, and I was back at

The Hermitage in time for lunch. After lunch, it being a full-moon day, I decorated the shrine in readiness for the evening puja and sermon. Not many people attended, but I gave what I thought was a good sermon, on 'Who is a Buddhist?' Joe was among those present, but after the meeting he became involved – rather inappropriately, I thought – in a long political discussion with a Bengali Hindu friend of mine.

Politics was, in fact, difficult to get away from, at least politics in the sense of having dealings with the local administration and the police. Film shows were entertainment. As such they were liable to entertainment tax. If we were to be exempted from having to pay this, on the grounds that our shows were for charity, then we would have to obtain an exemption certificate. I therefore saw both the Deputy Commissioner, who was in Kalimpong on tour, and the Sub-Divisional Officer, they being, apparently, the authorities concerned. I also dispatched Dawa to the *thana*, as the police had some (undefined) role in the business. With both Dutt-Majumdar and the youthful Bengali SDO I not only talked about the film shows, and found out just what was involved in obtaining the exemption certificate, but had a lengthy discussion regarding Christian missionaries and what was to be done about their undesirable methods of conversion, a delicate question I had already raised with Dutt-Majumdar when we met at Longview. In the SDO's case, I also discussed Miss Barclay's affairs and explored the possibility of Vaiśākha Pūrṇimā, the anniversary of the Buddha's Enlightenment, being declared a public holiday throughout the subdivision. With politics, or at any rate its administrative *avatāras*, out of the way, Dawa and I were able to meet the secretary of the Town Club and finalize the details of our bookings, and as the third week of March was succeeded by the fourth, preparations for the film shows started gathering momentum. Posters went up in the bazaar. Tickets were given to members and friends to sell from door to door. Volunteers were briefed on their duties at the Town Hall on the three nights of the film shows. Finally, to make assurance doubly sure, Dinesh was sent to Siliguri to check whether the precious cylinders had, in fact, been dispatched to us from there by ropeway.[106]

While these preparations were in progress I was also having to carry on with my usual work. There were letters to be written, the *Maha Bodhi* journal to be edited, and callers to be dealt with – not to mention my having to see to the day-to-day running of The Hermitage. There was also Sachin to be taught. Since my return from Darjeeling we had embarked on an intensive study of Shelley's shorter poems, such as 'When passion's trance is overpassed', 'To Jane: the keen stars were twinkling', and 'When the lamp is shattered'. As tended to happen when we studied poetry together, we were both sometimes left, at the end of a session, in a mood bordering on the ecstatic. There was also teaching of a more prosaic type to be done. Since my return from Darjeeling I had acquired two new pupils. One of these was the youngest of Sachin's three (younger) sisters; the other, Lobsang Phuntsok Lhalungpa, the young Tibetan aristocrat to whom Thubden Tendzin (Marco Pallis) had introduced me four years earlier and who had recently moved, with his wife and small son, into the Manjula cottage flat formerly occupied by Miss Barclay. Meera was twelve or thirteen and, like her brothers and sisters, strikingly good-looking. If Sheila, the eldest sister, could be described as handsome, and Beena, the middle one, as beautiful, Meera could best be described as extremely pretty. Though she seemed to enjoy her lessons with me she was not very bright, and was much more interested in new saris and the precise arrangement of her kiss curl than in her school books. That I had been asked to teach her (actually, to give her practice in English conversation whenever I happened to be at the Singh bungalow) was indicative of the increased closeness of my relations with the whole family. Sachin having spoken very warmly of the way in which I had looked after him in Calcutta during his illness, I was in fact for both his parents and his siblings now more *amicus familiae* than ever.

Lobsang Phuntsok was the son of the Nechung Oracle, the oracle consulted by the Tibetan government, and had been educated in Lhasa as a monk-officer. When I first met him he was still a monk-officer. Since then he had reverted to lay status and married, though whether he continued to be in the service of the Tibetan government was unclear. There was no doubt, however, that he was of a scholarly disposition and highly intelligent. Intelligence beamed from the broad, flat face, which often wore a look of amusement, and twinkled in the small, slit eyes. Mrs Lobsang – Darjeeling-born and half Bhutanese – was as beautiful as her husband was handsome. Among Tibetans, at least, she was reputed to be the most beautiful woman in the district, being even more beautiful than Princess Pema Tsedeun, the eldest daughter of the Maharaja of Sikkim, now past her prime. Unfortunately she had the habit of screwing up her eyes every few minutes, which rather detracted from the impression she made. Despite being such a belle, she was of

With Sachin's family

a friendly, obliging disposition, and though I had met her only once or twice I had no hesitation in giving her two or three books of tickets and asking her to sell them. As it happened, she sold more tickets for us than anyone else did, selling them mostly to Tibetan government officers who, I suspected, bought them more because they wanted to please her than because they wanted to support the work of the Kalimpong branch of the Maha Bodhi Society.

The week of the film shows was now, in fact, upon us. The cylinder containing the films had been collected from the ropeway station. Omiya had brought the ciné projector from Darjeeling, and on the morning of 3 April, immediately after breakfast, with Dawa and three or four volunteers, I conveyed the equipment by jeep to the Town Hall, where we spent the rest of the morning making the shabby, run-down old place as presentable as we could. With so much depending on the reliability of the projector, I took the precaution of getting Mr King, a Nationalist Chinese who had worked as an electrician in Lhasa, to come and check that it was functioning properly. He having assured me that it was functioning perfectly, and that I had nothing to worry about, I went home for lunch, returning to our temporary cinema an hour later. There was still much to be done, and the volunteers and I were kept busy right up to the time the doors opened. Despite all our efforts, however, the performance was a flop. Only seven tickets were sold, which meant that even allowing for the fact that a number of people had bought tickets in advance but not bothered to come, our first film show was a decided failure. Drastic action would have to be taken. Next morning I gave Mrs Lobsang more tickets to sell, and myself spent the remainder of the morning, and most of the afternoon, selling tickets from house to house and shop to shop in the bazaar. The result was that our second show was a success. The first performance (there were two performances this time) was very well attended, possibly because it was Sunday, though attendance at the second was less good. There being two performances, the show ended very late, and I did not get to bed until 2 a.m.

Most of the people attending the shows were Tibetans, of both sexes and all ages, and including a generous sprinkling of shaven heads and red robes. As I already knew, Tibetans were great cinema-goers, and few were the sturdy exiles from the Land of Snows who did not see every film that was screened at the town's (then) one and only 'bioscope'. As I also knew, the Tibetans were particularly fond of violent films. Thus it was not surprising that their favourite genre should have been the Western, in which there was a clearly defined conflict, in which plenty of blows and shots were exchanged, and which ended with dead bodies lying on the ground. If they had had the patience to wait for the last act, the Tibetans would probably have enjoyed *Hamlet*. Which genre – or genres – the two Raj Kapoor films represented I did not know, as I refrained from actually seeing them. They were certainly not Westerns, and in all probability contained little or no fighting. Some of the Tibetan members of the audience may, therefore, have been disappointed. One of them undoubtedly was, though whether because of the lack of violence or for some other reason was unclear. As I stood beside the door, waiting for the end of the performance, a burly figure strode out in disgust, loudly declaring that it was the worst film he had ever seen.

Despite this unfavourable verdict on the part of at least one of our patrons, I did not allow myself to be discouraged but did whatever I could to ensure the success of our third and last film show. As this did not take place until Wednesday, I had two clear days in which to boost the sale of tickets. On the Wednesday afternoon, however, when two volunteers had spent the morning giving the show extra publicity in the bazaar, Mr King discovered that the projector's exciter bulb had fused. Having failed to obtain a replacement either in the bazaar or at the Chinese School, I decided, as a last resort, to try Dr Graham's Homes. The Homes was, of course, a Christian missionary institution, and I had already tried, with no very great success, to sell tickets there, on the principle that if Christians could ask Buddhists and Hindus to support their work (as they frequently did) then there was no reason why Buddhists and Hindus should not ask Christians to support *theirs*. Mr Duncan, the whey-faced, tight-lipped superintendent of the Homes, obviously did not believe in such mutuality, and frostily told me, 'We do not approve of your activities,' though eventually he did agree, with the greatest reluctance, to accept a few tickets and even to put up a notice about them. Rubicund Mr Muir, the headmaster of the Homes' school, and his deputy Mr Ross, were more co-operative. They did not have a spare exciter bulb, but they did have a projector, and this they agreed to lend us. Back with it I therefore sped to The Hermitage, where the volunteers were waiting to take our equipment to the Town Hall and where I quickly finalized arrangements for the evening's show.

As if the fusing of the exciter bulb was not trouble enough, I also had to deal, that afternoon, with the problem of the *anagārika*. The volatile Frenchwoman had arrived with her two French friends soon after my own return from Darjeeling, the friends had stayed for two days, putting up at the Himalayan Hotel, and she had shown them the sights of Kalimpong and taken them to see Joe and Dr Roerich. On their departure for Calcutta, after I had conducted a special puja for them in the shrine, she was again thrown on her own resources, which meant that she took to spending more time at The Hermitage than was either convenient or desirable. She also took to handing me a written ‘confession’ after the evening puja, sometimes staying on to explain or discuss it. As I was planning to leave for Calcutta in the middle of the month, in order to see the Vaiśākha number of the *Maha Bodhi* journal through the press, and did not want her moving in to The Hermitage during my absence, as she had done before, I took the precaution of making arrangements for her to stay at Tirpai. When I tried to speak to her about these arrangements, however, after the volunteers had left for the Town Hall with our equipment, she burst into tears and wept bitterly for half an hour. I was therefore obliged to spend another half hour, and more, reminding her that the monastic life had its difficulties, and that she could not always have what she wanted, with the result that I was later leaving The Hermitage than I had intended.

On arriving at the Town Hall I found the place nearly full, and people still turning up. But if fortune, that fickle goddess, had decided to favour us that evening, she soon changed her mind. Despite our combined efforts, we could not get the Homes’ projector working, and at the end of three hours were forced to admit defeat. By this time the audience had become restive, even vociferous, and having made what excuses we could we had to send people home with the promise that there would be a (free) show the following evening. When they had gone we again tested the projector and eventually, at about eleven o’clock, managed to get it working. That night I did not sleep until the early hours. ‘Very trying day with innumerable disappointments and luck apparently dead against us,’ I noted in my diary, adding, ‘But we must carry on.’ In the immediate context, carrying on meant putting on a film show that very evening (the evening of Thursday, as it now was), and putting on a film show meant finding a new exciter bulb, for it was obvious we could not rely on the Homes’ projector and would have to fall back on Tilak’s. No exciter bulb being obtainable in Kalimpong, finding a new one meant making a trip to Darjeeling. In the morning I therefore caught the nine o’clock Land-rover, reaching my destination in the record time of less than two hours. After scouring all the radio and electrical shops in the town without success, meeting many friends on the way, I eventually located the bulb I wanted with a friend of Tilak’s. As I, too, was a friend of Tilak’s, and as this naturally made me *his* friend, and he mine, he was happy to let me borrow it, and I was back in Kalimpong, the elusive exciter bulb safe in my shoulder bag, a couple of hours before the film show was due to begin.

Ani-la receiving alms from Dinesh

This time fortune smiled on us the whole evening. The Town Hall was full, the projector gave no trouble, and the audience seemed to be satisfied. As I walked up and down outside, in the dark, waiting for the performance to finish, I felt relieved that we had been able to keep our promise, relieved that the film shows had proved not wholly unsuccessful, and relieved (I had to admit) that the last performance would soon be over and that I would soon be seeing the last of our present audience, at least in their cinema-going capacity. But had it really been worth it? Had all the trouble and worry been justified? In any case, I was a monk; I was trying to lead a spiritual life; yet here I was, organizing film shows, selling tickets in the bazaar, and running from place to place in search of exciter bulbs. Why was I doing this? True, the work of the Kalimpong branch of the Maha Bodhi Society had to be carried on, and its finances therefore placed on a secure footing, but was this really a sufficient reason for my becoming so deeply involved in what were, undeniably, worldly activities, and what was the significance of such involvement for my own spiritual life? Was I being (or trying to be) a good bodhisattva, engaging in worldly activities for the benefit, ultimately, of other people, or was I simply being a bad monk, allowing myself to be distracted from my true vocation of self-purification?

Whichever it may have been (and the two were not necessarily antithetical), the end of the film shows did not mean the end of the work connected with them. Films and projectors had to be returned, chairs in the Town Hall restored to their former positions, money collected from Mrs Lobsang and others, and full details of ticket sales submitted to the DC, the SDO and the police in connection with our application for exemption from entertainment tax. There were also the accounts of the film shows to be made up, and the extent to which the Maha Bodhi Society's Kalimpong branch had benefited from them ascertained. Unfortunately, it had not benefited as much as I had hoped it would – certainly not enough to place its finances on a secure footing even for a short period. This did not altogether surprise me. The sluggishness of ticket sales prior to the shows, and the piling up of unlooked-for expenses, had forewarned me that such would probably be the case and I had already taken action accordingly. The action had been drastic. I had sold the only objects of any monetary worth I possessed: my thangkas. These thangkas, a set of three depicting the sixteen *arhants* travelling by sea to China on the backs of various monsters, had been a farewell present from Marco Pallis,[107] and hence possessed a sentimental as well as a religious value for me, so that I was extremely loath to part with them. But part with them I did: in the circumstances, I had no choice. Fortunately I did not have to do the actual selling myself. Joe happening to mention that he thought he could sell them for me, I handed them over to him, and a few days later he brought me six hundred rupees. Neither then nor afterwards did he tell me to whom he had sold the thangkas, only assuring me that he had sold them, as I had stipulated, to someone who would treat them with proper respect. However, I knew that Prince Peter, for whom Joe had recently started working, currently had the Italian Ambassador staying with him, and drew my own conclusions.

Six hundred rupees was not a great sum, but together with what we had made from the film shows it would cover the branch's expenditure for the next few months. I could therefore prepare for my journey to Calcutta with a light heart, without having to worry about the immediate future of our work. Whether because the strain of organizing the film shows was now over, or for some other reason, during the week that preceded my departure light-heartedness was indeed the dominant mood among The Hermitage's little band of youthful habitués. Certainly it was the mood when Sachin and Dawa and I, together with half a dozen others, spent the day picnicking at Durpin, at the south-eastern end of the ridge on which Kalimpong was situated. Rain had recently fallen, and the haze being finer than usual we could see, 4,000 feet below, and bathed in the golden sunlight, a vast expanse of level countryside stretching away into the distance for forty or fifty miles, as it seemed, before finally merging with the overarching blue of the sky.

This picnic was not my only outing that week. One afternoon I had tea at Tirpai with Geshe Wangyal, a Mongolian monk who was a friend of Marco Pallis and had been his guest in England in the thirties. The Geshe, or 'Doctor of Buddhist Divinity', as some translated the title, was planning to leave Kalimpong. In fact he was planning not only to leave Kalimpong but to emigrate to America and teach Tibetan there in an institute of higher learning.[108] I had no such plans. I was happy in Kalimpong, and whatever the difficulties I would stay there and work for the good of Buddhism as my teacher had directed.

8

PROOF-READING AT 110°F

The Sri Gauranga Press was situated down a narrow lane behind the headquarters building. They were reputed to be one of the best printers in Calcutta, and the Maha Bodhi Society had dealt with them for many years. During the two and a half weeks for which I was in the City of Dreadful Heat,[109] as it now also was, seeing the Vaiśākha number of the *Maha Bodhi* journal through the final stages of its production, many a half hour did I spend in the Press's dark, cramped little front office checking last-minute corrections and signing print orders on the completed formes.

Most of my time, however, was spent in my room on the second floor of the headquarters building, whither there came to me, in rapid succession, first the galleys and then the proofs, brought while the ink was still wet by the Sri Gauranga Press's black-fingered printer's devil.[110] The galleys took the form of narrow strips of paper, often as much as eight or ten feet in length, on which was a single, continuous column of type. If there were more than forty or fifty misprints on a strip (the compositors did not know English, or knew very little), I sent it back with the misprints corrected and called for a second galley. Sometimes I had to call for a third. Otherwise – or when galley misprints had been reduced to no more than six or eight – the corrected matter came back to me in page-proof form and set up in the journal's traditional double columns. First page proofs did not often contain more than half a dozen misprints, so that I was usually able to give the print order on the second page proof, whether at the Press or in my own room, it being my practice to give this only after I had seen a perfectly clean proof. The Press, I had already learned, could not always be trusted, good as they were, to carry out my final corrections before printing (time was money) or, even if they did carry them out, not to make any fresh mistakes in the process. Since the Vaiśākha number comprised more than a dozen formes (there were eight pages to a forme), and since I was often reading the page proofs of earlier formes and galleys of later ones at the same time, my little table in front of the barred window was usually covered with proofs of different kinds, at their various stages of progress, the long strips of the galleys hanging over the edge of the table and trailing across the floor.

If the proofs came from the Sri Gauranga Press with the ink still wet, they often went back damp with my perspiration, which fell in great drops onto the paper from my forehead and soaked it from the palms of my hands and the underside of my wrists and forearms. On my arrival in the city, which I reached in mid-afternoon, the weather had been very sultry, with a hot wind blowing. Since then the wind had subsided, but it continued to be sultry, and before many days had passed the thermometer was standing at 110 °F.[iii] In Calcutta, it seemed, April was indeed the cruellest month, even if it was cruel, here, for reasons different from those which the author of the famous line proceeded to allege. I sat at my proof-covered table wearing only my inner robe (a sort of waist-cloth), the coarse cotton of which adhered uncomfortably to the seat of my chair and felt disagreeably tight about my middle. Every now and then I had recourse to the earthenware water pot that stood in the corner by the door, or, more occasionally, sent out one of the Society's bare-legged servants to a nearby tea stall for tea. Before lunch I doused myself, Indian style, in the bathroom on the opposite corner of the inner veranda, but ten minutes later I would be as hot and sticky as ever. On days when the heat was particularly trying I took a second bath in the afternoon, and even a third one in the evening. Great as the temptation might be, however, one had to be careful not to take too many baths, as this tended to deplete the skin's natural oils, with the result that one came out in an unsightly and rather painful rash. Since it was so hot I had little or no appetite, and found the Society's meagre breakfast of two slices of toast and its insubstantial, ante-meridian lunch (for the monks) of rice and curry, supplemented by the occasional tiny pot of sweet curds, more than sufficient for my needs. Night brought but scant relief. The atmosphere was close; I slept heavily, almost as though I had been drugged, and woke to the grey dawn light with a feeling of the oppressiveness of existence – a feeling that weighed not only on my eyelids but almost on my soul. By six o'clock, however, having meditated a little and had breakfast, I was seated at my table getting on with the work for which I had come to Calcutta at this, the very time of year I would least have wished to be there.

That work had started long before my arrival in the City of Dreadful Heat. For two months and more I had been collecting articles for the Vaiśākha number, reading them, corresponding with their respective authors, and preparing the articles themselves for the press. Now they were all passing through my hands in proof form and I was reading them once again, perhaps even more closely than before. As befitted the avowedly international character of the journal, indeed of the Maha Bodhi Society itself, the authors of the articles were of seven or eight different nationalities, belonged to both the East and the West, and represented – in the case of the Buddhist contributors – both the Theravādin and the Mahāyāna traditions. The authors of no fewer than five of the articles had previously been contributors to *Stepping-Stones*, my own minuscule journal of Himalayan religion, culture, and education; after its demise I continued to be in contact with them, and on my appointment to the editorial board had succeeded in enlisting them as contributors to the bigger and better known *Maha Bodhi*, then in its sixty-third year of publication. Perhaps the most prominent member of the group was Lama Govinda, with whose interpretation of Buddhism I was very much in agreement and who was now a personal friend. The lama, who had known Anagarika Dharmapala, and been actively associated with the Society in the early thirties, had of course contributed to its journal before; but disagreements having arisen between him and Devapriya Valisinha he ceased contributing and in fact virtually severed his connection with the Society. One of the disagreements between him and Devapriya-ji was of a personal nature, relating to Govinda's style, or distinguishing title. At first, at the time of his association with the Society, the future lama had styled himself Brahmachari Govinda, as he had done previously in Ceylon. Subsequently, however, he began styling himself first Anagarika Brahmachari Govinda, then Anagarika B. Govinda, and finally, after his initiation into Tibetan Buddhism and his marriage to Li Gotami, Lama Anagarika Govinda. Devapriyji had strongly objected to this latest development. How could a married man call himself an *anagārika*, he wanted to know. An *anagārika* was by definition homeless, and hence wifeless; he was one who, without being a *bhikkhu*, gave up all domestic ties and civic responsibilities in order to devote his life to the Dharma – as Anagarika Dharmapala had done. For Govinda to go on calling himself an *anagārika* after his marriage was highly improper. It was an insult to the memory of the Society's revered founder, who had been a *real anagārika*. Devapriya-ji, who as Dharmapala's personal disciple and chosen successor cherished his memory deeply, had therefore refused to print Govinda's articles in the *Maha Bodhi* journal as being by Lama *Anagarika* Govinda (he had once, I believe, blue-pencilled the offending title), with the result that Govinda had ceased to submit articles.

As the friend of both parties, as well as editor of the journal, I naturally was anxious to bring the disagreement to an end and for Govinda to become as regular a contributor to the *Maha Bodhi* as he had been to *Stepping-Stones*. Since neither the German lama nor the Sinhalese *upāsaka* would yield, a compromise had to be found. Devapriya-ji's insistence that Govinda was *not* an *anagārika*, and that he therefore could not be so styled in the pages of the official organ of the leading Buddhist society in India, had somehow to be reconciled with Govinda's claim (in his correspondence with me) that the dropping of 'Anagarika' from his title would seriously affect his interest in the copyright of *all* his writings. My solution to the dilemma was that contributions by Govinda should appear in the *Maha Bodhi* as being by 'Lama A. Govinda'. This solution having proved acceptable to both parties (I had arrived at it earlier in the year), I had already been able to print Govinda's poem 'The Buddha's Seat',[112] and now had an article from him for publication in the Vaiśākha number.

The article was entitled 'The Buddha as the Ideal of the Perfect Man and the Embodiment of the Dharma'.

> That the Buddha lived as a man among men gives us the courage to follow Him. That as a man he succeeded in overcoming the man within him, gives us the certainty that we also can overcome ourselves, that we also can transcend our human limitations and liberate ourselves from the shackles of death and rebirth.[113]

But though the Buddha was a man in the general sense of the word, he was not *only* a man, but something more, something that reached out into the timeless and infinite, where concepts like 'man' and 'not-man' lost their meaning. Buddhahood, the lama insisted, was in fact transcendental, and this 'transcendental' nature was in no way in conflict with the humanness of the Buddha. Being transcendental, the Buddha's nature was, in the words of the *Prajñāpāramitā Sūtra*, 'inconceivable' and only to be 'hinted at' in symbols. It was not to be communicated by creating a plastic image of the Buddha in the conventional-realistic style of Greek portraiture, an attempt which had resulted in 'the pathetic failure of Gandhara art' which, though of great interest to the archaeologist and art historian, was entirely devoid of religious inspiration and depth of feeling for the supramundane greatness of the Tathāgata. In Govinda's opinion it was fortunate that Gandharan statuary had died as quickly as it had come into existence and been soon superseded by a new wave of spiritual art, in which the symbolic value replaced the naturalistic tendency in the representation of the ideal form of Buddhahood. As with the visible representation of the Enlightened One, so with the treatment of the Buddha's life story. What was important to the Buddha's followers were not the material facts and their occurrence in time or chronological sequence, but the Buddha's spiritual quest, the development of his spiritual career, the psychological facts and inner experiences that led to his Enlightenment and the formulation of his teachings.

> These inner experiences were subsequently concretized into external occurrences in the description of the Buddha's life, and gave rise to the most beautiful and profoundly true symbolism of art and poetry which carried the eternal message of the Buddha into the farthest corners of the world and did more for the propagation of Buddhism than the learned treatises of philosophers and scholars.[114]

The transcendental also featured in an article on 'Conditions and the Unconditioned' by Edward Conze, another of the five contributors to the Vaiśākha number who had previously been contributors to *Stepping-Stones*. An object, Dr Conze pointed out, was swallowed up by the conditions which governed its presentation, and could not be separated from them. The same held good when we regarded a thing not as a datum but as a process or *event*, and considered the conditions which produced it. An investigation of conditions was of central importance for the Buddhist scheme of meditations, undermining as it did our belief in the fixity and ultimate validity of the sense-given distinctions between things around us. Buddhists meditated on conditions in order to win salvation from all conditioned things, with a wish to reject them in so far as they were conditioned, thereby winning through to the Unconditioned.[115]

In the articles by the three other members of the group the transcendental featured only by implication. Dr George Roerich wrote on 'Vanaratna – the Last of the Great Panditas', basing himself on the Tibetan *Blue Annals*, which he was then translating, while Marco Pallis wrote on 'Some Aspects of Buddhist Education' and HRH Prince Peter of Greece and Denmark on 'Buddhism and the Japanese Character'. Marco Pallis made, *inter alia*, much the same point with regard to the representation of the Buddha in art that Lama Govinda had made. Latterly there had appeared in the Buddhist world, he complained, a good many cheap prints showing episodes in the life of the Victorious One and other pious subjects, which had been copied, as far as style was concerned, from the 'naturalistic' atrocities which nowadays passed for religious art in Europe, and these were tending to replace the traditional models. It was forgotten that these models were the work of inspired craftsmen, who knew how to give form to the symbolical aspect of the thing they portrayed: the naturalistic image for its part stopped short at the perfunctory reproduction of surfaces.

> The true Buddhist iconography therefore is accurate in an 'essential' sense, which no 'photographic' image can ever be, and that is why it is able to evoke in the beholder those genuine intellections, but for which piety would rapidly degenerate into mere sentimentality, as it has done elsewhere.[116]

In view of the current Zen boom in America, echoes of which had reached me even in Kalimpong, Prince Peter's observations on the relation between Buddhism, particularly in its Zen form, and the Japanese character, were of special interest. A psychologist and anthropologist who had recently visited Japan, he believed that in that country the techniques of mysticism had been adopted without the mysticism. The average Japanese, endowed as he apparently was with an unusually liberal dose of fierce aggression which had, at all times, to be kept in check, looked upon the Buddhist teachings mainly as efficient precepts of self-discipline, of self-training in perfection, as the means by which one might obtain 'expertness' which causes a man to be completely absorbed in the tasks he has undertaken, eliminating the 'observing self' and giving him total dedication during action. Such training culminated in a supreme release from conflict, from the ever-present watchfulness of that which we in the West called our conscience.

> And that is where the special aspect of the Japanese character reveals itself. The everyday conflict between one's own terrific aggression and one's social obligations is so great with the Japanese that, in order to free themselves from it, they seek the techniques if not the meaning of Buddhism.[117]

This gave their conception of the Dharma a very special, national distortion, at which one could not help wondering.

Articles by former contributors to *Stepping-Stones* were, of course, in the minority, though it was noticeable that they were of a more substantial character than the rest. Prominent among the latter were D. T. Devendra's 'Where a Hero King was Born', an account of the excavation of a twelfth-century stupa in Ceylon, and Christmas Humphreys' 'The Menace of Belief', in which the founder of the Buddhist Society, London, 'speaking with thirty years of experience in the Western Buddhist field', declared that one of the great attractions of Buddhism was that it lacked the warlike voice of authority.

> No one School of Buddhism has the monopoly of the Dhamma, and woe betide the School or nation which claims it.[118]

Most of the remaining articles were very short, being in effect little more than expressions, on the part of well known Buddhists like Alexandra David-Néel and U Maung Maung Ji, and scholars like Dr Pachow and Dr Anukul Chandra Banerjee, of goodwill towards the Society and its work. The rest of the Vaiśākha number was made up of the journal's regular features, such as book reviews, the Notes and News section, and an editorial, as well as the 'messages' from sundry presidents and prime ministers to which the Society seemed to attach so much importance and with which I could willingly have dispensed.

The editorial, which as usual was from my pen, was headed simply 'Buddha Gaya'. But I was not concerned only to recall the Figure beneath the bodhi tree, radiant and victorious in the early morning sun, or even to remind readers of the fact that, after sixty years of agitation, the Buddhists of India still had less than half a share in the management of their own holiest shrine, and the millions of Buddhists in Ceylon, Burma, Siam, Cambodia, China, Japan, Tibet, and Nepal no share at all. I was concerned with the fact that, according to reports appearing in the press, Bodh Gaya was 'shortly to assume further importance in the eyes of the world' by having a *Samanvaya Mandir*, or centre for religious, cultural, and racial synthesis, built there by Acharya Vinoba Bhave, the veteran follower of Mahatma Gandhi, whose movement for the voluntary donation of land had recently attracted a good deal of attention and support. The attainment of Enlightenment by the Buddha, I commented, apparently did not suffice. Bodh Gaya would now be given full importance by having a Samanvaya Mandir built there by Sri Bhave. It was as though one should think to increase the importance of the Himalayas by building a sand-castle on their lower slopes. Not only was the importance of Bodh Gaya to be enhanced; the teachings of the Buddha were, it appeared, to be improved upon. '*Vedanta* and *ahiṃsā* (teachings of the Lord Buddha) were interlinked,' the press had reported the Acharya as saying, 'one could not exist without the other. Particularly *ahiṃsā*, non-violence, could never have [a] solid basis without the foundation of Vedanta', for '*Satya* (truth) was revealed in all its glory only in Vedanta.' That Sri Bhave's ideas were not without powerful backing was evinced by the fact that the digging of the well which would mark the centre of the Samanvaya Mandir had been inaugurated by the president of India, while the prime minister had made a donation toward the cost of sinking the well. The abbot of the Shaivite monastery at Bodh Gaya, whose predecessor had opposed by all means, fair and foul, the transfer of the Maha Bodhi Temple to Buddhist hands, had donated five *bighas* of land to the institution – a circumstance which must surely have aroused the worst suspicions of any Buddhist who had even the slightest knowledge of events in Bodh Gaya during the last sixty years. I concluded by wondering what would be the reaction of the Muslim world, or of the Roman Catholics, in similar circumstances, and asking what answer the Buddhist world was going to make to the challenge now being made to the very existence of Bodh Gaya as a centre for the dissemination of pure Buddhist religion and culture.[119]

When I wrote my editorial I was not aware that the press reports about Acharya Vinoba Bhave and his Samanvaya Mandir were all by-lined not from Bodh Gaya but from Sarvodayapuri. Overnight Bodh Gaya, which had borne that name for centuries, had become Sarvodayapuri – the City of Sarvodaya! Bhikkhu Silabhadra, one of the vice-presidents of the Society and a member of the editorial board, accordingly wrote to the editor of the *Hindustan Standard*, a leading English daily, protesting against the innovation; but his letter was not published, and I therefore inserted it at the back of the Vaiśākha number, together with a note to the effect that we were printing it there for the information of our readers,

Cover of the 1954 Vaiśākha number of the Maha Bodhi journal

as well as to show how difficult it was for the Buddhist point of view to find expression in a certain section of the press.

Besides the actual proof-reading, seeing the Vaiśākha number of the *Maha Bodhi* journal through the press meant commissioning an artist to produce a special cover, which he did to a design of my own, choosing the illustrations (this involved a visit to the Indian Museum in Chowringhee), and finding fillers for the blank spaces at the end of some articles. Finding fillers was less easy than one might have thought, but in the case of the present (double) issue of the journal I was fortunate, having just come across a copy of *The Path of Light*, L. D. Barnett's (incomplete) English rendering of Śāntideva's *Bodhicaryāvatāra*, a work I subsequently characterized as 'one of the brightest gems in the thickly studded tiara of Mahāyāna Buddhist literature.'[120] So delighted was I with this work, and so inspired by the combination of ecstatic devotion and penetrating insight with which the author celebrated the incomparable bodhisattva ideal, that I could not forbear sprinkling the pages of the Vaiśākha number liberally with quotations from it on such topics as the Thought of Enlightenment (as the translator called the *bodhicitta*) and the different *pāramitās*, the 'perfections' or 'transcendental virtues'. All this – reading proofs, commissioning a cover, choosing illustrations, and finding fillers – I had to do quite single-handed, sitting at my desk in front of the barred window, in my room on the second floor of the headquarters building, with the perspiration trickling down my body and dripping from my forehead. Devapriya-ji was not in Calcutta. He was in Japan, or at least was on his way there, having left Calcutta by steamer a few weeks earlier in order to attend the Pan-Pacific Buddhist Conference that was to be held in Tokyo. With him he had taken a portion of Buddha-relics and two bodhi tree saplings for presentation to the Buddhists of Japan. If he ever happened to think of me sweltering over the proofs of the Vaiśākha number in his stead he must have smiled to himself, and may even have recollected his comment to me the previous year, when the Society's predominantly Hindu governing body, having refused to accept his proposal that I should be formally appointed editor of the *Maha Bodhi* journal, reluctantly agreed to my becoming a member of the seven- or eight-man editorial board. I remembered his words very well. Himself excepted, he had said, the other board members would take little or no interest in the actual production of the magazine, though they might criticize it afterwards, and I would be left to do all the work. So far no criticism had been forthcoming from that quarter, but in other respects the little general secretary's prediction had proved accurate, and now that he was in Japan and I in Calcutta, seeing the Vaiśākha number through the press, it was proving more accurate than ever.

Devapriya-ji's was not the only familiar face missing from the headquarters building. Soratha, the Little Monk, was also away, so that there was no question of my being able to relieve the tedium of proof-reading by indulging in the lively verbal exchanges that had become customary between us. He and our common friend Venerable Sangharatana, the voluble and eccentric *bhikkhu*-in-charge of the Society's important Sarnath branch, had gone to Ceylon. With them had gone Anagarika P. Sugatananda (Francis Story), the English-born director of the rather grandly named Burma World Buddhist Mission, whom I had happened to meet on one of my earlier visits to Calcutta. I naturally had welcomed the opportunity of exchanging ideas with a fellow Western Buddhist, but the meeting turned out to be a great disappointment to me, as perhaps it was to him too. Sugatananda, who was a few years older than me and had like me served in the army, was a rationalistic neo-Theravādin, and his constant scoffing and sneering at the supposedly degenerate Mahāyāna was so little to my taste that I felt no inclination to pursue the contact any further. He indeed struck me as being a good example of a middle-class Englishman of the superior, supercilious type which had helped make the very name of 'Englishman' obnoxious to people in so many parts of the world, and I wondered how my two warm-hearted Sinhalese friends were faring in his company now that the three of them were travelling together in Ceylon.

But if Devapriya-ji and Soratha were missing from the headquarters building, Jinaratana, the High Priest, most certainly was not. In the absence of Devapriya-ji, who as general secretary ranked as his administrative, though not his religious, superior, his polished pate and yellow silken robe were more in evidence than ever, and even when he himself was not to be seen his harsh, discordant tones could be heard coming from some other part of the building as he gave orders, berated the servants, or greeted visitors of the more well-to-do sort. Since I could not in honesty regard him as being other than a bad monk, a bad Buddhist, and even, in certain respects, a bad man, and since he was aware of this, and aware of at least some of the reasons for my attitude, relations between us, though less awkward than they had been, were neither close nor cordial. For my part, I felt unable either to respect him as someone senior to me and more developed spiritually, on the one hand, or, on the other, to tell him what I really thought of his arrogance, his worldly way of life, and his wholesale hypocrisy. He, for his part, probably felt equally unable either to treat me as a junior monk or to be as open as he was (in their own language) with the other Sinhalese monks, for most of whom a *bhikkhu* was a *bhikkhu* and the question of his being a good or a bad one hardly arose, though of course appearances had to be kept up in front of the laity. With Devapriya-ji and Soratha away, however, and me seeing the Vaiśākha number through the press, we were thrown more into each other's company than usual; relations between us improved, and we somehow arrived at a *modus vivendi*, possibly as a result of our several times discussing the finances of the journal, of which Jinaratana was managing editor, with a seat on the editorial board and responsibility for subscriptions, advertisements, and dispatch and distribution. That relations between us had improved, and a *modus vivendi* arrived at, was both a source of satisfaction to me and a source of uneasiness. It was a source of satisfaction to me because it pained me to be on anything less than friendly terms with a brother monk, or fellow Buddhist, even a bad one, but a source of uneasiness inasmuch as I feared that in being on better terms with him I might in fact be condoning, or appearing to condone, certain (unsavoury) aspects of his behaviour, thus compromising, if not actually betraying, the very ideals I was pledged to uphold.

Though Jinaratana and I saw more of each other than usual, the self-styled High Priest was far from being my only source of company. I spent an evening or two with Sachin's relatives in Hindustan Building, attended a tea party in Park Street in the flat of Marguerite Allen, a friend of Irene Ray's, who was also present, where we discussed Tantric Buddhism and Sri Aurobindo's poetry (of which I did not have a very high opinion), and went for walks in the vicinity of College Square with Jayadev, another young ex-Untouchable protégé of Anand-ji's, who had once worked for him in Wardha and was now at a loose end. There were also meetings with old friends like Venerable Amritananda, the young-looking secretary of the Dharmodaya Sabha in Nepal, Dr Kajiyama, who was still studying with Kashyap-ji at Nalanda, and Phani Sanyal, who took me on another visit to his father, with whom I had a long discussion on the place of grace in Buddhism, as well as exchanges with a Bengali student on Communism and Socialism and with a Tamil student from Ceylon on Buddhism and Tamil literature. The greater part of my time, however, I spent in my room, with little company other than that of the black-fingered printer's devil who, three or four times a day, brought me a fresh batch of proofs and took away those I had corrected. Though the Sri Gauranga Press worked quickly, they did not work quickly enough for my liking. Not only did I want to get away from the heat of Calcutta; I was also anxious to be back in Kalimpong in good time to prepare for our Vaiśākha Pūrṇimā celebrations. I therefore fixed the date of my departure and gave them an ultimatum: either send me the remaining proofs by 5 May, while I was still in Calcutta, or be forced to post them to me in Kalimpong after that date – which of course meant that the printing would take more time and cost them more money.

The final page-proofs therefore came flooding in, with the result that my deadline was met, though not without my having had to proof-read right up to within half an hour of my departure from the headquarters building. Jinaratana came to the station and saw me off, as did Jayadev. With me in the reserved second-class compartment were Phani and his small nephew, my universalist friend having decided that he and his young relative would benefit from spending a few weeks in the comparative cool of the hills. Jayadev wanted to come too, but I already had one protégé of Anand-ji's staying with me at The Hermitage and did not really want another, the more especially as Dinesh had been misbehaving of late and I was expecting that after my arrival in Kalimpong I would probably have to ask him to leave.

9
SURVEYING BUDDHISM

The adage that 'one thing leads to another' may be seen as a homelier version of the basic Buddhist principle of *pratītya-samutpāda* or conditioned co-production, the principle that phenomena come into existence not by chance, or as a result of the decree of fate, but in dependence on a certain complex of causes and conditions. It was an adage that was certainly exemplified in the case of the circumstances that led to my being in Bangalore in the summer of 1954 and there delivering, under the auspices of the Indian Institute of Culture, the lectures which subsequently appeared in book form as *A Survey of Buddhism*.

The catena of these circumstances stretched back to the early months of 1947, when I was staying at the Ramakrishna Mission Institute of Culture in Calcutta and happened to come across a dusty pile of back numbers of the *Aryan Path*, a monthly magazine published from Bombay. Containing as it did articles on both Eastern and Western religion and culture I found the magazine of great interest and spent many a happy hour working my way through the pile. During my wandering days I read it whenever I chanced to light upon a copy, whether at an ashram or in someone's home, and after my arrival in Kalimpong not only arranged to receive it in exchange for *Stepping-Stones* but started contributing articles, poems, and book reviews. These contributions led to an exchange of letters with the editor, Sophia Wadia, who turned out to be connected with the Ananda Vihara, Bombay, and to have helped with the production of Dr N. K. Bhagwat's edition and English translation of the *Dhammapada*, a copy of which I had bought in Delhi within weeks of my arrival in India[121] and had carried around with me ever since. Sophia Wadia was in fact a theosophist and sympathetic to Buddhism, as was her husband B. P. Wadia, who wrote in the *Aryan Path* under the Buddhistic pseudonym of 'Shravaka'. They were not, however, Adyar theosophists. They belonged to a branch of the theosophical movement that repudiated as aberrations the Hinduizing and Christianizing tendencies of Annie Besant and C. W. Leadbeater and sought to return to the 'original' theosophy of Mme Blavatsky, which they believed to be closer to Buddhism. Such being the case, it was not surprising that they should be anxious to see a knowledge of Buddhism flourishing in India, and not surprising that they should want to have a series of lectures on Buddhism at the Institute they had established in Bangalore. This was where I came in. At the beginning of the year Sophia Wadia had sounded me out as to the possibility of my paying a visit to the Garden City, I had responded positively, further letters had been exchanged, and eventually B. P. Wadia had formally invited me to give four lectures at the Institute during the first half of July. The last two days of June therefore saw me travelling down the east coast of the subcontinent on the Calcutta–Madras Mail.

Soratha came with me to Howrah Station and saw me off, as did the scholarly Saddhatissa, who was studying for his BA at the Benares Hindu University and who four years earlier had been present at my *bhikkhu* ordination in Sarnath. I had spent little more than a week in Calcutta, and had barely had time to see the July issue of the *Maha Bodhi* through the press or listen to Soratha's accounts of how he and Sangharatana had fared in Ceylon with Anagarika Sugatananda. They had not fared very well, the Little Monk admitted ruefully, pursing his lips and shaking his head at the recollection of what he and his brother monk had had to endure. The *anagārika* undoubtedly possessed a good knowledge of the Dhamma, and was an excellent speaker, and the speeches he had delivered at twenty or more different parts of the island – speeches which he and Sangharatana had translated – had been received with great enthusiasm, but he possessed a foul temper, was extremely exigent, and quarrelled with almost everyone with whom he had any dealings. A hundred times a day he and Sangharatana had exclaimed to each other, 'If only we were travelling with Sangharakshita and translating for *him* instead of for Sugatananda!' As it happened, this could well have been the case. Only a few months earlier the Maha Bodhi Society of Ceylon had proposed that I should write a full-length biography of Anagarika Dharmapala and invited me to spend a few months at their Colombo headquarters for that purpose. Had I accepted the proposal (and so far I had not actually rejected it) I could have been leaving for Ceylon that afternoon instead of for Bangalore, and Soratha, instead of coming to the station to see me off, could have been accompanying me.

With me in the second-class sleeping compartment, in which I had a reserved berth, were three other passengers, all of them South Indians. Two were middle-aged businessmen, the third a Catholic priest. It was my experience that even travellers *not* occupying the more democratic third-class and inter-class carriages usually were not slow to enter into conversation, especially if their journey was going to be a long one, but on this occasion my friendly overtures met with little success. Neither of the two businessmen knew much Hindi (I knew only a few words of Tamil), while the priest was obviously wary of speaking to an Englishman who very evidently was not a Christian and might, for all he knew, actually be the Devil in disguise. I therefore took out Gide's *The Immoralist*,[122] which I had bought a few days previously, and soon was absorbed in 'Michel's adventure', as the author called his hero's story of his self-discovery, of the growth in him of a confused consciousness of untouched treasures somewhere lying covered up, hidden, 'smothered by culture and decency and morality', of the terrible cost of freedom, and of the burden that freedom itself could be. So absorbed was I in the story that I did not sleep that night until – long after the occupants of the other berths had switched off their lights – I had turned the last page of the book.

Whether because of my having spent the previous evening absorbed in *The Immoralist*, or on account of a difference in the air (we were not far from the coast), or simply because I had slept particularly well, when I awoke in the morning my mood was one of exhilaration. It was a mood that was enhanced by my enjoyment of the lyricism of certain passages in Gide's *Fruits of the Earth*, which I had bought at the same time as *The Immoralist* and into which, after an early breakfast, I started dipping. But though I enjoyed the French writer's lyricism, as a whole his prose style was too stilted and self-conscious – I had almost said too affected – for my taste, nor did I like his constant references to the Deity or appreciate the curious mixture, in *Later Fruits of the Earth*, of the Gospels and Communism.[123] For all his avowed hedonism, and his protestations that he called nature God, he struck me as being in some ways a very Christian – even a very Protestant – sort of writer, and after a while I laid the book aside and spent the rest of the morning looking out of the window. At every station at which the train stopped – and there were many stops – it was wonderful to see what a variety of things was being sold by the hawkers who marched up and down the platform crying their wares. There were cakes, biscuits, fruits, books and magazines in half a dozen languages (and half a dozen scripts), brightly painted toys, and fried delicacies hot and crisp from the pan, as well as lunches which came packeted in a plantain leaf and with each individual item, even the liquid ones, neatly wrapped in its own separate segment of rubbery green. One such lunch I bought. It cost me only a rupee and two annas, and was the best meal I had tasted for a long time. What a difference there was, I reflected, between the stations on the Calcutta–Madras[124] line and those on the Calcutta–Siliguri one, on which there were relatively few stations and where it was sometimes impossible to get so much as a cup of tea!

Nor was it only the stations, and the catering arrangements, that were different. The landscape, too, had changed, especially now that we had entered Madras state. Gone was the dense green vegetation, so rank and so profuse, of Bengal and Orissa – vegetation out of which there protruded, every few miles, the cluster of thatched huts that denoted a village. In its stead was a predominance of scrub and bare soil with, here and there, a line of areca palms silhouetted against the sky. We were in another climatic region, another culture, even another world, one that differed from the world of northern India in so many ways, and which I had not seen for more than five years.[125] Already Calcutta, and even the foothills of the Himalayas where I now lived and worked, seemed very far away, and as the warm afternoon wore on I found myself reviewing my activities over the last two months, from my return to Kalimpong after editing the Vaiśākha number of the *Maha Bodhi* to my arrival in Calcutta the previous week, almost as though they had been those of another person. May and June had been comparatively uneventful. I had continued to teach Sachin, Meera, and Lobsang Phuntsok, and to spend time with visitors; the Kalimpong branch of the Maha Bodhi Society had celebrated Vaiśākha Pūrṇimā, both with a religious function at The Hermitage and a public meeting at the Town Hall; Dinesh had left in a huff, after being told he must either mend his ways or find somewhere else to stay; and Sachin and I had spent a week in Darjeeling and Kurseong, in each of which places I lectured and conferred with local Buddhists, besides spending a night at Longview, where I renewed acquaintance with Dutt-Majumdar, the Deputy Commissioner, who with the District Superintendent of Police was then investigating a disturbance in a neighbouring tea estate.

But uneventful though May and June had been, there was one circumstance that was perhaps of greater significance, in the light of subsequent developments, than I realized at the time. This was the fact that prominent among the four or five local Buddhists whom I invited to address the Vaiśākha meeting at the Town Hall was the red-robed figure of Dhardo Rimpoche, the Gelug incarnate lama who lived in the Old Bhutan Palace at Eleventh Mile. We had met the previous year, when I went to see him in connection with a dispute that had arisen in Bodh Gaya between him, as abbot of the Tibetan monastery there, and the monk in charge of the adjacent Maha Bodhi rest house, and I had come away from the interview not only convinced that he was the innocent party but deeply impressed by his patent goodwill, candour, and integrity.[126] It was no surprise to me, therefore, that when I took Phani to see him, a few days before the Town Hall meeting, my spiritually-minded Bengali friend should have been equally impressed and have commented in the warmest terms on the Rimpoche's serene, friendly, and unassuming behaviour. As this was Phani's first experience of Tibetan Buddhism – and Tibetan Buddhists – I was delighted that his impression was such a positive one. His impression of Christianity, at least in its missionary form, was rather less positive. As we passed through Dr Graham's Homes one morning, on our way to a picnic at Dailo, I was mocked and jeered at over the wall of their cottage by a group of teenage Christian boys who evidently regarded a Buddhist monk as an interloper and an enemy. Usually I ignored such manifestations of intolerance, but on the present occasion I swept in through the gate, closely followed by Phani, the boys scattering in terror as I did so with cries of 'He's coming in!' Inside the cottage I found the house mother, as she was called, and severely upbraided her for not teaching her charges to show more respect for the representatives of other religions. The wretched woman stammered a half-apology, though she was not personally to blame for what was in fact still the ethos of the whole institution, despite Independence, and later on I sent Mr Duncan, the Superintendent of the Homes, a formal letter of complaint.

Recalling the incident that warm afternoon, as I reviewed my activities over the last two months, I wondered, not for the first time, what it was that made people intolerant of beliefs and practices other than their own and whether some religions were not intolerant by their very nature. Christianity appeared to fall within this category. All its major historical forms had on occasion proscribed and persecuted, even tortured and burned alive at the stake, and it was not surprising that the missionaries – inheritors as they were of this grim tradition, and surrounded as they believed themselves to be by the forces of darkness – should be narrow-minded and intolerant.... Christianity was said to have taken firm root in South India. Were the missionaries of Madras, I wondered, as intolerant as those of Kalimpong?...

Madras! After I had spent a second night in the train, here we were at Madras Central, and here was Venerable Jinananda waiting on the platform to welcome me and whisk me off to the Maha Bodhi centre in Kennett Lane for breakfast. Though quite large, the building in which I partook of that meal was old and inconvenient, and I noticed that there was no shrine-room. Like several other Maha Bodhi centres, the place was in fact not so much a temple or a monastery as a caravanserai for Sinhalese pilgrims on their way to the holy places of northern India. The *bhikkhu*-in-charge looked after the pilgrims, made merit for them by accepting their offerings ('making merit' was the principal object of a pilgrimage for old-fashioned Buddhists), and in his spare time he did what he could to propagate the Dharma among the more educated portion of the predominantly Hindu population. On the whole it was not a very inspiring life for a well-meaning monk, as Jinananda seemed to be, and in the afternoon, after I had written a few letters, he was glad to accompany me to the Ramakrishna Math at Mylapore, the Brahmin quarter of the city. Here I met Swami Kailashananda, the Math's rather saturnine president. I had met him in the same place seven years earlier, within days of my going forth 'from home into the homeless life', and when I was still rather conscious of my shaven head and saffron robes. On that occasion he had seemed dubious of the wisdom of the step I had just taken, but now, no doubt realizing that I had persevered in my chosen way of life, he welcomed me as cordially as his rather aloof temperament permitted and we had a very friendly conversation. Back in Kennett Lane, having found the city's leading English bookshop closed, I talked to a young monk who was studying at one of the local colleges, then left to catch the overnight train to Bangalore, Jinananda accompanying me to the station and seeing me off.

Bangalore was one of the pleasantest cities in India. From the fact that its central area abounded in beautifully laid-out parks and gardens, some of which dated from the Moghul period, it was known as the Garden City. In 1949 I had spent several weeks there,[127] on my way back to northern India and, I hoped, formal monastic ordination, and I thought I knew the city, but as the car that had met me at the station made its way through the busy streets to the Wadias' residence on a tree-lined avenue in a quiet suburb I failed to recognize a single landmark. Either Bangalore had changed a lot, as had so many Indian cities in the years following Independence, or I had seen less of it than I supposed. The residence in question was a substantial, Western-style building. As if to emphasize the owners' link with Buddhism it was called Maitri Bhavan, which could be rendered as 'the Abode of Loving-Kindness', *maitrī* or loving-kindness being the first of the four *brahma vihāras* or 'sublime (mental) states' to be developed, in meditation, by the Buddhist. B. P. Wadia was there to welcome me. We had not met before, but on one of my visits to Bombay I had been taken to Flora Fountain[128] to hear him speak on theosophy, and had a vivid memory of a packed hall and a powerful lecture that obviously impressed the audience deeply. In appearance he had not changed much since then. As his 'surname' indicated, he was by birth a Parsee (in fact, a member of the wealthy Bombay shipping family), but he was taller and bulkier than the average member of his community and wore, moreover, a beard which, together with his benign look and confident bearing, served to give him an appearance of almost regal dignity. After we had talked for a while, he escorted me to the Institute and there installed me in the guest room. For the rest of the morning I was left to my own devices, so that I was able to look at the extensive and well-equipped library, next to which the guest room was conveniently situated, and write a few letters. It was then time for lunch. This I had at Maitri Bhavan with B. P. Wadia, after which the car returned me to the Institute, where I rested and wrote more letters and where I received a visit from Dr and Mrs Doraiswamy, who it seemed were responsible for the day-to-day running of things. The former, as I already knew, and as he was not slow to remind me, was a cousin of my friend R. A. Padmanathan, the hospitable manager of Longview.

That evening I met Sophia Wadia, with whom I had been so long in correspondence. Younger than her husband, who must have been well over sixty, and the shorter by a head, she had a broad forehead, an earnest expression, and a resonant contralto voice that at times seemed too big for her frame, and she was dressed entirely in white, almost like a priestess. Annie Besant, as I remembered reading somewhere, had also dressed entirely in white, even her shoes being of that colour, so that it was possible for a Brahmin admirer to style her, on account of her erudition and eloquence, as Sarva-shukla-Saraswati or 'the All-White Saraswati', Saraswati being the popular Hindu goddess of education and learning.[129] There was no doubt that Sophia Wadia could also be so styled, at least as far as her appearance went. Whether she was comparable to the legendary Annie Besant in point of erudition and eloquence was another matter. Soon I had an opportunity of judging for myself, or at least of forming an initial impression. Maitri Bhavan, where we met, besides being the residence of the Wadias when they were in Bangalore, was the local centre, apparently, of the United Lodge of Theosophists, the branch of the theosophical movement to which the couple belonged, and it so happened that there was to be a study class that evening. I was invited to sit in on this class, which was led by Sophia Wadia and was on a section of Robert Crosbie's *The Friendly Philosopher*. The name of Robert Crosbie was new to me. As I discovered later, he was an American theosophist, under whose guidance and inspiration the United Lodge of Theosophists had been formed in 1909 in Los Angeles, California. He had worked closely with W. Q. Judge, joint founder with Mme Blavatsky and Col. Olcott of the Theosophical Society in 1875, and in the ULT his and Judge's writings were prized next only to the more voluminous but less immediately accessible output of Mme Blavatsky. Though I found *The Friendly Philosopher*, or rather the section of it chosen for study that evening, rather pedestrian, from her comments on the text, as well as from her replies to questions, it was obvious that Sophia Wadia had a thorough knowledge of the principles of theosophy and could explain them clearly. I noticed, however, that the dozen or so members of the class stood very much in awe of her, as they did of her husband, and that on account, presumably, of her French extraction she was addressed, deferentially, as 'Madame'.

As my lectures were not due to begin for three or four days I was able to take advantage of the library, and to read works to which I did not have access in Kalimpong or even in Calcutta. The Institute's library was, in fact, the best I had encountered since my time at Benares Hindu University with Kashyap-ji, when my kind teacher had allowed me to use his ticket to the university library, and contained many rare and valuable items collected by B. P. Wadia in the course of his travels in the West. Besides immersing myself in such authorities on Buddhism as Suzuki and E. J. Thomas,[130] I dipped quite extensively into Oscar Wilde, W. B. Yeats, and 'Æ' (George William Russell). A discovery of particular interest was *Literature and Occult Tradition* by Denis Saurat, an author of whom I had not heard before. There were also letters to write and members of the Institute to see, among the latter being S. K. Ramachandra Rao, with whom I had corresponded a couple of years previously and who was deeply interested in Buddhism. The two people of whom I saw most were, naturally, B. P. and Sophia Wadia, with whom I had lunch every day at Maitri Bhavan and, more often than not, a lengthy discussion. Most of our discussions centred on Buddhism, especially in its relation to the teachings of Mme Blavatsky, and although I sometimes disagreed with my host and hostess I could not but admire the purity of their devotion to theosophy and the sincerity with which they strove to apply its principles in their own lives. Lunch may have been served in some style, with a butler and other servants in attendance, but it was simple to the point of being spartan and the meal was always preceded by a reading from a religious text and a few minutes of silent recollection. On one occasion we discussed the missionary threat, and Roman Catholic dogmatism, about which both husband and wife felt very much as I did, and Sophia Wadia related how, when she was on a lecture tour in Argentina (she seemed to have South American connections),[131] she had been given police protection as the authorities had received information that the Jesuits might try to poison her. In the evening there was usually a function of some kind to attend, either at Maitri Bhavan or at the Institute. Thus I heard my white-robed hostess give an address on 'After Death – What?' at the former venue, while at the latter, a speaker having failed to turn up, two members of the Bangalore intelligentsia, M. K. Venkata Rao and K. Guru Dutt, gave brilliant extemporaneous talks on the philosophy of George Santayana. As the talented duo were not unrepresentative of the kind of audience I would shortly be addressing, I was thankful that I had prepared my lectures with even more than my usual care.

In a way I had been preparing the lectures for some months, at least in my own mind. It might even be said I had been preparing them for some years, in fact ever since I awoke to the fact that I was a Buddhist, and that between them they constituted a summation of all I had learned about Buddhism during the intervening period, whether from books, from my teachers, from discussions with friends (and foes, i.e. foes of the Dharma), and from my own independent reflection and meditative experience. B. P. Wadia's invitation indeed came at exactly the right moment for me, as well as at the right moment for the movement of Buddhist revival in modern India, then on the eve of experiencing a dramatic quantum leap, and presented me with both an opportunity and a challenge. With an opportunity, inasmuch as I would be communicating the Dharma to a predominantly Hindu audience which, cultured and intelligent though it might be, possessed for the most part only a superficial or a distorted understanding of the Buddha's teaching; with a challenge, inasmuch as I would be able to take full advantage of that opportunity only if I stood back and asked myself how I really saw Buddhism and what it really meant to me.

Work on the preparation of the lectures in the more specific sense had started only a month earlier, when B. P. Wadia wrote asking me to draw up a prospectus for distribution as part of the Institute's publicity. This entailed finding a title for each lecture, and therewith determining what material it should contain, as well as finding a title for the whole series, which eventually I decided to call 'A Survey of Buddhism: Its Doctrines and Methods Through the Ages' – with acknowledgements, as to the subtitle, to the excellent volume of Buddhist texts that had just appeared under the editorship of Dr Conze.[132] For a lecture (as distinct from a sermon of the traditional type, which I delivered extemporaneously) I was in the habit of making a few notes, covering in most cases only a page or two. On this occasion, however, I made several pages of notes for each lecture, for my view, like that of Observation in the opening lines of Dr Johnson's famous poem, was going to be an extensive one, and I would be surveying not, indeed, 'mankind, from China to Peru',[133] but Buddhism, from the Theravāda to Zen and Shin. Moreover, I would be surveying it not only in its breadth but in its depth, which meant seeing it in its deeper interconnections, both within itself and in relation to the

Dharma-life of the individual Buddhist. This called for a tremendous intellectual and spiritual effort on my part, an effort that the putting together of the notes, concentrative of my energies as this was, helped me to make. The notes for most of the lectures had already been written. In fact I had only the notes for the fourth lecture to write, those for the first three having been assembled during my week or so in Calcutta, which was why I could spend my first few days in Bangalore taking advantage of the library, seeing people, and attending functions at Maitri Bhavan and the Institute.

I started giving the series on Tuesday 6 July, four days after my arrival, when I spoke on 'The Buddha and Buddhism'. I spoke to a full hall, and under the chairmanship of Sophia Wadia, who after saying a few words of gracious introduction read my poem 'Taking Refuge in the Buddha'.[134] The audience being quite new to me, I fumbled for the first few minutes getting the 'feel' of it, so to speak, but once I had done this – and for me, getting the feel of an audience was a process so tangible as to be almost physical – I very quickly got into my stride and with the help of my notes spoke fluently for more than an hour and a half. In speaking about the Buddha I was concerned not so much to recount the story of his life, complete with legendary embellishments, as to place that life within its traditional cosmological context and, by so doing, to reveal in what the Buddha's greatness and role truly consisted. Similarly, in speaking of Buddhism, in the sense of the Original Doctrine, I did not want to dwell on specific ethical and spiritual teachings, important as those teachings undoubtedly were, so much as to lay bare the philosophical principle underlying them – the principle, that is to say, of universal conditionality, in its two modes, the 'cyclical' and the 'spiral'. In particular, I wanted to show that the Buddhist Nirvāṇa was not synonymous with a state of annihilation, as the Hindu critics of Buddhism believed, any more than the path leading to that Nirvāṇa consisted solely in the eradication of negative mental states. My second lecture, which followed two days later, was devoted to 'Hīnayāna and Mahāyāna'. In it I insisted on the 'transcendental unity' of all forms of Buddhism, traced the rise of the Mahāyāna, and dealt with some of the more important of its distinctive tenets. I was also at pains to emphasize the purely instrumental nature of the Dharma.

In between the giving of these two lectures I continued to see people and to attend functions at Maitri Bhavan and the Institute, besides going for a drive with the Doraiswamys' son, who showed me the famous Lal Bagh,[135] with its centuries-old trees, and took me into the city centre. Mrs Doraiswamy, his mother, for her part showed me round the Cosmopolitan Home, the student hostel the Wadias had built next door to the Institute and where there was a devotional meeting once a week led by B. P. Wadia. She was an Englishwoman by birth, and I was glad to find that she shared my own views regarding Christian missionaries. The Institute and the Bangalore ULT had, in fact, several English and Dutch members, some of whom were married to Indians. As in Singapore, where I had first encountered theosophists, in 1946, it was heartening to see people of different races and different national and religious backgrounds (the Institute even had a few Christian and Muslim members) associating on terms of friendship. Though I might not agree with some of the teachings of theosophy, I was certainly full of admiration for the way in which individual theosophists, both Adyar and non-Adyar, sought to practise the principle of Universal Brotherhood, the first of the three declared Objects of the parent Theosophical Society.

The next two lectures, which I gave on 12 and 14 July, were firmly based on the two previous ones. Having dealt with some of the more important of the Mahāyāna's distinctive tenets in my second lecture, I proceeded, in my third, on 'The Schools of the Mahāyāna', to deal in turn with the scriptures, teachers, and treatises of the Madhyamaka, of Devotional Buddhism, of the Yogācāra, and of Tantric Buddhism. Each school, I declared, had developed a specific aspect of Buddhism, and far from their being mutually exclusive the Mahāyāna itself could be understood only if they were viewed in their totality as complementary aspects of the Dharma. The fourth and last lecture in the series was dedicated to 'The Bodhisattva Ideal'. After describing the place of the bodhisattva ideal in Buddhist thought, and dealing with popular interpretations, I outlined the bodhisattva doctrine as presented in authoritative texts. I then gave an account – an account afterwards described as 'glowing' – of the six *pāramitās* or 'perfections' and the ten stages of the bodhisattva's career, and concluded by trying to communicate to my audience something of my own enthusiasm for the spiritual life as exemplified by the glorious bodhisattva ideal. Despite having notes to make, in between my third and fourth lectures I found time for two encounters of an ecumenical nature. The first of these was with the Jain community. At their invitation, I visited their temple, where they gave me a formal reception, complete with tea party and speeches of welcome, and where I spoke of my contacts with Jainism and on the Jain doctrine of *anekāntavāda*. My second such encounter, which was of a more intimate character, was with a bright-eyed, gnome-like Roman Catholic priest named Father Monchanin, one of the founders of the first 'Christian ashram', with whom I had a two-hour-long conversation on Buddhism, especially the Madhyamaka, the Vedanta, and comparative mysticism.

After the conclusion of the fourth lecture, and therewith the completion of my survey, the Wadias and I left for Maitri Bhavan, where fourteen or fifteen leading members and friends of the Institute later joined us for an informal celebration. Both B. P. and Sophia Wadia were highly pleased with the lectures, the former having asked me, after I had given my first lecture, to write them out for publication in book form. Indeed, from what I heard that evening I gathered the series had attracted a good deal of attention, and even been something of an event in the cultural and religious life of Bangalore. This did not surprise me. Throughout the series the hall, comfortably full at first, had become more tightly packed with each lecture, while the audience, greatly augmented though it was, had grown ever more attentive, and more concentrated. Thus by the time I gave the last lecture I had a very large – and appreciative – audience indeed, such as the Institute apparently had not seen before. It was an audience, moreover, with which I had succeeded in establishing a definite rapport. As I spoke, and they listened, time almost stood still, and it was as though we were transported to another world. To what extent they felt this I could not tell, but I certainly felt it very strongly, and whether on account of their receptivity, or on account of my own enthusiasm for the Dharma, or both, at the end of one lecture, in particular, I found myself in a very exalted state of consciousness.

That time should almost stand still was not without its disadvantages, even though the audience and I might be transported to another world. The Wadias, contrary to the usual Indian practice, were great sticklers for punctuality and keeping to schedule, and before the commencement of the series I was warned that I should on no account exceed my allotted sixty, or at the very most seventy-five, minutes, as this could seriously disrupt whatever other events might have been planned for the rest of the evening. Unfortunately, my first lecture exceeded even the more generous allotment by a full fifteen minutes, and subsequent lectures exceeded it by as much as half an hour or more. The fact was that I had so much material, and found that material so inspiring, that it was hardly possible for me to keep to the prescribed limit without doing a serious injustice to my subject and perhaps even to myself. Moreover, though Sophia Wadia kept glancing meaningfully at the clock when my time was up, as did her successors in the chair, it was clear the audience did not want me to stop, and both then and subsequently I ignored the signals and carried on. Each time this little drama between the speaker and the chair was enacted, smiles of amusement appeared on people's faces. Evidently they were by no means adverse to seeing protocol flung to the winds and the proceedings conducted in a manner that was more in accordance with Indian cultural traditions. As for my host and hostess, in the goodness of their hearts they refrained from taking me to task for my intransigence, though it was obvious that they ran the Institute and the ULT as very tight ships and were not accustomed to having their wishes disregarded.

Having made the notes for three of my lectures in Calcutta, I did not have much to do by way of preparation in Bangalore. None the less, during the week in which I was engaged in surveying Buddhism I had thought it best to avoid distractions as much as I could and stay close to base, my base being the double one of the Institute and Maitri Bhavan. Now, however, the lectures were over, and I was able to see more people and go out and about more. As the second city of a predominantly Kannada-speaking area that had once been under Muslim rule, Bangalore was a tolerant, cosmopolitan place, with a polyglot citizenry that included people from most parts of India and of many different faiths. Among those who came to see me, or whose hospitality I accepted, there were Bengalis and Kashmiris, Tamilians and Mysoreans, devotees of Swami Ramdas and disciples of Ramana Maharshi, followers of the Lingayat sect, Viśiṣṭādvaitavāda pandits, Muslims, Christians, and Jains – but not a single Buddhist, though after my first lecture a local man had come up to me and introduced himself and his wife as Buddhists. Most of those who came did so out of curiosity or to 'talk religion' in the platitudinous, pseudo-intellectual sort of way that was so common in India (I once observed that Hindus, in particular, discussed religion much as the English discussed the weather), or even to beg me, as one elderly Tamil Brahmin repeatedly did, to teach them some 'Tantric rites'. A few there were, however, whose interest was of a more serious nature. They included two young men, one of them a student, with whom I had several worthwhile discussions and to whom, at their earnest request, I explained the *ānāpānasati* or 'respiration-mindfulness' practice. Not that I usually taught meditation, or even thought of myself as a 'meditation teacher'. Though I now had been meditating for a number of years, my principal concern was still to deepen my own practice, and while I had no objection to explaining *ānāpānasati* to the occasional sincere individual, it was to be many years before I started teaching meditation on a regular basis or to more than one person at a time.

The fact that I saw more people and went out and about more, during my last few days in the Garden City, did not mean that I neglected my base. If anything, I had more to do with it than ever. To begin with, the lectures having created intense interest among the local intelligentsia, many of whom declared that it was the first time they had been given a complete and coherent picture of Buddhism, B. P. Wadia made arrangements for a special question-and-answer meeting. At this meeting, which was held under the chairmanship of his white-robed coadjutrix, I answered more than sixty written questions on the philosophy, history, literature, and spiritual practices of Buddhism. B. P. Wadia also arranged for me to give, under his own chairmanship, a lecture on *The Voice of the Silence*, the devotional treatise compiled and translated by Mme Blavatsky, allegedly from Tibetan Buddhist sources. I was quite fond of this little work, which I knew to be immensely popular with all theosophists, though in view of some of its terminology I found it difficult to regard it as being *in toto* an authentically Buddhist composition. Besides making these two additional appearances at the Institute, I gave several informal talks for the benefit of the occupants of the Cosmopolitan Home, B. P. Wadia apparently thinking that the students to whom he stood *in loco parentis* could not have too much of a good thing in the way of moral and religious instruction from visiting holy men of whatever persuasion. On other occasions I carried my base, as represented by the Wadias, with me when I went out – or my base carried me. Thus my host and hostess and I were guests at a lunch given by the Ghataks and spent a musical evening with the Lalkakas. Among the other guests at the lunch were Svetoslav Roerich, the younger brother of George Roerich, and his wife Devika Rani, the famous film actress, both of whom I had met a few weeks earlier in Kalimpong at a tea-party given by Mrs Tagore in honour of Dr and Mrs Liebenthal's fortieth wedding anniversary. I was seated opposite Devika Rani and we talked about her mother, a niece (or perhaps it was a grand-niece) of Tagore, whom I had known in Kasauli and who in fact was one of the last people to whom I spoke before going forth 'from home into the homeless life' in August 1947.

At the Lalkakas' the Wadias and I were the only guests. Major Lalkaka had served in the British – not the Indian – army, and though no longer wearing the Queen's uniform was very pro-British. He was also very pro-Western. So extremely pro-Western was he that he and his wife had not been content to adopt the language and social customs of their (former) rulers. They had gone so far as to adopt their religion too. Both were converts to (Roman Catholic) Christianity, and I noticed that running round the pointed arch of every door frame in their comfortable, European-style bungalow there was a text from the Vulgate, neatly executed in Gothic script and in the original Latin. Despite such apparent signs of orthodoxy, the kind and hospitable Lalkakas were not in the least bigoted, as converts to Roman Catholicism so often were, and I concluded that their Christianity was a matter of culture rather than of religion in the strict sense. Major Lalkaka was in fact a great lover of Western classical music, and in the course of the evening he played some of his favourite Bach and Mozart records for us on the gramophone. In my teens I had been passionately fond of classical music, and had listened to it (on the radio) as much as I could. During my years in India I had been able to hear it only in odd snatches, and by accident, and in any case there was a rule prohibiting members of the Theravādin monastic order from listening to music. As the ultra-orthodox Narada Thera had once remarked to Lama Govinda, in my hearing, a Buddhist monk was not allowed to appreciate beauty[136] – and classical music was certainly beautiful. Yet though I had been so fond of classical music in the past, and had listened to it so much, I did not miss it now, and never felt I was being deprived of something essential to my emotional wellbeing. I could therefore enjoy Major Lalkaka's Bach and Mozart without wanting to prolong or repeat the experience, and even when, on my departure, he presented me with two boxes of records, my only thought – apart from gratitude to him for his generosity – was that since I did not possess a gramophone I would have to give them to somebody who did. Perhaps Joe would like them.

Less harmonious than the musical evening at the Lalkakas', in principle at least, was the situation I encountered when Sophia Wadia and I, on the afternoon of my last day in Bangalore, went to see the vihara that was being built at Gandhinagar, in the older, western quarter of the city. It was being built by the Maha Bodhi Society of Ceylon, and was nearing completion, and we were shown round the place by A. R. S. Chari, the retired judge of the Bangalore High Court who had presided at my lecture on 'Hīnayāna and Mahāyāna'. Mr Chari, I gathered, was in overall charge of the building project. He was also chairman of the vihara committee. Or rather, he was chairman of one of the two committees then contending in the courts for control of the vihara. The dispute had been going on for some time, as a paper drawn up by the retired judge informed me, and had become quite complicated. Whether by accident or by design, the leading member of the other committee, one Ramaswami, was on the premises at the very time Sophia Wadia and I were being shown round, and later that day he came to see me at the Institute.

It did not take me long to get to the root of the problem. The root of the problem, as so often was the case in South India, was the deep-seated antagonism between Brahmins and non-Brahmins. Chari was a Brahmin, Ramaswami a non-Brahmin. Chari's committee consisted of Brahmins and other caste Hindus, Ramaswami's of members of the Scheduled Castes. Several of these latter were, it seemed, followers of Dr Ambedkar, who for years had been telling the Scheduled Castes peoples that there would be no improvement in their lot so long as they remained within the Hindu fold and that they would have to change their religion. Only recently there had been rumours to the effect that the Scheduled Castes leader was about to embrace Buddhism, together with his followers, and several of the questions handed in at my question-and-answer meeting had related to this burning topic. From the nature of the questions it was fairly obvious that the caste Hindus were opposed to any change of religion on the part of the Scheduled Castes peoples, and I was left with the impression that should Ambedkar and his followers ever take the drastic step of giving up Hinduism for Buddhism they could expect little sympathy or understanding from that quarter. Much as caste Hindus might appreciate Buddhism, to them it was only a branch of

Hinduism, and they saw no need for anyone born a Hindu to 'convert' to it as though it was a separate religion like Christianity or Islam. In their eyes Ambedkar was simply a politician, and his periodic threats of mass defections from Hinduism were no more than a political stunt.

Scheduled Castes South Indians like Ramaswami saw things differently. For them Ambedkar's threats were seriously meant and conversion to Buddhism was a real option. Caste Hindu insistence that Buddhism was not a separate religion but only a branch of Hinduism was intended, so they believed, to make it impossible for the Scheduled Castes peoples to escape from Hinduism and, therefore, from caste Hindu tyranny and exploitation. Chari's involvement in the affairs of the Bangalore branch of the Maha Bodhi Society had a similar purpose. He and his Brahmin and other caste Hindu friends knew that a revival of Buddhism was inevitable and they wanted to be in a position to contain it. According to no less an authority than Swami Vivekananda, Hinduism had killed Buddhism with a loving embrace,[137] and it would no doubt try to repeat the performance if its hated rival ever came back to life.

Thus the root of the conflict between the two vihara committees was not even just a conflict between Brahmins and non-Brahmins, or between caste Hindus and members of the Scheduled Castes. It was a conflict, also, between different attitudes towards Buddhism, even different ideologies. If those conflicts were not resolved, or even if they were, what would be the future of the vihara? What would be the future of Buddhism in Bangalore?

10
BUDDHISM AND THE NAGPUR BAR

Dharmacakra Day was the second most important festival in the Buddhist year. It was the day on which the Buddha, two months after his attainment of Enlightenment, 'set in motion the Wheel of the Law' or, less poetically speaking, started communicating the Truth he had discovered. Like Vaiśākha Pūrṇimā, Dharmacakra Day was a lunar festival, falling on the full-moon day of the month *Shravana*, corresponding to June–July of the Western calendar. This year it had fallen on Thursday 15 July, the day of my lecture on *The Voice of the Silence*. Arriving at Madras Central three days later, however, on the morning of Sunday 18 July, I found that the Madras centre of the Maha Bodhi Society had yet to celebrate the festival. Whether because a Sunday was more convenient than a weekday, or because I would then be in the city, the celebration had been postponed to that afternoon. There would be a public meeting at five o'clock, Venerable Jinananda informed me, after we had exchanged greetings. It would be held at Kennett Lane, there would be three speakers, and I would be presiding over the function.

At five o'clock I therefore took my place on the stage that had been set up in the courtyard, Jinananda administered the Refuges and Precepts to the hundred or so people – some of them Buddhists – who had assembled for the occasion, and the meeting proper began. The three speakers were all from South India, and all addressed the audience in excellent English, a circumstance that reminded me of the region's proud boast that although the English language might be forgotten in England it would never be forgotten in Mylapore. The second, and principal, speaker was R. Jayachandram, whom I had known when he was a boy in Travancore and who now was Lecturer in Philosophy at the Vivekananda College, one of the city's more prestigious educational institutions. We had renewed our acquaintanceship prior to the meeting, and reminisced about the time, six or seven years earlier, when he was a student and I one of the two long-haired, long-bearded wandering ascetics then staying at the haunted ashram on the outskirts of the little town of Muvattupuzha.[138] Some of my Buddhism had perhaps rubbed off on him. His lecture, which I was required to announce as being on 'The Life of the Buddha, not the story of an *avatāra*, but the story of a man's true emancipation', was not only very well delivered, in a highly poetical style, but also imbued with the speaker's strong feeling for the person of the Enlightened One, a feeling especially in evidence when he was describing the Buddha-to-be's disillusionment with mundane existence, his departure from home, and his early struggles for light. So vividly did Jayachandram describe these events, and to such a degree did he empathize with what he believed were the youthful Siddhārtha's thoughts and feelings at the time, that he seemed to have been almost an eyewitness – or even to be speaking from personal experience. If he now and again departed from strict historical accuracy, or showed rather too marked a tendency to sentimentalize the figure of the Buddha, no one appeared to mind, or even to notice, and when he sat down it was to warm applause.

One person there was who did not join in the applause. This was the third and last speaker. As the rather cumbrous title of Jayachandram's address had made clear, the young college lecturer did not believe the Buddha to be an *avatāra* or 'descent' of the god Vishnu, and he in fact had more than once been at pains to remind his audience that the founder of Buddhism was a human being who had attained Enlightenment by his own human exertions. His successor at the microphone, who from his 'surname' I knew to be a Brahmin, was of a different opinion. The Buddha *was* an *avatāra* of Vishnu, he insisted. He insisted on the point so vehemently, and criticized Jayachandram in such unreasonable terms, that the latter could not forbear retorting, and had I not intervened to restore order the stage might well have been the scene of an unseemly altercation. Rain in any case had started to fall, as if to cool hot tempers, and I proceeded to deliver my presidential address, in the course of which I underlined the principal points made by Jayachandram and spoke at some length on the danger of Christian missions, the avowed object of which was to destroy the religious and cultural traditions of India. By the time I finished it was raining heavily, and we were forced to retreat indoors. Here I talked with some of the South Indian Buddhists who had attended the meeting, as well as with two Italian travellers who had come to ask my advice about extending their visas. One of the Italians was eager to visit Tibet, but I assured him that with the Chinese Red Army occupying the country this was impossible.

At ten the next morning I gave a lecture at the Vivekananda College, which as its name suggested had connections with the Ramakrishna Mission, Swami Vivekananda, after whom the college was named, having been the founder of the Mission. The lecture was attended by about a thousand people, mostly students, and after five or ten minutes of Vedic chanting I spoke, by special request, on 'The Differences Between the Principles of Buddhism and Hinduism'. Who asked me to speak on this topic, which was obviously a controversial one (though a Hindu speaker would probably have denied that there was any difference between the two religions), I no longer remember, but whoever it was I had taken the request seriously, perhaps even as a challenge, and had sat up late the previous night writing my notes. After pointing out that both Hinduism and Buddhism were to be viewed against the wider background of Indian spiritual tradition, I went on to give a systematic – if somewhat black and white – account of the more important philosophical and ethical differences between them. This took me the best part of an hour, and paved the way for a vigorous attack on the caste system and on orthodox Brahmanism, the exclusiveness and bigotry of which I not only condemned in the roundest terms but contrasted with the spirit of universality and compassion shown by the Buddha. The attack came as a severe shock to the Brahminical part of the audience, and the principal of the college, who was in the chair, and who was himself a Brahmin, did not know what to say. Many of the students, however, were clearly pleased, and even some of the more orthodox remarked that the Buddhist point of view, though different from that of Brahmanism, was deserving of careful study.

The remainder of the day was divided between poetry and philosophy, the former being represented by one Krishnamurti, the poet-proprietor of an arts and crafts emporium, who already had presented me with his latest book of (English) poems, entitled *The Cloth of Gold*, and the latter by Jayachandram, with whom I spent the evening discussing Buddhism and other topics of common interest. In the morning, straight after breakfast, I went to see Dr Natarajan, the scholarly successor of the famous Narayan Guru, who as Jayachandram had informed me was then staying in the city. I had met Dr Natarajan – or Nataraja Guru, as he was also called – once before, in Travancore.[139] Circumstances had permitted only the briefest of exchanges, and on the present occasion, too, the interview had to be a short one, as I was seeing him on my way to the station and had a train to catch. There was time, however, for him to tell me about the radical new interpretation (and translation) of the *Bhagavad Gītā* on which he was then working and had, in fact, been working on for a number of years. At Madras Central I located my berth, bought a volume of English essays at the station bookstall, said goodbye to Jinananda, and settled myself for the journey. Punctually at 9.15 whistles blew, doors were slammed, and I was on my way – not to Calcutta but to Nagpur.

Nagpur, 500 miles from Madras, and situated at the exact geographical centre of India, was the capital of Madhya Pradesh. Though it lay on the main line between Bombay and Calcutta, and though I had passed through it several times, I knew little more about it than that it was the orange-growing capital of India and the headquarters of the Rashtriya Sevak Sangh or National Service Association, an ultra-nationalist, right-wing Hindu organization one of whose members had assassinated Mahatma Gandhi. In recent months I had become more aware of the place's existence. Venerable Silabhadra, one of my colleagues on the editorial board of the *Maha Bodhi*, had lectured there on 'Buddha and Buddhism' at the invitation of the local Ramakrishna Ashram, then celebrating its Silver Jubilee, and I had been in correspondence with A. R. Kulkarni, the Secretary of the Buddha Society, Nagpur, who was a supporter of the Maha Bodhi Society and an occasional contributor to its journal. Either Kulkarni suggested I might like to visit Nagpur, or I suggested the Buddha Society might like to invite me. Whichever it was, a visit had been arranged, and I now was making a grand detour and returning to Calcutta from Madras by way of Nagpur. During the whole day only three other persons entered the compartment, and I spent the time immersed in my volume of essays. At ten o'clock in the evening, as we were passing through Hyderabad state, a group of three

Muslims got in for an hour. It was a rather unusual group, consisting of a well-built police inspector, a handsome young man, and a very pretty boy. Soon the police inspector was arguing politics with a Tamil Brahmin who already occupied one of the berths, while his two companions, who may not have understood English, sat quietly beside him. Twelve hours later the train reached Nagpur.

Kulkarni was waiting for me on the crowded platform. A middle-aged man of medium height, he was simply clad in a white *kurta* and *dhoti*, and was shaven-headed, though without the crown lock that denoted the orthodox Hindu. As I later discovered, he saw himself as a Hindu follower of the Buddha rather than as a Buddhist, which explained why the organization of which he was secretary, and of which he was indeed the founder and moving spirit, was a Buddha society and not a Buddhist society. A taxi conveyed us to his residence in Dharampeth, which as its name indicated was or had once been a Brahmin locality, where I met his doctor brother and his two teenage nephews. The women remained in the background, cooking and washing clothes and drawing water from the well in the yard. After we had discussed the condition of Buddhism in Nagpur (it was not good), and I had had lunch and written a letter to Kalimpong, he took me with him to see various people who would, he thought, be interested in arranging lectures. We did not meet with much success. The registrar of the University, a UP Brahmin,[140] did not respond at all favourably to my host's suggestion that I should deliver a lecture in the Convocation Hall. Indeed, it was my impression that the forthrightness of Kulkarni's approach, and the bluntness of his manner, which made a suggestion seem very much like an order, rather disconcerted him, not to say annoyed him. The fact was that Kulkarni was by birth a Maharashtrian Brahmin, and Maharashtrian Brahmins, as I had yet to learn, were renowned for their harshness and militancy – though the Deshastha Brahmins, of whom Kulkarni was one, were much less harsh and militant than the Chitpavans. At the Ramakrishna Ashram, which we visited next and where we met the two resident swamis, one young and one old, we fared hardly better than we had done at the University. While Young Swami was interested in my giving a lecture there, Old Swami very clearly was not – perhaps because they had already had a lecture on Buddhism that year, or because Silabhadra's lecture had not been to his liking. In the end it was agreed that if it was possible for them to arrange a lecture they would let us know. With the theosophists we were more fortunate. A Bengali follower of Mme Blavatsky assured us that there would be no difficulty in arranging for me to speak at the local TS lodge, and promised to ask the lodge secretary to get in touch with us. The rest of the afternoon, as well as most of the evening, was spent visiting first the Buddha Society's library and reading room, then a temple where an image of the Buddha had been installed, and finally the headquarters of the State Congress. By the time we returned to Dharampeth I was feeling rather tired. Kulkarni, despite his fifty-odd years, was still full of energy, and bustled about preparing 'English tea' for me.

The following morning it became apparent that our labours of the previous day had not been in vain. From breakfast time until well after midday there was a constant flow of visitors, several of whom either wanted to arrange lectures or had already done so. The Principal of the Science College had arranged one for that very evening, the secretary of the TS lodge wanted to arrange one for the following Saturday (it was then Thursday), while a *brahmacāri* or novice from the Ramakrishna Ashram came with an invitation to speak there the following Sunday. Young Swami had somehow managed to persuade Old Swami! The result was that for that and the next three days I was kept busy preparing and giving what seemed an uninterrupted stream of lectures and addresses. Kulkarni, who was a lawyer by training, kept a faithful record of them all, and an article from his pen entitled 'Bhikshu Sangharakshita's Lecture Tour in Nagpur' eventually appeared in the *Maha Bodhi* and elsewhere. Many of the details of where I spoke, to whom, and what I said, had vanished from my recollection even before the article appeared. On the other hand, incidents of which he made no mention, and of which he probably was quite unaware, were indelibly impressed on my mind. Biography and memoirs supplement and correct each other, especially when the biographer writes about the memoirist from personal knowledge. Concerned as it was with my public activities rather than with my private ones, Kulkarni's article naturally began with my visit to the Buddha Society's library and reading room.

> On the very first day of his arrival Rev. Bhikshu Sangharakshita paid a visit to the Library of the Buddha Society, Nagpur, which is located in Sitabaldi in the magnificent building of Dada Saheb Dhanwale, known as Dhanwale Chamber. After this the revered

> Bhikshu paid a visit to the Siddhartha Bhagyodaya Library located in the Vithal Rukmini Deosthan temple, Sitabaldi, Nagpur. The revered Bhikshu was immensely pleased to notice the beautiful image of the Buddha installed in the temple in the heart of the Nagpur city. The revered Bhikshu then paid a visit to the Abhyankar Congress House and attended the mass common prayer conducted therein. Sri A. R. Kulkarni recited *Trisarana* and *Panchasila* and the revered Bhikshu made a short speech explaining their meaning. The audience was spellbound when the Bhikshu was delivering his sermon.[141]

Dhanwale Chamber may or may not have been a magnificent building, but the hundred or so Hindi, Marathi, and English volumes, some of them on Buddhism, that formed the Society's library, certainly could not be considered a magnificent collection. Running the library was, however, the Society's one permanent activity, and apart from Kulkarni's occasional lectures it had for some years past been virtually the only sign of Buddhist activity in Nagpur. More interesting to me was the image of the Buddha in the neighbouring Siddhartha Bhagyodaya Library. It was more interesting not on account of its beauty but because, as Kulkarni's article failed to mention, it had been installed there by the Scheduled Caste followers of Dr Ambedkar. How it came to be installed there, especially as the library was located in a Hindu temple, I was unable to discover. Whatever the explanation may have been, in view of the momentous change that was to take place in the lives of Ambedkar's followers only two years later, in that very city, it could be said that coming events were casting their shadow before.

> On the second day, i.e. on July 22nd, the revered Bhikshu gave a lecture in the Science College Hostel on 'Buddhism and the Modern World' under the presidentship of Dr. Krishnamurti, Principal, Science College, Nagpur. In his opening address Dr. Krishnamurti pointed out how Buddhism was the purified form of Hinduism. The learned Bhikshu told the science students how Buddhism inculcated a scientific attitude in man. Buddhism never believed in accepting anything on trust. 'Come and see for yourself' is the motto of Buddhism. It was for this reason the most rationalistic religion on earth. The learned Bhikshu aptly

> pointed out that there was never any conflict between Buddhism and science. The lecture had an abiding effect on the students who actually declared their faith in Buddhism by saying, '*Buddhaṃ saraṇaṃ gacchāmi*'.[142]

As my lecture lasted for an hour and a half, Kulkarni's account of it was not even a summary. Probably I was at pains to rebut Krishnamurti's assertion that Buddhism was a purified form of Hinduism, but I no doubt did this gently, as the Principal of the Science College was a friendly, likeable man, and I had no wish to injure his feelings. The attitude inculcated in man by Buddhism was, of course, 'scientific' only in the wider sense of its being objective, as I must have explained. Similarly, Buddhism's 'Come and see' meant not that it was rationalistic (a word I never used in this connection) but that it was rational – a very different thing. As for the dozens of students who, at the conclusion of my lecture, thronged round me with joyful shouts of '*Buddhaṃ saraṇaṃ gacchāmi!* I go for refuge to the Buddha!' – they were members of the Scheduled Castes, and followers of Dr Ambedkar. Once again, coming events were casting their shadow before.

> On July 23rd the revered Bhikshu delivered a learned discourse on 'Buddhism' in the Nagpur Mahavidyalaya under the auspices of the Philosophical Society of the College and under the presidentship of Prof. Ramnathan, Vice-Principal of the College. Earlier the revered Bhikshu had delivered a discourse on the Dharma Chakra under the auspices of the Harijan Sewa Sangh. The occasion was the mass spinning programme organized by the Sarvodaya workers of Nagpur to commemorate the eighty-sixth birthday of Mahatma Gandhi. The function was attended by Sri R. K. Patil, ex-Minister, Sri Rauka, Sri Wazalwar and other eminent Sarvodaya workers. The whole audience was highly impressed by the learned and illuminating discourse delivered by the revered Bhikshu. After questions and answers the function terminated. Sri R. K. Patil was also present in the evening function held in the Nagpur Mahavidyalaya.[143]

The fifty-odd Sarvodaya workers taking part in the mass spinning programme were the biggest collection of freaks and eccentrics I had seen for a long time. Old rather than young, and clad, or half clad, in coarse white homespun, they were wild-eyed, long-haired and, in some cases, long-bearded. Some tried to carry on hand-spinning when they stood up to address the audience. Others spoke with the most extraordinary gestures, at times touching the ground with one hand while simultaneously shooting the other towards the ceiling. The most sensible-looking person present was a local mill-owner in a white Gandhi cap who sat silent and impassive, and without a *charka*, to one side. The Sarvodaya workers were all disciples of Vinoba Bhave, whose proposal to enhance the importance of Bodh Gaya by building there a temple of his own I had recently ridiculed in the *Maha Bodhi*. Gandhi's economic ideals, of which Bhave was the principal inheritor and custodian, appealed to me strongly (the Mahatma's *Hind Swaraj* was one of the first books I read after my arrival in India),[144] but if those ideals depended for their implementation on Bhave's Sarvodaya movement, as represented by the present collection of crackpots, then I for one could not see them transforming Indian society.

> On July 24th the learned Bhikshu delivered at 5 p.m. a lecture on 'Buddhism the Gospel of Action' in the Hislop College, Nagpur, under the auspices of the Philosophical Society of that College. Sri Padhye, Professor of Philosophy, presided. The learned lecturer pointed out in the course of his stirring lecture how Buddhism was essentially a religion of action. This lecture created a favourable impression on the younger generation who mostly attended it. Immediately after this lecture was over the revered Bhikshu delivered at 6.30 at the Theosophical Lodge, Dhantoli, a lecture on 'Buddhism and Theosophy'. The learned Bhikshu pointed out the many common points between Buddhism and Theosophy and laid particular emphasis on the universal brotherhood of man which was an essential feature both of Theosophy and Buddhism. The Theosophical Lodge was packed to its full capacity and the entire audience was listening to the discourse with rapt attention. The simple but easy flowing style of the learned Bhikshu created a deep impression on the audience and they thought they were listening to something which they had not witnessed before. In fact the revered Bhikshu's lectures had created a sensation in Nagpur.[145]

The Hislop College lecture was delivered at the invitation of the students themselves, two of whom had come only that very morning to ask me to address them. Buddhism was a religion of action, but not of activism. It was a religion of action in that it recognized the law of karma, the law in accordance with which impure actions of body, speech, and mind were followed by suffering, and pure ones by happiness. Thus Buddhism was a religion of ethics. Meditation consisted, essentially, in an uninterrupted succession of ethically pure mental actions (or skilful volitions), that is, in an uninterrupted succession of mental actions free from greed, hatred, and delusion.

> On the morning of July 25th the revered Bhikshu went to the village of Bahadma at a distance of about 7 miles from Nagpur, to witness the anti-untouchability campaign launched by Sri Raukaji and others. On this occasion the revered Bhikshu delivered a speech before the villagers in English which was rendered into Marathi by Sri A. R. Kulkarni. In the course of his very simple but convincing speech the revered Bhikshu laid emphasis on unity in life and pointed out how disunity amongst them may lead to their ruin.[146]

For the last mile of the journey we had to walk, threading our way between the paddy fields along the narrow raised paths. On our arrival in the village we had breakfast with Sri Rauka-ji and other members of the Harijan Sewa Sangh in an Untouchable hut. (*Harijans*, or Children of God, was Mahatma Gandhi's name for the Untouchables, but many of them rejected the designation as a condescending euphemism.) While we were having breakfast I had an experience that affected me more strongly than anything else I saw or heard during my visit to Nagpur. We were seated directly on the beaten earth floor of the hut. In front of each of us was a *thali* and beside the *thali* a brass tumbler. On picking up the tumbler beside my own *thali,* and raising it to my lips, I found the water in it so thick with ochre-coloured clay as to be opaque. What was the reason, I asked. Apologetically, our host explained that Untouchables were not allowed to draw water from the village well. They were therefore obliged to take it from the river, which at that time of year was naturally very turbid. Not allowed to draw water from the village well! Not even during the rainy season! Those few simple words, spoken quietly and without bitterness, seemed to sum up all the wrongs the Untouchables had suffered, down the ages, at the hands of the caste Hindus. They haunted me for months afterwards, and I never forgot them.

> At 4 p.m. the revered Bhikshu recited the Mangala Sutta at the residence of Dr D. R. Kulkarni in the true Buddhist style and explained its meaning in English which was rendered into Marathi by Sri A R. Kulkarni. This was a sort of private informal function attended by the members of Dr. Kulkarni's family and his personal friends, viz., Rao Bahadur D. K. Mohoin and Sri M. Y. and Mrs Koli and others.[147]

Besides his two sons, Dr Kulkarni's family consisted of his wife and a grown-up daughter who was at medical college. The previous day the two women, together with the elderly maidservant and a little girl who may or may not have been a relation, had been formally presented to me. Dressed in their best saris, bejewelled, and with flowers in their hair, they had come forward one by one, had silently touched my feet, and then had withdrawn. During the whole course of my stay they did not address a single word to me, any more than I did to them, but they were very much aware of my presence in the house, as I well knew, and did their best to meet, and even anticipate, my material needs. With Dr Kulkarni and his sons I naturally had more contact, as I also had, to an even greater degree, with the indefatigable brother of the one and uncle of the others. More than once did I sit on the flat roof of the house with the doctor and his elder son, Krishna, discussing Buddhism, until long past midnight. My discussions with Kulkarni usually took place during the intervals between lectures, especially when the two of us were travelling by car or cycle rickshaw to the next venue, or when we were waiting for a bus. In the course of these discussions I learned, bit by bit, of the circumstances that had led him, a Deshastha Brahmin by birth and a lawyer by profession, to declare himself a follower of the Buddha and to dedicate his life to the task of making India 'Buddha-minded'. It was an interesting story, and began twenty years earlier in the Nagpur High Court.

A Hindu monk from the Punjab had come and taken up residence in a deserted Shiva temple in Nagpur. The monk belonged to the Mahanubhava sect, the members of which worshipped not Shiva but

Vishnu, particularly in his *avatāra* as Krishna, the preacher of the *Bhagavad Gītā* and lover of the *gopis* or cowherd maidens. After taking up residence in the temple, the Mahanubhava monk installed there an image of Krishna, as a result of which the Krishna temple, as it now was, became a popular place of worship for the local Hindus. At this point a Sanātanī or 'orthodox' monk who, as a follower of the non-dualist philosopher Śaṅkara, was a worshipper of Shiva, filed a civil suit against the Mahanubhava monk, contending that the temple had been built by his guru and that on the latter's death he, the plaintiff, was its rightful owner. He further contended that the temple was a Sanātanī temple and that the Mahanubhava monk, not being a Sanātanī Hindu, had no right to reside there and no right to manage the place as he was doing. Kulkarni appeared in the case for the defendant. He had already appeared for him in the criminal case that had preceded the civil suit and which the Sanātanī monk, then also the plaintiff, had lost. This case did not really form part of Kulkarni's story, and I in fact learned about it only much later, on one of my subsequent visits to Nagpur. In the civil suit there were three questions to be determined. What was a Hindu? Were Mahanubhavas Hindus? What was the difference between a Hindu and a Sanātanī Hindu? Under cross-examination the plaintiff defined a Hindu as one who believed in the authority of the Vedas; admitted that the Mahanubhavas were Hindus; and averred that a Sanātanī Hindu was one who, on the authority of the Vedas, believed – as the Mahanubhavas did *not* – in the caste system and untouchability. In support of his contention that the Mahanubhavas, though Hindus, were not Sanātanī Hindus, he called as witnesses a number of Brahmin pandits, the most eminent of whom Kulkarni cross-examined at some length. From this pandit he elicited statements to the effect that the caste system was based on birth, not on merit, that Tukaram, the famous poet-saint of Maharashtra, despite his spiritual attainments was to be classed as a Shudra (which he was by birth), not as a Brahmin, and that the Buddha was not an authority on religion.

These uncompromising statements shocked and distressed Kulkarni, the more especially as they represented the considered opinion of a Brahmin pandit well versed in the Hindu scriptures. He realized that in orthodox Hinduism there was no place for social justice, and that the very people who were supposed to teach the principles of true religion were themselves ignorant of those principles. The only remedy for such a state of affairs, he concluded, was the Buddha. Only the Buddha could remove the evils of caste, untouchability, and communalism from the present-day Indian society. With the help of friends and well-wishers he therefore founded in Nagpur, in 1944, a Buddha Society, with himself as Secretary. As I discovered later, the principal supporters of the little organization were all Maharashtrian Brahmins and all members of the legal profession. Between Buddhism and the Nagpur bar there seemed to be a definite connection. There was also a connection between Buddhism and the Nagpur bench, the President of the Society being a judge of the Nagpur High Court. The connection between Buddhism and the Nagpur bar, at least, was not a new one. Both then and in the course of my subsequent visits to Nagpur, Kulkarni was wont to reminisce not only about the Mahanubhava case but about some of his other experiences as a lawyer. In particular he reminisced about the legal giants, both British and Indian, who had dominated the Nagpur High Court in the days of the Raj. Prominent among these legendary figures was Sir Hari Singh Gour, about whose forensic battles Kulkarni had many a story to tell and whom he as a young lawyer had evidently much admired. The name of Sir Hari Singh Gour was not unknown to me. He was the author of *Spirit of Buddhism*, a substantial and scholarly work on the life, teaching, and influence of the Buddha that had been published soon after my birth and which, as a teenager who recently had realized he was a Buddhist, I had devoured back in the early forties.

Two years after the founding of the Buddha Society Kulkarni experienced a further shock. In order to popularize the Buddha and make the people of India Buddha-minded, as he put it, he had started celebrating Buddha Jayanti every year on the Vaiśākha Pūrṇimā (significantly, it had not been celebrated in Nagpur before), and in 1946 invited Tukloji Maharaj, the well-known musician-saint of Maharashtra, to sing *bhajans* or devotional songs on the thrice-sacred day. Tukloji Maharaj being extremely popular, and his *bhajans* greatly appreciated, the function was a huge success. 20,000 people attended. Afterwards, however, as the crowd dispersed, Kulkarni heard several people asking, 'Who is this Buddha whose Jayanti is being celebrated today?' These enquiries shocked and distressed him even more than the Brahmin pandit's uncompromising statements had done two years earlier. That the Buddha, who was the glory of India, should be unknown in the land of his birth, was intolerable. It was a stigma on the fair name of India. The stigma must be removed. Who would remove it? *He* would undertake to do so. A few weeks later he therefore gave up his practice as a lawyer and became a homeless beggar for the sake of the Dharma. When he came to this part of the story Kulkarni was so overcome that he shed a few tears, as he would do on future occasions when he related it to me, and I saw that he was a man not only of iron determination but of powerful emotions. Having given up his practice he paraded the streets of Nagpur every morning reciting the Refuges and Precepts, distributing pamphlets, and calling out, 'O noble sons of Bharat, arise, awake! Remove the thorn of misery and be happy! Destroy casteism, destroy communalism, destroy untouchability, destroy Brahmanism! Preach the Dharma of humanity! Love mankind and glorify the Buddha!' Though he had kept this up for several years, even extending his activities beyond Nagpur, the noble sons of Bharat had so far shown little sign of responding to his appeal. The Buddha Society had not grown, being still confined more or less to a handful of Brahmin lawyers. But Kulkarni was not disheartened. He still wanted to make the people of India Buddha-minded, and was overjoyed that I was visiting Nagpur and that my lectures were proving a success.

> At 7.30 p.m. the learned Bhikshu delivered his last lecture at the Shivananda Hall of the Ramakrishna Mission. The subject of this lecture was 'The Spiritual Path in Buddhism'. By this time the revered Bhikshu's fame had spread far and wide in Nagpur and therefore this lecture attracted a large audience. In fact the entire Shivananda Hall was packed to the full. The audience was easily about 300 and was a distinguished one which included many prominent persons. The meeting was presided over by Swami Bhaskeshwarananda. The revered Bhikshu in the course of his lecture pointed out how spirituality was of the essence of Buddhism, and how there could be no progress in spirituality unless we laid stress on ethics and on renunciation. An emphasis on the *Panchasila* was the right emphasis in life. The learned Bhikshu further pointed out that the regular practice of meditation was indispensable to the higher life, and that Nirvana could be attained only by the complete elimination of the concept of ego. The learned president in the course of his presidential

> speech profusely praised the lecturer and underlined the need for renunciation and meditation. After the lecture was over there was a rush towards the revered Bhikshu as everybody present wanted to have a look at the young English monk.[148]

People seemed to be struck as much by the speaker's youth as by the fact that he was a Westerner, as indeed had been the case in Bangalore. Not that I was really so very young. I was in my twenty-eighth year, though being shaven-headed probably made me look younger than I actually was. In India religious knowledge tended to be associated with age, notwithstanding the fact that youthful – even sixteen-year-old – gurus were not unknown to tradition.

> In fact many institutions in Nagpur wanted to arrange the lecture of the learned Bhikshu but they were disappointed as the Bhikshu had no time. The revered Bhikshu left Nagpur by the Calcutta Mail on July 26th.[149]

I had no time because there was an issue of the *Maha Bodhi* waiting to be brought out. Otherwise I would gladly have stayed longer in Nagpur. Not only could I then have given more lectures; I could also have spent more time with my host and his family and got to know them better. Short though my stay beneath their hospitable roof had been, there was already a good deal of warmth between us, and when the time came for us to say our goodbyes, soon after breakfast, they were all subdued and sad. Krishna and his brother Raja, particularly, were quite affected. Krishna was so affected, in fact, that he did not come to the station, and I was seen off by the two elder Kulkarnis and Raja. Rather unusually, the compartment in which I had a reserved berth, and where the three of them sat and talked with me until the train's departure, was otherwise unoccupied, so that for the early part of my journey I was able to sit back and think my own thoughts without fear of interruption. The visit had been a memorable one. I felt moved by all the devotion I had encountered, and wondered what I had done to deserve it. In the course of the day only two or three people got into the compartment, with one of whom, the Punjabi manager of a Birla concern, I had a little conversation before sleeping. The following morning, having enjoyed a good night's rest, I talked with some of the passengers who had joined us during the hours of darkness, including a young Bengali who turned out to be the nephew of someone I knew and an MP from Orissa who was deeply interested in Tantric Buddhism. Thus the time passed pleasantly, so that when the train reached Howrah Station I hardly noticed that we were three hours late. Soon I had crossed the mighty cantilevered span of Howrah Bridge and was making my way through the congested streets of Burrabazaar to College Square and the Maha Bodhi Society.

Within hours of my arrival at the headquarters building I received a nasty shock. While I was away a meeting of the editorial board of the *Maha Bodhi* had been held, and at this meeting, as a copy of the minutes informed me, decisions had been taken which were plainly designed to check me in my work for the journal and make it virtually impossible, in fact, for me to carry on. These treacherous and underhand proceedings angered me considerably. I flatly told Silabhadra, who was the prime mover in the business, that I proposed to take no notice of the editorial board's decisions and asked Jinaratana to call a special meeting of the board. I then made up the August issue and the following morning, after heated exchanges with my two yellow-robed colleagues (the third, the pacific Dharmaratana, was either away or remained in his room), began sending it to the press as usual, without going through all the channels I was now supposed to go through and without first obtaining the approval of all the people whose approval I was now supposed to obtain. The special meeting, held a week later, was a stormy affair, but despite Silabhadra's determined opposition I carried the day, and with the rather lukewarm support of Dr Kalidas Nag, the chairman of the board, and Dr Nalinaksha Dutt, managed to have the decisions previously taken rescinded. What with proof-reading and counteracting the machinations of Silabhadra and Jinaratana (at one stage they even tried to intercept my letters to members of the governing body), the time between my arrival and the holding of the special meeting was a busy one, so that with the exception of Soratha, who lived on the premises, I could see little of my Calcutta friends. After the special meeting, however, I was able to see more of them, especially Phani Sanyal and his father and Sachin's relations at Hindustan Building. I was even able to pay a visit to the Kamalalaya book department, where I bought a copy of Gide's *If It Die....*[150] None the less, the atmosphere at the headquarters building was such that I had no wish to stay longer than was absolutely necessary and accordingly left Calcutta after spending little more than a week there. Soratha, who had sympathized with me throughout, and who had written about my difficulties to Devapriya-ji, then still in Japan, accompanied me to Sealdah Station and saw me off.

During the daytime I talked with a Baptist missionary, and pointed out in very strong terms the shortcomings of the Christian missions. In the evening we crossed the Ganges, and from the upper deck of the paddle steamer I watched the rose-red disc of the sun drop with increasing rapidity beneath the grey horizon. That night it was very warm and my berth so infested with bedbugs I was unable to sleep. Between Siliguri and Teesta Bridge there were some forty landslides. Once I had to transship, scrambling knee-deep in mud along the mountainside for about thirty yards, with a sheer drop to the swollen waters of the river far below. At midday I reached Kalimpong – and The Hermitage. Hasta arrived soon afterwards with a companion, then Sachin's cousin Durga, whom I had recently started teaching, then Sachin himself with a big bundle of mail, and finally Anand-ji. I was relieved to be back and overjoyed to be once again surrounded by friends.

11
BRICKBATS – AND A BOUQUET

In the Notes and News section of the August issue of the *Maha Bodhi* journal there appeared an item that was of more than usual interest to me. It was headed 'Non-Theravāda Articles in the Journal' and had been written not by me but by Dr Nalinaksha Dutt, who had joined the editorial board a few months earlier. He had written it as a result of a letter that had been received from Joseph Alles, the editor of the *Buddhist World*, a fortnightly paper published in Colombo, complaining that the journal was publishing articles by Mahāyāna Buddhists, a practice Mr Alles seemed to think was not only an innovation but contrary to everything for which the Maha Bodhi Society and its journal were supposed to stand. As I was, effectively, the editor of the *Maha Bodhi*, the letter was obviously aimed at me and was not, in fact, the first brickbat to have been hurled in my direction by the occupants of that citadel of supposed Buddhist orthodoxy, Theravādin Ceylon. Indeed, it was not the first brickbat to have been hurled in my direction by the band of militant 'fundamentalist' Theravādins who were responsible for conducting the *Buddhist World*. They had been deeply upset, even outraged, by my appointment to the editorial board of what they insisted on regarding as a purely Theravādin publication, and had lost no time in attacking the appointment in the pages of their fortnightly, which of course meant attacking me. Joseph Alles's letter represented a continuation of the campaign.

The *Buddhist World*'s attack on me and my appointment, which was couched in that paper's usual intemperate style, was entitled 'Thus Are

We Misled' and was by Dhamma Mamaka, a pseudonym that concealed the identity of the wife of the founder and first editor of the paper, Major-General Tun Hla Oung. This article of hers was a good example of the kind of attitude that was, and unfortunately still is, characteristic of certain representatives of the modern Theravāda (as distinct from the Theravāda of the Pāli canon), and as Western readers of *A Survey of Buddhism* – as my Bangalore lectures became – and other writings of mine may have wondered whether my portrayal of the narrowness and bigotry of these people did not contain an element of exaggeration I reproduce Dhamma Mamaka's article here in full, together with a few comments. The article appeared in the *Buddhist World* of 28 April 1954, and was featured on the front page.

> THUS ARE WE MISLED
> *By Dhamma Mamaka*
> The *Mahabodhi*, Vol 62, no 2 announces an improvement in its editorial board consequent on the appointment of a Mahāyānist Bhikshu (not Bhikkhu) as one of its senior members, despite his *vas*. What improvement, we are entitled to ask, could be expected from association with one having vetulyan ideas? Is it not an insult to the memory of its revered Founder and the numerous Theravādins who have supported and maintained this journal for the past 62 years to publish in its pages articles by avowedly Mahāyānist contributors? It will be observed that all the four articles in this issue are by Mahāyānists!

'Vetulyan' meant heretical, the Vetulyavāda being a quasi-Mahāyānist, possibly Tantric, movement in early Sinhalese Buddhism that had been forcibly suppressed by the dominant Theravāda and whose name was regarded, by modern Theravādins like Dhamma Mamaka, as synonymous with every kind of doctrinal error and moral depravity. As for my having been appointed as one of the senior members of the *Maha Bodhi*'s editorial board 'despite my *vas*', i.e. despite my *vassāvāsa* or 'rains-residence', it was not clear what the writer meant by this objection. Did she mean despite the fact that, having received the higher ordination in 1950, I had observed the rains-residence only thrice, and was therefore a very junior monk, or did she mean despite the fact that for the duration of the rains-residence, which lasted for three months, a monk was not allowed to travel? In either case her objection was beside the point. My being a junior rather than a senior monk did not disqualify me from appointment to the editorial board, any more than my having been appointed to that body in January was really incompatible with my observing the *vassāvāsa* later in the year.

> The columnist 'Himavantavasi' hides under his pseudonym the Mahāyānist ideas of the Editor of this journal. Four columns of his article 'In the Light of the Dhamma' have been devoted for the benefit of one of his staunch supporters, who, as 'a sincere European Buddhist' makes the preposterous suggestion to turn the wheel of the Norm backwards. He actually dares to insult, and the columnist-editor apparently approves, the readers by asserting that the 'current Theravādin system that makes the present [year] 2497 is incorrect'. He had even gone to the extent of insulting the Burmese who are sparing no pains to make the Sixth Buddhist Council the great success it undoubtedly would be.

The 'Sincere European Buddhist' happened to be G. F. Allen (ex-*bhikṣu* Y. Siri Nyana), the scholarly author of *The Buddha's Philosophy*. He was not a supporter of mine, staunch or otherwise, but simply a regular reader of the *Maha Bodhi* who had written to me in my editorial capacity. His 'preposterous suggestion', which according to Dhamma Mamaka amounted to a turning of the Wheel of the Norm backwards, related to the chronology of the Pāli canon. Inasmuch as such traditional stories as that in which Lord Buddha is said to have taught Abhidhamma to his departed mother in Tuṣita heaven and returned to earth to expound it to mankind, and that the Tipiṭaka was rehearsed at the First Council held a few months after the *parinibbāna,* were not fact but legend, and inasmuch as there was in existence a copious library of scholastic research into the chronology of the Pāli canon, contributed over the last half-century by the finest scholars of Buddhism of both the East and West, did not the approaching Sixth Council offer an admirable opportunity for the best brains of the Buddhist world to face that vitally important subject in a rational and scientific manner, and work out an acceptable detailed chronology of the three *Piṭakas*? My well-meaning correspondent, who was himself a (liberal) Theravādin, ventured to offer two further suggestions for the Council's agenda: that a uniform system of referencing the Pāli canonical quotations be introduced, and that the Council agree upon a chronology of dates for the Buddhist era, the current system that made the year 2497 being incorrect.

Why this last suggestion should be regarded as an insult to the readers of the *Maha Bodhi* was unclear, unless the *Buddhist World's* fiery contributor was under the impression that the journal's readership was made up entirely of orthodox Theravādins, and unless she believed, likewise, that the Theravāda was incapable of being mistaken in its chronology. It was also unclear in what the insult to the Burmese consisted. In fact it was unclear whether it was the Sincere European Buddhist who had insulted them or his friend the columnist-editor, the writer's rage apparently having affected her ability to write coherently. But probably it was the columnist-editor. Earlier in the year I had upset some of the more conservative Burmese Theravādins by pointing out that the Burmese pronunciation of Pāli was incorrect,[151] as well as by suggesting, in an editorial, that the money being spent on building new shrines and gilding old ones should be devoted, instead, to propagating the teachings of the Buddha.[152] For the latter offence the Australian-born editor of *The Light of the Dhamma*, the official organ of the Union of Burma Buddha Sasana Council, threatened me with rebirth as a dwarf, while the *Buddhist World* attacked me on both counts in the most vitriolic terms. To these attacks I responded with two light-hearted squibs in my Himavantavasi column[153] and, more seriously, with an editorial on 'Controversy'[154] in which, after referring to the Buddha's warning against 'wordy warfare', I quoted at length from Addison's *Spectator* essay 'Modes of Disputing'. The *Buddhist World*, I observed, had discovered a mode of disputing unknown to Addison, which we might call 'arguing by abuse'.

> Whoever disagrees with its narrow, dogmatic and intolerant views is at once attacked in the vilest and most virulent language imaginable. 'Heretic', 'pseudo-Buddhist' and 'Devadatta' are among the milder epithets with which it favours anyone whose ideas do not coincide in every particular with its own. The leading Buddhist layman of Ceylon, who has done more for the revival of Buddhism than any other Sinhalese since Anagarika Dharmapala (who, by the way, had to face similar attacks even on his deathbed), is assailed with accusations so wild and abuse so

> gross that one wonders how the paper concerned can venture to describe itself as Buddhist. Of course it is not difficult for ill-nature to disguise itself as zeal for religion, or dogmatism to pose as '*saddhā*'. In fact, the paper's official description of its mud-slinging policy is 'radiating *mettā*'.[155]

But regardless of whether my response to their attacks was light-hearted or serious, it saddened me that I should be the object of abuse by fellow Buddhists. When I confided my feelings to Anand-ji, however, my cynical and worldly-minded elder brother in the order only laughed. 'If they want to make you famous why should you worry?' he wanted to know. But I preferred not to be made famous by such means.

> The 'Sincere European Buddhist' has asked his friend the columnist-editor to 'see your way to making the suggestion in the columns of the M. B. Journal, i.e. the premier and eldest mouthpiece of *our* (the italics are ours) Buddhist world – providing, of course, that you agree as to its importance – it might bear fruit.' We understand the agreement between these two friends. That is why so much space has been allowed in this journal. It will certainly bear fruit – the rotten fruit which should never have found a place in this journal. We would ask 'Himavantavasi' to disclose the name of his friend, the 'Sincere European Buddhist' or, is he ashamed or afraid to divulge it? 'Himavantavasi' and people of his ilk would do well to bear in mind that the *Mahabodhi* is a purely Theravada publication, supported and maintained by Theravadins all these long years, and that anti-Theravadin views should not be allowed to sully its pages.

I did not disclose the name of my alleged friend, the Sincere European Buddhist, as I did not wish to embroil him in my own disagreements with the *Buddhist World*. Had I disclosed it, Dhamma Mamaka might well have received a shock, G. F. Allen having spent several years in India and Ceylon as a monk and been highly regarded in Theravādin circles. His reference to 'our Buddhist world', to which Dhamma Mamaka took such exception, was simply an innocent acknowledgement of the fact that all Buddhists were members of a single ecumene. It did not represent a laying claim to the Buddhist world on behalf of the Mahāyānists, as Dhamma Mamaka seems to have thought. Whether the Maha Bodhi Society was a Theravādin organization, and its journal a purely Theravādin publication, was the principal point addressed in Dr Dutt's Notes and News item on 'Non-Theravāda Articles in the Journal', as shortly will transpire.

> It would, perhaps, interest readers to know what the editor of *The Western Buddhist* says about *Maha Bodhi*. Here it is: 'We value highly the encouragement given by many Buddhist periodicals, especially the most friendly welcome accorded us in the pages of *Maha Bodhi* at the pen of Ven. Himavantavasi. We should do our utmost to justify the welcome support of the Ven. Bhikkhu and to fulfil the prophecies he makes about us.' The Ven. Bhikshu is also a preacher of the western order!

The *Western Buddhist* was the organ of the Western Buddhist Order, founded about two years earlier by Robert Stuart Clifton, an American Buddhist, and its editor was Jack Austin, the young English bank clerk who was one of my most faithful correspondents. Though I did not agree with all Clifton's ideas, and had not been too pleased at my involuntary co-option into his order, I had, as Himavantavasi, indeed given the order's little journal a warm welcome on its first appearance.[156] Dhamma Mamaka evidently thought that this fact would interest her readers as constituting further evidence, if such were needed, of my Mahāyāna proclivities, the Western Buddhist Order being admittedly based on the Far Eastern (Mahāyāna) Sangha of Japan, for which and other shortcomings it had already been more than once castigated in the pages of the *Buddhist World*. She concluded her article by recurring to the theme that it was an insult to the memory of Anagarika Dharmapala that Mahāyānists should be allowed to control the *Maha Bodhi.*

> The Maha Bodhi Society of India must realize that it is an insult to the memory of its reverend Founder and its numerous supporters in all parts of the Theravada world to allow Mahayanists to control this valued Journal, and that the sooner they can get the 'Rakshita' to 'change his spots' the better it would be if its continuance is to be ensured for many, many years

> to come. This is the earnest wish of Theravadins. Otherwise, its knell would be sounded sooner or later, sooner perhaps than later. If this were to happen, it would indeed be a tragedy, and a success for the Bhikshu!

I did not change my spots,[157] or at least did not change them in the way Dhamma Mamaka had in mind, and continued to edit the *Maha Bodhi* journal and – *pace* her despicable suggestion that I was out to destroy it – managed to ensure its continuance as the leading English-language Buddhist journal until my final return to the West twelve years later. The history of the *Maha Bodhi* journal thereafter was one of steady decline. With 'Mahāyānists' no longer in control, its knell indeed sounded, and eventually it ceased publication.

But in 1954 all that was in the distant future. Though the August Notes and News section's item on 'Non-Theravāda Articles in the Journal' had been written as a result of Joseph Alles's letter, it in fact made no mention of that letter. Instead it took issue with Dhamma Mamaka's article in the *Buddhist World*. The truth of the matter was that the nature of Alles's letter had at first been seriously misunderstood, and the action which, as I discovered on my return to Calcutta from Nagpur, had been taken by the editorial board in order to restrict me in my work for the journal, had been taken on the basis of the misunderstanding. The letter had been received, apparently, by Silabhadra. At any rate, it was Silabhadra who had placed it before a meeting of the governing body, and Silabhadra who had informed the meeting that it was a complaint about the editorials that had been appearing in the Society's journal, editorials which were, as was well known, written by me. The result was that, without those present having actually read the letter for themselves, a resolution was passed upholding Alles's complaint and, by implication, criticizing me for writing the editorials. Armed with this resolution, Silabhadra was able to persuade the editorial board to pass a resolution of its own restricting me in my work for the journal and making me, in effect, a tool in the hands of himself and the other members of the board. But Joseph Alles's letter did not so much as mention my editorials, as I ascertained from a perusal of the minutes of the governing body's meeting, to which a copy of the letter was attached. His complaint was that the *Maha Bodhi* journal was publishing articles by Mahāyāna Buddhists, so that the resolution passed by the governing body was entirely beside the point. I therefore went to see Keshub Chandra Gupta, one of the Vice-Presidents of the Society, under whose chairmanship the governing body meeting at which this resolution was passed had been held.

Keshub Babu was a tall, dark-complexioned, saturnine Bengali in late middle age whom I had seen a few times at Society functions but with whom I was personally unacquainted. Besides being a prominent member of the Calcutta Bar, he was connected with several educational institutions, and was a regular contributor to leading Indian dailies and monthlies, both English and Bengali. He was, of course, a Hindu, though not a Brahmin, and I was not sure how sympathetic a hearing he would give to my representations, it being well known that I was no less critical of orthodox Hinduism than I was of fundamentalist Theravāda. I need not have worried. As I proceeded with my story Keshub Babu's heavy eyebrows elevated themselves in astonishment and he listened with increasing interest. The governing body had not understood the nature of Mr Alles's letter, I explained, nor grasped its implications. Mr Alles had not complained about my editorials, as Silabhadra had led it to believe. His complaint was that the *Maha Bodhi* journal was publishing articles by Mahāyāna Buddhists, which he seemed to regard as an innovation. The point to be decided by the governing body was, therefore, *whether articles by Mahāyānists, or contributions dealing with Mahāyāna Buddhism, were to be excluded from the journal or not.* In deciding this point it would have to bear in mind that neither the Society nor its journal were limited to any sect of Buddhism: both were international and inter-sectarian. Many members of the Society, including the President, were Mahāyānists. It would also have to bear in mind that articles by Mahāyānists, and articles dealing with Mahāyāna Buddhism, had appeared in the journal ever since its inception. The Founder himself had written several appreciative articles on Mahāyāna Buddhism, including one in the first issue of the journal (May 1892), and we were certainly not being unfaithful to his memory by continuing the practice of publishing such articles. The governing body might also like to take note of the fact, of which it had evidently been unaware (though Silabhadra had been well aware of it), that Mr Alles happened to be the editor of the *Buddhist World*, a fortnightly paper published from Colombo that was well known for the violence and virulence of its attacks on Mahāyāna Buddhism. In view of these considerations, I concluded, the governing body should pass a fresh resolution, to the effect that a reply be sent to Mr Alles – preferably over the signature of himself as chairman of the meeting – informing him that the Society and its journal were not limited to any sect of Buddhism, and that as the journal had published articles on Mahāyāna Buddhism (including some by the Founder himself) from the very beginning, his complaint on this score could not be entertained.

Experienced criminal lawyer that he was, it was not difficult for Keshub Babu to see the force of my arguments. Neither was it difficult for him to see that Silabhadra had acted in a less than straightforward manner. He therefore told me that he agreed with me on all points and that if I would write to him officially he would raise the matter at the next meeting of the governing body. Business thus having been dispatched to our mutual satisfaction, we turned to other topics, and spent the rest of the evening discussing Buddhism and literature.

My next step was to have the decisions that the editorial board had taken in my absence rescinded. This I did at the special meeting of the board that I had asked Jinaratana to convene, though I did not manage to do it without coming into violent conflict with Silabhadra, who was determined that the decisions should not be rescinded and who seemed, in fact, to share Joseph Alles's – and Dhamma Mamaka's – conviction that the *Maha Bodhi* journal was a purely Theravādin publication. In the course of our rather heated exchange I confronted him with the deception he had practised on the governing body, as well as on the editorial board itself, and took him severely to task for his treacherous and underhand behaviour. My language was rather strong, perhaps stronger than it should have been to such an old man (Silabhadra was more than twice my age, and was to die the following year), but I was outraged that one who did so little for the journal should seek to obstruct my own efforts on its behalf and exasperated, moreover, by the obstinacy with which he continued to maintain his position even when it had been shown to be without foundation.

The result of my meeting with Keshub Chandra Gupta, and of my having the editorial board's decisions rescinded, was that I was able to leave Calcutta for Kalimpong secure in the knowledge that I was still the *de facto* editor of the journal and free to operate without the restrictions Silabhadra had sought to impose on me. A few days after my return Sachin brought me, along with the rest of the mail, my copies of the August issue of the *Maha Bodhi*, in which there appeared, as the second item in the Notes and News section, Dr Dutt's 'Non-Theravāda Articles in the Journal'.

My scholarly colleague did not express himself as forcibly as I might have done, but he expressed himself forcibly enough, his contribution being in fact based upon an editorial on 'Our Policy' that I had sent Keshub Babu – along with the official letter for which he had asked – but which had not been used. Moreover, though he had given me only lukewarm support at the special meeting of the editorial board, soft-spoken, bespectacled Dr Dutt was, I knew, very much of my own way of thinking with regard to the *Maha Bodhi* journal. When I saw him in his room at the University, where he was Head of the Department of Pāli, the day after the meeting, he indeed went so far as to characterize Silabhadra's attitude as narrow-minded and bigoted. Thus it did not surprise me that although the item of which he was author could have been more forcibly written, he should have struck, in his opening paragraph, a sufficiently stern and decisive note.

A recent pseudonymous article published in the *Buddhist World* (28 April 1954) of Colombo, he declared, had dragged in the name of the Society's founder Anagarika Dharmapala without giving sufficient thought to the magnanimity of his outlook expressed in the early issues of the *Maha Bodhi* journal in these words:

> The Society representing Buddhism in general, not only single aspects of it, shall preserve absolute neutrality with respect to the doctrines and dogmas taught by sections and sects among the Buddhists. It is not lawful for anybody, whether a member or not, to attempt to make it responsible, as a body, for his own views. Membership being open to all, whether professed Buddhists or not, the Society is bound to guarantee them their rights as neutrals. It will be equally ready to publish expositions of all Buddhist sects, but without committing itself to any one.

Dharmapala's outlook had indeed been a magnanimous one, as I well knew, from having written about the *anagārika*'s life two years earlier, and the noble statement cited by Dr Dutt served to make it clear, once and for all, whether or not the Society and its journal were the exclusive property of the Theravādins. Dr Dutt also drew attention to the fact that the writer of 'Thus Are We Misled' had even shut 'his' eyes to the cover of the journal in which it was clearly stated that 'the Maha Bodhi is a monthly Journal of International Buddhist Brotherhood'. He then proceeded to show that out of the four articles complained of as being by Mahāyānists three established nothing but Theravādin points of view, while the fourth paper was a descriptive one, giving information about later Buddhism which, the editors considered, should be made known to the Theravādin Buddhists. As regards the particular exception that had been taken to the remarks of a 'Sincere European Buddhist' who had attached more value to the results of critical scholarship than to orthodox beliefs, such views admittedly might not appeal to all Buddhists but there were Ceylonese scholars like Prof. Malalasekera and others who adhered to the former views. (Dr Dutt was evidently unaware that along with Christmas Humphreys, Robert Stuart Clifton, and me, G. P. Malalasekera was one of the *Buddhist World's* principal *bêtes noires*, and that it was constantly attacking him.) Finally, though probably upset by the names of the contributors, the writer of 'Thus Are We Misled' should, on the contrary, have appreciated that so many foreigners had been attracted to Buddhism and had studied the Pāli texts in order to find out what Buddhism really was.

Thus my scholarly colleague. Though disappointed that my editorial on 'Our Policy' had not been used, I could see that it was better that Dhamma Mamaka's allegations should be refuted in the Notes and News section of the journal rather than in an editorial, which would have given the *Buddhist World* more importance than it deserved. In any case, my policy of printing articles by Buddhists of *all* persuasions had been amply vindicated, and the brickbats hurled at me from Theravādin Ceylon had fallen short of their mark.

But if brickbats were sometimes hurled in my direction I was also the recipient of the occasional bouquet. Not long after my return to Kalimpong there arrived at The Hermitage a copy of *The Mysorean*, self-described as 'a National Weekly with an International Outlook'. It contained an article by M. A. Venkata Rao, a literary member of the Indian Institute of Culture to whom, on my departure from Bangalore, I had presented a complete set of *Stepping-Stones*. Clearly the gift had not been wasted. The article, which was entitled 'Poison – But Also Nectar', bore the subtitle 'When East meets West the fruit is sometimes of uncommon value', and it was about me. Bhikshu Sangharakshita's lectures at the Indian Institute of Culture that year had shown him as a scholarly student of Buddhist lore with a remarkable gift for clear and attractive exposition, the writer was so good as to declare. But the puzzle remained as to why attraction towards ancient Buddhist teachings should have led a young Britisher to burn his boats and become a *bhikṣu*. Were not specialization, assimilation, and even exposition possible without accepting *saṃnyas* and formal monasticism and binding oneself to the limitations of historical dogmatical schools? Whatever the answer to that question, a glimpse into the discourses and poems contained in the twenty numbers of *Stepping-Stones* revealed, in the writer's opinion,

> a singularly attractive personality. One gets the impression that here we have one of the romances of the inner life of our times.

Though the meeting of East and West had generated much poison it had also brought forth nectar (as in the Purāṇic story of the churning of the ocean by gods and *asuras*),[158] the nectar of immortality.

Not that the *bhikṣu*'s case was unique. A whole series of earnest and inspired Westerners, touched by something deep and unfathomable in Eastern tradition, had devoted themselves heart and soul to the service of the Asian peoples. Such, in India, had been Sister Nivedita, C. F. Andrews, and Mirabhen, and such now were Sri Krishna Prem and Father Verrier Elwin.[159] What, then, made this British youngster come to India at the early age of nineteen at the height of the war of world powers (1944), casting out the pride of race and empire? And what sustained his resolve and carried him into the fold of Buddhist monasticism, in this age of secularism? Venkata Rao thought *Stepping-Stones* revealed much of the answer.

> The young bhikshu (he is now 29) is a poet and has a genuinely aesthetic temperament. His discourses and poems show a perfect and attractive fusion of poetic and spiritual strains. The appeal of beauty in life and nature overflows naturally into the sense of the transcendental. We find here a variant of the new kind of priest, preacher or interpreter of spiritual things, of which there is a great need everywhere. For the bhikshu has approached the Buddhist scriptures, not as an orientalist or unattached scholar but

> as a thirsty soul seeking the water of everlasting life. And the little magazine is full of the appealing result.

Though I had certainly not achieved a perfect fusion of the poetic and spiritual strains of my own nature, I could appreciate that there was a need for a new kind of priest, preacher, or interpreter of spiritual things, and it was interesting that my Bangalore friend should see me as a variant of such a figure. Lama Govinda, I knew, believed that religion and poetry – indeed religion and all forms of art – were closely connected. In his Introduction to *The Veil of Stars*, my little (as yet unpublished) volume of poetic aphorisms, he had expressed his belief that

> It was the poet in Sangharakshita that led him to the religious life, and it was the path of renunciation that enabled him to see the world in a wider and truer perspective, which is the hall-mark of genuine poetry.[160]

He had also gone on to quote the words of Novalis:

> Poets and priests were one in the beginning, and only later times have separated them. The real poet, however, has always remained priest, just as the real priest has always remained poet.[161]

In my essay 'The Religion of Art', written the previous year, I had affirmed my belief that art and religion overlapped, and that just as there was in religion a constituent that was aesthetic, so there was also in art a constituent that was religious. The essay indeed concluded with the declaration that the Religion of Art, as I called it, was peculiarly fitted to produce a kind of character, a type of spiritual personality, which would be the living embodiment of the fact that Religion and Art were in essence one, and that Beauty was not merely Truth, but Goodness as well.[162] Not that I thought of my own character or personality as constituting such an embodiment. I still saw myself as simply a monk who wrote poetry, even though there were moments when aesthetic experience and spiritual experience seemed to coincide. Perhaps I needed to redefine my identity.

Be that as it may, having given a thumbnail sketch of the young *bhikṣu*'s temperament Venkata Rao turned to Kalimpong, the place where he had settled, which he described at some length and in the most grandiloquent terms. Situated on a foothill of the Himalayan range, within sight of Kanchenjunga peak (which bore an unearthly purity and splendour when the clouds lifted), with the deep and narrow river flowing and turning upon itself, skirting deep gorges between hills, covered with evergreen forests of *sāl* and deodar, hills whose tops dotted the horizon all round, leading up on the north to the ice-clad Himalayan peaks in mid-sky, as it were, with houses peeping through foliage round the slopes of the hills at all levels, and the central road becoming the market road at the Tenth Mile – Kalimpong was a dream of restful and various beauty, wrapped in translucent, lambent radiance all its own. Beyond the Himalayas lay the mysterious land of Buddhist Tibet, 'fabled still to contain teachers of primeval wisdom'. From Tibet, via one of my poems, it was not difficult for the writer to make the transition to reincarnation and karma, and from these to some of the topics with which I had dealt in my discourses, as he called my articles, from the 'stepping-stones' of right conduct, meditation, and wisdom, to the bodhisattva ideal, and from the simple life to the nature of Buddhahood. Unfortunately, Venkata Rao's appreciation of my having worked out for myself 'an appealing form of Mahāyāna Buddhism through which a positive spiritual idealism gleams forth, not in technicalities but in terms of thought and feeling while seeking out the higher values of life' was vitiated, for me, by his typically Hindu insistence on seeing this as constituting a return, by an alternative route, to Upanishadic idealism. None the less I was pleased with the article. It really was a bouquet, even if among the flowers there was a weed or two. I particularly appreciated the writer's pointing out the way in which the sights and sounds of Kalimpong, besides forming a natural background to my thoughts, provided much of the symbolism and imagery of the 'discourses' and poems. And of course I appreciated his quoting from three of my poems, even if his attribution to 'Messengers from Tibet'[163] of a 'certain eerie lilt recalling Yeats and Walter de la Mare' rather puzzled me.

My poems were very much in my mind at the time. Forty-five of them, most of which had been contributed originally to various magazines, had recently been brought out by a Bombay publishing house under the title *Messengers from Tibet and Other Poems*, and notices had already begun to appear. The *Illustrated Weekly of India*, in an unsigned review that was probably by the English-born editor, Mr Mandy, characterized this my first publication in book form as ‘a pleasant volume, mainly religious and descriptive in tone’. The idiom was conservative and the rhythm mellifluent; there was no great depth of thought behind the imagery, which was purely factual for the most part, as for example in ‘Mountain Mist’, from which the reviewer proceeded to quote.

> A poet of gentle sentiments and wistful longings, Bhikshu Sangharakshita consistently employs straight rhymes, of a studiously correct and simple nature, and one feels that had he resorted occasionally to well-contrived assonance, the result would have been more effective.

I was best, the reviewer thought, in my shorter lyrics, some of which had ‘a strong flavour of the work of Walter de la Mare.’ Miss I. B. Horner, the distinguished translator of the Vinaya Piṭaka, reviewing the collection in the *Maha Bodhi*, concentrated on the fact that the author of ‘these charming and happy poems’, as she called them, was deeply in the debt and under the spell of India, that great and beautiful land, with her kindliness, patience, and age-old wisdom, the birthplace of ‘the Lord of Compassion’, that ‘Void-born Compassion diamond-hard and petal-tender’ to which I appealed in ‘Invocation’.[164] Several of the poems, she pointed out, had India,

> with her snowy mountains, her rivers, plains and villages, her flowers, her sunshine, mists and rain as the fount and as the symbols of man’s adventures as he strives and aspires to fulfil the spiritual growth for which the Teaching of the Buddha provides a Way, a Track of ‘sunward-mounting golden stages’.

She also drew attention to the fact that the poems were ‘happy’ because their inspiration stemmed from Buddhism, and in Buddhism there was nothing sad, dismal, or depressing.[165]

Having a book published, it has been said, is one of the all-time most satisfying experiences. A good part of the satisfaction lies in presenting copies to one’s friends. One of the first recipients of *Messengers from Tibet* was Clare Cameron, the pixie-like former editor of the Buddhist Society’s journal *The Middle Way*. The volume was in fact dedicated to her. Ten years earlier I had shown her the best of my youthful verses and she had given me, in the course of a walk in Kensington Gardens, the benefit of some very sound criticism for which I was still grateful.[166] Recipients of the volume nearer home included Sachin, Dawa, the *anagārika*, Joe, and, of course, Dr Hudson (still settled comfortably in Darjeeling), who had defrayed the cost of publication. When I handed Joe his copy the hypercritical *upāsaka* could not forbear heaving a small brickbat of his own in my direction. Glaring through his spectacles at the cream-coloured little volume as though it was something the cat had brought in, he professed himself extremely disappointed. Why, for the generous sum Dr Hudson had given me he had expected to see a handsome *dee* luxe edition, printed on the best hand-made paper, lavishly illustrated by a well-known Bombay artist, and with beautifully designed endpapers and a watered silk marker! But there it was. I had done things in my own way, as I always did. I had not consulted anybody, least of all him, with the result that the publishers had swindled me and Dr Hudson's money had been wasted.

Joe's outburst momentarily confounded me. Dr Hudson had given me 750 rupees, this being what the publishers had asked for bringing out my poems, and from what I knew of printing and binding costs in Calcutta their demand was not unreasonable. None the less I was sufficiently disturbed to write to Sophia Wadia, in whose *Aryan Path* a brief notice of *Messengers from Tibet* had appeared, asking her if she thought I had been swindled. Her reply was unequivocal. 750 rupees was not a great deal of money, and I could rest assured that the book had been produced to as high a standard as could be expected for that sum. Joe remained unconvinced, and not only refused to retract his brickbat but before long was assuring Dr Hudson that it was useless for anyone to give me money as I was totally impractical and always wasted it.

Brickbats and bouquets were, it seemed, an integral part of mundane existence. Sometimes there were more of the former, sometimes more of the latter, but one never experienced the one without sooner or later experiencing the other. The wisest course was to treat them as one should, according to Kipling's famous poem, treat those two impostors Triumph and Disaster, that is, 'just the same',[167] or else be, in the words of the *Maṅgala Sutta*, one of those 'whose mind does not shake' when touched by the 'eight worldly conditions' of pleasure and pain, gain and loss, praise and blame, fame and infamy.[168] Not that the wisest course was necessarily the easiest, especially to someone as sensitive as I was to people's emotional reactions to me and as liable, moreover, to fluctuations of mood – fluctuations which, more often than not, found expression only in my poetry. Nevertheless, conscious of the need to develop equanimity I did my best to be neither cast down by Dhamma Mamaka's (and Joe's) brickbats nor elated by Venkata Rao's bouquet, and carried on with my work for Buddhism and the local people. As usual, this included the giving of a good deal of personal tuition. After my return to Kalimpong I had resumed teaching Sachin and Meera (the latter at her home, whenever I happened to be visiting there) and had started teaching Durga, Sachin's sixteen-year-old cousin, History and English Literature. Sweet-natured but inclined to be taciturn, Durga lived near Sixth Mile, and in the evening, after giving him his lessons, I sometimes walked a mile or two down the road with him, instead of going up the road to Sachin's place. I also started teaching the *anagārika*, or Thupten Chhokyi as she now was, having been ordained as a *śrāmaṇerī* or novice nun by Dhardo Rimpoche that summer. In her case the lessons were meant to serve the double purpose of helping her improve her English and deepen her knowledge of Buddhism (not to mention satisfying her chronic need for attention), but they did not continue for long, as after a few weeks the ever-restless Frenchwoman decided she would be better off back in Darjeeling.

I was not sorry to see her go, for though intellectually stimulating she was extremely demanding, and had taken to complaining about the Rimpoche's supposed lack of interest in her in a way I did not like. Besides, I had not forgotten B. P. Wadia's request that I should write out my Bangalore lectures for publication in book form and wanted to set to work as soon as possible. This was not proving easy to arrange. Not that giving tuition was the only thing that took up my time. There were meetings to be organized, letters to be written (usually I wrote several a day), and visitors to be received, as well as the *Maha Bodhi* journal to be edited. Eventually, however, on the last day of August, I seated myself at the rickety gate-legged table that served me as a desk, spread out my lecture notes, and started writing. 'The importance of Right Motive, of a correct attitude of mind, is emphasized more strongly in Buddhism than in any other form of traditional teaching,'[169] I wrote. Work on the first chapter of *A Survey of Buddhism* had begun! Two hours later, having filled several foolscap sheets, I put down my pen and walked out into the garden. Despite the rain, the sun was shining brilliantly. Looking up into the sky, I saw a rainbow. According to Tibetan Buddhist belief the appearance of a rainbow was an auspicious sign. Double and triple rainbows had spanned my path when, almost exactly seven years ago, I had 'gone forth' from home into the homeless life.[170] *This* was a single rainbow. None the less, I hoped its appearance was auspicious and that, now I had started writing the *Survey,* I would be able to get on with the work without too many interruptions.

12
CRAIGSIDE

In a long autobiographical poem written in 1949, when I was staying with Kashyap-ji in Benares, I had described myself as roaming, after the havoc wrought by war,

> Without a friend, without a home,
> For many a year, with unquiet breast,
> Perplexed between the East and West.[171]

In this there undoubtedly was an element of hyperbole. I was perplexed between East and West only in the sense that, notwithstanding Venkata Rao's eulogy, I had not yet succeeded in integrating the East as represented by Buddhism, with the West, as represented by English (and European) literature, and in particular by English poetry. Though a keen student of the Pāli canon and the great Mahāyāna *sūtras*, of Śāntideva and Aśvaghoṣa, I was still an avid reader of Shakespeare and Milton, Wordsworth and Shelley, besides a host of lesser names. My spiritual life seemed to derive nourishment from both streams of inspiration. Though I had not roamed entirely friendless (had not Buddharakshita shared my life for two years and more?) since my departure from England ten years earlier I had certainly been without a home. Indeed, for the last seven years, ever since the be-rainbowed day on which I had 'gone forth' from home into homelessness, I had been formally pledged to being without one. None the less, from the time of my arrival in Kalimpong I had led a comparatively settled life. After six months as the (eventually unwanted) guest of the Dharmodaya Vihara and six months as the guest of the exiled Prince and Princess of Burma, I had moved into The Hermitage, where I had now lived for more than three years and which had become the centre of my activities. But if I was in any danger of forgetting that the semi-derelict frame building was *not* my home, and that I was in reality a homeless wanderer, I was soon to be given a sharp reminder of the true state of affairs. In the middle of October, when I had been working on the first chapter of the *Survey* for no more than six weeks, I received a curt message from the landlord. The Hermitage was going to be pulled down and rebuilt, and we would have to vacate the place.

Whether the landlord ever intended to rebuild, or whether he simply wanted us out so that he could accommodate some of the drivers of his expanding fleet of taxis and buses, I never discovered. There was certainly no rebuilding during my remaining years in Kalimpong, nor was it long after my departure before wild-looking men who may well have been drivers were to be seen occupying my old abode with their families. Whatever the landlord's real reason for giving us notice may have been, the fact was that I had to find fresh accommodation for myself and the Kalimpong branch of the Maha Bodhi Society. Fortunately this did not take me long, nor did we have to go very far. Jutting from the hillside on the other side of the road, directly opposite The Hermitage, there was a spur, and strung out along this spur, at increasingly lower levels, there were three bungalows. At the base of the spur, immediately below the road, stood Glengarry, the biggest of the three, which was surrounded by tall privet hedges and occupied by Mrs Hamilton, the elderly, grim-faced Anglo-Indian widow with whom I sometimes had morning coffee. On the far end of the spur stood an anonymous bungalow that was occupied, during the summer months, by a Bengali family from the plains. In between the two, but nearer Glengarry, whose well kept privet hedges towered like a green wall above its red roof-tiles, stood Craigside, a modest pukka building with a generous expanse of front lawn and a few rose bushes. Craigside was occupied by cheery, pipe-smoking Major Cummins, the retired commander of a Gurkha regiment, who strode about the town in khaki shirt and shorts and was much saluted by Nepalese ex-servicemen and others. We were not unacquainted; each occasionally dropped in on the other for a cup of tea, and soon after my return from Calcutta I had borrowed his gramophone in order to play some of Major Lalkaka's records. On my returning the device he told me that he would be moving to Darjeeling shortly, as he wanted to be nearer some of his old comrades-in-arms. At the time the information meant little or nothing to me, but on receiving our landlord's message I remembered it and at once went to see Major Cummins, who not only confirmed that he was moving to Darjeeling shortly, in fact that very month, but also gave me the address of his Marwari landlord. The upshot was that by the end of October Major Cummins had moved out of Craigside and I had moved in.

The business of moving did not take long. Apart from pictures and crockery, which with Major Cummins's agreement I had sent down separately a couple of days earlier, my worldly goods comprised little more than robes and bedding, a few aluminium cooking pots, several dozen bundles of *Stepping-Stones*, a typewriter, and the handsome glass-fronted bookcase I had recently had made for my growing collection of books. All the same, they filled the back of the jeep I had hired for the occasion, and as we negotiated the track leading to my new abode I could not but reflect, somewhat ruefully, that whereas I had arrived in Kalimpong with no more baggage than I could carry myself I now had fifteen or twenty times that amount. If one stayed very long in one place, it seemed, possessions had a way of multiplying, which was probably why the Buddha not only had restricted the personal belongings of his monk followers to just eight items[172] but had exhorted them, moreover, to spend the greater part of the year wandering from village to village and town to town.[173] That eventually the majority of them settled permanently in one spot, there to enjoy the use of corporate monastic property, was another story, and one with which I would be concerned in the second chapter of the *Survey*. But although my worldly goods now filled a jeep, they at least did not include any furniture, other than the glass-fronted bookcase. The Hermitage having been let to us furnished, that is to say, equipped with a table and chairs and two or three wooden bed-platforms, I had not needed to acquire any furniture. The same was the case with Craigside, which was also let furnished. The only difference was that the furniture in my new quarters was of a better kind, the table being a real dining room table and the beds real beds, with springs and mattresses such as I had not seen for years and with which I could well have dispensed. Better or not better, the furniture was soon rearranged, and within a few hours of their being unloaded my belongings had been distributed among the various rooms.

There were three principal rooms in the bungalow, which was L-shaped and flanked by an outhouse containing three much smaller rooms, the middle one of which was the kitchen. In the biggest room, which occupied the body of the L, I installed on a table beneath the casement window at the far end our three Buddha images, one standing and two sedent, thus transforming the apartment into our new – and much more spacious – shrine-room. This meant that we would be unable to have a games room, as there was no other room in the bungalow capable of accommodating our full-size ping-pong table. Not that I regretted the loss of the games room. On the contrary, I had for some time past been wanting to phase out our recreational activities, which in any case were a legacy from our earlier days as the YMBA, and to lay greater emphasis on the more specifically religious activities that were appropriate to our position as a branch of the Maha Bodhi Society. One of the results of our moving from The Hermitage to Craigside was that this could happen quite naturally, rather than it being the result of a definite decision on my part. Far from regretting that we now had no games room, I therefore did not even regret our having had to leave The Hermitage, despite the associations the place had come to have for me. In some ways I was even glad to leave. For the last few months relations with the angry-looking driver who, with his large family, occupied the tiny cottage at the far end of the garden, had not been very happy. On my return from Calcutta he complained that during my absence our members had torn up a number of letters that had arrived for him, a charge the latter all vigorously denied. Moreover, for the last eight or nine months he had refused to pay his share of our joint electricity bill (the cottage was supplied by an extension from The Hermitage, and the account was rendered in my name), alleging that the responsibility for paying it rested with the landlord, who was also his employer. The landlord apparently did not recognize any such responsibility, and if I was not to continue paying for the driver's electricity I had either to disconnect the extension or deduct his share of the bill from our rent each month, neither of which courses I was keen to pursue. The landlord's announcement that The Hermitage was to be pulled down and rebuilt, which served to resolve the impasse, therefore came as something of a relief. My only real regret at our leaving The Hermitage was for the loss of the garden up and down the gravel path of which I had so often walked, either thinking about my next lecture or composing a poem, or simply listening to the bird calls and enjoying the silent companionship of the flowering trees and shrubs.[174] If The Hermitage was pulled down and rebuilt the garden would, I hoped, be spared.

But man is an adaptable creature. Within a matter of days I had ceased to regret the loss of the garden, or even to think about it very much, and had begun to feel as though I – and the Kalimpong branch of the Maha Bodhi Society – had been at Craigside for years. This feeling was due partly to the fact that my personal routine continued virtually unchanged, as did the rhythm of our more public activities. On the very day after we moved in there was a *dāna* party. It was arranged by Dr Hudson, who a few weeks earlier had left Darjeeling to live a mile or so down the road at a house called Winston (there was another nearby called Churchill).[175] According to her, the *dāna* party was a traditional Buddhist institution, and she had come to know about it during a visit to Burma. In a letter sent out over her signature, our members and friends were invited to come and see our new premises (I had to type the letters, Dr Hudson's typewriter having broken down) and to bring with them gifts in cash or in kind. Not many people actually turned up, though a number sent gifts of one kind or another, from small sums of money to household items. Among those who did come were our two most generous donors, the fascinating Princess Pema Tsedeun ('Coo-Coo La'), the eldest daughter of the Maharaja of Sikkim,[176] and her husband Mr Pheunkhang. Though I knew Princess Pema Tsedeun fairly well, I think it was the first time I had met her husband, who had probably been away in Lhasa. Pheunkhang-se or Pheunkhang Junior, as he was known, his father being still alive, was a pink-cheeked, affable young Tibetan nobleman, the descendant of the families of *two* previous Dalai Lamas, who some years later, when we were near neighbours, became quite a close friend. The day after the *dāna* party I resumed work on the *Survey*, and a week after that we celebrated the full-moon day in our new shrine-room with an inaugural puja at which I spoke on the Buddha's famous 'Song of Victory'.[177]

Thus the days and weeks went by, and as autumn gave way to winter I was able to become more and more deeply involved in my writing. Sometimes I wrote sitting out on the little veranda, from which I could look up at the increasingly clear blue of the sky and at the dazzling whiteness of the ever more frequently visible snows. Not that I was never interrupted, even in the mornings, when I was supposedly incommunicado. More often than not, the interruptions took the form of visitors, both expected and unexpected. One of my earliest visitors was Vilasak, a novice monk from the Dharmodaya Vihara who had no money for necessaries and whom I promised to help. Another was Dr Ravi Singh, Sachin's cheerful and good-natured father, who came with Mrs Singh and Meera to see the new premises. There was also a visit, one fine morning towards the end of the month, from tall, white-haired Mrs Barnet, a widow who lived with her unmarried elder sister in a big house not far from Joe. According to the woman-wary *upāsaka*, she wanted to marry him and was always giving him opportunities of proposing to her. However, their *tête-à-têtes* were invariably interrupted by the flirtatious, girlishly-attired elder sister, who also had her eye on Joe and who, to Mrs Barnet's annoyance and Joe's relief, would come flouncing in at the critical moment.

My own acquaintance with the husband-hungry widow was much slighter, being more or less limited to the occasion when, two years earlier, she had invited me to lunch and shown me some black kittens for whom she was anxious to find good homes. When I enquired whether they were male or female she replied that she would have to ask the servants, as 'they always know about such things'. On the present occasion she had come not to dispose of unwanted kittens but to ask me if I would speak to Dr Hudson about renting her house. Like other United Kingdom citizens left high and dry by the retreating tide of the Raj she was worried about her future in an independent India, especially as a *femme sole* with a penniless sister to support, and wanted to let or sell her house and move to England. Eventually, Dr Hudson being already suited, she sold out to a local businessman, said goodbye to Kalimpong and her hopes of marrying Joe, and went to live in the Home Counties. Soon Joe was being inundated with heart-rending letters of complaint. England was unbelievably expensive. She and her sister were living in a top floor back room with no amenities and had to do all their own work, even to the extent of carrying buckets of water up three flights of stairs. Bitterly did she regret giving up her big house, her beautiful garden, and her band of devoted servants.

Mrs Barnet was an unexpected visitor. Around the middle of December I had a whole cluster of visitors whose arrival was not only expected but even, in the case of one of them, eagerly anticipated. This especially welcome visitor was Dhardo Rimpoche, who came accompanied by Lobsang Phuntsok. Like me, the Rimpoche had moved since our first meeting the previous year. He had moved, a few months earlier, from Sherpa Building at Tirpai, where he occupied a flat above the ground floor one formerly occupied by Joe, to the Old Bhutan Palace at Eleventh Mile. The Old Bhutan Palace, so called to distinguish it from Bhutan House further up the road, which had been built in the thirties, was a large, two-storey wooden structure in the traditional Bhutanese style of architecture. Once it must have been a magnificent sight. Now, though still impressive on account of its size and noble proportions, it was so shabby and in such a state of disrepair as to resemble the ruined mansion so graphically described in the *White Lotus Sūtra's* 'Parable of the Burning House'.[178] Dhardo Rimpoche lived in a suite of rooms on the first floor, where I had seen him the previous week and invited him to visit Craigside and give us his blessing. In two of the big downstairs rooms classes in Tibetan had been started, it being the Rimpoche's ambition to establish a school where Tibetan boys and girls could study both the Dharma and modern subjects through the medium of their own language, instead of being obliged, as so many of them were, to attend Christian missionary schools where non-Buddhist and even anti-Buddhist values were inculcated. Soon after his arrival at Craigside Dhardo Rimpoche was joined by Geshe Wangyal, who had not yet left for America and whom I had also invited. With the assistance of the Geshe and his personal attendant, a rather dour-looking monk who had been with him for many years, he then performed the traditional Tibetan ceremony of purification and blessing, after which he and Lobsang Phuntsok discussed with me their plans for a Tibetan school. I was already familiar with those plans. They were part of a bigger plan, for the creation of an Indo-Tibetan Buddhist Cultural Institute, also to be located, for the time being at least, at the Old Bhutan Palace. In fact I had already agreed, at Lobsang's request, to draw up the rules of the Institute. During the weeks that followed his and the Rimpoche's visit, the young ex-monk officer was a frequent visitor to Craigside, with the result that I not only became better acquainted with their plans for the Institute but agreed to give a fortnightly lecture under its auspices. I also promised to help him write the chapter on Tibetan

Buddhism he had undertaken to contribute to a book on the Path of the Buddha that was being brought out by an American publisher.

My most frequent visitor during this period, however, apart from my regular students, was Thupten Chhokyi, who having changed her mind about being better off back in Darjeeling was now again in Kalimpong. Restless as ever, she was staying up at Tirpai in someone's outhouse, and was hoping to be able to move into a cave she had discovered in the hillside just above the village, by the side of the track leading to Dailo. Meanwhile, she spent a good part of each day at Craigside, arriving as soon as it was light and joining me in my puja and meditation. In the week or so following my removal to the new premises she had a reason for being so much in evidence there, having taken on the responsibility for arranging the shrine-room and sewing the maroon silk hangings. This task she accomplished with her usual energy, and on the whole I was pleased with the result, even though there were perhaps rather too many frills and furbelows for some tastes. Unfortunately, the fact that she had worked so hard on the shrine-room led to her developing a proprietary attitude towards it and even towards Craigside. Sometimes I thought she was developing a proprietary attitude towards me. She certainly resented my spending so many hours a week teaching Sachin, Durga, and my other students, an activity she frankly regarded as being a sheer waste of time, especially as it meant I had less time to spare for her and her problems than I might otherwise have had. For Durga, in particular, she appeared to feel something akin to hatred, and would dart in his direction, whenever she saw me giving him a lesson, venomous glances that gave meaning to the expression 'if looks could kill'. Durga, for his part, remained unperturbed by the Frenchwoman's hostility, only remarking once, after she had gone, that he could not imagine anyone less like a Buddhist nun, who was supposed to be the very embodiment of gentleness and compassion.

Poor Ani-la (as the Tibetans called her, Ani-la or 'Reverend Auntie' being the customary way of referring to, or addressing, a female monastic), she was her own worst enemy! Though loud in her demands for help, especially for help with her Tibetan studies, and bitter in her complaints when that help was not forthcoming, she invariably acted in such a way as to frustrate the efforts of those who were trying to help her. At her request, Dhardo Rimpoche had arranged for her to read a Tibetan text with his dour-looking personal attendant. She soon tired of this, however, the text being of a simple, devotional character, and began plying the monk with questions about the Madhyamaka philosophy, a subject which he had not studied and which she, in any case, did not know Tibetan nearly well enough to be able to discuss properly. Moreover, she was in the habit, when having her lesson, of sitting as close to him as possible, sometimes squeezing herself up against him and even leaning so far across him as to be almost sitting in his lap. Such behaviour he, as a monk, found extremely embarrassing. So embarrassing did he find it that he eventually begged the Rimpoche to relieve him of the responsibility of teaching such a pupil. This the Rimpoche had no alternative but to do, with the result that Ani-la became more than ever convinced that Dhardo Rimpoche was not really interested in her and had no desire to help her.

She could not have been more wrong. During the last two or three months, ever since the discontinuance of her lessons with Gelong Lobsang, as the dour-looking personal attendant was called, Dhardo Rimpoche and Lobsang Phuntsok had more than once jointly consulted me, with every sign of concern, about the reason for the terrible mental states into which she tended to fall and what the three of us could do to help her become a better and happier person. So far we had been unable to come to any definite conclusion. But if our consultations brought no immediate benefit to Ani-la, they at least had the effect of strengthening the ties between Dhardo Rimpoche and Lobsang Phuntsok, on the one hand, and me on the other, and now that I was co-operating with them in their plans for a school and a cultural institute those ties were becoming stronger still. Not that Ani-la was left entirely without help. Somehow I found myself acting as an intermediary between her and the Rimpoche, especially when she wanted to communicate something which, she was convinced, he would not understand unless it was accompanied by detailed explanations from me. Once I was in the uncomfortable position of having to ascertain from him whether a certain activity, in certain circumstances, did or did not amount to (female) masturbation and, therefore, to a breach of the Vinaya or monastic code. Not that I felt particularly uncomfortable discussing such matters with the Rimpoche himself, but Ani-la was so anxious that he should understand the exact nature of her question that she insisted on communicating to me facts about the anatomy and physiology of the human female that I had no wish to hear and in fact found distasteful. Thereafter I was careful to steer the conversation away from sexual topics, which she seemed more eager to discuss than a nun ought to have been, though I continued to act as her intermediary with Dhardo Rimpoche. I also found myself acting, not long after the move to Craigside, as her unofficial meditation instructor. Since she found the mantra-recitation and deity-visualization practices into which the Rimpoche had initiated her too difficult, or at least not to her liking, I taught her the rudiments of the *ānāpānasati* or 'respiration-mindfulness' practice, at the same time pointing out that this did not make me her teacher and that I was not assuming any responsibility for her spiritual progress. She was Dhardo Rimpoche's disciple, I firmly reminded her, and whatever help I was able to give her was given in my capacity as friend and fellow Buddhist.

Towards the end of December, when despite visitors I had managed to write at least two or three foolscap pages of the *Survey* virtually every day for the past six weeks, I paid a short visit to Darjeeling. It was my third or fourth visit that year, and the second since my return from Calcutta and since my starting work on the first chapter of the *Survey* at the end of August. This time I was accompanied by Durga, who was currently in disgrace for having failed his yearly examinations and with whom his father, the municipality's gnome-like head fitter, was so angry that he very nearly refused to allow him to make the trip, relenting only at the last minute as a result of Sachin's intercession on his young cousin's behalf.

In Darjeeling I stayed at Chota Khagjhora, at the Gandhamadan Vihara, whose Bengali Buddhist supporters treated me with their usual hospitality. On my previous visit, which had taken place in September, when I had been working on the *Survey* for only six weeks, I had stayed in Bhutia Busti, the 'Tibetan' settlement on the hillside below the Chowrasta, on the other side of the town. My stay there had lasted two weeks, and I had been the guest of the local Young Men's Buddhist Association. The Bhutia Busti YMBA, as it was known, had no connection with its now defunct Kalimpong counterpart. It had been founded about twenty-five years earlier by Bhikkhu Jinorasa, a Sikkimese monk of noble family who had received ordination in Ceylon. After his death in 1931 the association's religious activities had come to an end, except for the celebration of Vaiśākha Pūrṇimā, and it was in the hope of my being able to revive these that I had agreed to stay in Bhutia Busti that autumn, at the YMBA's spacious but run-down premises. Besides giving a public lecture on the Three Refuges and Five Precepts, and presiding at the Mahatma Gandhi birth anniversary celebrations, during my stay there I took every opportunity of pointing out to the people of the locality, many of whom were Buddhists, the need for taking a more active interest in the Dharma. I also spent time with Dr Hudson, then still living in Darjeeling, who pressed theosophical literature on me, showed me the manuscript of her book on blood (not to be published, lest the information in it be used for purposes of black magic), and reminisced at great length, and to her own evident satisfaction, about her various record-breaking achievements in the early years of the century. On my happening to remark, in all seriousness, that she seemed to have had a wide experience of life, and to know a great deal, her craggy features lit up with a smile of amusement at my having only just woken up to the fact and she replied, with a complacent chuckle, 'Oh, I know *everything*!'

My most vivid memory of those two weeks, however, was of the weather. It was bitterly cold, much colder than in Kalimpong, which was only 4,000 feet above sea level to Darjeeling's 8,000, and I shivered in the mornings as I sat in my unheated room at the YMBA trying, with frozen fingers, to write a few more pages of the *Survey*. But there were compensations. If it was cold, it was also clear, and I had only to step outside to see piled up against the intensely blue sky, bigger and whiter than they were when seen from Kalimpong, the jagged sunlit masses of the eternal snows.

On the occasion of my present visit to the town, the fact that I was staying at Chota Khagjhora did not prevent me keeping up my contact with Bhutia Busti and its Young Men's Buddhist Association. Indeed, one of the reasons for my being in Darjeeling again so soon was that the secretary of the association, a Nepalese Hindu sympathetic to Buddhism, had invited me to preside at the annual prize-giving ceremony of the YMBA primary school. The function took place the morning following my arrival. After the pupils of the school had given a variety performance, Ani-la, who had left Kalimpong before me, distributed the prizes, and I gave an address on the importance of *dāna* or giving, explaining it in the traditional manner as the giving of material things, of education, and of the Dharma. In the course of my two remaining days in Darjeeling I received a visit from two leading mountaineers, one a Tamang and one a Sherpa (*not* the famous Tenzing Norgay), with whom I had an interesting exchange about mountaineering and

Buddhism. I also went to see Mankazi Lama, a Newar Buddhist who had confined himself to a tiny room for puja and meditation. Something about him must have impressed me. That night I dreamed that the two of us were in Gangtok and that he was giving me mantras. The morning after this dream I left for Kurseong, still accompanied by Durga, who had spent much of his time in Darjeeling learning to ride. In Kurseong, to which we travelled by the toy train, taking three freezing hours to cover a distance – as the crow flies – of about twenty miles, I presided at another prize-giving ceremony and gave, under the auspices of the Young Tamang Buddhist Association, a lecture on the bodhisattva ideal. From Kurseong it was only an hour, by jeep, to Longview, where Durga continued his riding lessons and where Padmanathan took me to view the site of a new temple he was planning to build.

Soon after my return to Kalimpong I received a visit from Anand-ji. He did not come alone. With him came Dinesh and Jayadev, now transformed into Naginda and Sumedha and wearing, rather shamefacedly I thought, the yellow robes of the Theravādin *sāmaṇera* or novice monk, Anand-ji having just ordained them. The ordinations came as a complete surprise to me, neither of the young men having shown the slightest interest in the monastic life, and I could only assume that my none-too-scrupulous elder brother in the order had ordained them simply as a means of enabling himself to keep them with him at the Dharmodaya Vihara. There were also visits from Ani-la, who had returned to Kalimpong before me. It did not take me long to realize that trouble was brewing. The first time she came she was extremely angry with me for going out without waiting for Lobsang Phuntsok, who had arranged to see me but was late; the second time she left in a huff, without staying for lunch as she usually did when she came in the morning, and the third time she handed me a note and her keys and went away without speaking. Understanding from this last action that she was thinking of committing suicide I called her back, as she no doubt knew I would, and did my best to reason with her. 'Like summer tempests came her tears',[179] though unlike the subject of Tennyson's poem she wept not for a real loss but out of self-pity and because of the frustration of her unreasonable demands. In the end, having talked with her for an hour or more, I succeeded in bringing her a little to her senses, and as it was by that time quite late allowed her to stay the night in Man Bahadur's room in the outhouse.

But if I had thought that my talking with her had produced more than a transient effect on Ani-la I was soon made to realize my mistake. A few days later there occurred an incident that illustrated, all too clearly, the recalcitrant nature of the material with which I had to deal. Dr Hudson, having noticed that the little table at which I worked stood on the cold cement floor, had brought me a small woollen rug and had herself spread it beneath my feet. Soon after her departure, when my lower extremities were beginning to feel pleasantly warm, Ani-la arrived. Her sharp, darting eyes immediately saw the rug. 'That's *much* too good for your feet!' she exclaimed, in shocked tones. 'Its proper place is in the shrine-room.' Whereupon she whipped it from beneath my feet and without further ado bustled with it into the apartment in question. Thinking the matter not worth arguing about, I said nothing and went on writing. Next time Dr Hudson came to see me she naturally wanted to know where her rug had gone. When I explained what had happened she was extremely annoyed, not so much with me for my weakness (as she saw it) in allowing Ani-la to have her own way as with the French nun for having had the temerity to interfere with her arrangements. Marching into the shrine-room, she retrieved the rug, replaced it beneath my feet, and sternly told me that it was on no account to be used for any other purpose than the one for which she had expressly given it. When Ani-la saw the rug again beneath my feet she became quite hysterical, crying, 'Oh the beautiful rug! You will spoil it! It must go into the shrine!' and attempted to take it from me. This time, however, I was firm with her and did not allow her to have her own way, with the result that she wept all through lunch and left Craigside looking crushed and miserable.

13
TWO FUNERAL PYRES

People taking up the spiritual life tend to fall into one or other of two categories. There are those who are drawn to the Unconditioned because they are disgusted with the conditioned, and there are those who lose interest in the conditioned because they are enamoured of the Unconditioned. The former, one might say, are pushed from behind by the sheer painfulness of mundane existence, whereas the latter are pulled from in front by the sheer beauty and attractiveness of the transcendental. So far as I could tell, I belonged more to the second than the first category, my overall experience of life having been positive rather than negative. One of the main reasons for the painfulness of mundane existence is that it involves separation, especially separation by death, from those who are near and dear to us. Though I had been geographically separated from my parents and my sister, as well as from my English Buddhist friends, for more than ten years, the circumstance of my having as yet suffered no serious bereavement meant that, while I knew I would die one day, the fact was not fully real to me. With the sudden death of Miss Barclay a year ago, however, it had assumed greater reality, the elderly Englishwoman having been a friend of sorts, despite all the trouble she gave me; and with the loss, during my first few months at Craigside, of two more members of my circle of friends and acquaintances in Kalimpong, it assumed greater reality still.

The first to go was Miss Rao's mother. Miss Rao was the tiny, fantastically dressed South Indian woman who from time to time came and poured out her woes to me, usually at great length and when I was busy. Often she could be heard coming in the distance, as it was her practice to start talking long before she actually reached my door and to continue talking, on her arrival, without pausing for breath and as though I had been listening to her all the time. She invariably addressed me not as 'Bhante', as everybody else did (except, of course, my seniors in monastic ordination), but as 'Swami-ji', which was the mode of address for Hindu renunciants. Bedaubed, bedizened little Miss Rao was in fact a universalist of the deepest dye, though from instinct rather than from intellectual conviction. For her there was no difference between Buddhism and Hinduism, all religions being one or, what amounted to the same thing, nothing but different forms of Hinduism. It was therefore not surprising that besides addressing me as Swami-ji she should have done her best, over the years, to make me look like a Hindu renunciant and my abode like a Hindu temple or ashram. At different times she presented me with sealed copper pots of holy Ganges water, a yellow silk 'Benares shawl' stamped in red with the name of Rama, a pair of wooden sandals, and a string of brass mango leaves. While I had no objection to hanging the string of brass mango leaves above my door, I drew the line at installing the pots of holy Ganges water in the shrine-room and at wearing the yellow silk shawl or the wooden sandals – particularly at wearing the wooden sandals. It was not simply that they were very uncomfortable (there was a peg to be gripped between one's great toe and its neighbour), or that it was generally the more orthodox Hindu renunciants who wore them. The black-maned, crimson-clad Bengali *tantrik* who lived at Eighth Mile sported a pair, creating a tremendous clatter with them as he walked up the road on market days, and I had no wish to resemble him in that or any other respect. Not that my reluctance to be Hinduized seemed to bother Miss Rao, if indeed she was aware of it at all (I sometimes thought that the Hinduization of Buddhist India had been as much the work of the Miss Raos of the time as of the Vedantic philosophers). She continued to inundate me with details of her financial difficulties, her brother's misbehaviour, and her differences with her landlady, and indeed to treat me as a combination of Roman Catholic father confessor and Hindu family priest. Thus it was that I had learned from her that autumn, when I was still living at The Hermitage, that her seventy-year-old mother was seriously ill. Would I mind going to see her?

Naturally I did not mind. During the next few weeks I went to see Mrs Rao a number of times, at first visiting her in the flat she and her daughter occupied in the High Street and then, her illness having taken a turn for the worse, in a private room at the Charteris Hospital, where she was attended by Dr Singh. Each time I saw her she seemed to have grown thinner and weaker, and her refined, aristocratic features – so different from those of poor Miss Rao – more transparent to the tiny flame that still flickered within. She made no complaint, her only anxiety being about her two children. But eventually even that anxiety received its quietus, and one morning, as I was about to have breakfast, I heard that Mrs Rao had died. I at once went to the hospital, where I consoled Miss Rao and her brother as best I could and gave instructions to the Nepalese Christian nurses about the laying out of the body. Returning to Craigside, I then sent Dawa up to Tirpai to inform the lamas of the Tharpa Choling Gompa of Mrs Rao's death and invite four or five of them to take part in the funeral. Normally, funeral arrangements were made by the older male members of the deceased's family, or at least (in the case of Hindus) by his or her caste-fellows, and had Mrs Rao died in South India this is undoubtedly what would have happened. In Kalimpong the Raos had neither relations nor caste-fellows, so that had I not taken on the responsibility for making the necessary arrangements, as the distraught brother and sister both begged me to do, the old Brahmin lady would probably not have had a proper funeral and her remains, in all likelihood, would have been unceremoniously disposed of by the hospital authorities.

As it was, at three o'clock that afternoon there issued from the hospital compound, where a small crowd had gathered to see Mrs Rao off on her last journey, a cortège consisting of a lorry and two or three other vehicles. In the back of the lorry with the coffin were Miss Rao's brother, the lamas in their red robes and yellow ceremonial headgear, and as many of our members and friends as were able to squeeze themselves in. Miss Rao had of course to be left behind, it not being the custom for women to be present at a cremation. She was in any case still hysterical with grief, and before we set out I asked Beena, the most good-natured of Sachin's three sisters, to look after her. From the hospital the little procession slowly made its way through the High Street down to Craigside, where the lamas and others were given tea, and then, rather less slowly, from Craigside down to the River Teesta.

The cortège having halted a few hundred yards short of Teesta Bridge, the coffin was manhandled down the narrow, zigzag track that led from the road to a stretch of white sand lying within a bend of the river. Here a shallow trench was dug, a row of stones placed on either side of the trench, and wood from the nearby bazaar laid, in alternate lengthwise and crosswise layers, on top of the stones to a height of two or three feet. Mrs Rao's body was then taken out of its coffin and lowered onto the pyre, more layers of wood were added, kerosene was sprinkled, and finally Miss Rao's brother, as next of kin and chief mourner, thrusting a lighted torch in among the wood set the whole structure on fire.

Soon a ruddy blaze was illuminating the foreshore and the faces of the twelve or fifteen people who, in little groups, sat watching the flames leap up and the smoke billow forth. At first very little was said, but as time passed everyone relaxed, and there was a distinct change in the atmosphere. Voices again rang out, cups of tea appeared, and there was the occasional burst of laughter. Even Miss Rao's brother, who sat next to me, seemed to be affected by the general change of mood, At any rate, he now had a more cheerful look, and we exchanged a few commonplace remarks. I had not really met him before, though I had seen him once or twice, but I had heard a lot about him from Miss Rao, according to whom he was the worst of sons and brothers, a drunkard, a wastrel, and an inveterate frequenter of bad company. In appearance he was admittedly not very prepossessing, being as thin and black, though not as saucer-eyed, as the *pretas* or hungry ghosts I had once seen at the haunted ashram at Muvattupuzha.[180] But he seemed inoffensive and well-meaning, and was evidently grateful for the help he had received in connection with his mother's funeral, and in any case I had always taken Miss Rao's denunciations of her sibling with a grain of salt.

By this time night had fallen, the stars had come out above the Darjeeling hills, and the pyre was beginning to burn low. There could hardly have been a more beautiful setting for a cremation, or one that was more appropriate, and I could understand the poetry of the old Indian custom of committing a body to the flames on the bank of a river, where the four elements to which it was being returned were all present in some of their sublimest forms. On the occasion of Mrs Rao's cremation we had all round us the steep, tree-clad slopes of the Himalayan foothills; between the foothills wound the river, glassily sliding down to join the Brahmaputra, and on the hither bank of the river stood the pyre, its last plumes of smoke slowly dissolving into the air. Even the fifth element, that of ether or space, was present, being represented by the dark blue inverted bowl of the sky, now 'thick inlaid with patines of bright gold'.[181] As I watched, a shower of golden sparks flew up from the pyre, so that for a moment I was unable to tell which were the sparks and which the stars.

The following morning I arranged for Miss Rao to spend a couple of weeks at the Singh family's bungalow, where she would have the company of Sachin's mother and sisters. This, I thought, would be better for her than going back to the cheerless flat in Chung Building, where she would be on her own most of the time, it being unlikely that she would want to see much of her brother, though he did not seem to have the same animosity towards her that she had towards him. In the event Miss Rao stayed with the Singh family for more than a month, and the arrangement worked quite well, at least at the beginning. As she recovered from the shock of her mother's illness and death, however, some of the more bizarre features of her character and behaviour started reasserting themselves. In particular she made herself ridiculous by addressing Sheila, the oldest of Sachin's sisters, as '*didi*' or 'elder sister', just as Meera and Beena did, even though that college-going young lady was little more than half her own age. What was worse, at least from my point of view, was that she managed to convince herself that her mother had on her deathbed entrusted the responsibility for looking after her to *me* and that I had accepted the responsibility. This was sheer fantasy, but it was a fantasy that gave her an excuse for visiting me several times a week, even several times a day, in order to consult me about even the most trivial matters. Eventually, Sachin's mother having warned me that the frequency of her visits to Craigside might give rise to misunderstanding on the part of 'uneducated people', I wrote and asked her not to come more than once or twice a month as I wanted to devote more time to the writing of the *Survey*. To her credit, she accepted the situation with a good grace and cut down on her visits, so that I was able to help and advise her, when she did come to see me, without laying myself open to the kind of misunderstanding to which Mrs Singh had referred.

Before all this happened I had, however, suffered the loss of the second member of my circle of friends and acquaintances to die during this period. Having just had breakfast, I was about to settle down to my morning's work on the *Survey* when Anand-ji came to tell me that

Burma Raja had died the previous night. The news affected me much more deeply than the news of Mrs Rao's death had done. Burma Raja, as he was popularly known, was Prince K. M. Latthakin of Burma, the nephew and son-in-law of ex-King Thibaw. I had been his guest for six months before moving to The Hermitage. In fact he had come to my rescue at one of the most difficult and painful times in my life, when the choleric Newar monk in charge of the Dharmodaya Vihara was trying to oust me from my room there and I had nowhere else to go. He and the Princess had treated me with great kindness during my stay with them and Burma Raja himself had become, indeed, a good friend.[182] After my removal to The Hermitage we still kept in touch. I went to see them from time to time, though less and less frequently, and very occasionally Burma Raja came to see me. For the last few months there had been no contact between us. I had not even known that Burma Raja was ill. The news of his death therefore came as quite a shock, and I at once set out for Panorama with Anand-ji.

During my stay with them Burma Raja and the Princess, together with their adopted son and their maidservant, had occupied the upper bungalow, or Panorama proper, and I had occupied the lower bungalow, or guest cottage, which stood on a lower level, in its own compound. Separating the two compounds there was a hedge, in which Burma Raja had made a hole so that he could come and see me – as he did nearly every morning – without having to go round to the front entrance. Since my last visit he and his little family evidently had shifted from the upper to the lower building. On our arrival Anand-ji and I found the Princess sitting out in the sun, in the little garden beside the guest cottage, smoking a cigar and having her long grey hair combed by the maidservant. She seemed quite unperturbed by Burma Raja's death, but was obviously glad to see me and indicated, in her quaint mixture of Hindi and Nepali, which sounded like gibberish to anyone who did not know her, that I would find Raja Sahib inside the cottage. Inside the cottage I indeed found him. I found him in the little room I had used as a bedroom. My old friend's face was so purple as to be almost black, his jaw had collapsed, and his wispy white hair, normally concealed beneath an imposing turban, lay scattered across the pillows. He looked as though he had died after a long and debilitating illness.

Within minutes I had dispatched notes to my lawyer friend Madan Kumar Pradhan, who was Vice-Chairman of the Municipality, and to the Second Officer of Kalimpong, informing them of Burma Raja's death and asking for their co-operation in making arrangements for his funeral. The Government of India had, I knew, inherited from its imperial predecessor a certain undefined responsibility for him and the Princess, and in fact paid them a modest monthly allowance, the Burmese Government having refused to pay them anything unless they returned to Burma, which Burma Raja steadfastly refused to do. He was safer in India, he declared. While I was writing my notes people started arriving, some of them with bunches of flowers and *khatas*, but it was not possible for them to pay their last respects as the body had not been laid out. After I had talked with Alaungyi, Burma Raja's adopted son, and with the maidservant, both of whom were evidently quite upset, I accompanied Anand-ji back to the Dharmodaya Vihara. On the way we met Madan Babu, who had received my note and was now hastening to Panorama. Money would have to be found for the funeral expenses, I told him, as according to Alaungyi the Princess was in debt, as she usually was, and there were only a few rupees at the bungalow. Madan Babu promised to see what he could do, and having left Anand-ji at the Dharmodaya Vihara I went home.

My lawyer friend was as good as his word. Soon after lunch, when I was typing an urgent letter to Devapriya-ji, he arrived at Craigside with the two thousand rupees he had drawn from the Kalimpong Treasury, as well as with Anand-ji, whom he had collected on the way, and the three of us set out for Panorama. By this time quite a number of people had gathered outside the guest cottage, as well as in the lane that led to the Panorama compound. Many of them were known to me, at least by sight, and now that money was available I asked some of these to help with preparations for the funeral. One of the first things to be done was to send to the Tharpa Choling Gompa for four lamas. No sooner had the burly, red-robed figures clambered out of the jeep, however, than difficulties arose. The Princess, who so far had shown no interest in the proceedings, seemed to take a dislike to them and refused to allow them to touch Burma Raja's body, insisting that it should be prepared for cremation by me and only by me. Eventually Madan Babu and I succeeded in convincing her that it would be impossible for me to do what was required single-handed, and she grudgingly allowed the lamas access to the body, on the strict understanding that I would remain in the room with them all the time and personally supervise everything they did. The Princess's reluctance was due not so much to the fact that the lamas were followers of Tibetan Buddhism, whereas she was a Theravādin, as to the fact that they were complete strangers and she was by nature suspicious almost to the point of paranoia.

Even with the help of four lamas the task of preparing Burma Raja's body for cremation was not an easy one. Nor was it a pleasant one. The old man could not have been properly cared for during the last few days of his life, and may even have died *before* the previous night. On removing the coverlet we found his sheets and nightshirt soaked in urine and faeces and stuck together in a solid mass that could not be separated from the body. Used as they were to such work, the four lamas were horrified by the sight, as I also was. There was no question of Burma Raja being laid out in the usual fashion. While Anand-ji remained in the background, looking very sick, we arranged the body as best we could, wrapped it, sheets and all, in the coverlet, and laid it in the coffin. The coffin was then loaded on to one of the waiting vehicles and the cortège – a rather more impressive one than had accompanied Mrs Rao's body – started moving up the lane and onto the road. As it left the Panorama compound Burma Raja's maidservant burst into tears. The Princess, however, remained unconcerned. Or rather, she was concerned about only one thing. As Anand-ji and I were about to board the vehicle with the coffin, she drew me aside and hissed vehemently in my ear, 'Raja Sahib must be cremated with sandalwood logs. Nothing but sandalwood logs. Members of the Burmese royal family cannot be cremated with anything else.'

On the cortège's arrival at the Tibetan cremation ground at Tirpai the vehicle containing the coffin came to a halt, not near the stupa-like structure in which Miss Barclay had been cremated but in front of the iron bedstead, as it seemed to be, lying on which those of the nobler sex were cremated. It did not take long to build a pyre, plenty of wood being available from the stall inside the entrance. There was no question of our cremating Burma Raja with sandalwood logs, which would have cost a fortune, though one or two Marwaris had bought packets of sandalwood powder. When the pyre was complete Alaungyi set it alight, and Anand-ji and I chanted Pāli *suttas* and other verses appropriate to the occasion. *Sic transit gloria mundi,*[183] I thought, as I watched the flames leap up, except that Burma Raja had not experienced much *gloria* in his life, despite having been born into a royal family. But if he had not experienced much *gloria* neither had he experienced much hardship. Judging by the tenor of some of his remarks to me, the happiest time of his life had been the years before the war, when the Raj paid him and the Princess a generous monthly allowance (generous in comparison with what the Government of India subsequently paid them) and when he had been a leading figure in the social life of Kalimpong, taking part in everything from tennis parties to tiger hunts.

As the evening was growing cold, it being mid-January, I left early, without waiting for Burma Raja's funeral pyre to burn itself out, and having had a hot drink at Sachin's place made my way back to Craigside. Ani-la was chanting in the shrine-room. When she came out I talked to her for a while, then finished typing my letter to Devapriya-ji and attended to *Maha Bodhi* journal work until it was time to go to bed.

A few days later came offerings from the Princess. Obviously I should go to see her; but I was busy, and kept putting the visit off, until one day I heard that she had left the Panorama guest cottage, together with Alaungyi and the maidservant, and gone to stay in an outlying village. She was living in a hut, and subsisting on greens from the garden. Though I made extensive enquiries, no one could tell me the name of the village or in which direction it lay, and I had no further news of her until I learned that she had moved to Calcutta. She was living with her sister, and Alaungyi was working in the Burmese consulate as a clerk. Though I never saw her again, this was not the end of my connection with the strange old woman. Two years later I found myself standing inside the very 'hut' in which she had spent her last days in Kalimpong, and the building thereafter came to occupy an important place in my life.

14
THE UNACCEPTABLE FACE OF COMMUNISM

When I went forth from home into the homeless life, on 18 August 1947, it was with the intention of renouncing the world in the fullest and most literal sense. For me *pravrajyā* or 'going forth' meant giving up family ties, social position, and national and racial identity, as well as mundane interests and activities of every kind. It meant giving up pleasure, and possessions, and whatever else might serve to aggrandize the ego or enhance the sense of separative selfhood. The only thing from which I did not go forth that day – not because I refused to go forth from it but because the idea of so doing did not occur to me – was my mother tongue, English, to which I was in fact (unconsciously) quite attached. Since then it had been borne in upon me that it was less easy to achieve a full and literal renunciation of the world than I, in my youthful enthusiasm, had imagined, and that the reasons for this were not merely subjective but also solidly objective. Because I had no identity papers and refused to declare my nationality, saying that as a renunciant I had none, I had not been allowed to enter Buddhist Ceylon,[184] and because I had no money, as I was trying to observe the precept of not handling gold and silver, I had been refused ordination by the time-serving Theravādin monks of Sarnath.[185] Eventually I had been obliged to make concessions. In Kalimpong I admitted to being English, though without going into details, and not only handled gold and silver, in the form of specie and banknotes, but engaged in at least some of the transactions of which this was an inseparable part.

But concessions were one thing, abandonment of principle quite another. Believing as I did that 'going forth' was of the essence of the spiritual life, I tried not to think of myself as an Englishman, did my best not to utilize whatever money came my way for the gratification of personal desires, and abstained as much as I could from mundane interests and activities. Thus I abstained from reading newspapers and from discussing politics, though at times it was difficult for me to stop my ears against Joe's violent denunciation of all the works and ways of Prime Minister Winston Churchill and President Dwight Eisenhower or even to refrain from questioning some of his wilder assertions. Largely because I did not read the newspapers I had little sense of what was going on in the wider world, or even in India. I lived for meditation and study, for my students, and for the work for the good of Buddhism that my teacher Kashyap-ji, before his departure from Kalimpong, had enjoined upon me. Nevertheless I was vaguely aware of vast events looming on the horizon. I was aware that in the West the Second World War had been succeeded by the Cold War between the Soviet Union and Eastern Europe on the one hand, and the United States and Western Europe on the other, and that in the East Tibet had been occupied by the forces of Communist China and its religion and culture ruthlessly suppressed. I was aware that the aim of Marxian Communism was world domination.

Unlike many others of my generation I had no sympathy with Communism, either as a philosophy or as a programme for social change, and no sympathy with its adherents as such. Why this should have been so I find it difficult to say. My lack of sympathy was instinctive rather than being the reasoned result of study and reflection. It was as though I sensed in Communism a threat to everything I held most dear, whether in the realm of ideas, the field of poetry and the fine arts, or the domain of ethics and spiritual life. Communism was the negation of truth, of beauty, of goodness. Not that I knew very much about Marxian Communism, factually speaking. As a fifteen-year-old evacuee in Barnstaple, during the war, I had read *Das Kapital*.[186] Why I read it I do not know, except that in those days I read everything on which I could lay my hands, but for me there was no Marxist equivalent of a 'road to Damascus' experience and I was not converted to the faith.[187]

A year or two later, having returned home towards the end of the Blitz, I discovered a left-wing bookshop near Tooting Broadway (probably it was the only bookshop in the whole of south-west London) and after a certain amount of hesitation bought and read Lenin's *The State and Revolution*,[188] which was more interesting than *Das Kapital* as well as being much shorter. At about the same time one of my colleagues at County Hall, where I was working, lent me a copy of David Guest's *Dialectical Materialism*.[189] This colleague was himself a Communist, but if he had expected David Guest to succeed where Marx and Lenin had failed he was disappointed and I remained unconverted. When I returned the book to him it was with the remark that in my opinion it was not Hegel (in whom I was then deep)[190] who was standing on his head, as the author alleged, but Marx, it being axiomatic for Marxist thought that Marx had found Hegel upside down and had restored him to his feet, that is, had given his idealism a materialist interpretation. Not long afterwards my colleague received his calling-up papers and our discussions came to an end. Before the time came for my own induction into the armed forces he was back in the department and doing his old job – minus both legs and on crutches.

The war was inflicting its terrible casualties, in both Europe and the Far East, and on service personnel and civilians alike. During those days I *did* read the newspapers, as well as listen to the wireless (as many people still called the radio), and though the full horror of what was happening was sometimes concealed from us we were aware that what was happening was dreadful beyond imagination. In particular we were aware, in the winter of 1942–3, of the long drawn-out battle for Stalingrad and of the sufferings of the Russian people as they endured, then resisted, and finally routed, the forces of invading Nazi Germany. With others in Britain I rejoiced at their victory and mourned their great losses, nor could I hear the soulful, not to say sentimental, popular ballad 'Russian Rose' (as I think it was called), with its promise of new life for the heroic Russian people, without the tears coming into my eyes and a lump rising in my throat. It was the Russian people who were victorious, not the Communists. Russia was not Trotsky and Lenin, Stalin and Beria. Russia was Pushkin, Lermontov, Gogol, Turgenev, Chekhov, Tolstoy, and Dostoevsky. In the very month that I had read *Das Kapital* I had also read *The Brothers Karamazov*,[191] and there is no doubt which of them had made the deeper impression on me.

It was the same in the case of China. To me it was not the Chinese people who had invaded Tibet so much as the Chinese Red Army. China was not Mao Zedong and the *Little Red Book*. China was Confucius and Laozi, Huineng and Zhiyi, Li Bai and Du Fu, as well as the great painters of landscapes and of flowers. I therefore felt for China and the Chinese people the same love that I felt for Russia and the Russian people, so that when, towards the end of February, the two young Nepalese organizers came with an invitation to speak at the inaugural meeting of the Kalimpong branch of the Indo-Chinese Friendship Society I was happy to accept, the more especially as the meeting was to be held under the presidentship of Anand-ji. Not that I accepted without having ascertained the exact nature of the gathering. Relations between democratic India and totalitarian China were then at their most cordial; on all sides the mantra *Hindi-Cheeni bhai-bhai*, or 'Indians and Chinese are brothers', could be heard. In these circumstances it was unlikely that a body whose objective was the promotion of friendship between the two Asian giants would not have at least a quasi-political agenda, and neither as a Buddhist monk nor as a foreign national residing in a sensitive border area did I wish to get involved in politics. I could take part in the meeting, I therefore informed the two young men, only if it was completely non-political. This would certainly be the case, they both hastened to assure me: the meeting was to be a purely cultural affair, without the least trace of politics; and Anand-ji, when I met him a few days later, gave me a similar assurance.

The afternoon of the first Sunday in March accordingly saw me leaving Craigside for the Town Hall soon after lunch. I did not really need to leave so early, but knowing Anand-ji's dilatory, dawdling ways it was my intention to call for him *en route* and make sure he was not late for the meeting. On entering the upstairs room he occupied at the Dharmodaya Vihara I found he was not alone. With him was Arun Karki, one of the young men who had invited me to speak at the inaugural meeting. This in itself was not surprising. What was surprising was that the two of them were engaged in finalizing the wording of some three dozen resolutions and that these resolutions, which were to be passed at the meeting, were each and every one of them strongly condemnatory of the policies and actions of the United States in this or that part of the world. Under cross-examination Arun Karki eventually admitted that the real purpose of the inaugural meeting was political, and that the Indo-Chinese Friendship Society was in fact a political organization, whereupon I told him that it would be impossible for me to attend. Anand-ji did his honeyed best to persuade me to change my mind, but I was not to be moved by his specious pleadings, and having reminded them that the meeting was at two o'clock and that they had five minutes in which to get to the Town Hall I left the building and made my way back to Craigside.

As I walked down the road I experienced a variety of emotions. I was annoyed that the young organizers should have attempted to gain my support for their society by deliberately misleading me as to its true nature, and annoyed that Anand-ji should (apparently) have seconded them in the attempt. At the same time I was relieved that their machinations had not succeeded, for had I spoken at the meeting (no doubt *before* the resolutions were read out) I would have been placed in a very awkward, indeed a quite false, position. To have supported the resolutions, if only by my silence, would have given the impression that I was anti-American and pro-Communist, while to have objected to them would have given the impression that I was pro-American and anti-Communist. In either case I would have become involved in politics, or at least have appeared to have become involved in them, which in a place like Kalimpong amounted to much the same thing.

My predominant emotion, however, as I made my way back to Craigside that afternoon, was one of satisfaction, almost of elation. I was glad I had not yielded to Anand-ji's pleas not to leave him in the lurch, or accepted his absurd suggestion that, as a compromise, I should sit with him on the platform but not actually speak. The knowledge that I had done what I believed to be right, regardless of possible untoward consequences, indeed had the effect of giving me an increased sense of energy and purpose. It was as though my refusal to take part in the inaugural meeting, after discovering its true nature, constituted an affirmation of my status as a moral agent and of the fact that in the last analysis, and irrespective of circumstances, the responsibility for my life and actions was mine and mine alone.

What explanation Anand-ji gave for my absence from the meeting I never really knew. According to one account he said I was unwell. According to another he joked about my having changed my mind at the last minute for unexplained reasons no doubt connected with the poetic temperament. Whatever he may have said, the fact that I had not attended the meeting was the subject of a good deal of comment and speculation in the town, especially as I had been billed as the principal speaker. So much was this the case that I decided, a few days afterwards, to make my position clear. What better way was there of doing this than through the medium of the local press? The press existed, after all, to keep its readers informed about matters of public interest. I accordingly wrote a letter to the *Himalayan Times*, the town's English-language weekly newspaper, describing exactly what had happened, and dispatched it to the editor with a covering note requesting him to publish it as soon as possible. He did not publish it, either that week or any other. If my experience with the Indo-Chinese Friendship Society gave me a glimpse of the unacceptable face of Communism (not that there was necessarily an acceptable face behind the unacceptable one), then my experience with the *Himalayan Times* gave me a glimpse of the unacceptable face of the press. As was to be increasingly borne in upon me in the years to come, newspapers and magazines, no less than Communist front organizations, had their own agendas, and the dissemination of truth did not always feature among them. Perhaps it was a measure of the extent to which I had 'gone forth' from the world and its ways – a measure of my ignorance of *real life*, Joe would have said – that it had not occurred to me that the organizers of a public meeting might want to mislead and deceive me or that the editor of a local newspaper might be unwilling to give space to a statement of the facts on a matter of public interest, especially when that statement clarified a confusion.

My refusal to speak at the inaugural meeting of the Indo-Chinese Friendship Society, or even to support Anand-ji with my silent presence on the platform, made no difference to my relations with my opportunistic elder brother in the order, as I knew would be the case. There was little that he did not regard with good-humoured cynicism, least of all the objections and reservations of his eccentric, over-idealistic young friend who, he was convinced (to the extent that he could be convinced of anything), was inclined to take his Buddhism far too seriously and to be much too rigid in his attitude towards such things as bending the truth a little in the interests of a good cause. A glimpse of just how cynical Anand-ji really was had been vouchsafed me only a few weeks earlier. Happening to call at Craigside one morning, and having entered my room without my noticing, he had looked over my shoulder to see what I was writing. I must have been working on the *Survey*, for I had written, that very moment, something about ethics, meditation, and wisdom being the means to the realization of Nirvāṇa. 'Why are you wasting your time on that old-fashioned stuff?' a sneering, contemptuous voice behind me wanted to know. The unfeeling words pierced me to the quick. It was as though Māra himself had released a poisoned arrow from his bow. However, out of respect for Anand-ji's seniority I made no attempt to justify myself, and welcomed the unexpected visitor in my usual fashion.

His characterization of ethics, meditation, and wisdom – the three great stages of the Buddhist spiritual path – as old-fashioned was no momentary aberration. For him 'old-fashioned' meant 'not to be taken seriously', even as 'new', 'modern', 'up-to-date', and 'advanced' meant 'to be taken seriously' – though not *too* seriously. As I already knew, Anand-ji was at least as much a progressivist as he was a Buddhist. Or rather, he was a Buddhist only to the extent that Buddhism could be seen as 'progressive', that is, seen as a rationalistic, scientific, and iconoclastic system that was in keeping with the times and in line with the latest contemporary thought. It was thus possible for him to give his support to a Communist front organization, and even to help draft anti-American resolutions, without feeling that this was in any way incompatible with his role as a Buddhist monk. At the same time, he was not so very much a Communist as to want actually to identify himself with Communism, or to risk a breach with me on its account. For my own part, I considered it no business of mine to correct one who had spent more than twenty years in the robes, and in any case, Anand-ji always treated me with so much friendliness, and evaded my attempts to draw him into serious discussion with such an engaging mixture of adroitness and good humour, that notwithstanding our differences of temperament and outlook I found it impossible to quarrel with him or even to get him to acknowledge any real divergence of opinion between us. Our first meeting after the Sunday afternoon debacle therefore passed off quite amicably. Anand-ji asked me to help him edit *Lumbini*, an English-language magazine devoted to the Buddha's birthplace that Gyan Jyoti wanted to bring out, and I agreed to do so. We also discussed, on this and several other occasions that month, his and Gyan Jyoti's plans for an evening college at the Dharmodaya Vihara. Most of these discussions took place in Anand-ji's room. He was usually writing when

I called, but occasionally I found him talking with a visitor or two, and an exchange that took place between him and a Newar devotee served to open my eyes to another side of his character, though without making it any easier for me to comprehend him.

In the vicinity of Tenth Mile, behind a row of open-fronted shops, stood half a dozen tumbledown wooden shacks. I knew these shacks well, having included them in my almsround in my early days in Kalimpong, when first with Kashyap-ji, then on my own, I had followed the time-honoured practice of relying for my one meal of the day on my begging-bowl. They were inhabited by poor but devout Newars, and it was between Anand-ji and one of these good folk, the supporter of a wife and five or six children, that the exchange in question took place. Cap clasped respectfully to his chest with both hands, the Newar, a grey-haired, shabbily dressed man of about forty, was kneeling in front of Anand-ji and regarding him with an expression of intense devotion. My elder brother in the order, for his part, sat on the edge of his bed and appeared to be contemplating one of his sandals, which was broken. For a while nothing was said. Anand-ji then mused, as though speaking to himself, 'Well, it's broken. I won't be able to wear *these* sandals again.... But how will a poor *bhikkhu* like me get a new pair, I wonder?' Whereupon the fish swallowed the bait. 'I'll get you a new pair, Bhante, if you permit me,' breathed the devotee, his eyes shining. But Anand-ji was too experienced an angler to pull on the line straight away. 'Well,' he sighed, 'it would be nice if somebody bought me a pair. Otherwise ...' This was permission enough for his interlocutor who, having made a triple prostration, left for the bazaar, returning half an hour later with a pair of sandals which he then presented, with another triple prostration, to a smiling Anand-ji. I was shocked. The sandals must have cost twelve rupees, and the Newar, a silversmith who was nearly always out of work, did not make more than forty-five or fifty rupees a month, whereas Anand-ji received a pension of 250 rupees a month from the Association for the Advancement of the National Language, whose General Secretary he had been for many years. Having glimpsed the unacceptable face of Communism, and the unacceptable face of the press, was I now being vouchsafed a glimpse of the unacceptable face of Theravādin monasticism? But while shocked, again out of respect for Anand-ji's seniority I said nothing, though I wondered for how much longer I would be able to remain silent. Anand-ji was not only a Buddhist. He was also a progressivist, and as such highly critical of any exploitation of the poor by the rich. Did he not realize that by representing himself as a poor *bhikkhu* who did not know where his next pair of sandals was coming from he was guilty of falsehood and guilty of taking advantage, moreover, of the faith of a poverty-stricken Buddhist layman? I myself, knowing the straitened circumstances of the Newar and his family, did not even accept their invitations to *bhojana-dānas* or ceremonial food-offerings, which I somehow managed to do without hurting their feelings. Yet here was the comparatively wealthy Anand-ji angling for a pair of sandals which, as he must have known, the donor could ill afford to give him. Had he, then, no heart, either as a Buddhist or as a progressivist?

But if I said nothing about the incident to Anand-ji, I could not help unburdening myself to Naginda, who knew his preceptor a good deal better than I did. The young ex-Untouchable had long since got over his resentment at the undue strictness, as he saw it, with which I treated him, and since his ordination had been to see me a number of times, usually in order to borrow money. Anand-ji was not exactly tight-fisted, he explained. It was not that he bought nothing that he could get another to buy for him, or that he never spent money on anyone. But his generosity was certainly selective. If you were one of his favourites, as Sumedha was, he could be very generous, but if you were not a member of that select band, as he himself was not, you got little or nothing. That was why he was always coming to me for money, Naginda added with a laugh. Anand-ji must have allowed the Newar to buy him the sandals so that he would have more money to spend on Sumedha, Gunakar, and Co., the second of whom, who was studying in Darjeeling, as I well knew, was costing Anand-ji quite a bit in college fees and pocket money. All the same, he agreed, it was wrong of his preceptor to have manoeuvred the Newar into buying the sandals for him, especially when he had two thousand rupees in his account with the Kalimpong branch of the Central Bank. How did he know this? Anand-ji had sent him to collect his pass book and on the way back to the vihara he had taken a peep inside and seen the amount.

Though Naginda's disclosure made Anand-ji's exchange with the Newar devotee seem even more shocking, I was as far as ever from comprehending my many-sided elder brother in the order. No doubt he was deceitful and manipulative, besides being a thorough cynic, and no doubt he did not scruple to exploit those who were less astute, or more principled, than he was himself. Yet he also possessed many admirable qualities. He was good-tempered, approachable, and without a trace of the arrogance and self-importance that characterized so many Theravādin *bhikkhus*. Moreover, he lived simply, without caring for fine robes or rich repasts, and he did not eat in the evening – though he always took a glass of hot milk before going to bed, which strictly speaking was against the Vinaya. Like me, but unlike the vast majority of our yellow-robed brethren in Ceylon, Burma, and Thailand, he was a vegetarian, probably as much because of early cultural conditioning (he had been born into a Brahmin family) as out of religious conviction. A 'progressive' journalist rather than a writer on Buddhism, he had contributed to the revival of Buddhism in India by translating the *Aṅguttara Nikāya* or 'Book of the Numerical Sayings' into Hindi and was now engaged in translating the entire *Jātaka* book.

Thus Bhadant Anand Kausalyayan, politician, Buddhist monk, journalist, and translator, champion of the national language and scourge of Hindu reactionaries, was a complex figure, and as such difficult of comprehension. Though he once had told me it was his ambition to be known as the Voltaire of India, there seemed to be no master principle, no dominant theme, no overriding motive – no *jiban-debata*, or 'life-god', in Tagore's language – which could be regarded as reconciling the different, even contradictory, sides of his character, and giving unity of purpose to his various activities. He was certainly not aiming at the attainment of Enlightenment in this life, but neither was he wholly bent on professional success, whether political, journalistic, or even religious. There were occasions when I thought he did not really believe in anything, and simply wanted to pass the time in as amusing a fashion as possible, even if this meant his having to stir up a hornet's nest or two.

Because I found Anand-ji difficult to comprehend I was not always sure how I should conduct myself towards him. I could hardly treat him as my monastic superior in the real sense, with all that this involved in the way of receptivity on my part and responsibility on his. Indeed, it was not always easy for me to regard him as a Buddhist. At the same time, there was no question of my being able to treat him simply as a politician or a 'progressive' journalist, or even as an ordinary fellow monk. I therefore compromised, outwardly showing him all the formal respect and deference due to a senior member of the order, but inwardly keeping my thoughts to myself, except when circumstances obliged me to reveal them by my actions, as had been the case that Sunday afternoon at the Dharmodaya Vihara when I had glimpsed the unacceptable face of Communism.

15
A LIFE IN THE DAY OF THE ENGLISH MONK

Ani-la, otherwise known as the French Nun, had received her *śrāmaṇerī* ordination from Dhardo Rimpoche in May the previous year. News of the event was not long in reaching the ears of the three elderly ladies who ran Les Amis du Bouddhisme, the Gallic counterpart of Christmas Humphreys' London Buddhist Society, for soon afterwards I received a letter from G. Constant Lounsbery, the American-born president, asking me for what was, in effect, a progress report on the former Dominique Delannoy. Miss Lounsbery was clearly troubled. She was troubled by Ani-la's periodic changes of tack, from Sanskrit to Indian Archaeology, from Indian Archaeology to Vedanta, and from Vedanta to Tibetan Buddhism and the Madhyamaka, and troubled above all by her recent ordination. What would happen, it seemed she was wondering, if the tempestuous nun were to return to France? What would be her position vis-à-vis Les Amis du Bouddhisme and what effect would her presence have on the tiny French Buddhist movement? I did my best to reassure my correspondent. Since her ordination Ani-la had definitely been more settled, I wrote, and in her red Tibetan robes, with shaved head, she was now a calm and dignified figure.

Unfortunately she did not stay settled for long, and more often than not she was neither calm nor dignified. Perhaps her most serious lapse from grace was when, some months after her ordination, she became so enraged with the driver of a Land-Rover who had let her down that she struck him a blow in the face with her fist, knocking out two or three of his teeth and causing the blood to flow. The incident occurred in Darjeeling, where she was then staying. She was of course overwhelmed with shame and remorse and wrote me a penitent letter the same day. While admitting that she had lost all self-control she at the same time pleaded extenuating circumstances and begged me to be careful how I treated her (this was a constant theme of hers), as in her present state she was sensitive to rejection and capable of killing herself for a trifle. If Dhardo Rimpoche and I were as clever as her (Catholic) Christian director had been, she concluded, we would 'make a docile sheep of this savage masculine compressed nature'. Dhardo Rimpoche certainly never succeeded in reducing Ani-la to a state of ovine docility, and I was able to do little better. For all her theatrical self-abasement and protestations of humility and submissiveness, neither before nor after her encounter with the Land-Rover driver (to whom she made amends with an apology and a tin of fifty cigarettes) was she really amenable to control or discipline – not even when performing the little penances which, at her insistence, I imposed on her from time to time. It was as though she was willing to be directed, but only on condition that she could tell the director exactly how he was to direct her. Perhaps the cleverness of her Christian director had consisted in his allowing her to think he was directing her in the way she wished to be directed when in reality he was doing no such thing. Be that as it may, the fact that I had been firm with her over the incident of the rug, which took place three or four weeks after her assault on the driver, and had not allowed her to have her own way, certainly did not mean that she had become more manageable or less liable to outbursts of temper or fits of sullen uncommunicativeness. Before long there was a crisis. The immediate cause was some remarks she made in front of Sachin and Miss Rao. The remarks were so unkind and so sarcastic, and showed her to be in such a state of rebellion against everything to which she was supposedly committed as a Buddhist and a nun that I at once wrote and handed to her a severe letter about her spiritual condition, it being customary between us to communicate in this fashion when we had anything of importance to say, as Ani-la felt she was at a disadvantage when it came to communicating orally in a language not her own. The letter had the effect of reducing her to a truly dreadful state of despair and self-accusation, and I was obliged to spend more than an hour dealing with the emotional frustration that underlay the unkindness and sarcasm of her remarks and restoring her to something like normality. Sachin and I then walked up the road with her as far as his house (Miss Rao had already left), from where a subdued French nun continued her journey up the hill back to Tirpai alone.

All's well that ends well, even if it is well only for the time being. As a result of Ani-la's crisis I took the initiative and consulted with Dhardo Rimpoche and Lobsang Phuntsok about what could be done to help her. This time our consultations bore fruit. Ani-la obviously needed help with her Tibetan studies and in her spiritual life, as well as needing, perhaps, more structured conditions under which to pursue both the one and the other. With the Rimpoche's approval, Lobsang undertook to give her Tibetan lessons four or five times a week. He would give them at Craigside, where she came practically every day, and where he himself had in any case started coming of an afternoon in connection with the article on Tibetan Buddhism he was writing and I revising. For my part, I undertook to conduct for Ani-la's especial benefit a regular evening session of puja, readings from the scriptures, and meditation. These arrangements, we hoped, would enable our unruly French nun to do greater justice to her vocation and to be more at peace with herself. When the plan was communicated to her, the object of our consultations responded, initially, with gratitude and enthusiasm, and Lobsang and I lost no time putting it into operation. For me this meant a few changes in my existing routine, but I did not mind. Though there were times when Ani-la's irrational behaviour exasperated me, I knew her sufferings were none the less real for being largely self-inflicted, and therefore sympathized with her and was glad to be doing something to help. She was a strange woman, I reflected, as I looked out suitable readings for the first of our evening sessions. What did she really want (Freud's famous question with regard to all women!)[192] and just why did she sometimes become so very upset? It was to be hoped that as she developed, under the influence of the new arrangements, into a better and happier person, answers to these questions would be forthcoming. Meanwhile, the concluding words of her letter provided me with a clue to at least part of her nature, and I would do well to bear them in mind in my future dealings with her, including those that were to be conducted, in the case of our evening sessions, in a formally religious context and with the sanction of her official guru.

Savage, masculine, and compressed were the terms she had used to characterize that nature of hers, and no doubt she knew herself well enough for them to be of significance. She was certainly *savage* in the (dictionary) sense of being 'wild; untamed', at times 'ferocious in temper', and in certain respects 'crude', though not – paradoxically – 'uncivilized'. Notwithstanding my having described her, to Miss Lounsbery, shortly after her ordination, as being a calm and dignified figure, her overall appearance tended to be expressive of the more savage side of her nature. A common friend, a cultivated European woman, was years later to aver that Ani-la had the physique of a French peasant and looked as though she had been made to do heavy farm work and produce lots of babies. Of medium height, and sturdily built, she had a red bulldog face that was capable of turning scarlet with indignation, rage, or sardonic mirth, and from which there looked out two blue-grey eyes that either blazed or glittered. Possessing as she did a peasant-like physique, it was not surprising that she should have been at home with animals. More than once, at the Gandhamadan Vihara in Darjeeling, I had found her sitting on the floor amidst her pots and pans surrounded by stray dogs and cats she had taken in and whom she allowed to push their noses into the very plate from which she was eating. Every now and then she would suddenly catch up one of the cats and press it to her capacious bosom, at the same time smothering it with kisses and squeezing it so tightly that the wretched creature struggled to escape. Brisk and decisive in her movements, except when overcome by feelings of despondency or despair, she was always 'on the go' and had a positive mania for rearranging things.

Masculine was for her more or less synonymous with 'intellectual', and having as she did a high opinion of intellect she naturally entertained a low opinion of women, whom she considered insufficiently endowed with that faculty. Members of her own sex, with few exceptions, she in fact regarded almost with contempt and thought talking to them a waste of time. Whether or not she was 'masculine' in the more accepted sense of the term (and certainly she had a few hairs on her chin) there was little doubt that hers was a highly intellectual nature. A former professor of Philosophy and Literature, she had become a Buddhist for reasons that were metaphysical rather than religious in the narrower, more emotional sense of the term. Disillusioned with

Catholic theology and mysticism, as well as with the Advaita Vedanta, she had found in Buddhism alone, especially as represented by the Madhyamaka of Nāgārjuna, the non-substantialism she had come to regard as constituting the true doctrine of liberation. My own reasons for becoming a Buddhist were less clear-cut, and less metaphysical. Nevertheless the exigent Frenchwoman and I had a lot in common intellectually, and I always enjoyed our discussions, at least when they related to Buddhism. She enjoyed them too, when she was in the right mood and not preoccupied with her personal difficulties. Once she went so far as to declare that with the possible exception of Dr Roerich (who was in her bad books, having refused to teach her Tibetan) I was the only person in Kalimpong who was her intellectual equal and the only person, therefore, with whom she could have a worthwhile exchange of ideas. As Kalimpong was a small place, this was not really much of a compliment. With her high, sometimes impossibly high, intellectual and academic standards, Ani-la naturally was an extremely critical person and very difficult to please. When she *was* pleased, however, she could praise lavishly, even excessively, her favourite term of approbation being 'formidable'. Thus Dr A. C. Banerjee, with whom she had studied in Calcutta, was a formidable Sanskrit scholar and Paul Mus's magnum opus *Borobudur*, a formidable study of Indian Buddhism.

Probably it was to the lack of opportunities for intellectual exchange, among other things, that Ani-la was referring when she characterized her nature as *compressed*. It was compressed in the sense that her intellectual and emotional energies were squeezed into a space that was much too small for them. They had no proper outlet, no adequate means of expression. Hence she felt frustrated, dissatisfied, restless. She was even 'compressed' linguistically, in that her command of English, let alone Hindi or Tibetan, did not allow her to express her thoughts and feelings as fully or as freely as she would have liked. It was noticeable that her spirits soared when she had someone to talk to in her own language, even if it was only Aryadeva, the Darjeeling-based French *sāmaṇera*, of whose mental capacities she did not have a high opinion. An intensely patriotic person, with a strong feeling for the French language and French culture, she evidently was no less ill at ease outside her native milieu than was the fish in the *Dhammapada* simile out of its watery home.[193] Sometimes I thought that her real ambition was to spend half a lifetime working on a truly stupendous piece of original Indological research and then, when it was finished, return in triumph to her own country. Having delivered before the Academy or the Sorbonne a formidably brilliant allocution on the extent and significance of her discoveries she would declare, amid tumultuous applause, that her humble efforts had all been for the glory of France.

This, then, was the person for whose benefit I had undertaken to conduct a regular evening session of puja, readings from the scriptures, and meditation, and for whom I was having, therefore, to make a few changes in my existing routine. Once those changes had been made, and the evening session incorporated into the structure of my day, the new routine remained virtually unchanged for several months, until my departure for Calcutta towards the end of March. So little did it change during this period, and so much was each day like every other, that to describe one day was to describe them all. In fact to describe one day was to describe my life at that time, so that a visiting journalist could well have written not of a day in the life of the English monk, or Imji Gelong as the Tibetans called me, but of a life in his day.

That day began before dawn, as people's day usually did in India. After a cup of tea I performed puja in the shrine-room, reciting (in Pāli) the Salutation to the Three Jewels, the verses for offering flowers, incense, and lighted lamps or candles, and verses invoking the blessings of the *devas* or shining ones. Sometimes I also recited such texts as the *Maṅgala* or 'Auspicious Signs' *Sutta* and the *Ratana* or 'Jewel' *Sutta*.[194] All this took ten or fifteen minutes, after which I meditated for an hour, concentrating my mind by means of the *ānāpānasati* or 'respiration-mindfulness' practice, and becoming absorbed, on some days at least, in the lower *dhyānas* or superconscious states. After puja and meditation came breakfast, which consisted of tea and buttered toast (without jam) and for which I was joined by Sachin. Examination time was approaching, and my young friend was staying with me so that he could revise subjects in which he was weak without being disturbed by siblings or visiting friends. On some days I helped him, after breakfast, with his revision. Otherwise I was at my writing table by eight o'clock, or earlier, and there remained, with Dr Hudson's rug beneath my feet, until it was time for lunch. Usually I wrote three or four foolscap pages, occasionally two or even only one. Besides the actual business of writing, there were quotations to be selected and references checked. At my request Marco Pallis had sent me, from London, several dozen volumes of important texts and studies that I did not have in my own small library, and which were indispensable. Thus for three or four hours I was totally immersed in the serene, radiant, and majestic world of the Dharma, or perhaps I should say 'of the Doctrine' (as distinct from the Method), for had I not also been immersed in that world, in a different kind of way, when performing puja and meditating?

Lunch was at twelve o'clock or even later. Strictly speaking, as a *bhikkhu* I was supposed to finish eating by noon, but for the last year or so I had been observing the *vikāla-bhojana* or 'untimely meals' rule in the spirit rather than in the letter. Not that I thought the letter unimportant or that I was in the least disposed to disregard it completely. Spirit and letter were closely connected, the latter being ideally an expression of the former and its observance, therefore, a means to the observance of the former. I had been shocked and disgusted, however, by the extreme formalism of many Theravādin *bhikkhus*, whose strict observance of the letter of the *vikāla-bhojana* rule was accompanied by a total disregard of its spirit, and had no wish to risk becoming one of that company. For me the principle behind the rule was *moderation in eating*, and there was no necessary connection between this and the particular hour at which one ate. Lunch was therefore at twelve o'clock or even later and for this meal, too, I was joined by Sachin. Our simple rice and vegetable curry repast was prepared and served by my new cook-bearer Padam Bahadur, a cheerful, competent thirty-year-old who at times struck me as being a Nepalese version of Sam Weller, Mr Pickwick's quick-witted Cockney servant.[195]

After lunch I gave Aniruddha and his companion Luparatna, Gyan Jyoti's cashier, a lesson in English grammar and composition. I had taught the Newar monk before, when his companion had been the hedonistic Mr Bhumiveda, and now that he was again back in Kalimpong he was continuing his studies with me. By this time relations between us were quite cordial, despite their having got off to such an unpropitious start five years earlier, and I had the impression that he had a better opinion of me than he had of Anand-ji, for some of whose ways he at times expressed strong disapproval. Aniruddha and Luparatna having departed, it was time for me to teach Durga and his school friend Mitra Kumar, a strapping young Hindu Newar whose family ran an orchid-growing business down at Seventh Mile. Sometimes I taught them Geography and Indian Administration, sometimes Civics and English Poetry. Occasionally they were joined by Lalit Shamsher, another of Durga's friends, who was also Mitra's cousin. The rest of the afternoon was spent writing letters, or editing the *Maha Bodhi* journal (including writing the editorial and Himavantavasi's column), and making up accounts.

At half-past five or six o'clock I took my place in the shrine-room, Ani-la sitting opposite me on the other side of the image table. She had arrived an hour or two earlier, and Lobsang had given her a Tibetan lesson while I was occupied with my students. After we had performed puja (the same Pāli puja that I performed in the morning) I read aloud a lengthy extract from a Theravādin or Mahāyāna canonical text, the idea being that we should listen as receptively as possible and allow every syllable of the *Buddhavacana* or Word of the Buddha (as these texts were, according to tradition) to sink into the depths of our consciousness. This was the first time I had experimented with reading (as distinct from chanting) the Buddhist scriptures in a liturgical context, and I soon discovered it to be a highly effective spiritual practice. A 'reading from the scriptures' always formed part of our full-moon day pujas, but as people's attention span was limited the text chosen was short and the impression it produced therefore correspondingly slight. From receptive listening to the *Buddhavacana* the transition to meditation was an easy and natural one. At least it was comparatively easy and natural for me. For Ani-la meditation was the least enjoyable part of the evening. Though not unused to the cross-legged posture, she was extremely restless, and could not sit still even for a minute. What kind of mental state she was in at such times I did not like to think. None the less I gave her further instruction in the 'respiration-mindfulness' practice, and did my best to clear up her various doubts and difficulties, though I took good care to do this only after we had finished meditating. Had I attempted to clear them up before we started we probably would not have got started at all, for Ani-la's doubts and difficulties were hydra-headed, and no sooner was one cleared up than two more appeared in its place.

That I found the transition from receptive listening to the *Buddhavacana* to meditation easy and natural did not mean that I necessarily found meditation itself easy. Though I had been meditating, fairly regularly, for seven or eight years, I still had to cope with wandering thoughts, with negative emotions, and, sometimes, with the sheer disinclination to sit down on the folded towel that served me as an *āsana*, to close my eyes, to watch my breath, and to calm and concentrate my mind. There were even periods of complete dryness, when for days on end I would be unable to concentrate properly and when Māra whispered in my ear that nature had not meant me for a yogi and I had better stick to books. Yet there also came, every now and then and sometimes when least expected, experiences that not only encouraged me to carry on meditating but pointed to the possibility that, eventually, Enlightenment would be attained. My whole body, especially the forehead, might be pervaded by an indescribable feeling of refreshment. Or I might 'see' the Buddha. Or the *kuṇḍalinī* might start bubbling in the *maṇipūra* chakra.[196] Or I might have a strong sense of the impermanence of all conditioned things. Whatever the experience, and however much it was welcome (and sometimes it was very welcome indeed), I told myself it was only a signpost, not the goal, and that I must press on. During the period of my evening sessions with Ani-la these experiences came to me more frequently than usual, especially experiences of *vipassanā* or 'insight' into – or, more literally, 'clear vision' of – the true nature of existence. This was probably due to the fact that I was meditating twice a day instead of once, and that when I meditated for the second time it was after performing puja and listening to the *Buddhavacana*. By traditional Buddhist standards, two hours of meditation a day represented a very modest achievement, but I had no doubt that in combination with other spiritual practices, and with the support of an ethical life, it really did conduce to progress towards Enlightenment.

The end of my session with Ani-la did not mean the end of my day. Sachin was waiting for me, and together we walked up the road and through the brightly lit High Street to his house. Here I gave Meera her lesson while he had his (non-vegetarian) evening meal, after which we returned to Craigside. Neither of us burned any midnight oil, but the lights were on in our respective rooms until quite late, as he did more revision and I concluded my day in the company of Rilke or Dostoevsky.

Yet though my routine, during the first three months of the year, changed so little that a journalist could well have written a life in the day of the English monk, that routine was by no means unpunctuated by interruptions. These interruptions usually took the form of casual visitors, either local people who were passing by and called to pay their respects, or sightseers staying at the Himalayan Hotel, or Darjeeling friends who were in Kalimpong for a day or two and wanted to see me. If I was writing or teaching I dismissed them as soon as I decently could – unless, of course, it was someone like Anand-ji, who could not be disposed of so easily. Otherwise, if I was free, I talked to them about the Dharma, about the Maha Bodhi Society, and (especially if they were Buddhists) about the need to revive Buddhism in India and spread the teachings of the Buddha as widely as possible. Thus the days passed, each one much the same as every other, until my work for the *Maha Bodhi* journal required me to go down to Calcutta. Sachin went with me. His examinations were over, and as he was confident of passing he wanted to look into the possibility of his joining one of the Calcutta colleges. Having said goodbye to the friends who had gathered at Craigside to see us off, we left Kalimpong on a cold, wet afternoon in the third week of March, and within twenty-four hours of catching the evening train at Siliguri were in hot, sticky, noisy, overcrowded, insalubrious Calcutta and unfastening our bedding rolls in my old room in the Maha Bodhi Society's headquarters building.

This time no nasty shock awaited me. Far from trying to check me in my work for the journal, as they had done the previous year, Silabhadra and Jinaratana received me almost with open arms and behaved as though we had always been on the best of terms. Their change of attitude was not entirely disinterested. As my friend Soratha, the Little Monk, soon privately informed me, they had been guilty of a serious dereliction of duty for which Devapriya-ji (now again out on tour) had taken the pair of them, Jinaratana especially, severely to task, and as a result of which they were in the governing body's bad books and very much on the defensive. The dereliction related to the licence under which copies of the *Maha Bodhi* were dispatched to the journal's subscribers all over the world at a special reduced postal rate. This licence had to be renewed each year and the responsibility for its renewal rested with Jinaratana, as Managing Editor, and to a lesser degree with Silabhadra. This year they had omitted to renew it, with the result that the Post Office had refused to accept copies of the February issue at the reduced rate. The cost of dispatching them at the standard rate being prohibitive, they had not been dispatched at all and were still piled up on the floor of Jinaratana's office awaiting a solution to the problem.

One of my first tasks after my arrival, therefore, was to accompany Jinaratana to the General Post Office and there lend him, for a space of

With friends and visitors

two hours, my moral support as he pleaded, argued, and expostulated with various officials. The situation was even worse than had appeared. Not only did the journal's licence have to be renewed each year. It had to be renewed within a certain time and each issue had to be posted by a specific date in the month in which it was brought out. Moreover, there had to be twelve issues a year, neither more nor less, which meant that there could be no Vaiśākha double number as in previous years. Somehow it was all sorted out, at least to an extent, and Jinaratana returned to his office to arrange for the copies of the February issue lying there to be dispatched at last and I to my room to start tackling the backlog of press work. The February issue having not gone out, the articles for the March issue had not been sent to the printers. These I now had to see through the press, as well as edit and proof-read the April and May issues – all within the space of three weeks. The May *Maha Bodhi* was, of course, the journal's Vaiśākha number. Though not a double number this year, it was sufficiently substantial in content, including as it did articles by Dr Conze and Lama Govinda, among others, as well as an extract from the second chapter of the *Survey* entitled 'The Transcendental Unity of Buddhism', and an editorial on 'The Reign of Law'.[197] There was also a special cover, designed by a Shantiniketan-trained Bengali artist, and a black-and-white frontispiece. The latter was an art photograph of a seventh-century bronze head of Śākyamuni from the Nara Museum. 'The gentle eyes, the powerful lines of the nose, and the benevolent expression of the face impart to this head a deeply religious feeling', the museum's guidebook observed. 'It is one of the finest creations of the earliest period (seventh and eighth centuries) in which Buddhist culture first permeated all Japan.'

My efforts on behalf of the Society's journal did not go unnoticed, or even unappreciated, and at a meeting of the editorial board held when I was nearly halfway through my stay its chairman, silver-haired and silver-tongued Dr Kalidas Nag, presented me with a small (verbal) bouquet. Under my editorship the *Maha Bodhi* had improved enormously, he declared, in his customary charming manner, and he and his colleagues – in fact all the Society's members – were deeply grateful to me for what I had done. The contrast between the present harmonious occasion and the stormy meeting that had taken place last time I was in Calcutta was striking, and I hoped it was indicative of a change of heart on the part of some of my colleagues.

The fact that I had to bring out three issues of the *Maha Bodhi* in as many weeks meant that I spent the greater part of the day (not excluding the evening) in my room, at a table strewn with galleys and page proofs, and had little time to spare for other things. Nevertheless I took part in some of the functions organized by the Society, even speaking at one and presiding over another, and delivered three lectures in the Society's hall, including one on 'The Recollection of Death' which I gave just after recovering from a bout of fever. The biggest and in its own way most successful of the functions held at this time was the public reception given to the ex-king of Cambodia, Prince Norodom Sihanouk Varma, in his capacity as leader of the Goodwill Delegation to India, which was attended by members of the Diplomatic Corps, Ministers of the West Bengal Government, prominent citizens of Calcutta, and other distinguished guests. On me, for one, the ex-king did not make a very favourable impression. A podgy figure in a white tunic and dark Cambodian-style sarong, he had crafty eyes and a suspicious expression that indicated, I thought, an unfriendly and deeply mistrustful nature.

Besides taking part in functions organized by the Society I talked with visitors to the headquarters building, lunched at the Grand Hotel with Dr Hudson, then on her way back to Kalimpong from Sarnath, visited the Sikh Cultural Centre and the Sri Aurobindo Centre, had my usual discussions with Phani Sanyal, and on two or three occasions accompanied Sachin to Hindustan Building to see his relations. There were also meetings with two highly regarded members of the Theravādin monastic order, one of whom was from Cambodia, the other from Ceylon. Venerable Veera Dhammawara, the Cambodian monk, had founded near New Delhi a vihara where he not only taught the Dharma but practised naturopathy for the benefit of the local people. Though more or less settled in India, he maintained links with his native land, and was said to be an adviser to the ex-king, whom he in fact had accompanied to the Maha Bodhi Society's reception. Venerable Ananda Maitreya, the Sinhalese monk, was a scholar, preacher, and educationist who was well known even outside Ceylon. Though both were very much my seniors (Ananda Maitreya had been ordained years before I was born), neither of them showed the least disposition to treat me otherwise than as an equal and I soon had the satisfaction of discovering that they were well-informed, open-minded men who were Buddhists first and Theravādins afterwards. Ananda Maitreya even displayed a knowledge of the Mahāyāna, indeed a positive sympathy with it, that in my experience was rare among Theravādins.

My most enjoyable meeting, however, was with my old friend Buddharakshita, the companion of my wandering days, who was passing through Calcutta on his way back to Burma. We had not met since 1949, when he left for Ceylon and I went to stay with Jagdish Kashyap at the Benares Hindu University. Letters had passed between us from time to time, and from his I had gathered that he was not having an easy time in the Copper-Coloured Island. The irresistible force that was Sinhalese Theravādin Buddhism had collided with the immoveable object that was Brahminical cultural conditioning (my friend had been born into a Bengali Brahmin family), and there had been an explosion. The explosion had blown him to Burma, where he had studied on a government scholarship, had learned Burmese, and was now serving as interpreter and liaison officer between the Burmese authorities and the Indian *bhikkhus* attending the so-called Sixth Buddhist Council. This Council, which was the brainchild of the Burmese prime minister, U Nu, was being held near Rangoon in a specially constructed artificial cave. Proceedings had begun in 1954 and were due to come to a close in 1956, the year of the 2,500th anniversary of Buddhism.

Buddharakshita was full of praise for the Burmese laity but rather critical of the monks, at least in certain respects. U Nu had made arrangements for the 2,500 *bhikkhus* attending the Council to be offered vegetarian, rather than non-vegetarian, food each day, judging this to be more in accordance with the nature of the occasion. The Burmese *bhikkhus*, who were very much in the majority, strongly objected. Unless they were given meat and fish, a delegation told him, they would withdraw from the Council *en masse*. U Nu had no alternative but to capitulate, even though this meant that hundreds of animals would have to be slaughtered every week to feed the *bhikkhus*, and even though consumption of the flesh of animals killed especially for their benefit was prohibited to *bhikkhus* by the Buddha in the very Vinaya Piṭaka whose text the Council was then engaged in reciting, checking, and 'purifying'. Buddharakshita's story did not surprise me. For some Burmese monks, I well knew, giving up meat and fish was equivalent to giving up Buddhism.

The morning after my meeting with Buddharakshita, and a few hours after I had sent the last corrected page proofs of the Vaiśākha number to the press, Sachin and I left Calcutta. Previously one had always had to cross the Ganges by the ancient, overcrowded paddle steamer. Now launches were plying, and in one of these we took our place. The result was that we reached the opposite shore ahead of most of the other passengers, secured seats in the connecting train without difficulty, slept for most of the night, and arrived in Kalimpong the following afternoon not too much the worse for our journey.

During my absence Anand-ji and Gyan Jyoti's plans for an evening college at the Dharmodaya Vihara had started to bear fruit. Classes were already being held. Before my departure I had agreed to teach the IA and BA classes English and Logic and having had tea and talked with Aniruddha and a few other early visitors I accordingly made my way to the Dharmodaya Vihara and took my first class. After the class I discussed the forthcoming Vaiśākha Pūrṇimā celebrations with Gyan Jyoti. This year, for the first time since my arrival in Kalimpong (perhaps for the first time ever), the dozen or more Buddhist organizations and institutions of the town were going to celebrate the thrice-sacred day jointly, as well as individually, a committee had been formed for that purpose, and I had been elected general secretary. For the next few weeks much of my time was therefore taken up with committee meetings, consultations with Gyan Jyoti, who had been made treasurer, and discussions with the stewards of the procession that was to be the main feature of the joint celebrations, as well as with the collection of funds for our own Maha Bodhi Society celebrations at Craigside.

Inevitably my routine was affected. Though I taught Aniruddha and Durga most afternoons, and took my IA and BA classes at the Dharmodaya Vihara three times a week, my mornings were broken into and it was more than two weeks before I could resume work on the *Survey*, and then only for a few days. There was no time for the evening sessions of puja, readings from the scriptures, and meditation. Ani-la was in any case in Darjeeling, and after her return to Kalimpong she evinced little or no interest in their being restarted. They had not benefited her as much as I had hoped they would. At the time of my departure for Calcutta she was still liable to black moods, still in the habit of silently handing me letters about her difficulties, and capable of announcing that she had decided to 'go away' and nobody would ever be bothered by her again. Now she was experiencing difficulties in connection with her living arrangements in Tirpai. Two or three months earlier she had moved from her quarters in someone's outhouse into a roomy natural cave in the hillside above the village. With the help of friends she furnished the cave, installed electric light, and made herself otherwise comfortable in her new abode. For a while the French Nun's wonderful 'electrified cave' was the talk of the town, with people walking all the way up to Tirpai from the bazaar just to see it. I had seen it once, when on an outing to Dailo, the wooded hill behind Tirpai, with some of our younger members. Recently, however, there had been friction between Ani-la and her neighbours, and shortly after returning to Kalimpong she tearfully informed me that it was impossible for her to go on living there. Her neighbours did not realize she needed peace and tranquillity for her studies; despite her pleas for silence they continued to shout and quarrel in the vicinity of her dwelling. Worse still, one of them wanted to cut down the row of bamboos that screened the entrance to the cave, thus depriving her of their protection and exposing her to the gaze of passers-by.

The evening sessions of puja, readings from the scriptures, and meditation not having been restarted, Ani-la was seen at Craigside less frequently than before. But Lobsang continued to come, even though there was no rebellious French nun for him to teach, and we continued to work on the article on Tibetan Buddhism he was writing. Not that he had actually written very much of the article. Weeks were to pass before he had produced a sufficient number of pages for me to be able to make a serious start on the work of revision – a work that was to last far longer than I had expected. Meanwhile, we spent our afternoons together discussing Tibetan Buddhism in general and trying to clarify terminology. Though Lobsang was writing the article, in a sense he was not its author, as the material for it was being supplied by Dhardo Rimpoche, for whose knowledge of the Dharma he had the highest regard and with whom he was in regular contact. The Rimpoche was aware, of course, that I was helping Lobsang and aware, therefore, that material supplied to the young Tibetan aristocrat was also material supplied, indirectly, to me, and that I would need to understand it thoroughly if I was to give the article an adequate revision. Sometimes Dhardo Rimpoche seemed to be communicating to me, through Lobsang, material not intended for the article or indeed for publication at all. Thus for four or five afternoons in succession, apparently at the Rimpoche's behest, Lobsang gave me a detailed account of the meditational practices of the *Guhyasamāja Tantra*.[198] So complex were these practices that as soon as he was gone I wrote down what I remembered of them, in this way accumulating quite a sheaf of notes on a highly esoteric subject. It was curious, I reflected. Ever since my first encounter with it, some years earlier, in an article written by a Bengali Indologist, the mere name of the *Guhyasamāja Tantra* had possessed a strange resonance for me. In Nepal a lay Tantric *yogin* had told me that together with the *Prajñāpāramitā* 'in Eight Thousand Lines' and the *Bodhicaryāvatāra* it was one of the three foundational texts of Nepalese (Newar) Buddhism. With the Prajñāpāramitā or 'Perfection of

Wisdom' literature and the *Bodhicaryāvatāra* or 'Entry into the Life of Enlightenment' of Śāntideva I was already familiar. Indeed, I prized them highly. Was there, then, a hidden spiritual connection between these two texts and the *Guhyasamāja*, and why had Dhardo Rimpoche chosen to reveal to me some of the secrets of Tantric Buddhist meditation?

Whatever the answer to these questions may have been, or even if the latter represented a misunderstanding on my part, one thing at least was clear. Just as our consultations about Ani-la had strengthened the ties between Dhardo Rimpoche and Lobsang, on the one hand, and me on the other, so my work on the article on Tibetan Buddhism was bringing me, through Lobsang, into ever closer contact with the kindly but, seemingly, aloof Gelugpa incarnate lama who was its true author. Thus when a situation arose in which I needed Dhardo Rimpoche's help I had no hesitation in approaching him directly. The situation related to the forthcoming joint Vaiśākha Pūrṇimā celebrations, now less than a week away. For several days rumours had been circulating in the bazaar to the effect that the (Gelugpa) lamas, of whom there were about a hundred in Kalimpong, were deeply divided, that tensions between the two rival parties were building up, that there was going to be a violent confrontation, and that the clash was due to take place on Vaiśākha Pūrṇimā Day, either in the course of the procession or at the public meeting that was to be held at the Dharmodaya Vihara afterwards. What had led to the division I never discovered, but as the two groups seemed to regard Dhardo Rimpoche and the abbot of the Tharpa Choling Gompa, respectively, as their leaders, it was these two dignitaries that I initially approached. Dhardo Rimpoche promised to intervene and restrain the lamas who claimed to be his followers, and the venerable old abbot, with whom I had been on friendly terms since my arrival in Kalimpong, gave me a similar undertaking. I also took the precaution of speaking to the representatives of the two *kidus* or lay associations, both of which had become embroiled in the dispute, and warned that any violence on the Vaiśākha Pūrṇimā, of all days in the year, would bring shame and disgrace on the Buddhists of Kalimpong and particularly on the members of the Tibetan community. These and similar meetings kept me busy for several days, but at length I was satisfied that no untoward incident would be allowed to mar the sanctity of the thrice-sacred day.[199] It was as well I had taken the action I did. Dhardo Rimpoche's followers, who were the more aggressive party and included monks belonging to the Tharpa Choling Gompa, apparently had been planning to attack the abbot at the meeting at the Dharmodaya Vihara and drive him from the platform.

Feelings within the Kalimpong Buddhist community could indeed run high. Besides the divisions among the lamas, there were serious differences between Tamang and Newar Buddhists, or at least between Dhanman Moktan and the Dharmodaya Vihara, and these, too, I had to settle before I could be certain that everybody would be taking part in the procession and the public meeting. Dhanman Moktan lived in Tirpai and was a dealer in grains. As I had long known, he cherished a violent hatred towards Newars, especially Buddhist Newars, and in particular towards the three (formerly four) Jyoti brothers, who were among the town's leading merchants and the Dharmodaya's principal supporters. For him no epithet was too bad to be applied to the unfortunate Newars. The reason for this inordinate hatred I had yet to discover, though over the years he had told me many a story purporting to reveal the arrogance, perfidy, and meanness of the entire Newar community. One of the more identifiable grounds for his differences with the Dharmodaya Vihara (though not for his unreasoning hatred) related to the ownership of the little one-room vihara situated a few doors from his grain shop. This had long been a bone of contention between him as the (self-appointed) representative of the Tirpai Buddhists and the Dharmodaya Vihara's Kathmandu-based parent body the Dharmodaya Sabha. If the issue was not resolved to his satisfaction, the irascible Tamang declared, he and his supporters would neither take part in any procession that started from the Dharmodaya Vihara nor attend any meeting held on the Vihara's premises. Fortunately I was able, as a friend of both parties, to get them to agree to a compromise. In return for Dhanman Moktan's recognition of the Sabha's ownership of the little vihara, Gyan Jyoti, on behalf of the Sabha, recognized the right of the Tirpai Buddhists to manage it. Thus the co-operation of Dhanman Moktan and his supporters in the joint Vaiśākha Pūrṇimā celebrations was assured.

Not that Gelug lamas, and Tamangs and Newars, were the only ones whose divisions and differences threatened to mar the unity of the Buddhist community. In Kalimpong there were only four Western Buddhists (or five if one included Dr Roerich), yet on the eve of the Vaiśākha Pūrṇimā two of them managed to get into a foolish quarrel that created, for a time, a quite unpleasant atmosphere. The two offenders were Ani-la and Joe. Both were keen to help decorate Craigside for our Maha Bodhi Society celebrations, but knowing that they were not the best of friends, and knowing, moreover, that they possessed very different artistic tastes, I had been careful to demarcate their respective areas of responsibility. Ani-la was to be responsible for decorating the shrine-room, where the morning celebrations would be held, and Joe was to be responsible for setting up the outside shrine, in front of which we would be holding the evening celebrations, when more people were expected to attend. Our younger members were given the responsibility of erecting the Tibetan marquee I had borrowed for the occasion from the Tharpa Choling Gompa. Having displayed, as I thought, truly Solomonic wisdom, I went to the Dharmodaya Vihara to see Anand-ji, leaving my helpers, young and old, to get on with their respective tasks. But even the wisdom of Solomon was unable to prevent the intransigent French nun and the prickly Canadian *upāsaka* from finding cause for disagreement. Though I had demarcated their respective areas of responsibility, I had omitted to define exactly where one ended and the other began. In particular, I had not made it clear to whose area the casement windows in the back wall of the shrine-room belonged, and during my absence a dispute arose between them over this important point. Ani-la claimed that as the windows were usually kept shut they formed part of the *inside* of the shrine-room and therefore fell within *her* jurisdiction, whereas Joe contended that as they opened outwards they should be considered as being *outside* it and therefore as falling within *his* jurisdiction. The reason for Joe's contention was that he had set up the outside shrine immediately below the windows; if the windows were opened, and the shrine-room's main image turned round, this would create a triptych-like effect, with the image forming the central panel of the triptych and the window-frames on either side of the image the two wing panels. Obviously the idea was a good one, and despite Ani-la's vehement protests Joe not only opened the windows but proceeded to line the inside – now transformed into the outside – of the window-frames with flowers. This high-handed behaviour, as she saw it (and Joe should really have waited for me to return and settle the dispute), infuriated Ani-la, and soon the two Western Buddhists were engaged in an unseemly altercation that dismayed and embarrassed the other helpers. Nor did the matter end there. After Joe had left, Ani-la climbed up onto the outside shrine and threw down the flowers with which he had lined the window-frames. At this point I returned. On learning what had happened I ordered Ani-la to replace the flowers and after the usual hysterics she obeyed.

Joe was very angry the next morning when he discovered what Ani-la had done to his handiwork, and Dr Hudson was even angrier on his behalf. 'Why was *that* woman allowed to interfere?' she kept demanding, of no one in particular, her bony frame trembling with rage. But this was not the time for anger or any other negative emotion. Vaiśākha Pūrṇimā Day had dawned clear and bright; from early morning more than a dozen pairs of hands (including Ani-la's) had been putting the finishing touches to the decorations, and soon it was time for us to welcome Dhardo Rimpoche, to invite him to hoist the five-coloured Buddhist flag, and to conduct him to his throne in the shrine-room. Here he performed puja in Tibetan and gave an address which Lobsang translated into English. I then administered the Refuges and Precepts to the gathering, led the chanting of the Salutation to the Three Jewels, and delivered a short sermon. Later in the morning, after an alfresco early lunch, our members and I went in a body to the Dharmodaya Vihara and took our places in the procession, which had just started moving. Anand-ji and I walked together immediately behind the palanquin containing the image of the Buddha. In front of the palanquin went the red-robed lamas in their yellow ceremonial headgear, some of them carrying flags and banners, others beating drums and clashing cymbals and blowing on various wind instruments, including a pair of twelve-foot copper trumpets. Behind us came a motley crowd of Tibetan, Nepalese, Sikkimese, Bhutanese, Chinese, and Indian lay devotees, many of them in national dress and carrying on their shoulders images and sacred books. The mile-long procession presented a colourful sight as slowly it wound through the High Street and Chowrasta, up past the Scottish Mission compound, and so along the ridge to the Tirpai bazaar and the Tharpa Choling Gompa, whence it made its way back to the Dharmodaya Vihara by a different route. The public meeting, which took place soon afterwards, though short was no less successful. I addressed the audience in English, after which Anand-ji addressed it in Hindi. On the platform with us, seated in two enormous armchairs, were Dhardo Rimpoche and the abbot of the Tharpa Choling Gompa. Though some of their respective followers exchanged unfriendly looks, and though the abbot was the object of a few aggressive stares, the two dignitaries greeted each other warmly on their arrival. I was reminded of the Hindu saying that however much Shiva's ghosts and Vishnu's demons might quarrel the two gods, their masters, remained the best of friends.

The evening celebrations at Craigside were held on the lawn, beneath the Tibetan marquee, and were attended by a couple of hundred people including the new Deputy Commissioner from Darjeeling and the Second Officer of Kalimpong. As in the morning, I administered the Refuges and Precepts, led the chanting of the Salutation to the Three Jewels, and delivered a sermon. This time the sermon was a long one. Taking as my text the words *sukho buddhanamuppado*, or 'Happy is the birth of the Buddhas', from the *Dhammapada*,[200] I emphasized the fact that the way to Enlightenment was also the path to supreme happiness. Then came a reading from the Pāli canon descriptive of Siddhārtha's attainment of Enlightenment beneath the bodhi tree, after which there followed a short period of group meditation. This should have marked the end of the proceedings, but such was the atmosphere that had been created that more than half the people, including the Deputy Commissioner, sat on, as though unable to tear themselves away. If the predominant mood of the morning celebrations had been one of joy, that of the evening celebrations was one of peace and tranquillity. Some sat with eyes still closed. Others contemplated the 'altar' Joe had set up at the far end of the marquee, against the outside wall of the shrine-room, where three tiers of butter-lamps burned and where, above the topmost tier, the sedent Buddha-image that was the focal point of the celebrations looked out from between banks of Madonna lilies.

16
GANGTOK, THE VILLAGE CAPITAL

Gangtok, the capital of Sikkim, was fifty miles from Kalimpong by road. I had visited the place once before, when at the invitation of Venerable Sangharatana I had joined the official delegation taking the relics of Śāriputra and Maudgalyāyana, the Buddha's two chief disciples, for exposition in Gangtok and at the Dungkara Gompa in southern Tibet, where the sixteen-year-old Dalai Lama was then staying. On that occasion the government of India, for reasons of its own, had prevented me from setting foot in Tibet, but I had at least seen Gangtok, where twice daily for a week I assisted Sangharatana and Kashyap-ji at the ceremonial expositions of the relics for the benefit of the faithful and where, in the evenings, I gave discourses on the Dharma.[201] Since then, Gangtok and Sikkim had become as remote and mysterious to me as the mythical kingdom of Shambhala, and I had expected to see no more of the Himalayan principality than the snows of Kanchenjunga and its other sacred mountains shining against the blue sky a hundred to a hundred and fifty miles away. Early in December, however, there had come a message from the Maharaj Kumar or Crown Prince. He would like to consult me before attending a meeting of the Maha Bodhi Society's governing body the following week. Would I mind coming up to Gangtok for a day or two? Not knowing at that time that the Indian authorities, who controlled access to Sikkim, gave invitees of the Palace their frontier passes automatically, I sent back a message to the effect that there might be a delay in my receiving permission to cross the Inner

Line.[202] Could His Highness not see me on his way down to Calcutta? He could and he would, and a few days later we accordingly met at Churchill, the Kalimpong home of his sister Princess Pema Tsedeun, where we had a long discussion about the Society's affairs.

The Maharaj Kumar must have found the meeting useful, for towards the end of May there had come a second message inviting me up to the village capital. Not only did the Maharaj Kumar want to consult me again about the affairs of the Maha Bodhi Society; he also wanted me to give a few lectures. The invitation, though welcome, did not come at the most convenient time. It was less than a month after the Vaiśākha Pūrṇimā celebrations, I had only recently been able to re-establish my daily routine of writing and teaching, and did not want to interrupt it yet again. Moreover, I had been rereading D. T. Suzuki's translation of the *Laṅkāvatāra Sūtra*,[203] as well as the three volumes of his *Studies in Zen Buddhism*. I had first encountered the great 'idealist' *sūtra* in the early forties, when I was still in my teens and still in England. Though I had encountered it in Dwight Goddard's shortened version *The Self-Realization of Noble Wisdom* (afterwards included in his well-known *Buddhist Bible*), its teaching had impressed me almost as deeply as that of the *Diamond Sūtra*, the reading of which, at about the same time, had made me realize that I was, in fact, a Buddhist, and always had been. Reading the work again now, after an interval of thirteen or fourteen years and with, perhaps, a better understanding of Buddhism, I found myself being plunged into a deeply introspective mood that I had no wish to disturb by a sudden change of scene. Nevertheless I thought it would not be right for me to refuse the Maharaj Kumar's invitation a second time, especially as on this occasion a refusal would mean not taking advantage of an opportunity to preach the Dharma. Nor were these the only considerations. Sikkim was a Buddhist state, with a ruler who was a Dharmaraja or Righteous Monarch, and though Buddhists were now outnumbered by (immigrant) Hindus Buddhism was still culturally and socially dominant and it behoved me to see as much of the principality as I could while the present regime was in place. I therefore accepted the Maharaj Kumar's invitation, and taking a volume of Suzuki's *Studies* with me for company left for the village capital at the beginning of June.

During the last few days it had been raining heavily, and though the road between Kalimpong and Gangtok was not blocked by landslides there was plenty of cloud and mist and I caught only an occasional glimpse of the darkly wooded slopes on the other side of the Teesta. At the little market town of Rangpo, where trains of Tibetan mules stood disconsolately around in the rain waiting for their packs to be searched for contraband, I alighted and showed my pass at the West Bengal police checkpoint, after which we were free to cross the frontier by the narrow, swaying suspension bridge. On the Sikkim side a friendly police constable waved us on with a smile that was in marked contrast to the sullen, suspicious looks of the Bengali sub-inspectors on the Indian side of the boarder. As we drove up into the hills clouds parted and mist cleared to reveal clusters of thatched huts and terraces already green with early rice and maize. Gangtok bazaar, where I was set down soon after midday, presented a depressing sight, consisting as it did of little more than a few rows of nondescript shops and miscalled 'hotels', most of them of the open-fronted Indian variety and most of them owned, judging by their names, by Indians. On the hillside behind the bazaar was a scattering of wattle and daub cottages with here and there a modern bungalow. It was not difficult to understand why Gangtok was called the village capital, for apart from the Palace and a few other buildings out of sight higher up the ridge what I saw before me *was* Gangtok, which with its two thousand inhabitants represented the biggest concentration of people in Sikkim.

Fortunately I did not have to contemplate the bazaar for long. A telephone call to the Palace to announce my arrival soon produced the khaki-clad Superintendent of Police to whom had been entrusted the responsibility of welcoming me on behalf of the Maharaj Kumar and conducting me to the state guest house. Hardly had this functionary gone, after seeing me settled in my quarters, than there appeared another, in the shape of a tall, rather nervous young Sikkimese in a black *chuba*.[204] This was the ADC,[205] who had come to make sure that I was comfortable and had everything I needed, as well as to inform me where and when I would be giving my lectures. The rest of the afternoon was my own. In the evening I had a visit from Rai Bahadur Densapa, also known as Berniak Kazi, Berniak being the name of his estate and Kazi his title as a Sikkimese nobleman. I had met him on my previous visit to Gangtok, as well as several times in Kalimpong subsequently, and knew him reasonably well. Like the ADC he wore a *chuba*, in his case brown, but unlike the ADC, who sported a Western-style haircut, he wore his uncut hair in the traditional Tibeto-Sikkimese manner, that is, plaited into two braids that were coiled tightly round the head. Tall and portly, with an exceptionally florid complexion, he was in fact a man of strongly conservative views and one of the pillars of the Sikkimese establishment. At one time or other he had occupied all the major posts in the administration (at the time of my visit he was, I think, in charge of the Department of Ecclesiastical Affairs), and was well known for his capacity for work, his personal integrity, and his loyalty to the ruling family – a loyalty that did not prevent him from offering, on occasion, unpalatable advice. He was also well known for his scholarship and for liking nothing more than a good discussion on Buddhist history, or doctrine, or literature. If this was indeed the case, and if it was the hope of having such a discussion that brought him to the guest house that evening, then probably he was not disappointed, for we talked far into the night and covered a good deal of ground.

The following morning came ebullient, irrepressible Tseten Tashi, the Maharaja's Private Secretary, whom I also knew reasonably well. He was at my reverence's service, he announced in his usual comical fashion, doffing his pork-pie hat with a flourish and making an exaggeratedly low bow, and had come to take me to the Palace. To the Palace we therefore went, at dizzying speed, and up a succession of hairpin bends, and in less than ten minutes I was being ushered into the Maharaj Kumar's private sitting-room. Here I found Rai Bahadur Densapa, and talked with him and Tseten Tashi until the arrival of the Maharaj Kumar, upon which they withdrew. Polden Thondup Namgyal, Crown Prince of Sikkim, was in his early thirties and of medium height. Like the members of his entourage, he wore a *chuba*, off-white in colour and with long sleeves into which he inserted his hands from time to time as if to conceal something. Apart from a pronounced stutter, his most noticeable feature were his eyes, which were black and beady, and could be said to twinkle, especially when he became animated, as he had in Kalimpong when we discussed Maha Bodhi Society affairs. On the occasion of our present meeting, which lasted for the rest of the morning, his eyes twinkled more brightly than ever, especially when we passed from the Society's affairs to the question of the revival of Buddhism in Sikkim, which evidently was very much on his mind.

The Dharma had been introduced into Sikkim in the seventeenth century, its introduction being especially associated with the name of

Lhatsun Chempo, a learned Tibetan lama. According to legend, the lama was guided across the mountains by the spirit of Kanchenjunga in the form of a white bird. Subsequently, monasteries sprang up at the spots where he had erected shrines. These monasteries, which eventually numbered more than forty, were divided fairly equally between the Nyingma and Karma Kagyu schools. Whatever they may have been like in the past, it was generally admitted that their present condition was on the whole one of serious decline. Hardly any of the lamas were celibate (according to Rai Bahadur Densapa, perhaps *one* of them was) and few lived in the monastery to which they were affiliated. Most lived nearby, with their wives and families, cultivated the land, and gathered at the monastery twice a month to perform rituals. Religious knowledge was minimal or non-existent, and drunkenness and sexual immorality were rife. With the clergy in such a state, it was hardly to be expected that the laity should be remarkable either for understanding or practice of the Dharma, Rai Bahadur Densapa being very much an exceptional figure in this respect. Clearly Buddhism needed to be revived in the state, and clearly it was fitting that the Maharaj Kumar, as the future Dharmaraja or Righteous Monarch, should be giving thought to the matter. There could however be no revival of Buddhism without Buddhist education, in the sense of regular, systematic instruction in the fundamentals of the Dharma, and he was therefore trying to ascertain how such instruction might best be given. In the case of the lamas it would probably have to be given with the help of qualified Nyingma and Kagyu teachers from Tibet, and it was to be hoped that from the lamas knowledge would trickle down to their largely illiterate peasant clientele. But what of the English-educated laity, who together with their Hindu counterparts now formed the most highly influential section of the community? How was the Dharma to be communicated to *them*? Since they were to a great extent alienated from their traditional culture, it would probably have to be communicated in terms that were rational rather than symbolic and not too obviously incompatible with their Westernized outlook. Probably it would even have to be communicated, at least for the time being, by a Western Buddhist, which was where the English monk of Kalimpong came in, the Maharaj Kumar apparently having not forgotten the enthusiasm with which younger Sikkimese Buddhists, in particular, had responded to the lectures I had given four years earlier, in connection with the exposition of the relics of Śāriputra and Maudgalyāyana.[206]

Thus it was that I was again visiting Gangtok, the village capital, and again giving a series of lectures there. The first lecture took place on the afternoon of the day following my meeting with the Maharaj Kumar, and the second and third on the two succeeding days. I gave all three of them in the secretariat building adjoining the Palace, in a room that with the help of Tibetan painted scrolls, lighted silver lamps, and incense, had been transformed into a veritable temple. Looking round, I could not but contrast the care taken here in Gangtok to create the right kind of atmosphere for my lectures with the very different way things were done in Calcutta. In Calcutta, when I lectured in the Maha Bodhi Society's shabby hall, no care whatever was taken to create the right kind of atmosphere. Jinaratana, who as Joint Secretary was in charge of such things, did not even bother to advertise the lectures properly. Half an hour before I was due to speak a board announcing the title of the lecture and the name of the speaker (invariably described as 'English monk') would be placed outside the entrance in the hope that passers-by would see it and wander in, which fortunately some always did, especially if it was raining. When there was a reception to be given to a visiting politician or other such dignitary, however, no trouble or expense would be spared to decorate the hall and send out invitations, even Devapriya-ji not being free from such opportunism. The fact that no care was taken to create the right kind of atmosphere for my lectures did not mean that I took any the less trouble preparing and delivering them, especially as I had, in addition to those who came in off the street, a small band of regular auditors; but when such care *was* taken, as in Gangtok it patently had been, it was a great encouragement to me and I felt more inspired than ever to give of my best.

Mindful that on the occasion of my previous visit, when I spoke on such basic topics as the Four Noble Truths and the Noble Eightfold Path, some of the younger Sikkimese Buddhists present had declared they had no idea Buddhism taught such wonderful things, I had decided that this time, too, I would stick to fundamentals. I therefore spoke on the Three Jewels, devoting my first lecture to the Buddha, the second to the Dharma, and the third to the Sangha, which enabled me to present the Buddha's teaching not only in its depth but in its breadth. According to a contemporary report, in the course of these lectures, none of which lasted for more than an hour, I gave a survey of practically the whole field of Buddhism.

> The unique status of the Buddha as not only the preacher but the discoverer of the path to Nirvāṇa, the Dharma as the means to Enlightenment, the treading of the threefold way, the practice of meditation, the duties and mutual obligations of monks and laymen, the wrongfulness of supporting Christian missions, the importance of the guru, and the need for properly trained and educated monks, were topics upon which the Ven. Bhikshu laid particular emphasis.[207]

That I should have laid such emphasis on them was not surprising, for they were among the topics with which I was dealing in the *Survey* and therefore very much in my thoughts.

Though the lectures were held in the secretariat building, which for those without means of transport meant a long uphill climb, all three were well attended, especially the second and third. My auditors included the Maharaj Kumar, Princess Pema Tsedeun, the new Dewan (a plump little Parsee from Bombay whom I had yet to meet), Rai Bahadur Densapa, and Tseten Tashi, as well as members of the Sikkimese nobility and officers of the state, both Sikkimese and Indian. Each lecture was followed by questions and the questions by a discussion which became at times, quite lively. Afterwards I mingled with the audience, greeting old friends and being introduced to people I had not met before. Thus I talked about Tibetan art with Kanwal Krishna, whom I had met in Kalimpong a few years ago and who had given lessons to Burma Raja and to the Maharaja of Sikkim, discussed the teachings of J. Krishnamurti with Moti Chand Pradhan, an elderly theosophist who once had been Sub-Divisional Officer of Kalimpong, and made the acquaintance of Apa B. Pant, the new Political Officer, who as the representative of the Government of India was the real if unavowed ruler of the little Himalayan principality. Having not forgotten that it was the Government of India that had prevented me, through a previous Political Officer, from accompanying the relics of Śāriputra and Maudgalyāyana to Tibet, I was inclined to treat the present agent of its authority – and ambitions – in the region with a certain amount of reserve. However, when we had chatted for a while Pant said he would like to have some discussion with me in Kalimpong and naturally I replied I would be happy to see him there.

In between the lectures, and when not busy working on my notes in the guest house, I was usually out and about seeing places and meeting people. The most interesting place I saw was Enchay Gompa, where I gave a short talk to the fifteen or twenty boy lamas studying at the Tibetan school there. They were a mixed bunch, some of them looking as though they were not at all suited to the religious life, but I gave them what encouragement I could, exhorting them to be faithful to the Dharma and to regard being a lama as a vocation rather than as a profession. The *gompa*, which was situated on the outskirts of Gangtok, was a large wooden building of the traditional type. As Rai Bahadur Densapa afterwards told me, it was about 200 years old and a branch of Pemayangtse Gompa in western Sikkim, which was the royal monastery and the biggest and most important Nyingma establishment in the principality. Despite its (indirect) connection with the ruling family, however, Enchay Gompa was in a state of considerable disrepair; some of its massive timbers were warped and decayed, and like the old Bhutan Palace in Kalimpong it reminded me of the ruined mansion described in the *White Lotus Sūtra's* Parable of the Burning House.[208] On the day I saw Enchay Gompa I also visited the Sir Tashi Namgyal High School, where Lama Kazi Dawa-Samdup, the translator of *The Tibetan Book of the Dead*, had once wielded the rod as headmaster. Here too I gave a talk, this time to a hundred or more boys who were *not* lamas, and discussed the curriculum with the staff. Discussion turned on religious education in schools and it transpired that only one teacher, a caste Hindu from Bihar, was against it. On other days I talked with a Superintendent of Police from Shillong, an American journalist, a friend of Phani Sanyal's, a Kazi friend of Ani-la's, and the weaving master from the Cottage Industries Emporium, as well as with various people whom I had known when they lived in Kalimpong. There were also more long discussions with Rai Bahadur Densapa, who seemed anxious to spend as much time with me as possible.

Despite all this external activity I did not altogether lose touch with the introspective mood into which I had been plunged, shortly before the arrival of the Maharaj Kumar's invitation, by the rereading of the *Laṅkāvatāra Sūtra* and the three volumes of Suzuki's *Studies in Zen Buddhism*. Whenever I could I had recourse to the volume of *Studies* I had brought with me to Gangtok, and one night, when I had been reading it and reflecting on its contents for two or three hours, I not only found myself in a deeply meditative state but had a new insight into the nature of Zen. This served to confirm my belief that external activity and inner spiritual experience were not necessarily incompatible, and that however valid the distinction between 'introvert' and 'extravert' might be on the psychological level it was one that was transcended by the bodhisattva's non-dual experience of the Wisdom that is Compassion and the Compassion that is Wisdom.

The confirmation was not untimely. Full as the last few days had been, my final day in Gangtok was to be even fuller. Four or five people came to see me at the guest house before breakfast, and straight after breakfast the Maharaja's Assistant Private Secretary whisked me off to the Palace for further discussions with the Maharaj Kumar about the revival of Buddhism in Sikkim. These discussions were interrupted by the arrival, at about 10.30, of R. M. Nehru, India's Secretary for External Affairs, and his wife, who were on their way to Bhutan and had decided to halt for half an hour at Gangtok. Mrs Nehru was European. In fact she had been born in Hungary, and was pleasantly surprised to learn that I was of partly Hungarian descent, my mother's paternal grandfather having emigrated from Hungary at an early age. The Nehrus were accompanied to the Palace by the Political Officer and the Dewan, whose name, I now learned, was Nariman K. Rustomji. When they had all gone the Maharaj Kumar and I resumed our discussion, which continued through lunch, which turned from Buddhism in Sikkim to Buddhism in the sense of the general principles of the Dharma, and in which Princess Pema Tsedeun and her husband Pheunkhang-se, and the Maharaj Kumari or Crown Princess, eventually came and joined. What with the friendly, cultivated atmosphere, and the sense that we were united in our common devotion to the Three Jewels, it was one of the most enjoyable discussions I had experienced for a long while, and I was sorry when the time came for me to say goodbye to them all and leave the palace and leave Gangtok. A fortnight after my return to Kalimpong the Maharaj Kumar sent me, through Princess Pema Tsedeun, offerings in the form of sacks of rice, tins of cooking oil, and other no less welcome additions to my scanty stores.

By that time I had again re-established my daily routine of writing and teaching, and was hoping to be able to keep to it, without any further interruption, all through the rainy season and into the autumn. In the event I was more or less successful in doing so. During this period the *Survey* made steady progress, I rewrote the greater part of Lobsang's lengthy article on Tibetan Buddhism, edited three or four issues of the

Maha Bodhi, produced the first two issues of *Lumbini* (after which the magazine ceased publication), and at the invitation of the editor of *2500 Years of Buddhism* started writing an essay on 'Cultural and Political Implications of Buddhism for the Modern World'.[209] Though I still gave Aniruddha, Durga, and a few other students individual tuition at Craigside, most of my teaching was done at the Dharmodaya Vihara, where I continued to take the IA and BA classes three times a week as part of the evening college. Besides taking the classes I corrected essays, set question papers, and marked the students' answers, all of which took time. There were also staff meetings to attend. These could be long and acrimonious, the longest and most acrimonious being the one at which my six or seven colleagues and I debated the issue of remuneration. So far we had all given our services voluntarily, it being understood that most of the students were not in a position to pay fees. At the meeting in question, however, Pandit Paramahans Misra, the uncouth, aggressive UP Brahmin who took the Sanskrit classes, not only raised the issue of remuneration but was adamant that we should all demand it as our right. The unabashed mercenariness of the Pandit's attitude embarrassed even the least philanthropic among us, though when his proposal was put to the vote only two of our number actually voted against it. The two were Bhaichand Pradhan, the young littérateur who taught Nepali and was the proposal's bitterest critic, and the English Buddhist monk from the Maha Bodhi Society's branch at Craigside who taught English and Logic.

Knowing as I did that any remuneration for the teachers would have to come from Gyan Jyoti, and that the latter's resources were not limitless, I was not very sanguine about the evening college's chances of survival. But it certainly survived long enough for the IA and BA classes I took there to form a substantial part of my routine all through the latter half of the year. For these five or six months my routine was in fact a very demanding one. I had never been as busy, nor worked so hard, in my life, and some of my friends, Ani-la in particular, were of the opinion that I was doing too much and that my health was suffering in consequence. The only variations from my routine were those provided by our full-moon day celebrations and other festivals – and by visitors and guests from overseas or from other parts of India.

17
BIRDS OF PASSAGE

A fine afternoon in the middle of May saw me leaving Craigside shortly after lunch and making my way to Sachin's place. For the last few days my young Nepalese friend had been ill in bed, suffering from what his doctor father thought might be appendicitis, and I was going to see him. Accompanying me on my visit was Venerable Saranankara, the slow-spoken, kindly Sinhalese monk with whom I had become acquainted in Calcutta and who for the last two or three weeks had been staying with me. On our arrival at the bungalow where he lived with his family we found Sachin no better than he had been the previous day, and Saranankara proposed that we should perform a *paritta* or 'protection' ceremony for his benefit. Such ceremonies were, I knew, popular in the Theravādin Buddhist world of South-east Asia, just as their more elaborate and colourful Mahāyāna counterparts were in China, Japan, and Tibet. I did not have much faith in them as remedies for actual disease, though willing to concede they might have a kind of placebo effect, but Saranankara was a firm believer in their efficacy, and as Sachin himself had no objection and as his mother and sisters rather liked the idea of a religious ceremony being performed in their house, I agreed to co-operate. A length of white thread and a brass pot filled with water were accordingly produced, the thread was passed round Sachin's bed and between his hands, and for the next twenty or thirty minutes Saranankara and I chanted the *paritta suttas*, all the while keeping hold of the thread, the ends of which had been allowed to hang down in the water inside the pot. By the time we finished Sachin was fast asleep, and having tied a portion of the thread round his wrist we departed. Saranankara was sure he would wake up feeling much better.

From the hospital compound we made our way not back to Craigside but a little further up the road, to Tenth Mile. Our destination was the Homes Studio, where we had arranged to meet Joe, Ani-la, Aryadeva, and Lilian Silburn for a group photograph. Whose idea the group photograph was I no longer recollect. Probably it was mine, in which case I must have thought it would be a good idea to have a record of some of the (mainly Western) Buddhists who were associated with me at that time. Joe, Ani-la, and I were now permanently resident in Kalimpong, though Ani-la and I, at least, were often out of town; but Saranankara, Aryadeva, and Lilian Silburn were birds of passage, spending the hottest weeks of the year in the comparative cool of the hill station. Saranankara and Aryadeva were in fact due to leave the following day, though Miss Silburn would be staying for another fortnight. In the photograph the three monks are seated on chairs. Saranankara, as the seniormost, sits in the middle, looking uncharacteristically glum, with an amused-looking Aryadeva on his right and a faintly smiling Sangharakshita on his left. Between Saranankara and me, a little to the rear, stands Joe, lips pursed as though he had just sucked a lemon and eyes looking piercingly through heavy spectacle-frames. Lilian Silburn, who wears a sari, sits cross-legged on the floor at my feet. Like me, she manages a faint smile. Ani-la, sitting at Aryadeva's feet, has the mournful, resigned expression of one who, in her own opinion at least, is obliged to put up with a good deal of ill usage. She fingers a rosary, but mechanically, her thoughts far away.

It being a studio photograph, none of us looks very natural, with the possible exception of Aryadeva, who appears about to crack a joke, as he often did. Though Ani-la's mournful, resigned expression was quite characteristic of her, she was in fact at that time happier than I had ever known her to be. She had abandoned her electrified cave at Tirpai and moved into a room on the ground floor of the Manjula cottage. As Lobsang and his wife were living in the upstairs flat that had once been Miss Barclay's she had easy access to Tibetan lessons, Lobsang having offered to teach her again. She was also studying daily with Tethong Rimpoche, a Gelug incarnate lama recently arrived from Tibet. But probably what contributed most to her happiness at this time was

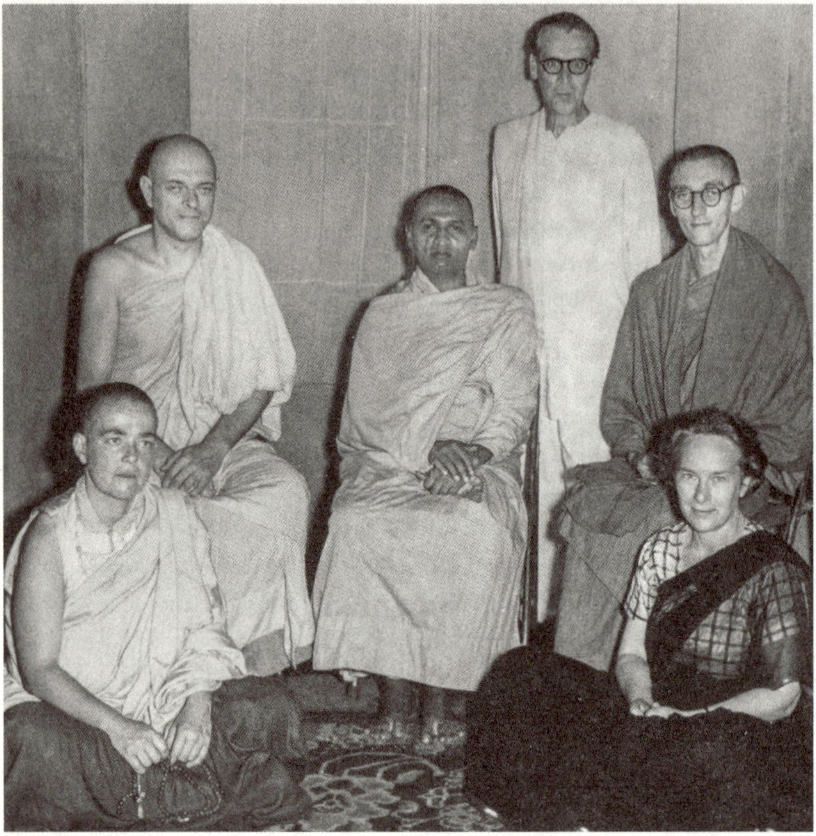

Group photo at Craigside: (back) Joseph Cann; (middle, l-r) Aryadeva, Saranakara, Sangharakshita; (front) Ani-la and Dr Lilian Silburn

the fact that with Aryadeva and Miss Silburn in Kalimpong she had two friends with whom she could communicate in her own language. Miss Silburn was indeed staying with her (Aryadeva was staying with me), so that the 'compressed' French nun had someone with whom she could share her thoughts and feelings on a day-to-day basis.

Lilian Silburn was almost the exact opposite of Ani-la, at least in temperament. A quiet, modest, unobtrusive Englishwoman, auburn-haired and of no particular looks, she was (or had been) a student at the Sorbonne and was working on a doctoral thesis on discontinuity in Indian thought, the discontinuity in question being that between the substantialist and non-substantialist philosophies. During the month she was in Kalimpong I saw a good deal of her, sometimes together with Ani-la and Aryadeva but more often on her own. Knowing that my mornings and afternoons were occupied she usually came and had lunch with me and then stayed on for a while afterwards. In fact I soon gave her a standing invitation to lunch, as she was intelligent and well-informed and I greatly enjoyed her company. The *Survey* being very much in my mind, I naturally told her about it and explained the general plan of the work. No less naturally, she told me about her thesis and we discussed some of the points with which she was having to deal. She also spoke of her researches into Kashmir Shaivism, one of the comparatively unexplored areas of Indian philosophy and religion – unexplored, that is, by Western savants and their Indian followers. Jagadish Chandra Chatterjee, the wily old Bengali pandit with whom I had been briefly associated in 1947, was one of the few modern scholars to have investigated this ancient tradition, apparently one of the richest and most complex in the whole field of Indian thought and praxis, and I had read his pioneering book on the subject.[210] Yet scholar though Lilian Silburn undoubtedly was (and her knowledge seemed well on its way to winning Ani-la's accolade of 'formidable'), her approach to Indian philosophy and religion was far from being academic in the pejorative sense of the term. She was as much a devotee as a scholar, though only towards the end of her stay did I learn that her affinities were with Hinduism rather than with Buddhism and that she had taken initiation from a Hindu guru.[211]

Among her more peripheral interests were Indian films, about which we had a long discussion, and graphology and other forms of character analysis. One day I selected from my files specimens of the handwriting of some twelve or fourteen correspondents who were personally known to me and asked her to tell me what she could about their respective characters. Her readings proved to be remarkably accurate. At least they accorded with my own knowledge of the persons concerned. Towards the end of the session, however, it was evident she was tiring and her analyses becoming less confident, as though the task of concentrating on so many different handwritings – and so many different persons – one after another demanded a degree of energy that could not be sustained indefinitely. The other forms of character analysis in which she was interested, and which she showed me, included one I had not encountered before. The subject or analysand was given a sheet of paper and a pencil and asked to draw a landscape containing houses, trees, bushes, ponds, bridges, and other such features. Several of our younger members were desirous of submitting themselves to this novel method of analysis. Saranankara, who like many Sinhalese monks was an amateur palmist, had already told their fortunes for them, and they were eager to learn more about their characters and future prospects. By far the most interesting of the drawings thus produced was the one made by Dawa. The faithful secretary of our little Maha Bodhi Society branch had depicted two solidly built houses, identical in size and every other respect but separated by a thick wall that ran right down the middle of the paper, dividing it into roughly equal halves. There was no door in the wall, and no means of climbing over. Miss Silburn was not surprised when I told her that Dawa's affections were divided between his mother, who had forbidden him to marry a non-Tibetan, and the Nepalese girl with whom he had long been in love and to whom he was secretly engaged. Not that I altogether escaped analysis myself, even if it was only self-analysis. At the intuitive little Englishwoman's suggestion I too drew a landscape containing all the prescribed features, but when I asked her to tell me what it revealed of my character she refused to do so, saying I would have to work it out for myself.

Neither Ani-la nor Aryadeva cared to have recourse to paper and pencil in this way, Ani-la indeed being inclined to pooh-pooh the whole idea of character analysis. Had they cared to have recourse to them the results would probably have been both interesting and informative, especially in the case of Aryadeva, whom I knew much less well than I knew Ani-la. In Ani-la's case I at least knew *what* she was like, even if I found it difficult to understand *why* she was like it, whereas in Aryadeva's case my knowledge of what he was like was limited. Though we had corresponded for several years, ever since his ordination as a *sāmaṇera* by my own teacher Jagdish Kashyap, we had spent very little time together. I had bumped into him once or twice in Darjeeling, and he had stayed with me at The Hermitage for a few days, and that was all. During his stay at The Hermitage he had been an object of great interest to our younger members, some of whom were positively fascinated by him. This was due partly to his height, on account of which his yellow-robed form towered above them all in a way at which they never ceased to marvel, and partly to the fact that he played the flute. His flute was in fact his constant companion, and he played it on the slightest provocation. Sometimes he replied to questions by producing on it a kind of derisory flourish. He did this with Ani-la in particular, especially when he thought she was becoming argumentative or too obsessed with her own problems. This annoyed her intensely. At the same time, he would look at her with an expression of such comical good humour that she could not help laughing in spite of herself. Aryadeva, I reflected, was very good for Ani-la. He handled her much better than I did, or at least handled her in a way that gave him less trouble than my way of handling her gave me. For her part, the French nun was quite fond of her flute-playing compatriot, even though she disapproved of his flippancy and had no great regard either for his mental capacity or his knowledge of Buddhism. Despite his having been ordained by Kashyap-ji, who was a scholar of the first water, Aryadeva's knowledge of Buddhism, as of Indian philosophy and religion generally, indeed was not only rudimentary but extremely patchy, though he made up for this by a perverted intellectual ingenuity which enabled him to detect all sorts of 'correspondences' in the fields of philology and comparative religion. One of the most outrageous examples of his ingenuity in this respect was his 'discovery' that the Abraham and Sarah of the Old Testament were none other than the Brahma and Saraswati of Hindu mythology, and this proved that Hebrew was derived from Sanskrit and that Judaism was a branch of Hinduism. For discoveries of this kind his little band of Hindu admirers in Darjeeling were accustomed to speak of him, much to Ani-la's sardonic amusement, as 'a very great scholar'.

So patchy was Aryadeva's knowledge of Buddhism, and so little interest did he evince in traditional Buddhist practices such as meditation and puja, that even after making all possible allowances for differences of background and temperament I still wondered, sometimes, if he was really a Buddhist. Nor was this my only doubt. So hysterical was his high-pitched, whinnying laughter, so bizarre his thought processes, and so manic the expression in his staring blue eyes, that I also wondered if he was entirely sane. But whether or not he was really a Buddhist, and whether or not he was entirely sane, he certainly regarded himself as a Buddhist (though he may have defined the term in his own way), and claimed to have been one even before leaving France for the East. In Paris he had attended meetings of Les Amis du Bouddhisme, and possessed a fund of anecdotes about the members of the formidable female triumvirate that ruled the tiny French Buddhist organization. One of his most amusing anecdotes related to an encounter between

Constant Lounsbery, the expatriate American president of Les Amis du Bouddhisme, and Alexandra David-Néel, the famous explorer and author, who was *not* one of the triumvirate.[212] The encounter took place on Vaiśākha Pūrṇimā Day, which Les Amis du Bouddhisme was celebrating in a grand, neo-classical building in the heart of Paris. Standing at the top of the steps, Mme Lounsbery was receiving, queenlike, members of the association and specially invited guests. Among the guests was Mme David-Néel, who came wearing her red Tibetan lama costume and brandishing a trumpet made from a human thighbone. Having climbed the steps, she halted directly in front of Mme Lounsbery and blew a blast on the trumpet right in the latter's ear. 'What do you think of *that*, madame?' she demanded triumphantly. 'I think it is not Buddhism, madame,' retorted Mme Lounsbery, quivering with indignation. Whereupon there ensued, according to Aryadeva, a violent argument between the two ladies as to what was, and was not, Buddhism. So violent was the argument that, if he was to be believed, the building rocked.

Though Saranankara, Lilian Silburn, and Aryadeva all spent the hottest weeks of the year in Kalimpong (and Darjeeling, in Aryadeva's case), birds of passage there were who descended on the English monk at other seasons. Some came earlier, some later, than the three with whom Joe, Ani-la, and I had our photograph taken that afternoon in mid-May, when Saranankara and I had visited Sachin and performed a *paritta* ceremony for his benefit. There were those who settled in the town – a few of them at Craigside – for weeks and months together, and those who came and went within a matter of days or even hours. Some were already known to me, either personally or through correspondence, while others were people of whom I had not heard but who had, apparently, heard of me and wanted to meet me. Some, again, were people who, regardless of the length of their stay or the extent of our contact, printed themselves indelibly on my memory – not necessarily to their advantage. Others, on the contrary, left on it only the faintest of traces. Among the latter was a Mr Hobson, of whom I remember only that he was an Australian theosophist, that he arrived early in the year, and that he stayed with me for several months. He must have given me no trouble (otherwise I would probably remember him better), for when I went down to Calcutta at the end of February I allowed him to stay at Craigside on his own. But if he gave me no trouble he apparently was giving it to someone else. While I was in Calcutta a woman came to see me who had been searching for him for several months and who was, she claimed, his wife. At my suggestion she travelled to Kalimpong to see him. What the result of the interview was I never learned, or have forgotten, but on my return to Kalimpong I found Mr Hobson still quietly living at Craigside.

The bird of passage who printed himself most indelibly on my memory, and by no means to his advantage, was a young Italian named Dosi Angelo. We had met in Calcutta, where I helped him obtain a renewal of his visa, and a week or two later he turned up on my doorstep with a lot of luggage and no money. As he spoke not a word of English, communication was difficult, but with Ani-la's help (either she knew a little Italian, or he a little French) I established that he was from northern Italy, that his family owned a bakery and would be sending him money, and that he had come to India in search of initiation into the mysteries of Tantric Yoga. 'La Yoga Tantrica' was a perfect obsession with him. As I had noticed in Calcutta, he could not meet a new person without asking, in an agitated manner, 'La Yoga Tantrica? La Yoga Tantrica?' as though he fully expected them to have the much coveted object somewhere about them and to be able to hand it to him on the spot, like one of his parents' pastries. Yet though the phrase 'La Yoga Tantrica' was constantly on his lips, and though apart from his creature comforts he seemed to think of nothing else, the twenty-three-year-old Italian gave the impression of being as devoid of religious feeling as he was of consideration for other people. With the possible exception of someone I had known in the army he indeed was the greediest and most selfish person I had ever met. At mealtimes he grabbed at food without waiting to be served, and on one occasion drank the entire contents of a jug of milk. When it was pointed out to him, with the help of gestures, that his action left the rest of us with no milk for our tea, he protested (in Italian, presumably, though his aggrieved expression made his meaning clear enough), 'But I *wanted* it!'

So disruptive was Dosi's infantile behaviour that when his money came through (and getting it for him involved me in protracted negotiations with the bank and the Sub-Divisional Officer) I insisted he moved to a hotel, which with a very ill grace he eventually did. During his last days with us he spent much of his time in the bazaar, making up for the deficiencies of our admittedly spartan diet. To the astonishment of passers-by, who had not seen a European behave in that way before, he would squat at the roadside cracking eggs on the kerb and dropping the contents into his upturned open mouth. At Craigside he spent his afternoons out on the lawn, reclining in the cane-bottomed armchair I had inherited from Major Cummins and eating the little cakes with the brightly coloured icing that he had bought from the itinerant *roti wallah* or bread man. The armchair was one of the old colonial type, with double-length wooden arms on which one could rest one's legs after the day's work. Having spaced out his cakes along these arms, five or six of them on each side, Dosi would pop them into his mouth one by one, a smile of satisfaction on his pink, rather rat-like features. After his departure for the Himalayan Hotel, where he stayed only long enough to obtain a pass for Gangtok, I did not see him again until, some years later, I ran into him in Calcutta. He still knew no English, though he had picked up a few words of Hindi, was again having trouble with his visa, and was as obsessed as ever with '*La Yoga Tantrica*'.

On the eve of Vaiśākha Pūrṇimā Day, some weeks after Dosi Angelo had left Craigside, I received an unexpected visit from a very different kind of person. She was small, bowed down with age and infirmity, wore the brown robe of an *anagārika* or 'homeless one', and was shaven-headed. It was Mother Vipassana, the Nepalese nun who had taken a great liking to Buddharakshita and me when, six years ago, we arrived at Kusinara in search of ordination as *sāmaṇeras* or novice monks. Not only had she looked after us, and arranged for us to meet U Chandramani, who we hoped would agree to ordain us. When the old man finally did agree, partly as a result of her intervention on our behalf, she also had constituted herself our *Dharma Mata* or 'Mother in Religion', organizing the preparation of our robes and making the customary food-offerings to U Chandramani and all the other monks (including our newly ordained selves) after the ordination ceremony and doing, in short, everything our biological mothers would have done had they been Buddhists and present on the occasion.[213] Now she had come to say goodbye. She did not have much longer to live, she explained, with a smile of the same peculiar sweetness that had lit up her worn features in Kusinara, and wanted to see me, and pay her last respects, before she died. I was deeply touched, but also a little surprised. Though I knew how devoted she was to Buddharakshita and me I had not imagined that almost the last act of her life, as it turned out to be, would be to travel all the way from Kusinara in order to see me for an hour and bid me farewell. Contrary to Theravādin tradition, I offered her something to eat before she left, and was glad when she did not scruple to accept. It was the least I could do. She had been a real Dharma Mata to me. Without her intervention, U Chandramani might not have agreed to ordain me, and had he not ordained me my life thereafter could well have been very different, and probably much more difficult. That apart, I honoured Mother Vipassana as one truly devoted to the spiritual life and would always cherish her memory.

Another *anagārika* who came to see me about this time was Magandiya. Like Mother Vipassana she was a disciple of U Chandramani, but unlike her older and more literate sister she lived not at Kusinara but on the hillside above Teesta Bazaar, where she had a cottage and piece of land which she cultivated herself, doing all the digging and planting with her own hands, and where I had once visited her. With her lived her father, the aged Sadhu Lama, who was not a lama in the Tibetan sense but one of the many Tamang Buddhists who were called 'Lama' on account of their forebears having belonged to the Tamang priesthood. In the course of my visit I asked what had led her to become an *anagārika*. '*Dukkha*, Bhante,' she replied, using the Pāli word, 'nothing but *dukkha*.' She did not elaborate, but no elaboration was necessary. The tone of her voice, and the look in her eyes, told me all. Suffering had been her teacher, not books. It was deep personal suffering that had made her turn to the Dharma, giving up all worldly ties and responsibilities save that of supporting and caring for her old father, who was unable to manage without her. Not that as an *anagārika* she had experienced no suffering. Her life was one of great hardship, even of privation, and I was therefore all the more surprised when she told me, probably during that same visit of mine, that she and Sadhu Lama were planning to make a pilgrimage to Lhasa, as the latter wanted to worship at the holy places there before he died. Lhasa being 300 miles away, and the passes into Tibet more than 15,000 feet up, I privately doubted if this was a very practicable proposition, especially as Sadhu Lama was seventy and Magandiya herself over forty. But months later, around the time of Mother Vipassana's visit, they came to see me at Craigside on their way back to Teesta Bazaar *from Tibet*. They had made their pilgrimage. Sadhu Lama had worshipped in the holy places of Lhasa and could die in peace, his last wish fulfilled. Yet the journey had not been an easy one. To begin with, like true pilgrims they had covered the entire distance on foot, walking there *and* back and taking, altogether, three months to do so. Then they had been snowbound, Sadhu Lama had fallen ill, and when their funds ran out Magandiya had been forced to support the pair of them by begging. But they did not complain, and after I had given them tea they set off down the road with stout hearts, seemingly none the worse for their adventure.

The old Tamang and his daughter were by no means the only people of my acquaintance to go on pilgrimage to Lhasa that year, nor was it only Buddhists, apparently, who went. Opening my door one morning I found crouching on the veranda a half naked sadhu or Hindu holy man. He was extremely dark-skinned, with aquiline features and a shock of black hair, so that I judged him to be from South India. Unlike most sadhus he had an excellent command of English, and was in fact an MA. We had not exchanged more than a few words before I realized he was in quite an abnormal mental state, though whether as a result of a nervous breakdown or of an overwhelming religious experience it was difficult to tell. Anyway I took him in, and after staying with us for a few days he set out for Lhasa. From various disjointed utterances I had gathered that he was looking for something (what it was he did not know, or could not say), that it was of supreme importance to him to find it, and that he was convinced he would find it in Tibet. Months later he, too, came to see me on his way back to the plains from Lhasa. This time he wore the maroon robes of a Tibetan lama and was shaven-headed. When I asked him if he had found what he was looking for he answered, simply, 'Yes.'

Like the birds of passage who visited me before Vaiśākha Pūrṇimā, some of those who winged their way to Kalimpong after the thrice-sacred day came from overseas and some from other parts of India. Gregory (as I shall call him) came from England and was a scion of a family well known in English history. Though he stayed with me for three months, leaving only when I myself left Craigside for yet another rented property, he seems to have made little impression on me, for had it not been for an incident that occurred halfway through his stay I might well have remembered him no better than I remember the shadowy figure of innocuous Mr Hobson.

The incident in question took place late one night. We had been talking for some time, probably about the Buddhist attitude towards psychic powers, when Gregory started to speak about black magic. He was evidently well acquainted with the subject. In graphic detail he described the black mass and other satanic rituals, some of which involved animal – and, he hinted, human – sacrifice. The principal centres of black magic in Europe were London, Paris, and Brighton. In all three cities lived powerful black magicians, some of whom were at enmity with one another and fought, by means of black magic, pitched psychic battles that in some cases resulted in the actual death of one or more of the participants – deaths that doctors and the police were unable to explain. These battles took place, I gathered, mainly between the French and the English black magicians, and so vivid a picture of this supernatural warfare did Gregory paint that, as he spoke, I could see in my mind's eye the psychic missiles winging their deadly way across the Channel from Paris to London and Brighton and from London and Brighton to Paris like so many satanic V-1s and V-2s.[214] There was something else I could see – in the literal sense. In the pupils of the young Englishman's eyes burned two tiny green flames. As he continued to speak, and I to listen, the flames grew steadily bigger and brighter, until eventually the entire room was engulfed in a brilliant green fluorescence. At this point, when I could see nothing but the fluorescence, I realized that something untoward was going on and started mentally reciting the mantra of Avalokiteśvara, the Bodhisattva of Compassion. Immediately the green fluorescence disappeared, and there was my clean-featured companion again, sitting on the other side of the table and still quietly speaking.

Sikkim was not a part of India, and it was certainly not overseas. It was an Indian protectorate and the larger state was represented, as in the days of the Raj, by a resident Political Officer who was the principality's *de facto* ruler. During my visit to Gangtok the new Political Officer, Apa B. Pant, had expressed a wish to have some discussion with me in Kalimpong, and one afternoon in August he accordingly came to tea and we talked at length about conditions in Sikkim and Bhutan and about Buddhism. He was particularly interested, it seemed, to ascertain the extent of Communist influence in the area, especially among members of the younger generation, and though he was responsible to the Ministry of External Affairs in Delhi, which was well known to be riddled with fellow travellers, I formed the distinct impression that personally he was anti-Communist rather than otherwise. He was also concerned to assure me that as Indian High Commissioner in Kenya he had not aided and abetted the Mau Mau terrorists, as alleged in the British press. The reason for his concern was not clear. I was in any case unaware of his having been High Commissioner in Kenya, and probably had not even heard of the Mau Mau before. Perhaps my visitor took me to be more British, or a greater reader of the newspapers, than I actually was.

18
BOMBAY REVISITED

Towards the end of August, when I had been living at Craigside for less than a year, the landlord informed me that the property had been bought by a wealthy Tibetan refugee and that the new owner wanted to move in right away. Though I had not been following events in Tibet very closely, I knew the Chinese were tightening their grip on the country and that the Tibetans were becoming increasingly restive. I also knew that members of the aristocratic governing class had started arriving in Kalimpong in greater numbers and that many of them were buying from the Marwaris, at vastly inflated prices, such English-style houses and bungalows as happened to be on the market. It was one of these moneyed new arrivals, I gathered, who had taken a fancy to Craigside and made our landlord an offer the latter felt unable to refuse.

The idea of our leaving Craigside did not disturb me personally, even though I knew that the move to new premises would mean an interruption to my work on the *Survey*. I had put down no roots in the place, and there was nothing about it I would regret as much as I had regretted the loss of the garden when we left The Hermitage. But if the idea of our leaving Craigside did not disturb me personally it certainly disturbed me in my capacity as *bhikṣu*-in-charge of the Kalimpong branch of the Maha Bodhi Society. Since my arrival in the town more than five years earlier I had conducted Buddhist activities at, and from, as many as five different premises, and well knew the disruptive effect a change of location could have on those activities. But there was no help for it. We had to leave Craigside, a new place had to be found, and I accordingly asked our members and friends to look out for a suitable property that was available at a rent we could afford. In the end it was Chunnilal, our landlord, who found our new home for us and persuaded the owners to let us have it for 130 rupees a month, which was still thirty rupees more than we were paying at present. Where the extra money was going to come from I did not know, but trusting it would come from somewhere, as it always did when really needed, I closed the deal and prepared to move.

Everton Villa was situated on the outskirts of the Development Area, not far from Panorama, which meant that it was about two miles from the bazaar. Like Panorama it occupied a broad hillside terrace, and like Panorama it commanded a magnificent view of the Darjeeling foothills, as well as the foothills of western Sikkim. Like Panorama, too, it was not overlooked by any other building and was strangely quiet, not only at night but even during the day. Oblong in shape, and with a roof of so low a pitch that it was almost flat, the isolated, unpretentious bungalow contained three large rooms at the front and three much smaller ones at the back. The middle room at the front, which was very large, opened on to a narrow veranda running the whole length of the building. Behind, there was a kitchen, storeroom, and servants' quarters, and on one side a square of lawn in the centre of which stood a small monkey puzzle tree. Access was by means of a flight of stone steps that from the pukka road connecting the Upper and Lower Cart Roads ran down to the square of lawn. When Chunnilal first took me to see Everton Villa I was not favourably impressed. It had been empty for a couple of years (why, I discovered only later) and presented a shabby, neglected appearance. The roof leaked, some windows were broken, and on the walls of the front rooms patches of mould had developed, so that the air indoors was damp and musty. However, the owners undertook to repair and decorate the place, within little more than a week the work was finished, and on a rainy day in mid-September I moved into our new abode, now smelling of paint and varnish and wearing a brighter, more cheerful look. A few days later came Anagarika Dharmapala's birth anniversary, which we celebrated under Anand-ji's presidentship with the usual speeches in honour of 'the greatest Buddhist missionary of modern times', and the following day I resumed work on the *Survey*.

Not that the work on the *Survey* was merely resumed. I actually put on a spurt, and in the course of the next few weeks not only succeeded in finishing chapter 3, 'The Mahāyāna Schools', but also made a good start on chapter 4, 'The Bodhisattva Ideal', with which the book concluded. What made it possible for me to put on the spurt was the fact that, though I still taught at the Dharmodaya Vihara's evening college, and still gave lessons to Durga and his friends, I was no longer having to devote time to the rewriting of Lobsang Phuntsok's article on Tibetan Buddhism, the handwritten draft of which had eventually come to comprise more than 300 foolscap pages. I had finished the work a week before moving into Everton Villa, and had handed the last typed corrected sheets to the grateful young Tibetan aristocrat with a feeling akin to relief. It was well that I had finished it when I did. Dr Kenneth W. Morgan, the American scholar who had commissioned the article, arrived in Kalimpong a few days later, and Lobsang was able to deliver the completed manuscript to him personally in Dhardo Rimpoche's and my presence. The following year, edited and drastically shortened, the article appeared in Dr Morgan's *The Path of the Buddha*,[215] which also contained an article by Kashyap-ji on 'Origin and Expansion of Buddhism'.

As the material for Lobsang's article had been supplied by Dhardo Rimpoche, and as the Rimpoche himself had been educated at Drepung, the manuscript delivered to the American scholar inevitably reflected the more intellectual Buddhism of the great Gelug monastic universities. Towards the end of September, and during the month of October, I became better acquainted with a very different kind of Tibetan Buddhism. This was the ethnic, almost tribal Buddhism of the inhabitants of the Tamang village at Seventh Mile. Despite their living just down the road, so to speak, for one reason or other I had seen much less of these rustic followers of Padmasambhava than I had of their more numerous co-religionists in Darjeeling, but recently they had invited me to give a lecture for their especial benefit in the village school. Down to Seventh Mile one afternoon I therefore went and spoke for an hour and a half on 'The Three Jewels'. So successful was this lecture, which was attended not only by the Tamangs themselves but by their Hindu neighbours, that in the course of the next few months I was invited to give two more lectures and accordingly spoke on 'Meditation and the Mantra *oṃ maṇi padme hūṃ*' and on 'The Buddhist World'. The first lecture having dealt with the fundamentals of Buddhism, of which I knew the Tamangs to be woefully ignorant, in the second I sought to elucidate a sacred formula with which they were familiar but of which they had little or no understanding, and in the third to give them an idea of the extent and diversity of the religion to which they belonged and of which their own tradition formed a part. At the conclusion of the third lecture I was taken to see the *gompa*, which stood a little apart from the village. It was very small, and comprised no more than a single whitewashed room at the far end of which, on a low platform, sat three life-size clay images. The images represented Buddha Amitābha, Bodhisattva Avalokiteśvara, and the Precious Guru, Padmasambhava – the traditional Nyingma triad. All three were of extremely crude workmanship and painted in colours which must have looked gaudy when new. The art of a religion, I reflected, tended to flourish or decline as the religion itself flourished or declined, and if images in a Tamang *gompa* were crude it was probably because the Nepalese followers of the Precious Guru had long been out of touch with the spirit of the Nyingma tradition.

After seeing the *gompa* I took tea at the house of a sympathetic Hindu Newar, with whom I discussed the possibility of buying land at Seventh Mile and building a monastery there, for remote as Everton Villa was from the bazaar a wealthy Tibetan refugee was just as likely to take a fancy to it as to Craigside, in which case we should be homeless again. Sooner or later, it seemed, the Kalimpong branch of the Maha Bodhi Society would have to acquire its own permanent premises. I therefore continued to think of buying land at Seventh Mile, and did so for some time, but nothing ever came of the idea. In any case, shortly after giving my lecture on 'The Buddhist World' I left for Bombay, and when I returned to Kalimpong six months later I had other things to think about.

There were two reasons for my making the trip to Bombay. Towards the end of 1952, after taking part in the re-enshrinement of the relics of the *arhants* Śāriputra and Maudgalyāyana at Sanchi, I had spent three weeks in the city as the guest of Raj Kapoor, the famous film star, who was planning to produce a film with a Buddhist theme and wanted to consult with me about it. During those weeks I struck up a friendship with Arjundev Rashk, the young Punjabi scriptwriter of the film, which was to be called *Ajanta*, after the famous cave temples, and we had kept up a desultory correspondence ever since. Recently he had been urging me to pay another visit to Bombay. Raj Kapoor was again thinking seriously about *Ajanta*, he wrote, and he himself was busy revising the script and badly in need of my assistance. Would I please come as soon as possible? The other reason for my going to Bombay was that the Wadias wanted me to give a couple of lectures there and that I needed, in any case, to discuss with B. P. Wadia the forthcoming publication of the *Survey*, now complete except for the last four sections of chapter 4. On 1 November, having delivered my usual full-moon day sermon the previous night, I therefore travelled down to Siliguri and caught the evening train to Katihar Junction. Fortunately I was not having to make the long journey across the subcontinent on my own, as Sachin had decided to accompany me. He had passed his IA examination, with honours, and after spending two weeks with me in Bombay would be joining college in Calcutta and reading for an Arts degree.

At Katihar Junction, which we reached at two in the morning, we had to wait twelve hours for our connection and it was another twelve hours before we reached Benares. Ten minutes earlier I had been surprised to see the pink sandstone tower of the Mulagandhakuti Vihara appearing above the trees, as I had not realized we would be approaching Benares from the Sarnath side. In the City of Ghats our train arrived after we had been waiting little more than an hour, and soon we were again on our way. Eighteen hours later, when we had enjoyed a good night's rest (Sachin on the luggage rack, I on the bench below), we found ourselves clanking slowly through the insalubrious suburbs of Bombay and steaming, at last, into the soot-blackened neo-Gothic splendours of the Victoria Terminus. My friend Soratha, the Little Monk, was there to meet us. In the absence of a permanent *bhikṣu*-in-charge he was spending his holiday, at Devapriya-ji's request, looking after the Ananda Vihara, one of the Maha Bodhi Society's two centres in Bombay, and it was to the Ananda Vihara that he joyfully took us to stay.

The modest, two-storey building was situated on a busy thoroughfare in the heart of the city, not far from Bombay Central railway station, and stood in a corner of the Nair Hospital compound. Vihara and hospital had been built in the twenties by the late Dr Anandrao Nair, a wealthy physician from South India who had become a Buddhist, or at least a very good friend of Buddhism, and who had organized the Buddha Society, Bombay. The hospital was, of course, much bigger than the vihara, and in fact seemed likely to squeeze the latter out of existence.

It was also much busier. Not more than half a dozen people came to the vihara from one week's end to the next, Soratha told me, whereas hundreds came to the hospital every day, as I could see for myself by looking out of the window. Moreover, in the centre of the common courtyard between the vihara and the main entrance to the hospital stood a small Hindu shrine, which may or may not have been built by Dr Nair. This was constantly thronged with worshippers, mostly women, either praying for someone's recovery or giving thanks for a cure. None of them even glanced in the direction of the vihara, much less entered its modest portals or sat quietly for a few minutes in front of the big alabaster Buddha, as Dr Nair apparently had hoped they would. The Ananda Vihara was in fact distinctly under-used. Vaiśākha Pūrṇimā was celebrated every year, and there was the occasional lecture, and that was about all. Soratha, however, was determined that the place should not be under-used while he was in charge, albeit temporarily, and least of all while I was in Bombay and available as a speaker. He had therefore made arrangements for me to give two lectures at the vihara. Quite a few people, it seemed, wanted me to give lectures for them that winter. So much was this the case that not long after my arrival, when I had met Mme Wadia, Rashk, and other friends and had an idea what I would be doing in Bombay, the Little Monk and I drew up a programme of my lectures for the next five or six weeks.

I gave my first two lectures at Aryasangha, the Wadia mansion on Malabar Hill, in what evidently had once been the ballroom. As they were held under the joint auspices of the PEN,[216] the Indian Institute of Culture, Bombay Branch, the Maha Bodhi Society of India, Bombay Branches, and the Indian Council for Cultural Co-operation, both lectures were attended by what the newspapers were accustomed to describe as the cultural élite of Bombay. In the first lecture, 'Buddhism as Doctrine and as Method', I emphasized that the criterion of Truth was pragmatic, and that as Doctrine Buddhism might be defined as a body of teachings the intellectual acceptance of which tended to lead to a course of action eventually resulting in the attainment of Enlightenment. As was famously illustrated by the Buddha's 'Parable of the Raft',[217] Doctrine had only a relative and provisional value, and it was because they were convinced of the relativity of their own doctrines that Buddhists could be undogmatic and, therefore, tolerant. The course of action following from acceptance of the doctrines of Buddhism, and resulting in the attainment of Enlightenment, was threefold, consisting of ethics, meditation, and wisdom. All the methods of Buddhism, comprising its entire practical side, could be included under one or another of these heads. As Method, Buddhism therefore comprised all those practices that were conducive to Enlightenment. After Enlightenment, doctrine or Wisdom meant the actual realization of Truth, and Method the dynamic compassion that caused us spontaneously to help others. Not that we needed to wait for Enlightenment before helping others. Buddhism included both the Path of the *arhant and* the Path of the bodhisattva, and helping oneself and helping others were systole and diastole of the spiritual life at *all* its levels.

My second lecture, 'Inspiration – Whence?', given a few days later, was of a more general nature. Though artistic inspiration might appear to come from without, in reality it came from within. The artist was not *wholly* passive; he had an active or creative aspect to his being. Creation meant expression, and expression meant communication, for which a common medium was necessary. Formerly, ideas derived from tradition, especially religious tradition, provided that medium. Not that the purpose of a work of art was to communicate ideas. Its purpose was to communicate feeling (for want of a better term); but feeling could not be communicated without ideas. Though there was no poetry, for example, without intellectual content, poetry was not identical with intellectual content. In modern times, because tradition was breaking down there was no proper medium of communication. We did not know what to believe, and hence there was chaos in the arts. Modern artists were open to low-level inspiration, with results that were often unintelligible, as in the case of Surrealism. The two great difficulties facing the artist today were (1) to remain open to high-level inspiration, which could be done with the help of yoga (the poet was, after all, the prophet), and (2) to have a philosophy of life. Ideally, inspiration should come from the highest possible level and be expressed in the most universal terms. Literature should elevate; nowadays it merely depressed.

Both lectures were well received by my cosmopolitan, not uncritical audience, and after each of them I was besieged by people who wanted to ask questions or simply to meet me. The second lecture indeed aroused a quite exceptional degree of interest. This was due partly to the nature of the subject, which was of special concern to the many people present who were involved with the arts, and partly to the fact that having taken the measure of my audience I spoke with considerable feeling and gave what in my opinion was a particularly good lecture. Among the people who besieged me afterwards there was a short, middle-aged woman in a Western-style frock who, being more pertinacious than the rest, was soon claiming my exclusive attention. So excited was she, and so voluble, that it was not easy for me to make out what she wanted to convey. Eventually I gathered that in my lecture I had given utterance to some of her own deepest beliefs, that she painted and meditated, that she considered herself a Buddhist, that she wanted me to meet someone called Dr Mehta, and that she would be coming to the Ananda Vihara in a few days' time and taking me to her place for tea. Thus began a connection that was to last many years and be the occasion, before long, of my making new friends and extending the sphere of my activities.[218]

After the lectures at Aryasangha came the lectures Soratha had arranged for me to give at the Ananda Vihara. I gave them the following weekend, and being held under the auspices of the same group of organizations as before they were attended by much the same kind of people, who, if they came in considerably smaller numbers, at least came out of a more definite interest in Buddhism. Unfortunately the atmosphere of the second meeting, when I spoke on 'Buddhist Meditation', was initially spoiled by some long-winded and unnecessary remarks from the chair. Mme Wadia had introduced my first lecture at Aryasangha by reading aloud one of my poems, Sir H. V. Divatia, the Vice-Chancellor of Ahmedabad University, had introduced the second with a few appropriate words, while the well-known Pāli scholar Dr N. K. Bhagwat, who had presided at the Ananda Vihara the previous day, when I spoke on 'Buddhism and the Future of India', had followed up my lecture by heartily concurring with my belief that Buddhism still had much to contribute to the land of its birth. Silver-haired Dr Kaikini, a tall, angular figure in a grey Western-style suit, chose to do things differently. His introduction was a rambling, incoherent discourse in which he perpetrated, in the course of half an hour, more blunders about Buddhism than I had encountered during the previous twelvemonth. Before I could speak on Buddhist meditation I therefore had to explain, *pace* the president of the meeting, what Buddhism did *not* teach. This unpropitious beginning did not prevent my lecture from being a success, and to judge by the length of the ensuing discussion Buddhist meditation was a subject in which many members of the audience were deeply interested. None the less I was dismayed that Dr Kaikini had been able to air his muddled views on such an occasion, especially as he was one of the leading members (an office bearer, I think) of the Ananda Vihara branch of the Maha Bodhi Society, as the Buddha Society had become after Dr Nair's death. If the tiny Buddhist movement of Bombay had many friends like Dr Kaikini, I reflected, it would not need enemies.

Not that the Ananda Vihara was the only Buddhist centre at which I had cause for dismay, or at least for disappointment, that week. Two days after giving my lecture on 'Buddhist Meditation' I spoke at the Bahujana Vihara, Parel, and at the Japanese Buddhist Temple, Worli. The Bahujana Vihara, the Maha Bodhi Society's other branch in Bombay, was situated down a side street in a working-class district dominated by factory chimneys. It consisted of a Sinhalese-style preaching hall, open on three sides and having a stupa at the far end, and a small bungalow for the accommodation of the *bhikṣu*-in-charge. Despite its name, which meant 'Vihara of (or for) the Masses', it did not enjoy much support among the local people, most of whom were in any case Hindus, and according to Soratha it was almost as under-used as its sister vihara in the Nair Hospital compound. Its principal function was to serve as a hostelry for Sinhalese Buddhists, and it was probably no coincidence that my audience that evening included a party of thirty-one monks on pilgrimage from Ceylon. I spoke on 'Dharma-Vijaya', or conquest by righteousness as opposed to conquest by force, and at the conclusion of my lecture I appealed to the monks – their lay guide interpreting – to come forward and assist in the propagation of Buddhism in India, which I said was severely handicapped for want of workers. My appeal fell on deaf ears. For all the response I received, I might as well have appealed to the stupa behind me. The faces of the thirty-one yellow-robed figures betrayed not so much as a flicker of interest. Most of them indeed seemed more dead than alive. At the Japanese Buddhist Temple, where I spoke on 'The Message of Buddhism' to a very attentive audience, the situation was hardly better. The Scheduled Castes Hindus who frequented the place had learned to chant *namu myōhō renge kyō*, 'Homage to the *Lotus Sūtra*', to the thunderous accompaniment of the big temple drum, and that was about all. What the *Lotus Sūtra* was, and why they were paying homage to it, they did not know, and as the Nichirenite monk or priest who banged the drum for an hour and a half every evening spoke only Japanese he was not in a position to enlighten them.[219]

With the Ananda Vihara being underused, or even misused, the Bahujana Vihara serving mainly as a hostelry for Sinhalese pilgrims, and the Japanese Buddhist Temple confining itself to drum-beating and chanting in Japanese, it appeared that Buddhism in Bombay was not in a very flourishing condition. I even began to suspect that it had been in better shape during the twenties and early thirties, when Dr Nair organized the Buddha Society and built the Ananda Vihara. This suspicion of mine was soon confirmed. Though Dr Nair had been dead more than twenty years his widow was still living in the city, and shortly after giving my Parel and Worli lectures I found myself partaking of a ceremonial food-offering in the block of flats that had once been the family mansion and listening to her rapturous accounts of what her philanthropic physician-husband had done for the poor of Bombay and for Buddhism. She was in fact very pleased to see me and overjoyed to be able to show me her Buddhist treasures, as she called the various works of Buddhist art Dr Nair had collected over the years. Treasures indeed they were, the collection including as it did magnificent bronze and alabaster Buddhas from Thailand and Burma, Gandharan sculptured panels, Japanese folding screens, Chinese porcelain pagodas, copies of Ajanta frescoes, and large modern oil paintings of scenes from the life of the Buddha, together with a hundred *objets d'art* in ivory, crystal, and sandalwood. Alas! they were all crammed into two or three shuttered rooms and covered in dust. After Dr Nair's death the family's fortunes had declined, Mrs Nair had been obliged to withdraw into a corner of the mansion, letting out the rest, and had neither the space in which to display her treasures nor the means to look after them.

By this time Sachin and I had been in Bombay a fortnight. While I lectured and met Buddhists and sympathizers with Buddhism, he had been looking up old friends who were either studying or working in the city, especially the film actress Malla Sinha and her parents, who were Nepalese and hailed from Kurseong. But now his holiday was over, and it was time for him to leave for Calcutta and for me to get back to the *Survey* and to start helping Rashk revise the script of *Ajanta*. On the evening of the day on which Mrs Nair showed me her Buddhist treasures I accordingly saw my young companion off at VT, as the Victoria Terminus was universally known, and the following day moved to Rashk's ground floor flat at Khar, a newish, middle-class suburb on the western side of the Bombay peninsula. I was sorry to say goodbye to

Sachin, especially as for the next two years we would not be seeing much of each other, and sorry to leave the Ananda Vihara, where Soratha and I had enjoyed our usual lively exchanges and where, moreover, I had made friends with a young Burmese monk who happened to be staying there. This young monk was exceptionally good-looking, and I was not surprised to learn that thereby hung a tale. He told me the tale not long after we had got to know each other, and though he told it in a simple, unaffected manner it was the kind of story to which only the colourful, impressionistic pen of a Lafcadio Hearn could really have done justice, in the sense of sketching in its idyllic background, exploiting its romantic interest, and bringing out the characters of the two people involved.[220]

The scene of the story was a small monastery on the outskirts of a village in the heart of rural Burma. There Visuddhisara or 'Essence of Purity', as the good-looking young monk was called, had lived with the learned elder under whose direction he was studying. Each morning, as the custom was, the two monks went into the village with their alms bowls, moving silently from door to door until they had collected enough rice and curry for their one meal of the day. On festival days and other special occasions, however, the villagers brought food to the monastery and served it to the monks on the broad veranda. Two of the villagers, a mother and her unmarried daughter, were especially assiduous in this respect. By the time Visuddhisara had been at the monastery a few months they were bringing food to him and his teacher every day, so that the two monks no longer had to go into the village with their alms bowls. One day the daughter came alone. Her mother was ill, she explained. As it happened, Visuddhisara's teacher had gone to visit a colleague in a neighbouring village, so that the young monk and the maiden had the veranda to themselves. When she had served him and he had eaten his fill and chanted a blessing, the maiden prostrated herself three times before him and asked him to excuse her presumption. She had a confession to make, she said – and a proposal. His good looks, and dignified bearing, had impressed her deeply – so deeply that she had fallen in love with him. As her mother's only child, she would inherit the house where they lived, along with some land. If his reverence wished, he could give up the yellow robe and marry her. He would not have to work, and they could live happily together for the rest of their lives. She would be a good and faithful wife to him, and he would have no cause to regret his decision. The proposal took Visuddhisara completely by surprise. He had never contemplated marriage, nor had he ever felt any romantic interest in the maiden. Since he kept his eyes lowered in the presence of women, as a monk should, he had not even realized before how beautiful she was. None the less he promised to consider her proposal. Whereupon she prostrated herself three times and left.

During the next few days Visuddhisara looked deep into his own heart. What he saw shining there, like a vein of gold in the depths of a mine, was a desire to be a monk for the rest of his life, and though tempted by the proposal he had received, and conscious that in Burma it was possible to leave the yellow robe without dishonour, he knew he had no alternative but to be true to that desire. When he and the maiden next had the veranda to themselves he therefore told her that much as he appreciated her offer he wanted to remain a monk and strive for Nirvāṇa. Deeply disappointed, she prostrated herself in silent acceptance of his decision. Nor was her proposal mentioned between them again. But she and her mother still came to the monastery every day, bringing food for him and his teacher, and continued to do so right up to the time of his departure for Bombay.

Simply and unaffectedly as Visuddhisara told his story, I found it difficult to know which to admire more, the firmness with which the young monk had rejected the maiden's proposal, or the good grace with which she had accepted that refusal. A Western woman, I reflected, might not have given up so easily. The manner in which the two actors in the little drama had acquitted themselves in fact reflected credit on them both, as well as on the traditional culture of Buddhist Burma, within which they had grown up and whose values had no doubt influenced their behaviour.

19
THE PRESENCE IN THE CORNER

The suburb to which I had moved was on the local railway line. From the station a road ran north, and from this road, at regular intervals, the still unmade-up roads extended east towards the middle of the peninsula and west towards the coast. Rashk's flat was located in a square white building, very similar to all its square white neighbours, which was situated near the end of Eighteenth Road, one of the last side roads to the west. It was a small flat, consisting, besides the usual offices, of a lounge, a bedroom, and a kitchen. The lounge was furnished, Western-style, with a sofa, two armchairs, a coffee table, and a bookcase containing, as I soon discovered, a stack of *Time* magazines, numerous American and Russian novels (*not* the classics), and the ten-volume official biography of Mahatma Gandhi. Here I was installed, Rashk having come and fetched me and my small luggage from the Ananda Vihara, and here for the next two months and more I stayed. The lounge was very quiet, as was the rest of the flat and, indeed, the whole building. This was due principally to the road not being a through road but coming to an abrupt end at the edge of a piece of waste ground, beyond which were only the huts of the dark-skinned fisherfolk who, until a few centuries ago, had been the sole occupants of the seven islands that were now the city of Bombay.

In circumstances thus propitious it did not take me long to settle down, and two or three days after moving to Khar I resumed work on the *Survey*. As my custom was, I worked on it in the morning, usually managing to complete three or four foolscap pages before lunch. After lunch I rested and read, dipping into Rashk's bookcase, and in the afternoon or evening – sometimes until late at night – my scriptwriter friend and I would discuss the story line, or the dialogue, of *Ajanta*, as well as the Hindi novelette he was writing. At least such was our routine initially. Before a week had passed Rashk was having to spend much of the day out on business of his own, sometimes leaving the flat early in the morning and not returning until 11 or 12 at night, to the ill-concealed annoyance of his young wife, who disliked spending the whole day with only the two teenage maidservants for company. For my part, I did not mind having extra time in which to work on the *Survey*, especially as B. P. Wadia was getting the manuscript typed and had started sending me bulky instalments of typescript for correction. Nor did I mind having extra time for the exploration of Rashk's bookcase, and besides reading several of the modern American and Russian novels, of which only Hemingway's *The Old Man and the Sea* really impressed me (I had not read any Hemingway before), managed to get through Kenneth Walker's *Venture with Ideas* and Axel Münthe's *The Story of San Michele* and to make a start on the multi-volume *Mahatma*.[221]

My exploration of his bookcase led to some lively discussions with Rashk, when he was at home, and I formed the impression that he was happier to talk about literature than to finish revising the script of *Ajanta*, to serious work on which we got down only several weeks later. His tastes were very different from my own, modern American authors being the principal occupants of his literary Valhalla, and William Faulkner the god of his particular idolatry. At that time my knowledge of American literature was confined to Emerson, Poe, Walt Whitman, and Harriet Beecher Stowe;[222] of the moderns I knew nothing, and if, years later, I got round to reading Faulkner[223] (and certain of his contemporaries) this was to some extent due to my discussions with Arjundev Rashk at Khar in the winter of 1955–6. Not that our discussions at his flat, and in taxis and Irani tea shops on our occasional joint forays into town, were by any means restricted to literature. They ranged over a variety of topics, from politics to sex, and from Buddhism to the Japanese film. We also talked about ourselves. At least Rashk talked about himself. As I already knew, his mother tongue was Punjabi, and his preferred literary medium Urdu, in which he had written poetry ('Rashk' was not his surname, i.e. caste name, but his poetic *nom de plume*, and as such rightly to be enclosed within quotation marks). What I did not know was that he had not been born in India. He had been born and brought up in Burma, in Rangoon. At the time of the Japanese invasion, when he was still in his teens, he and his family had fled as refugees to India, making the last part of their journey on foot through the jungles of Burma and Assam. In this connection he had a curious story to tell. Like the tale told me by Visuddhisara, it was one to which only the pen of a Lafcadio Hearn (in this case the Hearn of the late Japanese ghost stories), or perhaps, in a different style, the pen of a Somerset Maugham, could have done justice.[224]

A year or so before the invasion he had consulted an astrologer about his future. Not that he had much faith in astrology then, he explained, but most Hindus believed in it, even English-educated ones, and being on the threshold of manhood, and uncertain which direction in life to take (his real ambition was to be a poet), he thought he might as well find out what the stars had to say on the subject, if indeed they had, or could have, anything to say on it. To his surprise the astrologer, after making his calculations, professed himself extremely puzzled. He could tell his client what he saw, he declared, but not its meaning. What he saw was a broad track through dense jungle. On either side of the track, for its entire length, human skeletons were lying, and along this track, between the skeletons, his teenage client was walking, tired and hungry, with the sun blazing overhead and the vultures circling. A year or so later the prediction – for such it turned out to have been – was strangely and tragically fulfilled. With what remained of his family, Rashk told me, a more sombre expression than usual clouding his pleasant, irregularly-shaped countenance, he had found himself in just such a jungle as the astrologer had described, stumbling along just such a track, fleeing as fast as his failing strength permitted from the advancing Japanese troops. He must have passed thousands of skeletons, their bones picked clean by vultures – the remains of those Indian and European refugees, indistinguishable now in death, who had fallen exhausted by the wayside and perished before they could reach safety.[225] As a result of this experience, he said in conclusion, he had developed a certain amount of faith in astrology. At least he no longer dismissed it out of hand. There were good astrologers in Bombay, one of whom came to the flat every month and gave him the benefit of his – or the stars' – advice and guidance. That this was the case I already knew, having seen a thin, elderly Brahmin arriving one morning and being shown into the bedroom, where he remained closeted with Rashk an hour for what, the latter afterwards told me, was a professional consultation. What I did not know was that before I left Bombay I would be having, in connection with that same elderly Brahmin, a curious story of my own to tell.

As a Buddhist, I had no faith in astrology, in the sense that I did not believe that the relative positions of the stars and planets determined events on Earth, including events in individual lives. Had not the Buddha (as Bodhisattva, in the *Jātaka* book) scornfully demanded, in words my rationalist friend Anand-ji was fond of quoting, '*Kiṃ karissanti tārakā?* What can the stars do?'[226] Yet the resemblance between Rashk's experience, as he journeyed on foot through the jungles of Burma and Assam, and what the Rangoon astrologer had predicted, was too close to be explicable in terms of pure coincidence. A clue was perhaps to be found in the fact that the astrologer had, as it appeared, spoken of *seeing* the track through the jungle, the human skeletons, and his client walking between them. Perhaps it was a case, not of his having predicted Rashk's future in accordance with calculations made on the basis of a reading of the stars, but rather of his having 'seen' that future clairvoyantly by means of a precognitive faculty that had been brought into play as a result of the intense concentration the making of those calculations required. Be that as it may, one story about the occult led to another, as usually happened when that fascinating subject was broached, and I think it was on this occasion that I told Rashk about my own precognitive experiences as a teenager, when I 'saw' what was going to happen to me (though not was going to happen to others) half an hour or so beforehand,[227] as well as about my 'seeing' Buddharakshita clairvoyantly one night when he was several hundred miles away.[228] I did not, however, tell him about a strange experience that had befallen me much more recently, under his own hospitable roof, and in the very room in which we were sitting. I did not tell him about it, partly because it was not occult in the sense that clairvoyance and precognition were occult, being an experience of an entirely different order, and partly because I had no words with which to describe it.

It was an experience of Presence or, perhaps I should say, of *a* Presence. Though what was present was definitely not a thing but a person (not that Presence and person were really distinguishable), equally the presentness was not that of any particular person. Moreover, the Presence was spatially located. 'It' occupied a certain corner of the room, the one nearest the door, which, as I sat cross-legged on the sofa writing, was to my left. Objectively speaking, it was a strange experience, but though I recognized it, intellectually, as being strange, I never *felt* it to be so. There was nothing 'spooky' about the Presence, and when it was 'there', in its usual corner (not that it had any dimensions), I felt quite comfortable with it and at home. It always 'appeared' (not that I ever actually saw anything) when I was alone, perhaps when I had been alone for some time, and while I was writing. By now the end of the *Survey* was in sight, and I was working on the penultimate and antepenultimate sections of the last chapter, which dealt, respectively, with 'The Thought of Enlightenment' and 'The Ten Perfections'. As this whole chapter, and these two sections in particular, were devoted to the bodhisattva ideal, 'the perfectly ripened fruit of the whole vast tree of Buddhism',[229] as I then believed it to be, I could not forbear wondering, later on, if there had been a connection between my 'strange' experience and the lofty ideal about which I was writing. Might not the Presence have been that of a bodhisattva, or even of the Buddha? But this was only speculation *after* the event. What I experienced at the time was Presence, or *a* Presence. Not any particular person, good or bad, human or divine. Just personal-impersonal *Presence.*

The Presence appeared when I was *alone*, or rather, it did not appear when I was not alone. But I was not often alone, especially after Rashk, his outside business apparently concluded, started bethinking himself of the unfinished script of *Ajanta* and of the work we were supposed to be doing on it together. The time I was least alone, both before and after our getting down to serious work on the long-neglected script, was the evening, this being the time, usually, when Rashk's friends called on him and when we, though more rarely, went to see them. His friends were all men (at least I remember no women, though he appeared to be acquainted with some of the wives), and most of them belonged to, or were connected with, the film industry, whether as producers, directors, actors, scriptwriters, musicians, or artists. The friend of whom we saw most, and whom I got to know best, was tall, portly Jairaj, a South Indian in his early or middle forties who, Rashk told me, had played the hero in more than thirty Tamil 'mythological' films. What was of greater interest to me, he also happened to be a nephew (by marriage, I think) of Sarojini Naidu, the Nightingale of India,[230] on whose poetry, shortly after my arrival in India, I had written an article.[231] Like other members of Rashk's circle, he had a genuine interest in religion and philosophy, as his library attested, and we had more than one discussion on these subjects. Producers excepted, most of those who worked in the film industry were, I found, much less interested in their actual jobs than they were in doing other things. Rashk himself, I remembered, had told me, on my earlier visit to Bombay, that he wrote film scripts only because he could not afford to write poetry. Similarly, Achrekar, who was Raj Kapoor's art director (and designer of the *Maha Bodhi* journal's new cover) would rather have been painting pictures, and Abbas, a more successful scriptwriter than Rashk, would have preferred to be adding another popular novel to his œuvre.

Besides the people I met of an evening, there were those I saw in the course of my forays into town, both with and without Rashk. As my work on the *Survey* drew to a close (I must have finished it early in the New Year) these forays became not only more frequent but longer and more of the nature of excursions. On four or five of these I gave lectures, and on one of them presided over the World Religions Day meeting organized by the Bahá'í community. This last-named event, which went off even better than the organizers had dared hope, was attended by representatives of an astonishing variety of religions, sects, and cults. Bombay was not just a cosmopolitan city, not just a whole world in itself; it was a world within which there was a multitude of sub-worlds, religious, cultural, linguistic, and so on, most of which overlapped only to a limited extent. During the months of December and January I became acquainted, or better acquainted, with at least three of these sub-worlds, one cultural (if the film industry sub-world could indeed be so categorized), one religious, and one socio-religious, as well as with the three outstanding personalities by which they were severally dominated. As there was no overlap between the three sub-worlds, and as in each of them I appeared in a different capacity and functioned in a different manner (though still as a Buddhist monk), during this period I was leading, in a sense, three different lives, or part-lives, and expending my energies in three different directions. Often all three lives, or part-lives, were lived on different days of the same week, even at different hours of the same day, so that in the interests of consecutive narration each 'life' is best dealt with separately from the other two. As Ruskin observes in *Praeterita*, his autobiography:

> Whether in the biography of a nation, or of a single person, it is alike impossible to trace it steadily through successive years. Some forces are failing while others strengthen, and most act irregularly, or else at uncorresponding periods of renewed enthusiasm after intervals of lassitude. For all clearness of exposition, it is necessary to follow first one, then another, without confusing notices of what is happening in other directions.[232]

What is true of successive years may be equally true, sometimes, of the days and weeks of two successive months, even if in their case it might be a question not so much of forces failing and strengthening as of different forces being deployed at different times, according to circumstances.

The part I played within each of my Bombay sub-worlds was to a great extent determined, at least initially, by my relationship with its leading personality. In the film industry – certainly in the important part of it that was R. K. Films – the leading personality was Raj Kapoor. On my 1952 visit to the city, when he had shared with me his ideas for a film with a Buddhist theme to be called *Ajanta*, we must have met a dozen or more times. Miss Nargis, his principal leading lady, was usually by his side. This time we met only twice or thrice, and he was alone, in the sense that Nargis was not there. As before, we met at The Cottage, Raj Kapoor's private quarters at R. K. Studios, Chembur. At our first meeting, after I had gone onto the set and seen some shooting, discussion naturally soon turned to *Ajanta*. Though we discussed it at some length, indeed, until quite late in the night, I formed the impression that his mind was really on other things. This impression was not unconnected with the fact that in the course of the evening he had brought out from an inner drawer, with the air of a card-player revealing a winning hand, a sheaf of black-and-white photographs of his latest 'discovery' – an attractive Anglo-Indian girl whom he had met, quite by accident, in Delhi. She had the makings of a fine actress, he assured me, his eyes gleaming, and he had promised her a leading role in one of his films. On our way back to Khar Rashk enlightened me as to the background of the story. Relations between Raj Kapoor and Nargis were strained, and he was looking for a new principal leading lady. Whether she was to be given the leading female role in *Ajanta* he did not know. Personally, he did not think Nargis could be so easily replaced. But, with or without Nargis, Raj Kapoor would, he was confident, make the film. Achrekar had already designed costumes for it and created, in his room at R. K. Studios, a plaster and clay model of the main set. Rashk was also confident that the film would be a financial success and that Raj Kapoor would be happy to give me, out of the proceeds, the 20,000 rupees that would be required for the monastery I wanted to build in Kalimpong. Perhaps I would call the monastery the Ajanta Vihara!

The next time Raj Kapoor and I met at The Cottage he was in a very different mood, in fact in a very different mental state altogether. Nor was he alone. Not that it was Nargis who was with him. On this occasion he had for companion the bottle of Black Label on which it was his habit, apparently, to rely for moral support at times of crisis or when he was feeling particularly sorry for himself. The plain truth was that he was drunk, though not so drunk that we were not able to have a long, if rather inconsequential, discussion which he insisted on tape-recording for the benefit of posterity. The discussion was punctuated by maudlin outbursts in which he lamented the loss of his 'discovery' and upbraided her for her treachery, deceitfulness, and ingratitude. She had ruined his life, he declared, to heart-rending sobs. She had destroyed him. Once again it was Rashk who enlightened me as to the background of the story. The Anglo-Indian girl had come to Bombay (R. K. Studios had flown her there). Her screen tests had proved highly satisfactory, and Raj Kapoor had become more convinced of her talent, and more infatuated with her, every day. But last week there had come a message. Would he meet her in town at a certain fashionable restaurant? On entering the place he found, to his astonishment, that his 'discovery' was not alone. She was with a good-looking young man. He was still more astonished when she introduced the young man as her fiancé. They were going to be married quite soon, she said. 'But what about your film career?' a shocked Raj Kapoor had demanded, clutching at a straw. 'Oh my fiancé is a multi-millionaire,' she replied. 'He's ready to make as many films for me as I want.'

The leading personality in the Society of Servants of God was Dr Dinshah Mehta. This was the same mysterious Dr Mehta whom the short, middle-aged woman who had claimed my exclusive attention after the second Aryasangha lecture had been so anxious I should meet. True to her word, she had come to the Ananda Vihara a few days later and taken me to her Marine Drive flat for tea. There I learned that Dinoo Dubash, as she was called, was a Parsee by birth but a Buddhist at heart, that she was a Montessori teacher, having trained with Mme Montessori herself in Italy in the 1930s, that she was an insomniac, that the rest of the flat was occupied by her Montessori school, and that she wanted to give a thousand rupees for the Buddha Jayanti. In between she scolded the cook, gave me (or tried to give me) a sumptuous tea, and showed me her Buddhist books, many of them heavily underlined, as well as her watercolour paintings, among which there was a series of striking 'portraits' of the blue-eyed, golden-haired figure who had appeared to her in meditation and whom she believed to be the Buddha Maitreya. I also learned that Dr Mehta was by profession a naturopath, in fact a well-known one, that my hostess had once been a patient of his, and that he had founded the Society of Servants of God three years earlier. Originally it had been called the Society of Servants, Miss Dubash confided, not without a smile of good-natured amusement, but people thought it was a domestic servants' agency and kept telephoning about cooks and bearers, and Dr Mehta had been forced to change it. She herself was not a member of the Society (at least, not a member of the inner circle!), nor did she believe in all its teachings, or accept everything Dr Mehta said, even though it was supposed to come from God, but she liked the Society's emphasis on meditation and for that reason sometimes attended its meetings.

Despite her excitedness and volubility – her skittishness, even – Dinoo Dubash was, I could see, an essentially serious-minded person, with a genuine devotion to the spiritual life. She was like a little babbling brook, whose excess of foam, as it skips and dances down from the hills, conceals the depth and translucency of its water. I was therefore all the more disposed to treat seriously her reiterated wish that I should meet Dr Mehta and see what I thought of the Society of Servants of God, without allowing myself to be inhibited by the fact that its members were dedicated to the service of a being in whose existence good Buddhists did not believe. As it happened, I had already been approached by a stout, shifty-eyed young representative of the Society and invited to address the Servants of God on 'Love and Devotion in Buddhism', and one morning three weeks after taking tea with Dinoo Dubash accordingly found myself being escorted, by the same shifty-eyed young man, from Khar to the flat on Malabar Hill that was the Society's headquarters.

The flat was located on the ground floor of Mayfair, a block of luxury apartments not far from the Hanging Gardens. From the gloomy hallway there was a dark, narrow passage between what seemed to be wooden cubicles, and at the end of this passage a sunny room furnished, Indian style, with white-covered mattresses and bolsters. Opposite the door, his back against the far wall, sat a grizzled-haired, grossly corpulent figure in close-fitting muslin tunic and white cotton jodhpurs. On the floor beside him rested a telephone set, while in front of him a portable electric fan, swivelling energetically from side to side, sent a swathe of cold air in his direction. He welcomed me cordially, if with a certain solemnity, a smile of satisfaction on his grey, flabby features, after which the two of us got down to a serious discussion, mainly about meditation, that lasted for the remainder of the morning and well into the afternoon. Several members of the Society were present, as was Miss Dubash, but apart from the last-named, whose tongue could not be easily restrained, they were content to lean back against their bolsters and listen. After lunch, eaten from *thalis* in the same room and solemnly blessed before being served, Dr Mehta (for indeed it was he) read to me from what he called the Scripts. The Scripts, I gathered, were the written records of the 'guidance' he had received, over the last few years, when in a state of deep meditation. They were of various lengths, though none of them comprised more than a couple of thousand words. Some were in verse, some in prose. The verse Scripts, which were the shortest, reminded me, in their general tone and tenor, of the earlier, shorter suras of the Koran. But long or short, in verse or in prose, and regardless of their actual subject-matter, whether hortatory or consolatory, practical or deeply metaphysical, all the Scripts from which Dr Mehta read that afternoon were couched in the first person singular. Who, then, was the speaker? According to the Society, and indeed the Scripts themselves, it was none other than God. It was God who, through the Servant of Servants, Dr Mehta, directed the affairs of the Society and the lives of its members. The Scripts were thus a species of divine revelation, similar in content, if not in form, to the revelations vouchsafed by the prophets and founders of religions in the past, from Zoroaster to Mohammed.

That the members of the Society (at least the members of what Dinoo Dubash had called the inner circle) believed its affairs, as well as their own lives, to be personally guided by the Almighty meant that their involvement with it had a special significance for them. It also meant that the involvement had a certain depth of seriousness. Something of that seriousness was apparent in the faces of the thirty or more people who, later on in the afternoon, squeezed into the room to hear me speak on 'Love and Devotion in Buddhism'. I was glad to have the opportunity of speaking on this subject. Indeed, it may have been of my own selection. Even in a city like Bombay, supposedly the cultural as well as the commercial capital of India, the few who knew anything at all about Buddhism usually thought of it as a sturdy rationalism, or sterile agnosticism, in which there was no place for devotion, and I wanted to disabuse the Servants of God, at least, of any such idea, and in this way remove whatever prejudice they might have had against Buddhism. Love was of three kinds, depending on whether it was directed towards a person or an object superior, or equal, or inferior to ourselves. The first kind of love was called *śraddhā*, the second *maitrī*, the third *karuṇā*, and on each in turn I spoke at some length, giving examples from the Pāli scriptures and explaining how it was to be developed. In Buddhism the principal object of *śraddhā* or devotion was the Buddha, the Enlightened human teacher, the embodiment of Reality, just as in the theistic religions it was the Creator. I also emphasized that *śraddhā* was to be balanced by *prajñā* or wisdom, even though the predominantly emotional factors of bliss, joy, and equanimity played an important part in spiritual life right up to the attainment of Nirvāṇa. Nirvāṇa itself was both absolute wisdom and infinite compassion. Since the Buddha had no superior, and no equal, in relation to ordinary humanity it was compassion that was the most prominent aspect of Enlightenment. Compassion was characteristic of Buddhism – perhaps its most important teaching. It was because of the compassion he felt that the Buddha spent his life showing the Path to others. His actions had all been the spontaneous overflow of his love for sentient beings.

My talk was well received and followed by a discussion, initiated by Dr Mehta, on meditation as a source of nutrition. This enabled me to describe the four kinds of nutriment recognized in Buddhism,[233] as well as to relate how the Buddha, in the course of his early struggles for Enlightenment, had refused to allow the *devas* to provide him with celestial nourishment.[234] These particulars Dr Mehta seemed to find especially interesting. The Servant of Servants indeed had followed my talk with close attention, and a week or two later, when I attended a lecture on 'The Economic Structure of Islam' (in Urdu, which I could not follow very well), he asked me to give another talk and engaged me in further discussion about meditation. This second talk, which I gave a few days later, was on 'The Buddha and the Spiritual Life in Buddhism'. I spoke for nearly two hours, and whether on account of the concentrated, meditative atmosphere of the meeting, or because I was upheld by the sustaining power of the Buddhas and bodhisattvas, I gave what I afterwards thought was one of the best talks I had ever given, and probably the profoundest. At any rate, the audience was sufficiently impressed, and it was evident that some of its members, at least, were beginning to realize that there was more to Buddhism than they had imagined. In the weeks that followed I paid several more visits to Mayfair and had further discussions with Dr Mehta about meditation, as well as about Buddhism. He also read to me from the Scripts, of which there were about 2,000. At least this was the figure given by the youngish woman in a white sari who appeared to be Dr Mehta's chief disciple and who, I subsequently learned, ran the quality control business that was the Society's principal source of income. Sundri Vaswani, as her name was, also told me that a large proportion of the Scripts had been received in the first year or so of the Society's existence, when Dr Mehta had 'sat for guidance' several times a day. Nowadays he sat for it only occasionally, she said – a little regretfully, I thought. None the less, before leaving Bombay perhaps I would have an opportunity of being present when he sat and seeing him receive guidance in meditation.

It so happened that I did have an opportunity. There was no meeting at Mayfair that evening, and only the members of the inner circle were present in the room. Besides Dr Mehta himself, this consisted of Sundri Vaswani and her brother Hira (the shifty-eyed young man); Durgadas Birla, a minor member of the famous business family, and his bespectacled wife; and Father Mascarhenas, an elderly, disaffected Goanese Catholic priest who was fond of denouncing, at least within the walls of Mayfair, the iniquities of what he termed 'the Roman racket'. Proceedings began with a kind of group meditation. Dr Mehta then went into what appeared to be a trance state, turning up his eyes until only the whites were visible. After a while he closed them, his right hand was seized with a violent trembling, and snatching up a pen he began scribbling furiously on the top sheet of the stack of paper that had been kept in readiness before him. I was sitting beside him, on the same mattress, and observed that his eyes remained closed during the whole time he was writing and that he could not see what he was doing. Sheet after sheet he covered, Sundri snatching away each one as it was finished and making sure the sheet underneath was so positioned that his pen did not run off the paper. When seven or eight sheets had been covered he suddenly stopped, and his head slumped forward on to his chest. God had again spoken and given his guidance. Another Script had come into existence. When the light was switched on, I saw that the Servant of Servants' face was greyer than ever, and that he was bathed in perspiration.[235]

The socio-religious sub-world of the Scheduled Castes Federation was much bigger than the religious sub-world of the Society of Servants of God. I had met Dr B. R. Ambedkar, the leading personality of the Federation, in 1952, after having been in correspondence with him two years earlier. On that occasion we had met at Rajgir, his residence in Dadar, in the heart of industrial Bombay, and I had asked him, probably with his recent article 'The Buddha and the Future of His Religion' in mind, whether he thought Buddhism had a future in India.[236] His reply was an indirect one. *He* had no future in India, he declared bitterly (he was at that time in the political wilderness), as if his own future in India and that of Buddhism were inextricably interconnected. But his attitude, or at least his mood, had since changed. Having realized, after a lifetime of unsuccessful campaigning, that the caste Hindus were not going to give up their traditional inhuman treatment of the Untouchables, as the Scheduled Castes and Depressed Class people were popularly known, he had come to the conclusion that he and his followers would have to change their religion. They would have to become Buddhists, Buddhism being a religion that was of Indian origin, that was rational, and that treated men (and women) according to their worth, not their birth, i.e. not according to their (hereditary) caste. Within the last few months he had twice visited Buddhist Burma, and only days before our second meeting, which took place on 25 December, he had installed an image of the Buddha in the temple that had been built by members of the Scheduled Castes community at Dehu Road, near Poona.

We met not in Dadar but in the Fort area of Bombay, in Dr Ambedkar's office on the top floor of Buddha Bhavan, one of the buildings of the Siddharth College of Arts and Science.[237] In appearance he was greatly altered. At the time of our first meeting his demeanour had been belligerent, and his expression grim and lowering, and though inclining to corpulence he had seemed in good health. Now, three years later, he was quieter and more subdued, and so crippled by arthritis that, as he explained when apologizing for receiving me sitting down, he could stand only with difficulty. But though quieter and more subdued he had, as it seemed, made up his mind that he and his followers should become Buddhists, and was even now drawing up plans for the revival of Buddhism in India. These plans he explained to me at some length, adding, with evident emotion, that he intended to devote the rest of his life to Buddhism. Mrs Ambedkar, who stood beside him as he sat behind his desk, appeared to support his plans, and from time to time intervened to reinforce a point he had made, especially when his energy flagged. For my part I explained, in response to Dr Ambedkar's enquiries, that formal conversion to Buddhism consisted in 'going for Refuge' to the Three Jewels, i.e. the Buddha, the Dharma, and the Sangha, and in undertaking to observe the five basic principles of ethical behaviour. One could 'take' the Refuges and Precepts from any monk or other senior Buddhist. All the same, he and his followers would be well advised to take them from someone like U Chandramani of Kusinara, probably the seniormost monk in India, rather than from a junior monk like myself (Ambedkar had asked me if I would be willing to perform the conversion ceremony for them), as the Buddhist world would probably then take their conversion to Buddhism more seriously.[238] Before we parted the Scheduled Castes leader asked me to write to him recapitulating what I had said about conversion. He also asked me to explain to his followers what conversion to Buddhism really meant. On my acceding to both these requests, he promised to see that a talk was organized for me by his lieutenants in the city.

Dr Ambedkar was as good as his word, with the result that on New Year's Day I addressed a gathering of some 3,000 people on 'What it Means to Become a Buddhist'. It was not the first time I had spoken to members of the Scheduled Castes community on this burning topic, as it was fast becoming for all of them. Only days before my meeting with Dr Ambedkar I had addressed the residents of the so-called Harijan Colony at Khar, and had afterwards explained to its elders the implications of conversion to Buddhism. Compared with the meeting now organized for me by Dr Ambedkar's local henchmen this had been a very small affair, and it was clear that there would be no conversion to Buddhism, at least not on a mass scale, unless the Scheduled Castes leader himself took the first step. The meeting took place at Worli, on a piece of waste ground overlooked by a row of *chawls* or tenement blocks, and since many of Ambedkar's followers were factory workers who did not get home much before eight o'clock it did not begin until quite late. By that time there was a cold wind blowing, so that when I at last rose to speak I was shivering in my thin cotton robes. With the President of the Bombay branch of the Scheduled Castes Federation of Bombay giving a running translation into Marathi, I addressed the gathering for more than an hour, speaking as simply as I could and confining myself to fundamentals. Becoming a Buddhist meant going for Refuge to the Buddha, the Dharma, and the Sangha, I explained, just as I had to Dr Ambedkar, as well as undertaking to observe the Five Precepts, but one could not truly go for Refuge unless one understood what it was to which one went for Refuge. The greater part of my talk was therefore devoted to explaining that the Buddha was a human being who had gained Enlightenment by his personal efforts, not an *avatar* of the god Vishnu; that the Dharma or teaching of the Buddha was the principial way to Enlightenment, especially as represented by the three 'trainings' of morality, meditation, and wisdom, and by the Noble Eightfold Path; and that the sangha was the spiritual community of the Buddha's disciples – past and present, monk and lay.

In speaking about the Dharma Refuge I was at pains to emphasize that in Buddhism the word '*dharma*' possessed a meaning quite different from that which it bore in Hinduism. In the latter it meant one's duty as determined by the (hereditary) caste to which one belonged. If one had been born as a Brahmin, one's duty was to study the Vedas and receive offerings; if as a Shudra, to serve the members of the three higher castes. If one had been born as an untouchable then, of course, one's duty was to remove night soil and animal carcasses and to avoid polluting caste Hindus by coming into contact with them. According to Hinduism one could no more change one's *dharma* than one could change one's caste. It would be a sin even to try to change it. In Buddhism, however, the Dharma, in the sense of the way to Enlightenment, was the same for all human beings, regardless of caste, which in any case was not recognized by Buddhism. Becoming a Buddhist and practising the Dharma meant, among other things, breaking free from the caste system, and from untouchability, and following a path of ethical and spiritual development that was for the benefit of oneself and others.

Sitting there on the bare ground, my poorly clad and mostly illiterate audience followed my talk with the closest attention and in a silence that was broken only by the applause that greeted any remark of which they particularly approved. Not surprisingly, the greatest applause was reserved for my comments on caste and untouchability. From the warmth with which the organizers congratulated me on my talk after the meeting, I left Worli that night with the impression that provided Dr Ambedkar lived long enough Buddhism did have a future in India.[239]

20

NATURE CURE CLINIC

Dr Mehta's Nature Cure Clinic and Sanatorium occupied a spacious compound in a tree-shaded avenue immediately behind Poona railway station. It consisted of two buildings, one much larger than the other. The larger of the buildings was a tiled, barn-like structure consisting of a central hall surrounded by eight or ten suites of small rooms, hall and rooms alike being paved with black flagstones. The smaller building, which must once have been servants' quarters, was situated in a corner of the compound, on the same side as the front entrance of the larger building. It occupied an important place in the history of India, or at least in the history of the Independence movement, Mahatma Gandhi having stayed there a number of times in the forties, with his entourage, and taken treatment from Dr Mehta, who was his personal naturopathic physician and the manager of two of his three 21-day fasts. The smaller building was therefore called Bapu Cottage in his memory, Bapu or 'Father' being the name by which the Mahatma was known to his more intimate associates. The room where he had lived and worked was kept much as it had been in his day, and his bed, writing table, and spinning wheel could still be seen. Flush with the top of the rear wall of the compound was the stone platform from which he was wont to address the people who had gathered in the adjacent railway compound for his evening prayer meeting.

On my arrival at the Clinic, one day towards the end of January, I could not help noticing that the larger of the two buildings had a shabby, neglected look, and that the paths surrounding the garden between it and the rear wall were overgrown with weeds. Though the occasional patient still convalesced there, the Clinic had been inoperative for two or three years, Dr Mehta himself having not so much as visited the place during that period, despite the fact that his wife and his two small children were living at Bapu Cottage. But recently things had changed. God had spoken. Guidance had come to the effect that a branch of the Society of Servants of God should be established in Poona, at the Nature Cure Clinic, that the Union Government Minister of Planning, Sri Gulzarilal Nanda (a former patient of Dr Mehta's), should be invited to address the inaugural meeting, which was to be on a grand scale, and that Bhikshu Sangharakshita should be invited to preside. Even though I did not, indeed as a Buddhist could not, believe that the guidance received by Dr Mehta in meditation came from God (though I was willing to concede it *might* come from a source higher than his own conscious mind), the knowledge that I was the object of what the Servants of God regarded as nothing less than the personal attention of the Almighty gave me a peculiar sensation, the more especially as I also knew that the question of whether or not I would accept an invitation that had actually come for me 'in guidance' was one of intense interest and concern to Sundri and the other members of the inner circle. In the end, having consulted with Dinoo Dubash (who was of the opinion that the Society could do with a good dose of Buddhism), I decided to accept.[240] My decision was in no way determined by the fact that the invitation might have come from a higher source. The reason for my acceptance was that I was glad of an opportunity to visit Poona and, possibly, make contact with the Buddhists there, of whom I had heard there was a considerable number. Thus a day towards the end of January saw me arriving in Poona by Deccan Queen, being met at the station by Miss Dubash, and by her being conducted to the Nature Cure Clinic in Tadiwalla Road. Dr Mehta was already there, having arrived a few days earlier, together with members of the inner circle, and I was soon accommodated in a suite of rooms across the hall from his own.

The inaugural meeting of the Society's Poona branch was indeed on a grand scale, at least so far as the preparations were concerned. An enormous square stage, replete with white mattresses and bolsters, had been erected in the space – once a garden – between the main building and the rear compound wall. This was surmounted by a canopy, at the four corners of which hung curtains, so that from a distance the structure had the appearance of a four-poster bed of Brobdingnagian proportions. On the ground in front of the stage were row upon row of white mattresses. Strings of fairy lights hung between the buildings, and from branch to branch of the giant flame-of-the-forest trees. Yet despite the elaborate preparations the meeting was poorly attended. It must have been a long time since Gulzarilal Nanda, a wiry, Gandhi-capped figure with a black walrus moustache and a surprisingly bass voice, had addressed so small an audience. Even I usually had a bigger one. But though there could not have been more than seventy people down there in front of us on the white mattresses, the Union Minister for Planning made a cheerful speech, in which he eulogized Dr Mehta and the Society in very general terms, while I, for my part, spoke of the need for a sense of direction in life. People might talk about ideals, I declared, but a man could know what his ideal was only when he knew himself. Human beings lived on two levels, the animal and the rational, between which they oscillated. But beyond the rational mind there was the level of the superconscious, and beyond that the transcendental or divine. The aim and object of human life was to live at those higher levels, which were attainable through the practice of concentration and meditation. Those attending the present inaugural meeting would, I hoped, feel that they had been shown the way to a higher life.

In the evening there was a concert, the principal performer being a professional singer of devotional songs who, accompanied by her mother, had travelled from Ahmedabad for the occasion. Madhuribehn, as she was called, had a dark, pock-marked face and a pair of brilliant black eyes, and must have been in her middle or late thirties. In her green silk sari, and with flowers in her sleek black hair, she presented a distinctly queenly appearance as she sat facing the audience that had gathered in the flagstoned hall beneath the gently whirring ceiling fans. Her face, especially when she was singing, wore a kind of triumphant smile, such as one saw on the faces of certain gods and goddesses in ancient Hindu temples. She sang accompanying herself with a sort of *sistrum*,[241] as well as on a stringed instrument of a type with which I was unfamiliar but which was not a sitar, and from the first notes that the strong, rich voice plucked so confidently out of the air it was evident that Madhuribehn was a perfect mistress of her art. Song after devotional song she sang, with a vitality, and an intensity of expression, that raised

Dr Mehta and Sri Gulzarilal Nanda

the emotional temperature of the crowded hall by several degrees and no doubt brought some of her auditors nearer to a higher level of consciousness than I had been able to bring them with my presidential address. Though I had been privileged to hear some fine renderings of devotional songs, by singers both professional and non-professional, the present performance was of an entirely different order, and I could well understand why the saints and sages of the Hindu *bhakti* tradition should have come to regard sacred music as constituting an independent path to the realization of the divine.[242]

The Poona branch of the Society of Servants of God having been duly inaugurated, and the stage dismantled and taken away, the Nature Cure Clinic was a very quiet place. Besides Dr Mehta, Sundri, and Hira, the only persons left in the main building were me and Parvati, a middle-aged woman with permed white hair, dark glasses, and an exaggeratedly English accent who was, it seemed, still under Dr Mehta's care and semi-convalescent. Dr Mehta was staying on in

Poona because he had received guidance to this effect in meditation, and I was staying on because Dr Mehta had invited me to do so, though whether the invitation came from him or from God *through* him was unclear. Whichever may have been the case, I was glad to be there. Poona was very pleasant in winter. It was cooler than Bombay, and much less humid, and despite the blue skies and brilliant sunshine the heat was not oppressive. In subsequent years Poona was to become one of my favourite places in India, and one of the principal centres of my activities. On this first visit, however, I saw nothing of the city *proper* (as my Indian friends would have expressed it), being content to enjoy the peace and quiet of the Nature Cure Clinic, a peace and quiet broken only by the sound of the occasional train and the high-pitched, incessant note of the brain-fever bird, as well as to join the rest of our little community in the daily routine that had soon been established. There was a group meditation in Dr Mehta's room early in the morning, while it was still dark, followed by a second one after breakfast and a third in the evening. In between I read, talked with Dr Mehta, and took a constitutional stroll along the weed-grown paths that bordered what had once been the garden. Meals were taken out of doors, in the courtyard of Bapu Cottage, at a table set beneath one of the giant flame-of-the-forest trees. Thus the days and weeks passed. It was an idyllic existence, such as would not have been possible in strife-torn Bombay, which had been the scene, shortly before my departure, of serious disturbances in connection with the demand, by the Marathi-speaking section of the population, for a separate Maharashtra state with Bombay as its capital.[243] Rashk and I had happened to be in town at the time of the worst of these disturbances, when the police opened fire on a crowd of demonstrators at Flora Fountain, in the heart of the Fort area, killing six people and injuring many others.

In a letter to Dinoo, written in the fourth or fifth week of my stay at the Nature Cure Clinic, I gave my new friend a glimpse of what life was like there at the time. Though she was, I knew, eager to know how I was getting on at the place, it was not possible for me to satisfy her curiosity in a letter, or even in many letters. Having apologized for not writing earlier, and expressed the hope that we might meet in Bombay before she left for her pilgrimage to Ceylon and Japan, I therefore proceeded to give her more news of common friends than of myself.

> Dr is keeping quite well [I wrote]. He has been reading several extracts from Buddhist books, and repeatedly refers to the Buddha's life and teachings. He is even thinking of making a small Buddhist shrine here. Gulbehn is quite cheerful, and of course as active as usual. She and I have become well acquainted, and she too likes to hear about Buddhism. We chant the Buddhist prayers or verses from the *Dhammapada* together every day before meditation. You would like it! Mrs Rasma Mistri is coming every day. She too is very Buddhist-minded. Sundri and Hira are as busy as ever, and bear the main brunt of the work. Probably you have heard that the Society will be publishing a journal called 'Living Silence', and that Hira will be the publisher, Sundri editor, and myself associate editor. Parvati has not been keeping well and has been confined to her bed for several days. On the whole the atmosphere here is very good, with everybody friendly and cheerful.[244]

One of the reasons Dr Mehta was keeping quite well was, probably, that he had taken to joining me on my constitutional stroll round the garden, instead of remaining indoors on his *gaddi* all day as was his custom in Bombay.[245] At the time of my arrival at the Clinic Gulbehn, his wife, had not been at all cheerful. The fact that her long-absent husband had chosen to stay in the main building with his disciples, rather than at Bapu Cottage with her and the children, had hurt her deeply, and initially she had refused to have anything to do with the inauguration of the Society's Poona branch. Friends had interposed, however, and eventually she was persuaded to attend the evening concert. By the time I wrote to Dinoo she had more or less adjusted to the situation and, as mentioned in my letter, she and I had become well acquainted. At first, thinking I was a disciple, she had been a little wary of me, but on learning that this was not the case, and that I no more believed that the Scripts came from God than she did herself, her attitude had changed. Like Dr Mehta she was a Parsee, and like him she wore *khadi*, the coarse cotton handloom cloth that was the mark of the Gandhian true believer and which took, in her case, the form of a baggy, Gujarati-style sari that was really much too thick and heavy for such warm weather. Unlike her husband, however, Gulbehn was a follower of the way of Martha, rather than of the way of Mary,[246] being no less convinced of the importance of good works than he was of the value of meditation. She indeed was a kind, open-hearted woman, with a quite exceptional willingness to be of service to others.

Though Gulbehn attended the group meditations she always left straight afterwards, so that my principal contact with her was at mealtimes. These were pleasant, sociable occasions, over which Dr Mehta presided in patriarchal fashion, with his wife at his elbow and his servants in attendance. In the days when the Nature Cure Clinic and Sanatorium was a thriving institution, and he one of Poona's (and Bombay's) best-known physicians, he and Gulbehn had, it seemed, kept open house, and even now old friends and ex-patients would drop in at meal times and be invited to join us at the big round table. Sometimes Dr Mehta afterwards told me their histories. Many of them, like the Buddhist-minded Mrs Rasma Mistri mentioned in my letter to Dinoo, were Parsees, and many, I noticed, were more than a little perplexed by their host's transition from naturopath to divinely-guided guru and unsure how to relate to him in his new capacity. One who was not at all perplexed was Mr Bo, as everybody called him, a lean, hatchet-faced, jovial Italian who had been interned at Dehra Dun with Lama Govinda and who, after the War, had settled in Poona and made a living for himself as general handyman and amateur inventor. Mr Bo was not perplexed because he did not believe in God and could, therefore, cheerfully dismiss Dr Mehta's claims to divine guidance and continue to treat him as he always had done. He was in fact a militant atheist, an ardent socialist, and a sworn enemy of the Roman Catholic Church, with an inexhaustible fund of stories and jokes that were very much at the expense of popes, cardinals, bishops, priests, and the whole clerical fraternity. Some of his stories and jokes were extremely funny, and Mr Bo's comically fractured English and expressive gestures ensured that they lost nothing in the telling. Dr Mehta did not much relish these *jeux d'esprit*, though Gulbehn and I enjoyed them immensely, nor did he really like being treated as though he was still just the eminent naturopath and not, as he believed himself now to be, the recipient of God's guidance to the Society, India, and the world. Sometimes he tried to bring God into the conversation and assert his own new character, but with Gulbehn there to remind him of the past this was not always easy, especially when she produced, as she did on one occasion, photographs of the famous 'greek statue' posing performances he had given thirty years previously, when he was not only mad about body-building but a thoroughgoing agnostic. These trials the Servant of Servants bore with reasonable good humour, secure in the conviction that (as he used to tell me afterwards) a prophet had no honour in his own country, or at least in his own house,[247] and that this was proof positive of his being a prophet. Once he confided to me that he was sure the Buddha must have had difficulties with Yaśodharā, even though there was no mention of this in the Buddhist scriptures.

Our more serious discussions usually took place after the second meditation or when we were strolling round the garden later in the day. As Gulbehn was in the kitchen of Bapu Cottage, Sundri often away in Bombay on quality control business, and Hira out running errands in the bazaar, we were usually undisturbed. Though Dr Mehta did, no doubt, repeatedly refer to the Buddha and his teachings, more often than not in an attempt to discover parallels with his own experiences, our discussions covered a good deal of ground, from Nature Cure to the ethics of hunting (he confessed to having been a great *shikari* in his time), and from Indian politics to the Moral Re-Armament movement (he had known Dr Frank Buchman).[248] As a result of these discussions we became better acquainted, and I could not but acknowledge that while Dr Mehta's manner could be a trifle portentous there was a simple, human side to his character, and that whatever reservations I might have about the nature of the guidance he received he was, in fact, undoubtedly a man of broad sympathies, deep understanding, and great personal integrity. One day he told me the story of his conversion from agnosticism to a life of Godguidedness. Towards the end of what was to have been a fast to death he had heard a Voice. The Voice told him to terminate the fast, which he had undertaken because he was at the end of his tether intellectually, and terminate it on its fiftieth day. Many more such spiritual experiences followed, but on account of his agnostic convictions he was unable to accept them. The inner struggle had lasted seventeen years. In the end he had asked for a sign, a sign had been given him, and thereafter he had 'accepted' to follow the guidance vouchsafed him – by God, as he believed – when he was in a state of deep meditation. That was just over two years ago. Since then his whole life had gradually changed. He had founded the Society of Servants of God, and now all his activities were based on the guidance he received in meditation, as the activities of the Society also were.

Meditation, and the acceptance of the guidance received in meditation, indeed formed the principal themes of Dr Mehta's teaching. With much of what he said about meditation I was in complete agreement, especially as it was evident that he spoke more from personal experience than from books. Guidance was another matter. Though the actual content of the guidance received might be acceptable, it was acceptable, so far as I was concerned, only because it was in agreement with my own reason and experience and with the Buddha's teaching, *not* because it was said to come from God. And of course sometimes that content was unacceptable. Dr Mehta himself was inclined to see any refusal to accept guidance (that is, the guidance that came for one through him) as being simply a matter of the ego's resistance to divine grace. But as I pointed out, the fact that one did not follow the guidance that came through him did not necessarily mean that one's life was unguided. Take my own case. I was a Buddhist; I followed the guidance given by the Buddha in the Buddhist scriptures, and felt no need to look for guidance elsewhere. Rather grudgingly, Dr Mehta admitted that it was possible to be guided in this 'general' way, though he added that such guidance was much less reliable than that which came for one through a God-guided personality with which one was in actual contact. The *most* reliable kind of guidance was, of course, that which came to one directly from God, when one was in a state of deep meditation, which was the way his guidance came to him. But the vast majority of people were incapable of reaching such a state and their guidance had, therefore, to come to them indirectly. Those who were not God-guided had to submit themselves, unconditionally, to the guidance of those who were. This was one of the great laws of spiritual life.

The upshot of this exchange (and others like it) was that during the second half, especially, of my stay at the Nature Cure Clinic I made a special effort to deepen my meditation. Though I had been meditating for a number of years, my achievements in this field were far from commensurate with my aspirations. There were experiences of the bliss and peace of the lower *dhyānas*; there were visions, usually of the Buddha or Avalokiteśvara; there were flashes of insight, not always in connection with the meditation itself: and that was about all. What I now had to do, I felt, was to achieve a level of meditative experience which would enable me to receive whatever might be the Buddhist equivalent of Dr Mehta's 'guidance', for much as I rejected the possibility of guidance by God (a being in whose existence I did not believe) I was well aware that for real spiritual progress to take place the ego, or 'defiled mind-consciousness' (as the Yogācāra termed it) needed to open itself to the influence of what I was later to call 'the transcendental outpourings of the Absolute'.[249] Just how that deeper – or higher – level was to be achieved was not clear, but I trusted that if I was able to stay long enough in the lower *dhyānas* the inherent momentum of those states, together with my intense desire to be truly guided, would be sufficient to carry me further. Conditions were favourable. The Nature Cure Clinic was quiet and peaceful, I was meditating three times a day with a small group of spiritually-minded people, at least one of whom appeared to have an extensive acquaintance with 'meditative states', and I had no worries about my livelihood. In order to be able to review my daily and weekly progress (or otherwise) I started keeping a meditation diary. I had kept one once before, during my wandering days, but after two years it was so bulky that I discontinued it and eventually burned it. The present diary, which I kept from the morning of 1 February to the evening of 7 March, was a much less weighty affair. The entries were no more than rough notes, meant for my own eyes, but even so, like dried flowers long pressed within the pages of a book, they had the power to evoke in after years a sense of the experiences of which they were mementoes.

Though progress during those five weeks was by no means uniform (there were occasions when my concentration was poor), overall I succeeded in achieving higher states of consciousness than usual and staying in them longer. Often I experienced what I described in my diary as '*positive peace*', by which I meant a peace that was not merely the absence of conflict but which had a definite nature of its own, cool, refreshing, and vibrant. Sometimes this peace came percolating into my consciousness from a level even higher than the one I had attained, like water trickling down through the soil. At other times it was felt in the body. On the evening of 7 February, for example, as my diary records:

> Concentrated quite easily. Neither quite in nor quite out of ordinary mind. Experience of *positive peace* in crown of head. This descended and spread throughout whole body. Experience of ascending and descending at same time. All kinds of movements and explosions of energy in the body, though not exactly in the physical body. As though some healing, at the same time destructive, force, was pulling and stretching and kneading the mind.

Dr Mehta explained, when I told him about these experiences, that there was a conflict between grace descending through the topmost chakra and effort ascending through the lower chakras, the point of meeting being at the third or navel chakra. It may have seemed so, but nevertheless I did not find the explanation entirely satisfactory, especially as I tended, in any case, to be wary of employing the language of chakras and *kuṇḍalinī*. To me such language, together with its underlying philosophy, smacked not so much of Buddhism as of Hinduism. Be that as it may, besides positive peace I also experienced feelings of intense love and devotion towards the Buddha (especially in the form of Amitābha) and Avalokiteśvara, which was not often the case with me. Sometimes these feelings were accompanied by the corresponding visionary experiences, but more often there would be an awareness of the transcendental 'person' in question without my being conscious of any particular form. On several occasions this awareness was so strong that I was able to put questions and receive answers. Not that I heard any words, whether my own or the Buddha's. I pronounced the words of my questions sub-vocally, and those of the Buddha's answers were imprinted directly on my consciousness without being pronounced at all. The first such experience occurred on the morning of 11 February, the diary entry for which reads:

> Concentrated. Feeling of total dissociation between past and present life. Doubt. Awareness of answer: 'Whatever leads to etc ... is My Dharma'. Decided to ask more questions, as follows:
>
> Q. *What should be my attitude towards surroundings after returning to K.?*
> A. Absolute detachment. This detachment is positive. Must be detached even from the Buddha. Detachment as taught by the Buddha transcends both attachment and detachment in the ordinary sense.
>
> Q. *How behave towards people?*
> A. Buddha first and everyone else second. – Awareness of shortcomings in this respect.

> Q. *What about acquiring land etc.?*
> A. This will be settled after your return. You must be ready to be anywhere and nowhere.
>
> Awareness of the Buddha's presence, though rather faintly (*sic*). Reflected whether these awarenesses were genuine guidance. Concluded that since they were in agreement with the Scriptures and were not unreasonable they could be accepted.

The diary entry for the evening of the following day, 12 February, records a similar experience:

> Good concentration. Sensation of positive peace descending. Asked, 'What should I do?' Awareness of answer came at once – 'Nothing'. Experience of emptiness and stillness. Self reduced to an absolute pinpoint. This state lasted for some time. Awareness: 'Whatever works you may have to do later on, in the midst of them you will have to maintain this state of mind.'

Experiences on subsequent days included visions of 'flowers' made as though of flame, and of jewels of intense light, sensations as of a light trying to break through, as well as of vastness and emptiness, and an awareness of the importance and meaning of the *White Lotus Sūtra*. My predominant experience, however, especially during the second half of the month, was one of increasingly intense feelings of love and devotion towards the Buddha and Avalokiteśvara. On one occasion I felt in the region of the heart a love and peace so strong that I was unable to bear it and had to stop meditating for a while. There was also a sensation as of someone touching me on the heart, and an experience of my 'heart chakra' being suddenly opened. During this period the Bodhisattva of Compassion, Avalokiteśvara, featured no less prominently in my experience than did the Buddha, and it was not without significance that his name should be mentioned in my last diary entry, for the evening of 7 March, which ran:

> Fairly good concentration. Feeling of devotion. Awareness of universe as it appears in the eyes of A[valokiteśvara]. Again feeling of devotion. Consciousness of peace descending from a great height.

More often than not I discussed my experiences with Dr Mehta, and sometimes he told me about his own. One morning he had a vision of three monks meditating under the influence of the Buddha – which was probably indicative of his growing interest in Buddhism. But though we spent much of our time discussing meditation, and though meditation and the acceptance of the guidance received in meditation formed the principal themes of his teaching, the Servant of Servants' life had not changed so much since his conversion that he had forgotten the secular and humanist ideals of his unguided days. Whether owing to his Parsee family background or his Gandhian associations he still had an active social conscience. He continued, for instance, to be strongly opposed to the caste system, especially to its most abhorrent manifestation, the practice of untouchability. His opposition was not only theoretical but practical. As I had soon discovered, the servants at the Nature Cure Clinic, who had been with him and Gulbehn for decades, were Marathi-speaking members of the Scheduled Castes and, therefore, potential converts to Buddhism. Perhaps they would know whereabouts in Poona the Buddhists with whom I wanted to make contact lived. In the event they did not know, any more than did Mrs Mistri, or Mr Bo, or any of the other visitors I questioned on the subject, and I began to think that the 'considerable number' of Poona Buddhists of whom I had heard in Bombay had a purely mythical existence.

Dr Mehta was of the same opinion. At least, during all his years in Poona he had not come across a single Buddhist. He did, however, believe that conversion to Buddhism would be very much to the advantage of the Scheduled Castes people, and when I told him about my meeting with Dr Ambedkar he at once suggested I should write to the Scheduled Castes leader inviting him and Mrs Ambedkar to spend a few days at the Nature Cure Clinic and continue our discussions there. The place being a nursing home, whatever medical facilities he might require would be available. Whether because he could not spare the time, or because the institution's Gandhian associations did not appeal to him (he and Gandhi had been political opponents), Dr Ambedkar did not take up the invitation, and when we did meet, ten or more months later, it was in a different place, and under very different circumstances.

21

2,500 YEARS OF BUDDHISM

The Buddhist era has always been regarded as beginning with the *parinirvāṇa* or final passing away of the Buddha. According to the traditional Sinhalese reckoning, which is accepted by all Theravādin Buddhists but which modern scholarship has shown to be incorrect, the *parinirvāṇa* took place in the year 544 BCE. Thus the 1956 Vaiśākha full-moon day, which fell on 24 May, marked the completion of 2,500 years of Buddhism – the Vaiśākha full-moon day being the anniversary, according to late Sinhalese traditions, not only of the Buddha's attainment of Enlightenment but also of his birth and his *parinirvāṇa*. The year from the Vaiśākha full-moon day of 1956 to that of 1957 was accordingly celebrated as the year of the Buddha Jayanti by Buddhists all over the world, not excluding those whose own traditional chronologies differed from that of Ceylon but who, in the words of a Japanese scholar at the time, 'were glad to collaborate with Theravādin Buddhists in their 2,500th year ceremonies honouring the Buddha.'

India was not a Buddhist country, and its Buddhist population was tiny, consisting of perhaps a quarter of a million people scattered mainly along its northern borders. Moreover, India was a secular state. None the less, prime minister Nehru and his colleagues had decided that India should join the Buddhist countries of South-east Asia in celebrating the Jayanti and that the cultural, as distinct from the religious, celebrations should be sponsored by the Union government. Preparations had been set in train and a programme drawn up. On the eve of the Vaiśākha full-moon day Pandit Nehru would lay the foundation stone of a monument to the Buddha in New Delhi, thus inaugurating the nation's Buddha Jayanti celebrations, and the following day, 24 May, the President of the Republic, Dr Rajendra Prasad, would address a mass meeting. The occasion would be marked by special programmes on All-India Radio, by the publication of a volume entitled *2500 Years of Buddhism*, and by the issue of commemorative postage stamps. Foreign Buddhists visiting the Buddhist holy places would be able to travel on the railways for half the usual fare, and facilities at the holy places themselves would be improved. The main celebrations, however, would take place in the month of November, in the cooler weather, when an exhibition of Buddhist art would be held in New Delhi, as well as a meeting of UNESCO and an international symposium on 'Buddhism's Contribution to Arts, Letters, and Philosophy'. A documentary film on the life of the Buddha would also be released.

To a minority of orthodox caste Hindus the idea of the Government of India sponsoring the Buddha Jayanti celebrations even to a limited extent was anathema. One of their number, a certain Acharya Neminath of South India, went so far as to publish a pamphlet in which he accused the Government of violating the Constitution by spending public money on the celebration of Buddha Jayanti, called on them to 'keep themselves absolutely away from all religious functions', and incidentally admitted that it caused him 'heart burnings' to hear national leaders praising Buddhism as the best of religions. As usual, such people wanted to have it both ways. They wanted to be able to claim Buddhism as a branch of Hinduism; at the same time, they did not want Buddhism to be praised or patronized. Replying to the Government's orthodox Hindu critics, Dr S. Radhakrishnan, the Vice-President of India and Chairman of the Buddha Jayanti Celebrations Working Committee, pointed out that:

> When we call ourselves a secular State we do not mean by it that we are worshippers of comfort, security and worldly goods. We mean by it respect and appreciation of all faiths which have found a home in this country.[250]

Judging by the way in which preparations for the Jayanti were going on all over India the majority of Indians agreed with Dr Radhakrishnan. The state governments had drawn up programmes of their own, as had a number of public bodies. The Government of Bihar proposed to shower the Maha Bodhi Temple at Bodh Gaya with rose petals from a helicopter. More prosaically, the Government of Bombay planned to drop leaflets.

The Maha Bodhi Society's Buddha Jayanti celebrations were to take place mainly at its Calcutta headquarters and at its centres in Sarnath and Bodh Gaya, and unlike the government-sponsored celebrations they were to be of a predominantly religious character. The dozen or so other centres were expected to organize celebrations of their own, and Devapriya Valisinha, the Society's General Secretary, had toured the country visiting them and exhorting the *bhikkhus*-in-charge to rise to the occasion and enlist the support of the local people. He had not visited Kalimpong, which was off the beaten track, but on my returning there, towards the end of April, I found that a public meeting had been held in the Town Hall and a Buddha Jayanti Celebrations Committee set up with, as was usual on such occasions, Rani Chunni Dorji as Chairman, Gyan Jyoti as Treasurer, and Bhikshu Sangharakshita as General Secretary. I had been away six months. From Poona, after saying goodbye to Dr Mehta and the Nature Cure Clinic, I had gone to Bombay, and from Bombay I had made my way to Calcutta, though I did not leave the former city without spending a few days at Khar with Rashk. No doubt we discussed the script of *Ajanta*, and no doubt my friend gave me the latest news of Raj Kapoor, but my principal memory of those days relates to something of a very different order.

Before my departure for Poona I had given Rashk, at his request, the date, time, and place of my birth, and these details he had communicated to his personal astrologer, the thin, elderly Brahmin whom I had seen arriving at the flat one morning. The latter had drawn my horoscope and made certain calculations, and one afternoon, at Rashk's suggestion, he came to tell me what the stars had revealed. The first thing they had revealed was that I had broken my vow of *brahmacarya* or chastity. I had broken it on a certain date in February. When I told him categorically that I had done no such thing the old man became quite furious, declaring that the stars could not lie and that if he was proved wrong he would throw his books in the Ganges. I could only conclude that, supposing the stars *could* reveal the state of one's *brahmacarya* and that the Brahmin's calculations *were* correct, I must have got my birth hour wrong, which was in fact more than likely. The stars had revealed not only my immediate past but also my remote future. I would have many disciples, the Brahmin assured me, but when I was fifty (or it may have been sixty) I would give up being a monk and after that I would have more disciples than ever.

These revelations gave me food for thought as the train sped towards Calcutta. In the first place my friend's astrologer was a Brahmin, and orthodox Brahmin householders were notoriously hostile to non-Brahmin ascetics, especially if the latter happened to belong, as I did, to one of the great non-Vedic traditions. What better way could there be of undermining people's faith in such ascetics than by casting doubts on the purity of their morals? Rashk knew me well enough to believe me when I gave the stars the lie, despite his (qualified) faith in astrology, but others who came to know what the Brahmin had said might well think that I must have broken my vow of *brahmacarya* in Poona and was no longer a true monk. As for the revelation about my future, this could be understood as an attempt to induce me to give up the monastic life by appealing to my religious ambitions. But I had no wish to give up the monastic life, and no ambitions of the kind the stars' – or the Brahmin's – prediction seemed to envisage. Even if I had entertained such ambitions I would in any case have stood a better chance of realizing them by remaining a monk in my old age than by giving up being one. Elderly ex-monks, in my experience, were much more likely to lose such disciples as they had than to attract new ones in even greater numbers. However that might be, there was little doubt that astrology was a powerful weapon, quite irrespective of its truth or falsity, and that people could be manipulated by its means. Politicians of every party had their personal astrologers, just as Rashk had, and these were said to exercise, through the advice they gave their powerful clients, an enormous influence behind the scenes. Businessmen too had their astrologers, as did film actors and others connected with the cinema industry. Astrology in fact dominated large and important areas of Indian life, and to the extent that it tended to play on people's hopes and fears, on their greed, hatred, and delusion, those areas could be said to be dominated by the forces of Māra the Evil One. It was therefore no wonder that the Buddha should have included astrology among the 'low and lying arts' in which his monk disciples were not to engage.[251] – With reflections such as these did I beguile the tedium of my two-day journey.[252]

In Calcutta I stayed, as usual, at the Maha Bodhi Society's headquarters building, behind the Sri Dharmarajika Vihara in College Square, and as usual the greater part of my time there was spent attending to the work of the *Maha Bodhi* journal, the last five or six issues of which I had been obliged to bring out on the wing. The Vaiśākha full-moon day was fast approaching, and therewith the time for the appearance of the journal's special Vaiśākha number. It would be the third such special number I had brought out, and since it would also be the 2,500th Buddha Jayanti number I was anxious that it should be bigger and better than any of its predecessors. Despite the intense heat I set to work with a will, editing the articles I had collected, choosing the illustrations, which this year included two in full colour, commissioning a cover design, changing printers (for two issues only), reading proofs, and writing the editorial and much of the Notes and News section.

For the last four months my editorials had dealt, in one way or another, with the forthcoming Buddha Jayanti. The January editorial, which was entitled 'The Coming Year', drew attention to the fact that, as many indications showed, Buddhism was capable of meeting a very definite need, satisfying a spiritual hunger, not only in the East but in the West. The Vaiśākha Pūrṇimā of 1956 would therefore present the whole Buddhist world with a unique opportunity – and a challenge. It would present a challenge, because opportunities, besides revealing our strength, also exhibited our weakness.

> The great weakness of the Buddhist world today is lack of unity. By unity we do not, of course, mean mere external uniformity, much less still simply a keeping up of friendly social relations. We mean by unity an effective recognition of the fact that despite differences of presentation and interpretation, both *yānas* and all schools of Buddhism accept, teach, and follow that threefold path of morality, meditation, and wisdom, leading to Enlightenment, wherein consists the very essence of the Dharma of the Lord Buddha. The nearer we approach to actual practice of the essentials of the teaching the nearer we shall approach to each other. That 'unity is strength' is none the less true for being a truism. The nearer we approach to each other the more effectively shall we be able to take advantage of the opportunity, to meet the challenge which the coming Anniversary represents. Only a united Buddhism will be able to fulfil the old prophecy that from this year the Dharma will begin to overspread the whole earth.[253]

The editorial for February struck a different note. Entitled 'The Inner Preparation', it reminded readers of the *Maha Bodhi* that Buddhism had its origin in the fact that, five-and-twenty centuries ago, a man sat under a tree in the forests of north-eastern India and *meditated*. Buddhism had been able to spread so wide outwardly because the sources of its inspiration lay so deep within. In this fact there was an important lesson for us today. Preparations for the 2,500th anniversary of the *parinirvāṇa* had been going on for some time, and the celebrations promised to be the grandest with which the name of Buddhism had ever been associated, but there was one question which those who were in any way connected with these events had to ask themselves:

> What is the inner basis of all these manifestations of zeal for the Buddhist cause? Is it a love of pomp and circumstance, of the parade and pageantry of religion? Is it merely faith? Or is it, again, merely an opportunistic taking advantage of a particular conjunction of circumstances of the historical order?
>
> The tree of Buddhist revival can shoot high only if its roots are planted deep in the soil of our hearts. The modern Buddhist movement must be based not on faith, not on unreflecting enthusiasm – much less still on meaner motives – but on actual realization of the import of the Dharma.
>
> To such a realization there is only one way: meditation. The Buddhist texts are unanimous that the Truth can be discerned only by the mind which has been thoroughly purified by the systematic practice of meditation. Not to the intellect, not to the emotions, but only to the mind which is at equilibrium in *samādhi* do there arise these flashes of insight which destroy all wrong views, such as belief in a creator God and the reality of the ego-soul or *ātman*, and which eventually culminate in the attainment of that Aryan Knowledge which constitutes the Path to Supreme Enlightenment.
>
> Hence we urge upon all our readers the necessity of making, during the coming months, a special effort not only to study and propagate the Doctrine but to realize it through meditation.... On an occasion so auspicious as the one we shall be celebrating shortly, we should make every effort to raise our consciousness to the highest possible level. For only if it proceeds from within without will the modern movement of Buddhist revival be truly

> successful. Without underrating the part played by external organization, it may be said without fear of contradiction that it is the inner preparation which is the more important. To that inner preparation, therefore, let us devote ourselves during the coming months, so that the coming Vaiśākha Pūrṇimā will be an anniversary not merely in the history of Buddhism but in our own spiritual life.[254]

The March and April editorials suggested other ways of making a special effort in honour of the Buddha Jayanti. In the former, entitled 'Buddhism and the Indian Languages', I appealed to 'our friends in every corner of the Buddhist world' to inaugurate, as part of their Jayanti programme, a movement to have as much Buddhist literature as possible translated into as many Indian languages as possible,[255] and in the latter, entitled 'Buddha Jayanti Among the Birds', I pleaded for a measure of vegetarianism. A measure of vegetarianism, I pointed out, besides demonstrating our much-advertised *maitrī* for the animal creation, would go a long way towards enabling birds and beasts to participate in the Buddha Jayanti celebrations.

> Buddhist pilgrims to India in particular would be well advised to abstain from fish and meat during the period of their pilgrimage. Whether rightly or wrongly, the average Indian is deeply shocked at the spectacle of Buddhists, especially monks, who even while on pilgrimage are unable to control their palate to the extent of forgoing, even temporarily, this particular article of diet.[256]

Now, in my fifth editorial of the year, for the 2,500th Buddha Jayanti number, I was concerned to point out that the present anniversary did not mean that the Buddhist world, with twenty-five centuries of history behind it, was now justified in resting still more comfortably and complacently upon its laurels. Rather did it mean that, enriched by twenty-five centuries of experience, it could now prepare itself for a concerted effort to make the limits of the Dharma coterminous only with the limits of the globe itself. The May editorial was therefore entitled 'Ring in the New' and concluded, after referring to the duty of the Buddha's followers to spread the Dharma:

> Let us, therefore, on this unprecedentedly solemn and auspicious occasion, vow to make so great an effort for the world-wide dissemination of the Dharma that when, after two and a half millenniums, we celebrate the five thousandth anniversary of the *mahāparinirvāṇa*, we shall do so in a world united by a common allegiance to the Buddha, the Dharma, and the Sangha.[257]

The aspiration was a grandiose one, but what with the preparations for the Buddha Jayanti, and the rumours of the impending conversion of Dr Ambedkar and his followers to Buddhism, at the Maha Bodhi Society's headquarters at that time there was, perhaps, a whiff of triumphalism in the air.

Triumphalism or no triumphalism, the work of editing the 2,500th Buddha Jayanti Vaiśākha number, together with that of seeing two or three booklets through the press, left me with scant leisure for other things. I was able, none the less, to see a little of Soratha, now back in Calcutta after his spell as locum at the Ananda Vihara, and to spend a few evenings with Sachin. My Nepalese friend was now a student at St Paul's College, the prestigious Anglican missionary institution where Phani Sanyal was Professor of Economics and, I believe, at that time warden of the hostel where Sachin was staying. Talking with Sachin naturally brought the image of Kalimpong very vividly before my mind's eye, especially as we exchanged news of common friends and reminisced about the early days of the YMBA, and I longed more than ever to escape from the stifling heat of the plains to the comparative cool of the hills, and from the noise and bustle of the headquarters building to the tranquillity of Everton Villa. Fortunately it was not many days after writing my editorial on 'Ring in the New' that I was able to give the print order for the last forme of the Vaiśākha number, pack my bags, and summon a taxi to take me to Sealdah Station.

Once back in Kalimpong it did not take me long to slip into the duties my fellow citizens had assigned me and start organizing the procession and public meeting that was to be the town's principal contribution to the Buddha Jayanti celebrations. As I had organized functions of this sort before, and was well acquainted with the various people whose co-operation would be required, this did not prove difficult. Moreover, I had a regular assistant in the form of a young Thai *bhikkhu* from Shantiniketan. Khemasiri was in India to study English, but finding he did not make much progress at the Visva-Bharati University, where he and the other young Thai *bhikkhus* spent much of their time talking together in their own language, he had decided that the best thing he could do would be to go and stay with the English monk in Kalimpong for a few months. Quiet, modest, and diligent, he not only helped me organize the town's contribution to the Buddha Jayanti celebrations but thereafter spent several months with me as my assistant, friend, and companion. Not that Khemasiri's was the only help I received during the run-up to the Buddha Jayanti. Besides Dawa, Durga, and others of our members and friends there were occasional helpers from outside Kalimpong. One of these was Dr Kalidas Nag, the Chairman of the editorial board of the *Maha Bodhi*. Following Devapriya-ji's example, he was touring the Maha Bodhi Society's centres with a view to stimulating interest in the Buddha Jayanti. Unlike Devapriya-ji, he had included Kalimpong in his itinerary, and in the course of the two days he spent in the town his affable looks and charming manners captivated everybody he met. Another such helper was Narada Thera, the doyen of the English-speaking *bhikkhus* of Ceylon, whose public appearance, at least, was less than a complete success.

I had met Narada Thera in Kathmandu in 1951, and in 1952 I had shared a tent with him at Sanchi, where we had disagreed as to whether or not vitamin tablets counted as food and whether or not, therefore, a monk could take them after twelve o'clock without breaking the Vinaya. (According to Narada Thera they were not, and he could; according to me they were, and he could not.)[258] My last meeting with him had taken place in Calcutta, at the Maha Bodhi Society's headquarters building, where one evening he took me aside and pumped me for information about the strictness with which the Society's *bhikkhus* observed certain minor monastic rules. He also spoke about the higher stages of the Path, but in such a way that I formed the distinct impression that he wanted me to think he was an *arhant*. Be that as it may, he concluded by saying, in a confidential would-you-believe-it tone of voice, 'Do you know, Avuso, some people actually think I am a *hypocrite*.' (Avuso or 'Friend' was the correct mode of address from a senior to a junior monk.) 'Yes, Bhante,' I responded brightly, 'I have heard as much.' 'Oh dear, Avuso, have you really!' he exclaimed, shocked and momentarily flustered by this unwelcome confirmation of his worst suspicions. The truth was that although Narada Thera was a great favourite with the Theravādin laity, mainly on account of his pedantically strict observance of the Vinaya, he was not very popular with his fellow Sinhalese *bhikkhus*, the majority of whom tended to regard him as something between a joke and a fraud. Many were the stories that were in circulation about him. Soratha had told me a number of them, some of them very funny and to be appreciated only by those acquainted with the finer points of the Vinaya and the jealous, proprietary attitude of the Sinhalese laity towards its monks. Indeed, it seemed that all the stories ever told in the monasteries of Ceylon about hypocritical monks had come to be related, over the years, of the unfortunate Narada Thera, just as in India all the jokes ever told about dim-witted Sikhs had come to be related of Sardar Baldev Singh, Pandit Nehru's bearded and turbaned Minister of Defence.

Hypocrite or not, the elderly Sinhalese monk was a prominent figure in the Buddhist world, and on learning of his arrival at the Dharmodaya Vihara I at once went and invited him to give a public lecture. He accepted the invitation with alacrity, whereupon I not only publicized the meeting extensively but personally urged everybody I met to attend, saying that Venerable Narada was the most famous Buddhist monk in Ceylon, that he was well known as an author and speaker, and that he had lectured on Buddhism in many Western countries, all of which was perfectly true. When the time came the Town Hall was therefore crowded. Unfortunately what should have been one of the highlights of the run-up to our Buddha Jayanti celebrations turned out to be a near disaster. Narada Thera's lecture was dull and platitudinous in the extreme and delivered, from what were evidently old notes, in a high-pitched voice and with an air of benign condescension. People were bitterly disappointed, some of them afterwards going so far as to compare the Sinhalese monk's abilities as a lecturer with my own in a way that was by no means to his advantage. Friends wanted to know why I had praised Narada Thera so highly. But an incident which occurred before he began to speak created, perhaps, an even less favourable impression than the lecture itself.

As my custom was, I had arranged for the speaker and chairman (on this occasion me) to occupy the Town Hall's tiny stage and for the more distinguished members of the audience, including *bhikkhus* and lamas, to occupy the first two rows of chairs in the auditorium.

No sooner had Narada and I taken our seats on the stage, however, than my elder brother in the order insisted that the *bhikkhus* (but not the lamas) should join us there, nor was he satisfied until, with much hauling and scraping of chairs, and a good deal of confusion, the eight or ten *bhikkhus* in the audience were all squeezed together with us on the stage. But that was by no means the end of the matter. Narada Thera had not been speaking for more than a few minutes when a yellow-robed figure slipped into the hall and unobtrusively took a seat in the back row of the auditorium. It was Anand-ji's disciple Sumedha. He had been to see me in Bombay, and at my request Dr Bhagwat had agreed to teach him Pāli; but having no real interest in study he was now back in Kalimpong and again staying at the Dharmodaya Vihara. Not realizing that the meeting would be starting on time, he had turned up late. Narada Thera's eagle eye at once spotted the new arrival and, interrupting his lecture, he called upon him to come forward and take his rightful place on the stage. 'That's all right, Bhante,' protested Sumedha, in his uncultivated Hindi (which the Sinhalese monk did not understand), 'I'm fine where I am, thanks.' But Narada Thera, who was accustomed to having his own way, continued to call upon the recalcitrant *sāmaṇera* to come forward until the latter, deeply embarrassed to be the centre of everyone's attention, eventually made his way to the stage, where an extra chair was somehow squeezed in among the rest. Having seen him merged with the other yellow robes, Narada Thera turned to the audience and observed, in his blandest manner, 'I am glad to see that the good people of Kalimpong know how to show proper respect to the members of the Holy Order.'

This was not to be my last experience of Theravādin orthodoxy, as represented by the doyen of the English-speaking Sinhalese monks. Wishing to be hospitable, I had not only invited Narada Thera for lunch but made sure that Padam, my cheerful Nepalese cook-bearer, prepared a more elaborate meal than usual. Moreover, knowing what a stickler my guest was for the observance of the twelve o'clock rule (the rule that prohibited monks from taking solid food after midday), I had made sure that the meal was ready by eleven o'clock, for which time the Thera was invited. But eleven o'clock came and went, then 11.30, and still there was no sign of him. What could have happened? By 11.45 I was feeling distinctly worried on his account, as it was an unheard-of thing for an orthodox Theravādin monk to be late for a meal. Eventually, at 11.55, a panting, perspiring figure in yellow could be seen hastily descending the flight of rough stone steps that led from the road to Everton Villa. It was Narada Thera! Realizing that if he missed his lunch he would probably have to fast until the following day (except for vitamin tablets), and not wanting Padam's meal to be wasted, I told Naginda, who had invited himself to lunch that day (as he often did), to put the clock back half an hour and position it prominently on the dining room table. No sooner had he done this than in rushed a distraught Narada Thera. 'Avuso, Avuso,' he gasped, 'Am I late, am I late? I lost my way! Those Dharmodaya people misdirected me!' 'Don't worry, Bhante,' I replied, 'you're not *very* late.' Whereupon Narada Thera saw the clock. 'Oh!' he exclaimed, with evident relief, 'I thought it was later than that' – and lost no time in sitting down to the meal. He was careful, I noticed, not to look at his own watch. Even if Narada Thera was not exactly a hypocrite, there were clearly times when he regarded the apparent observance of the Vinaya as being of greater importance than its real observance.

But with the Vaiśākha Pūrṇimā almost upon us I had little time to think about such things. According to an ancient prophecy, the 2,500th Buddha Jayanti would mark the beginning of a period of revival for Buddhism, and if this was the case it was to be hoped that the pseudo-orthodoxy of the Narada Theras of the Buddhist world would soon dissolve like mist in the light of a truer understanding of the Buddha's teaching. Indeed, when at last the snows of Kanchenjunga flushed with the dawning of the great day, and as Khemasiri and I made our way up to the Tharpa Choling Gompa, it really did seem that the Buddhists of Kalimpong, like those of the rest of the Buddhist world, were ringing in a new cycle in the history of their religion. Five-coloured Buddhist flags fluttered everywhere, incense smoked from braziers in front of shops and houses, and on all sides the sound of chanting could be heard. On arriving at the *gompa* we found that two thousand people had gathered to take part in the procession, and it took me some time to organize them into their different sections. According to a report I subsequently wrote for the *Maha Bodhi*, the procession was led by more than a hundred Tibetan lamas,

> all magnificent in their ceremonial robes of silk brocade, who blew trumpets and clarinets, beat upon drums, and swung censers

With Khemasiri leading the Buddha Jayanti procession through the Kalimpong bazaar

> in which incense burned. A beautiful image of the Lord Buddha, pictures of His Holiness the Dalai Lama, and banners of victory, Buddhist flags and emblems were borne in the procession. Nearly a thousand devotees carried on their backs huge volumes of the Buddhist Scriptures in Tibetan.[259]

What I did not write was that although the procession was led by the hundred Tibetan lamas in their ceremonial robes of silk brocade, the lamas themselves were led, by popular demand, by Khemasiri and me

The Buddha Jayanti procession entering the Mela Ground

in our yellow cotton robes. Down from Tirpai to Eleventh Mile we led them, along the main road, through the narrow, shop-lined streets of the upper bazaar, and so to the Mela Ground. The Mela Ground was a level open space that had been cut out of the hillside between the High Street and the lower bazaar. As its name implied, it was really a fairground, though in my time only football matches were ever held there. It was surrounded on three sides by tiers of seats, also cut out of the hillside, and at intervals there were broad flights of steps. Down one of these flights of steps Khemasiri and I led the lamas, the rest of the procession behind them, and began following the lines of the maze which, with the help of Pheunkhang-se and two other Tibetan officers, I had marked out on the floor of the Mela Ground the previous day. Back and forth we went, from one side of the Mela Ground to the other, until by the time we had reached the end of the maze, and the tail of the procession was descending the steps, the entire space was a sea of red robes and colourful national costumes from which rose, like the masts and sails of ships, the still more colourful Buddhist flags and banners of victory.

In the afternoon the Mela Ground was the venue of a public meeting. Sri S. N. Roy, the current Sub-Divisional Officer, presided, and the guest of honour was Sri S. R. Das, the Chief Justice of India, who was a regular visitor to Kalimpong and with whom I was well acquainted. Speeches in various languages were delivered, including one in Tibetan by Jigme Dorji, the *de facto* prime minister of Bhutan, and one in English by me. Immediately after the meeting prayers – as one could not help calling them in English – were chanted by a large congregation of Tibetan lamas in front of the gilded and jewelled Buddha image that had been lent for the occasion by Rani Dorji, who was also responsible for the tasteful appearance of the shrine. Later, the Kalimpong branch of the Maha Bodhi Society and the other Buddhist institutions of the town held special functions in honour of the day at their own premises.

On the following day a meeting was held at the Town Hall especially for students, when the results of the Students' Essay Competition were announced and prizes distributed. A variety of entertainment, including dramatic sketches dealing with the life of the Buddha, was also given. Though I had organized the meeting I was unable to be present, as I was in Gangtok, taking part in the second and third days of the Buddha Jayanti celebrations being held there. Tibetan Buddhist chronology, which was followed in Sikkim, differed from that of Theravādin South-east Asia by several centuries, but in 1956, the year of the 2,500th Buddha Jayanti, the Tibetan *Shaga Dawa* or anniversary of the Buddha's Enlightenment, and the South-east Asian (and Indian) Vaiśākha full-moon day, happened to fall, miraculously, on the same date, so that Himalayan Buddhists could join in the Buddha Jayanti celebrations without feeling that they were being unfaithful to their own traditions. Besides services in all the monasteries of Sikkim, the previous day had seen a public meeting in Gangtok, and the next day, shortly before my arrival in the village capital, the Buddha's image had been taken in procession from the Palace Temple. I gave my first lecture that evening, and the second the following evening, both of them being given at the White Memorial Hall under the presidentship of the Maharaj Kumar. In the first I spoke on 'Tradition and Progress' and in the second on 'Buddhist Meditation'. Both lectures were well attended, members of the Sikkimese nobility and officers of the state being particularly prominent in the audience.

On my previous visit to the Village Capital I had been a guest of the Palace and had stayed at the Palace guest house. This time I was the guest of Apa B. Pant, the Political Officer, and stayed with him and his family at the Residency, where he lived in much the same style as his British predecessors, employing the same aged Lepcha butler and dining off the same silver plate on formal occasions. The Residency had been built some fifty or sixty years earlier, in a superior version of Himalayan Mock Tudor, and commanded a view of the snows that was unequalled even in Gangtok. It was surrounded by extensive lawns, the lawns were bordered by flower beds, and the flower beds were backed by shrubs and blossoming trees, behind which rose the dense enclosing mass of the Sikkim jungle. The space occupied by the whole *mise en scène* – house and outbuildings, lawns and flower beds – seemed to have been carved out of the jungle, so that as I looked across the front lawn at the tree ferns and giant rhododendrons I was reminded of the way in which, in the Garden of Eden as seen by the fallen Archangel in Book IV of Milton's great poem, 'the verdurous wall of Paradise up sprung'. Wandering in the grounds of the Residency, with their combination of the cultivated and the wild, it was easy to imagine oneself in the Garden of Eden, and I could not help wondering if any of Apa Sahib's English predecessors, walking there in the cool of the evening, had not been reminded of the lines in *Paradise Lost* describing that ideal scene.

I did not have much time to wonder. My stay was a short one, and I was soon back at Everton Villa, catching up with correspondence and attending to the work of the *Maha Bodhi*, for which I now had to write notices of some of the many special numbers that newspapers and periodicals of all kinds had brought out in honour of the 2,500th Buddha Jayanti. I did not have any classes to teach at the Dharmodaya Vihara. As I had feared, the strain of remunerating the teachers had eventually proved too much for Gyan Jyoti's limited resources, and during my absence in Bombay the evening college had collapsed, not without a certain amount of recrimination. For me personally the fact that I no longer had regular classes to teach was not without its advantages. It meant that I was now less tied to Kalimpong (not that I had been much tied even before), and in the course of the late summer and early autumn I was away twice, visiting three places and giving three series of lectures, while during the month of November I was away on pilgrimage to the Buddhist holy places with Dhardo Rimpoche and others as a guest of the Government of India.

In Calcutta, where I spent much of August attending to journal work, my lectures were given as three of the 'Thursday lectures on Buddhism' which now formed part of the regular activities at the Maha Bodhi Society's headquarters. On successive weeks I spoke on 'Buddhism and Modern Thought', on 'Buddhism and the Arts', and on 'Buddhism and the Social Order'. What prompted me to speak on the last subject, other than the simple desire to explore the relation between Buddhism and various departments of human life, I do not know, though the fact that Dr Ambedkar and his Scheduled Castes followers were, as it now seemed, about to embrace Buddhism, may have had something to do with it. However that may have been, the president at this lecture was my old teacher Kashyap-ji, in accordance with whose injunction I had stayed in Kalimpong to work for the good of Buddhism.[260] Having established the Pāli Postgraduate Institute in Nalanda, the site of the ancient monastic university, he was now editing the entire Pāli Tipiṭaka – the canon of Theravādin Buddhism – in *devanāgarī* characters for publication by the Government of Bihar. As we discussed this enormous project, which was to occupy him for many years, I recalled an incident which had occurred six or seven years earlier, when I was staying with him at the Benares Hindu University. Indicating the palm of his hand, he had one day exclaimed, with reference to the same forty-five-volume Tipiṭaka, 'Sangharakshita, I have it all *here*!' I certainly could not claim to have the Tipiṭaka, or even a small portion of it, in the palm of my hand, but texts like the *Sutta-Nipāta*, the *Udāna*, and the *Itivuttaka*, if not my constant companions, were often in my thoughts and had long been a major source of inspiration.

The three lectures I gave at Shantiniketan, in the first week of September, were given under the auspices of two different departments of the Visva-Bharati University and one of its campus organizations. At Cheena Bhavan, under the auspices of the International Club, I spoke on 'Buddhism as a Religion for Life', under the auspices of the English Department on 'Eastern Thought and English Literature', and under the auspices of the Philosophy Department on 'The Philosophical Interpretation of the Buddha's Personality'. The 'philosophical' interpretation in question was that of the subtle and mysterious doctrine of the *trikāya* or 'three bodies', according to which the Buddha possessed, in addition to the earthly body perceived by gods and men, a sublimely beautiful ethereal body that was perceived only by highly advanced bodhisattvas and other Buddhas, and an unmanifested body which, besides including the two previous bodies, was the Supreme Reality of all individual persons and things and the goal to be realized through transcendental wisdom. Lobsang Phuntsok had dealt with the *trikāya* doctrine in his article on Tibetan Buddhism, and my own exposition drew on his account, which was in turn based upon oral explanations given him by Dhardo Rimpoche. The *trikāya* doctrine was important, in my view, not least because it served to illustrate the fact that, enlightened *human being* though the Buddha was, his enlightened humanity possessed – as did the unenlightened humanity of all men potentially – dimensions undreamt of in the modern, secular conception of what constituted humanity.[261] That the Buddha possessed three 'bodies' was, of course, a distinctively Mahāyāna teaching, originally promulgated by the Yogācāra school on the basis of earlier, uncoordinated traditions, and it was mainly to the Mahāyāna that I devoted the two lectures I gave in Gangtok the following month. The first of these was on 'Hīnayāna and Mahāyāna', the second on 'The Six Pāramitās'. Both lectures were given in the White Memorial Hall, the Maharaj Kumar again presiding. To the Buddhists in my audience, including the Maharaj Kumar, the question of the relation between the Hīnayāna and the Mahāyāna was of more than academic interest. In recent years they had become increasingly aware that the Hīnayāna, as represented by the Theravādin *bhikkhus* with whom they came in contact in India, differed widely from the Mahāyāna, as represented by the Nyingma and Karma Kagyu lamas of Sikkim. Was the Hīnayāna the original Buddhism, of which the Mahāyāna was only a corrupt and degenerate form, as the *bhikkhus* (and some Western orientalists) tended to believe? Or was the Mahāyāna a higher, more developed form of Buddhism, to which the Hīnayāna was only introductory, as the more learned lamas asserted? Or, again, were the two *yānas* complementary?

These were questions which Western Buddhists, too, were having to face, and I had attempted to deal with them in chapter 2 of *A Survey of Buddhism*, on which the Gangtok lecture on 'Hīnayāna and Mahāyāna' was partly based.[262]

In between my visit to Calcutta and Shantiniketan and my visit to Gangtok, and my visit to Gangtok and my tour of the Buddhist holy places, I spent my time in Kalimpong organizing full-moon day meetings at Everton Villa, editing (and writing for) the *Maha Bodhi*, helping Khemasiri with his English, and doing my best to follow Dr Johnson's justly famous injunction that a man 'should keep his friendship in *constant repair*'.[263] I did more than follow it. Besides keeping old friendships in repair, whether through personal contact or by means of correspondence, in the course of the brilliant autumn days I made two new friends, who came to be as much associated, in recollection, with Everton Villa, as Sachin and Durga were with The Hermitage and Mitra and Lalit with Craigside. Autumn seemed to be the season of friendship, as spring was the season of love. In an essay written in the year of my arrival in Kalimpong, when I was still intoxicated with the mingled grandeur and loveliness of my surroundings, I had not only linked autumn with friendship but celebrated both in the highly lyrical terms that then came naturally and spontaneously to my exultant twenty-five-year-old heart.

> Beautiful indeed is the Indian Autumn [I wrote], but most beautiful of all here in the foothills of the Himalaya. The rains are over and gone, and one has no longer to huddle day after day within doors listening to the thunder of them on the roof, or watching the jagged lightning as it glares from end to end of the sky swollen with black clouds. Doors and windows are all open now, open to the warm golden sunlight glistening on the grass, on the long green hair of the earth, as she emerges from the rains as a naiad with dripping locks from the river. The human heart also expands and opens, unfolding petals of brotherhood and love. People meeting in the cool of the evening eagerly renew the acquaintanceship of last year, and friends who have not met for a season, turning aside from the highways and the heat at noon, lose themselves in the cool of the forest and once more wander hand in hand through the deep silence of innumerable trees.[264]

The friends who wandered hand in hand were friends in the strict, non-sexual sense of the term, not lovers, for in India it was possible for two men to hold hands in public without this giving rise to unwarranted suspicions. Whether Narayanmani and Taranath ever wandered hand in hand, in the forest or anywhere else, I do not know, but I became acquainted with them at about the same time. They were good friends, and they often came to see me together. Both were of Nepalese stock, Narayanmani being a Hindu Newar and Taranath a Chhetri. One was fair-complexioned, religious-minded, and cheerful; the other sallow-featured, philosophically inclined, and somewhat cynical. Though different in temperament, the two young men were not without common interests, the chief of these being Buddhism and English literature, which were the usual topics of discussion among the three of us and between me and one or the other of them when they came to see me independently. Both had been away at university for a couple of years, returning to Kalimpong only in the vacations, which was the principal reason we had not met earlier, though each had heard of me through friends or relations. Taranath, who was the elder of the two, had spent some time in Calcutta after graduation. There he had become engaged to an Anglo-Indian girl from Darjeeling. His engagement did not, however, prevent him from being something of a Don Juan, which, as he was extremely good-looking, he did not find it very difficult to be. Partly on account of their having seen a little of the outside world, both Narayanmani and Taranath possessed a greater degree of emotional and intellectual maturity than did their more stay-at-home contemporaries, so that in the course of our discussions I was often able to share my deeper thoughts and feelings in a way that it was not possible for me to do with anybody else in Kalimpong at the time.

Besides being religious-minded, in a devotional kind of way, Narayanmani was sensitive almost to the point of being psychic. Once, when staying at Everton Villa overnight, he woke me in the early hours of the morning by calling out to me, from the bed he occupied near my own, 'Bhante, who is that lady standing in the doorway?' I could see no lady, and thinking that he might be dreaming with his eyes open (though he sounded wide awake) I asked him to describe what he saw. 'She is not very young and not very old,' he replied, 'and she is wearing a white sari with a red border.' Enquiries subsequently revealed that Everton Villa had been occupied, some years previously, by a Bengali family; the lady of the house had died, and her ghost was believed to haunt the place, which was why it had remained unoccupied for so long. The white sari with a red border was typical of the Bengali married woman whose husband was living, the red border being torn off if she was so unfortunate as to become a widow. Narayanmani's experience may or may not have been connected with some odd experiences of my own. The room in which we had been sleeping, and in the doorway of which the ghost – if ghost it was – had appeared to him, was both my bedroom and study, and the table at which I worked stood directly beneath the window. When I worked there in the evening, as I usually did, I would hear a sound as of handfuls of gravel being tossed against the glass. When I went outside onto the veranda to look there was nobody there, neither was there so much as a speck of gravel to be seen on the ground beneath the window. After the first three or four nights I took no further notice of the phenomenon, and eventually came to accept it as a normal part of life at Everton Villa.

Not all the friends I made around this time were Nepalese, nor were they all from Kalimpong. Simmons and Marcia Roof were Americans, Vaidyasekera was Sinhalese, and Michael Junius was German, and so far as their immediate antecedents were concerned all four hailed from Shantiniketan. The precise nature of the Roofs' connection with that seat of the muses was unclear, but Vaidyasekera was a student there (he had organized my recent lectures), as was Michael Junius, who was studying Indian classical music at Sangeet Bhavan and learning to play the sitar. Simmons and Marcia, who as Americans were no doubt accustomed to comfort, stayed in a rented bungalow on the Homes Estate above Tirpai, while Vaidyasekera and Michael stayed with me at Everton Villa. The five of us (plus Khemasiri) met frequently, as there were few days when the American couple did not take a taxi to my place and spend a good part of the afternoon and evening there. Simmons was in his early or middle thirties. Tall and inclining to corpulence, he had a smooth manner and exuded complacency to a degree that bordered on the ludicrous. Only when we had been acquainted several weeks did I learn that he was a Unitarian minister and in India on a sort of study sabbatical. Marcia, who was of about the same age as her husband, was slim, nervous, and intense. As soon became evident, she was in love with Michael (a situation Simmons appeared to accept), who was at least ten years her junior and the veritable embodiment of blond Teutonic young manhood. For his part, Michael was not interested in Marcia, except as a friend, and was in fact soon in blatant pursuit of Taranath, who was then staying with me and who, on more than one occasion, had to take refuge in my room from the young German's importunity. Michael was, however, a pleasant enough companion, and already both an expert musician and a serious musicologist. Early each morning he played his sitar for an hour or more, starting while it was still dark, and I would wake up to the sound of the plangent notes of the appropriate raga coming from the shrine-room, where I had allowed him to practise and where, after he had finished, I would go and meditate.

Though the Roofs came to see me so often, the only visit of theirs of which I have a distinct recollection is associated, in my mind, not so much with the American couple themselves as with the figure of someone they very much wanted to meet and who, at their request, I had invited to have lunch with the three of us at Everton Villa.

Like others in India on a study sabbatical, Simmons Roof was gathering material for a book. It was to be a book about the spiritual life, as illustrated by his personal religious quest, and in this connection he was anxious to meet as many spiritual personalities, both Hindu and Buddhist, as possible. Being now in Kalimpong he wanted to meet a real lama. I do not know if he had met Dhardo Rimpoche, if indeed the latter was in Kalimpong at the time, but it so happened that I had recently become acquainted with a Nyingma lama who had impressed me greatly. I had become acquainted with him through Ani-la. On my return from Bombay I had found the volatile Frenchwoman in a state of great excitement. She had found a new guru! He was a most remarkable man, and she had met him in the strangest fashion!

Little by little the story of the meeting came out, Ani-la's words tumbling over one another in her eagerness to tell me everything at once. She had been wandering in the mountains of western Sikkim on her own, in a state of deep depression, thinking that life was not worth living and that the only course left her was to commit suicide. Thus wandering, not caring in which direction she went, she came upon a small clearing in the forest. A tent had been pitched in the clearing, and in front of the tent sat a shaven-headed, red-robed figure whom she at once recognized as a lama. Her curiosity aroused, she approached and saluted him in her best Tibetan, and the two got into conversation. The lama, it transpired, was from Tibet. He was on his way to Pemayangtse Gompa, the premier

Nyingma monastery of Sikkim, where he was to be installed as abbot. According to tradition, he had to enter the monastery on a certain auspicious day. That day had not yet come, and in the meantime he was staying on his own in the forest and meditating. Having satisfied the French nun's curiosity, he naturally expected her to satisfy his, a white woman in monastic garb no doubt being the last person he had expected to meet in the forest-clad mountains of western Sikkim. She was a *getsulma* or novice nun, Ani-la explained. Who had ordained her? Dhardo Rimpoche, a Gelug incarnate lama who lived in Kalimpong. Which *sādhana* or spiritual practice was she doing? She was doing the *sādhana* of Mañjughoṣa, 'He of the Gentle Voice', the Bodhisattva of Wisdom. So far the interrogation had proceeded along familiar lines,

At Everton Villa: back l-r: Durgaprasad, Kachu Rimpoche, Khemasiri, Kachu Rimpoche's secretary; front: a young boy, and (seated) Ani-la

but at this point the strange lama's expression changed. 'No,' he said, in a stern but kindly manner, 'you are *not* doing the Mañjughoṣa *sādhana*. You have not done it for six months.' Ani-la was overwhelmed. It was true. Being angry with Dhardo Rimpoche she had stopped doing the *sādhana* he had given her at the time of her ordination and had not done it for exactly six months. The lama must have read her thoughts. He was a real lama. She would become his disciple.

The upshot was that Ani-la had spent some time at Pemayangtse Gompa, after the lama's installation, and there received teachings from him. Nor was this all. Within weeks of my returning from Bombay and hearing Ani-la's account of how she had found her new guru, the lama himself had spent a few days in Kalimpong, and I had met him. On my not only telling Simmons Roof the French nun's story, just as she had told it to me, but adding the information that the lama was even now paying a second visit to Kalimpong, both he and Marcia begged me to arrange a meeting. Thus it was that I had invited the lama to have lunch with the three of us at Everton Villa.

Kachu Rimpoche was a cheerful, straightforward, down-to-earth person who certainly did not give the impression of being possessed of supernormal powers of any kind. He was undoubtedly very knowledgeable, however, and over lunch, and for some time afterwards, Simmons plied him with questions on a wide variety of topics, with me acting as interpreter and translating the Unitarian minister's questions from English into Nepali and the Nyingma incarnate lama's answers from Nepali into English. As the discussion progressed, the questions Simmons asked related to topics of a more and more abstruse nature. All the Rimpoche's answers, as well as his additional explanations, were clear and to the point, especially when the question related to meditation, of which he evidently had extensive personal experience. Sometimes the alternation of question and answer was so rapid that I had difficulty keeping up with my translations. Eventually, when Simmons had put a highly philosophical question regarding the nature of Nirvāṇa, I noticed the Rimpoche had started replying to it without waiting for me to translate it for him. He was replying not to the words of the question, which were in a language he did not understand, but to the thought (and possibly also to the feeling) behind the question, which it seemed he was able to comprehend directly, without having to rely on its verbal expression. For some reason Simmons failed to notice this, but after the Rimpoche's departure he and

Marcia expressed themselves entirely satisfied with the meeting, which had exceeded their expectations.

According to Buddhist tradition, *paracittajñāna*, knowledge of the minds of others, was one of the mundane *abhijñās* or super-knowledges. Though a sign of attainment in meditation, its development was not essential to the realization of Enlightenment. That Kachu Rimpoche was able to know Simmons' mind, if such indeed had been the case, did not in itself mean that he was far advanced spiritually. None the less, the meeting at Everton Villa left me more impressed by him than ever and anxious to continue the acquaintance, despite the fact that he was living in western Sikkim and I in Kalimpong. As it happened, he was of much the same mind, with the result that in subsequent years we met a number of times and he came to occupy an important place in my life as friend and teacher.

22
HOLY PLACES AND EMINENT BUDDHISTS

By the end of the thirteenth century Buddhism had almost disappeared from India as an organized religion. Assimilation by Hinduism, withdrawal of royal patronage, centralization of learning in grand monastic universities, and the destruction of those universities by Muslim invaders from the north-west, had all played a part in the process, though the relative importance to be attributed to each of these factors remains a matter of dispute among scholars. During the next 600 years the situation did not greatly change, so that when India achieved independence in 1947 Buddhist communities were to be found only in the border areas, principally those in the north (Ladakh and Himachal Pradesh) and in the north-east (Sikkim, Assam, and the North-East Frontier Agency).[265] As part of the Buddha Jayanti celebrations, some fifty representatives of these communities had been invited to tour the Buddhist holy places as guests of the Government of India and to spend four days in Delhi in the same capacity. Among the Eminent Buddhists from the Border Areas, as the invitees were officially designated, were two from Kalimpong, in the persons of Dhardo Rimpoche and me, for both of us had by that time resided in the town long enough, and played a sufficiently prominent part in its Buddhist activities, to be regarded as the *de facto* representatives of the place's rather heterogeneous Buddhist population.

The tour started from Calcutta, and it was outside the national tourist office in that city that we all assembled on the morning of 29 October.

Many of those who gradually filled the little compound were monks. There were shaven-headed, yellow-robed *bhikkhus* from West Bengal and Assam (none of them, unfortunately, known to me) and shaven-headed, red-robed lamas from Ladakh and NEFA, besides long-haired, red-robed figures from some indeterminate border region who may or may not have been monks and who presented, in some cases, a rather fantastic appearance. There were also laymen in a variety of national and regional costumes, from Nepalese coat and jodhpurs to Tibetan-style kaftan. Some of my fellow Eminent Buddhists were bewildered, even disoriented, by the experience of being suddenly plucked from a remote village or monastery and set down in the heart of the biggest city of India, especially as they knew neither Hindi nor English and could communicate, in a few cases, only in their own local dialect. This meant that the stylish young Bengali woman who was in charge of the tourist office and responsible, apparently, for getting us to Howrah Station, did not have an easy time ascertaining their identities and inducing them to board one of the waiting buses. At times, indeed, she was reduced to darting hither and thither, sari-end floating out behind her, pushing and shoving the more uncomprehending of them in the direction she wanted them to go – an unceremonious proceeding to which the more elderly and conservative among them clearly took exception. Eventually, however, she succeeded in getting everyone on board, and half an hour later we were being off-loaded at the station and escorted to the special train that was to take us to the holy places and which was to be our home for the duration of the pilgrimage.

In the course of the next week we visited Bodh Gaya, Rajgir, Nalanda, Sarnath, Kusinara, Lumbini, Sanchi, and Agra, as well as seeing two or three of the enormous dams the government was constructing as part of one of its ambitious hydroelectric power schemes. What with the time it took the train to get from one pilgrimage centre to another, and the time it took the coach to convey us from the railway station to the temple or archaeological site that was our objective, we rarely were able to spend more than an hour or two at any of the holy places we visited, with the result that in most cases my impressions of them are not very distinct. Of some of the most important holy places, including Bodh Gaya, I have indeed no recollection at all, at least so far as the present pilgrimage is concerned. My only really vivid recollections are of Sarnath and Kusinara, and these are recollections not so much of the places themselves as of certain incidents that took place in them, one of which was ultimately to affect the whole course of my life and thought as a Buddhist and as a monk. As for the dams we were taken to see, my only recollection of these is of standing in front of one of them with Dhardo Rimpoche and his shaking his head and remarking, with a smile, 'Such things don't *really* solve the problem of human suffering.' If the organizers of the tour had hoped that the Eminent Buddhists from the Border Areas would be no less impressed by the temples of modern India, as Pandit Nehru was fond of calling dams and power stations, than they were by the ruined shrines of the ancient Buddhist holy places, then they were doomed to disappointment.

Sarnath was one of the four principal places of Buddhist pilgrimage, together with Lumbini, Bodh Gaya, and Kusinara, the Buddha having preached there, to his five former companions, what had come to be known, in English, as his 'First Sermon', but which was much more likely to have been more of the nature of an informal talk.[266] In the course of the last seven years I had visited Sarnath at least four or five times, more than once staying there for a few days, and was familiar with its excavated area, dominated by the massive bulk of the Dhamekh Stupa, its two or three modern temples or monasteries, its archaeological museum, and its Birla *dharamśālā* or pilgrims' rest house, as well as with the half-dozen Sinhalese *bhikkhus* who ran the Maha Bodhi Society's activities there and cared for the Mulagandhakuti Vihara, the pink sandstone temple built by Anagarika Dharmapala in the late twenties and early thirties. Since my last visit much had been done in the way of improvement. Lawns and flowerbeds had been laid out, giving the whole place a serene, park-like appearance, and beyond the excavated area, not far from the Mulagandhakuti Vihara, a deer park had been created, Sarnath having been in the Buddha's day a place of refuge for deer and other wild creatures. As soon as we had paid our respects to the Dhamekh Stupa, which according to an ancient inscription marked the exact spot where the Buddha had delivered the First Sermon or, in traditional parlance, 'turned the Wheel of the Dharma', Dhardo Rimpoche and I and the rest of the Eminent Buddhists were led to the Mulagandhakuti Vihara. Here a reception by Venerable Sangharatana and his yellow-robed colleagues awaited us. Before it could begin there was a point of protocol to be settled. The Vihara consisted of a spacious rectangular hall, the walls of which were covered with frescoes, with a kind of chapel at the far end. The floor of the chapel, which contained a life-size gilded image of the Buddha, was a foot or so higher than the floor of the hall. On entering the Vihara the *bhikkhus* in our party automatically went and sat inside the chapel, where the Maha Bodhi Society *bhikkhus* were already seated, leaving the lamas to occupy the floor of the hall along with the laity. Some of the lamas, as Sonam Topgay Kazi, the Sikkim representative, was not slow to point out to Venerable Sangharatana, were however celibates, like their Theravādin counterparts. Would it not therefore be better, he politely enquired, if these lamas sat inside the chapel with the *bhikkhus*, rather than in the hall with him and the other lay members of the party? As I knew from my own acquaintance with him, Sangharatana was more open-minded than most Theravādin monks, and I was not surprised when, after he had briefly consulted with his colleagues, the celibate lamas were invited, to their evident satisfaction, to sit with the *bhikkhus* on the higher, more honourable level.

On the opposite side of the excavated area from the Mulagandhakuti Vihara stood the modest structure that was the Burmese temple. It was in this temple, almost exactly six years earlier, that I had received my *bhikkhu* ordination, and I naturally did not want to leave Sarnath without visiting the place, paying my respects to the resident monk, U Kittima, and renewing my commitment to the monastic life.[267] On entering the compound I saw a number of Burmese pilgrims, all in national costume and smoking cheroots, and either strolling about or squatting on their heels beneath the big, shady trees. But there was no sign of U Kittima, and no one seemed able or willing to tell me where he was or even if he was on the premises at all. At length there emerged from the servants' quarters the Brahmin woman who, as I knew, was U Kittima's cook, and the young man, her son, who acted as the temple manager. As soon as she recognized me the woman uttered a great cry and threw herself at my feet. Babaji wanted to throw her and her son out, she exclaimed, bursting into a flood of tears. She had served him faithfully for twenty years and more. She had been a good wife to him and now he wanted her and her boy to leave the place. Where would they go? What would they do? Would I please write to Big Babaji in Kusinara and ask him to tell Babaji not to turn her out? Would I speak to Babaji himself, who for the last two or three weeks had been staying in Benares and who had vowed not to return until she was gone? 'You all know Babaji and I were living together,' she pleaded. 'You all know my son is his son too. Please help us.'

I had not known that U Kittima's cook was also his concubine, though his brother *bhikkhus* in Sarnath (and Kusinara) had evidently been privy to what was going on. Nor had I known that the young man in the lungi who acted as the temple manager was the Burmese monk's son, though when I looked at him, as he stood there beside his mother, arms stoically folded, the resemblance was obvious. The distraught woman's revelations therefore came as a complete surprise to me and for some minutes I did not know what to say, especially as several Eminent Buddhists who wanted to see more of Sarnath had accompanied me to the Burmese temple from the Mulagandhakuti Vihara and were clearly wondering what was amiss. There was no question of my writing to 'Big Babaji', whom I was in any case hoping to meet the following day when the party visited Kusinara and who of course was none other than U Chandramani, from whom I had received my *sāmaṇera* or novice ordination in 1949. Neither was there any question of my speaking to U Kittima, whom I had always regarded as being very much my elder brother in the monastic order. When I had recovered from my astonishment I therefore simply assured the discarded cook-concubine of my sympathy, and expressed the hope that Babaji would change his mind and allow her to stay, after which I left the Burmese temple without having renewed my commitment to the monastic life and in a state of considerable perplexity.

That taciturn, scholarly U Kittima was, as it appeared, 'a layman in the guise of a monk' was not a matter that concerned him alone, or even one that concerned only him and the unfortunate woman he now wanted to dismiss from his service. It was a matter that concerned the whole Theravādin monastic order, or at least that branch of it to which he and I both belonged. It was certainly a matter that concerned me personally. U Kittima had been present at my *bhikkhu* ordination. He had taken part in it, sitting inside the *sīmā* or consecrated area with the other members of the ordaining chapter. It was he who, as presiding monk of the Burmese temple, had signed my ordination certificate, testifying that I was 'properly ordained as a Bhikkhu according to the Vinaya of Theravādin Bhikkhus.' If at the time of my ordination he was 'a layman in the guise of a monk' and if, as I had been told, the presence of such a person inside the *sīmā* as a member of the ordaining chapter invalidated the proceedings, then my ordination was technically null and void and I was not in fact a *bhikkhu*. What, then, was I? While I was certainly not 'a layman in the guise of a monk' in the way that U Kittima was, I was technically a layman none the less, in that according to the Vinaya I was neither *bhikkhu* nor *sāmaṇera* and there was no fourth category of male ecclesiastical persons to which I could belong. Yet I did not feel myself to be a layman. I was as much committed to the spiritual life, and to being a monk, as I had been before that fateful visit to the Burmese temple, and did not have the slightest wish to return to the life of the world. Indeed, I knew myself to be more committed to the spiritual life, and to being a monk in the true sense, than were many *bhikkhus* of my acquaintance, technically valid though their ordinations may have been. But if according to the Vinaya I was neither *bhikkhu* nor *sāmaṇera*, and if I did not feel myself to be a layman, then what was the basis of my commitment to the spiritual life? What was it that enabled me to live as a monk and work for the good of Buddhism? Such were the questions that passed through my mind as I rejoined my fellow Eminent Buddhists and boarded the coach that was taking us back to Benares, and it was to be many years before I found a satisfactory answer to them.[268] Meanwhile I had no alternative but to live as though I had, in fact, been validly ordained and was a *bhikkhu* in the technical Vinaya sense.

Kusinara was about 150 miles from Benares, and if we did not see the site of the Buddha's *parinirvāṇa* or 'final passing away' the following day we certainly saw it the day after that. Like Sarnath, it had been much improved since my last visit, and as that visit had occurred in 1949 there were even more changes for me to take note of here than in Sarnath.[269] In my eyes not all the changes counted as improvements. The brand-new temple with the big 'Ajanta-style' horseshoe windows that now housed the ancient thirty-foot-long recumbent image of the Buddha was no doubt a fine building, but it entirely lacked the atmosphere of the primitive structure, hardly bigger than the image itself, in the gloom of which, seven years ago, Buddharakshita and I had meditated each morning with only two or three flickering candles between us and the enormous face of the dying Master.[270] Other changes were even less welcome. The half-crazy Chinese monk who lived in a peepul tree, and who burned candles on different parts of his body, had come down from his tree. But he had not only come down. He had built himself a cottage, and was even now building a kitchen onto the cottage with bricks taken from inside the exposed rim of the newly excavated Angyar Chaitya, the mound marking the spot where the earthly remains of the Buddha had been cremated. A party of coolies was busy dislodging hundreds of bricks with crowbars and removing them in baskets. When some of us went and complained to the Archaeological Department overseer he flatly denied that anything of the sort was happening, whereupon we insisted on his accompanying us to the spot and seeing with his own eyes what the coolies were doing. Either there had been gross negligence on somebody's part or somebody had been bribed. Whichever it was, serious damage had been done to an ancient and important Buddhist monument.

Though Kusinara had been much improved since my last visit, few changes had taken place in the dimly-lit, sparsely-furnished ground floor room where Buddharakshita and I had been favoured with our first interview with U Chandramani and where my former preceptor now received as many of the Eminent Buddhists as could be squeezed into the limited space. Very little was said, conversation being hardly practicable in the circumstances and the visitors being for the most part content, in any case, simply to sit there and have the old man's *darshan*. At one point, however, as slowly he surveyed the different faces in the room, U Chandramani's gaze fell upon me. 'Is it Sangharakshita?' he asked wonderingly, as if unable to believe his eyes. I confirmed that it indeed was, but though he seemed pleased to see me there was no further exchange between us. We had not met for seven years. For my part, though *I* was pleased to see *him*, and though the occasion brought back poignant memories of my *śāmaṇera* ordination at his hands, the Brahmin woman's plea for help still rang in my ears and I was uncomfortably aware that U Chandramani, too, had known of U Kittima's liaison with her and had therefore been, in a sense, a party to it. Despite his eighty years he still presented a fairly robust appearance as he sat there, cross-legged, on the same old cane-bottomed armchair, but his face was more deeply furrowed and the flesh hung a little more loosely on his bones. He also looked a little tired. This was not surprising. He had not long returned from an exhausting trip to Madhya Pradesh, where on 14 October, in Nagpur, he had formally initiated Dr Ambedkar and his wife into Buddhism, after which the Scheduled Castes leader had himself administered the Three Refuges and Five Precepts, together with twenty-two vows of his own devising, to more than a quarter of a million of his followers, thus inaugurating the movement of mass conversion of Untouchables to Buddhism.[271] Before taking leave of U Chandramani the Eminent Buddhists, at Sonam Topgay's whispered suggestion, dug into pockets and shoulder bags with the result that we were able to place at his feet a small pile of currency notes.

Lumbini was not in India but in Nepal, so that in order to reach it one had to cross the border, but apart from having my photograph taken with Dhardo Rimpoche in front of the pillar that marks the spot where the Blessed One was born I remember nothing of our visit to the place. I do have a vivid recollection, however, of the evening the Rimpoche and I spent in Gorakhpur, where our special train was kept at the station for two nights in a siding and whence we were conveyed by coach first to Kusinara and then to Lumbini. Gorakhpur was an old-fashioned town with, it appeared, a predominantly Hindu population. At least that was the impression we formed as we made our way to the bazaar area, for there was a Hindu festival in progress and everybody was taking part. Night had already fallen and the houses and open-fronted shops, and the innumerable little wayside stalls, were all lit not by electricity but by the soft golden glow shed by myriads of tiny oil lamps. Despite the fact that a festival was being celebrated there was little noise, and an atmosphere of deep peacefulness prevailed. As though in a dream – a dream filled with the smell of incense and crushed flowers – we drifted down bylane after bylane and from stall to stall. Many of the stalls were selling beautifully painted and decorated wooden or clay figures a few inches high. Who or what the figures represented, or whether they had a connection with the festival, we did not know, any more than we knew what the festival itself was all about. Nor did we want to know. I myself was perfectly content simply to observe the scenes through which we passed, taking in colour, shape, and movement as it were for their own sake, without thinking about what I saw. 'In the seen only the seen, in the heard only the heard....'[272] Though we obviously were strangers to the town, nobody accosted us, or tried to sell us anything, or bothered us in any way. It was almost as though we were invisible, so that we returned to the train well pleased with our nocturnal outing and favourably impressed by Gorakhpur.

By this time the tour was more than half over, and something like a friendship had begun to develop between Dhardo Rimpoche and me, as well as between the pair of us and the two other occupants of our compartment. These were Sonam Topgay Kazi and S. Yhonzone. Sonam Topgay was a friend of the French nun, in fact the same Kazi friend who had come to see me in Gangtok on the first of my recent visits to the village capital. Small, light-complexioned, and invariably attired in the traditional *chuba*, he worked as a translator in Apa Pant's office, where he had acquired a reputation, I afterwards learned, for elusiveness. Though broad in his Buddhist sympathies, he was a convinced follower of the Nyingma tradition and the personal disciple of some of its most distinguished living masters. It was from him, in the course of one of our many conversations during the tour, that I first heard of Dzogchen, the highest Nyingma teaching. He possessed, in fact, a good general knowledge of Tibetan Buddhism and was acquainted with learned lamas of every school. In Benares he had taken me to see a Gelug lama whom he particularly esteemed, both for his learning and his asceticism. We found the lama, whose name was Tenzin Gyaltsen,[273] occupying a tiny whitewashed room whose sole contents were a mat, two or three Tibetan books, and a small tin suitcase that served him as a desk. He was overjoyed to see us and with Sonam Topgay as interpreter he and I were able to have a short conversation. All he wanted to do was study, he told me enthusiastically, his eyes shining. It was in order to study that he had come to Benares, as despite his advanced age (I judged him to be about fifty) he wanted to learn Sanskrit. On our taking leave of him he looked round the room for something to give me. But there was nothing there. Whereupon he looked inside the tin suitcase, but except for a few dried apricots it was empty. But he was not to be defeated. As though seized by a sudden inspiration, he broke the string of his rosary and gave me a bead, saying, 'Many millions of mantras have been said on this bead. Please accept it with my blessing.'

The fourth member of our quartet, S. Yhonzone, was a Tamang schoolmaster from Kurseong with whom I was already acquainted as a result of the visits I had paid to that place. Like Sonam Topgay, he was about my age, but unlike that staunch traditionalist he preferred Western dress, as did most English-educated young Nepalis in the Darjeeling area. For the purpose of the tour, however, he had decked himself out in a light blue coat and jodhpurs, complete with a black conical cap. Though a Tamang, and therefore technically a Nyingmapa, he knew little or nothing about the Nyingma tradition or, for that matter, about any form of Buddhism. Consequently he did not find it easy to join in the doctrinal discussions with which Dhardo Rimpoche, Sonam Topgay, and I passed the time between holy places, and when he did join in it was usually only to reveal an ignorance and a confusion that would have been laughable had they not been so lamentable. But though not very bright he was sincere and well-meaning, and in the course of the tour the three of us did our best to inculcate a few basic Buddhist ideas and to clear up at least some of his confusion. Occasionally our quartet received a visit from Dhondup Lhendup, the leader of the NEFA contingent, who had studied with me for a few months in Kalimpong, in the days when I was living as the guest of Burma Raja, and whose good looks had been much admired by Marco Pallis. Since then he had graduated, joined the Indian Administrative Service, and been posted to a subdivision in the depths of NEFA. There, I had heard, he exercised despotic sway, enjoying unlimited access to the local liquor and the local women. Absolute power had corrupted absolutely.[274] The first time he appeared in the doorway of the compartment I hardly recognized him. Gone were his looks, he had put on weight, his eyes were bloodshot, his gaze dull and vacant. In the crumpled navy blue suit he was wearing he looked like a middle-aged man, though he could not have been more than thirty. When I told Marco Pallis, a few years later, about the change that had taken place in my old pupil, he was quite distressed, and exclaimed, 'Oh, he was *so* good-looking!'

Whenever the Eminent Buddhists were ferried from a railway station to a holy place Dhardo Rimpoche and I would sit together in the middle section of the coach. Initially this occasioned astonishment, even indignation, on the part of the yellow-robed members of the party. Like most Theravādin *bhikkhus* they were great observers of protocol, and the first time we had to board a coach, which must have been when we visited Bodh Gaya, they made sure that they got on first and occupied the front seats. Their red-robed counterparts, on the contrary, motioned others to precede them with a polite 'After *you*.' When we were all on board, the leader of the Assam *bhikkhus* turned round in his seat, saw me sitting with Dhardo Rimpoche a dozen rows back, and called out, 'Come and sit in the front with us! You're a *bhikkhu* too!' But I stayed where I was, and as I sat with the Rimpoche for the rest of the tour he and the other *bhikkhus* eventually concluded that I was a renegade from their ranks and could not be relied on to help them maintain the prestige of the Theravādin monastic order. From our position halfway down the coach my companion and I could not only see what was going on in front of us but hear what was going on behind. Often we heard squeals and scuffles. These sounds came from the back seat, which extended for the entire width of the coach. In the middle of this seat, facing the aisle, sat a stout, youngish woman who, we had been told, was a Bhutanese nun. She wore a short, apron-like skirt that barely reached to her knees, leggings, a little jacket, and a conical hat with a feather in it, and her round, rosy face was always wreathed in smiles. On each side of her sat two or three shaven-headed, red-robed lamas. Every now and then one of the lamas would pinch her plump thigh (hence the squeals), whereupon she would turn in his direction and try to give him a slap (hence the scuffles). While she was thus engaged, a lama on the other side would pinch the *other* thigh, whereupon she would turn round and try to hit *him*. Everyone seemed to enjoy this little game, including the dignified Bhutanese abbess, said to be a relation of the king, who from a seat nearby regarded the proceedings with an indulgent smile. At any rate, both the lamas and the nun enjoyed it sufficiently to play it every time we were in the coach for more than a few minutes.

Friendship implies a degree of mutual knowledge, and the fact that something like a friendship had begun to develop between Dhardo Rimpoche and me meant that we had got to know each other better. In Kalimpong this had hardly been possible, as we met only at intervals and usually on some formal occasion. Moreover, we were both rather reserved, whether by nature or as a result of having had, in his case a Gelug monastic training, in mine an English upbringing. None the less, each had definite feelings of goodwill towards the other, while from my side there was an appreciation of the Rimpoche's unusual qualities. That appreciation naturally increased during the tour, as well as in Delhi afterwards, when the fact that we were constantly together meant that I got to know him much better than before, even as he, no doubt, got to know me better. Though he had many positive qualities, the two that impressed me most were his uniform kindness and generosity and his unfailing mindfulness. The latter consisted, not only in an entire absence of anything resembling forgetfulness or inattentiveness, but also in a degree of foresight and preparedness that was almost supernatural. In later years I was to say that Dhardo Rimpoche was never caught napping. On the tour itself there occurred an incident which strikingly exemplified this quality of his. The officials who were responsible for looking after the party and organizing its transport used to tell us each morning which places we would be visiting that day. One morning they told us we would be visiting a certain dam in the morning and in the afternoon, after returning to the train for lunch, a certain holy place. Unfortunately there was somehow a mix-up. An hour after leaving the train we found ourselves not at the dam, as we had expected, but at the holy place. This in itself did not really matter, but thinking that we would not be needing them until the afternoon none of us had brought any candles or incense sticks. None of us, that is, except Dhardo Rimpoche. As we were lamenting the fact that we would be unable to offer worship in the proper manner, he produced packets of candles and bundles of incense sticks from beneath his voluminous robes and smilingly distributed them among us. Strange to say, there proved to be enough candles and enough sticks of incense for everyone.

If Sarnath meant the Dhamekh Stupa, and Kusinara the colossal image of the recumbent Buddha, then Agra – our last stop before Delhi – meant the Taj Mahal. It was the first time either Dhardo Rimpoche or I had seen that 'one solitary tear hanging on the cheek of time', as Rabindranath Tagore characterized Shah Jahan's masterpiece.[275] Having seen so many photographs and paintings of the famous monument, not to mention the plastic models that were on sale at every railway station, I was more than half afraid that the beauty of the original had been spoiled for me and that I would be disappointed. Nor was it really to be expected that any building on earth could live up to the superlatives that had been heaped upon the Taj Mahal. In the event I was *not* disappointed. The Taj Mahal far exceeded my expectations. It was incomparably more beautiful than I had imagined it to be. It was also very much bigger. The perfect proportions of the building and its flanking minarets, as shown in a hundred pictures, had led me to think of it as small and dainty, but as the Rimpoche and I walked from the high red sandstone gateway, along one of the paths bordering the long watercourse in whose depths it was reflected, it grew steadily bigger until eventually the dazzlingly white marble mass loomed over us almost blotting out the blue sky. Inside it was cool and comparatively dark, especially in the crypt containing the actual tombs of the woman in whose memory the Taj Mahal had been built and the grieving emperor who had built it. A few months later, recalling the visit, I composed a quatrain in which the love and death – Eros and Thanatos – that were everything inside the crypt were contrasted with the life and hate that seemed to be everything outside it.[276] The fact was that I had visited the Taj Mahal at the time of the Suez Canal crisis,[277] when 'voices prophesying war',[278] ancestral and other, could be heard on all sides. But it was not only the prospect of war which dismayed me. I was also dismayed by India's adoption of the double standard. I had not expected this. Had there not been an ethical dimension to the freedom struggle, and had not independent India so far shown a marked tendency to occupy the moral high ground in international affairs? Yet here was Pandit Nehru, the prime minister, vigorously condemning the Anglo-French action in Egypt while at the same time responding to Soviet Russia's invasion of Hungary, and its crushing of that country's nascent reform movement, simply with a mild expression of concern. India's foreign policy, it seemed, was in reality no more guided by moral considerations than was that of less Pecksniffian nations.[279]

On our way back to the station from seeing the Taj Mahal and the Agra Fort a strange thing happened. Dhardo Rimpoche and I both saw the words 'Buddha Vihara' on the end of a small roadside building. This was not strange in itself, even though none of the other Eminent Buddhists on the coach saw them. What was strange, as we discovered afterwards when we compared notes, was that whereas the Rimpoche had seen the words in Roman script I had seen them in *devanāgarī*. Obviously we ought to investigate, for where there was a Buddha Vihara there were bound to be Buddhists and we had not expected to find any Buddhists in Agra. As none of our Eminent Buddhist colleagues was willing to accompany us, some of them indeed being of the opinion that both the Rimpoche and I had only *thought* we saw the magic words, the two of us got into a rickshaw and set off on our own. Finding the route taken by the coach did not prove easy, and it took us a long time to locate the area in which the building we sought was situated; but eventually we did so, and there it was, and there were the words 'Buddha Vihara' – in *both* scripts. It was a rather nondescript building, and consisted of little more than a single chamber and a veranda. Peering through the grille in the wooden doors, we saw inside a Buddha image of the traditional Burmese type. A Hindu temple had evidently been turned into a Buddhist place of worship. As there was no one to be seen, it being by that time about ten o'clock and very dark, I seized the rope of the large bell that hung, Hindu-style, inside the veranda, and gave it several sharp tugs, producing a corresponding number of loud clangs. Soon several dozen poorly dressed men, women, and children from the nearby hutments had gathered on the veranda. Despite the presence of the Buddha image on the shrine, which an elderly man now opened, they seemed uncertain whether they were Buddhists or not, nor did they know much about Buddhism, though I gathered that a few of the men had attended Dr Ambedkar's mass conversion ceremony in Nagpur the previous month. Though surprised by our sudden appearance in their midst, especially at such an hour, they were pleased to see us, and pleased when I gave them a twenty-minute impromptu talk on Buddhism. Dhardo Rimpoche and I therefore returned to the station well satisfied with the success of our expedition and glad we had followed our instinct in the matter.

In Delhi the Eminent Buddhists were guests of the Government of India for four days, after which we were expected to shift for ourselves. Some of us found shelter at the local branch of the Maha Bodhi Society and at the Ashok Vihara, Mehrauli, which had been founded by Venerable Veera Dhammawara, the Cambodian monk I had met in Calcutta the previous year, but which an Englishwoman married to a well-known Indian communist was trying to wrest from his control. During the days that we were still government guests we continued to live in our special train, whence we were conveyed each day not to a Buddhist holy place or a dam but to a meeting or reception. Our first meeting was with the President of India, Dr Rajendra Prasad, and it took place at his official residence, Rashtrapati Bhavan, the palace-like building that had once been the Viceroy's House. As it was his government that had invited us to tour the holy places as its guests, we naturally wanted to express our gratitude for the invitation to Dr Prasad, and I had been elected to perform this office on everybody's behalf. Besides thanking him, I made a number of requests. These requests had been agreed among the Eminent Buddhists beforehand, and related to such matters as facilities for worship at the *vajrāsana* in Bodh Gaya, the acquisition of land in Bodh Gaya by Border Area Buddhist organizations, the protection of the Angyar Chaitya in Kusinara, and the provision of scholarships for Tibetan-speaking border area Buddhists who wished to study Sanskrit, Hindi, and Pāli. To all our requests Dr Prasad gave a sympathetic response, promising to refer them to the appropriate authorities. Only

With Dhardo Rimpoche in front of the Aśoka pillar at Feroz Shah Kotla, Delhi

one request did he reject, and that was made not by me but by the leader of the Assam *bhikkhus*. Seeing the president was in what he must have thought was an indulgent mood, he asked if he and his fellow *bhikkhus* could stay on in the capital as the government's guests, and at its expense, for an extra two weeks. Dr Prasad could not help smiling at this absurd request, and stroking his walrus moustache replied, as gently as he could, that he did not think that would be possible, whereupon the *bhikkhu* sat down looking crestfallen and discomfited.

When I made the requests on which we had all agreed I noticed that as soon as I mentioned Bodh Gaya the president stiffened in his seat and his expression, hitherto kindly, became grave. He evidently thought I was about to raise the vexed question of the Bodh Gaya temple, control of which the Buddhists had been demanding since the time of Anagarika Dharmapala. But I knew it was unwise to ask for something the other party would never give, especially when the asking was likely to cause offence. Devapriya Valisinha had told me that Rajendra Prasad, though not a Brahmin, was a staunch Hindu, and that in pre-Independence days, when he was president of the Indian National Congress, he had once approached him regarding the Bodh Gaya temple. In the course of the interview Prasad warned him that if the Maha Bodhi Society persisted in campaigning for Buddhist control of the temple he would personally lead a counter-campaign and see to it that the Buddhists had no say at all in its affairs. People seemed to feel strongly about the Bodh Gaya temple, but while it was natural that Buddhists should want to be in control of their own holiest shrine it was difficult to understand why Hindus should want to hold on to a place that had come into their possession as a result of a series of historical accidents. When it became clear that I was *not* going to raise the Bodh Gaya temple question the president relaxed and his face resumed its previous kindly, almost fatherly, expression.

At our meeting with the Vice-President, Dr S. Radhakrishnan, we had no requests to make, and he did practically all the talking. Indeed, he treated us to a glib homily on the subject of the inseparability, even the unity, of *prajñā* and *karuṇā*, wisdom and compassion, which Sonam Topgay translated into Tibetan for the benefit of the Tibetan-speaking delegates and over which they afterwards shook their heads. That a non-Buddhist layman should take it upon himself to address Buddhists, including lamas, on one of the profoundest Mahāyāna teachings struck them as extremely odd. When we met Pandit Nehru there were neither requests from us nor any lecture from him. Dr Rajendra Prasad had received us in a sort of throne room, sitting on a dais and flanked by uniformed ADCs and attendants in scarlet tunics. At the meeting with Dr Radhakrishnan there had been much less formality, the Vice-President receiving us in his drawing room and addressing us from an easy chair. At Pandit Nehru's house, where we were given lunch and met Indira Gandhi and her two young sons, Sanjay and Rajiv, there was no formality at all.[280] After the lunch, for which we sat, Indian-style, at individual small tables decorated with flowers, Pandit Nehru took me

With Dhardo Rimpoche in front of the Maha Bodhi temple, Bodh Gaya

into the garden to show me the pair of giant pandas he had recently been given by the government of the People's Republic of China. Despite their keeper's enticements, they refused to come down from their eucalyptus tree and all I was able to see of them was two black-and-white patches high up amid the grey-green foliage. Much as one might disagree with Pandit Nehru's foreign policy statements there was no disputing the fact that he was a friendly and charming person and the perfect host.[281]

Dr Radhakrishnan's homily may have occasioned some head-shaking on the part of Tibetan-speaking Eminent Buddhists from the Border Areas, but he at least had attempted to meet us on our own ground. No such attempt was made at the reception we were given by the Hindu organizations of Delhi. The reception took place under a *shamiana*[282] in the grounds of the Buddha Vihara, the little temple that was part of the Maha Bodhi Society's Delhi centre and a sort of Buddhist annexe to the huge Lakshmi Narayan Temple next door, both of them having been built – the latter 'in grand and cakey style'[283] – by a philanthropic Hindu multi-millionaire. Evidently our hosts had decided to take the Buddhist threat seriously. The capital's seven or eight leading Hindu scholars and intellectuals had been invited to address us, with the result that we had to sit through more than two hours of speeches. There were speeches in Hindi and speeches in English, long speeches and short speeches. But regardless of whether they spoke in Hindi or in English, or for a longer or a shorter time, all the speakers harped on a theme that was only too familiar to me. They all told us, with varying degrees of emphasis, that Buddhism was only a branch of Hinduism and that there was no difference between the two religions. The Buddha himself had lived and died a Hindu, and his teaching was no more than a restatement of the teachings of the Upanishadic sages. Buddhists were really Hindus, and it was very wrong of them not to want to be included in the Hindu fold but to want, instead, to set Buddhism up as a separate, independent religion. They should give up their narrow-mindedness and intolerance, recognize that Buddhism was part and parcel of Hinduism, and allow themselves to be absorbed by the one true universal Hindu Sanātana Dharma.[284]

The message had not been repeated more than four or five times before the Eminent Buddhists, together with the other Buddhists in the audience, started becoming restive under the onslaught. There were signs of unease, even of indignation. Eventually two or three of my colleagues whispered to me that the Hindus ought not to be allowed to have things all their own way. I therefore sent a note up to the chairman asking if I might reply to the speeches (they were ostensibly speeches of welcome) and thank the organizers of the reception. Not suspecting anything, he agreed. I began innocently enough. We were grateful to the Government of India for inviting us to Delhi; we were grateful for having been given the opportunity of worshipping in the Buddhist holy places (I did not mention that as non-Hindus we had not been allowed to enter the Vishwanath Temple in Benares), and we were grateful to the Hindu organizations of Delhi for having arranged the present reception. All this I said at some length, and in the kind of language that was customary on such occasions. But having said it, I changed my tune. 'When you invite someone to your house for a meal,' I told the speakers, 'you offer them the food that they like. You do not offer them food that for one reason or another is unacceptable to them. For example, you would not offer a vegetarian non-vegetarian dishes. Now you know very well that Buddhists do *not* agree that Buddhism is "only" a branch of Hinduism, or that the Buddha lived and died a Hindu. You know that such ideas are quite unacceptable, even repugnant, to them. Yet having invited us to your house for a meal, so to speak, *this* is the fare you insist on setting before us. It is not a reception. It is an insult.' These words of mine created consternation on the platform. Several speakers started up to protest that they had not intended to hurt the feelings of the Buddhists, while the chairman, who had himself shown signs of unease during some of the speeches, did his best to conclude the proceedings on a conciliatory note. Next morning a report of the reception appeared on the front page of the *Statesman*, and though I was not quoted verbatim the report made it clear that Buddhists did not agree that Buddhism was a branch of Hinduism.

Once the meetings and receptions were over (and there were several others, of all of which I have only a faint recollection), the Eminent Buddhists from the Border Areas were free to go their separate ways. Dhardo Rimpoche and I, and the other two members of our quartet, continued to keep in touch and to go out and about in one another's company. A visit that Dhardo Rimpoche, Sonam Topgay, Yhonzone, and I made together ended in a way that was not only unexpected but also amusing and even instructive, as did a visit that Sonam Topgay and I made on our own. The first visit took the four of us back to Rashtrapati Bhavan, while the second took the two of us to the Ashoka Hotel, where the foreign delegates to the Buddha Jayanti celebrations had been accommodated. One of the President's ADCs was Yhonzone's cousin. This cousin had invited Yhonzone for lunch at his quarters, which were in Rashtrapati Bhavan. When the day came our Kurseong friend insisted that the rest of us should accompany him and that we should *all* have lunch with his cousin. As we had not been invited, Dhardo Rimpoche, Sonam Topgay, and I naturally demurred, but Yhonzone was so positive that there would be plenty for everybody, and that his cousin, with whom he was on the best of terms, would be very pleased to meet us, that in the end, rather against our better judgement, we allowed ourselves to be persuaded.

Plump, sleek, smiling Captain Tamang was indeed pleased to meet us, and an hour passed in light general conversation. But of lunch there was no sign. Half an hour more passed. Still there was no sign of lunch. Eventually, when the atmosphere had become rather strained, Yhonzone asked his cousin *sotto voce*, in Nepali, when he thought lunch would be ready. Captain Tamang replied, smoothly, that he had not expected so many people and that the chicken curry his cook had prepared would only be enough for two. 'Couldn't we divide it up and make it do?' asked Yhonzone in desperation. But Captain Tamang was afraid they couldn't. At this point, when Yhonzone was sweating with embarrassment, Sonam Topgay intervened, also speaking in Nepali. Obviously there had been a misunderstanding, he said, in his usual quiet, courteous tones. But there was no cause for concern. He would be happy to take the two venerable ones into the city and give them lunch at a restaurant. Leaving an apologetic Yhonzone and a sleek, still smiling Captain Tamang to enjoy their chicken curry (of which I, at least, would in any case have been unable to partake), we caught an auto-rickshaw to Connaught Circus and had a belated lunch at Gaylord's. Over the meal we chuckled, good-naturedly, at our well-meaning but naive friend's *faux pas*, and I was reminded of the famous apologue of the town mouse and the country mouse.[285] As Captain Tamang was doubtless explaining to Yhonzone at that very moment, the city was not the village, and the free and easy behaviour appropriate to backward, out-of-the-way Kurseong was out of place in sophisticated, cosmopolitan Delhi.

Not long afterwards it was Topgay and I who found ourselves in the position of country mouse, at least so far as political naivety was concerned. We had gone to the Ashoka Hotel to meet Narada Thera, whom we found well pleased with himself for having taught the youthful Muslim bearer not to offer him a banana without first removing the skin (*bhikkhus* were not allowed to peel their own bananas), and not to offer it without repeating the traditional Pāli formula. He had great hopes for the Dhamma in India, he told us. People were very receptive. After we had left Narada Thera it occurred to me that we ought not to leave the hotel without trying to meet at least some of the delegates from the Communist bloc countries. There was a Buriyat head lama from Soviet Russia, for instance. Having obtained his and his secretary's room numbers at the reception desk we made our way upstairs. The two rooms were adjacent to each other. Rather gingerly, we knocked on the right-hand door, which was the head lama's. After a second and a third knock it opened to reveal a burly layman who looked out at us with an unfriendly, even hostile, expression without saying anything. We had knocked on the wrong door. Or rather, we had knocked on the right door, but the right door was the wrong door, the secretary having installed himself in the room supposedly occupied by the head lama and vice versa. It was an old trick, and we had been taken in by it. None the less, Sonam Topgay asked the burly layman, first in Tibetan and then in English, if it would be possible for us to meet the lama, but he appeared to understand neither language, and after a few minutes shook his head and closed the door.

I had also hoped to meet the members of the Buddhist Association of China, but thinking I would probably have no more success with them than Sonam Topgay and I had had with the Buriyat head lama I abandoned the idea. In any case, the Association was little more than the willing or unwilling tool of Chairman Mao's regime, and its members' principal function, when travelling abroad, was to make, in the name of the Buddhists of China, statements supporting the regime's current position in international affairs. But if I did not meet any Chinese Buddhists I at least saw a good deal of ancient Chinese Buddhist art. The Government of India had sponsored an exhibition of Buddhist art as part of the Jayanti celebrations. Each of the participating countries had its own individual section, the contents of which had been selected and arranged by native experts. One thus was able to see that the Buddhist art of each country possessed a certain distinctive quality, which pervaded all its expressions and was found at all periods. Sikkimese and Bhutanese Buddhist art were usually subsumed under Tibetan Buddhist art, but seeing them in bulk, as it were (both sections took the form of a shrine), I was struck by the extent to which both differed not only from the art of Tibet but even from each other, Sikkimese art being more 'feminine', Bhutanese art more 'masculine'. But rich and varied though the exhibition was, many of the exhibits not having been seen outside their own country before, probably the biggest and most striking section was the one devoted to Chinese Buddhist art, and the most striking feature of that section, in my eyes, were the murals from Central Asia (or rather, from that part of Central Asia that was now part of the People's Republic of China). I had never seen anything like them, though they were not the originals but only full-scale copies and though they reproduced, apparently, the changes that had taken place over the centuries in the colour of the pigments that had been used. Unfortunately, picture postcards were not available, but images of the famous meeting between Mañjuśrī the Bodhisattva of Wisdom and the elder Vimalakīrti, as described in the *Vimalakīrti-nirdeśa*,[286] as well as of flying *apsarases* (or 'fairies') and angular Buddhas with extraordinary, multi-coloured haloes, lingered in my mind for many years afterwards.

It was a far cry from communist China, where Buddhism was in decline, to democratic India, where it was being revived and where, a month earlier, more than a quarter of a million people had been converted to Buddhism at a stroke. I had not been able to be present at the ceremony, as my invitation arrived late, when I had already made arrangements to visit Gangtok. Realizing the importance of the step Dr Ambedkar and his followers were about to take I had, however, sent a message to be read out on the occasion:

> In these days when there is so much lip-sympathy for Buddhism and so little real devotion, it is a refreshing and stimulating contrast to find a great national leader boldly breaking away from outworn creeds and obsolete dogmas and openly taking refuge in the Buddha, the Dharma, and the Sangha. Even if Dr Ambedkar stood alone today his conversion to Buddhism would be an event of epochal significance. But he does not stand alone. With him on this historic occasion are tens of thousands of his devoted followers, bent upon emulating his noble example. With him are Truth, Justice, and Compassion. With him, as he stands with his face towards the glorious Sun of Buddhism as once more it rises upon this land, are all those mighty spiritual forces which elevate the human mind and conduce to true progress. With him is the future of India.

I had also written an editorial about the forthcoming conversions for the October number of the *Maha Bodhi* journal. The editorial was entitled 'The Tide Turns', and in it I sought, *inter alia*, to remind readers of the background against which the conversions would be taking place.

> Let none think that Dr B. R. Ambedkar has taken this momentous step hastily or without due consideration, or that he had embarked upon this truly revolutionary course without full consciousness

Dr Ambedkar at the mass conversion ceremony, Nagpur, 14 October 1956

of its socio-religious implications and its far-reaching historical significance. It is perhaps five-and-twenty years since Dr Ambedkar first declared that though he had been born a Hindu he did not intend to die a Hindu. Twenty-five years is a big enough slice of anybody's life, and a period of time sufficiently long for the pondering even so momentous a step as the changing of one's religion. Brahmanical clamours to the contrary notwithstanding, Dr Ambedkar knows what he is doing, and his followers know what they are doing, too.

Not theoretical considerations merely but their own bitter experience of all the unspeakable cruelty, the soul-searing injustice and systematic relentless inhumanity through the ages has eventually convinced them that Hinduism is incapable of reformation and that the only course now open to them is to break away from it and embrace Buddhism.

Within the Buddhist fold they will find not only social

> emancipation but, what is even more important, a way of life conducive to the attainment both of happiness here and hereafter and that unshakeable deliverance of mind which is the gist of the Buddha's teaching. They will also find the hand of brotherhood stretched out to them from every side, not only welcoming but assisting and supporting them as they make their first step along the Noble Eightfold Path.[287]

My own hand was certainly stretched out to them, literally as well as metaphorically. Coming to know that Ambedkar was in Delhi, whither he had returned from Nagpur a few days after the conversion ceremony, I decided to go to see him and personally congratulate him on his great and historic achievement. Most of the Eminent Buddhists from the Border Areas were still in the city, waiting to receive the Dalai Lama and the Panchen Lama when they arrived at the end of the month, and I was able to persuade them to accompany me, even though many of them had not heard of Ambedkar before and did not know that he had been responsible for the conversion of hundreds of thousands of people to Buddhism.

Thus it was with representatives of several different Buddhist traditions that I descended, one fine morning in the second week of November, on Dr Ambedkar's modest residence in Alipore Road. As there was no room big enough for him to receive us all in, chairs were set out in the compound, and there, in a semi-circle, we sat facing our host in the hot sunshine. The Scheduled Castes leader – now a Buddhist leader – sat behind a small table, his wife at his side. I saw at once that he was far from well, and that the brown, pear-shaped face beneath the pith helmet looked tired and haggard. So tired and haggard did it look, and so full of suffering the dark eyes, that I apologized for disturbing him, saying that we had come simply to pay our respects and to congratulate him on his conversion to Buddhism. It had been my intention that we should stay no more than fifteen minutes, but in the event we stayed two hours. Ambedkar was unwilling to let us go. Or rather, he was unwilling to let me go, for it was solely to me that he addressed himself throughout the meeting, to the exclusion of Dhardo Rimpoche, Sonam Topgay, and the rest of the Eminent Buddhists. He was a deeply worried man. The movement of mass conversion had been successfully inaugurated, but what of the future? There was still so much to be done.... From the way he spoke, sitting there with arms resting on the table and lowered head, it was clear that the weight of his responsibilities had become almost too much for him to bear and that he wanted to transfer some of that weight to younger shoulders. Indeed, I had the distinct impression that the shoulders to which he wanted to transfer some of it were my own. Be that as it may, the meeting was undoubtedly tiring him. The broken sentences came from his lips with increasing difficulty, and at ever longer intervals. Eventually, when his head was already resting on his outstretched arms, his eyes closed in utter weariness. Whereupon, to his doctor wife's evident relief, we all quietly left.

If Dr Ambedkar was an old man who had started a new Buddhist movement, the Dalai Lama was a young man who represented an ancient Buddhist tradition. Whereas one was beholding the sun of Buddhism once more rise upon India, albeit amid clouds, the other would see that sun set upon Tibet for no one knew how long. Though it had been known for several months that the Government of India had invited the Dalai Lama to attend the official Buddha Jayanti celebrations in Delhi, only in October was it known that he would definitely be coming. Certain obstacles stood in the way, the Chinese authorities had declared, and it would not be possible for His Holiness to leave Tibet. But Pandit Nehru had intervened, the obstacles had been swept aside, and now it was certain that the Dalai Lama would be coming. He would be coming at the end of November, and the Panchen Lama would be coming too. The news was received with great satisfaction by the Indian public, and official and unofficial agencies alike prepared to give the two Grand Lamas a rousing welcome. They arrived in Gangtok on 24 November, and the following day the three planes carrying, respectively, the Dalai Lama, the Panchen Lama, and the Maharaja of Sikkim, touched down one after another at Palam airport, where tens of thousands of people had gathered to receive them. Each in turn was welcomed with the traditional white scarves, inspected a guard of honour, and was introduced to ministers of the Central Government and members of the Diplomatic Corps, some of whom also offered scarves. The Dalai Lama himself was welcomed by Dr Radhakrishnan and Pandit Nehru, and when the formalities were over, and the last diplomat had been introduced, he advanced towards the waiting *bhikkhus*. According to the newspapers, Delhi had never seen so many yellow-robed Buddhist monks as were then gathered on the tarmac. (There were no red-robed lamas, apparently because the authorities feared they might take advantage of the opportunity to demonstrate against the Chinese occupation of Tibet.) The monks came from all the South-east Asian Buddhist countries, as well as from India itself and from Nepal. There was even a yellow-robed figure from the United Kingdom. The only *bhikkhu* in Delhi who was *not* there was Narada Thera. The Dalai Lama was junior to him in monastic ordination, he had declared, and it would be highly improper for him to go to the airport to receive him. The Dalai Lama ought to come to *him*. None of the other *bhikkhus* seemed to be in the least bothered about who was junior in ordination and who senior, and as the Dalai Lama drew near everybody thronged joyfully round the youthful hierarch, catching him by the hands and reciting Pāli verses invoking on him the blessings of the Buddha, the Dharma, and the Sangha. For several minutes he remained standing there in our midst, blinking in the strong sunlight and smiling, a maroon island in a sea of brilliant saffron.

A day or two later, thanks to Sonam Topgay, I was able to meet the Dalai Lama privately and to exchange a few words with him. We met at Hyderabad House, where he had been taken from the airport after giving *darshan* there and making a short speech. It was also at Hyderabad House, I think, that I met him in company with two or three other British Buddhists, one of whom was Christmas Humphreys, Founder-President of the Buddhist Society, London, who had recently returned from Kathmandu after attending the fourth conference of the World Fellowship of Buddhists. I had already been to see him in his room at the Ashoka Hotel, and had been struck by his extreme coldness. Ten or twelve years ago in London I had not noticed it, but here in India, where Buddhists and Hindus alike tended to be warm and friendly rather than otherwise, it was very noticeable indeed. Besides being a cold person, the Founder-President of the Buddhist Society was a theosophist (not that the two things were necessarily connected), or was at least as much a theosophist as he was a Buddhist. When it was his turn to be presented to the Dalai Lama he not only sank to his knees in stately fashion, rather as a camel does, but produced a copy of Mme Blavatsky's *The Voice of the Silence* and asked the Dalai Lama to sign it for him. What was the book, His Holiness naturally wanted to know. 'It is a Buddhist scripture,' Humphreys replied. Whereupon the

Dalai Lama signed. Years later, when I was again in London, I heard him tell members of the Buddhist Society that *The Voice of the Silence* was a genuine Buddhist *sūtra* and that the Dalai Lama had personally authenticated it as such.

23
DEATH OF A HERO

At the time of my departure from Poona the previous March, Dr Mehta had urged me to see him again as soon as I could, and spend more time in his company, and this I had promised to do. Having attended the UNESCO Seminar on Buddhism in Delhi (which I did after paying a flying visit to Agra and Sarnath) I therefore decided not to return to Calcutta by the direct route but instead to make a detour and see the Servant of Servants in Bombay, where he was now staying. On 29 November I accordingly left the capital, and some forty hours later arrived at VT. Before going to Mayfair I spent a few hours with Dinoo Dubash, who recently had written to me expressing her disillusionment with Dr Mehta. In my reply I reminded her that she was a Buddhist, and that she had been attending meetings of the Society of Servants of God simply because she found it helpful to the leading of her own Buddhist life, particularly as regards meditation. The minute she found the association no longer helpful she was justified in breaking it off. Personally speaking, I added, I accepted Dr Mehta's 'guidance' only to the extent that it accorded with the Buddha's teaching, which meant that in *his* sense I did not accept it at all. Whatever was discordant I rejected, and before leaving Kalimpong I had written him a letter in which I made my position clear.[288] In the course of my meeting with Dinoo, which took place in her flat, I was able to reinforce these points, as well as to emphasize that if her disillusionment with Dr Mehta was accompanied by any emotional disturbance it meant that there was a personal attachment from which she should try to free herself. My words were not without effect, and I left my voluble Parsee friend less upset by her disillusionment with the Servant of Servants and more confident that in ceasing to attend the Society's meetings she had done the right thing.

At Mayfair I was welcomed very warmly by Dr Mehta and Sundri, as well as by Durgadas Birla and some of the other friends I had made there and at the Nature Cure Clinic earlier in the year. Dr Mehta's welcome, I could not help noticing, despite its warmth was not unmixed with something of the satisfaction a good shepherd feels on seeing a wandering sheep return at last to the safety of the fold. But there was no question of my having returned to the fold, for even if I could be regarded as belonging to the ovine species (which I rather doubted) I belonged to a different flock, had my fold elsewhere, and hearkened to the voice – however distant – of quite another Master. Though the pasturage at Mayfair was indeed green, and though I could happily have grazed on it for a while (Dr Mehta wanted me to go on a meditation retreat there), I knew that it was essential for me to be on my way and that I could not spend more than a few days with my Bombay friends. *How* I knew this I was unable to say, any more than I was able to say *why* it was essential for me to be on my way. I did not hear an inner voice, neither did I have a sudden intuition. It was simply that I knew, clearly and certainly, that *I had to be on my way*, and accordingly fixed my departure for 5 December. Dr Mehta was not at all happy that I would be going so soon, and did his best to persuade me to postpone my departure until later in the month. Indeed it would be good if I postponed it indefinitely. Making plans was nothing but a form of ego-assertion, he solemnly assured me, and the more one allowed the ego to assert itself the more difficult it became for one to surrender to the Divine and accept its guidance. As if to reinforce his words, a few days later there came a Script. It came in the usual manner, when we were all seated in meditation and Dr Mehta had gone into a kind of trance state, and among its various directives there was one for me. The Buddhist monk Sangharakshita, the mysterious entity behind the Scripts declared, should postpone his journey to Calcutta and remain at Mayfair, in the company of 'My Servant Dinshah' (i.e. Dr Mehta), for at least a few weeks.

Believing as Dr Mehta and the members of the Society did that the entity behind the Scripts was God, they naturally also believed that the 'guidance' given in these communications, whether for themselves or anyone else, was to be followed unquestioningly. Dr Mehta therefore renewed his efforts to persuade me to postpone my departure, and to his urgings Sundri added hers. Now that God himself had spoken it was in their eyes no longer simply a matter of my refusing to accede to the wishes of my friends but rather, what was an infinitely more serious matter, of my resisting – even rejecting – the 'guidance' that had come for me from the Divine through the Divine's chosen instrument, the Servant of Servants. Emanating as it did from such an exalted source, the guidance was obviously in my best interest, and any reluctance on my part to accept it must be due, they broadly hinted, to that root of all evil, ego-assertion, which despite my having committed myself to the Buddhist way of life evidently was still able to prevent me from surrendering wholeheartedly to the Divine. I did not blame Dr Mehta and Sundri for putting this construction on my failure to accept the guidance that had come for me. Believing as they did, it was hardly possible for them to put any other construction on it. Far from blaming them, indeed, I recognized that their efforts to persuade me, not so much to postpone my departure, as to *accept God's guidance*, were motivated by a genuine concern for my spiritual welfare and were the expression, therefore, of true, if misguided, friendship. Had I not known, with such clarity and certainty, that it was essential for me to be on my way, I would probably have stayed a little longer in Bombay, simply in order to please them. As it was, the fact that they were now pressing me to postpone my departure because I had been 'divinely guided' to do that meant that I had to confront the issue squarely and explain, as I had already explained in the letter I had written Dr Mehta from Kalimpong, that I did not accept the latter's 'guidance' unconditionally. In fact, I added, I was of the opinion that it was positively wrong to do so. Having made my position clear I felt much better, though I was not sure how Dr Mehta would take my plain speaking. In the event he took it quite well, probably because he was not unaccustomed to people 'resisting the guidance' (was not his own wife still resisting it?), and was prepared to be patient and wait for them to come round to his way of thinking. At any rate, he and Sundri stopped trying to persuade me to postpone my departure, and for the remainder of my stay at Mayfair I joined them in their thrice-daily meditation sessions, and talked with Dr Mehta, without reference being made to my unwillingness to accept divine guidance. I also arranged for one of the Society's evening meetings to be addressed by another Buddhist speaker.

The speaker in question was Christmas Humphreys. Having attended the Fourth Conference of the World Fellowship of Buddhists in Kathmandu, the Founder-President of the London Buddhist Society was now on his way back to the United Kingdom and making a brief stopover in Bombay. Besides being curious to know what the Society's members would think of Zen Buddhism (Humphreys' chosen topic, on which he had written several books), I had a Boswellian desire to see what two such dissimilar characters as the English criminal lawyer-cum-Buddhist and the Parsee naturopath-cum-guru would make of each other and how they would get on together. The audience at Humphreys' talk consisted of much the same kind of people as those who had attended my own talks a year earlier. Few of them had even heard of Zen before and though the tradition was, supposedly, of Indian origin, its 'style' was so foreign to them as to be virtually incomprehensible. As his custom apparently was, Humphreys emphasized the irrational, anti-intellectual, iconoclastic side of Zen (probably a useful emphasis in concept-ridden, tradition-bound India), illustrating his points with some of the more outrageous Zen anecdotes. He was a fluent and forcible speaker, at times even a fiery one, but the fire was the cold fire of the intellect, not the warm fire of the heart, and I could see that although the audience was impressed by his dramatic, not to say histrionic, manner of delivery, they were not moved. As for Dr Mehta, he sat through the talk motionless, eyes upturned so that only the whites were visible, and from the rambling, inconsequential nature of his summing up afterwards, in the course of which he spoke about '(sexual) union at the highest level', it was clear that there had been no meeting of minds between him and Humphreys and that he had perhaps not even been listening to what the latter said. The truth was that the two men could hardly have been more different. Despite his (reluctant) assumption of the prophet's mantle, Dr Mehta was very human, whereas there was something inhuman about Humphreys. If the former was easy to like (as Dinoo was later to observe, he had 'a way of melting one'), then to like the latter would, I imagined, be a rather difficult task. However that may have been, on my departure from Mayfair Dr Mehta's softer side was very much in evidence, and he bade me an almost tearful farewell; at the same time, he was full of dark forebodings about my failure to 'follow guidance' and predicted that all my plans would come to nothing.

Though sorry to part from my God-guided friend, I did not allow his forebodings to disturb me, and my predominant feeling as I caught the overnight train to Nagpur was one of satisfaction, even relief, that at last I was acting on the knowledge that it was essential for me to be on my way. Why it was essential for me to be on my way I did not know. Dr Mehta had predicted that all my plans would come to nothing; but it was not because I had plans that needed to be carried out immediately that it was essential for me to be on my way. I was on my way simply because it was essential I should be on my way. True, I was on my way to Calcutta, where I would be editing the next issue of the *Maha Bodhi* journal, and I would be breaking my journey in Nagpur in order to make the acquaintance of the newly converted Buddhists, who had invited me to spend a few days with them and deliver some lectures. But it was not because I had to do these things immediately that it was essential for me to be on my way. I could just as easily have edited the next issue of the *Maha Bodhi* journal in Bombay, and just as easily have given my Nagpur lectures two or three weeks later. I was on my way because it was, I knew, essential for me to be on my way, though why it was essential I did not yet know. Before leaving Bombay I wired the date and time of my arrival in Nagpur to A. R. Kulkarni, the elderly Brahmin advocate, and secretary of the Buddha Society, with whom I had stayed on my previous visit and who had arranged for me to speak at the University and elsewhere.

On the occasion of that visit, more than two years earlier, my arrival in Nagpur had attracted little attention. Only Kulkarni was waiting on the platform to receive me, and he had taken me to his – or rather his brother's – house in Dharampeth by taxi with a minimum of fuss. This time it was very different. As the train came to a halt I saw that the platform was a solid mass of excited, white-clad figures. There must have been 2,000 of them and I realized, with a shock of astonishment, that they were all new Buddhists and that they had come to receive me. Kulkarni was also there, and on my emerging from the carriage he and the office-bearers of the Indian Buddhist Society (which Ambedkar had founded a year or two earlier, and which had been responsible for the organizing of the mass conversion ceremony) pushed their way through the crowd towards me. I was profusely garlanded, and then to repeated shouts of 'Victory to Baba Saheb Ambedkar!' and 'Victory to Bhikshu Sangharakshita!' was led to the waiting car and escorted to Dharampeth and the Kulkarni residence. Since my previous visit Krishna, Kulkarni's elder nephew, had married, and as he and his wife now occupied the room where I had stayed I was accommodated in the wooden outhouse that Kulkarni had built for himself at the end of the back yard. Here I was left to undo my bedding roll and spend the rest of the afternoon recovering from my journey.

But this was not to be. I had arrived in Nagpur at one o'clock. Less than an hour later, when I was still settling into my new quarters, there was a sudden commotion in the yard outside and a few seconds later three or four members of the Indian Buddhist Society burst into the little outhouse. 'Baba Saheb' was dead. He had died in Delhi the previous night. The bearers of these dire tidings were not only in a state of deep shock but utterly demoralized. They were barely able to tell me that the Society's downtown office was being besieged by thousands of grief-stricken people who, knowing of my presence in Nagpur, were demanding that I should come and speak to them. Obviously it would be impossible for me to address so many people without a microphone and loudspeakers. I therefore told my visitors to organize a proper condolence meeting. They should organize it for seven o'clock that evening. I would address the meeting and console people for the loss of their great leader as best I could. There being no time to lose, my visitors departed without further ado, taking with them others who had arrived after them, and I was left to consider my own reactions to the news of Ambedkar's death. Though shocked, I was not surprised. At the time of our last meeting he was evidently a very sick man, and I had been astonished to learn, before my departure from Delhi, that he had flown to Kathmandu in order to attend the Fourth Conference of the World Fellowship of Buddhists. There, as I afterwards heard, he was given a standing ovation by the assembled delegates and addressed them, by popular demand, on 'Buddha or Karl Marx'.[289] Returning to Delhi on 1 December, he visited the exhibition of Buddhist art, attended a meeting in honour of the Dalai Lama, and passed some time in the Rajya Sabha or Council of States, of which he was a member. The evening of 5 December was spent receiving a deputation of Jain leaders, listening to a record of his favourite Buddhist devotional song and, apparently, working on the preface to his book *The Buddha and His Dhamma*.[290]

At 6.30 the following morning, when I was on my way to Nagpur, his wife had entered his bedroom to find him dead.

The condolence meeting was held in the Kasturchand Park, which was little more than a large open space part of which was occupied by a small pavilion. Roads apparently debouched into it from a number of directions, for on my arrival there at seven o'clock, by which time night had fallen, it was the dark centre of a gigantic wheel the golden spokes of which were formed by the lighted candles carried by the long columns of mourners who were converging on the place from all over the city. As the columns entered the park I saw that the men, women, and children carrying the candles were all clad in white – the same white that only seven weeks ago they had worn for the conversion ceremony. Whether on account of their demoralized state, or because there was not enough time, the organizers of the meeting had done little more than rig up a microphone and loudspeakers. There was no stage and, apart from a petromax or two, no illumination other than that provided by the thousands of candles. By the time I rose to speak – standing on the seat of a rickshaw and with someone holding the microphone up in front of me – about 100,000 people had assembled. Under normal circumstances I would have been the last speaker, but on this occasion I was the first. In fact as things turned out I was the only speaker. Though some five or six of Ambedkar's most prominent local supporters one by one attempted to pay tribute to their departed leader, they were so overcome by emotion that, after uttering only a few words, they burst into tears and had to sit down. Their example was contagious. When I started to speak the whole vast gathering was weeping, and sobs and groans filled the air. In the cold blue light of the petromax I could see grey-haired men rolling in agonies of grief at my feet.

Though deeply moved by the sight of so much anguish and despair, I realized that for me, at least, this was no time to indulge in emotion. Ambedkar's followers had received a terrible shock. They had been Buddhists for only seven weeks, and now their leader, in whom their trust was total, and on whose guidance in the difficult days ahead they had been relying, had been snatched away. Poor and illiterate as the vast majority of them were, and faced by the unrelenting hostility of the caste Hindus, they did not know which way to turn and there was a possibility that the whole movement of conversion to Buddhism would come to a halt or even collapse. I therefore delivered a vigorous and stirring speech in which, after extolling the greatness of Ambedkar's achievement, I exhorted my audience to continue the work he had so gloriously begun and bring it to a successful conclusion. 'Baba Saheb' was not dead but alive. To the extent that they were faithful to the ideals for which he stood and for which he had, quite literally, sacrificed himself, he lived on in them. This speech, which lasted for an hour or more, was not without effect. Ambedkar's stricken followers began to realize that it was not the end of the world, that there was a future for them even after their beloved Baba Saheb's death, and that the future was not altogether devoid of hope.

While I was speaking I had an extraordinary experience. Above the crowd there hung an enormous Presence. Whether the Presence was Ambedkar's departed consciousness hovering over the heads of his followers, or whether it was the collective product of their thoughts at that time of trial and crisis, I do not know, but it was as real to me as the people I was addressing.

In the course of the next four days I visited practically all the ex-Untouchable 'localities' of Nagpur, of which there must have been several dozen, and addressed nearly thirty mass meetings, besides initiating about 30,000 people into Buddhism and delivering lectures at Nagpur University and the Ramakrishna Mission. My locality speeches were rendered simultaneously into Marathi by Kulkarni, who despite being nearly twice my age not only kept pace with me but did full justice to the energy and passion with which I spoke. As he had done on the occasion of my previous visit, he maintained a detailed record of my engagements which he afterwards wrote up in article form.[291] When the time came for me to be again on my way I had addressed altogether 200,000 people and forged, incidentally, a very special link with the Buddhists of Nagpur, indeed with all Ambedkar's followers. As I wrote to Dinoo from Calcutta a few weeks later:

> I think I can say without vanity that I created a tremendous impression. Dr Ambedkar's followers told me that they felt my being there at that critical juncture was a miracle and that I had saved Nagpur for Buddhism. Had I not been there, there is no knowing what would have happened. At first people felt that the end of the world had come. But after listening to my speeches – which were very strong indeed – they felt full of hope and courage

> and determined to work for the spread of Buddhism. On the last day of my visit I gave no less than eleven lectures. The last meeting was held at 1.30 in the morning, when fifteen thousand people were converted to Buddhism.[292]

Nor was that all. The events of the last four or five days had had their effect on me as well as on my auditors. My letter to Dinoo continued:

> My own spiritual experience during this period was most peculiar. I felt that I was not a person but an impersonal force. At one stage I was working quite literally without any thought, just as one is in *samādhi*. Also, I felt hardly any tiredness – certainly not at all what one would have expected from such a tremendous strain. When I left Nagpur I felt quite fresh and rested. Now let us see about the rest of the programme.[293]

By the rest of the programme I presumably meant the work that had been awaiting me at the Maha Bodhi Society's headquarters, where I spent six or seven weeks seeing the December 1956 and January 1957 issues of the *Maha Bodhi* journal through the press, as well as bringing out my dialogue 'Is Buddhism for Monks Only?'[294] and an essay 'Buddhism and Art'[295] in booklet form with funds provided by Dinoo. A considerable portion of the Notes and News section of both the December and January issues of the journal was taken up by reports of the arrival in India of the Dalai and Panchen Lamas,[296] their participation in the Buddha Jayanti celebrations in Delhi, and their subsequent pilgrimage to the principal Buddhist holy places. Newspaper coverage of the activities of the two hierarchs was extensive. People were fascinated by the exotic visitors from beyond the Himalayas. The fascination was due partly to the Lamas' extreme youth (both were in their early twenties), partly to their being celibate monks, and partly – perhaps above all – to the fact that after being surrounded for centuries with an aura of remoteness, inaccessibility, and mystery, the Dalai and Panchen Lamas of Tibet were now treading the soil of India and could be seen and heard and even photographed. Despite the Chinese Government's efforts to ensure equal treatment for the two visitors (efforts which so far as official protocol was concerned were entirely successful), the Dalai Lama inevitably attracted more attention than the Panchen. The press regularly – and incorrectly – referred to him as the God King of Tibet ('God King Worships Relics' was a typical headline). Commentators also observed that the Dalai and Panchen Lamas were markedly different in temperament, the former being jovial and outward-going, the latter thoughtful and reserved. During their stay in Delhi Pandit Nehru had given them a choice of films. The Dalai Lama, characteristically, had asked to see a Marx Brothers film, while the Panchen Lama, no less characteristically, wanted to see *War and Peace*.

By the time the Lamas came to Calcutta, which was when they had been in India for about two months, a note of criticism had started to creep into the newspaper coverage, which hitherto had been uniformly favourable, even adulatory. Many people were shocked to learn that two such great religious personalities as the Dalai and Panchen Lamas were not vegetarians, as were the vast majority of Hindus, all Jains, and some Sikhs. But as I well knew, vegetarianism formed no part of Tibetan Buddhism, though the Tibetans did not maintain, as some Burmese did, that one could not be a (Theravādin) Buddhist *and* a vegetarian. There also were complaints that the two Lamas lived in a lavish style more appropriate to secular princes than to religious leaders and exemplars – a contradiction perhaps inherent in the very nature of their position in theocratic Tibet. An instance of this lavishness which excited particular comment occurred while they were in Calcutta. They were staying at the Grand Hotel, the best hotel in the city. One day they both decided they needed haircuts. A barber was accordingly sent for, and with the aid of a pair of clippers soon reduced their redundant locks to the regulation monastic length. For this service they each tipped him two thousand rupees. The size of the tip excited comment because if the Lamas gave two thousand rupees each for a haircut (in Kalimpong I gave one rupee, which was the top rate), then the rest of their expenditure was, presumably, on a correspondingly grand scale, which meant that each of them would be spending lakhs of rupees every month. What the two Lamas and their advisers seemed not to realize was that in India, unlike in Tibet, spirituality tended to be associated, in most people's minds, with poverty rather than riches, simplicity rather than ostentation.

It was in his suite at the Grand Hotel, after he had received his haircut, that I had my second private meeting with the Dalai Lama.

Having learned that he (though not the Panchen Lama) would be spending a week or so in Kalimpong before returning to Tibet I wanted to invite him to Everton Villa for a reception in his honour by our branch of the Maha Bodhi Society. Probably as much on account of the name of the Maha Bodhi Society, with which he was by this time well acquainted, as for any other reason, he accepted without demur. The reception was to be held on 27 January, four or five days after his arrival in Kalimpong. As this was not far off, I left Calcutta as soon as I conveniently could, which happened to be the very day the Dalai Lama himself left. Before my departure I had written the editorial for the January issue of the *Maha Bodhi*. It was headed simply 'Dr Ambedkar'. After giving a résumé of his eventful career, I wrote:

> A lifelong student of religions, Dr Ambedkar had step by step come to the conclusion that [Hindu] orthodoxy was incapable of reformation, and that the victims of age-old socio-religious oppression and exploitation in India could be freed from their disabilities only by embracing Buddhism. Towards this consummation he gradually bent more and more of his energies. Some, even among his own people, opposed him, feeling perhaps that no mere 'religion' could solve a problem of such tremendous complexity. But Dr Ambedkar's faith in Buddhism stood firm as a rock. With characteristic boldness, he declared that he was going to become a Buddhist even if nobody else became one. But when the time for taking the momentous step came far from taking it alone he carried hundreds of thousands with him. All over India, wherever the name of Dr Ambedkar was honoured, people gathered in their thousands and in their tens of thousands to take refuge in the Buddha, the Dharma, and the Sangha.
>
> Before the movement of mass conversion could reach its height Dr Ambedkar, worn out by the labours of a lifetime, died. Some there were who thought that with his death the movement would come to an end, or at least receive a serious setback. Never were prophets more false. The ashes of his funeral pyre were hardly cold before the movement gathered a momentum beyond the expectations of the most wildly optimistic. Nay, even as all that was mortal of him was consigned to the flames the sacred chant '*Buddhaṃ saraṇaṃ gacchāmi*' rose spontaneously from the

lips of tens of thousands of mourners there. Since then reports have come in of mass conversion ceremonies at Nagpur, Poona, Ahmedabad, Agra, and a score of other important centres. Great as Dr Ambedkar's influence was during his life, evidently it is greater still in death.[297]

24
'WHERE THE THREE YĀNAS FLOURISH'

One of the first things I did after my return to Kalimpong was to buy a special cup and saucer for the Dalai Lama. It was the Tibetan custom to offer a guest three cups of tea, and when the guest was an important incarnate lama the Chinese-style cup would be of porcelain or jade and its stand and lid of gold and silver studded with semi-precious stones. The Kalimpong branch of the Maha Bodhi Society possessed no such cup, neither did it have the means of purchasing one, but at least we should serve the Dalai Lama tea in a brand-new cup and saucer, I thought, and that cup and saucer should be the finest the Himalayan Stores was able to supply. We also erected a throne of the traditional type, consisting of five (or was it seven?) square Tibetan-style mattresses piled one on top of the other, covered with a rug, and backed by a brocade cushion the upper edge of which was draped with a white ceremonial scarf. This throne was set up in the shrine-room of Everton Villa, the walls of which were hung with silk for the occasion. There was also an archway of greenery and bunting at the entrance to the building.

The Dalai Lama arrived on the morning of the appointed day, which happened to be a Sunday, accompanied by the current Sub-Divisional Officer and by members of his entourage. On his arrival I, Khemasiri, Dr Singh, and Dawa offered him ceremonial scarves on behalf of the Reception Committee and conducted him down the flight of steps leading from the road to our centre. At the bottom of the steps I had stationed monk-musicians from the Tharpa Choling Gompa, and it was to the sonorous rumblings of their giant trumpets that the Dalai Lama passed between the rows of assembled members and friends who, with lighted incense-sticks in their hands, lined the path between the steps and the entrance to Everton Villa. On entering the shrine-room he prostrated himself three times before the image of the Buddha (the standing one Lama Govinda had given me), performing each prostration in the elaborate Tibetan manner. Having rearranged his voluminous upper robe, he then remained standing for about ten minutes as he chanted Tibetan verses in praise of the Enlightened One. He chanted in a deep, resonant voice, smilingly scattering grains of rice as he did so. When he had finished he took his seat on the improvised throne and Dawa poured him his first cup of tea. As I afterwards discovered, in Tibet it was considered a great honour to be allowed to pour tea for the Dalai or Panchen Lama, and those who had enjoyed that privilege were permitted to wear their cap turned up at the side in a particular manner. How aware of all this our young secretary was I do not know, but he certainly filled the Dalai Lama's cup slowly and mindfully, with the lowered eyes and deferential inclination of the body that were second nature to a Tibetan in such circumstances.

Our guest having taken a few sips of tea, as etiquette prescribed, I read out the address of welcome I had prepared. To this the Dalai Lama replied in Tibetan, an English version of his speech being supplied by Sonam Topgay, whose services the Government of India had, it seemed, placed at the Tibetan hierarch's disposal. In the course of his reply the Dalai Lama expressed his satisfaction at finding a 'young branch' of the Maha Bodhi Society at Kalimpong and exhorted its members to follow the teachings of the Lord Buddha. I then presented him, on behalf of the branch, with an ancient palm-leaf manuscript of a Pāli Abhidhamma work and a complete set of our publications in English and Nepali, including a two-volume bound set of the twenty issues of *Stepping-Stones*. The Dalai Lama spent the remainder of his visit, which lasted for about an hour, bestowing individual blessings on all those present, who filed past him for that purpose, offering white scarves and flowers as they did so. I noticed that he blessed everybody with the 'double-handed blessing', that is, by placing both hands firmly on each individual head, at the same time smiling broadly. In Tibet itself, apparently, he would simply have touched them lightly with a bunch of coloured ribbons fastened to the end of a stick. Among the recipients of

Dalai Lama in procession, Khemasiri and Sangharakshita behind. Ani-la behind Khemasiri

the double-handed blessing were a number of local Tibetans who, having got wind of the fact that the Dalai Lama was visiting our centre, had taken advantage of the opportunity to have the *darshan* of their revered leader. After his departure they drank up what remained of his third cup of tea (actually, the third topping up), sharing the precious drops among themselves with the kind of devotion with which, I imagined, pious Catholics took holy communion. Before leaving they thanked me warmly for making it possible for them to have such close contact with His Holiness. They could not have had it otherwise, they averred, as the members of Kalimpong's Tibetan community were finding it difficult to get so much as a glimpse of him.

On my arrival the following morning at Bhutan House, where the Dalai Lama was staying, I saw that this was indeed the case. There was a police guard on the gates, and Tibetans who had come for the Dalai Lama's *darshan* were being refused admission. This was because the Chinese Government wanted that there should be as little contact as possible between the Dalai Lama and the Tibetan population of Kalimpong, who were known to be strongly in favour of independence for Tibet and opposed to the continued occupation of their country by the Red Army. I and the rest of the little party from the Maha Bodhi Society's branch had no difficulty gaining admission, as the Dalai Lama had asked us to call that morning. We found him seated in the Dorji family's richly appointed chapel, where he was apparently putting up, and where, four years earlier, Anand-ji and I had recited *suttas* over the dead body of Raja S. T. Dorji and I had delivered the funeral sermon. The Dalai Lama received us with his usual cordiality, and after a few minutes' conversation presented me with a Buddha-image, block prints of two Tibetan scriptures (the *Prajñāpāramitā* or *Perfection of Wisdom* 'in Eight Thousand lines' and the smaller *Lamrim* or *Stages of the Path* by Tsongkhapa), and a signed and sealed photograph of himself, plus a cash donation. We were then smilingly dismissed.

While there were people in Kalimpong who wanted to see the Dalai Lama but could not, there were others who, although they had no wish to see him, were nevertheless obliged to do so. The Government of India was eager that the Dalai Lama should visit a modern educational institution, just as it had been anxious that the Eminent Buddhists from the Border Areas should see dams as well as holy places. In Kalimpong what better institution was there for him to visit than the famous Dr Graham's Home, where 500 orphans of mixed descent were housed, clothed, fed, and educated, and which was in many respects a model of its kind? The Homes authorities were therefore informed, through the Sub-Divisional Officer, that the Dalai Lama would be visiting the place and that he was to be shown round. To the Scottish Presbyterians who ran the Homes this was far from being welcome news; many of the teachers and house-parents were convinced that Tibetan Buddhists were devil-worshippers and practised black magic. Now they were being required to welcome the chief devil-worshipper himself onto their premises. But there was no help for it. Christian missionaries were being attacked in the press, restrictions had already been placed on some of their activities, and the Homes authorities dared not risk incurring the Central Government's displeasure by refusing to receive the Dalai Lama who was, after all, a state guest. If only something would happen to prevent his coming to the Homes! Perhaps God would prevent it if they prayed hard enough. The more bigoted teachers and house parents therefore held an all-night prayer meeting before the Dalai Lama was due to arrive, but their united prayers no more availed to keep him away from the Homes than the Tantric 'rites of destruction' ordered by the Lhasa Government in 1950 had availed to halt the steady advance of the Red Army into Tibetan territory. The chief devil-worshipper came the next day as planned, breakfasted with Mr Duncan, the whey-faced Superintendent of the Homes and his family, saw the school, met the children, and by all accounts thoroughly enjoyed his visit.

The Dalai Lama was not the only important Tibetan religious leader I saw in the New Year, nor the one with whom I had the most contact. Happening to meet Sonam Topgay in the bazaar one day, a few weeks after the Dalai Lama's return to Tibet, I learned that there was a celebrated Nyingma lama staying at Tirpai and that my Sikkimese friend had come from Gangtok in order to see him and pay his respects. The lama's name was Sangye Dorje (Buddhavajra in Sanskrit), but he was commonly known as Chattrul Sangye Dorje. 'Chattrul' meant something like 'without affairs' or 'without concerns' and the sobriquet had been bestowed on him on account of his complete indifference to such things as organized monasticism and ecclesiastical position. It was not even clear whether he was a monk or a layman. He roamed freely from place to place, no one knowing where he was going to turn up next or how long he would stay. He was an accomplished yogi, having spent many years in the solitudes of eastern Tibet, meditating; and if popular report was to be believed, he possessed many psychic powers and was a great magician. Despite his indifference to organized monasticism and ecclesiastical position, Sonam Topgay added, and his frequently bizarre and eccentric behaviour, Chattrul Sangye Dorje was highly esteemed by several prominent members of the Gelug hierarchy. Once, when in Lhasa, he had bestowed a number of esoteric Tantric initiations on the Regent of Tibet (whether this was Reting Rimpoche or his successor my friend did not say). At the conclusion of the ceremonies, which lasted several days, the Regent made the customary offerings which, his position being what it was, were extremely valuable. Chattrul Sangye

Dorje swept them all on to a cloth, tied the cloth up into a bundle, and handed the bundle to the Regent, saying, 'Look after it for me'. Whereupon he resumed his wanderings.

Sonam Topgay's account intrigued me. In fact I was fascinated by his picture of the unconventional lama whom, it was evident, he very much admired. (Later I discovered that Chattrul Sangye Dorje, though not an incarnate lama, was widely revered as one of the three great Nyingma gurus of the century.) Seeing my interest, Sonam Topgay observed that it would not be difficult for me to meet the lama, who notoriously did not stand on ceremony and who was very accessible – once you had succeeded in tracking him down. He moreover hinted that although Chattrul Sangye Dorje was highly unpredictable, and one could never be sure how he would respond to a particular request, he *might* be willing to give me Tantric initiation. In any case, I ought not to miss the opportunity of meeting so great a lama and obtaining his blessing.

The result was that a day or two later, on Friday 8 March, I left Everton Villa soon after breakfast and made my way through the bazaar and up to Tirpai. With me was the French nun, who had stopped by early that morning and who, on learning I was going to see Chattrul Sangye Dorje, had asked if she might accompany me. Though I would really have preferred to go without her, I raised no objection, as she was again experiencing 'difficulties' in connection with her Tibetan studies and I thought the lama might be able to help her, especially as she was by this time beginning to be no less disappointed with Kachu Rimpoche than she had been with Dhardo Rimpoche. What I had expected the famous Nyingma lama to look like I cannot say, but on meeting him I received a shock. He was of indeterminate age, perhaps somewhere between thirty and forty,[298] his coarse black hair was cut short, like a monk's, and he was clad in a nondescript maroon garment lined with what appeared to be grubby sheepskin. What I was most struck by however was his face, which was coarse and unrefined almost to the point of brutality, and could easily have passed for that of a horny-handed peasant with no thought beyond his pigs and poultry. At the same time, his whole being communicated such an impression of strength and reliability that one could not but feel reassured, and it was not long before the two of us were deep in conversation. As was proper, Chattrul Rimpoche (as my Sikkimese friend respectfully called him) took the lead, and asked me a number of questions, first about the Vinaya or Monastic Code and then about the Abhidharma. This seemed to be the standard procedure in Tibetan religious circles. At my first meeting with the abbot of the Tharpa Choling Gompa, I recalled, the old man had questioned me closely about the Vinaya before moving on to more abstruse topics.[299] Apparently the idea was that one should make sure one was operating within the same universe of discourse as the other person, and that the two of you had a common medium of communication (a medium that was not merely linguistic) and only *then* proceed to engage in serious discussion. On the present occasion I must have answered Chattrul Rimpoche's questions to his satisfaction, for from the Abhidharma we progressed – through what intermediate steps I no longer recollect – to meditation and meditational experiences, and eventually I found myself telling him about Dr Mehta's 'guidance' and asking him to what extent he thought this could be accepted. Perhaps not surprisingly, as we were both Buddhists, his reply was in agreement with my own conclusions. Teachings and directives received in a state of trance, whether by oneself or by another person, were not to be accepted uncritically but were to be subjected to the test of reason and experience and compared with the *Buddhavacana*, or Word of the Buddha, as explained by the enlightened masters of India and Tibet.

By this time I had developed considerable confidence in the Rimpoche, and I therefore asked him to tell me who my *yidam* or tutelary deity was. Though unable to accept Dr Mehta's 'guidance' on his (or its) own terms, I had taken very much to heart his insistence that in the spiritual life the best and most reliable guidance was that which came from beyond one's ego. For me it could not come from God, but perhaps it could come from one or other of those transcendental beings who according to the Buddhism of Tibet (as of that of China and Japan) were the different, infinitely various, aspects of the Buddha's *sambhogakāya* or 'body of glory' – the supra-historical 'body' in which he communed with advanced bodhisattvas and they with him. Chattrul Rimpoche showed no surprise at my request. In fact he seemed rather pleased, and after a moment of inner recollection told me that my yidam was Dolma Jungo or Green Tārā, the 'female' bodhisattva of fearlessness and spontaneous helpfulness, adding that Tārā had been the tutelary deity of many of the great pandits of India and Tibet. In other words, I had an *affinity* with Green Tārā, in the sense that she was the transcendental counterpart of my own mundane nature and that I could, therefore, more readily come to a deeper understanding of myself through devotion to her. Having told me my yidam, the Rimpoche proceeded to bestow the appropriate initiation. First he gave me the ten-syllabled mantra, which he pronounced very forcibly in the Tibetan manner, after which he explained the *sādhana* or spiritual practice that would enable me to visualize Green Tārā and call down her blessings on myself and all sentient beings. The latter he did at some length, so that it was mid-afternoon when I finally bade him a grateful farewell, having spent more than four hours in his company. My mood was one of considerable elation. Before leaving Tirpai I called on the aged Tibetan artist who lived there and commissioned from him a thangka or scroll painting, which I would be needing as an aid to visualization. The French nun, for her part, was more cheerful than she had been for a long time, Chattrul Rimpoche having spoken to her about her Tibetan studies and persuaded her to give up the fast on which she had embarked in order to force someone to do something about the difficulties she was experiencing in connection with them.

A few days later the Rimpoche came to see me at Everton Villa. Though he probably arrived unannounced, he must have been accompanied by Sonam Topgay, for he explained the Green Tārā *sādhana* to me again and gave me further instructions about its practice. I had already committed his previous explanations to writing and therefore was able to check what I had written with him and make sure I had got the details of the *sādhana* absolutely right. As soon as the thangka I had commissioned was ready I would start practising. A new phase in my spiritual life was about to begin. Hitherto I had been a Theravādin monk practising meditation with the help of the Theravādin tradition of *ānāpānasati* or respiration-mindfulness. From now on, while remaining a Theravādin monk, I would be practising meditation with the help of the Mahāyāna-cum-Vajrayāna tradition of mantra-recitation and deity-visualization. This did not mean that previously I had not valued the Mahāyāna and Vajrayāna, any more than it meant that in future I could afford to dispense with the practice of respiration-mindfulness. I had always valued the Mahāyāna and Vajrayāna very highly. Mahāyāna scriptures like the *Diamond Sūtra* and the *Laṅkāvatāra Sūtra* and Vajrayāna works such as *The Life of Milarepa* and *The Golden Rosary of the Precepts of the Gurus* had been important sources of inspiration from very early on in my Buddhist career.[300] It was after reading the *Diamond Sūtra* at the age of sixteen that I realized I was a Buddhist and in fact always had been one.[301] But though the Mahāyāna and the Vajrayāna meant so much to me, and though I had derived abundant inspiration from their respective canonical literatures, I had not practised any of the distinctively Mahāyāna or Vajrayāna methods of meditation. Now I was taking up the Green Tārā *sādhana*, and the fact that I was so doing marked an important transition in my spiritual life.

Changes of a more external nature were also imminent. In the course of his visit Chattrul Rimpoche elicited from me the information that Everton Villa was only a rented property, that our lease would expire in September, that it would be difficult for us to find an equally suitable property that was to let, and that although my real aim was to establish a permanent monastic centre in Kalimpong there seemed at present little likelihood of my being able to do so. The centre, I explained, would be dedicated to the study, practice, and dissemination of the total Buddhist tradition, for I had long been convinced that, in the noble words of Dr Edward Conze,

> the doctrine of the Buddha, conceived in its full breadth, width, majesty and grandeur, comprises all those teachings which are linked to the original teaching by historical continuity, and which work out methods leading to the extinction of [ego-]individuality by eliminating the belief in it.[302]

The Rimpoche's response to this information was as categorical as it was unexpected. There was no doubt that I would establish a permanent monastic centre in Kalimpong, he assured me. In fact I would establish it quite soon, and I should call it 'The Vihara Where the Three Yānas Flourish (or Blossom)'. Having given the as yet non-existent monastery its name in what I afterwards described as a mood of high spiritual inspiration, Chattrul Rimpoche addressed to me the Tibetan original of the following stanzas:

> In the sky devoid of limits, the teaching of the Muni is
> The sun, spreading the thousand rays of the three *śikṣās*
> [i.e. morality, meditation, and wisdom];
> Continually shining in the radiance of the impartial disciples,
> May this Jambudvīpa region of the Triyāna be fair!

In accordance with his request, [made] in the Fire-Monkey Year
On the ninth day of the first month by the Mahā Sthavira Sangharakshita,
This was written by the Śākya-upāsaka, the Vidyādhara Bodhivajra: [may there be] happiness and blessings!

Notwithstanding what was said in the first line of the second stanza, the stanzas were not in response to any request of mine. The Rimpoche produced them quite spontaneously. That he should cast them in the form of a response to a request was probably no more than literary convention, even as his styling me Mahā Sthavira or 'Great Elder' when I was only a simple *bhikṣu* was just the normal Tibetan politeness.

The fact that Chattrul Rimpoche had named my future monastery *of his own accord* greatly impressed my Tibetan friends, especially those of the Nyingma persuasion. According to Kachu Rimpoche, who came to see me shortly afterwards, it was exceptionally auspicious, as whatever Rimpoche Chattrul Sangye Dorje named was sure to prosper. I was pleased to hear this, but before the Triyana Vardhana Vihara – as I had decided the place should be called in Sanskrit – could prosper it had to come into existence, and as yet there was no sign of this happening. It was not that I doubted the reliability of the Rimpoche's prediction, but 'quite soon' was a relative term and could as well mean next year as this year, or even the year after next.

In the event, my dream of a permanent monastic centre was transformed into a reality much sooner than I had dared hope. The turning point in its fortunes came less than six weeks after Chattrul Rimpoche's visit, when I was in Calcutta, having flown to the City of Dreadful Heat (as it now was) from Cooch Behar after a short lecture tour in the Dooars, an important tea-growing area near the Bhutan-Assam border where there were many thousands of Nepalese Buddhists. In Calcutta I saw the Vaiśākha number of the *Maha Bodhi* journal through the press, gave weekly lectures in the hall of the Sri Dharmarajika Vihara, and spent time with friends like Soratha and Sachin. One day I received a batch of redirected mail from Kalimpong. Among the letters there was a rather disturbing communication from the landlord of Everton Villa. Though our lease did not expire till September, he wrote requiring us to move out by 15 May, as the property had been bought by a Tibetan who insisted on immediate occupation as one of the conditions of the sale. It looked as if the Maha Bodhi Society's Kalimpong branch would soon be homeless. The next letter I opened was from Marco Pallis, and in it my old friend promised very substantial assistance towards the realization of my plans. Having been buffeted one minute by the 'worldly wind' of loss, I was being assailed the next by that of gain, and it was not easy for me to contain my feelings of joy, thankfulness, and relief. We would not be homeless, after all, and I would be able to establish my permanent monastic centre! The plans to which Marco Pallis referred were, of course, the ones I had already outlined to Chattrul Rimpoche and which had prompted him not only to give the monastery its name but to predict its establishment 'quite soon'. Earlier in the year I had written to four or five people asking for their help in acquiring a place of our own in Kalimpong, as owing to the influx of Tibetans, who were buying up properties right and left, it would be impossible for me to find another suitable place when the lease on Everton Villa expired. So far the only response to my appeal had come from Dinoo, who had promised a thousand rupees.[303] On the strength of Marco Pallis's promise of very substantial assistance (he did not mention the actual figure) I was in a position to start looking for a property and entering, perhaps, into preliminary negotiations.

There were three properties which I knew to be for sale and which were, severally, suitable for conversion into a small monastic centre, besides being of a price that might be within my reach. Two of the properties were situated down at Seventh Mile, not far from the Tamang village, the other at Chebo Busti, on the Lower Bridle Road, a mile or so beyond Chitrabhanu and Manjula. On my return to Kalimpong on 21 April, after spending exactly a month in Calcutta, I viewed each one of these in turn. It did not take me long to make up my mind. The Chebo Busti property was far and away the most suitable, and the most attractive, comprising as it did a stone cottage, sheltered on the north and south by magnificent Kashmir cypresses, and four acres of terraced hillside land. The cottage, which was perched on a rocky spur high above Fifth Mile, faced due west and commanded a panoramic view of the foothills of both the Darjeeling and Sikkim sides of the River Rangit. The only drawback was that the property's asking price was somewhat higher than I had expected.

Fortunately, in the course of our occupancy of Everton Villa I had got to know the landlord's plump Bihari manager. Taking him into my confidence, I told him I was willing to move out of Everton Villa by 15 May provided I could move into the Chebo Busti property at the same time, but that I would be able to move into the latter only if I bought it and that I would be able to buy it only if the price was right. As his employer stood to make a very handsome profit if the sale of Everton Villa went through, and was therefore desperate to have me out by the stipulated date, Ramsingh promised to do what he could to help. The result was that there followed ten or twelve days of intensive negotiations, with Ramsingh acting as intermediary between me and the Marwari owners of the Chebo Busti property, and, I suspected, between the latter and the landlord of Everton Villa as well. At the end of that period I found myself accompanying Ramsingh to Lakhmichand Kaluram's High Street office and there making my final offer in person. 'Nineteen thousand rupees,' I said, as previously instructed by the plump Bihari; 'nineteen thousand and not a rupee more.' 'No, I can't let it go at that price,' protested the yellow-turbaned figure behind the desk. Whereupon, as also instructed by Ramsingh, the organizer of this little comedy, I rose to my feet, expressed regret at our inability to reach an agreement, and strode briskly to the door. Before I was halfway there I was called back. My offer was accepted, and I was free to move into the property even before all the formalities had been completed.

A few days later, on 13 May, the Maha Bodhi Society's Kalimpong branch held its last full-moon day meeting at Everton Villa. It was the full-moon day of the month Vaiśākha, the anniversary of the Buddha's attainment of perfect Enlightenment, and therefore marked the end of the Buddha Jayanti year – the year celebrating twenty-five centuries of Buddhism. For the tiny movement of Buddhist revival in India – a movement now augmented by hundreds of thousands of converts from among the followers of Dr Ambedkar – it had been a memorable year, even though it remained to be seen how deep or how lasting an impression the government-sponsored celebrations had made on the national psyche. It had been a memorable year for me too. In fact it had been a veritable *annus mirabilis*, a year of wonders. I had visited the principal Buddhist holy places in the company of Dhardo Rimpoche, I had met the Dalai Lama, I had forged a special link with the newly-converted followers of Dr Ambedkar, I had received Tantric initiation from Chattrul Rimpoche, and I had been enabled to establish in Kalimpong a vihara that would serve both as my personal headquarters and as a centre of living Buddhism. Nor was that all. *A Survey of Buddhism*, brought out a few months earlier by the Indian Institute of Culture, was already attracting highly favourable notices – notices that were to culminate in its publication being hailed by one Buddhist reviewer of Ceylon, a leading scholar, as the principal event of the Buddha Jayanti year.

The week following the full-moon day was spent making the newly-acquired property habitable, as it had been left unoccupied for more than a year and was badly in need of repair and decoration. In the course of these proceedings I discovered that it was to Chebo Busti that the Burmese Princess had gone to stay after the death of my old friend Burma Raja, and that the hut in which she was then supposedly living, subsisting on greens from the garden, was none other than the substantial, oak-panelled cottage that I was about to transform into the Triyana Vardhana Vihara. But there was no time for reminiscence. On Thursday 23 May, assisted by the friends who were staying with me, I dismantled the shrine with its much-travelled standing Buddha image and set it up in its permanent quarters, in this way formally marking the move from the old to the new premises. Next day I was off to Gangtok, where I was to give a series of lectures, leaving the others to finish the business of moving. Having completed its first two and a half millennia, Buddhism had entered upon its second, which according to tradition was to culminate in the appearance of Maitreya, the Buddha of Love; and I, a tiny cell in the multi-dimensional body of the sangha or spiritual community, was about to enter upon a new period in my Buddhist life.

Precious Teachers

PREFACE TO THE FIRST EDITION

During my years in India I had the good fortune to receive instruction and initiation from some of the most eminent Buddhist teachers of their day. With one exception, I first met them in Kalimpong, a hill station in the state of West Bengal, thirty miles to the north-east of the bigger and better known hill station of Darjeeling.

Ranging in elevation from less than 4,000 feet at one point in the town to more than 5,600 in another, Kalimpong occupies the ridge between the Dailo and the Rinkingpong hills, high above the east bank of the River Teesta. A road runs along this ridge for some two to three miles, and from this road there straggle down the hillside the streets and lanes of the Kalimpong bazaar. The climate of the place is mild, the rainfall moderate, and for much of the year there is a fine view of the snows of Kanchenjunga and the other peaks of the eastern Himalayas.

I lived in Kalimpong from the spring of 1950 to the summer of 1964. At that time the population of the town and the surrounding hamlets must have been about 20,000. Besides the indigenous Lepchas, Bhutia, and Nepalese of various tribes and castes, it included people from many other parts of India and from several foreign countries. Kalimpong was thus a cosmopolitan and polyglot place, where any day of the year one could see a dozen different national and regional costumes and hear as many languages and dialects.

It was against the colourful background provided by this little hill station, which from the diversity of its religions and cultures well deserved its sobriquet of 'The Town of the Seven New Years', that I lived my life and first came into contact, especially during my last seven years there, with most of the teachers who are the principal subject of these memoirs.

I have sometimes been asked if among my teachers there was one who was spiritually more developed than the rest. A similar question was once put by a disciple to one of the members of the celebrated trio of spiritual masters that was made up of Chattrul Rimpoche, Jamyang Khyentse Rimpoche, and Dudjom Rimpoche, all of whom feature in the following pages. The master replied, 'One of us is indeed more spiritually developed than the others, but you disciples will never know which one it is.'

For my part, I have never tried to find out how my teachers compared with one another, spiritually speaking. Indeed, I never thought in such terms. It was enough that they were vastly superior to me in wisdom and compassion and that, by a strange combination of circumstances, I had come to be in contact with them and could benefit from their teaching and spiritual influence. Though only some of them were actually styled *rimpoche* or 'greatly precious one', they were all alike my precious teachers and I remain deeply indebted to them and hope that in this account I have been able to give the reader at least a glimpse of them. I am grateful to the team at Windhorse Publications for overseeing the production of this book, to Shantavira for his meticulous copy-editing and for a number of helpful suggestions, and for compiling the index, and to Dhammarati who, despite his many responsibilities, found time to design the cover. Above all, I am grateful to Nityabandhu, to whom, in the course of many evenings, I dictated this work and without whose cooperation it would not have seen the light.

Sangharakshita
Madhyamaloka
Birmingham
26 March 2007

As the gods worship Indra, so should one
Worship the man from whom one learns the Dharma

The Buddha[304]

I
A RED-ROBED VISITOR

I arrived in Kalimpong in 1950. With me was the venerable Jagdish Kashyap, the learned Buddhist monk with whom I had been studying Pāli, Abhidhamma, and Logic at Buddha Kuti, his cottage on the campus of the Benares Hindu University, where he was professor of Pāli and Buddhist Philosophy. He had been professor there for twelve years and in January, when I had been with him for seven months, he decided he needed a change of scene. We would both have a holiday, he declared. He would show me some of the holy places of his native Bihar, and from there, perhaps, we would go up into the foothills of the eastern Himalayas, to a place called Kalimpong.

Spring had already come to the plains of Bihar. The sky was a tender blue, the air soft, and where the early crops were coming up the sunlit earth was a chequerboard of different shades of green. Beginning our pilgrimage at Patna, the ancient Pāṭaliputra, Kashyap-ji and I travelled via Bihar Sharif to the very extensive ruins of the great monastic university of Nālandā, where 10,000 monks had once studied, and thence to Rajgir, where the Buddha had often lived and taught. From Rajgir we visited several places of Buddhist interest in the vicinity, the most important of them being the Vulture's Peak, on which, according to Mahāyāna tradition, the Buddha had revealed the *White Lotus Sūtra*. We spent about a month in Bihar. In the course of our travels we lectured at a college, addressed public meetings, went for alms in the traditional manner, met an eccentric American follower of a Hindu sect, and were more than once accosted by young men who, on learning that we were Buddhist monks, begged us to build a temple and propagate the Buddha's teaching.[305] It was not until March that we reached Kalimpong, which turned out to be a pleasant hill station with a 'Norman' church, neat European-style bungalows, a colourful bazaar, and splendid views of the snows of Mount Kanchenjunga.

We were accommodated in a building belonging to the town's Newar Buddhist community, one of whose members, a young trader, Kashyap-ji had once met in Calcutta. Soon we had established a daily routine. After I had had my Pāli lesson we walked through the High Street to the same trader's office, where we had lunch, on our way there passing Nepalese, Tibetans, Bhutanese, and Indians in their distinctive national or regional costumes. In the evening we received visitors, of which there were at least two or three every day. But Kashyap-ji was still restless. We had not been three weeks in Kalimpong when he informed me that he would not be returning to the Benares Hindu University. Instead, he would spend some time meditating in the jungles of Bihar, where a yogi whom he knew had a hermitage. Perhaps, as he meditated, it would become clear to him what he ought to do next. I was to remain in Kalimpong. 'Stay here and work for the good of Buddhism,' he told me as he left the following morning. 'The Newars will look after you.'

I was twenty-four, and though I had been a Buddhist for seven or eight years I did not feel experienced enough to work for the good of Buddhism, especially as I was not yet fully ordained. I also doubted whether our trader friend and his fellow Buddhist Newars were quite so ready to look after me as Kashyap-ji supposed. But the word of the guru was not to be disobeyed, and I bowed in silent acquiescence.

Though I did not know it at the time, I was to spend fourteen years in Kalimpong.

In *Facing Mount Kanchenjunga* and *In the Sign of the Golden Wheel* I have told the story of my first seven years in the town, in which I soon became a well-known figure. During those seven years I started a Young Men's Buddhist Association, edited two monthly Buddhist journals (one of them short-lived), organized Buddhist events, made many friends (and one or two enemies), studied and meditated, and wrote *A Survey of Buddhism*. I also produced a good deal of poetry, much of it inspired by the scenery in the midst of which I was living,

Jagdish Kashyap

as well as by the lives of the local people. On the whole it was a happy time. I was happy in my friendships, happy in my literary activity, and happy in my work for the good of Buddhism.

But though much was achieved, I also had to face many difficulties. My biggest difficulty was that I had no permanent base, so that I was obliged to function from a succession of borrowed or rented premises. In March 1957, exactly seven years after my arrival in Kalimpong, I was living at Everton Villa, a roomy bungalow situated in a quiet spot about a mile and a half from the bazaar. I had taken it on a year's lease, and the lease was due to expire in six months' time. Before that, I would have to find somewhere else to stay. This would not be easy, since owing to the influx of wealthy Tibetan refugees into the town it had become more and more difficult to find a house or bungalow that was to let. It was at this point that I received a visit from a celebrated Nyingma lama whom I had met a few days previously, and with whom I had already formed a strong spiritual connection. On learning that my aim was to establish in Kalimpong a permanent monastic centre dedicated to the study, practice, and dissemination of the total Buddhist tradition, but that there seemed to be little likelihood of my being able to do so, my red-robed visitor assured me, in the most emphatic manner, that I would undoubtedly establish such a centre in Kalimpong. I would establish it quite soon, and I should call it 'The Vihara Where the Three Yānas Flourish'.[306]

Less than six weeks later, when I was in Calcutta in connection with my editorial work, I received a batch of redirected mail. Among the letters was one from the landlord of Everton Villa. Though my lease did not expire until September, he wrote requiring me to move out by 15 May, as the property had been bought by a Tibetan who insisted on immediate occupation as one of the conditions of the sale. The next letter I opened was from Marco Pallis, of whom I had seen a good deal when he was in Kalimpong in the early 1950s, and who was one of the friends to whom I had written for help. In it he promised very substantial assistance towards the realization of my plans. The result was that I was in a position to buy a small property situated on the southern outskirts of the town, about two miles from the bazaar, and on 23 May, with the help of friends who were staying with me, I moved in. The property comprised a stone cottage sheltered on the north and south by magnificent Kashmir cypresses, and four acres of terraced hillside that included a bamboo grove and a hundred orange trees. The cottage, which was perched on a rocky spur, faced due west, and commanded a panoramic view of the foothills on both the Darjeeling and Sikkim sides of the River Rangit.

The Triyana Vardhana Vihara, as I called it (this being the Sanskrit equivalent of the Tibetan name it had been given before it even existed), was to be my base for the next seven years – indeed, for the rest of my time in India.

The celebrated Nyingma lama who had predicted its establishment was Chattrul Sangye Dorje. I had met him through my Sikkimese friend Sonam Topgay Kazi, who was a great admirer of the lama and had come from Gangtok to see him and pay his respects. *Chattrul* meant 'without affairs' or 'without concerns', Sonam Topgay explained, and he was commonly known as *Chattrul* Sangye Dorje on account of his complete indifference to such things as organized monasticism and ecclesiastical position. It was not even clear whether he was a monk or a layman. He roamed freely from place to place, no one knowing where he was going to turn up next or how long he would stay. He was an accomplished yogi, having spent many years in the solitudes of eastern Tibet, meditating; and if popular reports were to be believed he possessed many psychic powers and was a great magician. Despite his indifference to organized monasticism and ecclesiastical position, Sonam Topgay added, and his frequently bizarre and eccentric behaviour, Chattrul Sangye Dorje was highly esteemed by several prominent members of the Gelug hierarchy. Once, when in Lhasa, he had bestowed a number of esoteric Tantric initiations on the Regent of Tibet. At the conclusion of the ceremonies, which lasted several days, the Regent made the customary offerings which, his position being what it was, were extremely valuable. Chattrul Sangye Dorje swept them all onto a cloth, tied the cloth up into a bundle, and handed the bundle to the Regent, saying, 'Look after these for me.' Whereupon he resumed his wanderings.

Sonam Topgay's account intrigued me. In fact, I was fascinated by his picture of the unconventional lama who, as I later discovered, was widely revered as one of the three great Nyingma gurus of the century, the two others being Jamyang Khyentse Rimpoche and Dudjom Rimpoche. Seeing my interest, Sonam Topgay observed that it would not be difficult for me to meet the lama, who notoriously did not stand on ceremony and who was very accessible – once you had succeeded in tracking him down. He moreover hinted that although Chattrul Sangye Dorje was highly unpredictable, and one could never be sure how he would respond to a particular request, he *might* be willing to give me Tantric initiation. In any case, I ought not to miss the opportunity of meeting so great a lama and obtaining his blessing.

Thus it was that, on the morning of 8 March, I found myself in the presence of Chattrul Rimpoche, as he was also called, who was staying at Tirpai, a village on the other side of the town, on the way up to Dailo Hill. I do not know what I had expected the celebrated Nyingma lama to look like. But in any case I received something like a shock when we met. He was of indeterminate age, perhaps somewhere between thirty-five and forty-five or even fifty, his coarse black hair was cut short like a monk's, and he was clad in a nondescript maroon garment lined with what appeared to be grubby sheepskin. What I was most struck by, however, was his face, which was coarse and unrefined almost to the point of brutality, and could easily have passed for that of a horny-handed peasant with no thought beyond his pigs and poultry. At the same time, his whole being communicated such an impression of rock-like strength and reliability that one could not but feel reassured, and with Sonam Topgay as interpreter it was not long before the two of us were deep in discussion.

As was proper, Chattrul Rimpoche took the lead, and asked me a number of questions, first about the Vinaya or Code of Monastic Discipline, then about the Abhidharma. I must have answered the questions to his satisfaction, for from the Abhidharma we progressed – through what intermediate steps I no longer recollect – to meditation and meditational experience, so that I was able to tell him about the Bombay friend who received, in a state of trance, teachings and directives which he believed came from God. To what extent did he think these could be accepted? Chattrul Rimpoche's reply was in agreement with the conclusion at which I had already arrived. Teachings and directives received in a state of trance, whether by oneself or by another person, were not to be accepted uncritically but were to be subjected to the test of reason and experience and compared with the *Buddhavacana*, or word of the Buddha, as explained by the Enlightened masters of India and Tibet.

By this time, I had developed considerable confidence in the Rimpoche, and I therefore asked him to tell me who my *yidam* or tutelary deity was. Far from showing surprise at my request, he seemed quite pleased, and after a moment of inner recollection told me that my *yidam* was Dolma Jungo, or Green Tārā, the 'female' bodhisattva of fearlessness and spontaneous helpfulness, adding that Tārā had been the tutelary deity of many of the great pandits of India and Tibet. He then proceeded to bestow on me the appropriate initiation, first giving me the ten-syllable mantra, which he pronounced very forcefully, after which he explained the *sādhana* or spiritual practice which would enable me to identify myself with Green Tārā and call down the blessing of the bodhisattvas on myself and on all sentient beings. The latter he did at some length, so that it was mid-afternoon when I finally bade Chattrul Rimpoche a grateful farewell, having spent four hours in his company. My mood was one of considerable elation.

A few days later, Chattrul Sangye Dorje came to see me at Everton

Chattrul Sangye Dorje

Villa. Though he probably arrived unannounced, he must have been accompanied by Sonam Topgay or another interpreter, for he explained the Green Tārā *sādhana* to me again and gave me further instructions about its practice. I had already committed his previous explanations to writing and therefore was able to check what I had written and make sure I had got the details of the *sādhana* absolutely right. It was in the course of this visit that Chattrul Rimpoche, having elicited from me the information that Everton Villa was only a rented property, assured me that I would soon be able to establish the permanent monastic centre of my dreams and that I should call it 'The Vihara Where the Three Yānas Flourish'. He then addressed to me, in what was evidently a mood of high inspiration, the Tibetan originals of the following stanzas.

In the sky devoid of limits, the teaching of the Muni is
The sun, spreading the thousand rays of the three *śikṣās*
[i.e. morality, meditation, and wisdom];
Continually shining in the radiance of the impartial disciples,
May this Jambudvīpa region of the Triyāna be fair!
In accordance with his request, [made] in the Fire-Monkey Year
On the ninth day of the first month by the Mahā Sthavira
Sangharakshita,
This was written by the Śākya-upāsaka, the Vidyādhara
Bodhivajra: [may there be] happiness and blessings!

That the stanzas were couched in the form of a response to a request probably was no more than a Tibetan literary convention, even as his styling me Mahāsthavira or 'Great Elder' when I was a simple *bhikṣu* was just the normal Tibetan politeness. That Chattrul Rimpoche should have referred to himself as the 'Śākya-upāsaka' meant that technically speaking he was not a monk but a layman. Later I learned that he was not a *tulku* or 'incarnate lama', which made the esteem in which he was held by many who were *tulkus* all the more remarkable.

There was a reason for my asking Chattrul Sangye Dorje to tell me who my *yidam* or tutelary deity was. For at least seven or eight years I had been greatly preoccupied with the problem of what I called 'getting beyond the ego' (not that there really was an ego, or any question of literally getting beyond it). In fact, I had written an essay entitled 'Getting Beyond the Ego', in which I declared Buddhism to be 'satisfied with nothing less than the absolute renunciation of the ego-sense in its subtlest no less than in its grossest formulations'.[307] One way of getting beyond, or renouncing, the ego, at least to an extent, consisted in preferring the will of another to one's own, especially the will of one's teacher or guru. Inspired by a passage in Thomas Merton's *Seeds of Contemplation*, according to which the disciple should surrender his will absolutely to the will of his spiritual superior,[308] I resolved to apply the idea to my relations with Kashyap-ji. This I did from the time I read Merton's book, which was during our pilgrimage to the holy places of Bihar, to the time my teacher left Kalimpong for the plains, and it was because I was still applying the idea to my relations with him that I was able to obey his injunction to stay in Kalimpong and work for the good of Buddhism. Had I not obeyed it, I most likely would never have met Chattrul Rimpoche or any other great lamas who, after the Chinese occupation of Tibet, started arriving in the town as refugees.[309]

One could also get beyond the ego by opening oneself to the transforming influence of one or other of the transcendental beings who according to the Buddhism of Tibet (and of that of China and Japan) were the different infinitely various aspects of the Buddha's *dharmakāya* or Body of Truth. That Green Tārā, the 'female' bodhisattva of fearlessness and spontaneous helpfulness, was my tutelary deity meant that she was a transcendental counterpart of my own mundane nature. In other words, I had an *affinity* with Green Tārā, and it was on account of that affinity that I could, by devotion to her – by *becoming* her – most readily gain access to the transcendental realm to which she belonged.

Chattrul Rimpoche did not stay long in Kalimpong. Shortly after visiting me at Everton Villa he resumed his wanderings, and we next met when both of us happened to be in Darjeeling. By that time he had picked up some Nepali, of which I also had a little knowledge, so that we had no need of an interpreter. At least, I have no recollection of anyone else being present. At one point he opened his hand to reveal a little heap of what seemed to be seed pearls. They were holy relics, he told me. When he was in Nepal he had thrust his hand inside an ancient, ruined stupa and this was what he had found. For the rest of the time I was with him he spoke in a strange, enigmatic manner that I did not find easy to follow, and the bizarre, magician-like side of his character was much more in evidence than it had been at our previous meetings.

2

THE FRENCH NUN – AND THE ḌĀKINĪ

Tibetan friends who came to know that the Triyana Vardhana Vihara had been given its name by Chattrul Sangye Dorje were greatly impressed. Whatever the Rimpoche blessed was sure to prosper, they told me. One of these friends was Kachu Rimpoche, the abbot of Pemayangtse Gompa, the premier Nyingma monastery of Sikkim. I first heard about Kachu Rimpoche from the turbulent and demanding Thupten Chhokyi (formerly Dominique Delannoy), known throughout the area as 'the French Nun' or, to those who knew her personally, as 'Ani-la'. Recently she had returned from a visit to Sikkim in a state of great excitement. She had found a new guru, she told me. He was a most remarkable man, and she had met him in the strangest manner.

Little by little the story of the meeting came out, Ani-la's words tumbling over one another in her eagerness to tell me everything at once. She had been wandering in the mountains of western Sikkim on her own, in a state of deep depression, thinking that life was not worth living and that the only course left to her was to commit suicide. Thus wandering, not caring in which direction she went, she came upon a small clearing in the forest. A tent had been pitched in the clearing, and in front of the tent sat a shaven-headed figure, whom she at once recognized as a lama. Her curiosity aroused, she approached and saluted him in her best Tibetan, and the two got into conversation. The lama, it transpired, was from Tibet. He was on his way to Pemayangtse Gompa, where he was to be installed as abbot. According to tradition, he had to enter the monastery on a certain auspicious day. That day had not yet come, and in the meantime he was staying on his own in the forest and meditating.

Having satisfied the French Nun's curiosity, the lama naturally expected her to satisfy his, a white woman in monastic garb no doubt being the last person he had expected to meet in the forest-clad mountains of western Sikkim. She was a *getsulma* or novice nun, Ani-la explained. Who had ordained her? Dhardo Rimpoche, a Gelug incarnate lama who lived in Kalimpong. What *sādhana* or spiritual practice was she doing? She was doing the *sādhana* of Mañjughoṣa, 'He of the Gentle Voice', the Bodhisattva of Wisdom. So far the interrogation had proceeded along familiar lines, but at this point the strange lama's expression changed.

'No,' he said, in a stern but kindly manner, 'you are *not* doing the Mañjughoṣa *sādhana*. You have not done it for six months.'

Ani-la was overwhelmed. It was true. Being angry with Dhardo Rimpoche she had stopped doing the *sādhana* he had given her at the time of her ordination. The lama must have read her thoughts. He was a real lama. She would become his disciple. The upshot was that Ani-la spent some time at Pemayangtse Gompa after the lama's installation, and there received teachings from him.

Not long after my hearing the excited Frenchwoman's account of how she had met her new guru, Kachu Rimpoche paid a short visit to Kalimpong and I was able to meet him myself. Unfortunately I remember nothing of that first meeting. I do, however, have a vivid recollection of my second meeting with him, as well as of the way it came about. At that time I was on friendly terms with an American couple, Simmons and Marcia Roof, who happened to be spending the hot season in the cooler atmosphere of Kalimpong. Simmons was a Unitarian minister who was in India on a study sabbatical. He was collecting material for a book on the spiritual life, as illustrated by his personal religious quest, and in this connection he was anxious to meet as many spiritual personalities as possible. When I told Simmons Ani-la's story, adding that the lama was just then paying a second visit to Kalimpong, he and Marcia begged me to arrange a meeting. I therefore invited Kachu Rimpoche to lunch, with the result that a day or two later my two American friends found themselves face to face with their first Tibetan lama.

Kachu Rimpoche must have been about forty at the time. Cheerful, straightforward, and down-to-earth, he certainly did not give the impression of being possessed of supernormal powers of any kind. There was no doubt that he was very knowledgeable, however, and over lunch, and for some time afterwards, Simmons plied him with questions on a wide variety of topics, with me acting as interpreter and translating his questions from English into Nepali and Kachu Rimpoche's answers from Nepali into English. As the discussion progressed, the questions Simmons asked related to topics of a more and more abstruse nature. All the Rimpoche's answers, as well as his additional explanations, were clear and to the point, especially when the questions related to meditation, of which he evidently had extensive personal experience. At times, the alternation of question and answer was so rapid I had difficulty keeping up with my translations. Eventually, when Simmons had put a highly philosophical question regarding the nature of Nirvāṇa, I noticed that the Rimpoche had started replying to it without waiting for me to translate it for him. He was replying not to the words of the question, which was in a language he did not understand, but to the thoughts (and possibly also to the feelings) behind the question, which it seemed he was able to comprehend directly without having to rely on its verbal expression. For some reason, Simmons failed to notice this, but after Kachu Rimpoche's departure he and Marcia expressed themselves entirely satisfied with the meeting, which had exceeded their expectations.

According to Buddhist tradition, *paracittajñāna*, knowledge of the minds of others, was one of the mundane *abhijñās* or super-knowledges.[310] Though a sign of attainment in meditation, its development was not essential to the attainment of Enlightenment. That Kachu Rimpoche was able to know Simmons' mind, if such indeed had been the case, did not in itself mean that he was far advanced spiritually. Nonetheless, that day's meeting left me deeply impressed by him and anxious to continue the acquaintance, despite the fact that he was living in western Sikkim and I in Kalimpong. As it happened, he was of much the same mind, with the result that in subsequent years we met a number of times and he came to occupy an important place in my life as friend and teacher. I wish I could say he came to occupy a similar place in the life of the French Nun. Unfortunately, she soon became no less dissatisfied with him than she had been with Dhardo Rimpoche, even though she was permitted to stay again at Pemayangtse Gompa and received more teachings. One of her bitterest complaints, to which I had to listen more than once, was that the Rimpoche spent far too much time talking with his brother, who was also a monk and lived at the monastery and was, according to the exigent Frenchwoman, a thoroughly bad influence on her guru. As I knew only too well, Ani-la regarded time spent talking to others which could have been spent talking with *her* as time wasted. Another complaint was that at Pemayangtse alcohol was employed in the monastery's ritual, this being in accordance with Nyingma tradition. Once, when Kachu Rimpoche was sprinkling the images of the Buddhas and bodhisattvas with a few drops of whisky, she had, by her own admission, protested against the desecration (as she considered it to be) in a way that was highly disrespectful both to the Nyingma tradition and to her guru. It was not surprising, therefore, that not many months after her unexpected meeting with Kachu Rimpoche she should have found herself not only again without a guru but pouring out her troubles to Jamyang Khyentse Rimpoche, who had recently arrived in the district and was staying in Darjeeling. For this she was gently rebuked by Princess Pema Tsedeun of Sikkim.[311] The Rimpoche had his own worries, the princess told her (he was unwell at the time) and she should not bother him.

By this time I had met the great Nyingma guru myself. I met him not in Darjeeling but in Kalimpong, at Panorama, the guest cottage where I had lived for six months in 1951 as the guest of Prince K. M. Latthakin, the nephew and son-in-law of the last king of Burma.[312] My first impression of Jamyang Khyentse Rimpoche was that he was very much a *monk*. With his closely cropped white hair, long ear lobes, and deeply lined face, he indeed looked more like a Burmese *mahāthera* or 'great elder' than a Tibetan incarnate lama. On my entering the room with Sonam Topgay he looked up from his book and asked me, when I had been introduced, 'Do you know anything about dancing?' I was obliged to admit that I was completely ignorant of the subject. Slightly disappointed, the old man explained to Sonam Topgay, and Sonam Topgay explained to me, that he had been reading about dancing, there being a dozen or so works on dance in the Tengyur, the voluminous collection of non-canonical texts of various kinds. The works on dance, all translated from Sanskrit, were the choreographic basis of the Tibetan so-called 'lama dances', and this was why the Rimpoche was studying them. As well as being an accomplished yogi, he was a polymath who

With Kachu Rimpoche

had taken all Tibetan knowledge for his province and was ready, moreover, to acquire information even from a casual Western visitor.

The next time Kachu Rimpoche was in Kalimpong I was therefore able to tell him that I had met Jamyang Khyentse Rimpoche. He was delighted to hear this, for he had a boundless admiration for the celebrated old lama, whom he regarded as his guru. But it was not enough, he told me bluntly, to meet a great guru like Jamyang Khyentse Rimpoche. I should ask for a *wongkur* (literally 'empowerment') or Tantric initiation, and since the Rimpoche, as his name indicated, was regarded as a manifestation of Jamyang or Mañjughoṣa, the Bodhisattva of Wisdom, it was for initiation into the following of that bodhisattva that I should ask. Kachu Rimpoche spoke so earnestly, and was so evidently desirous of my spiritual welfare, that I could not but heed his advice. Nonetheless, I did not want to be like those Tibetan Buddhists who collected *wongkurs* in much the same way as English schoolboys collected postage stamps, rare specimens being especially prized by both sorts of collectors. *Wongkurs* were empowerments to *practise* a *sādhana*, and I had to be sure I wanted to take on another *sādhana*, in addition to the one I had received from Chattrul Rimpoche. Eventually I decided I did want to, and that I ought to approach Jamyang Khyentse Rimpoche without further delay.

In the third week of October 1957 I therefore left for Darjeeling, where the great Nyingma guru was then staying. Kachu Rimpoche was also staying there, though not with Khyentse Rimpoche but with a Tibetan family in the bazaar, and in the afternoon I went to see my warm-hearted lama friend. We talked for a while, after which I sat while he performed a Lakshmi puja, it being the birthday of Tsering Chodron, Khyentse Rimpoche's *ḍākinī* or spiritual consort. I was familiar with Lakshmi as a popular Hindu goddess, the granter of wealth and prosperity, and I was therefore not a little surprised to find a Tibetan incarnate lama performing a lengthy puja in her honour. I subsequently discovered that the four-armed goddess had been absorbed into the Buddhist pantheon, and that under the name of Śrī she featured in the *Suvarṇaprabhāsa Sūtra* or '*Sūtra of Golden Light*', a Mahāyāna scripture on which I was to give a series of lectures many years later.[313] The following morning, having spent the night at the house of a Bengali doctor I knew, I called on Kachu Rimpoche at his lodging and together we made our way to Cooch Behar House, which the Maharaja of Cooch Behar had placed at Khyentse Rimpoche's disposal. After we had talked with the Maharani of Sikkim, who was also staying there, we were ushered into the presence of the great guru, who received us with his usual kindness and dignity of manner. Kachu Rimpoche spoke for me, as I think had been arranged between us beforehand. The English monk wished to ask the venerable master for a *wongkur*, he said, speaking in the flowery Tibetan appropriate to the occasion. Would the venerable master please grant his request. Khyentse Rimpoche's expression showed that the request had pleased him. He would give me not one *wongkur* but three or four, he told me. I should come back on Thursday, as he would have to get the books he needed for the ceremony from Gangtok. It was then Saturday.

On Wednesday night I slept badly, though not because I was excited at the prospect of receiving initiation from Khyentse Rimpoche but because for the last two days I had been suffering from an extremely painful swelling of the gums. Nonetheless, I had travelled up to Darjeeling that afternoon so as to be quite sure I was not late for the ceremony the following day. I was still in considerable pain when on the morning of 24 October Kachu Rimpoche and I made our way to Cooch Behar House for the second time that week, and the right side of my face was badly swollen.

The initiation was an intimate affair, with Khyentse Rimpoche presiding grandfather-like over his spiritual family. He sat cross-legged on a kind of throne made up of three or four big, square Tibetan cushions placed one on top of another; in front of him was a narrow table on which were arranged a *dorje*[314] and bell, a pot with a long, curved spout, a small pot filled with rice, and other ritual implements. On the guru's left, on a single cushion, sat 'the Ḍākinī', as she was respectfully called, and on *her* left, also on a single cushion, sat the Maharani of Sikkim. On the right of the guru were his personal attendant, another monk, Kachu Rimpoche, and my good Dharma-friend Sonam Topgay Kazi. My place was immediately in front of the Rimpoche. (I was later told that in the Hīnayāna one kept one's eyes respectfully lowered in the presence of one's teacher, but that in the Vajrayāna one looked the guru in the face.) Partly because the proceedings were in Tibetan (though Sonam Topgay translated whatever I was required to repeat after Khyentse Rimpoche), and partly because I was in pain, I remembered little of the elaborate ceremony, which lasted from 10.00 a.m. to 2.00 p.m. I did, however, remember offering Jamyang Khyentse a mandala or symbolic representation of the universe, and noticing with what reverence his attendant monk offered him the pointed red pandit hat which he donned at certain key points in the ceremony. Above all, I remember the rapt, beatific expression with which he looked up as he invoked the bodhisattvas whose *wongkurs* he was conferring upon me. It was as if he actually saw their diaphanous, rainbow-like forms floating in the air before him. Whether or not it was the Mañjughoṣa initiation which Kachu Rimpoche had asked Jamyang Khyentse to give me I do not know, but Mañjughoṣa was invoked first, then Avalokiteśvara, next Vajrapāṇi, and finally Tārā, so that by the time the last tinkle of Khyentse Rimpoche's ritual bell had died away I had been empowered to practise the *sādhana*s of all four bodhisattvas.

In order to practise the *sādhana*s I would need to have the texts describing them, and these the Maharani undertook to provide. She would have copies made when she returned to Gangtok, she said, and would send them to me. They arrived a few weeks later. Naturally they were in Tibetan, which I did not understand, least of all the classical Tibetan in which the texts were composed. Luckily I had a friend who did understand it and who, moreover, was willing to translate my texts for me. The friend was John Driver, an English scholar of about my own age who was doing research into the Nyingma tantras for a doctoral thesis. Dreamy and absent-minded (or at least appearing so), he lived with his wife Anne and their two – later three – daughters in a house within the Scottish Mission compound called the White House, but which, for the purposes of our correspondence, we renamed the White Tara House. It did not take John long to translate the *sādhanas* of Mañjughoṣa and Avalokiteśvara, but for reasons I no longer recollect he never got round to translating those of Vajrapāṇi and Tārā, even though he made for me English versions of several other Tibetan Buddhist texts.

I had now received altogether five tantric initiations, one from Chattrul Rimpoche and four from Jamyang Khyentse Rimpoche. For the last eight months I had been practising the Green Tārā *sādhana* given me by the former, and to this I now added the practice of the Mañjughoṣa Stuti Sādhana. I practised them early each morning, in the order in which I had received them, after chanting the traditional Pāli verses in praise of the Buddha, the Dharma, and the Sangha.[315] Later on, I came to see the two *sādhanas* as being not mutually exclusive but complementary, inasmuch as Green Tārā and Mañjughoṣa, like Avalokiteśvara, Vajrapāṇi, Kṣitigarbha, and the rest, were aspects or emanations of the Buddha's *dharmakāya* or Body of Truth. The fact that I was now practising tantric meditation did not, however, mean the complete abandonment of *ānāpānasati* or respiration-mindfulness, which had been the sheet anchor of my spiritual life for nine years or more. Though I did not practise it regularly, as I had previously done, I had recourse to it, as to an old and tried friend, whenever I found it necessary to calm and concentrate my mind before proceeding to *sādhana* practice. Mindfulness in the broader sense I continued to cultivate assiduously, doing my best to remain aware of whatever I thought, said, did, and felt throughout the day.

Three weeks after receiving the four *wongkurs* from Khyentse Rimpoche I saw him again, this time in Kalimpong. He was staying at Arunachal, the Kalimpong home of Princess Pema Tsedeun and her

Tibetan husband Pheunkhang-sey, who like his two incarnate lama brothers was well known to me. Arunachal was situated not far from the Vihara, and from its position high above the road commanded an even finer view. I found Khyentse Rimpoche walking stiffly in the garden, enjoying the warmth of the late autumn sunshine. The Ḍākinī was with him, as was Kachu Rimpoche, who was staying with me at the time and had preceded me. As I very much wanted to have a photograph of my guru I had arranged for a professional photographer to be present and Rimpoche agreed to sit for him. He sat in an armchair in the garden, upright and dignified, his hands resting on his knees, and gently smiling. At my request the Ḍākinī, too, agreed to sit for her photograph. I gathered that this was a great favour, as normally she did not allow herself to be photographed. But in view of her close spiritual relationship with Khyentse Rimpoche, I was keen to have a photograph of her as well, and perhaps she had understood this.

Kachu Rimpoche had been at pains to assure me that the relationship between Khyentse Rimpoche and the beautiful young woman was not a sexual one, though the thought that it might be of such a nature had not so much as crossed my mind. No one who had seen them together could imagine the relationship to be other than a spiritual one. Some years ago, so Kachu Rimpoche told me, an astrologer had predicted that the Rimpoche would die at the age of fifty-seven. Other senior lamas, as well as his own disciples, had therefore begged him to 'take' a *ḍākinī* or spiritual consort, since according to tantric tradition the taking of a *ḍākinī* could prolong a lama's life, thereby enabling him to continue benefiting humanity by teaching the Dharma. Fortunately, a *ḍākinī* was at hand, in the person of the daughter of Khyentse Rimpoche's secretary, and a year or two ago he had 'married' her.

Now I could understand that a sexual relationship with a *ḍākinī* might well have a rejuvenating effect on an elderly lama, and even, perhaps, prolong his life. Such a relationship would be marriage in the ordinary sense of the term, and the '*ḍākinī*' would simply be the lama's wife. But how could a purely spiritual relationship with a *ḍākinī* have the effect of prolonging the life of the lama who took her as his consort? For the members of Khyentse Rimpoche's spiritual family, his consort was not only 'the Ḍākinī'; she was also his chief disciple and a spiritual personality in her own right. She was ever calm and serene, never seeking to draw attention to herself or putting herself forward.

Jamyang Khyentse Rimpoche

Above all, she was deeply devoted to Khyentse Rimpoche. Her devotion was not of the emotional, quasi-erotic kind that some female disciples direct towards their guru. I cannot remember seeing her actually looking at the Rimpoche, or, for that matter, him looking at her, in a way that suggested there was something special between them. It was as though she felt his presence in her heart and that was enough. Was it, then, the strength and purity of her devotion that was prolonging Jamyang Khyentse's life, if indeed that was what was happening? But Kachu

Rimpoche and the other disciples were also deeply devoted to him. Could not their devotion have the same kind of effect, or was the Ḍākinī's devotion qualitatively different from theirs? On the other hand, it might be that by having a purely spiritual relationship with a *ḍākinī* a lama could not, in fact, prolong his life, and that although Khyentse Rimpoche ostensibly had taken a *ḍākinī* for the traditional reason, his relationship with her was really of a quite different kind.

Before leaving Kalimpong, the guru paid a visit to the Triyana Vardhana Vihara. He came escorted by Kachu Rimpoche, who brought him by car, as he was not able to walk even the comparatively short distance from Arunachal to the Vihara. With him he brought the plump, eight-year-old Sogyal Rimpoche, whom I had already seen at Arunachal, who was shaven-headed like his elders and wore a junior version of their maroon robes. A throne had been prepared for Jamyang Khyentse in the shrine-room, and when he had taken his seat the dozen or more friends and students of mine whom I had invited to meet the Rimpoche and obtain his blessing offered him white ceremonial scarves or *khatas*, as did I and the other inmates of the Vihara. Rimpoche then gave me, of his own accord, the *lung* or 'permission to read' a certain devotional text, after which he performed a ritual of purification and blessing for the benefit of the Vihara and those who were gathered there. I then escorted him back to Arunachal. He had spent altogether an hour with us.

My next two meetings with Khyentse Rimpoche both took place in Gangtok, which I visited from time to time and where I frequently lectured on the Dharma, sometimes at the invitation of the Maharaj Kumar of Sikkim and sometimes at the invitation of Apa Sahib Pant, the Government of India's Political Officer in Sikkim. Both meetings took place, moreover, at the white-walled, yellow-roofed palace *lhakhang* or temple, where the Rimpoche was then staying and where he died in 1959, aged sixty-seven. On each occasion I went simply to pay my respects, and each time I received a gift from him. The first gift was a thangka or painted scroll, resplendent with the traditional border of rich Chinese brocade and mounted on rollers. The big central figure was that of a saffron-coloured Mañjughoṣa, who with his right hand whirled aloft a flaming sword of insight while with his left he grasped the stem of a white lotus flower on whose open petals rested a sacred book, understood to be that of the Perfection of Wisdom. He was flanked on his right by a white, four-armed Avalokiteśvara, and on his left by a dark blue Vajrapāṇi in his wrathful form. Below Mañjughoṣa was Green Tārā, and above him, in three tiers, a couple of dozen human teachers of whom I recognized only the Buddha and Milarepa. Two wrathful deities, one blue and one red, occupied, respectively, the left-hand and right-hand bottom corners of the painting, while to the right of the book of the Perfection of Wisdom there was a range of snow-covered mountains. In two of the mountains there was a cave, and in each cave sat a tiny yellow-robed figure.

The painting was not so well executed as he could have wished, Jamyang Khyentse told me, though it was the work of the best artist he had been able to find in Gangtok; and indeed, the work was clumsily if painstakingly done, the rays of rainbow light that emanated from Mañjughoṣa's body terminating in a ring of solid-looking rainbow balls. But I was too deeply moved by the Rimpoche's kindness in giving me the thangka, which had been painted in accordance with his directions, to be much concerned about any shortcomings it might have. Moreover, there was a special significance in his giving me the thangka. As he proceeded to explain, through the initiations he had given me he had transmitted to me the essence of the teachings of the great masters who were depicted in it. I was now their spiritual heir and successor. Smiling, he then pointed to the yellow-robed figures in their caves, one meditating and one teaching. Both were me.

The second gift I received from Khyentse Rimpoche was one he may not have been aware he was giving, though in my eyes this did not render it any the less a gift. On my arrival at the palace temple that day I was asked to wait, as the Rimpoche was engaged. I must have waited for half an hour or more, and when he eventually emerged from an inner room, he apologized for having kept me waiting. A lama who was an old friend of his had just died, he explained, and he had been reciting the Vajrasattva mantra for his benefit. Reciting the Vajrasattva mantra! The words took an immediate hold on me. It was as though Khyentse Rimpoche was giving me a teaching. The teaching was to the effect that the Vajrasattva mantra should be recited for the benefit of the dead. Thereafter, following my guru's example, I recited it whenever I heard that someone connected with me had died.

3
A DAMSEL IN DISTRESS

Towards the end of 1957 I received a letter superscribed 'In Confidence'. It was from Ronald Boughen, a courier at the UK High Commission in New Delhi. We had met in the Indian capital, and he had visited Kalimpong. A large, sandy-haired man of about forty, he was a Buddhist of the devotional rather than the intellectual type, and though we were not exactly friends he wrote to me frequently, sometimes at considerable length, and often on official notepaper. He usually wrote about his personal problems, especially those that tended to arise in connection with his relationships with various youthful protégés. This time, however, he wrote to inform me that Mme Marie-Elise Langford-Rae had told him that she would be in Kalimpong later that month. She was married to the Kazi Dorje of Chakhung, who had come to Delhi to see the President, and who was involved, so he understood, in the Sikkim-Tibet trade. Mme Langford-Rae, or the Kazini Sahiba of Chakhung, as she now called herself, was very worried about her stay in Kalimpong, for she felt someone might cause her some trouble. 'I do not know on what grounds she bases her fears,' Ronald wrote. 'However, if anything does go amiss I should be grateful if you would keep me in the picture.'

The person who was the subject of this rather mysterious letter was not unfamiliar to me, at least by sight. A blonde, smiling woman in her forties, she had been in Kalimpong in 1950, staying at the Himalayan Hotel, and I had more than once seen her driving around with Mr Lha Tsering, the much-feared boss of the Kalimpong branch of the Central

Intelligence Bureau, who was a staunch supporter of mine.[316] The Kazi Sahib I had met once, in Darjeeling, and I remembered him as a 50-year-old man who wore Western dress and spoke very little English. How had the former Mrs Langford-Rae come to marry him, and why, if she was coming to join him in his Kalimpong home, should she be so worried about her stay in the town? I was soon to find out.

A few days after the arrival of Ronald's letter I received a note from the Kazini Sahiba. It was written from Arcadia, a bungalow situated on the main road into Kalimpong. In it she begged me to come and see her as soon as I conveniently could as she was badly in need of help and advice. I left the Vihara almost immediately and was soon with her. She was still blonde, but she certainly was not smiling. Indeed, she tended to act the 'damsel in distress', and with her long black gown seemed almost to have dressed for the part. I quickly realized that beneath the histrionics she was genuinely worried about what Ronald had tactfully termed her 'stay in Kalimpong'. No doubt it was because she was worried about this that she had brought with her a companion in the shape of a short, fierce-looking old lady with a pure white quiff. This was her dear, dear sister – her adopted sister – Helen, the Kazini Sahiba explained, throwing her arms round the old lady, who out of loyalty and devotion had come with her all the way from Delhi and would be sharing her new life in Kalimpong.

Rather to my surprise, the Kazi Sahib was not with them, and it soon transpired that Arcadia was not his own house, as I had assumed, but a place he had rented for his new wife and her companion. His house was situated in another part of the town, and under its roof there still lived a woman whom the Kazini described as a despicable creature for whom the Kazi had once cared, and whom he was unable, or unwilling, to throw out. Apparently the Kazi had neglected to be off with the old love before he was on with the new.[317] Or perhaps he had not considered what effect his marriage to the Kazini might have on his existing domestic arrangements. In any case, the Kazini was insistent that the other woman should be evicted forthwith and herself installed as mistress of the house, and the help and advice she wanted from me was with regard to this end. Since I did not really know the Kazi, having met him only once, I did not feel able to intervene in connection with so personal a matter. I therefore confined myself, then and subsequently, to counselling patience and giving the Kazini what moral support I could in her predicament, the humiliating nature of which she felt keenly. How long she and Helen had to stay at Arcadia I do not remember, but eventually the day came when, escorted by the Kazi and me, the Kazini and her companion were driven to their new home, smuggled in through the front door, and hurried into two rooms at the rear of the building. The Kazini had achieved one, at least, of her objectives, but only one, and it was hardly a glorious victory. The other woman still occupied the front bedroom of the bungalow.

In the course of the next few days I came to understand the situation better, though I never understood it completely. The Kazi had been married to the woman in the front bedroom for some thirty years. She belonged to the same aristocratic land-owning class as himself, and the marriage had been celebrated in accordance with Sikkimese customs. They had no children. She had been of no help to him in his business and political activities, and no comfort to him personally, and they had long since ceased to be effectively married. It was not surprising, therefore, that the Kazi should have seen the articulate, highly educated and well-informed Mme Langford-Rae as an ideal partner in every way and have wanted to marry her. Thus it came about that, at the start of the New Year, Kazi Lhendup Dorje, as he was generally known, had the old love and the new love under his roof at the same time. What was to be done? The present situation could not be allowed to continue. It was highly unsatisfactory, especially to the Kazini, who could not be expected to remain confined indefinitely to the two back rooms like a prisoner. In the end, tradition came to the rescue in the form of a *panchayat*.

A *panchayat* was a group of five persons who judged disputes and disagreements between two parties. Each of the parties would nominate two members of the *panchayat* and jointly nominate the chairman, usually someone of position or prestige in the community. The *panchayat* was an institution well known in the villages of India, and known also, as I now discovered, to the local Sikkimese and Tibetans, though I believe they did not strictly follow the Indian model. In the present instance the *panchayat* consisted of Lha Tsering, now retired from Government service, myself, two Tibetans, one of whom I knew slightly, and Gergen Tharchin, the genial Ladakhi Christian editor of the *Tibet Mirror* ('the only Tibetan newspaper in the world') whom I had met on a number of occasions.[318] Lha Tsering and I had been nominated by the Kazini, though it was not clear to me in what way she was a party to the dispute, which was really between the Kazi and the woman in the front bedroom, who must have nominated either the two Tibetans or one of the Tibetans and Tharchin.

The *panchayat* met in the Kazi's comfortable lounge. It met daily for nearly a week, each session lasting three or four hours and involving the consumption of numerous cups of tea and, I suspect, after my departure, a very different kind of liquid refreshment. The Kazi was present throughout in his double capacity as host and as one of the parties to the dispute, *de facto* if not *de jure*. The proceedings were conducted by turns – sometimes simultaneously – in Tibetan, Hindi, Nepali, and English, so that at times it was not easy for me to follow the debate. In the course of the first two sessions I gradually realized that the separation between the Kazi and the woman in the front bedroom had already taken place, and that, Sikkimese customs being what they were, this had required little more than the consent of both parties. What the debate was really all about was money, or money and property, and what the *panchayat* had to decide was the amount of the compensation (if that was the right word) to be paid by the Kazi to the woman who, after all, had been his wife – in the eyes of their world – for thirty years.

This naturally involved a good deal of discussion, as the *panchayat*'s decision had to be unanimous, and agreement was not quickly or easily arrived at. There were two interruptions to the proceedings. During one of the sessions there suddenly came from the back rooms the doleful sound of the Kazini's raised voice. 'They want to kill my Kazi,' she wailed. 'They want to kill my Kazi.' We all froze. Who 'they' were was not apparent, nor did the Kazini afterwards explain what she meant. But the wailings were not repeated, and after a few minutes we resumed our discussions as if we had heard nothing, for the Kazini should not really have been on the premises. During another session the Kazi suddenly burst into tears. 'He still loves her!' exclaimed Tharchin, meaning the woman in the front bedroom. 'He still loves her!'

Whether because he was a warm-hearted, kindly man, or whether because, as a minister of the Gospel, he believed in the indissolubility of marriage, even marriage between heathen Buddhists, he evidently would have liked to see a reconciliation between the Kazi and his former wife. This was the last thing anybody else wanted, and Lha Tsering quickly intervened to head off any move in that direction. To me it seemed that the Kazi's tears were forced from him by long-repressed bitterness over his marriage, and relief that it was now over. Be that as it may, he soon recovered himself, and by the end of the next session the *panchayat* had come to a decision. The Kazi was to give his former wife 20,000 rupees (the Vihara had cost only a little less) together with a house he owned in Darjeeling.

The *panchayat*'s decision having been communicated to the lady, she emerged from the front bedroom, the door of which opened directly into the lounge. I had not seen her before. She was a tall, gaunt woman, and wore the traditional long Sikkimese (and Tibetan) ankle-length gown or *bokku*, which in this case happened to be dark blue. As was the custom, the Kazi immediately handed her the 20,000 rupees in cash, whereupon she stuffed the thick bundle of currency notes into the bosom of her *bokku* and, accompanied by a handsome young nephew of the Kazi who had been helping her with her packing, left by jeep for Darjeeling.

The Kazini was now able to emerge from her seclusion with propriety. She emerged alone – without Helen. She and her dear sister had quarrelled, and the latter had returned in high dudgeon to Delhi, though not before the Kazi had given her a first class railway ticket. I had once had a brush with the haughty old lady myself, in connection with an argument she had got into with the Kazini. She was being unreasonable, I told her, with rather more frankness than tact. '*Me? Unreasonable?*' she shrieked, her white quiff quivering with indignation.

The days following the former wife's departure were days of discovery. The servant discovered under the bed in the front bedroom a dozen or more empty whisky bottles, and the Kazini discovered that her predecessor had been having an affair with the handsome young nephew. What was more, she discovered that the Kazi had known about the affair all along. This both surprised and angered her, and she upbraided the Kazi for his having parted with 20,000 rupees and a house when, the woman having committed adultery, he could have thrown her out of the house without giving her a single anna. But the Kazi was unrepentant, and refused to discuss the matter with her. He had handled the situation in the way he thought best, he seemed to be saying, and there was nothing more to be said.

My own discovery, a week or two later, was that the Kazini's original fear that someone in Kalimpong might cause her trouble was not entirely baseless. We were walking round the bungalow's garden one morning, talking, when suddenly an arrow whizzed past the Kazini's head missing her by inches. On another occasion I was with her in the back room she had made into a study for herself. She was standing near the open window. Suddenly she leapt back with a scream. A woman with a knife was crouching outside the window, ready to stab her as soon as she turned her back. Though the Kazi and the servant searched the garden they could find no trace of the woman, and I could see that the Kazi was inclined to think that the Kazini had imagined the whole thing, just as previously he had been inclined to regard the arrow as a random shot not intended for her. The Kazini, on the other hand, was convinced that on both occasions her life had been threatened and that behind the threat there lurked the vengeful figure of the discarded wife.

Owing to the nature of the circumstances under which we first met, I soon got to know the Kazi and Kazini very well, especially the Kazini, the Kazi being often away in Gangtok in connection with his business and political activities. In fact, there developed between the three of us a strong friendship. 'When shall we three meet again?' the Kazini would chant[319] whenever I went up to Chakhung House (as she had renamed the bungalow) to say goodbye to them before leaving Kalimpong for one of my extensive preaching tours in the plains.[320] Even in the early days of our friendship, it was obvious to me that the Sikkimese aristocrat and the European lady were very different in character and temperament, and even if theirs was not a case of opposites attracting each other there were, nonetheless, sufficient points of difference between them to ensure that the sparks would sometimes fly. The Kazini was outspoken, tended to be sweeping in her judgements, saw things in black and white, and was inclined to exaggerate and dramatize, though I never knew her be untruthful.[321] Moreover, she never gave anyone the chance to deceive her or let her down twice. 'If they will do it once, they will do it again,' she would say firmly. The Kazi, being both businessman and politician, did not always say what was in his mind, rarely adopted an extreme position, was patient and forbearing, and believed in giving those who had disappointed him a second and even a third chance. He was also ready to do even a political opponent a good turn if he could, which was an attitude the Kazini found difficult to understand.

I therefore was not surprised when I learned that in his younger days the Kazi had spent some time in a monastery. He had been head lama of Rumtek Gompa, which was the premier Kagyu monastery in Sikkim, just as Pemayangtse was the premier Nyingma one. He had been deprived of his position, on false charges, in order to make way for someone else. This happened to be the future Maharaj Kumar of Sikkim, who was not then the Maharaj Kumar or Crown Prince as his elder brother was still living. The injustice he had suffered continued to rankle with the Kazi, and it was one of the reasons for his hatred of the Maharaj Kumar – a hatred to which he rarely gave open expression – and his determination, as a politician, to see the overthrow of the Namgyal dynasty and the establishment of democracy in Sikkim. Yet despite his long immersion in politics and business, and his Western dress, he had not altogether ceased to be a lama. When at home he would often finger his *mālā* or rosary, at the same time murmuring a mantra, or read to himself from a little Tibetan book. One day I asked him what the book was. It was the *Dorje Chopa,* he replied, rather to my astonishment, for the *Dorje Chopa* was the Tibetan translation of the *Vajracchedikā* or 'Diamond Cutter' *Sūtra*, also known simply as the *Diamond Sūtra*, a text belonging to the Prajñāpāramitā or 'Perfection of Wisdom' class of Mahāyāna scriptures. As I well remembered, it was on my encountering the *Diamond Sūtra*, some twelve or fourteen years earlier, that I had realized I was a Buddhist and had, in fact, always been one.[322]

The Kazini knew nothing of Buddhist doctrine, but she had lived in Burma and had been deeply impressed by what she saw of the Buddhist way of life there. Now that she was married to a Buddhist, she ought, she felt, to take the religion more seriously. She ought, in fact, to study it. For the next few months, therefore, she spent much of her time reading the books I lent her. She also talked about the Dharma with her husband, but neither his English nor her Hindi was good enough for them to be able to discuss the finer points of the Buddha's teaching. For that kind of discussion she relied on me, as well as relying on me for basic instruction in meditation. It soon became evident that she was drawn more to the rational and ethical aspects of Buddhism than to its devotional and contemplative aspects. Not that this really mattered. By the time the anniversary of the Buddha's attainment of Enlightenment came round she was ready to declare herself a Buddhist, which she did at the Vihara in the traditional manner. At my suggestion, she wrote a report of the event for the Buddhist monthly journal I edited. It appeared under the heading 'Kazini Sahiba of Chakhung Initiated into Buddhism' and read, in part, as follows.

> Kazini Elisa-Maria Dorji-Khangsarpa of Chakhung took the Pancha Sila at the Triyana Vardhana Vihara in Kalimpong on the Vaisakha Purnima Day, Saturday the 3rd May, 2502, after having studied with her guru, the Venerable Sangharakshita, Bhikshu-in-Charge of the Vihara. The wife of the Kazi Sahib of Chakhung, Sikkim, Kazini Sahiba was born in Scotland, but brought up in Belgium where she was educated, later returning to Edinburgh University for advanced studies. She has studied and travelled in many parts of the world, and, on completion of her studies in Europe, she went to live in Burma, where she was first attracted to Buddhism.
>
> Travelling throughout the length and breadth of Burma, the Chinese frontier on one side, the Chin Hills, the Kachin Hills, the Manipur border, she was always deeply impressed by what she saw of the way of the life of Buddhists. Later, in her travels which took her to China, Malaya, Thailand, Morocco, Turkey, Egypt, and even to Iceland, she always felt influenced by what she had seen of Buddhism in Burma.[323]

This was the nearest the Kazini ever came to telling the story of her life, parts of which were shrouded in mystery. From time to time, however, she told me things that enabled me to fill in some of the gaps. In Burma, for instance, she and her first husband had known the future author of *Animal Farm* and *Nineteen Eighty-Four*. They had known him not as George Orwell but as Eric Blair.[324] He was then in the Burma Police, and every now and then she and Langford-Rae would find themselves handing over to him, or taking over from him, as they were posted to different towns around the country. Nor was George Orwell the only famous person she had known. She had interviewed Mussolini and had lived for two years in the palace of Kemal Ataturk, from whom she had received more than two hundred letters, all now deposited with a bank. In recent years (it was not clear for how many) she had lived in Delhi, teaching French at a school run by the Christian Brothers, and moving in diplomatic and political circles.

Several of the Kazini's Delhi friends knew me. One of these friends was Ronald Boughen of the UK High Commission who had written to me before her arrival in Kalimpong, asking me to keep him in the picture if anything went amiss. Something had indeed gone amiss, at the beginning of the Kazini's stay, and I had kept Ronald in the picture both then and subsequently. Thus the ball of our correspondence was kept rolling between us. I continued to hear about what he called his domestic problems and, eventually, about his plans to visit Kalimpong, which he did the following year. In the course of this visit he had a curious experience, about which he wrote to me after his return to Delhi. Just after his arrival in Kalimpong something had gone wrong with him, he wrote, and he had suffered a mental breakdown.

> The previous evening I had gone to see Joe Cann. He spoke to me of tantricism and mentioned that the Nepalese were not all they were meant to be. He spoke of many things and in a mysterious way; from then I hated everyone who was not Buddhist. I came back to Delhi in a state of collapse. Now I am again well, I have had to think over things and realize how awful I must have seemed.... I assure you on everything that is Holy, that I was the victim of some form of Auto Suggestion. It is not my way or my nature to be a person who hates anything.... I am however convinced that I was in a sick state from the time I left Joe Cann's place. Is it possible that something he said played on my mind? I feel that this was so, for also I became quite unwell and could not reason the thing at all.

It was not my way or my nature to be a person who hates anything. It was a *cri de cœur* and I knew it to be true. Ronald was of a kindly, generous disposition. I also knew that Joe Cann was just the opposite.[325] Thin, irritable, impatient, and highly strung, the chain-smoking sexagenarian was an inveterate backbiter and scandalmonger and had the most venomous tongue in Kalimpong. He had arrived in the town soon after me, and for a short time was associated with me in my work for the Dharma. But his attitude towards me had always been highly ambivalent, and it was not long before I found myself the object of his barbed attacks, mainly on account of what he saw as my refusal to accept the advice and guidance of those older and wiser than myself. Where had all this bitterness and hatred come from? I concluded, eventually, that Joe Cann suffered from a chronic inferiority complex. The fact that someone was better than, or superior to, himself in some way – socially or educationally, for example – made him painfully conscious of his inferiority not only in that respect but in general. So painful was that consciousness, indeed, that he felt compelled to criticize, disparage, and denigrate the person concerned, and in this way bring them crashing to the ground. It may therefore have been some perceived superiority of Ronald's that had prompted Joe Cann's negative remarks about the Nepalese, knowing as he did that the close friend who had accompanied Ronald to Kalimpong was Nepalese and, what was more, not a Buddhist. On the other hand, Joe Cann had within him such a store of pent up bitterness and hatred that it needed no prompting to break out. Probably it was not something he said that had played on Ronald's mind, as the latter felt, so much as the intensity of the negative emotions to which he had been exposed in the course of his evening with the chain-smoking old man. As I knew from my own past experience, to listen to Joe Cann's tirades for any length of time was to be injected with a kind of psychic poison that could leave one feeling physically ill.

Shortly after his visit to Kalimpong there began to appear in Ronald's letters passing references to 'the Lady of Kulu'. As I came to know afterwards, this mysterious personage was the widow of an old friend of Ronald's, a British army officer who, after his retirement from active service, had settled in the Kulu Valley, a particularly beautiful part of Punjab, bought an estate there, and married a local woman. The widowed lady was now writing to Ronald, whom she had known during her husband's lifetime. She wrote making him an offer the nature of which was unclear and Ronald therefore asked the Kazini to correspond with her on his behalf and sort things out. The fact was that on her husband's death the Lady of Kulu had inherited the estate and she wanted that on her own death it should go to Ronald. It had come to her from an Englishman, so she declared, and it was right that it should go back to an Englishman. Whether this involved Ronald marrying her I never knew. I knew only that he had moved to the Kulu Valley and was living on the estate with the lady. According to the Kazini, to whom Ronald wrote more about the business than he did to me, they were not happy together and quarrelled violently. Though the lady was seventy-five (this may have been one of the Kazini's little exaggerations) she wanted to be told she was still beautiful, and Ronald found it difficult to do this. She died, however, and Ronald came into possession of the estate. Unfortunately, the lady's nephew and niece, who had expected to inherit the estate themselves, accused him of having murdered their aunt. He was arrested, kept in prison, in shackles, and it was many months before he could be released, there being no evidence against him. As he may well have reflected, his stay in the Kulu Valley had gone far more amiss than had the Kazini's stay in Kalimpong.

4
THE OLD BHUTAN PALACE

There are people with whom we become friends at the first meeting, and others with whom we become friends only after knowing them for a long time. Similarly, there are gurus with whom we immediately form a strong spiritual connection, others with whom we develop such a connection only gradually. In my own case, Chattrul Rimpoche was an example of the first kind of guru, Dhardo Rimpoche of the second.

Dhardo Rimpoche was a monk of the Gelug school,[326] also known as the Yellow Hats on account of the yellow pandit hats they wore for certain ceremonial purposes, as distinct from the red hats worn by members of the three other schools of Tibetan Buddhism.[327] As it happened, Dhardo Rimpoche set eyes on me before I set eyes on him. I was then in Bodh Gaya, where the Buddha had attained Enlightenment, staying at the Maha Bodhi Society's rest house.[328] Rimpoche was staying at the nearby Tibetan *gompa*, of which he had recently been appointed abbot by the Tibetan government. Looking out of the window of his room one day, he espied me on the flat roof of the rest house. So astonished was he to see an Englishman in yellow monastic robes that he called to his attendant. 'Look!' he exclaimed, 'the Dharma has gone as far as the West!'

This was in 1949, and it was not until 1952 that we actually met. There had recently been a dispute in Bodh Gaya between Dhardo Rimpoche and the young Sinhalese monk who ran the Maha Bodhi Society's rest house, and the authorities of the Society, knowing that the Rimpoche was now back in Kalimpong, had asked me to see him about the matter. This I was glad to do, as I did not want the dispute to develop into a permanent breach between the Tibetan Buddhists and the Maha Bodhi Society. The next morning, therefore, I set out for Tirpai, where the Gelug lama was staying, taking with me as my interpreter a highly intelligent young Tibetan whom I had known for a year or more. This was Lobsang Phuntsok Lhalungpa, a former monk official, who was a close associate of Dhardo Rimpoche and anxious that I should meet him. The Rimpoche occupied the first floor of Sherpa Building, the ground floor being occupied by Joe Cann, who on the strength of his having given the Rimpoche a few English lessons had developed a rather proprietary attitude towards him and had assured me, on more than one occasion, that he was far too important and busy a lama to have time for me. Dhardo Rimpoche did, however, have time for me. In fact, he was very pleased to see me, especially as he recognized in me the yellow-robed figure he had seen on the roof of the Maha Bodhi Society's rest house in Bodh Gaya.

After we had exchanged the usual amenities, I told the Rimpoche the reason for my visit. He at once became very serious, and proceeded to give me a full account of the dispute between himself and the young Sinhalese monk, who I knew to be hot-headed and given to using intemperate language. As the Rimpoche spoke, I received such an impression of sheer goodwill, candour, and integrity that when I wrote to the General Secretary of the Maha Bodhi Society the following morning I had no hesitation in assuring him that Dhardo Rimpoche was in no way at fault and that the blame for the dispute rested solely with the Sinhalese monk.[329]

Thus began a friendship that lasted for the rest of my time in India, and which did not cease with my departure for England. It was a friendship in the course of which Dhardo Rimpoche and I worked closely together for the good of Buddhism, especially in Kalimpong. It was a friendship which culminated, moreover, in my receiving from him the bodhisattva ordination in 1962 and the White Tārā 'long-life' initiation the following year, so that from being my friend he became also my teacher.

In 1954 Dhardo Rimpoche moved to the Old Bhutan Palace, and it was there that we had our second meeting. He was then thirty-six, which meant that he was my senior by seven years. Of medium height, and rather slightly built, he wore an informal 'indoor' version of monastic dress consisting of a fawn underskirt and a sleeveless shirt of orange silk. His black hair was cropped instead of his being shaven-headed like a Theravādin monk, and a few long hairs on his upper lip gave promise of a wispy moustache. The Rimpoche spoke very little English, but he had command of a fluent if ungrammatical Hindi, and it was in that language that we conversed. During the years in which we were in personal contact there developed between us a sort of patois in which our common Hindi was freely mixed with English words and phrases as well as Tibetan, and even Sanskrit, religious and philosophical terms. Thus we were able to discuss almost any subject, from politics to the

Dhardo Rimpoche

doctrine of voidness, and from *sādhana* practice to the production of books and pamphlets. Such discussion was facilitated by the fact that there was in our communication an intuitive element, almost telepathic in its nature, that supplemented, or even bypassed, the words we spoke.

At our first meeting Dhardo Rimpoche had been serious, as befitted the matter I had come to discuss with him. On the present occasion, too, he was serious, but in a more animated way and with regard to a subject of a very different kind. This subject was the school he was planning to start. Lobsang Lhalungpa, Pheunkhang-sey, and others were helping him, and the school would be housed there in the Old Bhutan Palace, on the upper floor of which he was now living. The huge, rather ramshackle wooden building had, it seemed, been placed at his disposal by Rani Chunni Dorji, the wife (later widow) of Raja S. T. Dorji, the effective prime minister of Bhutan and Kalimpong's leading Buddhist citizen. The school would teach Tibetan and Buddhism in the morning, Dhardo Rimpoche explained, and modern subjects in the afternoon. There were many refugee children in Kalimpong, and he was anxious that they should grow up with a knowledge of their own religion and culture. At the same time, he realized that they had to be equipped to meet the demands of life in the modern world. From the way in which he spoke I could see that he had the interests of the children very much at heart, besides being deeply concerned for the preservation of the language, literature, and religion of his native land.

It was in the course of this meeting, I think, that Dhardo Rimpoche invited me to cooperate with him in establishing the Indo-Tibetan Buddhist Cultural Institute School, as it came rather grandly to be called, and to give a series of fortnightly lectures under its auspices. Both invitations I was happy to accept. I do not remember how many lectures I gave, but I gave them at the Old Bhutan Palace itself, in a large room on the upper floor where the Thirteenth Dalai Lama had once stayed. Thereafter I was a regular visitor to the school whenever I was not out on tour and when Dhardo Rimpoche himself was not in Bodh Gaya. This meant quite a long walk for me, as the Old Bhutan Palace was situated some distance beyond the bazaar, below the road that led, eventually, to Lhasa. From this road a broad track paved with cobbles as big as small boulders led down to an open space that had once been the Palace courtyard and was now the school playground. On my arrival I would be given tea, and the Rimpoche and I would talk. He might then show me what was happening in the different classrooms, or ask me to translate a letter. From time to time he came to see me at my own place, usually bringing with him something for me to type, in which case he also brought his own stationery and carbon paper. On such occasions he wore the usual maroon monastic dress, and his faithful monk attendant Gelong Lobsang, who accompanied him wherever he went, followed a few steps behind. Lobsang was younger than his master, but looked older. He had stiff black hair which, since he did not keep it very short, stuck out from his head on all sides. His habitual expression was one of extreme dourness, but sometimes, as when a remark was addressed to him, his face would light up with a delightful smile.

In 1956 Buddhism was 2,500 years old, reckoning from the date of the Buddha's *parinirvāṇa* or 'final passing away', and the occasion was celebrated all over the Buddhist world. Though India was not a Buddhist country, the Buddha Jayanti, as it was called, was widely celebrated here too. Indeed, it received official patronage and support on cultural grounds, much to the disgust of some orthodox caste Hindus. As part of the celebrations, some fifty representatives of the Buddhists of Ladakh, Sikkim, Assam, the North-East Frontier Agency, and so on were invited to tour the holy places as guests of the Government of India and to spend four days in Delhi in that capacity. Both Dhardo Rimpoche and I were among the invitees, presumably as representing the Buddhists of Kalimpong. The Eminent Buddhists from the Border Areas, as we were officially styled, were given a special train, where we ate and slept, and from which we were taken every day by coach to either a holy place or an important government project. In this way we visited Bodh Gaya, Rajgir, Nalanda, Sarnath, Kusinara, Lumbini, and Sanchi, all of which I had seen before, as well as several huge dams that were under construction. We also visited Agra, where I saw the Taj Mahal for the first time. In Delhi we met the President, Dr Rajendra Prasad; met the Vice-President, Dr Radhakrishnan; had lunch at the prime minister's house, where Pandit Nehru took me into the garden and showed me his giant pandas, and were among the tens of thousands who gathered at the airport to welcome the youthful Dalai Lama (with whom I later had a private interview) and the no less youthful Panchen Lama.[330]

During the week that we were on tour, and the four days we were in Delhi, Dhardo Rimpoche and I occupied the same compartment in the train, which we shared with my Sikkimese friend Sonam Topgay and with S. Yhonzone, a young Tamang Buddhist from Kurseong, a small hill station near Darjeeling, with whom I was already acquainted. Living as we did in such close proximity, sharing meals and going on excursions together, the four of us naturally got to know one another better than we might otherwise have done. I certainly got to know Dhardo Rimpoche better. I saw that he was adaptable, that he did not stand on his dignity as an incarnate lama (it was the first time he had travelled without Gelong Lobsang), and that he had a lively sense of humour. Above all, I saw how uniformly kind he was, how unfailingly mindful. His mindfulness consisted not merely in an absence of anything resembling forgetfulness or inattention, but also in a degree of foresight and preparedness that was almost supernatural.

There occurred an incident which strikingly exemplified this particular quality of his. It was the custom of the officials who were looking after the party and organizing its transport to tell us which places we would be visiting that day. One morning they told us we would be visiting a certain dam in the morning, and in the afternoon, after returning to the train for lunch, a certain holy place. Unfortunately there was somehow a mix-up. An hour after leaving the train we found ourselves not at the dam, as we had expected, but at the holy place. This in itself did not really matter, but thinking we would not be needing them until the afternoon none of us had brought any candles or incense sticks. None of us, that is, except Dhardo Rimpoche. As we were lamenting the fact that we would be unable to offer worship in the proper manner, he produced packets of candles and bundles of incense sticks from beneath his voluminous robes and smilingly distributed them among us. As I was to say in later years, Dhardo Rimpoche was never caught napping.

Back in Kalimpong, both the Rimpoche and I had work to do. In his case, besides having the school to run, which was quite a responsibility, he had to decide what was to be done about Ani-la. It was two years since the turbulent Frenchwoman had cut off contact with him. During that period she had behaved more and more outrageously, so that she was now notorious throughout the district and was bringing the whole Buddhist community into disrepute. Since she refused to come and see him, he felt he had no alternative but to deprive her of the *getsulma* or 'female novice' ordination he had conferred on her four years earlier, and in July 1958 he drew up a document to this effect. With his help, I produced an English version of this document, a copy of which, signed and sealed by him, was to be given to his erstwhile disciple. In it Dhardo Rimpoche declared that she had been proved guilty of grave offences against the monastic law, that by virtue of the authority vested in him by the Dalai Lama he was depriving her of her ordination, and that she was no longer entitled to the support of the lay community. Ten offences were enumerated. She had refused to submit herself to the lawful monastic authorities; had openly blasphemed the Holy Dharma; had grossly slandered sundry incarnate lamas and members of the sangha; had gravely slandered prominent lay persons of the locality; had declared in writing that she was not a Buddhist and that she was wearing the monastic robe for the sake of worldly acquisition; had publicly declared her intention of writing a book against Buddhism; had misappropriated religious books; had been guilty of an act of violence; had conducted herself publicly in an unseemly manner; and had by her behaviour been a source of scandal and brought the whole Buddhist community into contempt and disrespect.

Unfortunately, all this was not only true but also a matter of public knowledge, and even of public record, as in the case of the scathing article on Himalayan Buddhism that Ani-la had published in the town's little English weekly paper. Some of her offences had been committed in front of me, as well as in front of others, and some she herself told me about. Among the latter was the act of violence of which she had been guilty. The act had been committed in Darjeeling. The taxi she had ordered having arrived late, she struck the driver a blow in the face with her fist, knocking out two front teeth. She apologized to him afterwards, and gave him a tin of fifty cigarettes by way of compensation. The incident was an ugly one, and the police had become involved. A European had assaulted an Indian. What was more, the perpetrator of the assault was a Buddhist nun. In telling me about the incident, Ani-la pleaded extenuating circumstances, saying that she had arranged to meet a visiting French scholar at his hotel, and the taxi was to have taken her there. By making her late for her appointment the driver had lowered her in the eyes of her compatriot, who would think her an uncivilized person, and this thought so infuriated her that when the driver at last appeared she had lashed out at him. As she was a strong, sturdy woman, a blow from her fist was no light matter, and I was not surprised that it should have knocked out two of the unfortunate man's teeth. The Kazini Sahiba, to whom the French Nun was able to pour out her troubles in her own language, was of the opinion that she had the physique of a peasant and that Nature had meant her to do hard farm work and have lots of babies. She was also convinced that Ani-la's talk of suicide could not be taken seriously, especially in view of what the latter had once told her. It had been one of those times when, feeling deeply depressed and thinking that life was not worth living, she had walked into the forests of western Sikkim with the intention of committing suicide there. 'But you know what these cheap Bata shoes are like,' she told the Kazini, 'I hadn't gone very far when they started leaking. So I turned back.'

The Kazini found the idea of someone being prevented from committing suicide by leaking shoes quite ludicrous, and she could not help smiling as she told me the story. For my part, I found the incident not only ludicrous but pathetic, and despite her bad behaviour I felt sorry for the French Nun. Her life in Kalimpong had begun so well! From being a student of Hindu temple architecture and Sanskrit she had become first a Theravādin *anāgarika* or 'homeless one' and then a *getsulma* or novice nun. It was evident from the beginning, however, that she was by nature extremely demanding, so that if what she considered to be her legitimate intellectual and spiritual needs were not met, or not met in the way she wanted, her face would assume an aggrieved, sullen, resentful expression, and sooner or later there would be an explosion. I witnessed several such explosions, and heard about others (sometimes from the aggrieved party herself, if she was in a repentant mood), for even those who were most anxious to help Ani-la did not find it easy to do so and consequently incurred her wrath. I used to say of her that she would ask a guru to teach her as she prostrated herself before him, then tell him just how he ought to do this as she rose to her feet, which was in fact not far from the truth. Naturally she was disappointed, and this led to her becoming increasingly frustrated, disillusioned, and bitter, and more and more inclined to blame everyone for her unhappiness except herself. Her behaviour also changed, especially after she left Kachu Rimpoche, eventually becoming so much at variance with the kind of behaviour expected of a Buddhist nun that Dhardo Rimpoche was obliged to take action against her.

Dhardo Rimpoche might deprive Ani-la of her ordination, and even draw up a document to that effect, but he could not compel her to stop wearing the monastic robe, as he would have been able to do in

Tibet. Indeed, he found it difficult to get a copy of the English version of the document delivered to her. He therefore decided to hand it to her himself. On learning that she was visiting friends at the Himalayan Hotel, he took up position beside the front gate and waited for her to emerge, thinking that when she did so he would speak to her and get her to accept the document. When she did at length emerge, however, she rudely thrust him aside as he attempted to greet her and proceeded on her way without a word. I was deeply pained when I heard how Ani-la had behaved towards Dhardo Rimpoche, who had treated her so kindly and endured her vagaries with such patience. The picture of him standing beside the front gate of the hotel, waiting for her in the darkness, haunted my imagination for a long time. The Rimpoche himself did not complain, but he must have wondered how an educated European woman could act so rudely. In Tibet, one was expected to treat everybody, even an enemy, with the courtesy that was due from one human being to another. Good manners were part of Buddhist ethics.

Grave as were the offences Ani-la had committed, and for which she had been deprived of her ordination, one of the worst things she did found no place in Dhardo Rimpoche's document and was not, I think, known to him. It was in connection with George Roerich, the Russian Tibetologist, who lived in some style in a mock-Tudor villa in the best part of Kalimpong. Ani-la had once asked him to teach her Tibetan. He had refused, and since then she had borne him a grudge. One day she came to see me, breathless and trembling with excitement. She had discovered Roerich's secret, she announced triumphantly, her eyes gleaming. She had found out where his money came from. The story, as she then proceeded to tell it to me, was that she had been eating in a restaurant in the bazaar when she heard two men talking on the other side of the partition separating her banquette from theirs. They were talking in Tibetan. More than two years had passed since Roerich's refusal to teach her, and during that period she had acquired enough colloquial Tibetan to be able to follow their conversation. They had come from Mongolia, she gathered; they had some gold with them, and the gold was meant for Roerich. Having told me all this, she declared her intention of going to Chandralok, the tall, isolated building that housed the area headquarters of the Central Intelligence Bureau, and telling them what she had learned. I strongly advised her not to get mixed up in the business, but she refused to listen. Roerich had refused to teach her

Tibetan, she reminded me, and now she was going to have her revenge. And off she went to Chandralok as fast as her legs could carry her. A week later I heard that Roerich had suddenly left Kalimpong. When next heard of, he was in Moscow.[331]

I do not remember how long it was after Roerich's departure that Ani-la, too, disappeared from the scene. For the few weeks that she remained in the area after being deprived of her ordination she continued to wear the monastic robe, but when next heard of she was in Calcutta, where she was seen with bobbed hair, in a short skirt, and puffing a cigarette.[332]

5
THE SECRET ORDER OF THE POTALA

When I moved into the stone cottage that was to become the Triyana Vardhana Vihara, some of my friends wondered what I would do with the four acres of terraced hillside land that went with it. I had no experience of gardening, let alone of farming. But I told them not to worry. If an uneducated Nepalese or Lepcha peasant[333] could grow crops, I was sure I could do so. Give me a year, I said, and I would know as much as any of them.

The property's most valuable asset, apart from the cottage, were its orange trees, of which there were about a hundred. The trees had been neglected by the previous owners and stood in need of some attention. I therefore had the soil round each one of them loosened, care being taken not to damage the roots, and manure dug in. The oranges were of the small, sweet, easily peeled variety that in my childhood appeared in the shops at Christmas time and were known as tangerines. They were grown throughout the Kalimpong subdivision, as well as in Sikkim, and were an important cash crop. As soon as the trees had fruited the middlemen would come round, going from orchard to orchard and buying up the entire crop in advance, except for the two or three trees one reserved for one's own consumption. The secret was not to accept the first offer that was made but to wait until the orange season was in full swing and the wholesale price had peaked. Some orange growers could not afford to wait, and the middleman, taking advantage of their need for ready money, would drive a hard bargain. During my time at the Vihara the price I got for my oranges rose steadily, so that the price I got for them in 1964 was ten times what it had been in 1957. I also started growing buckwheat between the orange trees. Its crimson stalks and pink-and-white flowers created a sea of colour out of which the trees seemed to rise.

So far as I remember, the buckwheat was not sold. The crop was never a big one, and in any case the other community members and I all enjoyed our Lepcha cook's fried buckwheat cakes. We did have another cash crop besides the oranges, however. This was maize or Indian corn, locally known as *makkai*. It was cultivated for us by a sharecropper inherited from the previous owners of the property, and thanks to his labour the handsome plant with the long green leaves and purple-tasselled pods covered more than two-thirds of the land. The sharecropper was a bent, shambling old Nepalese Brahmin with yellow, decaying teeth and a long, thick *tiki* or ritual crown lock that hung halfway down his back. He liked to come and chat with me from time to time, squatting on the veranda in his dirty clothes, and smelling of sweat, manure, and cheap country tobacco. At first I used to offer him tea, but he always refused, as our cook was a non-Brahmin and the caste-conscious old man would not accept even water from his hand. As he was by birth a member of the priestly caste, he was invariably addressed by Hindus and Buddhists alike as Bhaje, which meant something like 'your worship'. This did not mean he was always treated with deference. 'Come here, Bhaje, you old rascal,' someone might shout to him.

When the year's *makkai* crop had been divided equally between us, I would sell the greater part of the Vihara's share of the pods, the rest being stored in a sort of miniature haystack mounted on stilts. This kept them out of the reach of rats. The haystacks were of two kinds, the round and the oblong, the Nepalese and the Lepcha, though which kind was associated with which community I no longer remember. When one wanted a few pods, all one had to do was reach up and pull them out of the stack. Coarsely ground, the parti-coloured grain could be made into a sort of porridge, so that we had no need to buy packaged breakfast cereals. There was also plenty of corn on the cob to eat, especially early in the season when the grain was small, soft, and sweet.

Growing vegetables was a matter of trial and error, as I quickly discovered. The soil, which was full of mica, did not suit either potatoes or cauliflowers. Such potatoes as we managed to produce were hardly bigger than marbles, while our cauliflowers were not only stunted but preyed upon by caterpillars to such an extent that their leaves were reduced to skeletons. The pumpkin, on the other hand, required little or no attention and was extremely prolific. One was always coming across fruit hidden beneath the big leaves, and the plant's tender leading shoots made an excellent green vegetable. The *karela*, or bitter gourd, was no less prolific. It bore tiny yellow flowers, and the green, crinkled gourds, rarely more than six inches in length, dangled at the end of a long string by which it was connected with the parent vine. As it ripened, it became a beautiful golden yellow colour, eventually bursting open to reveal brilliant scarlet seeds. Both the flowers and the dangling gourds themselves emitted a strange aroma that I found not unpleasing.

The banana trees and the bamboos, like the pumpkin, required little or no attention. There were thirty or more bamboos, all thick as a man's arm and rising to a height of thirty or forty feet. They grew close together, so that when the wind blew, and the slender tops nodded, they knocked against one another, producing sounds that were almost musical. Since the bamboo is a species of grass, they died and grew afresh every year. In the rainy season they grew with great rapidity, as did the banana trees and the *makkai*, sometimes achieving as much as eight or nine inches of growth in a single night. There was a constant demand for bamboos in the locality. They were used in building construction, sections of them could be made into vessels for drinking home-brewed beer, and split lengthwise they were the means by which water could be channelled from a higher to a lower terrace, in a process sometimes even crossing the road high overhead. Hence there were few weeks that I did not sell a bamboo to a neighbour, who would chop it down himself with his *kukri*[334] and march away with it balanced on his shoulder.

The bamboo grove, as I liked to call it, was situated a little beyond the orange trees, on a lower terrace. I used to go down from time to time and stand among the bamboos admiring their smooth greenness, inhaling the smell of the fallen leaves underfoot and, if there was a breeze, listening to the sounds they made as they knocked against one another.[335] Once, on my way down to the terrace, I caught sight of a strange bird in the grove. About the size of a pheasant, it was a deep emerald green from its head to the tip of its long tail. By the time I reached the grove it had disappeared and I never saw it again. None of the people to whom I described it could tell me what it was, and some of my friends thought I must have imagined it. Real or a product of my imagination, to me the mysterious bird was the spirit of the bamboo grove, even of the little hillside property itself.

'If you have a loaf of bread,' the prophet of Islam is reported as saying, 'sell half and buy a rose'.[336] The Vihara had plenty of oranges and plenty of *makkai*, but I also needed flowers for the shrine-room, where I meditated each morning and evening and where members and friends of the Vihara celebrated the full-moon days. But at the time I moved in, the only flowers to be seen were the small pink-and-yellow ones on the lantana bushes bordering the property. I therefore created a little garden on the terrace immediately below the cottage, and soon we had plenty of French marigolds and zinnias, besides a few gerberas, which Tibetan friends told me had been the favourite flowers of the Thirteenth Dalai Lama. I had half a dozen big flowerpots made, grew geraniums in them from cuttings, and placed them at intervals along the veranda. On the steep bank behind the cottage I created a kind of 'orchidarium'. Exotic and expensive as orchids might have been in Europe, in the part of the world in which I now lived they grew in abundance, and were little regarded by the local people.[337] If one wanted a few plants, all one had to do was to send a man into the forest with a *tokri*, the big, cone-shaped wicker basket in which the Nepalese, men and women alike, carried loads on their backs. He would climb up into the trees and gather the plants until he had a full *tokri*.

This was dangerous work, for the orchids grew high on the trees, preferring branches that were rotten and therefore unsafe. Hence there were two ways of paying the man. One could either give him two rupees, and pay his family a hundred rupees if he fell from the tree and was killed, or one could give him five rupees and be free from any such liability. I opted for the first alternative, sent a man into the forest one morning, and by the evening had several dozen plants. These I attached to bits of rotten wood, then thrust the wood into holes that had been dug in the bank behind the cottage. Before many months had passed, long sprays of orchids appeared from among the green leaves, some snowy white, some golden yellow. They were the most common varieties, knowledgeable friends told me. Joe Cann in particular was very dismissive of my orchids. *He* had some extremely rare specimens, he assured me, for which he had paid a lot of money. But I did not care.

I loved orchids, as I loved all other flowers, for their beauty, not for their rarity or their monetary value.

The orange trees and the *makkai*, the vegetables and the flowers, all required a certain amount of attention from me, even if this meant only that I directed the labour of others. The work of the farmer and the gardener was never done, it appeared, even when the area under cultivation was no more than four acres. Yet there was at least one project which I began soon after moving into the property and succeeded in finishing shortly afterwards. This was the construction of a five-roomed guest cottage. I had always had visitors from distant places, and I had usually been able to put them up for a night or two at the rented premises I happened to be occupying at the time. The stone cottage that was the Vihara proper was quite small, and though a visiting monk might be accommodated in the shrine-room and other guests in a loft above what had once been a cowshed, something better was badly needed. I therefore decided to build. There was no question of my building in stone, which would have been difficult and expensive; but there was no reason why I should not build with wood and bamboo, as the villagers did. For this I had the means and, I hoped, the capacity.

First I drew a ground plan of the building, and decided on its dimensions. I then hired a carpenter, discussed with him what materials would be needed, and sent him to the bazaar to buy wood and to hire four coolies. A site adjacent to the Vihara having been levelled, the foundations of the cottage were laid and the work of construction could begin. I have no recollection of the different stages of the work, but it progressed steadily, and by the end of the second week the wooden frame of the cottage stood complete. At the time I was busy, as I usually was, writing articles and book reviews, but every half hour or so I would leave my desk and go outside to see what my workmen were doing. The Nepalese carpenter, Lal Bahadur, who acted as foreman, was a good worker, but the coolies slacked or disappeared if an eye was not kept on them. The frame of the cottage being in place, the spaces between the vertical and lateral beams of the outer and inner walls had to be filled in with what in England would have been called wattle-and-daub, the 'wattle' being split bamboo and the 'daub' clay mixed with chopped jute sacking. This work was done by the coolies, while Lal Bahadur got on with making doors, window frames, and beds. Finding the reeds with which the cottage was to be thatched proved difficult.

Reeds were in short supply, it seemed, and in the end they had to be brought up from somewhere near Teesta Bridge by bullock cart. They came in bundles which, laid side by side in layers, made a roof a foot thick. It would last for three years, I was told. In fact it lasted for the rest of my time in Kalimpong. All that now remained for Lal Bahadur to do was to hang the doors and glaze the windows. This having been done, the walls of the cottage were whitewashed, and the doors and windows painted bright yellow.

It was the local custom that on the completion of a house the builder should give the workmen a feast on the site. I had no objection to going along with this custom. Thanks to my five workmen, the Vihara now had a five-roomed guest cottage capable of accommodating eight persons. The work had proceeded smoothly; the cottage had been built in a month, and it had cost me just over a thousand rupees, which was a little more than a twentieth of what I had given for the stone cottage and its four acres of hillside land. But though I had no objection to giving the workmen their feast, I declined to provide the customary meat and liquor. Lal Bahadur and the four coolies had a merry time nonetheless, chatting and laughing, and eating as much food as they could. On their departure I gave them some extra money, which they no doubt spent on liquor in the bazaar.

The Vihara's modest guest cottage was occupied, over the years, by a number of people. One of the earliest of them, and the most unusual, was a visitor who arrived unexpectedly in the summer of 1958. I was in my sitting room one morning, reading, when I was told there was a sahib to see me. He was tall and heavily bearded, and carried a pipe. Over a cup of tea he said he had come from Bodh Gaya, from Dhardo Rimpoche, who had told him that the English monk in Kalimpong would be able to teach him what he wanted to know. The Rimpoche had been wearing a skirt, he added, laughing uproariously, as if the idea of a man wearing a skirt was the funniest thing in the world. What, then, did he want to know, I enquired, when the guffaws had subsided. He wanted to know how to read people's thoughts, he replied unhesitatingly, and how to see what was happening at a distance. But before I could ask him why he wanted to acquire those powers he produced a newspaper cutting from his wallet and silently handed it to me. From it I learned that my bearded, pipe-smoking visitor was in fact a woman. Born in 1915, he had been orphaned at an early age, had been brought up by two maiden aunts, had gone to Oxford, and between 1945 and 1948 had undergone a series of operations that had given him the outward appearance of a man, thus enabling him to pass as such. He had then qualified as a doctor, and until recently had worked as a ship's doctor on a British liner, resigning only when the discovery of his change of sex by a reporter had led to its extensive coverage in the press. The press was still on his trail, he explained, though he believed he had shaken them off in Calcutta. Could he stay at the Vihara until things had blown over? I assured him he could stay as long as he wished. Within half an hour of his arrival, therefore, my unusual visitor had been installed in the guest house and was arranging his scanty belongings. To make it difficult for the press to track him down he shaved off his beard and I gave him a Buddhist name, so that Michael (née Laura) Dillon became Jivaka, which had been the name of the Buddha's personal physician.

Later he told me he had been greatly impressed by the fact that I had read the newspaper cutting without turning a hair, as he put it, as well as by the readiness with which I had agreed to his staying at the Vihara. If I did not turn a hair on learning of Jivaka's sex-change, it was partly because I was familiar with the phenomenon from my reading of the Buddhist scriptures, where it was represented as occurring spontaneously.[338] In Jivaka's case the change had not occurred spontaneously but as the result of a series of surgical operations. He liked to talk about these operations, of which there had been thirty-six, spread over a period of three years. They had begun with the removal of his unwanted breasts, two semicircular scars being still visible when he went bare-chested in hot weather. The plastic surgeon who had carried out the operations was a pioneer in the field, I gathered, and it was evident that Jivaka regarded him with admiration and gratitude. He was especially grateful for his artificial penis, of which he was immensely proud. One day he offered to show it to me, assuring me that it was 'a beautiful piece of work'; but I declined the offer. Despite all the operations he had undergone, however, Jivaka's change of sex was far from being either complete or final. He was still having to take hormone tablets to promote the growth of facial hair and suppress menstruation. The change from female to male would in fact never be complete. Jivaka was essentially a woman whom modern surgical techniques and modern drugs had enabled to act the part of a man on the stage of life. The beard, the pipe, and so on, were all so many stage props. There were times when he overacted the part, as when he laughed uproariously at the idea of a man wearing a skirt. At other times he could behave like an overgrown schoolboy, as when he astonished other members of the community, who thought he had gone mad, by suddenly gyrating up and down on the veranda, waving a letter and shouting at the top of his voice, 'Oxford's won the Boat Race! Oxford's won the Boat Race!' For although he had gone to Oxford before having his mastectomy, and had belonged to one of the women's colleges, he thought of himself as being very much an 'Oxford man'.

The fact that he was the first female-to-male transsexual to have modern surgery and hormone treatment was not the most interesting thing about Jivaka, at least so far as I was concerned. He was also a disciple of the notorious Lobsang Rampa, author of the best-selling *The Third Eye*, who was not a Tibetan lama at all but a plumber from Plympton with a vivid imagination and a racy style.[339] A few weeks after his arrival at the Vihara, Jivaka confided to me, with a solemn air, that Lobsang Rampa had initiated him into the Secret Order of the Potala and invested him with its robe and girdle. There were only thirteen members of the Order, including the Dalai Lama, and every Tibetan who saw him wearing the robe – however highly placed – would immediately prostrate himself before him. He had worn the robe when he went to see Dhardo Rimpoche, he added, but strange to say, the Rimpoche had not prostrated himself. Perhaps he was a low-ranking lama who had not heard of the Secret Order of the Potala.

Naturally I wanted to know if Jivaka had brought the robe with him. He indeed had, he assured me, and at my request not only showed it to me but demonstrated how it was to be worn, wrapping it round himself in the most extraordinary fashion and tying it with what appeared to be a length of dressing-gown cord. 'But Jivaka, it's an ordinary Burmese monk's robe!' I exclaimed, with genuine astonishment. 'No, it's not,' he retorted angrily. 'It's the robe of the Secret Order of the Potala.' Fortunately I had just such a monk's robe in my cupboard, presented to me by Burmese pilgrims whom I had met in one of the holy places. It was of the same yellowish-brown colour as the one Jivaka was wearing, consisted of the same number of patches, and bore in one corner the same manufacturer's label in Burmese script.

Jivaka was dumbfounded by the discovery. Even so, I had a hard time convincing him that Lobsang Rampa was not, as he claimed, a

With Jivaka on the veranda of the Triyana Vardhana Vihara

lama who had spent many years in Lhasa and been initiated into the deepest mysteries of Tibetan Buddhism, and that the Secret Order of the Potala existed only in his fertile imagination. Eventually, however, I did convince him, whereupon he wrote to Rampa, who was then living in Ireland in a house bought for him by Jivaka, a letter of indignant remonstrance. To this the supposed lama only replied that evidently some evil person had been undermining his faith.

Jivaka's faith in his erstwhile master was indeed undermined, but not his faith in his own high spiritual destiny – a faith that had enabled him to regard membership of the Secret Order of the Potala as being no more than his due.

'I *know* that I am a teacher, a teacher with a capital T,' he told me not long after his disillusionment with Rampa.

'In that case you ought to have something to teach,' I responded, not without irony.

Jivaka failed to notice the irony. 'I never thought of that,' he said, quite seriously.

What a teacher ought to have, he seems to have thought, were psychic powers – especially a teacher with a capital T. This was why he wanted to be able to read people's thoughts and how to see what was happening at a distance. For on my asking him, earlier, why he wanted to know these things he had replied that it was because they would be helpful to him in his work. What that work was he refused to tell me, only observing, rather portentously, that when the time came for it to be known I would know it. That time had now come, it seemed. By his work he had meant his work as a Teacher, for that was what he 'knew' himself to be. Later he went so far as to speak in a mysterious, oracular manner that suggested he believed he was a reincarnation of Jesus Christ. In the meantime, however, his energies were being applied to the study of Buddhism. A Teacher ought to have something to teach!

As I had discovered soon after his arrival, Jivaka was acquainted with the ideas of Gurdjieff and Ouspensky,[340] but he knew nothing about Buddhism, least of all about Tibetan Buddhism, despite – or perhaps because of – his association with Lobsang Rampa. I had a small Buddhist library, and from this I selected books for him to read, mark, learn and, I hoped, inwardly digest.[341] He certainly read them (he was a very fast reader), and he may have marked and learned to an extent, but nothing was inwardly digested. It was as though what he read went straight into his head without passing through his heart. He had no understanding of the need for reflection and assimilation, especially in the case of the Buddhist scriptures, and he grumbled that I doled out books to him instead of allowing him the run of my library. He also grumbled about the hard wooden bed, about the monotonous vegetarian diet, and about the difficulty of sitting cross-legged for the morning and evening puja and meditation. Nonetheless he was cheerful, perhaps even happy, for he had escaped the press and was living quietly in a Buddhist monastery which he seemed increasingly disposed to regard as home. At any rate, despite my being ten years younger than himself, he insisted on calling me 'Daddy', which I heartily disliked. Beneath the outsized pseudo-masculinity, the wilfulness, and the spiritual ambition, I detected, I thought, a rather infantile craving for affection.

Jivaka not only read fast; he also wrote fast. Letters poured from his pen, all addressed to the few friends in England who knew of his sex-change and who could be trusted not to reveal his whereabouts to the press. Articles also poured from his pen, as did an autobiography to which he gave the title *Out of the Ordinary*.[342] It was written at my suggestion, and later he returned the compliment by suggesting that I, too, should write my autobiography. His life had indeed been an extraordinary one, and reading about it was an interesting experience. I could not but be impressed by the courage and tenacity he had shown, however misguidedly, in choosing to undergo a series of difficult, painful, and potentially dangerous operations, and I asked him why he had been so desperately anxious to change his sex. There were two reasons, he replied. One reason was that he had always felt that he was a male soul trapped in a female body, and he wanted to bring his body into line with his soul. The other was that he was sexually attracted to women and thought that if he had a male instead of a female body 'it would be all right', the implication being that lesbianism was immoral and therefore out of the question. He did not say if it ever had been 'all right', and in the autobiography there was no mention of any sexual relationship.

'He's a strange man, your Jivaka,' one day remarked the Kazini, to whom I had introduced the Vihara's new guest and to whom he was indebted for the occasional non-vegetarian meal. 'There's something wrong with him but I can't put my finger on it. It's as though his sex had gone rotten within him.'

She was a very perceptive woman, and for a moment I thought she must have guessed Jivaka's secret. But she had not, which was fortunate, for she would have found it difficult to keep such a titillating piece of information to herself.

The future transsexual's childhood had been an unhappy one, the autobiography made clear. The two elderly maiden aunts who had brought him up were women of narrow, conventional views who had sought to mould the tomboyish girl, as Jivaka then was, into an upper-class young lady who would make a good marriage. Both aunts were extremely miserly. Though they had sizeable private incomes, they had somehow managed to convince themselves that they were very poor and barely able to afford necessaries. Reading about their curious, penny-pinching ways, I could not help wondering if Jivaka had inherited something of his aunts' attitude to money. It had been agreed at the beginning of his stay that the Vihara should charge him five rupees a day for his board and lodging (the Himalayan Hotel charged twenty), but he seemed to think that the one hundred and fifty rupees to which this amounted each month was a huge sum, and that he was being incredibly generous in paying so much.

Jivaka had not been with us for many months when I left for a preaching tour of central and western India. On my return I found that during my absence there had been serious trouble between Jivaka and Dupchen Lama, one of the younger members of the community. Dupchen was from the Dooars, a densely forested area that marched with the southern border of Bhutan and formed part of Assam. I had gone there at the invitation of the local Tamang Buddhists, some of whom were concerned that they knew so little about their ancestral faith. Besides giving Dharma talks and holding discussions, I suggested they should give me a young man to teach and train at my monastery in Kalimpong. To this they readily agreed, and I chose a bright-faced young man of about twenty who had listened to my Dharma talks with particular interest and had already expressed a wish to study with me. He would join me in Kalimpong in three weeks time, his family promised.

Three weeks later there arrived at the Vihara a small, scared boy of ten or eleven. It was Dupchen. He brought with him a letter from his uncle, who informed me that the young man I had chosen was not able to come, after all, and that he was sending Dupchen in his place. Though I was disappointed and suspected I was being taken advantage of, I did not have the heart to send the boy back to the Dooars, especially after learning that he was an orphan and that his uncle, with whom he had been living, did not want to have any further responsibility for him. I therefore assigned him a room in the guest cottage, and had him admitted to the local government boys' school.

He was not very bright, and did not do well at school. More than once I had to discuss his lack of progress with the headmaster, whom I happened to know. But Dupchen seemed happy enough. He had friends both at school and at the Vihara, and apart from his unsatisfactory school reports he gave me no cause for concern. It was not to be expected, though, that he would not sometimes get into mischief, especially when

I was away, and one day he had amused himself tormenting the Vihara cat. For this Jivaka had chastised him with a slipper, a terrible indignity by local standards. Dupchen had been very angry, and he had threatened to knife his assailant. He would not have minded had Jivaka beaten him with his hand or even with a stick, he told me, for he knew he should not have tormented the cat; but the shame and humiliation of being beaten with a shoe was more than he could bear. I had therefore to explain to Jivaka what being struck with, or even touched by, another person's shoe meant in Indian (and Nepalese) culture, whereupon he apologized to Dupchen and insisted on shaking hands with him to the accompaniment of 'No hard feelings, I hope.' I could see that Dupchen was puzzled by this strange public school ritual, but he shook hands nonetheless, and peace was restored to the Vihara.

The next time I went out on tour, I took the precaution of taking Jivaka with me as far as Sarnath, where I arranged for him to stay until my return, as I did not want to risk any further trouble between him and Dupchen. Sarnath was one of the four principal holy places, for it was here that the Buddha had set in motion the wheel of the Dharma. Besides ancient monuments, it had temples and monasteries, and a small body of Theravādin monks who looked after the needs of the pilgrims, and I thought Jivaka would in any case benefit from a wider range of Buddhist contacts. From the letters beginning 'Dear Daddy' that followed me round central and western India I learned that he was helping out in the dispensary, that he had given nicknames to all the monks (my old friend Sangharatana was 'Sammy'), and that he was writing a book on Buddhism for children.[343] On my returning to Sarnath, however, I received a shock. No sooner had I arrived than Jivaka took me aside and told me that the monks had agreed to his ordination as a *sāmaṇera* or novice provided I, too, agreed. The ceremony was to take place the following morning. This put me in a quandary. I did not want to disappoint Jivaka, but neither did I want to connive at the deception of my brother monks, the very thought of which was abhorrent to me. In the end, I decided to say nothing about Jivaka not being really a man. Strict rules governed ordination as a *bhikkhu* or monk proper, but in the case of *sāmaṇera* ordination a degree of irregularity was, I knew, permitted, or at least tolerated. There was also the fact that it would be difficult to veto Jivaka's ordination without giving a reason, especially as the other monks were all very much in favour of it. Such were the sophistries with which I sought to soothe my uneasy conscience.

The following morning I arrived at the Sinhalese Temple late, and took my seat at the back, behind the other monks.

'Come and sit in the front,' the abbot called out to me. 'You're his teacher.'

In the front I therefore had to sit, though my heart was not in the proceedings, and afterwards my congratulations lacked warmth.

Jivaka failed to notice this. 'The next step is *bhikkhu* ordination,' he declared with evident satisfaction.

In normal circumstances, *bhikkhu* ordination would indeed have been the next step, but in Jivaka's case the circumstances were not normal. However, I did not remind him of this. Instead I simply asked him why he was so anxious to become a *bhikkhu*.

'It's because I want to be able to ordain my own disciples,' he replied unhesitatingly.

'But you won't be able to ordain others until you've been a *bhikkhu* for at least ten years,' I pointed out.

His face darkened. 'I'm not going to bother about a little thing like that,' he retorted.

'*Jivaka will have to be stopped*,' I said to myself, for it was obvious that the erstwhile disciple of Lobsang Rampa was dominated by spiritual ambition and that ordination was for him only a means to the attainment of essentially egoistic ends. By his own admission, he was a great believer in the fait accompli, and I now knew he did not scruple to act in accordance with that belief. He had caught me out once, but he would not catch me out a second time.

Thus resolving, I left for Kalimpong. I cannot be certain whether Jivaka accompanied me and returned to Sarnath later, or whether he stayed behind and never saw Kalimpong again. Whichever it was, he was certainly in Sarnath by the summer of 1959, a year after his arrival at the Vihara, and letters beginning 'Dear Daddy' were again pouring from his prolific pen. They were often full of complaints, as well as requests. One of his biggest complaints was about the amount of money he had to spend on postage stamps, for he appeared to be carrying on an extensive correspondence with various editors and publishers. The letters were suspiciously silent on the subject of *bhikkhu* ordination. One day, however, I heard on the monastic grapevine that he had asked the Sarnath monks to allow him to take the 'next step'. Evidently another fait accompli was being planned for my benefit. I therefore at once wrote officially to the abbot and his brother monks, informing them that Jivaka was a transsexual, apologizing for having not informed them before, and leaving it to them, in their wisdom, to decide whether or not he qualified for ordination as a *bhikkhu*. This was towards the end of 1959.

Jivaka was furious. In a bitter, angry letter he accused me of betraying secrets confided to me 'under the seal of the confessional'. He seemed to be rather fond of the phrase, for he used it more than once in the letter, as well as subsequently. I replied that I was not a Roman Catholic priest and that there was no question of any 'confessional'. Nonetheless I had kept his secret faithfully, even to the extent of keeping silent about it so that he could be ordained as a *sāmaṇera*, despite my misgivings. But *bhikkhu* ordination was an entirely different matter, and now that he had asked for it, as I had heard, I could no longer remain silent. I was his friend, and I wished him well, but my loyalty to the order of *bhikkhus*, as represented by Sangharatana and the other Sarnath monks, took precedence of my loyalty to him. Jivaka was unable to accept this, as was obvious from his reply. In his view, my loyalty to him took precedence over all other loyalties, so that in revealing his secret to my fellow *bhikkhus* in Sarnath I had been guilty of a shameful betrayal for which there could be no forgiveness. Though he did not compare me to Judas Iscariot, the tone of his letter suggested that this was the kind of light in which he now saw me. Thus from being good, kind Daddy I became, almost overnight, the wicked, cruel stepfather who had unaccountably prevented poor little Jivaka from getting something he badly wanted.

All the same, he continued writing to me. He wrote less frequently than before, and his letters now began 'Dear Sangharakshita'. A few weeks after the 'betrayal' he assured me he was not angry, and that his faith in human nature had long been weak. Most of his letters contained the familiar complaints, and in some of them he was sarcastic at my expense. In the articles he published, and in the correspondence columns of the English-language press, he made a point of disagreeing with me, or criticizing me, whenever he could. Perhaps this was an example of what I was to term, years later, 'delayed adolescent rebellion'. In one of his letters he assured me that in not becoming his guru I had missed a wonderful opportunity. In another he ascribed my treatment of him to jealousy. I was jealous of him, he claimed, because he came from an aristocratic family (which he did), because he was better educated (which he was), and because he was spiritually more advanced (which was at least debatable), and I wanted to hold him back lest, endowed as he was with these advantages, he should become better known than myself as a Buddhist writer and teacher.

During the three years that followed, Jivaka left the Theravāda for the Mahāyāna form of Buddhism, was re-ordained as a Tibetan *getsul* or novice, took the name of Lobzang (sic) Jivaka, and wrote a popular abridgement of Dr W. Y. Evans-Wentz's *Tibet's Great Yogi, Milarepa*, which was published by Murray in the well-known Wisdom of the East series.[344] In 1960 he spent three months in a Gelug monastery in Ladakh, in the western Himalayas. Unfortunately, he was refused permission to re-enter Ladakh which was in a prohibited area, and reluctantly returned to Sarnath.

In the spring of 1962 I received a review copy of *Imji Getsul: an English Buddhist in a Tibetan Monastery*. It was not *Out of the Ordinary,* as I had at first thought. Neither was it, apparently, one of the three versions of his autobiography which, Jivaka had told me, he had recently prepared for publication. One version showed me in a favourable light, one in a very unfavourable light, and one in a light that was neither favourable nor unfavourable. Which version was published, he informed me, would depend on whether or not I cooperated with him. What this 'cooperation' meant he did not say, but I assumed it had something to do with the higher monastic ordination, which I knew him to be still desperately seeking.

Imji Getsul, it turned out, was mainly a quite interesting account of the three months Jivaka had spent at Rizong Gompa. There was even a photograph of him with some of the other monks, looking not very happy. But there was no mention of the sex change, nor of Lobsang Rampa, nor of the Secret Order of the Potala, nor of his wanting to acquire psychic powers. Since there was no mention of the sex change there could be no truthful account of the circumstances which had brought him, eventually, to Kalimpong, nor of how he had come to be called Jivaka. I appeared briefly in the book simply as 'the English *bhikkhu* in Kalimpong', my name not being given, and his account of me could be said to fall into the 'not very favourable' category. I had taught him nothing, had not allowed him to read any books from my library except those I selected, and had made him work all day. 'What was behind this policy I never discovered,' he wrote in an evident plea for the reader's pity.

I at once wrote to Jivaka, reproaching him for his ingratitude and reminding him of some of the things I had taught him. Nor did I fail to mention that it was I who had opened his eyes to the fact that Lobsang Rampa was not a genuine Tibetan lama and that the Secret Order of the Potala was no more than a product of the latter's fertile imagination. Whether Jivaka ever received my letter I do not know. On 15 May he died at the Civil Hospital, Dalhousie (Punjab), after less than two days of illness, and his body was immediately cremated. No one knew why he was in Dalhousie, and the cause of his death remained a mystery.

6
FAMILY FORTUNES

There are people who insert themselves into our lives by imperceptible degrees, and whom we can remember knowing without being able to recall when we first met them. Such a one was Rigdzing Wangpo, a Lhasa-born Tibetan who lived up at Tirpai in a wooden bungalow not far from the residence of Gergen Tharchin, the proprietor of the Tibet Mirror Press and editor of the *Tibet Mirror*, whose first wife was Rigdzing Wangpo's sister. Though I knew him for seven years or more, he seemed not to change during that period but to have remained the same thin, 45-year-old man with a long, lean face deeply furrowed down both sides, an amused expression, and a huge carbuncle on his left cheek. As a young man he had studied Pāli in Ceylon, besides working for two years at the School of Oriental Languages in London, and Tibetan friends told me he was a fine poet and writer in his native tongue. By his own admission, he was something of a womanizer, and well-acquainted with the pleasures and pains of love. Recently, however, he had resolved to lead a more regular life, married a young Tibetan girl, and settled down with her in the wooden bungalow. A daughter was soon born to them, but when the child was a few months old, the young mother, who was only seventeen and rather wild, suddenly walked out on Rigdzing Wangpo, taking the baby with her.

This gave Rigdzing Wangpo food for serious thought, and he eventually concluded that the time had come for him to renounce the world and its false delights. He therefore asked me to ordain him as a

Theravādin *sāmaṇera*, for by this time we were well acquainted. At first I refused point-blank, for I thought it would be inappropriate for me to be in a formal guru-disciple relationship with someone so much older than myself. Moreover, Rigdzing Wangpo was a Tibetan, and it seemed strange that he should not want to be ordained within the Tibetan monastic tradition, especially as he was on friendly terms with Dhardo Rimpoche and did, I knew, respect him highly. Naturally I explained my position to him, but the would-be *sāmaṇera* remained politely adamant. He wanted to be ordained, and he wanted to be ordained by nobody but me. In the end I relented, especially as it had become clear that although he was not openly critical of Tibetan Buddhism, he had serious reservations about some aspects of it and definitely wished to be ordained within the Theravādin monastic tradition. He was ordained on 20 July 1958, in the shrine-room of the Vihara, and I gave him the name Prajnaloka or 'Light of Wisdom'. For a few months all was well. The new *sāmaṇera* occupied himself with teaching and translation work, dividing his time between the Vihara and his bungalow at Tirpai, but spending most of it at the Vihara. Then one day, when he was at the bungalow, his truant wife unexpectedly appeared with the baby. She did not want the bother of looking after it any longer, she declared. He was the father, and now *he* would have to look after it. Whereupon she left, leaving the baby with Prajnaloka. It all happened so quickly that Prajnaloka, who at the best of times was slow of speech, had no time to say anything. He could only sit staring through the open door at the retreating form of the young woman, trying to grasp what had happened to him. Here he was, newly ordained, but now with a young child to care for and bring up!

Once he had got over the initial shock, Prajnaloka accepted the situation philosophically. No doubt he was experiencing the fruit of the bad karma he had created by his affairs with women, he told me with a rueful smile the next time we met. A similar reflection may well have occurred to a Newar *sāmaṇera* who appeared in Kalimpong around this time and who soon found himself in a predicament not unlike Prajnaloka's.

Ananda was about the same age as myself, but shorter, plumper, and, like many Newars, very fair-skinned. Though I have referred to him as a *sāmaṇera* I am not sure if he really was one. He certainly wore a yellow robe, as did his two wives, who apparently had 'gone forth' from home into the homeless life when he did. All three were shaven-headed. On their arrival in Kalimpong the little group did not receive a very warm welcome from their Newar co-religionists, some of whom jeered at Ananda, saying that one who, as a layman, was so lustful that he needed two wives, could hardly be expected to make a success of the religious life. Ananda bore their scoffs and jeers patiently, as did the two women, and I more than once saw the three of them quietly going for alms in the bazaar, as I myself had once done.

One day he came to see me. He came alone, and as the visit was repeated a number of times during the next few weeks I quickly got to know him quite well. He was an enthusiastic meditator, with some experience of higher meditative states. Meditation seemed, in fact, to be the only aspect of the Dharma in which he was interested. Before long he was urging me to accompany him into the forest. We would stay there together, devoting all our time to meditation. (He did not say what his two women would be doing while we were thus engaged.) But I was not convinced that the forest would provide me with better conditions for meditation than did the Vihara; in any case, I did not yet feel ready to be a full-time meditator. Ananda did, however, persuade me to take up a special form of *ānāpānasati* or 'respiration mindfulness', with the traditional form of which I had long been familiar. I had practised the new form for only a few minutes when I experienced a sudden upsurge of *prīti* or 'rapture' so unbearably intense that it almost knocked me from my seat and left me gasping for breath. Shortly after this experience of mine, one of Ananda's wives gave birth to a child, which was soon to be seen wrapped in a piece of yellow cloth. I did not know when the three had 'gone forth', and it was possible that the woman was pregnant at that time. The other Newar Buddhists took a less charitable view. Ananda was heaped with abuse for having broken his vows, and life was made so difficult for them that in the end the little group of wanderers left Kalimpong. I never heard of Ananda again, though I made enquiries after him for several years.

Unlike Ananda, Prajnaloka did not have to leave Kalimpong. There was some amusement at the way karma had caught up with him, but he had broken no vows, and most of those who knew him could not but feel sympathy for a man who, no longer young, and only recently ordained, had been unexpectedly saddled with the responsibility of single-handedly bringing up a child. Not that this new responsibility

Prajnaloka's ordination at the Triyana Vardhana Vihara

changed Prajnaloka's way of life completely. He continued to be based at Tirpai, continued to teach his students, continued to wear the yellow robe with which he had been invested only a few months earlier, and greeted friends he passed in the street with the same amused smile. Only in one particular was there a change in his outward aspect: the disfiguring carbuncle had disappeared. It disappeared either just before or just after his ordination, but in any case during the time Jivaka was with us, for it was Jivaka who had performed the operation. I might well have forgotten the incident, had I not learned from it something about myself. We had laid Prajnaloka out on the dining-room table, and having given him a local anaesthetic Jivaka was hacking away at the carbuncle with a razor blade while I caught the blood in a basin. There was a lot of blood. I experienced no conscious revulsion at the sight, but my stomach seemed to turn a somersault, and I had to rush to the bathroom and vomit, returning a minute later to hold the basin again. Thus I learned that my stomach had a life, even a mind, of its own, and that I had no more control over it than I had over my heart or my lungs. When Jivaka had stitched up the wound with an ordinary needle and thread, Prajnaloka sat up and asked to see the carbuncle. Jivaka gave it to him, whereupon he held it in the palm of his hand, studied it carefully for a while, and at length took it away with him. In a few weeks the wound had healed and there was no scar.

Prajnaloka not only kept the carbuncle but showed it to his friends and related to them the whole story of the operation. In his unhurried, deliberate way he was an excellent raconteur, with a sly sense of humour, and people enjoyed listening to him no less than he enjoyed entertaining and instructing them with his anecdotes and reminiscences. His favourite theme, especially after his wife deserted him, was the fickle, vain, unreliable, deceitful, treacherous, superficial, manipulative, and generally unsatisfactory nature of the female sex. This was also the subject of a long poem he was writing in classical Tibetan, verses from which he would sometimes read aloud for the benefit of those who understood Tibetan and translate for the benefit of those who did not. It was not that Prajnaloka was a misogynist, of course. He was simply giving expression to the traditional monastic view of women, especially as illustrated by his own experience over the years. Besides having a favourite theme, he had a favourite audience. This consisted of the young men, both Nepalese and Tibetan, who came to the Vihara from time to time, whether to see me or to take part in our regular full-moon-day pujas. Some were former students of mine, others the sons and nephews of people I knew. Among these young men were Durgaprasad and Budhkumar, two friends of about the same age who often came to the Vihara together. Like the others, they listened to Prajnaloka's anecdotes and admonitions with great interest, but in the case of one of them, at least, they did not benefit from what they heard as much as they could have done.

I had known Durga, as he was generally called, since he was fifteen, when he accompanied an older cousin who was studying with me to the semi-derelict wooden bungalow in which I was then living.[345] He was somewhat below average height, tended to be uncommunicative, and from beneath drooping eyelids surveyed the world with a lazy, contemplative gaze. His father, Setu Singh, who was the Kalimpong municipality's head fitter, was well known to me. An active, gnome-like little man in traditional Nepalese dress, complete with black pillbox, he had a weather-beaten face, a worried expression, and a big nose – a nose that Durga, unlike his brothers, had inherited. Whenever we met, which was usually when he came to read the Vihara's water meter (we had mains water but no electricity), Setu Singh would complain to me in an injured tone about his son, whom he always referred to as 'Mr Durga'. His complaint was to the effect that Durga was lazy, neglected his studies, spent too much time roaming the bazaar, and disregarded his father's wishes. In all this there was a good deal of truth, as I well knew; but there was another side to the story, as I also knew.

Nepalese fathers believed in being strict with their sons, even to the point of harshness, and were convinced that such treatment was in their sons' best interests. As a result, there was often little confidence between father and son, and little communication. Durga, I knew, avoided his father as much as he could, and if he wanted to ask him something he did so through his mother, a pious Hindu lady who occasionally came to the Vihara to see me and to pay her respects to the Buddha. Yet Setu Singh was a kindly, helpful man who loved his unsatisfactory son and could be hurt by the latter's avoidance of him, even though that avoidance was the result of his own treatment of him. When Ronald Boughen invited Durga to spend a week with him in Delhi (this was before Ronald's migration to the Kulu Valley) he said nothing to his father about the trip. His father knew he was going, however, and on the morning of his departure tucked a five rupee note into the breast pocket of his jacket, with the intention of giving it to Durga when he came to say goodbye. But Durga never came. The disappointment must have rankled, for the next time we met, Setu Singh told me about the incident with evident emotion.

While it was true that Durga spent too much time roaming the bazaar, as his father believed, it was no less true that he probably spent too much time at the bungalow where the older cousin through whom he had met me lived with his parents, younger brother, and three sisters. The family was well known in the town, the father being the popular 'Nepali doctor' at the Scottish Mission Hospital as well as the subdivisional civil surgeon. All five children were strikingly good-looking, had many friends, and readily took part in such social life as was available to the Westernized younger generation. Old-fashioned members of the community to which the family belonged were of the opinion that their parents allowed the three girls far too much freedom, and they were therefore not at all surprised when Meera, the youngest of the three, was found to be pregnant. I had known Meera for as long as I had known Durga. When she was twelve or thirteen her parents

Sachin and Durgaprasad

asked me to give her practice in English conversation whenever I happened to be at their place. She seemed to enjoy her lessons with me, but she was far from being as bright as she was pretty, and did not profit from them very much. I noticed, however, that she was always eager for news of Durga who, she knew, sometimes visited me, and did not hesitate to question me about what he had been doing. As she was so young, I naturally thought that she had no more than a cousinly interest in him. Yet she must have conceived a definite liking for him even then. That liking must have persisted and grown stronger with the passing of time, and eventually, four or five years later, must have been actively reciprocated, for it was Durga who was responsible for Meera's present condition.

The culprit was severely criticized by both the extended families involved. It was not simply that he had seduced an unmarried girl. Though he and Meera were not first cousins, and though in their community the rules governing such matters were less strict than they were in the higher castes, the two were near enough in blood for their conduct to be regarded as scandalous.

But Durga was unrepentant. 'They know what young men are like,' he grumbled to me. 'If they don't want their daughters to get pregnant they should keep them locked up.'

It was much too late for anyone to think of locking Meera up now that she was pregnant, but it was not too late for her to be rehabilitated, at least to an extent. Rehabilitation meant getting her married to Durga before the child was born. The elders of the two families therefore agreed that on a certain day Durga should go to the house where Meera's mother now lived with her daughters and then, when it was dark, take Meera by the hand, so to speak, and conduct her to her new home under his parents' roof. Meera's mother, however, was adamant that they should be escorted by a responsible elder, for she was convinced that otherwise Durga would throw her daughter into a ditch at the first opportunity and run away. Nor was this all. Since Meera's father had recently died, and since her elder brother was working in Calcutta, she was insistent that I should be that responsible elder and make sure that Meera arrived safely at her destination. I did not want to take on this responsibility, which was more suited to a layman than a monk, but in the end I agreed to do so, for I was fond of Meera, and though I knew she was in no danger of being thrown into a ditch, I also knew that Durga did not really want to marry her and probably would not be a very agreeable companion that evening.

There was no moon when the three of us set out, and it was quite dark. We walked up to the T-junction where the High Street began, and from there down the winding hillside road that led, eventually, to Teesta Bridge. It was not long before Durga, without saying a word, detached himself from Meera and me and walked on ahead as though he had nothing to do with us, from time to time disappearing round a bend in the road. Meera was evidently pleased with how things were turning out for her, and chattered gaily all the way. After walking for nearly an hour we left the road and with some difficulty made our way down the terraced hillside that fell away to the right, Durga all the while keeping well ahead. Ten minutes later we saw a shadowy form disappear into a no less shadowy cottage, and shortly afterwards we were inside it ourselves. There was no sign of Durga. Someone lit a kerosene lamp, and Durga's two sisters called Meera to their room, where the three of them could be heard talking and laughing. Presently Durga's parents appeared. Both were in a sombre mood, and little was said. When I had drunk a cup of tea Setu Singh called Durga and rather sharply ordered him to see me up the road. In little more than an hour I was back at the Vihara.

A month or so later, Durga and Meera were married. The wedding was a very modest affair, I was told, with only close relations and a few friends attending. When her time came, Meera returned to her mother's house for the delivery, as the custom was, but the child was stillborn, and Durga and Meera gradually drifted apart.

Though Durga was averse to marriage, he had no objection to his friends getting married, and was even prepared to help them in this connection. He was certainly prepared to help Budhkumar elope with the girl he wished to marry, despite the fact that both his own parents and the girl's were absolutely opposed to the match. I had known Budhkumar as long as I had known Durga, but until recently we had met only intermittently, as he was usually at college down in the plains, studying civil engineering. He was a cheerful, good-natured extrovert, who was interested in body-building and would confess, laughingly, to being a victim of a bad habit of chewing tobacco. Quite early in our friendship he confided to me that he was in love with a beautiful, modest, well-behaved girl who belonged, as he did, to the Hindu Newar caste. In their caste, however, marriage was strictly prohibited between those having a common ancestor up to seven generations back. He and Radha were related in the fifth degree, that is to say, they had a common ancestor five generations back, so the future seemed dark. I did my best to cheer him up, which was not difficult, and the following day I addressed to him a sonnet beginning,

Your sorrow is my sorrow, friend, and so

When yesterday I saw you, wan with grief,
I yearned to give some comfort or relief,
And thus it was, the reason of your woe,
Not merely curiously, I sought to know.[346]

The poem concluded with a reference to the rainbow that had appeared in the sky as we were talking, and which I saw as a symbol of hope. Nonetheless, as the prospect of his marrying Radha was so remote, I asked Budhkumar one day why he did not marry the older of Meera's two elder sisters, with whom, as I knew, he had long had an illicit relationship. He was quite shocked. 'Oh, I wouldn't want to marry a girl of bad character!' he exclaimed.

Radha was not kept locked up, as Durga believed daughters ought to be, but her parents made quite sure that she and Budhkumar never had an opportunity to meet. The most they could hope for was a distant glimpse of each other on the occasion of some big family gathering such as – ironically – a wedding. But love will find a way, and Budhkumar had for some time been carrying on a clandestine correspondence with Radha through the agency of a small boy whom he bribed to smuggle letters to her and bring back her replies, and it was in the course of this correspondence that the elopement had been discussed, agreed upon, and planned. The plan was simple. The house in which Radha lived with her parents and other members of the family was situated on the other side of town, a mile or more beyond the Old Bhutan Palace. This house had a garden, and between the garden and the road there was a hedge, and in the hedge, not too near the house, there was a gap. At two o'clock in the morning, on a certain moonless night, Radha would tell the aunt or sister who slept with her that she needed to visit the toilet, which was an outside one, and located a few yards from the gap in the hedge. Budhkumar and Durga would be waiting for her with a jeep on the other side of the gap. She had only to squeeze through it, and they would be off.

The two friends spent the earlier part of the night at the Vihara, leaving at 1.30 for their rendezvous with Radha. Budhkumar was excited and anxious, Durga a little more communicative than usual.

In the morning I received a visit from Budhkumar's father, a choleric old gentleman whom I had once met at his own place. He came accompanied by his youngest son, who was in Budhkumar's confidence and who evidently was saying nothing. I was unable to tell my visitor where his son was, for I did not know. He must have suspected I was keeping something back, for he did not leave without remarking that it was common knowledge Budhkumar did nothing without consulting me. Two days later Durga came to see me. Things had gone according to plan, he reported, and Budhkumar and Radha were now staying in the Dooars. Later I heard that they were married and living in Gangtok, where Budhkumar was working as a civil engineer. In due course a child was born, whereupon intermediaries set to work, and a reconciliation between Budhkumar and his family was arranged. He and Radha fell at his parents' feet and begged their forgiveness. Tears were shed all round, and the two old people had the satisfaction of seeing their first grandchild.

7
POETRY AND PROSE

Although I was living on the outskirts of a small town in the foothills of the eastern Himalayas, I experienced no sense of isolation from the wider world. As Avalokiteśvara, the Bodhisattva of Compassion, in the form of a cuckoo, tells the other birds in James H. Cousins' *A Tibetan Banner*, written many years earlier while the Irish poet was visiting Kalimpong,

> Who seeks the world, his heart beclouds
> In the thick solitude of crowds;
> But he who seeks a peak apart
> Must hold the world within his heart.[347]

That I experienced no sense of isolation from that wider world, and at times could even hold it within my heart to an extent, was due largely to my being in correspondence with fellow Buddhists in the West, in South-east Asia, and in other parts of India, some of whom wrote to me regularly and at great length. Particularly when I was not on tour, a good deal of my time was therefore spent replying to letters, for I enjoyed replying to them almost as much as I enjoyed receiving them. Some letters gave news of Buddhist activities in London, or Paris, or Budapest, while others invited me to speak at this or that inter-religious conference, or put questions about the Buddha's teaching, or asked me to accept the writer as a disciple. Regardless of whether or not I was on tour, there was always the next issue of the Buddhist monthly journal to be brought out, which meant selecting and arranging the articles I had received, finding fillers and illustrations, and writing my editorial for the month.

These editorials dealt with a variety of topics and were unsigned. In 'The Buddhist World' (October 1959) I argued that a Buddhist should be acquainted with all forms of Buddhism; in 'Spreading the Dharma' (January 1959) I urged lazy Buddhists to bestir themselves, and in 'A Serious Matter' (August 1961) I deplored the practice of ordaining *sāmaṇeras* but not teaching them anything, for unless it was abandoned 'we may have people in yellow robes but we shall not have a sangha'. Some editorials were concerned with what was happening in this or that Buddhist country. 'Stop the Rot' (August 1960), written in the wake of the assassination of the prime minister of Ceylon by a Buddhist monk, called upon the new government to take the management of ecclesiastical properties out of the hands of the monks, while 'A Disturbing Dispute' (March–April 1961) commented on the differences that had arisen in Korea between the celibate *bhikkhus* and those who, during the Japanese occupation, had become Japanese-style married priests. I occasionally allowed myself to be a little controversial, even polemical, as I did in 'Religion vs God' (June 1960) and in 'Stars and Stupidity' (February 1962), the 'stupidity' being that of the millions of Hindus who were engaged, that month, in burning food-offerings in the sacred fire and feeding Brahmins in order to avert the terrible disasters predicted by the astrologers.

There were also months when I drew the attention of the authorities to the way in which certain ancient Buddhist sites were being vandalized. In 'More Vandalism' (June 1961), for example, I complained that at Karle a Hindu temple had been erected immediately in front of the entrance to the main Chaitya Cave, the largest and most magnificent of its kind in India. What was more, the deity installed in the temple was a blood-thirsty local goddess to whom fowls and goats were regularly sacrificed, being slaughtered *within the protected area of the cave itself*.

From time to time I struck a more reflective note, as in 'Rainy Season Retreat' (August 1958), in 'Meditation on a Flame' (October 1958),[348] and in 'Words and Meaning' (September 1959), in which I observed,

> Much unnecessary dust has been raised by people, not excluding experienced scholars, confidently writing and speaking about Buddhism without first ascertaining what its main keywords are and what are their respective meanings.[349]

The ascertaining of these keywords and their meanings was one of the things I had tried to do in *A Survey of Buddhism*, published in 1957, and which I also tried to do, on a smaller scale, in the second and third of the three books I wrote, or began to write, during my time at the Vihara. The first was *The Rainbow Road from Tooting Broadway to Kalimpong*, on which I started when Jivaka was staying with us.[350] He had just finished writing his own autobiography, *Out of the Ordinary*, and one day he asked me why I did not write *mine*.

'But what would be the point?' I protested, 'I haven't had nearly such an interesting life as you. In fact, my life has been quite ordinary, and even if I did manage to write my autobiography who on earth would want to read it?'

'Nonsense!' retorted Jivaka, in his usual brusque fashion, 'You've had a *very* interesting life, and if you were to write your autobiography a lot of people would want to read it. It might even become a best-seller.'

I remained unconvinced. I had suggested that Jivaka should write his autobiography because there were, I suspected, things he needed to get off his chest, and writing his autobiography seemed a good way for him to do this. In my own case no such consideration applied. There was nothing of a personal nature of which I particularly wanted to disburden myself. However, Jivaka returned to the attack, pointing out that I wasn't very busy just then, and the following morning I sat down at my desk and cast my mind back to faraway Tooting.

I wrote rapidly, as the memories came to me, without giving much thought to the arrangement of my material, and with little regard for literary style. Each morning I handed over to Jivaka what I had written the previous day, and he typed it for me, a service he rendered for as long as he remained at the Vihara, after which I had to do my own typing. In his usual high-handed fashion, he did not hesitate to edit my work as he thought fit. He particularly objected to what he called my book lists, by which he meant my detailed account of my early reading, and cut them ruthlessly. This did not bother me, as at this stage I had no thought of publication, and I continued to write for the sheer joy of writing. Since I had no old letters or diaries to help me, I had to rely entirely on my memory. What I was writing was therefore not my autobiography, in the sense of a complete, well-documented account of the events and circumstances of my life so far, but simply my *memoirs*. Thus I remembered, and wrote about, my childhood in

Tooting, about my confinement to bed for two years with supposed heart disease, about my indebtedness to the *Children's Encyclopedia*, about my involvement with the Boys' Brigade, about the Blitz and my evacuation to Devon with my school, about the break-up of my parents' marriage, about the two years I spent working for the London County Council, about my realization that I was a Buddhist and had always been one, about my four years in the army, which took me to India, Ceylon, and Singapore, about my leaving the army and teaming up in India with a Bengali friend, about our encounter with Anandamayi and her fractious disciples, about our 'going forth' together as freelance wandering ascetics, and about the multiple rainbows that spanned the road as, shaven-headed and clad in our new saffron robes, we walked from the Punjab hills down to the plains.

As I wrote, I was astonished how much I remembered. It was as though I had in front of me a huge library or archive of materials and had only to reach out and take down the next volume. Thus it was not surprising that within two years of my starting work on *The Rainbow Road* I should have produced well over a 100,000 words.[351] Not that the production of those words had proceeded without interruption. During the same period I undertook a number of extensive preaching tours in the plains, some of which kept me away from Kalimpong for months together. Then in 1962 I received an invitation to contribute a series of articles on Buddhism to the *Oriya Encyclopaedia* and put the memoirs aside in order to concentrate on the new assignment. I was sorry to put them aside, for in the process of working on them I was learning a lot about the art and craft of writing; but I thought it better to spend my time making the Dharma available to Oriya-speaking people than to spend it writing about myself.

The *Oriya Encyclopaedia* was one of the fourteen regional language encyclopaedias then being sponsored by the Government of India, and the invitation to write the articles on Buddhism came from the Oriya poet and dramatist Mandhar Mansinha, who was already known to me. I had met him in Sambalpur, a town in the state of Orissa. He took the chair when I gave a lecture at the local college, of which he was principal, and we had remained in touch ever since. In inviting me to write the articles, Dr Mansinha had left me free to treat the great subject in my own way, and I therefore set to work with a will. I began by writing the articles on the Buddha, the Dharma, and the Sangha respectively, then went on to write those on the scriptures of Buddhism, and on its numerous sects and schools. As with *The Rainbow Road*, in the course of two years I produced well over 100,000 words, despite the usual interruptions. This was far in excess of what was wanted, and only a few of the articles I had written were, therefore, translated into Oriya and included in the encyclopaedia. As it was, by allotting to Buddhism even as much space as this, Dr Mansinha incurred orthodox Hindu wrath, and eventually resigned his position as editor-in-chief.

Though only a few of the articles I had written found a place in the *Oriya Encyclopaedia*, I did not think the time I had spent on the assignment wasted. As I quickly realized, the thirty-nine articles I had produced fell quite naturally into three groups. The first group consisted of the articles on the Buddha, the Dharma, and the Sangha, and these went to form parts 1, 2, and 3 of *The Three Jewels: An Introduction to Buddhism*, published in 1967.[352] The Three Jewels were the triple embodiment of an ideal, and it was commitment to the realization of that ideal by following a certain way of life in the company of others similarly committed that made one a Buddhist. This was what was traditionally known as 'Going for Refuge' to the Three Jewels, which, as I wrote in the preface to the volume, was

> an act which, though it may find ceremonial expression, is essentially a profound inner experience, a spiritual rebirth or 'conversion', as a result of which one's whole life is transformed and reoriented.[353]

The second group of articles consisted of those on the Buddhist scriptures, from the Monastic Code to the tantras, preceded by those on Buddhism and language and on the oral tradition. These articles went to make up *The Eternal Legacy: An Introduction to the Canonical Literature of Buddhism*, published in 1985.[354]

The third group of articles, and by far the smallest, consisted of the three I had written on the sects and schools of Buddhism. There were to have been many more, but I never got round to writing them, mainly because I had been invited by the Oxford University Press to write the article on Buddhism for their new edition of *The Legacy of India*, an assignment I managed to complete before leaving for England in August 1964.[355] The articles making up the third group, both written and unwritten, were provisionally entitled 'The Pattern of Development in Buddhism'. According to the first article in this group, that pattern would be revealed if certain principles of classification were to be systematically applied to the different Buddhist traditions. There were seven such principles, each of which I discussed briefly. They were: (1) geographical provenance, (2) *yāna* membership, (3) spiritual faculty (*indriya*) emphasized, (4) principal Buddha-form revered, (5) canonical basis, (6) doctrinal position, and (7) line of transmission from master to disciple. Thus the Nyingma school, for example, would be described as a Tibetan form of Vajrayāna which emphasizes meditation, revered Samantabhadra as principal Buddha-form, had its canonical basis in the Nyingma Tantras and the *Rinchen Terdzen*, taught *ati-yoga* doctrine, and traced its line of transmission back to the three men of Kham (the so-called Lower Vinaya) in respect of *upasampadā* or *bhikṣu* ordination, to Nāgārjuna and Śāntideva in respect of bodhisattva ordination (*saṃvara*), and to Padmasambhava in respect of *abhiṣeka* or Tantric initiation.

The remaining articles in the third group were not the only ones I did not get round to writing. I had also planned to write articles on meditation in the three *yānas*, and on forms and functions of Buddhist art. Together with *The Three Jewels* and *The Eternal Legacy*, and the completed 'Pattern of Development in Buddhism', they would, I hoped, eventually make up a series of five independent volumes under the general title of 'The Heritage of Buddhism'. But alas for the aspirations and ambitions of men! Events and circumstances prevented me from finishing the third volume and from even starting on the fourth and fifth. For me, as for Abt Vogler, it was a case of 'On the earth the broken arcs; in the heaven, a perfect round.'[356]

The writing of *The Three Jewels* and *The Eternal Legacy* involved a good deal of reading and re-reading, both of the canonical texts and of modern scholarly works. This was particularly so in the case of *The Eternal Legacy*. Reading and writing about the *Āgamas/Nikāyas* and the great Mahāyāna *sūtras* I felt myself transported to another world. It was not always the same world. At one time it might be the world of ancient India, a world of green paddy fields, of vast, dark forests, of little groups of thatched mud-walled huts, of women walking to the well with earthenware pots balanced on their heads – a world of farmers and artisans, Brahmins and wandering ascetics, merchants and princes. It was the world in which the Buddha had lived and taught twenty-five centuries ago, now in a village moot hall, now beneath the spreading branches of a banyan tree, now to invisible presences in the silence of the night. I had visited some of the places where the Buddha had taught, and it was therefore not difficult for me to imagine what they looked like in his day. Nor was it difficult for me even to imagine what the Buddha himself looked like, at least to the outward eye. I did not see him as he was depicted in the popular religious art of South-east Asia and India, where he appeared looking like a modern Theravādin *bhikkhu* – well groomed, clad in brand-new yellow robes, and carrying an embroidered shoulder bag. I saw him, instead, as a man who looked much more like some of the Hindu sadhus I had encountered during my wandering days – unshaven, clad in ragged, dust-stained garments, and with few or no possessions. It was therefore small wonder that – as the texts I was reading attested – people sometimes failed to realize that this man was none other than the Buddha, the Enlightened One.

At another time I might be transported not to the world of ancient India and the human, historical Śākyamuni, but to an archetypal world inhabited by innumerable Buddhas and bodhisattvas and resounding with the sublime tones of the Dharma. Or I might be transported to a transfigured Vulture's Peak, where a transfigured Śākyamuni relates for the benefit of the assembled bodhisattvas, *arhants*, divinities of various orders, and human beings, a series of magnificent parables, and where various wonders take place. Then again, I might find myself in the legendary world of Laṅka and the ten-headed Rāvaṇa, lord of the demons, and there hear the Buddha discoursing to Mahāmati, the great bodhisattva, on the self-realization of noble wisdom (*āryajñāna*), the store-consciousness (*ālaya-vijñāna*), and mind-only (*cittamātra*), and on many other subtle and abstruse aspects of the Dharma.[357]

From the world, or worlds, of the great Mahāyāna *sūtras* in particular, I would not always find it easy to turn my attention to a world in which one had to keep accounts and pay bills, even for a Vihara. Sometimes a good book would help me to make the transition. One such book had been given me by a European friend in Bombay. 'You'll like this book,' he told me, with a smile, 'It's just like a Mahāyāna *sūtra*.'

The book was Olaf Stapledon's *Star Maker*.[358] I did like it, and despite the absence of Buddhas and bodhisattvas it really was like a Mahāyāna *sūtra*. This could not be said of any of the other books

I was reading at this time, though all of them contained elements of insight and imagination that were not incompatible with the spirit of the Dharma. Most of them had been given me by friends, and they included such classics of Western literature as *Don Quixote*, *The Faerie Queene*, the *Poetical Works of Robert Burns*, Eckermann's *Conversations with Goethe*, *Hard Times*, *The History of Henry Esmond*, and *Anna Karenina*.[359] They all made a strong impression on me, in their different ways, and some of them remained favourites for the rest of my life. To me, it was not strange that I should read the classics of Western literature as well as the Buddhist scriptures, though my more austere Theravādin colleagues in Calcutta and Sarnath might raise their eyebrows to see me with a volume of English poetry in my hand. Both were necessary to me and I saw no reason why I should have to choose between them, as some people thought I should.

Ten years earlier, when I was staying at Buddha Kuti with Jagdish Kashyap, I had once received, by the same post, letters from two such people, one of them a Buddhist monk, the other a Buddhist laywoman. Both must have been reading my latest contributions to the Buddhist magazines of Ceylon. When I could write such excellent articles on Buddhist philosophy, the monk demanded, why did I waste my time writing those foolish poems? The laywoman took exactly the opposite view. When I could write such beautiful poems on Buddhism, she asked, why did I spend so much time writing those dry, intellectual articles? I agreed – and disagreed – with them both. The conflict was not so much between the philosophically-inclined monk and the poetry-loving laywoman as between the two sides of my own nature, the monastic-intellectual and the poetic-emotional, which I had not yet succeeded in reconciling and harmonizing.[360] It was not until some time later, during my early years in Kalimpong, that I began to see not only the possibility of reconciliation and harmonization but also that the dichotomy on which the conflict was based was not so real as I had supposed.

I happened to be explaining Shelley's 'The Cloud' to three or four students who were preparing for the Intermediate Arts examination. They were all very attentive, there was a good rapport between us, and I found I was able to go more and more deeply into the meaning of the poem. The more deeply I went into it, the profounder and more universal that meaning seemed to be. After a while, as I plumbed depth upon depth of significance, the thought suddenly struck me that I was not simply elucidating Shelley's poem: *I was teaching the Dharma.* It was not that I was using the poem as a hook on which to hang an exposition of the Dharma. I had given myself to the poem; I had plunged into it as into an ocean, and the ocean had yielded up the pearl of the Dharma, a pearl that was already there, hidden in the depths, only waiting to be discovered. However, it was because I was already acquainted with the Dharma that I was able to recognize it when I encountered it in the poem. Indeed, if one was acquainted with the Dharma, and looked deeply enough, one could encounter the Dharma not just in Shelley's poem but also in other works of Western literature as well, perhaps, in painting and sculpture, and even in musical compositions. Not that one should go looking for the Dharma in any of them in a self-conscious and deliberate manner. One should simply give oneself to the poem, or painting, or song, and forget about the Dharma for the time being.

It was during my early years in Kalimpong, too, that I produced two essays in which I sought to determine the nature of the relation between religion and art and, in particular, between Buddhism and art. The two essays were 'The Meaning of Buddhism and the Value of Art' and 'The Religion of Art'.[361] In both of them I used the word art in the wider sense, as including not only painting, sculpture, and architecture, but also fiction, drama, and music. In the first I argued that every genuine work of art enlarged the circle of our consciousness and it was in this enlargement that the value of art, from the spiritual point of view, consisted. Similarly, in the second I argued that art and religion overlap, inasmuch as there is in religion an element which is aesthetic and in art an element which is religious. The writing of these two articles made it clear to me, once and for all, that my love of poetry was not incompatible with my commitment to the Dharma. Henceforth I read – and enjoyed – the classics of Western literature, as well as the Buddhist scriptures, despite the frowns of puritanical fellow Buddhists.

8
A BANNER OF VICTORY

I do not remember when or where I first heard the name of Padmasambhava, the great Indian scholar and yogi who, in the eighth century CE, was mainly responsible for the initial dissemination of Buddhism in Tibet, was the founder of the Nyingma tradition, and about whose extraordinary personality there soon gathered a mighty corpus of myth and legend. I do, however, remember when and where I first saw a representation of Padmasambhava. It was not a picture I saw but an image, and I saw it in Darjeeling, in the Tamang Buddhist Gompa, towards the end of my first year in the eastern Himalayas. The *gompa* was situated in the heart of the Darjeeling bazaar and was, in fact, not a monastery but a temple of the typically Nepalese pagoda type, and I was taken to see it by some local Tamang Buddhists with whom I had become acquainted. I had not seen a Nyingma temple before, and I did not know quite what to expect. As I have written elsewhere, in words I cannot now hope to better,

> As I entered the temple, all the greater was the shock, therefore, when I saw in front of me, three or four times larger than life, the mighty sedent figure of the semi-legendary founder and inspirer of the Nyingma tradition, a skull cup in his left hand, a staff topped with skulls in the crook of his left arm, and the celebrated 'wrathful smile' on his moustached face. All this I took in instantly, together with the 'lotus hat', the richly embroidered

> robes, and the much smaller flanking figures of his two consorts, one Tibetan and one Nepalese. Having taken it in, I felt that it had always been there, and that in seeing the figure of Padmasambhava I had become conscious of a spiritual presence that had in fact been with me all the time.[362]

In other words, that magical figure had activated, at a very deep level, a part of me that hitherto had lain dormant and unrecognized. Though I had not seen it before, it was strangely familiar. It was familiar as my own self, yet at the same time infinitely mysterious, infinitely wonderful, and infinitely inspiring. Familiar, mysterious, wonderful, and inspiring it was to remain. Indeed, the Precious Guru was to occupy a permanent place in my spiritual life.

During the next few years I visited the Tamang Buddhist Gompa more than once, and got to know many members of the Tamang Buddhist community, especially two brothers, one of them an inspector in the West Bengal police who came to see me whenever his duties took him to Kalimpong. Unfortunately, neither of the brothers could tell me anything about the life and teaching of Padmasambhava, nor could any of the other Tamangs I happened to meet, whether in Darjeeling itself, in Kalimpong, or in the Dooars. At the same time, there was no doubting the fact that, despite their almost total ignorance of their ancestral faith, the Tamangs strongly identified themselves not just as Buddhists but as *Nyingma* Buddhists, and no doubting the strength of their devotion to the figure of Guru Rimpoche, the Precious Guru. As I was beginning to realize, the ordinary Nyingma Buddhist, like the ordinary followers of the other forms of Tibetan Buddhism, was not historically-minded. He did not look *back* to Śākyamuni and Padmasambhava. Rather did he look *up* to a supra-historical 'archetypal' realm in which he saw the figures of a transfigured Śākyamuni, Padmasambhava, Avalokiteśvara, and Amitābha, the Buddha of Infinite Light, together with other divinities. In the Tamang Buddhist Gompa in Darjeeling the mighty sedent figure of Padmasambhava, flanked by his two consorts, occupied the central chamber on the ground floor, the 1000-armed Avalokiteśvara a smaller one on the first floor, and Amitābha a still smaller one on the second floor. Between them they represented the specifically Nyingma version of the Mahāyāna doctrine of the three bodies (*kāya*) of the Buddha, Padmasambhava being the emanated body (*nirmāṇakāya*),

Avalokiteśvara the glorious body (*samboghakāya*), and Amitābha the body of Truth (*dharmakāya*).[363]

In the little one-room Tamang *gompa* situated half way between Teesta Bridge and Kalimpong, the three figures were arranged in a row, on a low dais, Padmasambhava being in the middle, with a four-armed Avalokiteśvara on his right and Amitābha on his left. All three figures were of clay, life-sized, and painted in colours that had long since faded. On the one occasion when I set foot in the *gompa* I had the impression that in the eyes of the Tamang villagers who had built it, probably with their own hands, the three figures it enshrined were little more than the 'gods' of the Tamang community, to whom they made offerings and to whom they addressed their prayers. Even so, although the middle figure was of clumsy workmanship, as were the two others, it was instantly recognizable as that of Padmasambhava. There was the same lotus hat, the same wrathful smile, the same staff topped with skulls in the crook of the left arm, as in the very much larger figure in the Tamang Buddhist Gompa in Darjeeling, as well as in the figures, both large and small, in all the other Tamang *gompas* in the area. The Precious Guru's presence was in fact strongly felt throughout the entire Himalayan region. Not only were there *gompas* with his image wherever there were Tamangs or any of the other hill people who adhere to the Nyingma tradition. There were remote mountain caves in which the Precious Guru had meditated, and in which his image had been installed, so that the pilgrim, on looking in, would feel himself to be in the very presence of the Master. Places there also were, where the Precious Guru had performed miracles, or with which he was associated in other ways. According to Yogi Chen, the Chinese hermit who lived on the edge of the lower bazaar, with whom I was later to become acquainted, it was in Kalimpong that there had taken place the famous meeting between Padmasambhava and the King of Tibet, when Padmasambhava had demonstrated his superiority and the king had given his queen to be the Guru's consort.[364] He had seen it all in his meditation, Yogi Chen told me. He also told me that beside the road, on the way to Tirpai, there was a large boulder. A demon had thrown it at the Guru, but the latter had headed it 'like a football', as Yogi Chen put it, and sent it flying.

Whatever the truth of these stories, Kalimpong was undoubtedly a special place, with a special atmosphere. Indeed, soon after my arrival there I was told that repeating a mantra once in Kalimpong was equivalent to repeating it a hundred times elsewhere. I was also told that in the atmosphere of Kalimpong an individual's true qualities, whether good or bad, developed more freely than anywhere else, and could more clearly be seen. Such being the case, one would have thought that among the Tamang Buddhists of Kalimpong there would be at least a few who were true inheritors of the Nyingma tradition, but so far as I could tell there were none. Though they definitely regarded themselves as Nyingmapas, and though they maintained some of the outward forms of their religion, they knew as little about the life and teaching of Padmasambhava as their co-religionists in Darjeeling and elsewhere.

The principal reason for this ignorance, it appeared, was that on their migrating from southern Tibet into Nepal, and acquiring the *lingua franca* of that country, the Tamang people had gradually lost their command of the Tibetan language and, in consequence, their ability to read the Tibetan scriptures and other religious works, including the very extensive literature of the Nyingma school. It therefore followed that if there was to be a renaissance of the Nyingma form of Buddhism among the Tamangs, there would also have to be a revival of Tibetan learning. What was no less important, they would need to have personal contact with the eminent lamas who had lately arrived in India as refugees from Chinese-occupied Tibet, especially with those who were versed in the Nyingma tradition. Jamyang Khyentse Rimpoche had, I knew, given teachings to local Buddhists while he was in Darjeeling, and no doubt his example was being followed by other lamas.

I do not know whether the Rimpoche ever visited the Tamang Buddhist Gompa during that time, or saw the mighty sedent figure of Padmasambhava that had affected me so deeply seven years earlier. But regardless of whether or not he saw it, at the time of his giving me the *abhiṣekas* of Mañjughoṣa, Avalokiteśvara, Vajrapāṇi, and Tārā, the figure of the Precious Guru must have been present to his illumined consciousness, for not long afterwards he directed Kachu Rimpoche to bestow on me the Padmasambhava *abhiṣeka*. I do not remember when Kachu Rimpoche told me he had been so directed, but in any case it was not until 1962, three years after Khyentse Rimpoche's death, that I received the initiation. In the meantime I kept up my friendship with Kachu Rimpoche, or perhaps I should say he kept up his friendship with me, for he was more often with me at the Vihara than I with him at Pemayangtse Gompa. In fact, I visited him there only once. This was in November 1958. I was in Gangtok at the time, and at the invitation of Apa Pant, the Political Officer, had delivered five discourses on the *Hṛdaya* and *Vajracchedikā Prajñāpāramitā Sūtras*.[365] These discourses were attended by the Maharaja of Sikkim, the Maharaj Kumar, Apa Pant, the Dewan of Sikkim, and officials of the Governments of India and Sikkim, besides a number of leading citizens of Gangtok. Among those who attended was tall, ruddy-complexioned Rai Bahadur Densapa, Chief Secretary to the Government of Sikkim, a staunch traditionalist with whom I was on very friendly terms.[366] When I told him I wanted to visit Pemayangtse Gompa, he at once offered to provide the transport.

A day or two later I was riding up into the mountains of western Sikkim on a pony. This was only the second time in my life that I had ridden a pony, and despite the magnificence of the scenery by which I was surrounded, I did not enjoy the journey from the spot where I had left Densapa's jeep, the track being no longer motorable, to the ridge on which stood Pemayangtse Gompa, which I reached some hours later. This was not the fault of the pony, who seemed to know the way and carried me on and up at an even pace. The fact was that Theravādin cotton robes were not adapted to equestrian pursuits. Strictly speaking, the Theravādin monk should not even ride in a vehicle drawn by a horse, let alone ride one. Nonetheless, I had tied my inner robe like a dhoti, so as to be able to sit astride more easily. But this did not really help, as the saddle was simply a piece of sacking. By the time I arrived at my destination I was extremely sore, and moreover had the return journey later that day to look forward to.

Pemayangtse Gompa, 'Monastery of the Glorious Lotus', had been founded in the seventeenth century by Lhatsun Rimpoche, the learned Tibetan lama who was mainly responsible for the introduction of Buddhism into Sikkim, though according to legend Padmasambhava had been there before him and had, moreover, hidden, in different parts of the country, written teachings which certain gifted individuals would discover in future times when the world was in need of them. Lhatsun Rimpoche was a remarkable man. He was depicted in the religious art of Sikkim, I subsequently learned, as an ascetic. His blue-coloured body is almost bare. He is seated on a leopard-skin, his right hand makes the gesture (*mudrā*) of teaching, his left holds a skull cup, while in the crook of his left arm rests a staff like that of Padmasambhava. Besides introducing Buddhism into Sikkim, and founding Pemayangtse Gompa and other monasteries, Lhatsun Rimpoche started a line of *tulkus* or 'incarnate lamas' that continued down to the present, Kachu Rimpoche being the latest 'incarnation' and the eighth in the series. Though I was glad to see my friend, I was especially glad to see him at his abbatial seat. He was no less glad to see me, and received me warmly. In the course of my short visit I did not see the shrine-room of the monastery, so far as I remember, but in an upstairs room I did see a wonderful three-dimensional mandala in the form of a celestial palace. About six feet high, and made of wood, it was overarched by a painted wooden rainbow. As we were drinking tea in his room, Kachu Rimpoche pulled out from under his bed a large silver head of Padmasambhava. It was strikingly lifelike, for besides being a talented painter and sculptor the Rimpoche was a skilled metallurgist. Jamyang Khyentse Rimpoche had instructed him to make a life-size silver image of the Precious Guru, he explained. It was to be housed in a special roadside chapel, near the border with India, and its presence there would protect Sikkim from danger. We also discussed certain obstacles to the expansion of Buddhist work in the state, and in this connection Kachu Rimpoche informed me that a four-month refresher course for lamas was currently in progress at the monastery. The course was sponsored by the Sikkim Durbar,[367] and seventeen lamas were attending it.

One of the texts the lamas on the course may well have been studying was the traditional biography of Padmasambhava by his chief disciple, Yeshe Tsogyal. But be that as it may, in 1954 I received a review copy of a book which, to my surprise and delight, contained an epitome of the same traditional biography. The book was *The Tibetan Book of the Great Liberation*, the fourth volume in W. Y. Evans-Wentz's famous Oxford Tibetan series, and the epitome was the work of two Darjeeling-born Tibetans, the Sardar Bahadur S. W. Laden La and Lama Sonam Senge. Naturally I read the epitome before reading Evans-Wentz's long introduction to the volume, for I was eager to find out more about the facts of the Precious Guru's life than was already known to me from scholarly histories of Buddhism. With biographical fact in the ordinary sense, however, the epitome was little concerned. Its eighty-odd pages were replete with marvels and miracles, some of them quite bizarre, as when a *ḍākinī* swallows Padmasambhava, having first transformed him into the syllable *hūṃ*, and gives him the secret Avalokiteśvara initiation inside her stomach. In the review I wrote of the book as a whole I regretted that it had not been possible for the first comprehensive account in English of the great Guru's career to present him in a more balanced and, I believed, truer way as a thinker and saint rather than as a 'culture hero' and thaumaturgist. After all, numerous texts of great spiritual value were ascribed to Padmasambhava, one of them being included in *The Tibetan Book of the Great Liberation*, along with the epitome. The 'Great Liberation' of the volume's title in fact referred not to the colourful events of the epitome but to the goal of the meditative practices described in this text.

Though Laden La's epitome failed to enlighten me as to the historical biography of Padmasambhava, it nonetheless made me better acquainted with the 'symbolical' biography and more vividly aware of Padmasambhava the Myth, as distinct from Padmasambhava the Man. One might even say, as my friend Lama Govinda wrote to me, that so deeply did the great Guru impress the people around him that in their urge to convey his greatness to future generations they resorted to the superhuman and the miraculous. To Kachu Rimpoche the Precious Guru was not just a historical person, nor even a figure of myth and legend; he was a spiritual reality, and it was as a spiritual reality that he experienced him when he gave me the Padmasambhava *abhiṣeka* on 21 October 1962. By this time it was twelve years since my momentous first visit to the Tamang Buddhist Gompa in Darjeeling, and eight years since I read *The Tibetan Book of the Great Liberation*, and although the Precious Guru may not have been a spiritual reality to me, as he was to Kachu Rimpoche, I was at least beginning to have a sense of his spiritual presence.

The initiation took place in the shrine-room of the Vihara. Kachu Rimpoche came a few days earlier, bringing with him an attendant lama, as he usually did. His nephew Namzey, who was a little older than Dupchen, was already staying with me and attending the local high school. Both boys were on holiday just then, for it was the Hindu festival season, and as the Rimpoche and I talked there could be heard coming from the bazaar the faint sound of fireworks. He had arrived early, partly in order to spend time with me, and partly because a day or two would be needed to make arrangements for the ceremony. These arrangements were in the hands of the attendant lama, who spent many hours making *tormas*, offerings sculpted from barley-flour dough, and decorated with discs of butter, each divinity having a *torma* of a particular size and shape. The butter-discs, I noticed, had to be moulded under water, since otherwise the warmth of the hands would cause the butter to melt. When finished, they were placed on a special table in front of the shrine, along with the other offerings and a variety of ritual objects. Among the ritual objects there was a beribboned arrow symbolizing Amitāyus, the Buddha of Eternal Life (a form or aspect of Amitābha, the Buddha of Infinite Light), whose *abhiṣeka* Kachu Rimpoche would also be giving me. At length all was ready, and the Rimpoche and I took our seats on either side of the shrine, facing each other, the Rimpoche's seat being higher than mine and having in front of it a little desk for his dorje and bell and the other ritual items he would be needing in the course of the ceremony.

I cannot say that I remember much of the proceedings, which lasted two days. For most of the time I sat with closed eyes, simply allowing myself to become absorbed in the atmosphere of the occasion, an atmosphere to which the rather hoarse sound of the Rimpoche's voice as he chanted, the occasional tinkle of his bell, and the sharp scent of Tibetan incense, all contributed. I was very conscious of the fervour of the Rimpoche's devotion to Padmasambhava, and to the spiritual tradition of which the Precious Guru was the founder. I had once told Kachu Rimpoche that some Western scholars termed the Nyingma school the 'unreformed' school, as distinct from the other major schools of Tibetan Buddhism, all of which were 'reformed'. He replied that the Nyingma school was unreformed because it had never needed to be reformed, it having remained faithful to the teachings that had come from India during the first diffusion of Buddhism in Tibet. His devotion to the Precious Guru was very much in evidence when, towards the end of the second day, he explained to me how I was to visualize him in meditation. It was also at this time, I think, that he introduced me to the practice of the *mūla* (or 'foundation') *yogas* of the Vajrayāna, and particularly to the Going for Refuge and Prostration practice and the Vajrasattva visualization and purification practice.[368]

It certainly was at this time that the Rimpoche – now my teacher as well as my friend – bestowed on me the name Urgyen (or Orgyen), the Tibetan variant of Uḍḍiyāna, the name of the country to the north-west of India where Padmasambhava was born – according to legend – from the calyx of a lotus flower.[369] On this account he was known as Urgyen Padmasambhava, as well as being known by many other names. I was delighted to receive the name, which served to confirm my connection with the Precious Guru, as the *abhiṣeka* itself had done, besides suggesting that my true home was in the mysterious land of Uḍḍiyāna.

The morning after the ceremony I went to the bazaar, taking with me one of the Vihara's younger members. As I sometimes did, I had a look at a spot beyond the vegetable stalls where the Tibetans had a little street market. A man, probably a refugee, was squatting at the side of the road with a few items spread out in front of him on a piece of sacking. One of the items was a bundle of small Tibetan woodblock prints. As the man was asking only a few rupees for them, on an impulse I bought them, even though I could not read them and did not know what they contained. On my return to the Vihara I at once showed them to Kachu Rimpoche. They were all Nyingma texts, he told me, and the fact that I had come across them so soon after receiving the Padmasambhava initiation was a very auspicious sign. What was more, the longest of the texts was the well-known *Tharpe Delam* or 'Smooth Path to Emancipation', the author of which was a famous nineteenth-century Nyingma lama. It described the general and special preliminary practices of *ati-yoga*, to several of which Kachu Rimpoche had already introduced me. Before his departure the Rimpoche gave me further instruction regarding the Going for Refuge and Prostration practice. I was to do it 20,000 times, though 100,000 times was desirable. He also gave me permission to make an English version of the *Tharpe Delam* with the help of Dhardo Rimpoche.[370]

I knew that there was a certain amount of rivalry between the Nyingma school, to which Kachu Rimpoche belonged, and the Gelug school to which Dhardo Rimpoche belonged, but I nonetheless had no hesitation in asking the latter's help in making an English version of the *Tharpe Delam*, a Nyingma text. Apart from the fact that we were friends, and that I knew him to be free from sectarian exclusiveness, the *tulkus* of the line to which he belonged had been Nyingmapas until the time of his immediate predecessor, who had been educated as a Gelugpa on the orders of the Thirteenth Dalai Lama. He therefore readily agreed to help me with my task, and in the course of the next few months we spent many hours working together on the project, eventually producing a rough English version of the rather cryptic Tibetan text. Meanwhile, I made a start on the preliminaries to which Kachu Rimpoche had introduced me, beginning with the Going for Refuge and Prostration practice. This was a quite strenuous practice, I found, and it was a couple of weeks before I could make a hundred prostrations straight off without becoming breathless and exhausted. But I persevered, and by the time I left for England I had accumulated the 20,000 prostrations that Kachu Rimpoche seemed to think was the minimum number required. Long before that, I had added to the Going for Refuge and Prostration practice, the Vajrasattva visualization and purification practice, and the practice of offering to Padmasambhava a mandala or symbolic representation of the universe. I also continued to do the Green Tārā *sādhana* I had received from Chattrul Rimpoche and the Mañjughoṣa Stuti Sādhana I had received from Jamyang Khyentse Rimpoche. All these practices required a good deal of time, as did the literary work in which I was engaged. I therefore decided that I had no alternative but to cut down my preaching tours in the plains. The result was that for the best part of two years I remained in Kalimpong, spending much of the day either at my desk or in the shrine-room.

My coming across the Nyingma woodblock prints so soon after receiving the Padmasambhava *abhiṣeka* may be regarded as an example of what Jung termed synchronicity,[371] or 'the simultaneous occurrence of events which appear significantly related but have no discernible connection'. But as though one was not enough, there occurred around the time of my initiation another example of the phenomenon. One morning, a poorly clad Tibetan, evidently a refugee, came to the Vihara carrying a set of thangkas he wanted me to buy or, as he would have said, 'ransom', for things sacred were not to be bought and sold like so much merchandise. So far as I remember, he wanted a hundred rupees for the set. As gently as I could, I explained that I was not in a position to buy any thangkas just then, but the only result was that he lowered his price, thinking I was bargaining. This went on for some time, with me continuing to plead poverty and the wretched Tibetan again and again lowering his price. Eventually he reached a rock-bottom forty rupees. As it happened, forty rupees was all the ready money I had in the world at the time, but as the man was obviously desperate for money I bought the thangkas, feeling ashamed that I was getting them for so little and wishing I could have given more. There were eight thangkas in the set, and on unrolling them I found that they depicted the eight manifestations of the Precious Guru, one of them being none other than Śākya Seng-ge, the historical Buddha, who according to Nyingma tradition was the teacher of the *sūtras*, whereas Padmasambhava had taught the tantras. Though I knew very little about thangkas, I could tell from the style that they were old, probably eighteenth century or earlier. They were mounted in tattered brown silk brocade, which in some places hung in strips. After inspecting them carefully, I hung them on the walls of my study-bedroom, five on one wall and three on the other, where they remained for the rest of my time in India.

In those days, refugees were arriving from Tibet all the time, some of them after experiencing terrible hardships on their way to the Indian border and safety. Officials and members of the aristocracy were often able to bring with them bullion and jewels (several bought houses in the town), but the common people and the monks had only the clothes they stood up in and, perhaps, their most valued possessions. These were generally of a religious nature, and included small portable shrines, thangkas, and images of Buddhas and bodhisattvas. Some of the monks had with them quite large images that had belonged to their monastery and which they had managed to save from destruction by the Chinese troops. But whether lay people or monks, in Kalimpong there were no official arrangements to receive the refugees and no organized relief. Neither was there any work for them, though two enterprising monks who had been cooks at Drepung Gompa, the biggest monastery in Tibet, opened a restaurant that quickly became the most popular in town.

Some of the refugees left Kalimpong for the plains, some begged, and some (a very few) turned to dacoity. But regardless of whether they stayed or went, most of them were forced, sooner or later, to sell even their most valued possessions for whatever they could get. It therefore was not long before the bazaar was flooded with images, thangkas, and other religious artefacts of every description. Most of them were bought by local Indian merchants for eventual sale in the West and in Japan. One such merchant took me to see his godown, which I found filled from floor to ceiling with rolled up thangkas. On another occasion a poorly clad Tibetan drew me into a dark front room and showed me a standing Tārā, three feet high, with one of the most beautiful faces I had ever seen. He, or his master, wanted 2,000 rupees for it, but for all the money I had, he might just as well have asked for two lakhs. The refugees, I found, like other Tibetans, often gave me first refusal when they wanted to sell something that had been consecrated, as they knew that being a Buddhist I would treat it with respect. For the first time in my life I found myself heartily wishing that I had more money and was able to ransom at least some of the many beautiful images and thangkas I was offered, for it grieved me to see them passing into the hands of non-Buddhists and being treated as though they were just another Tibetan export, along with wool, yak tails, and musk. At the same time, I was aware that even the most beautiful images and thangkas were simply aids to devotion and meditation, and that for me, as for every Buddhist, the most important thing in life was to get on with practising the Dharma and not waste time in idle regrets.

I was therefore glad when Kachu Rimpoche came to stay for a few days and see what progress I was making with the preliminary practices, thus reminding me what my true priorities were. It was in the course of this visit, I think, that I was reminded of the fact that my teacher was a visionary, and that he acted on his visions. One day he told me at breakfast that in his early morning meditation he had seen a banner of victory on the roof of the Vihara, and as soon as the meal was over he hurried off to the bazaar with his attendant lama. In the bazaar he went to a carpenter and had the six-foot cylindrical frame of the banner made; went to the cloth merchant and chose the red, green, blue, yellow, and white silks; found a tailor and had the silks made up into the flounces that would hang round the cylindrical frame; and finally returned in triumph with the banner and erected it himself on the roof of the Vihara with the appropriate ceremonial blessings. Hitherto, the only outward sign that our modest stone cottage was a Buddhist monastery was the Burmese gong that hung on the veranda and was struck at six in the morning and six in the evening every day, thus giving the time to the villagers who lived further down the hillside. But now we also had the five-coloured banner of victory, which proclaimed to all who saw it not any earthly conquest but the Buddha's victory over the forces of greed, hatred, and delusion.

9
THE SHADOW ACROSS SIKKIM

On the mantelpiece in the front room that was the Kazini's office there stood a framed head-and-shoulders photograph of an elderly gentleman of decidedly military appearance. There may even have been a row of medals across his chest. It was not long before the Kazini informed me that this imposing personage was Field Marshal Mannerheim, the father of modern Finland, and that he was her uncle. It was in fact he who had brought her up, and throughout her life she had been greatly influenced by him. Later still she confided to me that he was not her uncle, as she had been led to believe when young, but her father, and although she did not actually say so it appeared she was illegitimate. She always spoke of her supposed uncle, or real father, with great emotion, and seemed to have had a stronger feeling for him than for any other person in her life.[372] She never spoke of her mother, but she often mentioned her sister (perhaps a half-sister) who lived in Edinburgh and with whom she was in regular correspondence. Her first husband she referred to only in passing, and always in connection with their life in Burma. I never learned his given name, for she invariably spoke of him simply as Langford-Rae, nor did I ever learn whether she was a divorcee or a widow when she met the Kazi. There was, however, a son of about my own age called Roderick, who worked in a tea garden in Assam, and who must have been born when the Kazini was in her early or middle twenties.[373]

It was not easy to imagine the Kazini as a mother, either as a young woman or as the middle-aged woman she had become. There was very little that was motherly about her, though she was capable of showing genuine concern for those of whom she was fond. She once told me she had no maternal feelings and was quite indifferent to her son, whom she had probably handed over to the care of a Burmese ayah soon after he was born.[374] Just how indifferent she was to him became evident when news came that Roderick had been killed in a road accident in Assam. His death had not affected her in the slightest, she assured me the next time we met, in a tone, and with an air, that suggested the event was of absolutely no interest to her.[375]

She had displayed a similar lack of interest some months earlier, when Roderick came to see her in her new home. The Kazi received him kindly, and was his usual hospitable self, but the Kazini took no more notice of him than if he had been the most casual of casual visitors. So far as I remember, he stayed at the Himalayan Hotel, but though he came several times to Chakhung House, where I met him once, after the first visit it seemed he came to meet the Kazi rather than to see his mother. What was more, during his short stay in the town he somehow struck up a friendship with Joe Cann, whom he probably met in the lounge of the Himalayan Hotel, to which the scandalmongering old man was a frequent visitor. The Kazini had refused to have anything to do with him, for she knew, as I did, that during her 1950 visit to Kalimpong he had spread scurrilous stories about herself and Lha Tsering, and she thought it best to see as little as possible of one who possessed such an evil tongue.

Besides the photograph of the Field Marshal, there was also in the Kazini's office, and elsewhere in the house, another photograph in a silver frame. This was a studio portrait of a benign, gently smiling Kazi in traditional Sikkimese dress. It was the Kazini's favourite portrait of her husband, and it was she who had made him sit for it. She had made him sit for it not just out of wifely devotion but also in her capacity as his publicity officer, and over the years she must have distributed hundreds of copies of it among journalists, editors of newspapers, and other possible supporters. Unlike the Kazini, the Kazi never spoke about his father, nor did he ever mention his mother, but there were several occasions on which he talked to me about his two uncles, Phodang Lama and Khangsa Dewan, who I gathered had been powerful and influential figures in the Sikkim of their day and whom the Kazi evidently admired. He also talked to me about Chakhung, his estate in western Sikkim, with its orange gardens and its cardamom fields, and he once took me there for a couple of days. There were only servants living in the roomy old timber mansion, and when showing me round the Kazi directed my attention to the enormous brass *thalis*, more than two feet in diameter, that hung on the wall. Members of the family would eat from one of these giant plates, which would be carried into the room piled high with rice and meat. When they had eaten their fill it would be taken back to the kitchen, where the servants and other dependants would eat what was left.

Despite his feudal, aristocratic family background, the Kazi felt for the sufferings of the common people of Sikkim, regardless of whether they were of Tibetan, Lepcha, or Nepalese descent, and wanted to do what he could to improve their condition. This was one of the main reasons for his being in politics, the other reason being his hatred of the Maharaj Kumar, or Crown Prince, who now acted for his father, the Maharaja, and whom the Kazi was determined to 'finish off', as he once put it to me with uncharacteristic ferocity.

Before becoming friends with the Kazi and Kazini, I knew nothing about Sikkimese politics, even though I had been to Gangtok a number of times, but after becoming friends with them I came to know quite a lot. But perhaps I should say I *heard* quite a lot about the politics of Sikkim, especially from the Kazini, for I had no real interest in the subject and much of what I heard was soon forgotten. Nonetheless, there were things I heard so often I could not but remember them. Thus I knew that the political party to which the Kazi originally belonged had collapsed, that a new party had been formed, and that the Kazi was president of this party, that the party was opposed to the rule of the Maharaj Kumar, and that it was campaigning for the establishment of a democratic Sikkim. I also knew that the Kazi had the support of the Nepalese, who were the majority community in Sikkim, his two powerful uncles having encouraged Nepalese immigration into the country, that there existed a political party that supported the Maharaj Kumar, that the little Himalayan kingdom was a protectorate of India, and that the biggest player in the messy game of Sikkimese politics was the Government of India.

The Kazini was much more aware of the Indian dimension to Sikkimese politics than was the Kazi, even though it was he who went to Delhi for the purpose of explaining his party's position to officials in the Department of External Affairs. Besides being widely travelled, during her years in the Indian capital she had moved in political and diplomatic circles, had met many people, and was remarkably well informed. Like quite a few British officials in the days of the Raj, she preferred Muslims to Hindus, and for a time had been married to a Muslim, Dr Khan. They were married according to Islamic law, she told me, but since he would not agree to have a civil ceremony as well, she had refused to consummate the marriage and had left him. She was also decidedly pro-Pakistan, which meant she was correspondingly anti-Hindustan, and she admired the Socialist Party and its leaders much more than she admired the Congress Party and its leaders. Mahatma Gandhi she disliked, and in this connection she had a story to tell.

She had once attended one of the Mahatma's prayer meetings in the grounds of Birla House, where he was subsequently assassinated, and had found herself sitting directly behind him. As he listened to the scripture readings, she had studied him closely, eventually saying to herself, 'No, I don't like you.' Thereupon the old man had turned round and said, with a smile, 'You don't like me, do you, Madame.' She had been utterly astonished, and had not known what to say. It was as though he had read, or felt, her thoughts as she studied him. The Kazini told the story very well, wrinkling up her nose and shaking her head as she described how she had felt towards the Mahatma, for she was an excellent raconteuse, and could be very entertaining. She was also an excellent mimic, and I well remember her hilarious imitation of Pandit Nehru, the prime minister, absent-mindedly picking his nose as he presided over a public function. All things considered, it was not surprising that at their first meeting the Kazi should have been quite dazzled by the mature charms of the lively, articulate woman of the world, the like of whom he had not encountered before, though he was not so dazzled that he could not see she could be of great help to him in his political career.

In the event she proved to be a greater help to him that he could possibly have imagined. Besides being his public relations officer, she drafted his petitions and proclamations, did all his typing, and very soon was advising him and his colleagues on policy and tactics (one of the Kazi's favourite English words) and giving them the benefit of her legal knowledge and her intellectual acumen. In short, she threw herself wholeheartedly into what she had at first termed, rather disparagingly 'Kazi's politics', and identified herself with them to such an extent that she became, over the years, as great a force within the party as the Kazi, and at times a greater one. She was especially popular with the younger party activists, who were often at the house, for they liked the intemperate manner in which she denounced the Maharaj Kumar as a dictator and a tyrant and called upon them to overthrow his corrupt and oppressive regime. Like the Kazi, she spoke the language of democracy and human rights, but it was not a language that was natural to her; unlike the Kazi, she had no real feeling for the sufferings of the common people of Sikkim. She was very much the *grande dame*, and had she dazzled the Maharaj Kumar with her mature charms and married him instead of the Kazi (an unlikely event in view of the disparity between their ages) she would no doubt have thrown herself into *his* politics no less wholeheartedly than she had thrown herself into the Kazi's, and probably with greater satisfaction. Yet, here she was in Chakhung House, Kalimpong, and not in the Palace, Gangtok, and denouncing not Kazi Lhendup Dorje as a dangerous revolutionary but the Maharaj Kumar as a power-crazed dictator. She denounced him as a dictator so often and, to my mind, so unfairly, that one day I asked her how many political prisoners there were in Sikkim. This took the wind out her sails, for she was obliged to admit that there were no political prisoners in Sikkim. On another occasion the Kazi and I accused her of being a far bigger dictator than the Maharaj Kumar. We spoke laughingly, but she could see there was truth in the accusation all the same, and joined in the laughter, even though it was at her expense.

Although she worked tirelessly for the Kazi, and was such a force within his party, the Kazini did not appear openly on the stage of Sikkimese politics. She worked behind the scenes, preferring to help shape the script rather than to play any of the parts, even an important one. Letters over her signature did, however, appear frequently in the correspondence columns of the English-language Calcutta dailies. The letters were written in a lively, entertaining style, and often ridiculed the Maharaj Kumar's plans for the benefit of his country, and even the unfortunate ruler himself. The Maharaj Kumar felt this ridicule keenly, and whenever I was in Gangtok and staying at the palace guesthouse he would complain to me bitterly about the Kazini's letters as soon as we met. He knew I could do nothing about them, nor did he expect me to, but was simply giving vent to his feelings. I did, however, once manage to convince the Kazini that a certain letter was libellous and should not be published. The Maharaj Kumar also once complained to me about the behaviour of Apa Pant, the Political Officer, a Chitpavan Brahmin from Poona and a staunch Hindu. Pant had actually had the audacity to install, in the grounds of the Residency, a giant image of Hanuman, the Hindu monkey god. I already knew this, Pant having taken me to see the image the last time I stayed with him. The image faced north, he had explained, in the direction of Tibet, and the god's club was grounded, not shouldered, as a sign that India's intentions towards China were peaceful. But the Maharaj Kumar was not concerned with how Hanuman bore his weapon. What concerned him, and excited his indignation, was the fact that at a certain hour of the day the giant image's shadow fell across the Palace. 'Some people will think it's just foolish superstition,' he told me, 'but Pant believes in these things and he knows that *we* believe.'

I could not say that I believed in them, but I knew that India's shadow had fallen across Sikkim, and that in the eyes of the Maharaj Kumar the shadow across the Palace symbolized that bigger and darker shadow. Independent India was in expansionist mood, despite Hanuman's grounded club, and I very much feared that sooner or later, by one means or another, Sikkim would be absorbed into the Indian Union and lose its separate identity. I also feared that the Kazi and Kazini were unwittingly helping to facilitate this process with their activities. For his part, the Maharaj Kumar was bent on preserving Sikkim as a Buddhist kingdom with its own cultural and religious tradition and its own political structures, and in this he had my full sympathy.

Just as the Maharaj Kumar would complain to me about the Kazini's letters to the press, had any appeared since our last meeting, so whenever I returned from Gangtok she would want to know if I had met the Maharaj Kumar and, if I had met him, what had passed between us. She was not interested in our discussions about Buddhist activities in Sikkim, or the revival of the country's traditional arts and crafts. All she wanted to know was whether the Maharaj Kumar had talked about her and, in particular, whether he had complained about her letters to the press, for if he complained it would mean that their purpose – which was to hurt him – had been fulfilled.

The Sikkimese prince and the European lady indeed seemed to be obsessed with each other, even though they had never really met, as the Kazini was *persona non grata* at the Palace, and as the Maharaj

Kumar, though he sometimes came to see me at the Vihara, never called at Chakhung House. Even the Kazi sometimes felt that the Kazini's preoccupation with the Maharaj Kumar's misdeeds, real or imagined, was excessive. Hers was indeed a character of the obsessional type, and during the time I was in regular contact with her it was with politics, in the sense of party politics and political intrigue and gossip, that she was obsessed, and apparently always had been. Outside politics she had, in fact, few interests. She was hardly ever seen in the bazaar, had no real social life, and seldom relaxed. If she did relax, it was either over a *thumba*, or bamboo beaker, of home-brewed millet beer, or over a book from her personal library. This little collection, which she had brought with her from Delhi, consisted mainly of political biographies and diplomatic memoirs. Her favourite author was Daniele Varè, a retired Italian diplomat, whose biography of the Dowager Empress of China she particularly praised.[376]

The Kazini's obsession with politics, especially Sikkimese party politics, did her little good. Though she retained her robust appearance and her upright, almost regal bearing, it was an obsession that not only made her restless and anxious but soured her temper and frayed her nerves. Each time I returned from one of my preaching tours, which generally lasted four or five months, I could not help noticing that despite the powder and paint, her features were more drawn and haggard than when I had last seen her. She was always glad, even relieved, to see me, and although we had corresponded regularly during my tour she lost no time in telling me what had been happening in my absence, with special reference to the Maharaj Kumar's misdeeds and the Kazi's reluctance to follow her advice. There had already been differences between her and the Kazi with regard to what he and his party should do next, whether in the way of responding to events or precipitating them, and in course of time these differences became more pronounced and led to some angry exchanges. If the Kazini was a sledgehammer, the Kazi was a rock on which she often found it difficult to make an impression, which meant she was often an extremely frustrated woman. The frustration showed itself in a constant nervous drumming with her fingers on the table, or on the arm of her chair, and in the fact that she was irritable and impatient with her husband in minor domestic matters. Occasionally the frustration reached such a pitch that there would be an explosion, a stream of violent reproaches and angry recriminations would be directed at the Kazi, and he would find it impossible to reason with the Kazini or to calm her down. When this happened he would send a servant down to the Vihara with a verbal message requesting me to come up as soon as it was convenient for me to do so. I could always tell something was amiss from the way the servant spoke, and would therefore drop whatever I was doing and go up straightaway.

On my arrival at Chakhung House, the Kazi would disappear into the kitchen to order tea for me, leaving me alone with the Kazini, whom I once found prostrate on the drawing-room carpet, as though she had been biting it in her rage. On this occasion, as on the others when I had been sent for, she at once launched into a litany of complaints against the Kazi, the chief of which were that he never heeded her advice, that he listened too much to other people, and that he was incapable of making up his mind about anything. As I usually did, I listened to her for a while without saying very much, allowing her anger to exhaust itself, then gradually led the conversation away from the subject of the Kazi and into more peaceful and productive channels. Within little more than an hour she was her normal self. There were no traces of tears to be wiped away, for unlike other women she did not cry when she was frustrated, which was probably a mistake on her part, for the Kazi was a soft-hearted man, and tears might have had a greater effect on him than the tenth repetition of her point of view. Be that as it may, now that she was herself again the Kazi reappeared, a smiling servant brought in *thumbas* for him and the Kazini and more tea for me, and the three of us spent a pleasant hour together. The Kazini probably reminisced about her glamorous life in Delhi, and may even have referred to the Maharaj Kumar without too much acrimony.

Had the episode taken place in the summer of 1962, we must have talked about the Maharaj Kumar's forthcoming marriage to Hope Cooke, a young American socialite whom he had met in Darjeeling two years previously. I was not interested in the marriage itself, which was attracting international attention and would no doubt be a colourful affair, but only in the fact that hundreds of pigs, chickens, and other living creatures were to be killed for the wedding feast. Since Sikkim was a Buddhist kingdom, with a Chogyal or Dharmaraja for its ruler, this seemed quite inappropriate, and I therefore wrote to the Maharaj Kumar protesting against the slaughter, as well as against the amount of alcohol that had been ordered. He replied at some length, maintaining that the number of animals to be killed, and the amount of alcohol that would be consumed, had been greatly exaggerated, and that age-old customs and traditions had to be kept up. This did not satisfy me, and the correspondence continued. While it was still in progress I happened to run into Princess Pema Tsedeun in the High Street. 'Why are you writing those dreadful letters to my brother?' she demanded, half-angrily and half-tearfully.

The Maharaj Kumar himself took my criticism in good part, and it was not long before I was having tea at the Palace with him and his new wife. What the Kazini wanted to know when I returned from Gangtok this time was not whether the Maharaj Kumar had talked about her and her letters, but whether I thought he and Hope Cooke were in love, for it was widely believed that he had married her for political reasons. He was obviously very much in love with the lady, I told her, but whether she was in love with him I was quite unable to say.

10
TIBETAN *TULKUS*

I once asked Dhardo Rimpoche how many *tulkus* or 'incarnate lamas' there were in Tibet. He replied that there were about two thousand who were recognized as *tulkus* by the Tibetan government, plus an indefinite number who were regarded as such within their own district or their own monastery. Since the word '*tulku*' was the Tibetan translation of the Sanskrit word *nirmāṇakāya*, and since '*nirmāṇakāya*' meant the manifested or emanated body of a Buddha, I then asked the Rimpoche how many incarnate lamas were *tulkus* in this more exalted sense. After reflecting a moment he said, 'Perhaps six or seven'. The Dalai Lama and the Panchen Lama were the best known members of this much smaller group of *tulkus*, the Dalai Lama being the emanation of Avalokiteśvara, the Bodhisattva of Compassion, who was virtually indistinguishable from a Buddha, and the Panchen Lama of Amitābha, the Buddha of Infinite Light. All the rest of the two thousand, and perhaps some others, were *tulkus* in that they had been identified as the 'reincarnation' of a famous teacher or abbot who had recently died and who might, of course, have been far advanced on the path to Buddhahood. I later learned that a great teacher might decide to reincarnate in more than one body, Jamyang Khyentse Rimpoche, for example, being one of the five simultaneous reincarnations of the original Khyentse Rimpoche, the great nineteenth-century master.

During my fourteen years in Kalimpong, and especially during my time at the Triyana Vardhana Vihara, I had the good fortune to come in contact with many *tulkus*, and to receive initiation from some of the greatest of them. Even those from whom I received neither initiations nor teachings, but with whom I was simply on friendly terms, had a positive effect on me by virtue of their kindness and generosity. On the whole, *tulkus* were, I found, noticeably superior to the ordinary monks and lamas, some of whom were very rough characters indeed. Not only were *tulkus* more deeply versed in the Dharma: they were more cultured, and more refined in their behaviour. From the Tibetan point of view this was no more than was to be expected. After all, they were *tulkus*, with all that the word implied in the way of higher spiritual attainment.

I saw things a little differently. Though I did not doubt that at least some *tulkus* were what they were believed to be, I knew that *tulkus* were taken from their mothers at an early age, that they were brought up with the greatest care, and that they were surrounded by the constant loving attention of guardians and tutors who felt a deep respect for their young charges, and it seemed to me that all this must have played an important part in making them the exceptional human beings most of them were. Had they not been brought up in that kind of way, the spiritual qualities they had inherited from their previous lives might not have been able to find expression through the new psychophysical organism. I knew that the Sixth Dalai Lama had led a dissolute life. This was owing, it was generally believed, to the fact that for political reasons his birth had been kept secret for many years, with the result that he had not received the education that was customary for a *tulku*. Even the highest *tulkus*, it seemed, needed the right kind of education.

But regardless of whether or not it was the special education that had made them what they were, I counted myself fortunate in being in contact with so many incarnate lamas. What made it possible for me to be in contact with them was the fact that they were all in Kalimpong, where, thanks to Kashyap-ji, I happened to be living, and most of them were in Kalimpong as refugees. Like thousands of others, they had fled to India in order to escape from the Chinese army of occupation. The most important of these refugees was the Dalai Lama, whom I had the opportunity of seeing when his train stopped at Siliguri for an hour when he was on his way to exile in Mussoorie, in the Punjab hills.[377] Three years earlier, when he and the Panchen Lama visited India in connection with the 2,500th Buddha Jayanti celebrations, I had not only seen him but met him several times – in Delhi, in Calcutta, and finally in Kalimpong, where I gave a reception for him at Everton Villa, where I was then living.[378] Now he was again in India, this time as a refugee.

The story of his escape was a dramatic one. He had left Lhasa in the midst of the confusion created by the March 1959 uprising, when hundreds, perhaps thousands, of Tibetans were killed by the Chinese troops. He had left in disguise, under the cover of darkness, accompanied by his mother, his two tutors, and a few senior officials. For some days the world did not know where he was, or even if he was still alive. It was a time of intense anxiety on his behalf, especially among the Tibetans in Kalimpong and elsewhere, and I shared that anxiety. For many years I had not looked at the newspapers, but now I scanned them every day for news of the Dalai Lama. We eventually learned that after a difficult journey he and his little party had reached the safety of the Indian border, that they were in Assam, and finally that his train would be arriving in Siliguri the following day. The Kazi and Kazini and I drove down to the hot, dusty little township in the hope of our being able to see him, as did hundreds of Tibetans from Kalimpong, Darjeeling, and Sikkim.

It was a strange sight that met our eyes when we reached our destination. An enclosure had been built near the railway station, and within it stood the tall, maroon-clad figure of the Dalai Lama. Indian officials and their wives strolled in and out of the enclosure, talking among themselves, and taking no particular notice of the Dalai Lama, but no one else was allowed to enter. The Tibetans who had come to pay their respects to their leader were kept back by a barrier, which prevented them from coming anywhere near the enclosure. They could only gaze at him from a distance in mournful silence. For his part, the Dalai Lama could only gaze back at them. He had, I thought, a bewildered look, and I felt extremely sorry for him. 'He's not a refugee, he's a prisoner,' remarked the Kazini, rather loudly, probably in the hope that some of the Indian officials would hear her.

Not all the high lamas who were living as refugees in India, or in Sikkim, had escaped from Tibet in the same dramatic manner as the Dalai Lama. Some of them had left earlier, before the turmoil and bloodshed of the Lhasa uprising, and had made the journey without much difficulty. One of the most eminent of these was the Sixteenth Gyalwa Karmapa, who according to his followers ranked third in the Tibetan Buddhist hierarchy, immediately below the Panchen Lama. His escape was a highly organized affair, and he arrived in Bhutan with a large entourage, and bringing with him many images, thangkas, and other precious items from his monastery in Tsurphu. For political reasons he was not allowed to settle in Bhutan, even though the Bhutanese were Kagyupas, as was the Karmapa, but he was allowed to settle in Sikkim, where he established himself at Rumtek. On his first – and so far as I know his only – visit to Kalimpong he stayed at the house of a wealthy Newar merchant, and it was there that the Kazi and Kazini and I met him. The Kazi had some business to transact with the Karmapa, and the Kazini and I were able to study him as the two men talked. He was of my own age, but decidedly corpulent, and he had, I thought, rather a shifty look. When the Kazini and I compared notes afterwards, we agreed that he seemed more like a successful businessman than a high lama.

This unfavourable impression did not prevent me from going to see the Karmapa when I happened to be in Gangtok at the same time that he was staying at the Palace Temple, where I had once met Jamyang Khyentse Rimpoche. He received me kindly, and at the end of the interview he presented me with a *dorje* and bell. They had been cast at Rumtek, he told me, and were from the first batch to be produced there under his direction. Unfortunately, despite his generosity, my impression of him remained unchanged. Tibetan Buddhists would no doubt have said that it was my own mental defilements that had prevented me from seeing the Karmapa as a Buddha, a fully enlightened being, and of course they might have been right.

There was no question of my seeing – or not seeing – Khamtul Rimpoche as a Buddha. Like the Karmapa he was a Kagyu incarnate lama, but unlike him he was a *tulku* of the middle rank, so to speak, and he lived unpretentiously with a close friend, who was also a Kagyu incarnate lama, in a little whitewashed monastery they had built at Rinkingpong, on a site from which one could see, in the far distance, the sunlit plains of West Bengal. Both were of my own age, perhaps a little younger, and both were by nature lively and friendly. I enjoyed their company, and I think they enjoyed mine. Once, when they were having lunch with me at the Vihara, a discussion arose about the Vinaya or code of monastic discipline. In the course of the discussion it transpired that my two friends were only *śrāmaṇeras* or novices, not fully ordained monks as I had supposed, and this astonished me. They, for their part, found my astonishment highly amusing, and could hardly contain their laughter. When I enquired the reason for their mirth, Khamtul Rimpoche spluttered, 'The Karmapa is only a *śrāmaṇera*,' and more laughter ensued. The Kagyupas, like the Nyingmapas, attached more importance to asceticism and the practice of meditation than to the observance of rules, though this was not to say that fully ordained monks were not to be found among them.

Rechung Rimpoche was the latest reincarnation of Milarepa's wayward disciple of that name, to whom the great poet-yogi addressed a number of songs, and at whose request he related the amazing story of his life.[379] Thus he belonged to a line of Kagyu *tulkus* but, like Dhardo Rimpoche's predecessor, he had been educated as a Gelugpa despite his non-Gelug spiritual affiliations, though whether on the orders of the Dalai Lama I never learned. During the two years or more that he spent in Kalimpong, he stayed at Arunachal with my friend Peunkhang-sey, whose brother he was, which meant that he was often at the Vihara. Slightly built, with a pale face, and a worried look, he was of a scholarly bent and for a while had worked in London as a translator of Tibetan texts. So far as I remember, he returned to the West before my own departure from India. Though not himself a yogi, he was acquainted with the theory, at least, of weather-making, and once explained to me how rain was produced and how storms could be averted. He also gave me a *dorje* and bell. The handle, he said, was Tibetan, but the bell was Indian, having been cast at Nālandā centuries ago and brought to Tibet. The bell was smaller than the one presented to me by the Karmapa and had, I thought, a more silvery sound. On another occasion Rechung showed me a wad of thick black hair, about an inch in length. It was his teacher's hair, he told me, in a reverential tone. Unfortunately, I could not help exclaiming, 'It looks like a dog's hair!' Rechung said nothing, but I could see I had hurt his feelings and felt a pang of regret. But words once spoken cannot be recalled, and one has to live with the consequences – sometimes for the rest of one's life.

There was a third Peunkhang brother who, like Rechung, was a *tulku* and a Gelugpa, and who also lived at Arunachal. But that was the extent of the resemblance between them, and one would never have thought the two were brothers. Peunkhang Rimpoche (as I shall call him, having forgotten his name) was tall, heavily built, and slovenly, with a shock of stiff black hair that stood out from his head on all sides. As he came to me for English lessons, I soon discovered that he was not very bright. I also discovered that he was mentally disturbed. This was perhaps not unconnected with the fact that he believed he was not really an incarnate lama. 'No, I'm not a Rimpoche,' he more than once assured me, mournfully shaking his big head.

As I knew, the Peunkhang family belonged to the highest Lhasa aristocracy, and monks would sometimes identify a boy of such a family as the *tulku* of the late abbot as a means of ensuring the family's patronage for their monastery. This was probably what had happened in the case of my two friends, but whereas Rechung was able to act like a *tulku*, at least to an extent, his shock-headed brother seemed quite unable to do so.

Peunkhang Rimpoche was not the only *tulku* to have been wrongly identified, if that was indeed what had happened. In Darjeeling there was a refugee incarnate lama who had become a Christian and been given the baptismal name of David. I first heard about him from some of my Tibetan friends, who were scandalized that an incarnate lama, of all people, should have taken such a step, and they begged me to go to Darjeeling and convert him back to Buddhism. The next time I was in Darjeeling, therefore, I went to see David Rimpoche, as he was now known, and found him to be a healthy-looking young man whose principal interest was in body-building. Yes, he was a Christian, he acknowledged, but he didn't like the New Testament. He liked the Old Testament much better: it was full of fighting. The avowal did not surprise me, for I knew that the Tibetans in Kalimpong liked those films best which contained a lot of violence, such as the Westerns. David Rimpoche also disclaimed any wish to love Jesus. 'How can I love Jesus?' he demanded, 'I'm a man, not a woman.'

He evidently had a rather idiosyncratic understanding of Christianity, and I wondered what his understanding of Buddhism had been like. A few weeks later he was in Kalimpong, and I went to see him. This time he was not alone, but had an American woman sitting on his knee. I did not stay long, and we did not meet again.

With one exception, all the incarnate lamas I knew had been born in Tibet. The exception was Tomo Geshe Rimpoche, who had been born in Sikkim, and who was the *tulku* of a famous wonder-working lama who had died three or four years earlier. I first heard the name of this lama, the original Tomo Geshe Rimpoche, soon after my arrival in Kalimpong, when I visited the Tharpa Choling Gompa, the Gelug monastery at Tirpai, and saw in the main shrine-hall a photograph of his embalmed body. Two years later I heard much about him from Lama Govinda, who had been one of his disciples,[380] and in 1961 I met the Rimpoche's 24-year-old reincarnation. He had been a prisoner in Lhasa for three years, and his arrival first in Gangtok, and then in Kalimpong, created a sensation in the area, for the name of Tomo Geshe Rimpoche was a name to conjure with not only throughout Tibet but throughout the entire Himalayan region.

We soon met, and soon became friends. He was probably the strangest and most mysterious person I have known. His form was that of a 12-year-old boy, but his behaviour was that of an old man, while the overall impression he created was one of innocence, wisdom, and gentle charm. More often than not a little smile of amusement played about the corners of his mouth. I sometimes visited him at his cottage near the Tharpa Choling Gompa, where he lived with his attendant monks and his little dogs. One day he showed me, in the narrow chapel behind his room, the meditation box in which his famous predecessor had spent so much of his time. The monks, I noticed, all went very much in awe of him, and though he spoke very quietly he was obeyed instantly, almost as though he had cracked a whip. Sometimes he visited me at the Vihara, especially after he had started studying English with me, when he came more regularly. Like all Tibetans and Sikkimese, he believed that whatever differences in rank and position there might be between them, the pupil always went to the teacher, not the teacher to the pupil. He already knew a little English, and made good progress. One day, quite spontaneously, he told me a little about himself and about his life as a prisoner of the Chinese.

He was born in 1937, he said, and at the age of seven had been sent to Sera, the Gelug monastic university near Lhasa, where he studied until 1959 and where he took his Geshe degree. He then moved to Lhasa, but hardly had he done so when the whole population rose against their Chinese oppressors, thus allowing the Dalai Lama to make his escape. As he happened to know many Amdopas, Khampas, and other Tibetans, the Chinese accused him of supplying them with life-giving *ribus* or 'magic pills', as well as of criticizing the Communist regime, encouraging opposition, and plotting with the Dalai Lama and other great lamas and with people in India. For this he was thrown into prison. What they said was true, he added, with a little smile. He *did* distribute *ribus* to many people. As I knew, both the old Geshe Rimpoche and the new were famous for their *ribus*, which were widely believed to have powerful protective qualities, and it is quite possible that the Chinese, despite their Communism, were still superstitious enough to have regarded them as a kind of alternative weapon and to have feared them – and their distributor – accordingly.

A prisoner of the Chinese for two years and three months, Geshe Rimpoche continued, he was being kept in different jails in Lhasa, and in one just outside Lhasa, a converted army barracks, where there were about 6,000 prisoners, some of them *tulkus* like himself. During his time as a prisoner he underwent two spells of solitary confinement, the first for fifteen or twenty days, the second for two months. His cell was about five feet square, and had neither a window nor a bed. Food was given to him through a hole in the door, which was kept locked, as was the door at the end of the passage. The guards told him he was being given the best food, such as no other prisoners were getting, for he was an Indian, and China was the friend of India. The food was rice and vegetables without salt. As the cell was of stone, he also suffered from the cold. After his first spell of solitary confinement he and about two hundred officials were kept together in three rooms. They were not allowed to talk about anything except the work they were doing for the Chinese, and they had to work all the time, with only a day or two off a month. He had worked for three months as a gardener, five months as a swineherd, four months as a washerman, and two months making envelopes, besides which he had stitched woollen belts, built and repaired walls, and worked in the fields.

The gardening work was fairly easy, though he and another man had to pull a heavy cart filled with earth. He also had to take out and put back a hundred heavy flower-pots, and he had to do this every day. (In Tibet, Geshe Rimpoche explained, flowers were always grown in pots.) He also had to water the flowers, and if any of them withered the Chinese would blame him. When he worked as a swineherd, he and another man had 200 pigs to look after, especially when they produced young. The pigs lived in five sties, and the sties had to be cleaned out every day. He also had to cook both for the pigs and himself. As a washerman he had to wash the clothes of the military, both the men's and the women's. It was then winter, the water froze, and his hands became covered with sores. At first the clothes were washed in the river, but two prisoners who were working with him committed suicide by drowning, after which they had to wash the clothes in the streams. The clothes had to be perfectly clean, but if they used too much soap they were abused. When he was making envelopes he had to produce between 500 and 600 a day, and when he was stitching woollen belts he had to produce 120 a day. He stitched from six in the morning until ten at night. The work was difficult and affected his eyes.

At this point Tomo Geshe paused. It was difficult to relate all his experiences, he said quietly, a few moments later, and perhaps he had said enough. There was another pause, and I thought he must have finished, but at length he resumed his account of life as a prisoner in Chinese-occupied Tibet.

The Chinese made them work sixteen hours a day. They were given food only twice a day, morning and evening, together with a little water. One hour in all was allowed for eating. When he cooked for other prisoners, all he could give them was dried peas boiled in water. They not only had to work very hard; they had to work quickly. The implements with which they worked in the fields were of very poor quality, and soon broke; but when the implements broke they were accused of misusing the People's property and their rations were halved. Religious practice of any kind was absolutely prohibited. They were not allowed to eat while working, and the Chinese were always on the watch. Bad meat, which was not fit for consumption by the soldiers, was given to the prisoners. Though they could not sleep for hunger, they still had to work. The food was never enough. Sometimes they ate wild garlic while working in the fields. By eating it they could get a good night's sleep.

Geshe Rimpoche told me all this in a quaint mixture of Hindi, Nepali, and English, and in a quiet, matter-of-fact manner. As I listened to him, it seemed incredible that one so small and weak-looking could have endured so much hardship. It was no less incredible that in telling me about his life as a prisoner he should have shown not the slightest sign of ill will towards those who were responsible for his – and his country's – sufferings. On the contrary, he twice told me that the work he did for the Chinese had been 'first class' (he used the English expression). It was as though he felt a quiet satisfaction in being able to work well under those appalling conditions, regardless of the nature of the work, for it showed he could rise above these conditions.

Tomo Geshe Rimpoche

His story – though not his country's – had ended happily. Having been born in Sikkim, which was a protectorate of India, he was an India-protected person, and the Government of India had eventually been able to secure his release. Among those who heard, some months later, of Geshe Rimpoche's arrival in Kalimpong, was Lama Govinda, in his ashram in distant Almora. On coming to know that I was in personal contact with the Rimpoche, he wrote asking for more detailed news of his teacher, whom he had last seen, as a boy of nine or ten, in Gyantse in 1947, when they happened to pass each other in the street.

In particular, he wanted to know whether Tomo Geshe remembered him, his old disciple, and whether he had recognized him at Gyantse. I replied at length, and was able to assure my friend that I had put his questions to Tomo Geshe, and that he had replied, quietly but firmly, 'I know him.' I also included in my letter a full report of the account Geshe Rimpoche had given me of his life as a prisoner of the Chinese, a report I wrote up from notes I had taken at the time. Lama Govinda used some of this information in the concluding chapter of *The Way of the White Clouds*, on which he was then working, and which after its publication in 1966 soon became a classic.[381]

Geshe Rimpoche continued to study English with me until my departure from India. Before I left, he gave me a waistcoat that had belonged to, and been worn by, his famous predecessor. This was not a waistcoat of the ordinary Western type but a heavy woollen garment, maroon in colour, of the kind normally worn by Tibetan monks, with projecting shoulder-pieces and long lapels, one of which crossed the other. As befitted so great a lama, there were insets of red and gold brocade back and front. I do not know why my friend gave me the waistcoat, which most Tibetans would have regarded as a holy relic. Perhaps he thought it would keep me warm in the English winter, or perhaps he wanted me to have a link with his 'previous body' as well as with himself.

Tomo Geshe Rimpoche was not the youngest incarnate lama I knew. The youngest was the 16-year-old Pabongkhapa Rimpoche, the *tulku* of the great Gelug scholar of that name, who had been the teacher of Trijang Rimpoche, the junior tutor of the Dalai Lama, and of many other eminent Gelug lamas of the day. A strict follower of the Gelug intellectual and spiritual tradition, he was reported to have thrown Nyingma books and images into the river, but when I questioned Dhardo Rimpoche about this he was positive that Pabongkhapa Rimpoche had done no such thing. Photographs showed him to have been enormously fat, and his reincarnation, although so young, seemed to be well on his way to achieving a comparable girth. But he had a pleasant, open face, and was very bright. I once asked him which picture of the world was correct, the modern scientific one, or the traditional Buddhist one, with its Mount Meru, its four islands, and so on. Both pictures were useful, he replied, but they were useful for different purposes. I would have liked to see more of him, but he and his little party were on their way to one of the big refugee camps in South India, and they did not stay long in Kalimpong. Unfortunately, within six months of his arrival at the camp this promising young *tulku* died. The news of his death saddened me, and I wondered how long it would be before he was reborn.

Although I was in contact with many incarnate lamas, they were not always in contact with one another. In the case of some of them, this was because they belonged to different schools of Tibetan Buddhism, and had no previous experience of such contact. In the case of others, even those of the same school, it was bound up with questions of protocol, the strict observance of which was a feature of all aspects of Tibetan life. Who, for instance, was to make the first advance? Who was to call on whom, and with what degree of ceremony? I was exempt from all this. To the Tibetans of Kalimpong I was simply Imji Gelong, the English Monk, and contact with me was no more problematic for my *tulku* friends than contact with them was for me. Originally, some Tibetans had wanted to know whether I was a Mahāyānist or a Hīnayānist, for to all appearances I was a follower of the lesser path of individual emancipation. But once I had made it clear that despite my yellow robes I accepted the bodhisattva ideal, and was a follower of the greater path of universal emancipation, I was warmly welcomed as a co-religionist.

One day it struck me that there ought to be more cooperation among the incarnate lamas I knew, especially the younger ones. They ought to work together for the good of Buddhism, and in this way encourage others in the area to do likewise. After consulting with Dhardo Rimpoche, I therefore invited twelve of them to the Vihara for a meeting. They all accepted the invitation, and on the appointed day all turned up as promised. Since at the Vihara they were on neutral ground, so to speak, there was no protocol to be observed, and they mingled happily with one another without regard to precedence. Some of them had not met before. I addressed them briefly, explaining why I had called the meeting, outlining my ideas about their working together, and appealed to them to give serious thought to the matter. My words were well received, and it was agreed that we should meet again in a few weeks' time for a fuller and more detailed discussion. That discussion was doomed not to take place. News of the meeting having reached the ears of the Tibetan officials in

Dharamsala, to which the Dalai Lama had moved from Mussoorie, the Drunye Chenmo, or Lord Chamberlain, arrived in Kalimpong, called the *tulkus* together, and severely reprimanded them for presuming to hold a meeting without the permission of His Holiness. The *tulkus* were aware that the Dalai Lama probably knew nothing of the meeting at the Vihara, but the Drunye Chenmo spoke in his name, and there was no question of their arguing with him, or trying to explain their position. They could only hear and obey.

Dhardo Rimpoche, at least, was not surprised by the setback. He had his own experience of Tibetan officials, some of whom had tried to squeeze the Indo-Tibetan Buddhist Cultural Institute school out of existence and have the Rimpoche himself deported to Tibet on the grounds that, his father having been Chinese, he was a Chinese national. He had managed to avoid deportation by taking Indian citizenship. Later he went to Dharamsala, and in a private audience gave the Dalai Lama a full account of how the officials had harassed and persecuted him, speaking with a directness not at all in accordance with protocol. On hearing what the officials had done, the Dalai Lama's eyes had reddened with anger, Dhardo Rimpoche told me, and he had thrown up his hands in despair, exclaiming, 'But what can I do? What can I do?' On another occasion, when I had expressed a degree of astonishment that a certain incarnate lama should have in his entourage a man of rather dubious character, the Rimpoche added to my astonishment by declaring, 'The greater the lama, the worse the people by whom he is surrounded.' In the old Tibet, the great lamas – especially the major incarnate lamas – were powerful and wealthy figures, and those who hankered after power and wealth, whether monks or laymen, would often attach themselves to such lamas with an eye to their own advantage.

Apart from two or three who had studied English with me for a while, I was not acquainted with any Tibetan officials, though I often saw them walking through the High Street. They were easily recognized, not from anything distinctive in their appearance but from the way ordinary Tibetans behaved towards them, especially those newly arrived from Tibet. On passing an official, they would doff their hats, bend themselves almost double, and hasten past the lordly one with every sign of deference and submission. The official, for his part, would appear not to notice them. I observed, however, that after five or six months in India, the Tibetans no longer showed their officials such extreme respect. This was symptomatic of wider changes within the Tibetan diaspora. The officials had originally maintained that the Government of India should deal with the refugees only through them. They wanted the diaspora to be, in effect, a state within a state – a state that would be ruled by them in the name of the Dalai Lama. But this was an attitude that could not survive long in Nehru's India. The Drunye Chenmo belonged to a dying breed.

11
THE ANNIHILATOR OF HELL

I first saw Dudjom Rimpoche at Rinkingpong. He had decided to build a three-storeyed Nyingma temple there, not far from the little Kagyu *gompa*, and I had been invited to attend the ceremony that marked the beginning of work on the project. This involved the burying of the earthenware pot containing various consecrated items at the spot where the temple was to stand, and it was Dudjom Rimpoche himself who performed the ceremony. Hundreds of people must have been present on that occasion, but I remember only the comparatively small figure of the Rimpoche, in his dark blue *bokku*, standing hatless in the bright sunshine on the edge of the hole in which the pot had been buried. He stood absolutely still, and I had the distinct impression that it was not just his bodily stillness. His mind, also, was absolutely still, as though the various winds that usually agitate the surface of our consciousness had in his case ceased to blow and he was at peace, in the deepest sense of the phrase, with himself and with the world.

Though I well remember where I first saw Dudjom Rimpoche, I have no recollection of when this happened. Probably it was towards the end of 1958. Even before that, however, I had heard much about the Rimpoche, who lived in somewhat regal style in a large house in the Development Area and was not often seen in public. In fact, an atmosphere of mystery surrounded him, and his name was generally pronounced in tones of awe. Though he was not the official head of the Nyingma school, he was widely regarded as its greatest living master and had many disciples, including some who were themselves eminent gurus. One of his disciples was my friend Sonam Topgay Kazi, who was also related to him in a more mundane way, having married the Rimpoche's stepdaughter. It was probably Sonam Topgay who told me that before the workmen started digging the ground for the foundations of the new temple, Dudjom Rimpoche had solemnly requested all the ants and worms to depart lest they be killed or injured. Believe it or not, my friend added, the workmen later reported that in the course of their digging they had failed to come across a single ant or worm, whereas they would normally have expected to come across hundreds.

Sonam Topgay also told me, as did other Nyingmapas I knew, that Dudjom Rimpoche's *wongkurs* or Tantric initiations were particularly powerful and that this was well known. What they meant by 'powerful' in this connection was not altogether clear to me, and I suspected that the Tibetan word, like the English one, had acquired connotations which were not wholly in accordance with the Dharma. The Sanskrit term for Tantric initiation was *abhiṣeka* or 'sprinkling', but the pioneer Tibetan translators of the Tantric texts chose not to translate the term literally. Instead, they rendered it as *wongkur*, which meant 'giving power' or 'empowerment'. When I started taking an interest in the Vajrayāna, soon after my arrival in Kalimpong, *wongkur* – *wong* for short – was one of the first terms I heard in this connection, and I naturally wanted to know what it really meant, especially as I heard it so often. All that my lama informants were able to tell me, however, was that '*wong*' meant becoming like a king, an explanation which left me no wiser than before. Eventually I discovered that the term *abhiṣeka* derived from the ancient Indian coronation ceremony, in the course of which water was poured over the king from four jars, thus investing him with the power to exercise the royal authority. Similarly, the bestowal of a *wong* empowered the disciple to study and practise the Tantra and thus attain Buddhahood more quickly than would otherwise have been possible. Some Tibetans, it seemed, believed that Tantric initiation involved a literal transmission of power from the guru to the disciple, so that the latter was more 'powerful' after the ceremony than he had been before it took place. I certainly did not experience a literal transmission of power when I received initiation from Chattrul Rimpoche and Jamyang Khyentse Rimpoche, nor was I to experience it later when receiving initiation from Dudjom Rimpoche and other eminent lamas. When I received the Vajrasattva *abhiṣeka* from Dudjom Rimpoche there was, however, a point at which I definitely felt something pass from him to me, but it was not something that could be described in terms of power.

I received the *abhiṣeka* on Saturday, 18 April 1959, a most auspicious day, for being the tenth day of the Tibetan month it was sacred to Guru Rimpoche. I did not receive it alone but in company with four other Buddhists, two of whom were Chinese and two English. The two Chinese, who came from Hong Kong, were Wu Chien, a monk, and Liu Fu Ken, a businessman. I did not know either of them, and I gathered that having heard of the efficacy of Dudjom Rimpoche's *wongs* they had come all the way from Hong Kong in order to receive initiation from him. Quiet, unassuming John Driver was already well known to me, but I had only recently made the acquaintance of John Blofeld. The latter was a tall, rather heavily-built man in his mid-forties, with a broad, florid face and a hearty, bellowing laugh. A lover of the East, especially its women, he worked for the British Council in Bangkok, had married a Chinese girl, and had two children who were at school in Darjeeling. It was in order to see these children that he was in the area from time to time. Previously he had always stayed with Joe Cann, who dissuaded him from coming to see me on the grounds that I knew nothing about Buddhism and was not worth meeting anyway. When *A Survey of Buddhism* appeared John therefore had a big surprise, came to see me the next time he was in the area, explained why he had not come before, and thereafter stayed with me whenever he visited Kalimpong.

On the present occasion he stayed with me for three weeks, walking with me up to Madhav Nikunj, Dudjom Rimpoche's residence, on the morning of 18 April and on the two following mornings. He had long been interested in Zen (in its Chinese rather than its Japanese form), as well as in Taoism, but having increasingly felt the need for a more devotional form of religious practice he had become interested in Tibetan Buddhism, and in particular in the Vajrayāna. Receiving initiation from Dudjom Rimpoche would, he hoped, be the means of introducing him to that more devotional form of practice. John Driver was taking the initiation because he wanted to experience the Nyingma tradition from within, as a practitioner, as well as understand it from the outside as a Western scholar. Liu Fu Ken, the businessman, believed that the practice of the Vajrayāna would bring him greater wealth and prosperity. What

Wu Chien expected to gain from the *wong* I did not know, but as he was a monk it must have been a spiritual rather than a material benefit that he was after. For my part, I welcomed the opportunity of forming a spiritual connection with a lama of Dudjom Rimpoche's eminence, about whom I had heard so much and who had made such a strong impression on me that day at Rinkingpong. Thus it was five people with very different backgrounds, histories, and aspirations who gathered in Dudjom Rimpoche's shrine-room that Saturday morning in readiness to receive the Vajrasattva *abhiṣeka*. It was Liu Fu Ken who had requested the initiation, and the rest of us had been invited to receive it along with him.

The Rimpoche sat on a kind of throne, his *dorje* and bell and other ritual implements within easy reach, while we, his five disciples, sat on the floor in front of him in a semicircle. The *abhiṣeka* proper, which in fact consisted of four separate *abhiṣekas*, did not take very long to complete. Like other *abhiṣekas*, it authorized those who had received it to study and practise a certain Tantric *sādhana*. Having given us the *abhiṣeka*, Dudjom Rimpoche therefore spent the rest of that first day, and practically the whole of the next two days, giving us a detailed exposition of the text of the *sādhana* to which the *abhiṣeka* pertained. According to John Driver, who provided us with a running English translation of the Rimpoche's exposition, the Tibetan title of this text could be rendered as 'The Essence of Profound Meaning: Being the One-Mudrā Sādhana of Him Who Annihilates Hell'. In this context, 'Hell' signified not only the hell realm proper but also the animal realm and the realm of the *pretas* or 'hungry ghosts', in both of which there is more pain than pleasure. Similarly, 'Him Who Annihilates Hell' stood for Vajrasattva, the Diamond – or Adamantine – Being. He 'annihilates' Hell for those who have broken their vows and Tantric commitments by purifying them of the deep-seated mental defilements that were responsible for the infringements – defilements which, had the offenders not been purified of them, would have resulted in their being reborn in the lower realms. An exclusively Tantric figure, Vajrasattva was a Buddha appearing in bodhisattva form. He was the Sixth Buddha, transcendent over time and space, and whether as the central figure of one of the *mūla yogas* or as the central figure of the Hell-Annihilator *sādhana*, he was associated with purification in the deepest and most radical sense of the term.

Dudjom Rimpoche

As we soon discovered, 'The Essence of Profound Meaning' was a very rich text, and Dudjom Rimpoche's exposition was not only eloquent and imaginative but scholarly. In the course of those three days we were introduced to the marvellous world of Mahāyoga Tantra, one of the three divisions of *Anuttarayoga* Tantra. In the preliminary part of the *sādhana*, having recited a version of the Sevenfold Puja, one entered that world by invoking, then identifying oneself with, Vajrasattva in his wrathful *heruka* form, dark blue in colour and in union with his light blue consort. From the point of contact between them, there springs a host of Wrathful Ones who, spreading and filling the sky, drive off and destroy all hindrances. They then coalesce to form an enormous *vajra*-tent, beyond which are three mighty barriers, the first of raging fire, the second of swirling black wind, and the third of violently agitated ocean waves. These fill the void in all directions, safely isolating one for the practice of the main body of the *sādhana*. This began with the production of the two *bodhicittas*, the relative and the absolute, the meditation on the three *samādhis*, and the generation of the Mandala of the Container and the Contained. From this point onwards, the *sādhana* consisted of a series of complex and colourful visualizations, all evoked by means of mantras and accompanied, in most cases, by *mudrās* or 'hand gestures' of various kinds. The culminating visualization was that in which streams of nectar from the Buddhas of the Ten Directions and the Four Times, all in union with their consorts, fall upon the practitioner, purifying him of his mental defilements. His body, speech, and mind are then transformed into the body, speech, and mind of all the Buddhas, and his five *skandhas* or psychophysical aggregates into the five Buddha-wisdoms. The Hell-Annihilator *sādhana* concluded with the practitioner reciting the hundred-syllable Vajrasattva mantra and dissolving Vajrasattva, that is to say himself, into the void.

At the end of the third day, having finished his exposition of the Essence of Profound Meaning, Dudjom Rimpoche bestowed on us the fourfold *abhiṣeka* of Ekajaṭī, Rāhu, and Vajrasādhu, the principal guardian deities of the Nyingma tradition, explained how offerings were to be made to them, and gave us a copy of offering-prayers of his own composition. His work, in a sense, was finished; but ours had just begun. John Driver made a literal translation of the Tibetan text of the Essence of Profound Meaning, which John Blofeld turned into proper English, keeping as close to the original translation as English syntax permitted. The latter some years afterwards drew on this material for a book on the Vajrayāna to which he gave what I considered the unfortunate title of *The Way of Power*.[382] Our Chinese *wong*-brothers, for their part, made a Chinese version of the Hell-Annihilator *sādhana* which was published in book form. I took no part in these literary activities, except that I typed John Driver's translations of the offering-prayers and other material relating to Ma, Za, and Dor, as the Nyingmapas generally called the guardian deities of their tradition. I also commissioned small paintings of the Hell-Annihilator and the three guardian deities from an old Tibetan artist, a refugee whom Dudjom Rimpoche had recommended to me.

The Driver-Blofeld version of the Essence of Profound Meaning comprised twenty typed foolscap pages plus notes. I was glad to have it, and I was grateful to my two friends for their willingness to share with me the fruits of their joint labours. But much as the reading of it inspired me, reminding me as it did of our guru's exposition of the *sādhana*, I soon realized it was too long for me, especially as I was already practising two other *sādhanas*. I therefore went to see Dudjom Rimpoche and laid my difficulties before him. He responded with sympathy and concern, and at once promised to compose a shorter, simpler version of the *sādhana* for my especial benefit. He was as good as his word, and it was not many weeks before he gave me, written with his own hand, a copy of the promised text. John Driver, who was still in Kalimpong, translated it for me, on second thoughts replacing 'Hell-Annihilator' with the more euphonious 'Confounder of Narak'.

In the course of the next few months, I visited Dudjom Rimpoche several times, each time putting questions to him about the 'Order of Preliminaries to the Confounder of Narak', as my new *sādhana* was called, and each time received from him prompt and clear replies. Sometimes it was John Driver who accompanied me and acted as translator, sometimes it was my Tibetan disciple Prajnaloka. More than once we arrived at Madhav Nikunj to find scores of people – men, women, and children – camping in the grounds or respectfully circumambulating the house, rosaries in their hands and mantras and prayers on their lips. Most of them were Sherpas, some of whom had come a long way in order to see Dudjom Rimpoche and obtain his blessing, for the whole Sherpa community was deeply devoted to the Rimpoche and regarded themselves as his disciples. How this had come about I did not know. He had evidently made a strong impression on them, but whether on account of his character and personality, or his great reputation as a Vajrayāna master, or his being the current representative of a line of gurus to which they traditionally owed allegiance, it was not easy to tell.

Dudjom Rimpoche had certainly made a strong impression on me, both at Rinkingpong and as he expounded to my four *wong*-brothers and me the visualizations and other practices of the Essence of Profound Meaning. At Rinkingpong it was his absolute stillness which had impressed me, but in the Madhav Nikunj shrine-room it was his liveliness and spontaneity. These qualities showed themselves in his graceful, harmonious gestures, in the joyful, amused expression that lit up his soft, almost feminine features, and in the modulations of his rather hoarse voice. At Rinkingpong he had worn the simple, dark blue *bokku* that was his usual outdoor costume, but at home he permitted himself more freedom. Once or twice, when the weather was hot, he slipped his arms out of his *bokku* and sat with empty sleeves knotted round his waist in the rather swashbuckling style favoured by some Tibetan men. On another occasion – it may have been when giving the Vajrasattva initiation – he sported a stetson and a colourful Hawaiian shirt, into the breast pocket of which was stuffed a thick wad of currency notes. His long hair was usually plaited into a braid and wound round his head. Sometimes he wore it spread out on his shoulders, which accentuated the rather feminine cast of his features, and sometimes, again, he tied it in a topknot like a yogi.

If at Rinkingpong Dudjom Rimpoche had seemed to be at peace, in the deepest sense, with himself and with the world, at Madhav Nikunj it was as though he took delight in being alive. It was a delight that had nothing to do with craving or attachment but was a purely spiritual emotion that had its source in a profound insight into the ultimate truth of things. He could be compared, in fact, to a great ocean, the depths of which were absolutely calm, but on whose surface innumerable waves danced and sparkled in the sunlight.

As well as answering my questions about the Order of Preliminaries, Dudjom Rimpoche explained that the text of the *sādhana* was extracted from one of the sections of a Nyingma tantra of the Māyājāla class. The literal meaning of the Sanskrit word *māyājāla* was 'net of delusion' or 'magic net', but its actual meaning, in the context of the Vajrayāna, was 'assembly (or multitude) of *nirmāṇakāyas* and *sambhogakāyas*'. The *abhiṣekas* for the practice of the *sādhana* were included in the Māyājāla *abhiṣeka* but not vice versa. They were therefore properly styled Confounder of Narak *sādhanas*, *not* Māyājāla *sādhanas*. Those who wished to practise the Māyājāla *sādhanas* had to obtain the *abhiṣekas* of the hundred or so wrathful and peaceful deities, all of whom were emanations of Vajrasattva, who was the central figure of the Māyājāla mandala.

In order to make perfectly clear to me the place of the Order of Preliminaries within the Nyingma system, the Rimpoche skipped down from his throne and, sitting beside me, drew on a blank page in my notebook a kind of genealogical tree showing how the Order of Preliminaries was affiliated to the Essence of Profound Meaning, this to one of the eighteen 'elephant' tantras, and these to the Māyājāla Tantra, one of the 'great' tantras, which itself belonged to a subdivision of Mahāyoga Tantra, one of the three divisions of *Anuttarayoga* Tantra. He also explained that there were two lineages of bodhisattva ordination, one going back to Nāgārjuna and Āryadeva, the other going back to Asaṅga and Vasubandhu. The first was called the 'Profound View' lineage, the second the 'Extensive Activity' lineage. He also took the trouble of showing me how to make the *mudrās* that accompanied the various offering mantras, demonstrating them in a graceful, fluid manner I could not hope to emulate.

For a year or two after this, I saw nothing of Dudjom Rimpoche, probably because I was away on tour for much of the time. I did, however, have news of him from time to time, and was one day shocked to hear that he had been arrested by the West Bengal police and was being held in custody in Siliguri. News of the arrest spread like wildfire among the Buddhists of the area, many of whom were not only shocked but puzzled and alarmed. Convinced that he had done nothing wrong, and that the authorities must have made a mistake, they demanded his immediate release. The Sherpas, faithful as ever, circumambulated the jail in which their guru was being held. Such of them as were familiar with the legendary biography of Padmasambhava may well have been reminded of the episode in which, having been falsely accused to the king, he is arrested, beaten, and bound to a stake and the wood heaped up around him set on fire. He is delivered by a miracle, Buddhas and deities coming to his aid.[383] No miracles delivered Dudjom Rimpoche, unless it was by virtue of the fervent prayers of his disciples. He was released after a month without charge. Why he had been arrested in the first place nobody knew, but there were many rumours in circulation. One rumour was to the effect that Dudjom Rimpoche's wife had quarrelled with the Maharani of Sikkim and that the latter had engineered the Rimpoche's arrest in order to get even with her. According to another rumour, the arrest was due to sectarian rivalry, it having been brought about by Kusho Bakula, the Ladakhi incarnate lama who was both a Gelug monk and a Deputy Minister in the Government of India. I found it difficult to credit either of these explanations, or indeed any of the others I heard. The reason for Dudjom Rimpoche's arrest and incarceration remained a mystery to me, as did so much that went on within the Tibetan diaspora in Kalimpong.

In 1961 I renewed my contact with Dudjom Rimpoche, if indeed it had ever really been interrupted. He already knew about my work among the followers of the late Dr Ambedkar in the plains, and visiting him one afternoon in May, shortly after returning from my latest preaching tour, I asked him what would be the most suitable form of meditation for newcomers to Buddhism. In asking this question I had in mind those followers of Dr Ambedkar who had recently converted to Buddhism from Hinduism, in which they were treated as Untouchables, and who wanted to practise Buddhist meditation. The Rimpoche replied that according to the tantras there were three types of practice, corresponding to the three types of practitioner: low, middling, and superior. He then proceeded to give a brief explanation of each of the three types of practice in turn. The first type consisted mainly in the development of compassion for all sentient beings, inasmuch as in the course of the beginningless round of births and deaths, all beings have at one time or another been our fathers and mothers. In the second type, the practitioner visualizes a deity (a Buddha or a bodhisattva) in front of him, then visualizes light coming from the deity's heart and entering him through the crown of his head. He also practises the four *brahma vihāras* or 'divine abodes'. In the third, the practitioner identifies his body, speech, and mind with those of the deity and reflects that all forms are the deity's forms, all speech the deity's mantra, and all mental states the deity's mind. All three types of practice begin with mantra recitation and conclude with dedication of merits.

Like all my Tibetan teachers, Dudjom Rimpoche, though he adhered firmly to his own tradition, was able to respect, even to appreciate, other forms of Buddhism. Thus when I asked him to be one of the speakers at a public meeting I was organizing in connection with the death anniversary of Jetsun Tsongkhapa, the founder of the Gelug school, he readily consented. That year the anniversary fell on 2 December. On that day the famous golden image of Tsongkhapa was taken in a colourful, mile-long procession from the Tharpa Choling Gompa, Tirpai, to the Town Hall, where the meeting took place. The chief speaker was Trijang Rimpoche,[384] who was then visiting Kalimpong, and whom I met several times. Also present on the platform, along with Dudjom Rimpoche, were Mindoling Doong Rimpoche, the titular head of the Nyingma school, Khamtrul Rimpoche, Dhardo Rimpoche, Tomo Geshe Rimpoche, Pabongkhapa Rimpoche, and the new abbot of Tharpa Choling Gompa,[385] who was studying English with me. Most of these lamas addressed the gathering, as did Parashmani Pradhan, a well-known figure in the Nepali literary world, Prajnaloka, and myself. In the course of his speech, Trijang Rimpoche remarked that a celebration of that kind had not been possible even in Tibet. It was, in fact, the first time that Tsongkhapa's death anniversary had been celebrated in India, and the significance of the occasion was marked by a truly record attendance. So great was the crowd that a thousand people, unable to gain admittance, had to listen to the speeches through the loudspeaker system outside the building. On the following day the image, having been reverently kept in the Town Hall all night, was taken in procession back to the Tharpa Choling Gompa, where a small function was held. I subsequently received a letter of congratulations from the Dalai Lama, who had probably heard about the celebration from Trijang Rimpoche.

12

ARRIVALS AND DEPARTURES

The Triyana Vardhana Vihara was not a very big monastery; indeed, it consisted of little more than a four-roomed stone hermitage to which guest accommodation, in the form of a six-roomed thatched cottage, had been added. Running the Vihara nonetheless involved a good deal of work, especially as it was the centre of my Buddhist activities not only in Kalimpong but throughout the surrounding area and beyond. I therefore needed a helper, or at least someone who would look after the domestic side of things, supervise the cook, and deal with visitors when I was away.

The first of these helpers was Khemasiri, a Thai monk who had been staying with me at Everton Villa and moved to the Vihara with me. He was one of a group of four or five Thai *bhikkhus* who were studying at Shantiniketan, the rural international university started by Rabindranath Tagore, the famous Bengali poet, novelist, and dramatist. They were at Shantiniketan ostensibly to improve their English, but most of their time was spent together, when they spoke only Thai, with the result that, whatever else they may have learned, there was little improvement in their English. Khemasiri was very dissatisfied with this state of affairs. More single-minded than the other monks, and more determined, he realized that if there was to be a real improvement in his English he would have to give up his studies at Shantiniketan and move to a place where there were no Thais and where he would be forced to speak English. He had therefore come to join me at Everton Villa in 1956, arriving in time to help me organize the celebrations with which the Buddhists of Kalimpong marked the 2,500th Buddha Jayanti.

Khemasiri was a man of about my own age. Hard-working, and conscientious to a fault, he had a worried look that would deepen into a frown when he was concentrating. During his time at Everton Villa I helped him with his English, which improved considerably, and he was happy to assist me in various ways. When I moved to the hillside property that became the Triyana Vardhana Vihara he moved with me, for he valued our association no less than I did and wanted it to continue. Unfortunately, we had not been many weeks in residence when Khemasiri was taken ill. Tuberculosis was diagnosed, and he was admitted to the TB Sanatorium in Kurseong, a small hill station situated between Siliguri and Darjeeling. He was not at all happy there, and in a long letter to me he complained bitterly about the noise and confusion of the place and about the amount of quarrelling that went on. He was adamant that he did *not* have tuberculosis, despite the continued bleeding, and in letter after letter he spoke of his wish to return to Kalimpong and help me in my work, possibly accompanying me on my preaching tours in the plains. But it was not to be. Khemasiri's condition deteriorated, and the Thai consul in Calcutta made arrangements for him to be flown back to Thailand. The next letter I received from him was dated from the 'Hospital for Monks' in Bangkok. His health had improved, he wrote, and he was thinking of returning to India. I did not hear from him again.

For some months I was without a helper; but one turned up in the end, in the person of Sugatapriya, a young Theravādin monk from Assam. Like Khemasiri, he wanted to improve his English. Unlike Khemasiri, however, he was not very hard-working, and spent much of his time either lying on his bed or gossiping in the kitchen with the cook. He was one of those who appeared to believe that if they lived with me, their knowledge of the English language would increase automatically, and that they would absorb its grammar and vocabulary by way of a kind of pedagogical osmosis. Nonetheless, he made himself useful in various small ways, such as making out the weekly shopping lists, and for this I was grateful. He left the Vihara after little more than a year, no doubt thinking he had absorbed enough English for the time being. For the next two years I had no permanent, live-in helper, and had to make do with such occasional assistance as was forthcoming from Prajnaloka and from visiting Thai *bhikkhus*.

The Thai *bhikkhus* came from Shantiniketan and were the same group to which poor Khemasiri had once belonged and which he had felt obliged to leave if there was to be a real improvement in his English. They came during their summer vacation, for Shantiniketan, a hundred miles north of Calcutta, was at that time of year unbearably hot and humid, and they were glad to escape to the cool of the hills. Junior to me in years, though not necessarily in ordination, they were, possibly with one exception, more like students in yellow robes than real monks. But they were sociable and friendly, helped me in whatever ways they could, and joined me in the shrine-room twice a day for puja and meditation. With one of them in particular I became good friends. This was Maha Prom, a big, jovial, moon-faced Thai who was a little older than the rest, and who, after returning to Thailand a few years later, disrobed and became an officer in the Thai police. He and his companions often spoke of Thailand, which they very much wanted me to visit. Unlike India, it was a Buddhist country; monks were highly respected there, and were provided by a generous laity with every comfort and convenience. Good preachers were especially appreciated, popular ones being showered not just with robes and shoulder bags but with fountain pens, watches, cameras, radios, televisions, and, in short, with whatever was not expressly prohibited by the Vinaya. If I was to go to Thailand and deliver a few sermons, so they assured me, I would be richly rewarded, instead of having to give them for nothing, as in poverty-stricken India.

Thailand was a veritable paradise for Buddhist monks, it seemed! But I had no wish to go there, despite the tempting prospects held out to me by Maha Prom and the others; and I had no doubt, in any case, that Buddhism in Thailand would get on quite well without me. At the same time, I was intrigued by what I had heard. Did Thai lay people *really* give the monks television sets? And in that case, what kind of programmes did they usually watch? The lay people indeed gave the monks television sets, I was told. Nothing was too good for the monks, since they had given up the world (at least for the time being). Every monastery had a television set, at least in Bangkok, and the favourite programmes were those devoted to Thai kick-boxing – a vicious and potentially lethal sport.

Besides Thai monks from Shantiniketan, during the summer months the Vihara put up, at different times, two Vietnamese monks from the Nalanda Pali Institute (as it was then called) and a Ladakhi monk from Sarnath. Though all three were followers of the Mahāyāna, they wore, as more in keeping with the climate and culture of India, the yellow cotton robes of the Theravāda. Both Thích Minh Châu and Thích Thien Châu, the two Vietnamese monks, were studying Pāli with my own teacher, Jagdish Kashyap, who, shortly after leaving me in Kalimpong with the parting injunction that I was to stay there and work for the good of Buddhism, had returned to his native Bihar and there established, not far from the ruins of the great Nālandā monastic university, its modest modern successor, the Nalanda Pali Institute. Minh Châu, who was very much the senior of the two, stayed for only a few days, but Thien Châu stayed for a much longer period. In fact he came more than once, and was with me during my final months in Kalimpong. A gentle, kindly soul, who got on well with the other members of the Vihara community, he not only gave me a good deal of help but gave it in an unobtrusive, sensitive manner which made it doubly acceptable. In short, I found in him the ideal helper, and I hope he found in me someone worth helping. Like Minh Châu, he would have liked me to visit Vietnam, both of them having assured me that I would be welcome to teach at Van Hanh Buddhist University in Saigon.

Vietnam was traditionally a Buddhist country, its Buddhism being a combination of Chan and Pure Land teaching and practice. Since 1954 it had been divided into communist North Vietnam, led by Ho Chi Minh, and pro-Western South Vietnam, led by Ngo Dinh Diem, neither of which could be described as a paradise for Buddhist monks of any persuasion. President Diem was a Roman Catholic, as was his younger brother who was in charge of Intelligence and the Secret Police. His elder brother was the Catholic Archbishop of Hué. It was therefore not surprising that under the despotic regime of this unholy trinity, as under French colonial rule, the Catholic minority should have been supported and encouraged, while the less organized Buddhist majority was discriminated against, suppressed, and finally systematically persecuted. In 1963 things came to a head. On 6 May President Diem issued an order prohibiting the Buddhists of Hué from flying the Buddhist flag on the Buddha's birthday two days later, even though a few days earlier, on the occasion of a Catholic festival, the

Vatican flag had been flown all over the city. On 8 May, their leaders having failed to get the order rescinded, the Buddhists of Hué protested against the ban by going in procession from Tu Dam Pagoda to the radio station. Government troops broke up the procession with tear gas, then fired on the crowd, killing twelve people and wounding more than fifty. The monks, nuns, and lay people of South Vietnam then presented the Government with five requests, namely, (1) that the Government rescind the order prohibiting the flying of the Buddhist flag, (2) that Buddhism benefit from the same special treatment granted to the Roman Catholic missions, (3) that the Government stop arresting and terrorizing Buddhists, (4) that the Buddhist clergy and laity be free to practise their faith and to spread it, and (5) that the Government pay equitable compensation for the people killed and punish those responsible in a fitting manner.

These requests formed part of a manifesto, the concluding sentence of which read, 'We are ready to sacrifice ourselves until these reasonable requests are granted.' Diem did not find the requests reasonable, and events soon showed him and the other members of the Catholic oligarchy that the Buddhists meant what they said. As I have written elsewhere,

> On 11 June a 67-year-old monk burnt himself to death in a crowded Saigon thoroughfare in protest against the Government's persecution of the Buddhists. The monk, Thích Qảng Đức, struck a match after his saffron robes were drenched with petrol, and sat motionless in the meditation posture while the flames enveloped him.[386]

It was an image that was flashed round the globe. Like thousands – perhaps millions – of other people I was struck by the erect posture of the old monk and his apparent insensibility to the flames swirling around him. Examples of such self-immolation for the sake of the Dharma were not unknown in the annals of Chinese Buddhism, of which Vietnamese Buddhism was largely an extension, the scriptural basis for the practice being a passage in the *White Lotus Sūtra* in which a monk makes himself into a living lamp in honour of the Buddha.[387] These accounts could be dismissed as mere legends, or as not meant to be taken literally. But it was not possible so to dismiss Quảng Đức's act of self-sacrifice. That act had not been performed in an age remote from our own, nor did it feature in the colourful pages of an ancient sacred book. It had taken place in the middle of the twentieth century, had been witnessed by hundreds of people, and had been captured on film by a Western photographer. It was not easy to imagine the depth of spiritual practice that had enabled the 67-year-old Quảng Đức to perform such a calm, deliberate act of self-immolation for the sake of the Dharma. I knew that I was devoted to the Dharma, and that for ten years and more I had worked for the good of Buddhism as enjoined by Kashyap-ji. But I was nonetheless aware that I did not possess a tithe of Quảng Đức's faith and devotion, and I doubted if I would ever have been capable of making the supreme sacrifice he had made.

Be that as it might – for one never really knew what one was capable of – South Vietnam's Roman Catholic oligarchy remained unmoved by Quảng Đức's death. 'If any more monks want to barbecue themselves,' Mme Nhu, the president's sister-in-law, told reporters, 'I'll be happy to provide the petrol and a match.'

More monks did want to 'barbecue' themselves, and in the course of the next few months, as the Diem government declared martial law, desecrated and destroyed major pagodas throughout South Vietnam, imprisoned thousands of monks and nuns, and held demonstrating students in concentration camps, eight more monks and one nun followed Quảng Đức's heroic example. These events, which were widely reported in the Indian press, stirred me deeply, and I could not but empathize with the anguish of Minh Châu and Thien Châu as they heard of the sufferings of their fellow countrymen. But worse was to come. On 1 August the Diem government was overthrown by a military *coup d'état* in which both the president and his younger brother were killed. The United States government and the CIA were behind the *coup*, for Washington had become convinced that by persecuting the Buddhists, Diem was undermining South Vietnam's – and the United States' – fight against Communism. By the time I returned to England in 1964, the United States had begun its military involvement in the Vietnam war – an involvement that was to turn the country into an inferno.

Before that, however, on 22 November 1963, John F. Kennedy, the president of the United States, had been assassinated in Dallas, Texas. Like countless other people, I can remember where I was when I heard the news. It was a fine winter's day, with brilliant sunshine, cloudless blue skies, and a perfect view of the snows of Mount Kanchenjunga.

I was on my way to the bazaar, and on passing the entrance to the Himalayan Hotel I caught sight of Annie Perry, the hotel's elderly proprietress, standing in the front garden. 'Have you heard the news?' she called out to me, 'President Kennedy has been shot.'

Though I have no similar recollection of the circumstances in which I first saw the picture of Quảng Đức meditating amid the flames, that image nonetheless remains vividly present to me, a permanent reminder of what devotion to the Dharma really means. This devotion can express itself in a number of different ways, most of them much less dramatic than the old Vietnamese monk's. Lama Lobsang, the Ladakhi monk from Sarnath, expressed his devotion to the Dharma by acting as the guardian and teacher of the Ladakhi Buddhist boys who were students at the Maha Bodhi High School at Sarnath. When he came to stay with me he did not come alone. With him came another monk and more than a dozen of his young charges. I made the guest cottage over to them, so that they formed a separate unit within the Vihara community, doing their own cooking, and with their own daily routine of classes and outings and sessions in the shrine-room. Lama Lobsang was a Gelugpa, and a disciple of Kusho Bakula. Short, active, and good-humoured, he was perhaps ten years younger than me. I admired the way he handled the boys, who, it seemed, were all destined for the monastic life. Though he was a bit of a disciplinarian, not hesitating to cuff or slap them if they misbehaved, I could see that he loved them dearly and was utterly devoted to their welfare. He and the other monk were not of any help to me during their stay. Indeed, they were not in a position to be of help. But I was glad of their company, which made the Vihara feel more like a monastery and less like my own private hermitage.

I was also glad of the company, for three weeks, of Sister Amita Nisatta, who so far as I remember was the only woman ever to stay at the Vihara. Born in Sweden some forty years earlier, she had worked as a nurse, and was now a Theravādin nun, with a shaven head and yellow robes. As I had been relieved to discover, she was in temperament and behaviour very different from the turbulent and exigent French Nun, being calm, dignified, and undemanding. Though she spent much of her time either studying the Pāli scriptures in her room in the guest cottage, or meditating in the shrine-room, she was by no means unsociable, and in the course of her stay we had a number of serious discussions about the Dharma – or Dhamma, as she would have said – and about the practice of meditation. These discussions seem to have made a deep impression on her, for she kept in touch with me until her death in Stockholm many years later. For my part, I remember her homely red face, and her warm smile, with considerable affection.

Sister Amita Nisatta may have been the only woman to have stayed at the Vihara, but she was not the only Western woman to have seen the place or even the only Western Buddhist nun to have done so. There was Sister Vajira, formerly Miss Eileen Robinson, from England. I had been familiar with her name since my earliest days in India, for she had published from Sarnath English versions of the first and second parts of the *Sutta-Nipāta*, and these were among the first books I bought after my arrival in the subcontinent in 1944.[388] She was not a very educated woman, however, or even particularly literate. Having been left some money by an old lady she had nursed through her last illness, she had moved to India before the War, built herself a cottage at Sarnath, and become a Theravādin nun, her preceptor being a Sinhalese monk with whom I subsequently became well acquainted. By the late 1950s she was living in Darjeeling, and it was there that I first met her. She wore the maroon woollen robes of a Tibetan Buddhist nun, though I never knew whether she had received a Tibetan ordination or was simply adapting to the climate of the hills. Her straight grey hair was cut short, just covering her ears, and from behind her spectacles she looked out on the mad doings of the world with an expression of amused tolerance. After that first meeting I went to see her whenever I was in Darjeeling, and we corresponded regularly. From time to time she would enclose a small cheque with her letter, for she was a kind, generous woman who did much good in Bhutia Busti, the village on the outskirts of Darjeeling where she had settled.

It must have been through me that Sister Vajira came to know Jivaka. In any case, the transsexual English doctor confided his secret to her, presumably under the same 'seal of the confessional' that he had confided it to me. She had not been able to keep the secret for long. On one of her visits to the Kazi and Kazini, with whom she occasionally stayed, she had communicated it to the Kazini. According to the latter, it had slipped out one evening when Sister Vajira had partaken of her second *thumba*. The Kazini was less surprised to learn that Jivaka was a transsexual than she was mortified to discover, the next time we met, that I had known about it all along, and she reproached me for not having shared the information with her, an omission she seemed to regard as a breach of friendship. That Sister Vajira had communicated Jivaka's secret to the Kazini did not mean that the two women were at all close. Sister Vajira's plebeian manners jarred on the Kazini's more aristocratic sensibilities, while the high-handed way in which 'dear Kazini' dealt with people made Sister Vajira feel uncomfortable.

I was not surprised to learn that the English nun had partaken of a *thumba* when staying at Chakhung House. More than once, on my going to see her, she had appeared to be not quite herself. I had thought nothing about it at the time, but later I came to know that she was in the habit of following St Paul's advice and taking a little wine for the good of her stomach,[389] except that the wine was whisky. This certainly did not lower her in the estimation of the local Buddhists, who being Nyingmapas did not have the same abhorrence of alcohol as their Gelug – and Theravādin – co-religionists. Indeed, the elderly head lama of Bhutia Busti Gompa, which was a sort of branch monastery of Pemayangtse, invited her to move into the *gompa* and live with him there as his consort. She accepted the invitation, and for two years she had a recognized place in the religious life of the local Nyingmapa community. At the end of that time she left the *gompa* with as little fuss as she had entered it, and moved into the wooden hillside chalet she had built for herself nearby. It was there that I saw her for the last time. She was an unusual woman, even a remarkable one, and I wish someone had written her biography. Her life ended tragically. She died when her chalet was swept away by a landslide in which dozens of people were killed.

After the departure of Sugatapriya, my second full-time helper, the Thai *bhikkhus* from Shantiniketan, Thien Châu from Nalanda, Lama Lobsang and his boys from Sarnath, and Sister Amita Nisatta all contributed to the ongoing life of the Vihara community, as did a number of other short-term guests from different parts of India and from abroad. It was only with the arrival on the scene of Lobsang Norbu and Thubden that I had the regular, full-time help I needed – had it, in fact, twice over, in that I now had two such helpers instead of one. Both were Gelug *getsuls* or novices, though only Thubden, the younger of the two, kept his head shaved and wore the maroon monastic robes. Lobsang Norbu had long since abandoned his robes and adopted Western dress. This was perhaps not surprising. In Tibet he had been a *dubdor* or 'fighting monk', with long hair on one side of his head, a smoke-blackened face, and robes worn in a distinctive way. He was proud of having been a *dubdor*, however. The *dubdors* were the true monks, he once assured me, very earnestly. Their only possessions were the clothes they wore and a small thangka of their *yidam* or tutelary deity. When I asked him what weapons they had, he replied, with great simplicity, that they had sticks and stones. They practised stone throwing every day and he himself had been quite good at it. If they happened to kill anyone they had to disrobe and could not be a *getsul* any more. The *dubdors* were strict observers of the monastic law. They never went with women, though some of them had boys. He had never been anyone's boy, though he had been asked many times. The new abbot of Tharpa Choling Gompa, who knew him well, would bear him out in this. I was not surprised that he should have been 'asked many times', for at twenty-seven or twenty-eight he was still good-looking, with a broad smile that showed his magnificent white teeth, and as a young *dubdor* he must have been doubly so, despite his soot-blackened face.

Thubden was recommended to me by his uncle, real or adoptive, with whom he had been living in the bazaar. This uncle, a small-time trader, was an ally of Dhardo Rimpoche in his resistance to the officials and a leader of one of the Tibetan factions in Kalimpong. He came to the Vihara one afternoon, bringing Thubden, and begged me to take him on. I was not anxious to have another mouth to feed, but reflecting that he must have consulted Dhardo Rimpoche about his nephew, and be acting in accordance with the Rimpoche's advice, in the end I agreed to give Thubden a place at the Vihara. It was not long before I was glad I had done so. Thubden turned out to be a very willing worker. In fact he enjoyed work. He particularly enjoyed serving me, whether it was washing my robes, cleaning and tidying my room, or airing my books, which in the damp weather quickly became mildewed. He and Lobsang Norbu worked well together, though there was a certain amount of rivalry between them, and I sometimes thought that Thubden was a little jealous of his older and more experienced colleague.

Lobsang Norbu was also recommended to me. In his case the recommendation came from Rechung Rimpoche, whose *chunzu* or estate manager he had once been. Having been connected with the Rimpoche, and through him with the aristocratic Peunkhang family, he was well versed in Tibetan etiquette and in the niceties of ecclesiastical protocol, and was therefore of great help to me in my dealings with incarnate lamas whom I did not know very well and who had to be treated with a certain amount of ceremony. He knew how many cushions should go to make up a particular incarnate lama's throne, and on what occasions a *khata* or ceremonial white scarf ought to be offered. Though still young, he had travelled widely in Tibet and had worked for a variety of masters. A monk was the best kind of master, he had found; the work was light, and you would be well treated. An unmarried layman was the next best; the work might be heavier, but you would not be treated too badly. The worst kind of master was a married man, for his wife would scold you and beat you, never allow you to rest, and try to get as much work out of you as she possibly could.

Lobsang's duties at the Vihara were certainly light, and I believe I treated him well. By Tibetan standards I probably treated him very well. He generally accompanied me when I went to the bazaar, walking a step or two behind me. He was always pleased when I went to see Dhardo Rimpoche, as I frequently did, for besides having a great respect for the Rimpoche he was on friendly terms with Gelong Lobsang, the Rimpoche's attendant monk, and liked to hobnob with him while the Rimpoche and I talked. One day we arrived at the Old Bhutan Palace to find, chained up on the veranda of the upper floor where the Rimpoche lived, a fierce-looking Tibetan mastiff that lunged at us as we passed, barking furiously. Lobsang Norbu's eyes gleamed. 'That very good dog,' he whispered to me in English, 'If you ask Rimpoche, he give you that dog.'

I did ask Rimpoche, and he did give me the mastiff. He was not sorry to part with it, for it refused to live peaceably with the Rimpoche's little Tibetan terriers, which it clearly would have liked to tear to pieces, and its furious barking frightened the pet mynah the Rimpoche had taught to say '*oṃ māṇi peme hūṃ*'. Strange to relate, Lobsang had no sooner threaded a rope through the mastiff's spiked collar than it seemed to know we were now its masters and made no attempt to attack us. On the way back to the Vihara, though, it gave us a lot of trouble, especially when we passed through the High Street. It wanted to stop and fight every dog we encountered, so that it had to be dragged along bodily at the end of Lobsang's rope. I did not keep it for long, as it had to be kept chained up and Lobsang and I were the only ones who could go anywhere near it. Fortunately, we were able to find it a master who needed a fierce Tibetan guard dog more than the Vihara did.

Both Lobsang Norbu and Thubden could turn their hand to cooking in an emergency, as when the cook happened to be unwell, but they were rarely called upon to do so. The Vihara's first cook was Padam, an active, talkative Nepalese in his thirties who had worked for me when I was living at Everton Villa. He was a good cook, but too fond of the *thumba*, and a few months after Khemasiri and I moved into the Vihara I dismissed him for drunkenness. I remember him chiefly on account of his father, who was a *jhakkhri* or sorcerer. The old man once came to the Vihara to see his son. He was very decently dressed in traditional Nepalese costume, with a long black coat and a black pillbox hat. Whether due to age or illness he walked stiffly, yet he was very erect, and gave an impression of sinister dignity. The expression of his gaunt face and glittering eyes was very strange, and the Scottish Presbyterian missionaries who lived on the other side of town would probably not have found it difficult to believe that the withered old man was in league with the Evil One, or even that he was the Evil One himself. He died while Padam was still working for me, leaving his son with the problem of what to do with the paraphernalia of his sorcery. In the end, greatly fearing, he tied everything up in a cloth and threw it into the River Teesta.

Belief in sorcery was widespread among the Nepalese; there were many practitioners of the art, and it took many forms. One day, Durgaprasad came and told me that large stones, each of them marked with a cross or the figure 4, had been falling on the roof of their house out of a clear sky. His mother was greatly alarmed, he said. She believed that the family was being attacked by means of black magic and she appealed to me for help. He did not believe in black magic himself, my young friend added, but he had seen the stones falling and they definitely came from the sky. Having told him to assure his mother that I would do what I could to help, I went to see Dhardo Rimpoche. Someone was trying to harm the family, he said, after listening carefully to my account. The cross and the figure 4 both meant death. I was to leave it to him; he would see what he could do.

When Durga came to see me a few days later it was with the news that the showers of stones had ceased. But when I asked Dhardo Rimpoche what he had done he only laughed merrily and said, 'I just did a little puja.' Tibetan white magic had proved stronger, it seemed, than Nepalese black magic.

Padam was succeeded in the kitchen by a series of three or four short-term cooks, one of whom was known as Kazi. He was extremely dark, and so short that he had to stand on a stool in order to do the cooking on the kitchen range. He also had an unusually deep base voice. What I did not know when I engaged him was that he wanted to be a sorcerer. It therefore was not long before I heard coming from the kitchen, in the evening, the sharp 'tap tap' of a little drum. Kazi was trying to work himself up into a state of trance in which he would levitate, so I was told; but he never succeeded in doing this, and left after a few months – presumably to apprentice himself to a sorcerer. It was only with the appearance of Kaila that the Vihara had a permanent cook, that is to say, one who stayed for the remainder of my time in Kalimpong. Kaila was a 20-year-old Lepcha with a light, yellowish complexion and a shock of black hair. Like his predecessors, he did not live at the Vihara but came in each day. He was quiet and efficient, and besides being a reasonably good cook he knew a lot about crops and cultivation, which added to his usefulness. The Kazini strongly suspected that he colluded with my old Brahmin sharecropper and that between them they cheated me of my full share of the *makkai* harvest. She was probably right, but I had learned not to look too closely into such matters. Complete honesty was no more to be found in the hills than in the plains.

13
THE CHINESE HERMIT

Sitting in my room one summer afternoon, I heard footsteps coming down the steep track behind the Vihara, and went out onto the veranda to meet whoever it might be. A few minutes later I was greeting, and being greeted by, a strangely assorted pair. One was a short Thai of indeterminate age, the other a thin, angular young Westerner who overtopped his companion by at least a head and a half. Both wore Theravādin monastic robes and carried begging-bowls.

The Thai visitor was Phra Vivekananda, with whom I was already acquainted. Though a student at the Nalanda Pali Institute, he was very different from the other Thai monks studying in India. Unlike many of them, he had not been made a novice as a boy but had become a monk when of mature age, after a rather turbulent secular life in the course of which he had been a professional kick-boxer. He was still very fit, and liked to demonstrate kicks and jumps to anyone who was interested. Friendly and unpretentious, and deeply devoted to the practice of meditation, he was in many ways an ideal monk. His young companion turned out to be English. As I soon learned, his name was Jivaka, he was twenty-seven years old, and a year earlier he had been ordained in London as a Theravādin novice by a senior Sinhalese monk who had taken part in my own *bhikkhu* ordination in 1950. He had already visited Sarnath, Bodh Gaya, and Nalanda (where he had met Vivekananda), and he and Vivekananda had just spent a month travelling in Assam with other monks and meeting the local Buddhists.

The two visitors stayed for only a few days. Jivaka would have liked to stay longer, but he had promised the abbot of the Thai temple at Bodh Gaya that he would spend the Rains Retreat there, and the rainy season was fast approaching. Eighteen months later, however, he came and stayed with me for a much longer period. By this time – November 1961 – he had accompanied me on one of my winter preaching tours in the plains, had spent nine months in Bangalore with Buddharakshita, the companion of my early wanderings as a freelance ascetic, and had there been ordained as a *bhikkhu* and given the name Khantipālo, 'One Who Keeps Patient'. During his three years in India, Khantipālo spent altogether a year or more with me, either on tour in the plains or at the Triyana Vardhana Vihara. His time at the Vihara was interrupted by a three-month pilgrimage in Nepal, from March to June 1962, in the course of which he not only walked from Kusinara to Palpa Tansen, as Buddharakshita and I had done in 1949, shortly after our ordination as *sāmaṇeras*, but had continued on to Pukhara. Many of the Buddhists he met remembered me and my companion, and on one occasion Khantipālo was mistaken for me.

As I quickly realized, Khantipālo had been well-named by Buddharakshita. He indeed was one who 'kept patient', though I suspected he did not always find this easy. I also found him to be sincerely devoted to the monastic life, industrious, and willing – even eager – to learn. His only real weakness, so far as I could tell, was that he was rather lacking in self-confidence. Whether on tour in the plains or living at the Vihara we got on well together. Years later, in *Noble Friendship: Travels of a Buddhist Monk*, Khantipālo was to give a circumstantial account of life at the Vihara during his stay, including a detailed description of my daily routine.[390] He had evidently been pleased to find in me an experienced senior monk who could communicate with him in his own tongue. 'It would be hard to imagine', he confesses, 'what my own development in Dharma would have been like without [Sangharakshita's] example or his clear communication of the principles of the Dharma in a language that we shared.'[391] Khantipālo also generously acknowledges that my explanations of Mahāyāna practices had immensely widened his horizons, and that his Dharma life had been enriched by living with me and slowly absorbing my teachings.

The relationship was by no means so one-sided as these comments might suggest. I gained a lot from Khantipālo's presence at the Vihara, and

On teaching tour with Khantipālo

when we were on tour, at least, he was of real help to me. Though differing in character and temperament, our social and cultural backgrounds were similar. Both were converts to Buddhism, and both were practising the Dharma in a foreign land and within the context of the monastic life. Thus we had a good deal in common. What we had most in common in the circumstances, apart from the fact that we were both Buddhists, was that we had the same mother tongue, English. Khantipālo was glad to have found a teacher who could communicate the principles of the Dharma to him in his own tongue. I was no less glad to have found someone *to whom* I could communicate the Dharma in my own language. This was not to say that Khantipālo had never 'heard the Dharma' from the lips of English-speaking Sinhalese and Thai monks, nor was it to say that I had never imparted the Dharma to English-educated Indian audiences through the medium of my own language. What it meant was that – other factors being equal – the Dharma was best communicated when speaker and audience, teacher and disciple, had the same mother tongue and were well nurtured in that tongue. Where this was not the case, either because the teacher was imparting, or the disciple was hearing, the Dharma in a language not his own, the Dharma would be less well communicated than it might otherwise have been and, unless special care was taken, misunderstandings would be bound to occur.

I loved to communicate the Dharma. Communicating the Dharma was one of the greatest joys of my life, especially when the communication was through the medium of the spoken rather than the written word. But I found it frustrating when I was not able to give full expression to my understanding of the Dharma, such as it was, because English not being the mother tongue of my English-educated auditors there was a limit to the extent to which they could follow me and a limit, therefore, to the extent to which I could communicate the Dharma to them. With Khantipālo there was no such limit, which made his companionship all the more welcome.

In his account of our life at the Vihara, Khantipālo notes that our devotion to the Dharma was expressed mostly through speech (puja, Dharma talk) and mind (meditation, contemplation) but little through the body. For me, at least, this was to change (or perhaps had already changed), as I took up the Going for Refuge and Prostration practice under the direction of Kachu Rimpoche. Our devotion to the Dharma was also expressed through literary work. At the time, I must have been writing the group of articles that became *The Three Jewels*, as well as producing, as usual, editorials and book reviews for the Buddhist monthly journal I edited. Khantipālo was no less busy. During his first few months at the Vihara, before he left for his Nepal pilgrimage, he was giving a final shape to *Tolerance, A Study From Buddhist Sources*, his first published book,[392] materials for which he had started assembling while staying in Bangalore with Buddharakshita. The subject was one in which I was particularly interested, and I was therefore happy to discuss it with Khantipālo and to make a few suggestions.

There was a reason for my interest. It had not taken me long to discover, after my arrival in India, that on the subject of toleration, Hindus, in particular, had some confused and misleading ideas – ideas to which they clung tenaciously and which they did not like to have challenged. According to them, tolerance meant accepting that religions were all equally true, or were one in essence, or were all paths to the same ultimate goal (the variations on the theme were many), from which it followed that intolerance meant refusing to accept this 'essential unity of all religions' as it had been termed by one of its leading modern proponents. Hindus often criticized me for refusing to agree that there was no difference between Buddhism and Hinduism, for I found it difficult to believe that *ātman* and *anātman* – self and no-self – were really the same thing, or that theism and non-theism were different aspects of the same truth. Nor was that all. Intolerance also meant criticizing other religions, as I indeed sometimes did, the assumption apparently being that such criticism was sure to be followed, sooner or later, by violence towards the followers of those religions.

In an essay entitled 'The Nature of Buddhist Tolerance',[393] written ten years before my discussions with Khantipālo, I had sought to show that this was not true of Buddhism. Since they did not believe that all religions were true, the preachers of the Dharma felt free to criticize the false views (*mithyā-dṛṣṭi*) maintained by the religions and philosophies they encountered, as the Buddha himself had done.[394] At times they criticized them vigorously, drawing on all the resources of logic. Yet although they believed in the truth of their religion as ardently as any Christian bigot or Muslim fanatic, they never sought to impose it by force. The reason for their restraint was that Buddhism sees violence as springing from hatred, and hatred from ignorance. This ignorance was not merely intellectual, but spiritual, and consisted in the erroneous conception of 'things' and 'persons' as mysteriously ensouling an unchanging principle of individuality by which they were irreducibly differentiated from all other 'things' and 'persons'. By living in accordance with the Dharma, and practising its successive stages of ethics (*śīla*), meditation (*samādhi*), and wisdom (*prajñā*), the disciple transforms ignorance (*avidyā*) into Enlightenment (*bodhi*), and hatred (*dveṣa*) into compassion (*karuṇā*), which by its very nature cannot issue in violence. In the words of that early essay of mine,

> Buddhism, since it annihilates the erroneous conception of unchanging separate selfhood, stifles as it were ignorance, lust, and hatred in the womb, and permanently precludes the possibility of violence being used even for the advancement of its own tenets. The Dharma of the All-Enlightened and All-Compassionate One spares us the contradiction of spreading the gospel of love by means of the sword, and the paradox of burning alive men, women, and children who entertain religious opinions different

from our own, to show how tenderly we care for the salvation of their souls.[395]

Tolerance, A Study from Buddhist Sources, was not the only product of Khantipālo's pen during his stay at the Vihara. Like myself, he wrote articles and book reviews, some of them at my suggestion. He also wrote at least one letter to the press. In this he drew attention to the fact that certain Christian missionaries in Kalimpong were attempting the forced conversion of Tibetan refugee children. The letter was also signed by Sister Amita Nisatta, though I have no recollection of her staying at the Vihara at the same time as Khantipālo. After giving a colourful account of Dhardo Rimpoche's school at the Old Bhutan Palace, with its atmosphere of Tibetan culture and its cheerful-looking pupils in Tibetan costume, the letter continued,

> Contrast this with another school we saw, where instead of education in the rich tradition of Tibet, advantage is taken, by the Plymouth Brethren missionaries in charge of the orphans taught there. The missionaries admitted to an emissary of the Tibet Society, London, that they were not interested in educating the children or in teaching them handicrafts; they wanted only to convert them to Christianity. So that they are able to convert others, the children are taught Tibetan, Nepali and English.[396]
>
> The fifteen children we saw looked miserable and were ill-clad in European cast-off clothing. The atmosphere of the school-cum-orphanage seemed cold and cheerless. The children are kept strictly segregated from other Tibetans. Part of their time is occupied with the menial work of re-making the garden, though we were told that they were 'taught gardening'.
>
> Worst of all, many of the school and house walls displayed vile anti-Buddhist posters which were banned from public hoardings in Kalimpong by the Deputy Commissioner, Darjeeling. They are calculated to ridicule Buddhism in these Buddhist children's eyes and flaunt the claims of this narrow Christian sect as the only way to Salvation.

I had seen two of these posters a few weeks earlier. They were prominently displayed on the side of a little wooden building that I passed on my way to see Dhardo Rimpoche – a building I knew to be connected with one of the various Protestant missions. As I could not remember seeing the posters before, I stopped to take a closer look. Both were large and printed in black and red. One of them depicted a deep gorge, through which there flowed a mighty torrent. Two bridges spanned the gorge – one spun by a spider, the other a solid timber structure. A Tibetan lama pointed to the first bridge, above which was written, in Tibetan and English, 'Bridge of Good Works', while a Christian preacher pointed to the second bridge, on which was written 'Bridge of Faith in Jesus Christ'. Similarly, on the torrent was written 'Sin', on the cliff on the near side of the gorge 'the World', and on the cliff on the far side of the gorge 'Salvation'.

The other poster depicted a more dramatic scene, and needed no such explanations. On the left was a huge cross, cut deep into the solid rock. A young Tibetan girl was running towards the cross, and had almost reached it. Close behind her, also running, came an evil-looking Tibetan monk. He carried a knife, which he was about to plunge into the girl's back before she could take refuge inside the cross.

Tibetans who saw the posters were deeply shocked by them, as were other Buddhists of the town. They were particularly shocked by the second poster, with its infamous suggestion that Tibetan Buddhist monks were prepared to murder people in order to prevent them from becoming Christians. But though they were shocked by the posters, the Tibetans were reluctant to protest publicly against the denigration of their religion. Many of them were refugees, and they did not want the authorities to think of them as troublemakers. It therefore fell to me to do something about the posters. What I did was to write to the Deputy Commissioner, Darjeeling, whom in any case I knew, complaining that the posters were hurtful to the feelings of the Buddhists and requesting his intervention. I also pointed out that such posters were not conducive to harmony between the different communities of the town. The result was that the Deputy Commissioner wrote to the Subdivisional Officer, Kalimpong, whom I also knew, directing him to take action in the matter. The next time I passed the little wooden building, on my way to see Dhardo Rimpoche, I saw that the posters were no longer there.

Commenting on *Tolerance* forty years after its final shaping at the Triyana Vardhana Vihara, Khantipālo remarks, in *Noble Friendship*, that

> it is distinctly set against the view that Theravāda represents the one true Buddhism as propounded to me by Buddharakkhita, for one, while presenting a very liberal view of all Buddhist traditions, in line with Sangharakshita's thought.[397]

That liberal view was to be reinforced, during the months he spent with me after his return from Nepal, by our joint association with someone who, while generously sharing his knowledge of the Dharma with all who found their way to him, also refused to regard himself as a teacher or to accept disciples.

I must have first heard mention of Mr Chen in the mid-fifties, four or five years after my arrival in Kalimpong. Not that I then knew his name; all I heard was that a strange Chinese Buddhist was living in one of the larger buildings in the High Street, that he kept very much to himself, and that he was, in fact, a kind of hermit. An atmosphere of mystery surrounded the unknown Chinese Buddhist, at least so far as I was concerned. Joe Cann, who had met him once, told me that he did not welcome visitors, and that I should on no account try to see him. Some months later I learned that he had left his room in the High Street and was living in a bungalow situated on the edge of the Lower Bazaar. By this time I knew his name, and that he spoke English, and I resolved to call on him, despite Joe's warning. The worst that could happen was that he would scold me for disturbing him, or even refuse to see me. In fact, he greeted me cordially when I appeared on his doorstep late one afternoon, and invited me in.

Yogi Chen, as he came to be known, bore no resemblance to the austere, emaciated yogi of Buddhist and Hindu tradition. He was short and stout, with a chubby face that frequently wore a broad smile, and though no longer young he gave an impression of health and vigour. Far from being half-naked, he was decently clad in the Chinese-style shirt and baggy Chinese trousers that were, as I later discovered, his usual costume, though there were times when he would don the black gown and black skullcap of the Confucian scholar, or appear in the splendour of a sky-blue anorak and bright red baseball cap. He indeed spoke English, but his accent was so strong, and his mispronunciations were so frequent, that at times I found it difficult to follow him. Similarly, he did not always find it easy to make out who I was talking about when I mentioned the name of some Chinese Buddhist worthy of former times.

'Oh, you mean *so-and-so*!', he would exclaim, when he had puzzled it out, pronouncing the name in question very forcibly, with the correct tone. Out of politeness I never laughed at his mispronunciations, but Yogi Chen had no such inhibitions and laughed heartily at mine, which he seemed to find highly amusing.

These little difficulties over pronunciation did not really obstruct the flow of communication, and that evening I learned quite a lot about Yogi Chen. I learned that he never left the 'Five Leguminous Tree Hermitage', as he called his tiny bungalow after the five such trees that once stood before it, in whose place there were now five bamboo poles with prayer flags; that he spent the whole day meditating, except for the half-hour he devoted to literary work; that he had published several books in Chinese, including a volume of poems; that he had studied with many Tibetan gurus; that he was vehemently opposed to Communism; that for him Red China was 'Slave China'; and that he did not encourage visitors. Before I left, however, he told me I was free to visit him from time to time, and that I should come in the late afternoon or early evening. During the next four or five years, therefore, few months passed without my paying Yogi Chen a visit, if I was in Kalimpong, and I learned to appreciate the extent and variety of his meditative experience and the clarity and precision of his understanding of Buddhist doctrine. Occasionally, with his permission, I would take someone to see him, and thus it was that late one afternoon in the summer of 1962 I made my way to the Five Leguminous Tree Hermitage not alone but accompanied by Khantipālo.

The three of us probably discussed meditation, for it was either on this occasion, or shortly afterwards, that Yogi Chen undertook to give Khantipālo and me a talk on the subject. Whether this was his own idea, or the result of a request by his two yellow-robed visitors, I no longer recollect. Whichever it was, the talk proved to be a long one. It was given in weekly instalments, over a period of more than four months, and five years later it came out in book form as *Buddhist Meditation, Systematic and Practical. A Talk by the Buddhist Yogi C. M. Chen.*[398] That the talk could be thus enabled to reach a much wider audience was almost entirely due to Khantipālo. It was he who took down Yogi Chen's words in longhand, sometimes scribbling furiously in order to keep up, and whom our host therefore designated the Writer. My task was to listen carefully to the talk, with a view to supplementing, and if necessary correcting, Khantipālo's written record, and I was accordingly designated the Listener. Yogi Chen's own designation, as the giver of the talk, was the Speaker. A photograph taken by Lobsang Norbu through the window of the room where our sessions took place shows the three of us at work. Two vertical window bars divide the photograph into three panels. The middle panel of this triptych is occupied by Yogi Chen, who sits on a small *moira* or wicker stool. His head is bowed, as though in thought, and he holds a prayer-wheel. The right-hand panel is occupied by me, in profile, and the left-hand one by Khantipālo, who is bent over his notebook; we both sit on chairs. There is a certain dynamic in the picture. I am turned fully towards Yogi Chen, who is turned slightly towards Khantipālo, who, though he looks down, is half-turned towards Yogi Chen.

Khantipālo and I always arrived at the Five Leguminous Tree Hermitage for our weekly session at about 5 o'clock. Sometimes we came through the rain, for the rainy season had now set in. If we happened to be a little late, we would catch a glimpse of Yogi Chen peering round the curtain of his shrine-room window, on the lookout for us. The sessions lasted for between two and three hours, depending on how long Yogi Chen spoke and how much discussion took place, after which the Writer and the Listener had a forty-minute walk back to the Vihara, either through more rain or, perhaps, under the stars. The next day, the subject still being fresh in mind, Khantipālo converted his notes into a rough draft which he gave to me for my comments. After being revised in accordance with my suggestions, the draft was typed and then taken along to our next meeting with Yogi Chen. He read it carefully, adding and deleting where necessary. In this way a faithful version of what he had said was finally arrived at.

Buddhist Meditation, Systematic and Practical contained seventeen chapters, each chapter corresponding to a talk, or – as Yogi Chen saw it – to an instalment of one and the same talk. The seventeen chapters covered the principal meditations of the Hīnayāna, the Mahāyāna, and the Vajrayāna, which Yogi Chen, in common with the followers of all schools of Tibetan Buddhism, regarded as successive stages of the path to realization of the three 'bodies' of a supreme Buddha. One of these chapters covered meditations of the Chinese Mahāyāna schools, another covered Chan ('Is Chan a meditation? No!'). Before he gave his first talk on meditation, however, Yogi Chen gave the Writer and the

Listener an outline of his biography. It would be a good introduction to his explanations of practice and realization, he told us. Though it was only an outline, it took Yogi Chen a whole evening to deliver it, and when *Buddhist Meditation, Systematic and Practical* was published it made a useful introduction to the book. In accordance with Tibetan literary practice he divided his biography into four parts: (1) outward biography, (2) inward biography, (3) secret biography, and (4) most secret biography.

The outward biography was the shortest of the four. That is, Yogi Chen spent less time talking about it than he did talking about any of the others. There were eight children in the family, four girls and four boys, of whom he was the youngest. Most of his siblings died young, and one day an itinerant fortune-teller told his mother that he, too, would have a short life. His parents frequently quarrelled, for his father not only took a second wife but was always running after the wives of others and squandered the family income on women and drink. For these reasons Yogi Chen grew up with two fears, the fear of death and the fear of poverty. One of his duties when young was to look after his grandfather, who had a shop, and the old man became very fond of him on account of his diligence. But he became nearly blind, and practically everything had to be done for him; he also developed consumption, and when Yogi Chen was ten he died. As a young prince, the Buddha-to-be saw the four sights – the old man, the sick man, the dead man, and the wandering ascetic – in the city outside his home – the Speaker told us with evident emotion – but *he* had seen three of them *inside* his home. The fourth, a *bhikṣu*, he did not see at that time.[399] He had no need of the Hīnayāna scriptures to convince him of the first noble truth, the truth that conditioned existence is suffering. Nonetheless, he could not give up the world, as there was no one else to look after his parents.

The inward biography was the story of his secular and religious education. It began when he studied with a teacher well-versed in the Confucian classics. As he had a good memory, he was always placed first in the class of ten boys. After finishing his study of the five classics, he joined the town's newly opened Government Primary School. While the school taught the usual range of subjects, he liked to study and recite poetry with a young man who had risen to official eminence through the old imperial examination system but had renounced it all in order to live as a hermit in the mountains, as he afterwards did. His poems were a mixture of Buddhism and Taoism, with a strong element of his own renunciation. After attending primary school and high school, the young Chen went for six years to the Normal School in Changsha, the capital of Hunan Province. Since he wanted to learn everything, there was little he did not put his hand to, even playing the piano! His room had no light, so during the night he studied in the one place where a light was always burning – in the latrines. Though his health suffered, he was in this way able to graduate well and to obtain a post as a teacher in the High School. Later he was appointed Secretary to the Provincial Education Committee, a post for which altogether 142 candidates from all over the province had competed. The appointment gave him access to the provincial library, which was an extensive one, and he had the opportunity to read widely. He particularly liked the Taoist authors, with their promises that there were many different methods for prolonging life. One day he consulted a Taoist diviner, who predicted that if he followed their teachings not only would his life be prolonged but he would become immortal. This was a turning-point in his life, Yogi Chen solemnly assured us. From then on he was less concerned with worldly things.

The library contained the works of Taixu, the leading Chinese Buddhist monk of his day, and he read them with enthusiasm, for with their blend of the modern scientific attitude and ancient wisdom they were easy for an educated young man to read. At that time there was no lay Buddhist organization in the province, and at the urging of a group of *upāsakas* he wrote to Taixu, inviting him to come and help them form one. A correspondence ensued, in the course of which Taixu gave him a Buddhist name and told him he should become his disciple. Two or three months later, the famous monk arrived in Changsha and a lay Buddhist association was formed and soon flourished. A temple for the worship of Amitābha was built, and Taixu himself founded a Buddhist college, in which his new disciple worked under his direction. It was around this time, Yogi Chen subsequently wrote to Khantipālo, that he began studying the *Avataṃsaka* or 'Flower Ornament' *Sūtra*, being particularly interested in the chapter on pure conduct, which explains how all the activities of daily life are to be accompanied by the *bodhicitta*. So captivated was he by this chapter that he wrote it out in a fine, vigorous style of calligraphy so that many copies could be printed for free distribution. Nonetheless, the Speaker sadly confessed that evening, he still continued to oscillate between Buddhism and Taoism, for he thought that, good as the Hīnayāna was, it could not prolong his life. Though he had taken the Buddhist Refuges, he really forsook them when he met a Taoist guru and learned some life-prolonging practices from him. The guru had the face of a little boy, though he was very old, and he had taken no food for twenty years. Though initially sceptical, after staying with the guru for a few days he could believe what he was told. He himself was then eating only vegetarian food and living apart from his wife (the Speaker had not mentioned her before).

During this period, he met a teacher belonging to the Gelug tradition, Gelu Rimpoche by name. Being a Gelugpa, he laid great emphasis on the observance of the Vinaya or code of monastic discipline, as well as on the four foundation yogas of the Vajrayāna. As taught by him, the four were Going for Refuge, Prostration, Reciting the Hundred-Syllable Mantra of Vajrasattva, and the Offering of the Mandala. Since he could not do these practices while living in the midst of his family, he went to live in a shrine in his teacher's temple. Each of the foundation yogas had to be performed 100,000 times. In the course of two or three years he was able to perform the first three foundation yogas 100,000 times each, but he had time to perform the fourth, the Offering of the Mandala, only 10,000 times in that place and he was still engaged in making up the total here in his hermitage in Kalimpong.

Gelu Rimpoche had heard that in the Guangxi region there was a great Nyingma guru who lived as a hermit, and he went to see him. On his return he would not reveal to him and the other disciples what he had learned, and Yogi Chen therefore decided that, although it would leave his family short of money, he would go and see the guru himself. While he was with him, Lola Hutuktu, as the guru was called, gave him many instructions regarding the practice of meditation, including Mahāmudrā and Dzogchen. Lola Rimpoche predicted that he would have a daughter, and told him to eat meat and live with his wife. He also told him to practise Chan, for its realization went very deep.

Yogi Chen's inward biography concluded with his telling us that he had had altogether four kinds of guru. They were the outward guru, the inward guru, the secret guru – who gave instruction in meditation and in dreams – and finally the guru of the *dharmakāya*, which was the wisdom of non-guru. This guru was not a personality, but from it he had obtained many teachings. So saying, the Speaker rose from his seat and went to a glass-fronted cupboard packed with books. Taking out a good pile of them, he brought them to us to see. In all there were twenty-two volumes, the pages of each one of them covered with closely written Chinese characters. They were examples of what the Tibetans called 'mind-treasures' and were on a variety of subjects, including the chakras and bodily health.

Coming to his secret biography, Yogi Chen began by emphasizing the importance of understanding that we must achieve perfect renunciation, and that our desire to practise must always be strong. When he was working as a teacher, for example, he used to spend the summer vacation and the Christmas holidays as a hermit. He did this for many years. When the time came for him to return to school he always wept, for at school there would be little time for meditation, but he knew he must earn money to support his aged parents and his own family. Many times he tried to leave home and live like Milarepa, the Tibetan solitary, and he often wanted to become a *bhikṣu*, but each time worldly obligations held him back.

On one occasion the Heruka Ḍākinī came to him when he was half awake and told him, 'Go to Sichuan.' He went there and received detailed teachings of the Vajrayāna. At another time, while he was meditating, the Five Sisters, emanations of Buddha Amitāyus, told him to go to Xikang. Fortunately, he was able to raise the money for the journey and set out for Xikang where, on the snowy mountain, he received instruction from the famous Ganga Guru. He stayed with him for a hundred days, constantly practising his teachings, and left only when his money ran out. While he was staying there, the Karmapa appeared to him in a dream and told him to come to him at Derge, in Tibet. Weituo, his guardian deity, promised him 50,000 Chinese dollars to meet the expenses of the journey (the Speaker laughed heartily at the recollection), and in fact he was able to raise exactly that amount. Before he arrived at Derge he had a vision, one night, of Jamyang Khyentse Rimpoche, who was the teacher of the young Karmapa. In Derge he received many teachings from the Rimpoche, teachings that were not always imparted to the other disciples. From this time onward he gathered numerous *abhiṣekas* and instructions from seven different schools of Tantra in Tibet. The practices had their corresponding texts, which might be read and studied only by those who had been given

Yogi Chen in his hermitage

the *abhiṣekas* for the meditations they described. Naturally, such texts were never published, their contents being meaningful only to those who had received instruction in them. It was also worth noting, Yogi Chen added, that not all his teachers were famous or enjoyed established reputations. The majority were little known, lived in remote, wild places, and had few disciples, if any. Those who were not *tulkus* might, by their efforts in this lifetime, establish a line of *tulkus*. Very often the deepest teachings were to be found among gurus of this type.

At the end of this period of seclusion, his gurus asked him to return to his home province to rescue his family from the turmoil of Second World War. This he did, and after he had settled his family in a safe part of the country, he spent two years living in a cave. A wealthy supporter who wanted to go on pilgrimage to India suggested that they should go together. This they did in 1947, when they made the pilgrimage to the principal Buddhist holy places. His kind supporter then returned to China, but Yogi Chen stayed on in India, where he spent one week meditating in each of the holy places in order to find out what would be the best place for his practice. Finally, his supporter helped him to remain in India, so he came to Kalimpong and to the hermitage in which he was now living.

The subject of the most secret biography was realization. This had three divisions, Yogi Chen explained, corresponding to the three *yānas* of Tibetan Buddhism. The three were the attainment of cause, in which renunciation was most important; the attainment of path or course, in which understanding of impermanence was necessary; and attainment of consequence, in which there was certainty of Enlightenment. Under these headings, Yogi Chen described how he had practised renunciation, how he had lived as a hermit for altogether eighteen years, and how the practice of meditation had brought glimpses of Truth.

Chapter 1 of *Buddhist Meditation, Systematic and Practical* was entitled 'Reasons for Western Interest in the Practice of Meditation'. It corresponded to Yogi Chen's first talk on meditation, the previous week's talk – on his biography – having been of an introductory nature. There were four reasons for this interest on the part of Westerners. (1) The *dharmakāya* embraced the *dharmadhātu*, and neither East nor West was outside it. All could receive its blessing and all, wherever they happened to be, could practise Buddhist meditation. (2) Many Buddhist sages had predicted that Buddhism would spread to the West, where a basis for it already existed in the form of the ethical teachings common to all religions. (3) Christianity was in decline in the West. (4) Western daily life was very stressful.

Chapter 2 dealt with the real and ultimate purpose of meditation, while chapter 3 was concerned with the exact definition of terms relating to meditation, both its theory and its practice. The ground having been cleared, the fourteen remaining chapters covered between them the entire field of Buddhist meditation, from the five basic meditations, which are the antidotes to the five mental poisons, to the highest meditations of the Tantra. Each chapter began by paying homage to a particular Buddha or bodhisattva, guardian deity, or guru, or to a particular group of such beings, just as Yogi Chen had done before he gave the talk on which the chapter was based. Chapter 9, for example, which was on the four foundations of mindfulness, began with a homage to Je Tsongkhapa, the four *Āgamas*, and the five hundred *arhants*. Both the Writer and the Listener noticed that these acts of homage on the Speaker's part were no mere formality but gave expression to a very real sense of devotion. Besides recording Yogi Chen's words, Khantipālo introduced each chapter with a short paragraph or two in which he set the scene, as it were, for the evening's talk. He also interpolated short accounts of any discussions that had arisen in the course of the talk, as well as any comment by me.

Shortly after completing his work on *Buddhist Meditation, Systematic and Practical*, Khantipālo left for Thailand, there to pursue his study and practice of the Dharma under traditional Theravādin auspices. Before his departure, we were associated in two events which in their different ways were of special significance to us both. Quite early in his stay, I had introduced Khantipālo to Dhardo Rimpoche, whom he soon came to admire for his kindness and generosity, and for the way he looked after the 200 or so pupils of his school, many of whom were the children of refugees.[400] When I told him that Dhardo Rimpoche had agreed to give me the bodhisattva ordination, therefore, he was moved to ask the Rimpoche if he, too, could take the ordination.

I had been attracted to the bodhisattva ideal for almost as long as I had been a Buddhist,[401] and I had been a Buddhist for twenty years. During that period, texts like 'The Vows of the Bodhisattva Samantabhadra', which forms part of the *Avataṃsaka Sūtra*, and Śāntideva's *Śikṣā-samuccaya* or 'Compendium of Instruction [for novice bodhisattvas]' had thrilled and inspired me,[402] and my feelings had found expression in poems and articles,[403] as well as in Chapter 4 of *A Survey of Buddhism*. There were two reasons for my being so strongly affected. As I have written elsewhere,

> In the first place, there was the sheer unrivalled sublimity of the bodhisattva ideal – the ideal of dedicating oneself, for innumerable lifetimes, to the attainment of supreme Enlightenment for the benefit of all living beings. In the second, there was the fact that, as enjoined by my teacher Kashyap-ji, I was 'working for the good of Buddhism', and that I could not do this without strong spiritual support, the more especially since I received very little real help

> or cooperation from those who were supposedly working with me. This spiritual support I found in the bodhisattva ideal, which provided me with an example, on the grandest possible scale, of what I was myself trying to do within my own infinitely smaller sphere and on an infinitely lower level.[404]

Thus it was not surprising that on 12 October 1962 I should have received the bodhisattva ordination, especially as by that time I had been working for the good of Buddhism for twelve years, both in Kalimpong and the neighbouring hill towns and in the plains. It was also not surprising that I should have received the ordination from Dhardo Rimpoche, whom I had known since 1952 and whom I had come to revere as a living bodhisattva. This was not to say that my other Tibetan teachers were not bodhisattvas, but I had known Dhardo Rimpoche longer than I had known any of them, had spent more time in his company, and in our odd mixture of Hindi, Tibetan, and English I had a serviceable medium of communication such as I did not have with any of them. He had never given me an outline of his biography, as Yogi Chen had done in his first talk to Khantipālo and me, but from the conversations we had had over the years I had come to know something about him. I knew that he had been born in Dhartsendo, in eastern Tibet; that his father was a merchant; that at an early age he had entered Drepung Gompa, the great Gelug monastic university near Lhasa; that he had passed all his examinations with great credit; that his teacher was strict but kind; that a breakdown in his health had prevented him from completing his studies at the Tantric College, where the routine was demanding and conditions harsh; that in 1947, at the age of twenty-nine, he had come to India in search of health; and that on his return, after he had been back only eighteen months, the Dalai Lama's government had appointed him abbot of the Tibetan monastery at Bodh Gaya, thus obliging him to make the long and arduous journey to India for the second time.[405]

It was at Bodh Gaya, in 1949, that our paths had first crossed (though I did not know this at the time), when looking out of the window of his room Dhardo Rimpoche saw me standing on the flat roof of the Maha Bodhi rest house nearby. Since then we had met, had become friends, and had worked together for the good of Buddhism in various ways, so that I was more than compensated for the disappointments I had suffered at the hands of those who in my early years in Kalimpong were supposedly working with me. In 1956, the year of the 2500th Buddha Jayanti, Dhardo Rimpoche and I toured the principal Buddhist holy places as guests of the Government of India.[406] This marked a definite stage in the development of our friendship. In the course of the tour I got to know the Rimpoche better, and the better I knew him the more I liked and respected him. I saw how unassuming he was, how kind, and how mindful in everything he did. Later, in Kalimpong, I had many opportunities, over the years, of observing his great and noble qualities. I saw how helpful he was to visiting Western scholars, how utterly devoted to the welfare of the pupils of his school, how patient with his irascible old mother, and how independent in his dealings with Tibetan officials, most of whom expected from other Tibetans only subservience. In short, Dhardo Rimpoche manifested in his life to a high degree the 'perfections' (*pāramitās*) of generosity (*dāna*), ethics (*śīla*), patience (*kṣānti*), energy (*vīrya*), concentration (*samādhi*), and wisdom (*prajñā*), the practice of which for the benefit of all beings made one a bodhisattva, and I rejoiced at my good fortune in being able to receive the bodhisattva ordination from such a person.[407]

The ordination took place at the Old Bhutan Palace. I do not remember the details of the ceremony, which was in Tibetan, but I do recollect having a strong sense of the Rimpoche's presence on his throne in front of me and of Khantipālo's presence at my side, as well as a strong sense of there being a bond between the three of us.[408] After the ceremony, I felt I was no longer merely an admirer of the bodhisattva ideal. I was now committed to the realization of that ideal in my own life. In other words, I had been formally enrolled as a member of the Mahāyāna sangha. This did not mean that I had abandoned the Hīnayāna, into one of whose schools I had been ordained as a monk, but only that the Hīnayāna had been integrated into the much wider context of the Mahāyāna. Indeed, it was one of the bodhisattva precepts (*saṃvara-śīla*) that the bodhisattva should refrain from disparaging the Hīnayāna. Dhardo Rimpoche later went through the precepts with me, explaining the eighteen major and forty-six minor precepts, and helped me to make an English version of them.[409] I sent a copy of this version to Khantipālo, who was then in Bangkok.

While he was still in Kalimpong, there took place the second of the two events that were of special significance to us both. This was the ceremonial planting of the bodhi tree sapling he had brought with him from Bodh Gaya, where it had been grown from seed by the monks of the Thai temple. The planting formed part of the Vihara's celebration of Shaga Dawa, the anniversary of the Buddha's Enlightenment according to the Tibetan calendar. I wielded the spade, while Khantipālo firmed the roots of the sapling, which was about two feet high, and filled in the hole. Despite the poverty of the soil, it flourished.[410]

14
HINDI-CHEENI BHAI-BHAI

On 23 October 1962, the Government and people of India experienced a rude awakening from a dream – the dream of *Hindi-Cheeni bhai-bhai* or 'Indians and Chinese are brothers'. The awakening came when well-equipped Chinese troops crossed, without warning, the border between north-east India and Tibet. They crossed it in force, and eventually attacked along the whole 550-mile border. At a number of points their advance units made deep incursions into Indian territory, routing the Indian troops, taking many prisoners, and causing a mass exodus of the local people, most of whom were tribals. It was not until 1963, after a meeting between the Indian and Chinese prime ministers, that the invaders withdrew to the McMahon Line, as the *de facto* boundary between India and Tibet was known. By that time, Indian public opinion had turned against the peddlers of the *Hindi-Cheeni bhai-bhai* dream, which had lulled the country into a state of complacency and unpreparedness.

I was in Kalimpong at the time, having decided to suspend my preaching tours in the plains for a year or two, and at first I heard only rumours of fighting in the north-east, five or six hundred miles away. There had been such rumours before, but nothing had come of them, and like the rest of Kalimpong I saw no cause for concern. I realized that the situation was a serious one only when I awoke one morning to find that during the night the whole Chinese community had been arrested and taken away. Some of them were shopkeepers, and the next time I walked through the bazaar I saw that the authorities had boarded up their shops in order to prevent looting. How many Chinese had been living in Kalimpong I did not know. There may have been a hundred of them, or even two hundred. In any case, there were enough children for them to have needed a Chinese-language school. During my early months in Kalimpong, I had visited the school more than once and had got to know the tall, thin headmaster, a Mr Shen, who was an artist, and who made a series of ink drawings in traditional Chinese style for an illustrated edition of my poems that I was hoping to bring out. He was later replaced by a nominee of Beijing, and I gathered that there had been a struggle between the Nationalist and Communist factions within the community for control of the school. As it happened, the majority of the town's Chinese inhabitants were Nationalists, but this had not prevented the Government from arresting and removing the whole community, probably out of fear that they might act as a fifth column. The only Chinese person not to be arrested and removed that night was Yogi Chen, who probably was spared either because he was a holy man or on account of his well-known antipathy to Communism.

The situation was indeed a serious one, as the drastic nature of the action taken against Kalimpong's Chinese community suggested, and it became more serious every day; even every hour. Every day brought news of fresh defeats suffered by the Indian Army and of further advances by the invading Chinese. The Chinese troops seemed to be irresistible, and people began to wonder how deep into Indian territory they intended to penetrate. Soon it was rumoured that their objective was Kalimpong, for had not Peking Radio denounced Kalimpong as the place where reactionary Tibetan aristocrats and imperialist American agents conspired against the Tibetan people and their Chinese friends? Later it was rumoured that the objective was not Kalimpong but Teesta Bridge, which was of obvious strategic importance. But this was almost immediately superseded by another rumour, to the effect that the objective was Siliguri, the nearest railhead. Finally it was rumoured that the ultimate objective of the invasion was Calcutta, the possession of which would give Chinese-occupied Tibet access to the Bay of Bengal and the Indian Ocean.

As the rumours became ever more alarming, something like panic began to be felt in the town, at least in some quarters. The potential fifth column had already been rounded up and taken, as I afterwards learned, to an internment camp in Dehra Dun, and now Government officials started sending their families away to the safety of the plains. Some of the yellow-turbaned Marwari merchants did likewise, while middle-class Bengalis who had been spending the traditional Hindu holiday season in Kalimpong thought it prudent to return to Calcutta. The Kazini, who seemed to hear every rumour that was afloat, and who scanned the newspapers with even more than her usual intensity, was convinced that the Chinese troops had Kalimpong in their sights and that nothing could stop them reaching the town. She and the Kazi had a jeep and a driver on standby all the time, she told me, in case they had to leave in a hurry. The jeep was stocked with provisions, and there would be room in it for me. We would escape by way of the track which ran past the Vihara down to the Lepcha village of Chebo Busti and thence to the Dooars, thus avoiding Teesta Bridge, which would surely be blown up by the Indian Army to prevent the Chinese pushing further south. Though the Kazi acquiesced in his wife's plans for a dramatic, last-minute escape, he appeared to think they were in no real danger. The Kazini strongly suspected that the reason for his equanimity was that through secret channels of his own he was in contact with the Chinese and had come to some kind of understanding with them. But though she more than once questioned him on the subject, the enigmatic Kazi would neither affirm nor deny that this was the case. He would only laugh and rub his hands together.

The authorities must have been concerned lest there should be a mass exodus from Kalimpong, as there had been from towns and villages further east. This would create its own problems, and one morning I received a visit from Inspector Mukherjee, the Frontier Officer, who was in charge of the Foreigners Registration Office, to which all foreigners, including Tibetan refugees, had to report on their arrival in the town. I had had no official dealings with him, for I was a UK citizen, not a foreigner, but we had friends in common, and I knew him fairly well. Like many of his colleagues he was corrupt, and was known to accept bribes from Tibetan refugees desperate to be allowed to stay in India. He was in uniform, and after we had chatted for a few minutes he told me that he had just been with the Subdivisional Officer and that the latter had two requests to make of me. The first was that I should not leave Kalimpong, and he would be conveying a similar request to Dhardo Rimpoche. The Rimpoche and I were highly respected by the people of Kalimpong, and if we left many of them would follow our example, thinking that we could be trusted to know whether or not it was safe to remain. I had no thought of leaving, any more than Dhardo Rimpoche had, and I told Mukherjee as much. What I did not tell him was that even if Dhardo Rimpoche and I were to leave Kalimpong, our departure would not in my opinion be the signal for a general exodus as the authorities seemed to believe. Government officials, Marwari merchants, and holidaying Bengalis might fear the approach of the Chinese Communist troops, but the bulk of the population, which was ethnically Nepalese, regarded it with a degree of equanimity. The truth of the matter was that the Government officials, the Marwaris, and the Bengalis, all came from the plains, and that many hill people saw them – and often experienced them – not as fellow citizens of India but as oppressors and exploiters, and therefore tended to look upon the Chinese as liberators. For them it was not 'Indians and Chinese are brothers' but 'Hillmen and Chinese are brothers'. '*You* are slit-eyed; *we* are slit-eyed,' Chinese agents had for years been telling the peasants and tea garden labourers of the area. 'We are from the same stock. We are brothers.' And the lesson had sunk in.

The SDO's second request was that I should organize a spontaneous demonstration against China's unprovoked attack on India. The Deputy Commissioner had telephoned the SDO, Mukherjee confided. There had been a spontaneous demonstration in Darjeeling, he had told him. Why had there not been one in Kalimpong? The speakers at the demonstration should say that the territory invaded by the Chinese troops was definitely part of India, Mukherjee warned me, and that China had definitely committed an act of aggression. It was particularly important that the word 'aggression' should be used. I found nothing to cavil at in this, and lost no time in going to see Dhardo Rimpoche and inviting him to speak at the demonstration, which I had decided should take the form of a public meeting at the Town Hall. I also invited other prominent citizens to speak, hired the Town Hall, and arranged for the meeting to be announced by beat of drum throughout the bazaar.

When the day came, the Town Hall was packed to capacity, and I was glad that I had arranged for loudspeakers to relay the proceedings to the crowds gathered outside. Dhardo Rimpoche and I were the principal speakers, he in Tibetan and I in English. Of the other speakers, two of them spoke in Nepali and one in Hindi. I saw to it that Dhardo Rimpoche was allowed more time than anyone else, for, as I had expected would be the case, the audience consisted mainly of Tibetans, most of whom understood only their own language. Neither the Rimpoche nor I felt any qualms about heeding Mukherjee's warning. China had invaded territory that was definitely part of India, we declared, and therefore China had definitely committed an act of aggression.

Years later I discovered that there was another side to the story, and that the situation was not quite so straightforward as I had been led to believe. At the Simla Conference of 1913 (according to the *Encyclopaedia Britannica*) the representatives of Great Britain, China, and Tibet had agreed that the McMahon Line should be accepted as marking the boundary between north-east India and Tibet. Two days later, however, the Chinese republican government disavowed its plenipotentiary and refused to sign a covenant. After the independence of India in 1947, Communist China made claims to a huge swathe of territory south of the McMahon line, on the grounds that the boundary had never been recognized by China and was the result of British aggression. Some maps showed the disputed territory as Chinese, some showed it as part of India, and some as part of Tibet.

From declaring that China had committed an act of aggression against India, it was only a short step to denouncing China for invading and occupying Tibet, and it was a step that neither Dhardo Rimpoche nor I hesitated to take. Both condemned, in the strongest terms, the barbarous behaviour of the invaders. We condemned the destruction of monasteries, the torture and killing of monks, the desecration of sacred books and images, the brutal suppression of the Lhasa uprising of 1959, and the virtual enslavement of the entire Tibetan people. In the heady days of *Hindi-Cheeni bhai-bhai* it would have been difficult to speak in this way at a public meeting. Communists and fellow travellers, whether Indian or Nepalese, would have denounced one as a warmonger or an American agent, and probably no Tibetan refugee would have dared to attend. But the situation had changed dramatically, and now Dhardo Rimpoche and I were free to speak our minds. In the course of my own speech I was unable to resist the temptation to refer in a rather pointed fashion to the change that had taken place. When the Chinese invaded Tibet we were not allowed to talk of aggression, I said, but now that China has invaded *India*.... I did not need to complete the sentence, which in any case was interrupted by laughter and applause by those who understood English. Whether Dhardo Rimpoche made a similar allusion I do not know, but from the expression on the faces of his Tibetan auditors I could tell that what he was saying was very much to their liking.

Over the years, Dhardo Rimpoche had developed into a very good public speaker, admittedly with the help of a little coaching from me. In Tibet there was no tradition of public speaking, or of lecturing, in the Western sense, though learned lamas might sometimes give expositions of particular sacred texts. The lack of such a tradition in the old Tibet was glaringly obvious at the Tsongkhapa death anniversary meeting I organized, which was attended by many eminent lamas. One of the speakers was Dudjom Rimpoche, but he spoke, or rather read from a prepared text, in a kind of rapid whisper which was audible only to those who were sitting in the front row of the auditorium. According to Tibetan notions of etiquette, by speaking in this way one showed respect for one's auditor or auditors, and Dudjom Rimpoche was known for his refined, aristocratic manners. By contrast, Dhardo Rimpoche had mastered the art of public speaking as this was understood in the West. Not only did he speak loudly and clearly; he spoke with vigour, and he dealt in a simple, straightforward manner with such matters – whether secular or religious – as were of serious concern to his audience. The Tibetans of Kalimpong had come to look forward to the Rimpoche's speeches. They attended in large numbers whenever he gave one, and listened with close attention.

This was very much the case on the day of our 'spontaneous demonstration', as Dhardo Rimpoche denounced China for invading and occupying Tibet and condemned the barbarous behaviour of its troops. Not that he spoke only in this vein. From condemning the Chinese he soon passed to exhorting the Tibetans, or at least those Tibetans who filled the Town Hall and who were gathered outside. He urged them to preserve their culture, to practise their religion, to make sure that their children learned Tibetan, to live peaceably in India, which had given them a refuge from the oppressive rule of the Chinese, and not to give up hope that Tibet would one day be free again. Above all, he urged them not to quarrel among themselves, but to live in unity.

Though I understood very little Tibetan, it was not difficult for me to catch the drift of Dhardo Rimpoche's speech. Not only did I have a good idea what he was going to say; I was familiar with his manner of speaking, and I could follow the changing expressions on the faces of his hearers as grief gave way to resignation, resignation to confidence, and confidence to hope. At that time, the Tibetans of Kalimpong were in need of hope, especially the refugees, who were very much in the majority. They had heard with increasing dismay of China's invasion of Indian territory, of the steady advance of the Chinese troops, and that – as it was rumoured – the objective of those troops was Kalimpong. Having escaped from Tibet with so much difficulty, would they be forced to flee from the Chinese a second time?[411] In the circumstances it was natural that some of them should turn for guidance and encouragement not only to the spiritual leaders, such as Dhardo Rimpoche, but also to a certain class of gods. These were the gods who, when ritually invoked by a qualified person, would deliver a message, or answer a question, through the mouth of a medium while the latter was in a state of trance. Their utterances were taken down by an amanuensis and printed from wood blocks. There were several such oracles in circulation among the Tibetans of Kalimpong. One of them came into my hands, and with Prajnaloka's help I made an English version of it. The second half of the oracle ran as follows.

> The position of the East Red Pig will not last long, but will vanish like a rainbow. Then a change will take place, and the Pig's harvest will be devoured by the Dog. The angry Tiger of the South is lying on the border. After a time the great storm of delusion will come, so don't believe it. The Snake and the Frog of the West will advance and withdraw in various ways. They don't see that they themselves will be ruined. The Cobra of the North is stretching out two tongues. It is somewhat dangerous to all beings. The sufferings of our Chintamani of the Himalayas will become clear like the sun.

The sufferings of 'our Chintamani of the Himalayas' (the Dalai Lama) may or may not have become clear as the sun, but there was no doubt that there was a change in the position of the East Red Pig. On 21 November, as suddenly and unexpectedly as they had crossed the McMahon Line a month earlier, the Chinese forces declared a unilateral ceasefire. Though it would be some months before they disappeared like a rainbow, the conflict was definitely at an end. Or rather, the invasion was at an end, for the Indian Army had put up so ineffective a resistance that a conflict could hardly be said to have taken place. At the time of the ceasefire, the Chinese were in a very strong position. Having overrun an area more than half the size of England, they could easily have continued their advance and threatened, within a matter of days, the entire Assam Valley. Why, then, had they not done so? No one seemed to know, and in the absence of knowledge, speculation flourished. Some people were of the opinion that the Chinese wanted to give the world an example of magnanimity in victory; others thought they were concerned lest the winter snows should block the high Himalayan passes, interrupting their supply lines and making it impossible for them to return to Tibet until the following year. There was also the theory that the invasion was China's way of nudging a reluctant India towards the negotiating table and to a discussion of the territories in dispute between them in both the north-east and the north-west.

There was perhaps an element of truth in all these speculations. My own view was that the Chinese had come to resent India's assumption that it was the natural leader of Asia, and the invasion was meant to remind India that within the continent there was a power no less important than itself. The reason why the Chinese troops had not continued their advance was that they had made their point. *Hindi-Cheeni bhai-bhai* did *not* mean that India was the big brother and China the little brother.

15
INITIATION, AND AN INVITATION

The Bhutanese Gompa was situated not far from the Old Bhutan Palace, and like the latter it must have been built a hundred or more years ago, when Kalimpong was still part of Bhutan. A square, solid-looking structure with a corrugated iron roof, the *gompa* stood flanked by a few dark pines in the middle of its modest compound, which was surrounded by a low stone wall. The place had a deserted, neglected look. Except for the caretaker, who was rarely seen, it was unoccupied; nothing ever happened there, it seemed, and in the course of my years in Kalimpong I had only once been inside the shabby old building, the doors of which were kept firmly shut.

One day I heard that an incarnate lama was staying at the Bhutanese Gompa. I do not remember if his name was mentioned to me at the time, though even had it been mentioned it would then have meant very little to me. Since the newcomer was an incarnate lama, it was not long before I went to see him, taking Prajnaloka with me as my interpreter. We found the lama living not at the *gompa* but in a small cottage situated just inside the compound gate, to the right of the path leading to the *gompa*. As Prajnaloka explained the purpose of our visit, which was simply to pay our respects, I noticed that although the Rimpoche wore the maroon robe he had the long hair that betokened the lay tantric yogi. I noticed, also, that he was exceptionally tall, for despite his being seated cross-legged on his bed, his grey head bent over the Tibetan xylograph volume in his lap, this was immediately obvious. When his wife came in with the customary

Tibetan tea she, too, turned out to be exceptionally tall, as did their two lanky grown-up daughters, who stood in the doorway for a few minutes regarding the visitors with undisguised curiosity. The average height of this family of giants must have been nearly six and a half feet. But the most remarkable thing about the Rimpoche himself was not his height but his smile, which was of extraordinary sweetness, without the least trace of sentimentality, and seemed to come from within, suffusing his soft features with a kind of glow.

How much I got to know about Dilgo Khyentse Rimpoche on that first visit I cannot say. Probably he told me that he and his wife and daughters had arrived in Kalimpong only recently, having escaped from Tibet to Bhutan, whence they had made their way to Sikkim. He would not have told me that he was – as I later discovered – one of the five *tulkus* of the great Jamyang Khyentse Wangpo, one of the leading figures in the Rimé or 'non-sectarian' movement in nineteenth-century Tibetan Buddhism, my own Jamyang Khyentse Rimpoche being also one of the five. He was therefore a very eminent lama indeed, and one who moreover was greatly revered by many people, especially those who were followers of the Kagyu and Nyingma traditions. Yet despite his being so eminent a lama, and so revered, it would have been difficult to find a more unassuming person than Dilgo Khyentse Rimpoche, or one who was more approachable. It was therefore not many months before I was visiting him regularly, accompanied sometimes by Prajnaloka and sometimes by Lobsang Norbu, for I never felt that I was being intrusive, or that I was wasting the Rimpoche's time. On the contrary, I felt that I was more than welcome. I always found the Rimpoche sitting cross-legged on his bed, a Tibetan xylograph volume in his lap. On my entering the tiny front room, he always looked up from his book with a little smile of recognition and pleasure, and his wife always came in after a few minutes with the Tibetan tea and, perhaps, some Tibetan bread. After a few such visits I observed that the Rimpoche never gave the impression of being disturbed or interrupted in what he was doing. His attention seemed to pass smoothly and seamlessly from one thing to another, as though all were equally interesting, equally important, and equally enjoyable, whether it was reading his book, answering a question from me, or drinking his tea.

It was no different when, on 9 May 1963, he transmitted to me the *phowa* or 'consciousness transference' of Amitābha, an oral tradition of the Nyingmapas. Once again I was able to observe how seamlessly his attention passed from one thing to another, passing on this occasion from whatever it was he had been doing before to the business of explaining to me the details of the practice and performing the simple ritual within whose context the transmission took place. The practice belonged to the *Anuttarayoga* Tantra, Khyentse Rimpoche told me. It was an oral tradition, having never been committed to writing, and was the simplest and easiest of all the *phowa* practices. It could be done anywhere and at any time but, for the time being at least, I was not to discuss it with anyone except Yogi Chen, though I was permitted to make notes for my personal use. Since the *phowa* included a visualization of Amitāyus, the Buddha of Eternal Life, it was not necessary for me to do the long-life practice separately.

Though I was still visiting the Rimpoche regularly, it was not until 6 October that he visited the Vihara. Unfortunately, I have no recollection of this visit, though a note I made at the time informs me that we discussed the *Tharpe Delam*, one of the texts I had chanced to come across after receiving the Padmasambhava initiation from Kachu Rimpoche. The author of the *Tharpe Delam* was a celebrated Nyingma lama, Khyentse Rimpoche informed me, and the text itself was very well known among Nyingmapas. The work was written about 150 years ago, the author having died at the age of 87 in the early years of the reign of the Thirteenth Dalai Lama. The latter had once expressed his regret at not being able to meet the author, as he himself lived in Lhasa and the author in Kham.

Two weeks later, on 28 October, Khyentse Rimpoche initiated me into the *sādhanas* of Kurukullā, a dancing red *ḍākinī* form of Tārā, and Jambhala, the stout golden-yellow bodhisattva of material wealth and spiritual riches. Like the *phowa* transmission, the ceremony took place in the Rimpoche's room in the cottage inside the Bhutanese Gompa's compound. Since there were only three of us, the third person being my interpreter, and since the smallness of the room obliged me to sit quite close to the guru, an atmosphere of intimacy prevailed. Indeed, it did not feel like a formal initiation at all. As on the occasion of the Amitābha *phowa* transmission, Khyentse Rimpoche resembled an affectionate father who was telling his son, quietly and confidentially, something that would be of immense value to him throughout his life.

With Dilgo Khyentse Rimpoche

Neither of the *sādhanas* required a full Tantric *abhiṣeka*, only a lesser initiation or special kind of blessing. I had asked for them at the instigation of Yogi Chen, who was overjoyed that the *phowa* transmission had given me a spiritual connection with the great Dilgo Khyentse Rimpoche and wanted me to strengthen the connection by taking further initiations from him. Kurukullā and Jambhala would help me in my work for the Dharma, he declared. Kurukullā belonged to the Lotus family, of which Amitābha was the head. She embodied one of the four principal Buddha activities, that of attraction or fascination, the three other activities being, respectively, those of maturation, pacification, and destruction. Jambhala belonged to the Jewel family, the head of which was Ratnasambhava. There were three Jambhalas,

Yogi Chen explained – the white, the yellow, and the black. The white Jambhala was a Buddha, the yellow Jambhala a bodhisattva of the eighth stage appearing in the form of a god, and the black Jambhala a *dharmapāla* or protector of the Dharma. The yellow Jambhala was the main one, and it was *his sādhana* that Khyentse Rimpoche would give me if I asked. The black Jambhala was hardly Buddhist, for he was worshipped for the acquisition of wealth by forcible means. When the Dalai Lama needed money he would get the Bön priests to worship the black Jambhala on his behalf. The white Jambhala had a special connection with the Karmapa.

October 1963 was an important month for me as regards initiations, especially as in the course of it I also received an initiation from Dhardo Rimpoche. On 25 October he initiated me into the *sādhana* of Vaiḍūryaprabhā or Blue Radiance, the blue-bodied Buddha of Healing, which like the Kurukullā and Jambhala *sādhanas* required only a lesser initiation or special kind of blessing. I had been drawn to the figure of the Medicine Buddha, as he was also called, after reading a translation of the Chinese version of the Mahāyāna *sūtra* that bears his name.[412] According to this popular scripture, prior to becoming a Buddha he had made twelve vows, and it was by virtue of these vows that those who worshipped him were guaranteed healing.

The fact that I was visiting Khyentse Rimpoche regularly, as well as Dhardo Rimpoche and Yogi Chen, meant that I often passed through the bazaar, on my way to or from the Bhutanese Gompa, or the Old Bhutan Palace, or the Five Leguminous Tree Hermitage. Nine months had passed since the withdrawal of the last Chinese troops from Indian territory, but signs of the alarm that the invasion had created were still to be seen. Chinese shops and business premises were still boarded up, and so far as anyone knew their unfortunate owners still languished in an internment camp or worse. But if there were no Chinese on the streets of Kalimpong, there were plenty of military personnel in their black berets and jungle greens. They came from the army camp which had been established at Rinkingpong, not far from the little Kagyu *gompa* and Dudjom Rimpoche's unfinished temple, both of which were now difficult of access. One day I happened to pass two *jawans*, as the ordinary soldiers were called, who like myself were on their way to the bazaar.

'We've got the atom bomb,' I heard one *jawan* say it to the other. 'If the Chinese give us any more trouble we'll drop it on Lhasa.'

India did not then have nuclear weapons, but the troops may have been told by their officers that she did have them in order to bolster their morale, which after their defeat at the hands of the Chinese was said to be very low.

But if Mother India did not have the atom bomb, she had plenty of other weapons. Gazing down the hillside from the Vihara garden I could make out, far below, the ant-like procession of trucks, artillery, and even tanks crawling along the road that zig-zagged its way from Teesta Bridge up to Kalimpong. As I discovered when I made an unscheduled flying visit to Darjeeling, Teesta Bridge itself was now protected by a battery of anti-aircraft guns, their barrels protruding disconcertingly from their half-camouflaged emplacement beside the road, and on both sides of the river there were swarms of green-clad *jawans*.

The flying visit was on account of Lobsang Norbu. At breakfast that morning I had been told that the Vihara's young manager had disappeared. Inquiries revealed that he and a good friend of his who worked at Arunachal had talked of joining the irregular force that Jigme Norbu, the Dalai Lama's eldest brother, was organizing for action against the Chinese troops in Tibet. According to Thubden, the two friends had probably gone to Darjeeling, where Jigme Norbu was based, in order to enlist. Even in the days of *Hindi-Cheeni bhai-bhai* there had been a surreptitious trickle of men and money from India to the legendary Khamba guerrillas, and now that India and China were no longer such good friends the operation could be carried on much more openly, albeit without the official sanction of the Indian government. Jigme Norbu's agents would travel round the area meeting young Tibetan men; they would talk to them about the importance of carrying on the armed struggle against the Chinese occupation, appeal to their patriotism, and, finally, assure them that if they volunteered they would be properly trained and equipped. Apparently Lobsang and his friend had been recruited in this way.

On arriving in Darjeeling I went straight from the motor stand to the Foreigners Registration Office, but no Lobsang Norbu had reported there, I was told. This left me wondering how best to continue my search for the runaway, and in the end I decided to consult a Bengali friend who had a watch repair shop on the main road into the town. I had not gone more than a hundred yards in that direction when I saw coming towards me through the crowd the familiar figure of Lobsang. He was not surprised to see me, nor was he surprised when I gave him a good scolding for having left the Vihara without telling me or anybody else that he was going, which was hardly in accordance with Tibetan good manners. That afternoon he accompanied me back to Kalimpong – and the Vihara. Though I admired the courage of the Khambas and other guerrillas, I believed that the cause for which they were fighting was a lost one, and I did not want to see Lobsang or any other young Tibetans sacrifice their lives for such a cause, however noble they might believe it to be. Lobsang later told me what he had learned about Jigme Norbu's force of irregulars. Those who volunteered to fight the Chinese were flown to a foreign country. He did not know the name of the country, but it was very far away, and the people there spoke English. The volunteers spent three months in that country. They were well treated, and were taught how to use rifles and other weapons. He did not know what happened to the volunteers once they had completed their training. No doubt some way was found of getting them into Tibet so that they could fight the Chinese.

When I repeated to the Kazini what Lobsang had told me, she expressed a degree of scepticism. She doubted if Jigme Norbu's guerrillas were trained in an English-speaking country. It was more likely, in her opinion, that the training took place at an American base where, of course, English would be spoken. The base was probably located somewhere in Pakistan. As I knew, the Kazini was more favourably disposed to Pakistan than to India, and the fact that it was cooperating with the Tibetan diaspora against Communist China would certainly have done it no harm in her eyes. Since the events of the previous year, she was more critical of India than ever, and would not have been sorry had her friend General Cariappa[413] led a military coup against the corrupt and inefficient Congress government, as at one time it was rumoured he might. The Kazini was also tired of living in Kalimpong. The place had changed, she declared, and she would have left had she not been married to the Kazi and the Kazi not been married to his politics.

Kalimpong had indeed changed in the course of the last few years. The fresh influx of Tibetan refugees, the rumours of impending invasion by the Chinese, and the presence of troops and tanks on the streets, had all affected the atmosphere of the town. What was more, the authorities had become more suspicious of foreign visitors, especially Europeans and Americans, seemingly finding it difficult to believe that anybody could come to Kalimpong simply for the sake of the view. This meant that one's movements were watched, one's letters were intercepted and, though personally I had nothing to fear, I was glad that I now had a British passport.

I had not always had a passport. On my 'going forth' as a homeless wanderer on 18 August 1947 I had not only given away my worldly possessions, not only donned the traditional saffron robes of the world-renunciant. I had also destroyed my identification papers. Like the friend who went forth with me, I believed that nationalism was one of the greatest evils of the modern world, and that in becoming a homeless wanderer I had renounced not only all domestic ties and social obligations but all national loyalties as well. Believing this as I did, I had vowed never to admit to having any particular nationality. I was a citizen of the world![414]

It was not long before I found it impracticable to maintain, in all its youthful uncompromisingness, the attitude I had adopted. World citizens belonged to an ideal realm, not to the real world. Much as I might believe that I had no nationality, there were plenty of people – not all of them officials – who believed I *did* have a nationality and wanted to know what it was. In the end, more than two years after my going forth, I wrote to the UK High Commissioner in New Delhi asking him to place my name on his Record of UK Citizens. This he did, giving me a serial number and requesting me to notify any change of address. For the next ten years his letter served me in lieu of a passport, and whenever I was required to give my passport number I gave my serial number on the High Commissioner's Record of Citizens. In 1962 I applied for a passport.

The reason I applied for one was that the English Sangha Trust had invited me to spend some time in England, and I had accepted the invitation. In accepting it I had made it clear that I would not be staying for more than four months, possibly six. At the time I saw myself as being permanently settled in India, which I had come to regard as my spiritual home. In Kalimpong, within sight of the snows, I had a peaceful hillside hermitage, the Triyana Vardhana Vihara, where I could meditate, study, write, and receive my friends, and from which I sallied forth on my preaching tours in the plains and to which, when I needed to recoup my energies, I could return. Above all, I had spiritual teachers of exceptional attainments, with most of whom I was in regular personal contact, and

Sangharakshita in front of the Triyana Vardhana Vihara

from whom I derived not just knowledge but inspiration. Thus there was little incentive for me to return to the land of my birth, much as I loved its language and its literature, and at first I was undecided whether or not to accept the Trust's invitation. Khantipālo was with me when it arrived, however, and when he pointed out that it was my duty to help spread the Dharma in England, inasmuch as I had been born and brought up there, I could not but recognize the force of his argument. I also reflected that the trip would enable me to see my parents and my sister, as well as to meet the various English Buddhists with whom I was in communication.

Between my acceptance of the English Sangha Trust's invitation and my departure from India there was an interval of two years. During this period the greater part of my time was spent meditating, or writing, or visiting such of my teachers as were in Kalimpong. I also went on a short preaching tour in the plains, leaving the Vihara in the care of Thien Châu, who was paying his annual visit to the hills. On my return some weeks later, I found that thieves had broken into my room the night before and that seven silver puja bowls were missing from my personal shrine. Thien Châu, Lobsang, and Thubden were asleep at the time and had heard nothing. When I told the Kazi and Kazini what had happened the Kazini was horrified, but the Kazi took a more philosophic – and more Buddhist – view of my loss. The robbery was a good omen, he assured me, especially as my life was about to enter on a new phase. It meant that a karmic debt had been paid and that I was now free to move forward without it hanging over my head.

Dhardo Rimpoche, too, was concerned that I was free to move forward. He was concerned, in particular, that I should not be held back by any threat to my life-force. Thus he had given me, not long before, the *abhiṣeka* of White Tārā, the female Bodhisattva of Longevity, and with his help I had started making an English version of the text of the relevant *sādhana*. I wanted to complete a first draft of this version before leaving for England, and the Rimpoche and I spent many hours working on the project together. We worked in the evening, in the Rimpoche's quarters in the Old Bhutan Palace, and sometimes it seemed that there were three of us in the room, and that White Tārā was looking down on our labours with a smile.[415] We worked up to the very eve of my departure, so that when I packed my bag that night I was able to include the exercise book containing the completed draft.

The following morning the Kazi and Kazini arrived with their jeep, having offered to drive me down to Siliguri and see me onto my train. As we left the Vihara, a Nepalese woman carrying a churn of milk happened to cross the road directly in front of us. This was a very good omen, the Kazi announced happily. My trip was sure to be a success.

With Allen Ginsberg in Kalimpong

Allen Ginsberg in India, 1962

Our first meeting with a person often seems of special significance, especially in retrospect. This was certainly the case with my first meeting with Allen Ginsberg, which took place in Kalimpong, a small town in the foothills of the eastern Himalayas, in June 1962. Allen was on his first visit to India, and had been touring the holy places of Hinduism and Buddhism and making friends with Indians of all classes and creeds. I had lived in India for more than fifteen years, of which the last twelve or more had been passed in Kalimpong, after I had spent two years in South India as a wandering ascetic and a year in Benares studying Pāli and Buddhist philosophy. In 1957 I had established, on the outskirts of Kalimpong, a small monastery which was already well known as a centre of interdenominational Buddhism, and it was in the sparsely furnished sitting room of this monastery that Allen and I had our first meeting.

Allen had already published *Howl* and *Kaddish*[416] and was probably the most outstanding – certainly the best known – of the Beat Poets,[417] but of all this I then knew nothing. Though I had read and written poetry from an early age, and was still reading and writing it at intervals, I was quite unaware of the more recent developments that had taken place in this field, whether in Britain or in the United States. In any case, my tastes were traditional rather than modernist, and it is doubtful if I would have felt much sympathy with the attitudes of the Beat Generation, at least so far as these were expressed in literature. Be that as it may, the fact that I knew nothing of the Beat Poets, and that Allen Ginsberg was not even a name to me, meant that when the slouching, dirty, dishevelled, hirsute figure appeared unexpectedly on my veranda one afternoon I could meet and greet him simply as a fellow human being.

How he came to know about 'the English Buddhist monk in Kalimpong' I do not remember. It may have been from Gary Snyder,[418] with whom I had corresponded (about Zen Buddhism) in the early fifties, or it may have been from Sister Vajira,[419] the elderly and somewhat eccentric English Buddhist nun he had met in Darjeeling a few days earlier. Most likely he had heard about me from Devapriya Valisinha, the General Secretary of the Maha Bodhi Society of India, whom he had met in Calcutta, when he visited the Society's headquarters. Calcutta had, it seemed, affected him deeply. He and his friend Peter had spent two or three uncomfortable weeks there, I gathered, but since Peter had fallen ill he had had to make the trip up to Darjeeling and Kalimpong on his own. 'Peter's my wife' he added, by way of explanation. At first I thought that I had either misheard my visitor or that Peter was in fact not a man but a woman. After all, there were female Lesleys and Robins and so on, especially in America. Why should there not be a female Peter? I had yet to discover that Peter definitely was a man and that Allen was nothing if not frank.

My initial impression of Allen, however, appearances apart, was that he was very American. That was indeed obvious as soon as he opened his mouth and began talking. Crouched uncomfortably on the edge of one of the bamboo armchairs that constituted almost the sole furniture of my little sitting room, and glancing uneasily out of the window from time to time in the direction of the blue Darjeeling hills, Allen indeed talked quite a lot that afternoon. Much of what he said was rather incoherent, and he rambled a good deal, but I gathered that he was interested in Buddhism, especially Tantric Buddhism, and that he had come to Kalimpong – as so many other Westerners had come – in search of Tantric initiation, the more powerful the better. While we were talking Lobsang Norbu, the young Tibetan manager of the monastery, brought in the tea and started pouring it out. Allen looked up from the apathy into which it seemed he had sunk for a moment. 'Wow, he's a good-looker!' he exclaimed, goggling up at Lobsang admiringly. Lobsang, who had spent the greater part of his life in a Tibetan monastery (he was still technically a novice, though he insisted on wearing Western dress) was not ignorant of what such admiration meant, but his only response was a broad smile that showed his magnificent white teeth. I began to think that perhaps I had not misheard my visitor and that Peter might, after all, be a man.

While we were drinking our tea I gathered that the balding American hunched opposite me was interested not only in Buddhism but in poetry. In fact, he was a poet. As though to prove it, he dove into a travel-stained cloth bag that he had dumped on the floor beside him and produced two small, dog-eared volumes. These were *Howl* and *Kaddish*, the latter of which had been published only the previous year. One volume he inscribed and presented to me (which one, I can no longer recollect), while the other he offered to leave with me to read overnight since he had no other copy with him in India and was therefore unable to give it to me. From the way in which he handled the two volumes, as well as the way in which he spoke about their contents, it was clear that Allen cared very deeply about his poetry, and that in making me a gift of the one volume and offering to lend me the other he was in fact giving expression to his willingness to share with me the deepest and most precious part of himself. Suddenly he seemed very open, very vulnerable, and very human.

That night I sat up quite late, after my usual meditation and puja, reading *Howl* and *Kaddish* by the light of a kerosene lamp. Before Allen's departure it had been agreed that he should come again the following afternoon to collect the volume he had left with me, and that I should tell him what I thought about his poetry. It had also been agreed that I should take him to see my friend C. M. Chen, the Chinese Buddhist yogi, who I felt might be able to help him in his search for Tantric initiation.[420] Poring over the two dog-eared volumes by the yellow light of the kerosene lamp, I could not but be struck by their raw energy and their directness, but I found it difficult to think of them as poetry and could not help wondering what I was going to say to Allen the following afternoon.

I need not have worried. When we met he was preoccupied (in an obsessive, unhealthy way, I thought) with the idea of Tantric initiation and on my returning the volume he had left with me the previous day he stuffed it into his cloth bag almost absent-mindedly. What I said about his poetry I do not know. Probably I got away with telling him that I found it very interesting, which was true enough. As we walked into Kalimpong along the Upper Cart Road he plied me with questions about Tantric Buddhism, especially about the exact nature of its sexual practices. I was describing these as best I could, and going into a certain amount of detail, when my companion suddenly stopped dead in his tracks, seized me by the arm, and with a voice hoarse with excitement demanded, 'Say, can you do it with a *boy*?' I had to confess I did not know if you could do it with a boy, and that he would have to ask Mr Chen. I was now quite sure that Peter definitely was a man.

Mr Chen's hermitage was situated at the farther, lower end of the Kalimpong bazaar. When we reached it half an hour later, and were sitting in the tiny reception room with its numerous pictures of Tantric divinities locked in (hetero-)sexual embrace, Allen lost no time in putting his question. *Could you do it with a boy?* Rather to my surprise, Mr Chen showed every sign of extreme embarrassment. No, you certainly could *not* do it with a boy, he replied shortly, and at once changed the subject. Allen's visit was not a success. When I saw Mr Chen a few days later he referred to the strange American I had brought to see him, and to his outrageous question, in terms of horror and disgust. How could anyone even *think* of 'doing it with a boy'! So far as the Chinese Buddhist yogi was concerned the sexual practices of the Buddhist Tantra were, it seemed, essentially and unalterably heterosexual, which I could not help thinking was rather a limitation.

Nevertheless, though the visit had not been a success it had not been a total failure either. Mr Chen had advised Allen to seek Tantric initiation from Dudjom Rimpoche, who was then living in Kalimpong, and I believe Allen did in fact meet the Nyingmapa hierophant before rejoining Peter in Calcutta. Whether he succeeded in obtaining Tantric initiation, or in finding an answer to the question that had puzzled me and embarrassed Mr Chen, I never discovered, for Allen and I did not meet again for three or four years. When we did meet (in London, on the morning after the famous Albert Hall poetry reading)[421] it did not occur to me to ask him how he had fared in Kalimpong after our visit to Mr Chen.[422] Nor has it occurred to me to ask him since. If he reads these lines perhaps they will jog his memory.[423]

NOTES

FOREWORD

1 *The Religion of Art*, Windhorse Publications, Cambridge 2010, p. 91 (*Complete Works*, vol. 26).
2 John Ruskin, *Praeterita*, para. 195. Oxford University Press, Oxford 1978, p. 159.
3 *Peace is a Fire*, Windhorse Publications, Birmingham 1995, p. 86 (*Complete Works*, vol. 26).
4 Saṅgharakshita's reflections continued over decades culminating in *Forty-Three Years Ago: Reflections on my Bhikkhu Ordination*, *Complete Works*, vol. 2. See also *Was the Buddha a Bhikkhu?* in the same volume.
5 *The Rainbow Road from Tooting Broadway to Kalimpong*, *Complete Works*, vol. 20, p. 149.
6 *Garava Sutta*, *Saṃyutta Nikāya* i.139. C. A. F. Rhys Davids (trans.), *The Book of the Kindred Sayings*, part 1, Pali Text Society, London 1979, pp. 175–6; or Bhikkhu Bodhi (trans.), *The Connected Discourses of the Buddha*, Wisdom Publications, Boston 2000, pp. 234–5.
7 The bodhisattva's *saṃvara-śīla* or sixty-four precepts are included in the appendix to *Complete Works*, vol. 2, pp. 657–9.
8 *Best Minds: A Tribute to Allen Ginsberg*, Lospecchio Press, New York 1986.
9 *Beating the Drum: Maha Bodhi Editorials*, *Complete Works*, vol. 8; *Dear Dinoo: Letters to a Friend*, *Complete Works*, vol. 21; *Complete Poems 1941–1994*, Windhorse Publications, Birmingham 1995 (*Complete Works*, vol. 25).

IN THE SIGN OF THE GOLDEN WHEEL

10 From *Jiban Smriti (Reminiscences)* of Rabindranath Tagore (1861–1941) quoted in Krishna Kripalani, *Rabindranath Tagore: A Biography*, Oxford University Press, London 1962, p. 211.

11 'The Religion of Art' is published along with three other essays on that theme, in *The Religion of Art*, Windhorse Publications, Cambridge 2010 (*Complete Works*, vol. 26).

12 Lama Govinda had presented Sangharakshita with this image at the end of his stay in Kalimpong in the autumn of 1951.

> It was about a foot-and-a-half in height, and though the rather flat wooden body was carved and painted with a simplicity that was almost primitive, the gilded face, hands, and feet, which were of clay, were of unusual delicacy and refinement.

Facing Mount Kanchenjunga, Complete Works, vol. 21, p. 261.

13 1. 'Joe' was Major Joseph E. Cann, or Upāsaka Joseph E. Cann as he preferred to be styled. He moved to Kalimpong from Lucknow to help the newly founded Young Men's Buddhist Association, arriving there in the summer of 1950. He is a prominent figure in *Facing Mount Kanchenjunga, Complete Works*, vol. 21, see especially pp. 45–8.
2. Miss Rao lived in Chung Building. She was the daughter of Mrs Rao, a Hindu lady from Mysore, with whom Sangharakshita sometimes had tea. Mrs Rao was a lady 'of great dignity and sweetness of character who had evidently suffered much'. The diminutive Miss Rao, however, seemed to be in every way the opposite of her mother. See ibid., pp. 226–8.

14 Man Bahadur was Sangharakshita's Nepalese cook-bearer. See *Facing Mount Kanchenjunga, Complete Works*, vol. 21, p. 432.

15 Krishnalok was in Ringkingpong, and was the home of Prince Peter and Princess Irene of Greece who had moved there from nearby Tashiding where Sangharakshita first visited them for afternoon tea and caused great offence to his hostess by not accepting a piece of cake (as a monk he did not eat after noon). See *Facing Mount Kanchenjunga, Complete Works*, vol. 21, pp. 253–4. He was later forgiven and wrote an epitaph for her squirrel when it died. See ibid., p. 319. 'Epitaph on Krishna, Princess Irene's Squirrel' is in *Complete Poems 1941–1994*, Windhorse Publications, Birmingham 1995, p. 175 (*Complete Works*, vol. 25).

16 Mrs Charu Mitter had her summer residence at Manjula where she 'gave tea parties, entertained women friends and relations from the plains, and pulled numberless small strings in the world of (predominantly) Bengali officialdom'. She was a close friend of Pratima Tagore, daughter-in-law of the poet; and something of a matchmaker. See *Facing Mount Kanchenjunga*, *Complete Works*, vol. 21, pp. 148–54.

17 Lama Govinda, *The Way of the White Clouds*, Hutchinson and Co., London 1969, p. 197.

18 Sangharakshita 'went forth' on 18 August 1947. He describes the occasion in his first volume of memoirs:

> As we left Kasauli it was raining, but, as in the course of our descent we emerged from the clouds into the bright sunshine below, we saw arching the road, at intervals of a few dozen yards, not only single but double and triple rainbows.

The Rainbow Road from Tooting Broadway to Kalimpong, *Complete Works*, vol. 20, p. 226.

19 In the Classical Greek tradition the Fates or *Moirai* were the three white-robed sisters who controlled destiny: Clotho, the spinner, who spun the thread of life; Lachesis, the allotter, who determined the length of the thread; and Atropos, the inevitable, who cut the thread with her shears. In Norse mythology the controllers of destiny were known as the Norns. They spun the threads of fate at the foot of Yggdrasil, the tree at the centre of the world.

20 Miss Delannoy, 'a short, untidy Frenchwoman with an anxious expression whom I had already met in Calcutta' first appears on the scene in Kalimpong at the end of 1952 or beginning of 1953 when

> for the next two weeks she came to see me every day, and we had some interesting discussions on such topics as the *Perfection of Wisdom Sūtras*, meditation, and the spiritual life, as well as on poetry and the relative claims of religion and art.

Facing Mount Kanchenjunga, *Complete Works*, vol. 21, p. 445.

21 The educational institution at Shantiniketan, Visva-Bharati (translated variously – for example 'the communion of the world and India'), was founded by the poet Rabindranath Tagore. It was given official government recognition as a university in 1951. The Cheena Bhavana (Institute of Chinese Language and Culture) was founded in April 1937. Sangharakshita describes his impressions of Shantiniketan in chapter 4.

22 The *Bhaiṣajya-guru-vaiḍūrya-prabhā-rāja Sūtra* or *Sūtra of the Lord of Healing* (also known as the *Medicine Buddha Sūtra*) tells how Bhaiṣajyaguru makes twelve

great bodhisattva vows and on reaching Buddhahood becomes the Buddha of the eastern Pure Land, Vaiḍūryanirbhāsa, or Pure Lapis Lazuli. Originally composed in Sanskrit, the *sūtra* was translated into Chinese by Dharmagupta in 615 CE and by Xuanzang in 650 CE.

23 Sangharakshita met Tibetologist George Roerich soon after his arrival in Kalimpong in 1950. He was the son of the artist Nicholas Roerich, 'a plump, ruddy-faced man in riding boots and breeches' who became a contributor to *Stepping-Stones*, the monthly journal of Himalayan religion, culture, and education that Sangharakshita published from July 1950 to February 1952. See *Facing Mount Kanchenjunga*, *Complete Works*, vol. 21, pp. 33–4 and 49. Roerich (1902–1960) is known for his translation of the fifteenth-century history of Tibet, *The Blue Annals* (1949).

24 When staying at the Anandashram of Sri Ramdas (1884–1963) in Kanhangad in 1949, Sangharakshita copied out the whole text of *The Awakening of Faith in the Mahāyāna*.

> Though I had read it before, the compactness of its style and the profundity of its teaching now impressed me more than ever.

The notebook into which he copied the work had been inscribed for him by Ramdas. See *The Rainbow Road from Tooting Broadway to Kalimpong*, *Complete Works*, vol. 20, p. 332.

25 Sachin was one of a small group of students whom Sangharakshita came to know well.

> Just as the little fraternity gave a lead to the rest of the students, so there was one member of the group who seemed to give a lead to the group itself. This was a seventeen-year-old Nepali called Sachindra Coomar Singh.

Facing Mount Kanchenjunga, *Complete Works*, vol. 21, pp. 72–3.

26 Sangharakshita set up the Kalimpong branch of the Young Men's Buddhist Association (YMBA) in May 1950 soon after his arrival in Kalimpong. As well as lectures, debates, and recreational activities, there were free tutorials to help with examinations on which the futures of the many young men from diverse backgrounds who came along depended. See *Facing Mount Kanchenjunga*, *Complete Works*, vol. 21, pp. 36–8. In December 1952, on returning from several weeks at the Calcutta headquarters of the Maha Bodhi Society, writing a biographical sketch of the Society's founder, Anagarika

Dharmapala, Sangharakshita decided, for financial and other reasons, that the YMBA should affiliate to that Society and it became the Kalimpong branch of the Maha Bodhi Society. See ibid., pp. 427–8.

27 Two of the great English Romantic poets: William Wordsworth's poem, whose full title is 'Ode: Intimations of Immortality from Recollections of Early Childhood', has eleven stanzas. It was completed in 1804. Percy Bysshe Shelley's 'Ode to the West Wind' in five cantos was written in 1819.

28 The initial hospitality shown by Gyan Jyoti to Jagdish Kashyap and Sangharakshita when they arrived in Kalimpong – and the complications that followed – is described in *Facing Mount Kanchenjunga*, *Complete Works*, vol. 21, pp. 8–10.

29
> I cannot see what flowers
> are at my feet,
> Nor what soft incense
> hangs upon the boughs,
> But, in embalmèd darkness,
> guess each sweet...

From John Keats' 'Ode to a Nightingale', written in 1819.

30 *Two Leaves and a Bud* is a novel by Indian writer Mulk Raj Anand (1905–2004) set in a tea plantation in Assam, and concerned with issues of exploitation of the poor.

31 'The cup that cheers but does not inebriate': from William Cowper's 'The Task: A Poem in Six Books' (1785). The themes of everyday life and the English countryside figure in Cowper's poems heralding the emergence of English Romantic poetry. He was also a writer of Christian hymns.

32 The popular slogan describing Indian Chinese relations in the mid-1950s was '*Hindi-Cheeni bhai-bhai*'.

33 The individual cases of three such young men are recounted in *Facing Mount Kanchenjunga*, *Complete Works*, vol. 21, pp. 364–6.

34 Sangharakshita first saw the image during a trip to Darjeeling in October 1950, when he was also accompanied by Sachin. On entering the temple

> I saw in front of me ... the mighty sedent figure of the semi-legendary founder and inspirer of the Nyingma tradition, a skull cup in his left hand, a staff topped with skulls in the crook of his left arm, and the celebrated 'wrathful smile' on his moustached face.... Though I had never seen the figure of Padmasambhava before, it was familiar to me in a way that no other figure on earth was familiar ... yet at the same time infinitely mysterious, infinitely wonderful, and infinitely inspiring.

Facing Mount Kanchenjunga, *Complete Works*, vol. 21, p. 93.

35 In 1971 Sangharakshita took up the theme of 'The Jewel in the Lotus' in a series of lectures on 'Parables, Myths, and Symbols of Mahāyāna Buddhism in the *White Lotus Sūtra*'. An edited version of this talk can be found in *The Drama of Cosmic Enlightenment*, chapter 7, *Complete Works*, vol. 16. That same year he also spoke on 'The Symbolism of Colours and Mantric Sound' in the series 'Creative Symbols of the Tantric Path to Enlightenment'. An edited version of the talk can be found in *Creative Symbols of Tantric Buddhism*, chapter 7, in *Complete Works*, vol. 13, pp. 276–95.

36 Sangharakshita I wanted to enjoy the beauty of nature, to read and write poetry, to listen to music, to look at paintings and sculpture, to experience emotion, to lie in bed and dream, to see places, to meet people. Sangharakshita II wanted to realize the truth, to read and write philosophy, to observe the precepts, to get up early and meditate, to mortify the flesh, to fast and pray

The Rainbow Road from Tooting Broadway to Kalimpong, *Complete Works*, vol. 20, p. 451.

37 The story of the battle with Rani Dorji over where the Sacred Relics might be stationed in Kalimpong and the reason for her intense opposition to their being lodged at the Tharpa Choling Gompa is described in *Facing Mount Kanchenjunga*, *Complete Works*, vol. 21, pp. 196–203.

38 See note 26.

39 Anagarika Dharmapala's birthday fell on 17 September. It was celebrated annually by the Maha Bodhi Society, and what was now the Kalimpong branch of the Society was therefore also marking the day. Anagarika Dharmapala was born to Buddhist parents in 1864 in the city of Matara, Ceylon (Sri Lanka), then a British colony. He founded the Maha Bodhi Society in 1891 to work for the restoration of the Maha Bodhi temple at Bodh Gaya (which was in a state of terrible disrepair and being used as a Hindu shrine) and other Buddhist holy sites, and for the propagation of the Dharma. It was at that time the only functioning Buddhist organization in India. See *Anagarika Dharmapala: a Biographical Sketch, and Other Maha Bodhi Writings*, Ibis Publications, Ledbury 2014 (*Complete Works*, vol. 8).

40 Sangharakshita describes the Dharmodaya Vihara or 'Monastery of the Rise of the Teaching' where he spent his first months in Kalimpong, and introduces the Vihara's librarian who had once been a monk in *Facing Mount*

Kanchenjunga, *Complete Works*, vol. 21, pp. 17–20.

41 Thus do the 'Brothers of the Shadow' – the murderers of their Souls, the dread Dad-Dugpa clan.

> H. P. Blavatsky, *The Voice of the Silence*, para. 228, Theosophical Publishing House, Adyar 1953, p. 185.

42 Hans-Ulrich Rieker (1920–1979) was a German actor and writer and a disciple of Lama Govinda. He was initiated by Lama Govinda into the Arya Maitreya Mandala (AMM) order which he had founded. In 1952 Rieker started a European branch of the AMM. Sangharakshita is quoting from Hans-Ulrich Rieker, *Beggar Among the Dead*, trans. Edward Fitzgerald, Rider and Co., London 1960, pp. 77 and 96–7. A review of the book by Sangharakshita was published in the *Maha Bodhi*, vol. no. 8 (August 1961) pp. 252–3. See *Anagarika Dharmapala: a Biographical Sketch, and other Maha Bodhi Writings*, Ibis Publications, Ledbury 2014, pp. 170–1 (*Complete Works*, vol. 8).

43 Bhadanta Ananda Kausalyayana, 'On the Verge of Death', *Maha Bodhi*, vol. 63, no. 2, February 1955, pp. 75–9.

44 The state of Madhya Pradesh (which means 'central province') was created in 1947 after India's independence, with Nagpur as its capital. In 1956 there was a reorganization so that Madhya Pradesh lost the Marathi-speaking Vidarbha area but gained three other areas (former states) to become the largest state in India with Bhopal as its capital. (Since a reorganization in 2000 it has been the second largest state.)

45 'The Bodhisattva's Reply' in *Complete Poems 1941–1994*, Windhorse Publications, Birmingham 1995, pp. 178–9 (*Complete Works*, vol. 25).

46 Described in chapter 6 of *Facing Mount Kanchenjunga*, *Complete Works*, vol. 21.

47 The Laughing Buddha, known as Budai in Chinese and Hotei in Japanese, is a legendary figure of popular Far Eastern Buddhism. He is depicted as a monk with an enormously fat belly and laughing face. His happy smile symbolizes contentment and his fat belly abundance. 'Buddha' here simply means that he is Enlightened.

48 Ang Tsering came to work for Sangharakshita in 1952 and was found to possess

> all those qualities of adaptability and resourcefulness which had gone to make the Sherpas of Nepal an essential part of every Himalayan expedition.

Facing Mount Kanchenjunga, *Complete Works*, vol. 21. pp. 325–6.

> Having served me faithfully for a year and accumulated a small capital, [he] left to set himself up in business as a pig breeder.

Ibid., p. 432.

49 The Musée Guimet was founded in 1879 by Émile Étienne Guimet, a French industrialist who travelled in the Far East bringing back many Buddhist, as well as non-Buddhist, images and artefacts which became the foundation for the museum. It moved from Lyon to its premises in Paris in 1889.

50 Pratima Devi's summer residence was Chitrabanu, near the house of Burma Raja, at whose guest cottage Sangharakshita was invited to stay after being forced to leave the Dharmodaya Vihara. He was introduced to Pratima Devi by another neighbour, Mrs Mitter (see note 16). Pratima Devi had

> a quality of transparency and luminosity ... which, combined with her dignity and sweetness, her perfect courtesy, and her refined, aristocratic manners, created the impression of a being from another world.

Facing Mount Kanchenjunga, *Complete Works*, vol. 21, pp. 153–6.

51 The visit of Lama Govinda and Li Gotami to Kalimpong is described in *Facing Mount Kanchenjunga*, *Complete Works*, vol. 21, ch. 13. In Lama Govinda especially Sangharakshita felt he had found a kindred spirit. Their friendship continued even after both men had left India. Lama Govinda's last letter to Sangharakshita, written from California, was dated 10 January 1984. 'What a joy to have your dear long letter...' he wrote. He died just four days later.

52 Krishna Kripalani, *Rabindranath Tagore: A Biography*, Oxford University Press, London 1962, p. 267. The motto Tagore gave to Visva-Bharati was '*yatra visvam bhavatieka nidam*' which means, 'where the whole world meets in one nest'.

53 Mary Wollstonecraft Shelley published the first edition of her husband's poetry with notes and a preface two years after his untimely death under the title *The Posthumous Poems of Percy Bysshe Shelley* (June 1824). Two further editions followed.

54 Robert Browning (1812–1899) was one of the most admired poets of the Victorian era. Sangharakshita mentions first reading the poems of Elizabeth Barratt Browning, Robert's – also famous – wife, at the age of eleven. See *The Rainbow Road from Tooting Broadway to Kalimpong*, *Complete Works*, vol. 20, p. 34.

55 Physician Havelock Ellis (1859–1939) was one of the first to study and write about human sexuality. He co-authored a medical text book published in 1897 on 'sexual inversion' i.e. homosexuality. His *Studies in the Psychology of Sex* in six volumes were published 1900–1910. *The Psychology of Sex*, an overview of human sexuality in one volume, was published in 1933.

56 This influx of refugees was a result of the Partition of the Indian subcontinent at the end of British rule in 1947, division being along religious lines, with the aim of creating separate Hindu and Muslim states so that East Bengal became East Pakistan which resulted in millions of Hindus fleeing. The catastrophic impact of Partition on the lives of millions of people is one of the great calamities of the twentieth century. (In 1971 East Pakistan became the independent state of Bangladesh.)

57 Sangharakshita first visited the Sri Dharmarajika Vihara in 1947. (See *The Rainbow Road from Tooting Broadway to Kalimpong*, *Complete Works*, vol. 20, p. 136). In the autumn of 1952 he spent several weeks there writing his biographical sketch of Anagarika Dharmapala as recounted in *Facing Mount Kanchenjunga*, *Complete Works*, vol. 21, chapter 18.

58 Calcutta (now Kolkata) is famous for festivals of the Hindu goddesses Saraswati, the goddess of learning, in the month of Magha (January-February), and Kali, 'the devourer of time', in the autumn, coinciding with Diwali, the festival of lights.

59 Robert Clive (1725–1774), known as Clive of India, established the political power of the East India Company in Bengal, paving the way for British rule. Siraj ud-Daulah (1733–1757) was the last independent Nawab of Bengal. In 1756 he laid siege to the British army at their Calcutta garrison known as Fort William. Many were taken prisoner and held overnight in such cramped conditions that the majority of them died. The place became known as 'the black hole of Calcutta'. In February 1757 Clive, who was by then a lieutenant-colonel of the British army, oversaw the recapture of Fort William and the surrender of Calcutta to the British.

60 William Carey (1761–1834) was a Baptist missionary, author of *An Enquiry into the Obligations of Christians to Use Means for the Conversion of the Heathens* who arrived in Calcutta in 1793. He translated the *Bible* into Bengali and several other Indian languages and translated Indian scriptures from Sanskrit into English.

Warren Hastings (1732–1818) was the first British governor of Bengal. Over a period of ten years he developed the British Raj, building on what Clive of India had begun.

61 William Makepeace Thackeray (1811–1863), author of *Vanity Fair* and other works, was born in Calcutta. (His father worked for the British East India Company.) Colman Macaulay (1849–1890) worked for the Indian civil service in Bengal. He died in Calcutta 'due to excessive heat during the railway journey from Bombay'.

62 Sri Ramakrishna (1836–1886), originally given the name Gadadhar Chattopadhyay, is known as the Bengali mystic whose teachings were the inspiration for the Ramakrishna Mission founded by his disciple Vivekananda. Ramakrishna became priest at the Dakineshwar Kali temple in Calcutta at a young age. His life and teaching was dedicated to Hindu devotional and tantric practices, and a philosophy based on the Advaita Vedanta of the great eighth-century Hindu philosopher, Śaṅkara.

Swami Vivekananda (1863–1902), whose given name was Narendranath Datta, was a chief disciple of Ramakrishna and largely responsible for bringing the Ramakrishna Mission to the attention of Westerners. He gave a speech introducing Hinduism to America at the Parliament of World Religions held in Chicago in 1893 (which was also attended by Anagarika Dharmapala). He founded the Mission in 1897 which has become known for its dedication to social work. Sangharakshita first came into contact with the Ramakrishna Mission in Colombo, Ceylon, as a young soldier. (See 'With the Swamis in Ceylon', chapter 11 of *The Rainbow Road from Tooting Broadway to Kalimpong*, *Complete Works*, vol. 20.) Contact with the Mission swamis greatly encouraged him in his own spiritual aspirations. During this time he read all the Mission's literature. Later, however, when he was staying at the Mission in Calcutta, he came to see the sinister implications of the Advaita Vedanta philosophy they espoused and subsequently had no further dealings with it (ibid., p. 164).

63 1. The Tagores were for generations a leading family in Calcutta with exceptionally talented individuals who contributed to business, social and religious reform, and literature, art, and music.
2. Rajendra Mullick (1819–1887) built the famous Marble Palace of Kolkata.

64 The Victoria Memorial is a grand marble building (today a

museum) built 1906–1921 on the banks of the Hooghly river in what was then the capital of India. It was a tribute to the Empress Victoria who had died in 1901.

The Ochterlony Monument is a tower, 48 metres high, erected in central Kolkata in 1828 in memory of Major-General David Ochterlony, commander of the East India Company, and to commemorate his victories over Indian uprisings. It was rededicated in 1969 and is now known as the Shaheed Minar or Martyrs' Monument in memory of those who lost their lives in the Indian Independence Movement.

65 The Hindu Mahasabha, a Hindu nationalist organization, was formed in 1909 after the formation in 1906 of the All-India Muslim League. In 1921 it became the All-India Hindu Mahasabha.

66 The month spent with the Maha Bodhi Society in Calcutta in 1947 is related in *The Rainbow Road from Tooting Broadway to Kalimpong*, *Complete Works*, vol. 20, chapter 17.

67 Sangharakshita's request for ordination as a novice monk to the Maha Bodhi *bhikkhus* at Sarnath is recounted in ibid., pp. 388–91.

68 Sangharakshita's *bhikkhu* ordination took place on 24 November 1950 as related in *Facing Mount Kanchenjunga*, *Complete Works*, vol. 21, pp. 107–9.

69 The preparations for the reception of the Sacred Relics in Kalimpong is described in *Facing Mount Kanchenjunga*, *Complete Works*, vol. 21, chapter 10. Chapter 11 describes the trip to Gangtok with the Sacred Relics, and how Sangharakshita was denied entry to Tibet. It also describes the successful reception of the Sacred Relics in Kalimpong (pp. 206–15). Chapter 14 relates how Sangharakshita accompanied the Sacred Relics to Nepal.

70 Jinaratana's 'unmonklike' behaviour included hoarding chocolate and fountain pens, 'rapping out orders', and cruelty towards the elderly Miss Albers. See *The Rainbow Road from Tooting Broadway to Kalimpong*, *Complete Works*, vol. 20, pp. 165 and 170–1 where he is referred to simply as 'His Holiness' – an honorific Jinaratana had decided to adopt for himself.

71 Sangharakshita's three meetings with Dr Ambedkar are described in *Ambedkar and Buddhism*, *Complete Works*, vol. 9, chapter 2.

72 Good Deeds is one of the allegorical characters in the late fifteenth-century English morality play, *Everyman* (more correctly, *The Summoning of Everyman*). When the eponymous central figure asks Good Deeds to accompany

him on his journey with Death to face God's judgement, she replies:

> Here I lie cold in the ground;
> Thy sins hath me sore
> bound,
> That I cannot stir.

Only when Everyman has repented his sins and scourged himself is she strong enough to go with him. Sangharakshita read the play in his teens, and saw Leslie French's ballet *Everyman* based on the morality play, which premiered in London in 1943.

> So deeply was I impressed that when I tried to write an appreciation of *Everyman* I found my feelings too strong for expression.

The Rainbow Road from Tooting Broadway to Kalimpong, *Complete Works*, vol. 20, p. 86.

73 Himavantavasi's column 'In the Light of the Dhamma' first appeared in the *Maha Bodhi* in the summer of 1953 and continued until December 1955. Himavantavasi's interests were broad, ranging from 'Buddhism and Astrology' to the question of 'To Film or Not to Film' and to 'Amiel, Schopenhauer, and Buddhism'. His *Maha Bodhi* contributions were collected together many years later and are included in *Anagarika Dharmapala: a Biographical Sketch, and other Maha Bodhi Writings*, Ibis Publications, Ledbury 2014 (*Complete Works*, vol. 8).

74 The monthly editorials written by Sangharakshita as editor of the *Maha Bodhi* began in January 1954 with 'Ancient Buddhist Site in Danger' (about the irrigation scheme that threatened to submerge Nagarjunakonda) and continued until June/July 1964. They cover an astonishingly wide field of interest from 'The Menace of Horror Comics' to reflections on meditation to the need for reform in the Buddhist world. The editorials are collected together in *Beating the Drum*, Ibis Publications, Ledbury 2012 (*Complete Works*, vol. 8) with an extended Introduction giving a detailed description and history of the publication.

75 See Book 3, Champai 36 in A. G. Atkins (ed.), *The Ramayana of Tulsidas*, vol. ii, Birla Academy of Art and Culture, Calcutta 1966, p. 573.

76 The *Maha Bodhi* for January 1954 lists the editorial board as follows: Dr Kalidas Nag (Chairman), Bhikshu Sangharakshita, Bhikkhu Dharmaratana, Bikkhu Silabhadra, N. Jinaratna Thera (Managing Editor), and Sri D. Valisinha (Secretary). Over the next decade the editorial board changed but little. A notable addition was in July 1954 when Dr Nalinaksha Dutt appears for the first time. Not

only Dr Dutt but also the full list of Dr Dutt's academic and other credentials: M.A., PhD., D.Litt., P.R.S., B.L., and M.P. As if to keep up, Dr Nag now also has a string of letters after *his* name and even Bhikkhu Dharmaratana and Sri D. Valisinha are awarded a B.A. Only Bhikkhu Silabhadra and Bhikshu Sangharakshita are there with neither portfolio nor academic qualifications.... Silabhadra died in 1955, being listed for the last time in the July issue (an obituary appears in August). He was not replaced. From June 1956 there was, however, an important addition to the otherwise masculine bastion of the board: Mrs A. A. G. Bennett of 9 Portland Square Mansions, London, joins as 'Editorial Representative in Europe and the Americas'. See *Beating the Drum*, Ibis Publications, Ledbury 2012, p. 65 (*Complete Works*, vol. 8).

77 Sangharakshita's stay at the Anandamayi Ashram, along with his friend Banerjee, is described in chapters 21–2 of *The Rainbow Road from Tooting Broadway to Kalimpong*, in *Complete Works*, vol. 20. A description of one such scene of hysterical devotion occurs on pp. 188–9.

78 The visits with Phani Bhusan Sanyal to Udbodhan and the shrine of the Holy Mother are described in *The Rainbow Road from Tooting Broadway to Kalimpong*, *Complete Works*, vol. 20, p. 136. Sangharakshita found the room where she had lived and which was now her shrine to be 'the purest and most peaceful place in Calcutta.'

79 See 'With the Swamis in Ceylon' in *The Rainbow Road from Tooting Broadway to Kalimpong*, *Complete Works*, vol. 20, chapter 11.

80

> I recoiled from the Mission like one who, when a lamp is lit, sees that he had been about to step on a snake in the dark.

The Rainbow Road from Tooting Broadway to Kalimpong, *Complete Works*, vol. 20, p. 164.

81 Irene Ray, like Sangharakshita, was born in Tooting, South London. He met her in Kalimpong when she was on retreat at the Ramakrishna ashram. A serious student of Advaita Vedanta and married to a Bengali doctor, she 'wore Bengali saris,... spoke the Bengali language,... cooked and ate in Bengali style.' *Facing Mount Kanchenjunga*, *Complete Works*, vol. 21, p. 156.

82 'The Meaning of Buddhism and the Value of Art' was published as a pamphlet in late 1956 or early 1957, funded by Sangharakshita's friend, Dinoo Dubash (referred to in *Dear Dinoo*, Letters 2, 10, and 12; see *Complete Works*,

vol. 21). 'The Meaning of Buddhism and the Value of Art' is included in *The Religion of Art*, Windhorse Publications, Cambridge 2010 (*Complete Works*, vol. 26).

83 'Buddhism and the Parliament of Religions' in *Maha Bodhi*, vol. 62, no. 2, February 1954, pp. 56–7; and *Beating the Drum*, Ibis Publications, Ledbury 2012, p. 98 (*Complete Works*, vol. 8).

84 As described in Homer's *Iliad*, book 17. The epic poem is usually dated to the eighth century BCE.

85 *Khata* can be translated as 'ceremonial scarf'. It is usually white and made of silk.

86

> A Lady, the wonder of her kind,
> Whose form was upborne by a lovely mind

appears in the garden to tend the plants in part 2 of Percy Bysshe Shelley's poem, 'The Sensitive Plant' published in *Prometheus Unbound and Other Poems* (1820).

87

> That time of year thou mayst in me behold
> When yellow leaves, or none, or few, do hang
> Upon those boughs which shake against the cold,
> Bare ruin'd choirs, where late the sweet birds sang.

William Shakespeare (1564–1616), Sonnet 73.

88 The Fable of the Fox and the Grapes comes from Aesop, a Greek slave and storyteller who is thought to have flourished 620–564 BCE. In this story the fox, unable to reach the grapes he longs to eat, remarks that they are sour and he didn't want them anyway – thus the expression 'sour grapes'.

89 Raj Kapoor had invited Sangharakshita to R. K. Studios in Bombay to advise him on a film he intended to make which was to be called 'Ajanta', featuring a Buddhist monk (to be played by himself). See *Facing Mount Kanchenjunga*, chapter 20, in *Complete Works*, vol. 21.

90 Jean Racine (1639–1699) is one of France's great dramatists, known for his tragic plays, such as *Phèdre*, which he composed using the French alexandrine, a poetic meter of twelve syllables divided into two by a ceasura or break.

91 The Kamakhya Temple is a sixteenth-century Hindu temple in the Kamrup district of western Assam. In one version of the legend, the god Shiva, mad with grief, dances through the cosmos with the corpse of his wife, Sati. Parts of her body fall to the ground, her vulva falling on the spot on which this temple is built.

92 Sangharakshita met Buddharakshita, originally Robin Banerjee, in Singapore in 1946 (see *The Rainbow Road from Tooting Broadway to Kalimpong*, *Complete Works*,

vol. 20, pp. 146–7). They went on to spend two years together as wandering ascetics, including fifteen months in a haunted ashram. During these years they met some of the great Indian spiritual masters of the time. Together they received *śāmaṇera* ordination at Kusinara in May 1949 before going their separate ways (see ibid., chapters 16–47).

93 This was Kamalashila, 'a very thin, very dark, very talkative Bihari of about my own age', who had been ordained by Jagdish Kashyap. See *Facing Mount Kanchenjunga*, *Complete Works*, vol. 21, pp. 85–6.

94 See *The Rainbow Road from Tooting Broadway to Kalimpong*, chapter 17, *Complete Works*, vol. 20, p. 166 where he is referred to as the quiet and meek Bihari *bhikkhu*.

95 *Dhammapada* 183. For an alternative translation see Sangharakshita (trans.), *Dhammapada: the Way of Truth*, Windhorse Publications, Birmingham 2001, p. 67 (*Complete Works*, vol. 15). I have not discovered the commentary which tells the story of the 1,250 monks who came together spontaneously and for whose benefit the Buddha spoke those words, but it seems to be a widespread tradition and is mentioned, for example, in Edward Irons, *Encyclopedia of Buddhism*, Facts on File Inc., New York 2008, p. 199 in a listing for Thailand, Magha Puja Day.

96 Although no record of this lecture survives, some of Sangharakshita's thoughts on education can be found in 'Buddhism and Education', a talk given at Siddharth College, Mumbai on 9 February 1982. See *Complete Works*, vol. 9, pp. 435–48.

97 Sangharakshita first met Colonel John Warren Swale Ryan in Sarnath. He later arrived in Kalimpong in 1950 as a guest of the Jyoti brothers. See *Facing Mount Kanchenjunga*, *Complete Works*, vol. 21, pp. 23–4. Swale and Joe Cann, the other YMBA helper, did not get on and eventually he ceased to work for the YMBA and left Kalimpong (ibid., pp. 151–2).

98 For this reason when in October 1956 Dr Ambedkar led the mass conversions from Hinduism to Buddhism of nearly half a million ex-Untouchables he created twenty-two vows (*pratijñās*) which the new converts made in addition to taking the traditional three refuges and five precepts. These twenty-two vows include: (1) I shall not consider Brahma, Vishnu, and Mahesh as gods, nor shall I worship them; (2) I shall not consider Rama and Krishna as gods, nor shall I worship them; (3) I shall not believe

in 'Gauri', Ganapati, and any other gods and goddesses of Hinduism, nor shall I worship them; (4) I do not believe that god has incarnated; (5) I do not and shall not believe that Lord Buddha was the incarnation of Vishnu. I believe this to be sheer madness and false propaganda. All twenty-two can be found in the Appendix to *Complete Works*, vol. 2, p. 656 and vol. 9. pp. 541–2.

99 Among the books sent by Dr Irene Bastow Hudson was a copy of Addison's *Essays.* Joseph Addison (1672–1719), together with his friend Richard Steele, brought out *The Spectator* six days a week from 1711 to 1712. (Addison revived it for six months in 1714.) Its aim was, 'to enliven morality with wit, and to temper wit with morality', and to bring philosophy 'out of closets and libraries, schools and colleges, to dwell in clubs and assemblies, at tea-tables, and in coffee-houses.' More than 3,000 copies were published daily.

100 Edward Conze, *Buddhism: Its Essence and Development*, Windhorse Publications, Birmingham 2001, p. 42. Conze cites Asaṅga's *Yogaśāstra* in which monks are allowed to possess gold, silver, and silken clothes, because 'such possessions allow them to be more useful to others, and to help them.' (Ibid.)

101 'L'Albatros' in C. Baudelaire, *Fleurs du Mal*, second edition, 1861. Baudelaire compares the ungainly albatross caught by mocking sailors on the deck of a ship with the albatross who flies with great wings majestically through the heavens. The final verse begins, 'The poet resembles this prince of cloud and sky'.

102 *The Illustrated Weekly of India* was a leading English-language magazine for more than a century. It began (in 1880) as the weekly edition of *The Times of India* changing its name in 1923. It ceased publication in 1993.

103 This was the multi-millionaire industrialist and philanthropist Jugal Kishore Birla (1883–1967) who had also financed the construction of Buddha Kuti, Jagdish Kashyap's residence on the campus of the Benares Hindu University where Sangharakshita stayed for his 'academic interlude' in the second part of 1949. See *Facing Mount Kanchenjunga*, *Complete Works*, vol. 21, pp. 316–17.

104 'April is the cruellest month…' is the opening line of T. S. Eliot's poem 'The Waste Land' (1922).

105 The *Aryan Path* was a theosophical journal founded in 1930 and published in Bombay. Its first editor was B. P. Wadia.

106 A ropeway is a form of naval lifting device used to transport

light stores and equipment across rivers or ravines.

107 Marco Pallis (1895–1989) was a Tibetologist and author of *Peaks and Lamas*, the book which introduced Sangharakshita to the figure of Milarepa and gave him his first insight into Tibetan Buddhism back in his army days in Singapore (see *Facing Mount Kanchenjunga*, *Complete Works*, vol. 21, p. 159). He first met Pallis, who was also known under his Tibetan Buddhist name as Thubden Tendzin, in his first year in Kalimpong and the older man became something of a 'guide, philosopher, and friend' – as well as interpreter – when dealing with the local Tibetan Buddhists (ibid., pp. 176ff). Pallis was required to leave Kalimpong due to activities connected with the Tibetan resistance movement. Before he left he gave Sangharakshita a number of presents including the beautiful thangkas which were 'not aids to visualization so much as an incitement to the living of the spiritual life in the widest sense'. They are described in detail in *Facing Mount Kanchenjunga*, ibid., p. 30.

108 Geshe Ngawang Wangyal (1901–1983) was of Kalmyk origin. He studied at Drepung monastery in Tibet, spent time in China, and worked as translator for the British Political Officer, Sir Charles Bell. After the Chinese invasion of Tibet in 1950 he escaped to India and in 1955 went to America where he established the Labsum Shedrub Ling monastery in New Jersey teaching many Western students. He was highly influential in the spread of Tibetan Buddhism in the USA.

109 After the poem *The City of Dreadful Night* (1874) by the Scottish poet James Thomson (1834–1882). It evoked in bleak and pessimistic tones the city of London. Rudyard Kipling used the title for a short story.

110 When printing was still done mechanically, the 'forme' was a body of type secured in a chase, or steel frame, for printing. The galley proof had the text before it was set into pages in a single column, often with an extra wide margin for inserting corrections. The printer's devil was an apprentice who ran errands and did small tasks at the printers.

111 110 degrees Fahrenheit is just over 43 degrees Celcius.

112 Lama A. Govinda, 'The Buddha's Seat (In the Ruins of the "Perfumed Chamber" at Sarnath)', *Maha Bodhi*, vol. 62, no. 2 (February 1954), pp. 33–4.

113 Lama A. Govinda, 'The Buddha as the Ideal of the Perfect Man and the

Embodiment of the Dharma' in *Maha Bodhi*, vol. 62, nos. 5–6 (May–June 1954), p. 151.

114 Ibid., p. 155.

115 Edward Conze, 'Conditions and the Unconditioned' in *Maha Bodhi*, vol. 62, nos. 5–6 (May–June 1954), pp. 159–164.

116 Marco Pallis, 'Some Aspects of a Buddhist Education' in *Maha Bodhi*, vol. 62, nos. 5–6 (May–June 1954), p. 186.

117 H. R. H. Prince Peter of Greece and Denmark, 'Buddhism and the Japanese Character' in *Maha Bodhi*, vol. 62, nos. 5–6 (May–June 1954), p. 171.

118 Christmas Humphreys, 'The Menace of Belief' in *Maha Bodhi*, vol. 62, nos. 5–6 (May–June 1954), p. 198.

119 'Buddha Gaya' in *Maha Bodhi*, vol. 62, nos. 5–6 (May–June 1954), pp. 224–7; and *Beating the Drum*, Ibis Publications, Ledbury 2012, pp. 110–13 (*Complete Works*, vol. 8).

120 *A Survey of Buddhism*, *Complete Works*, vol. 1, p. 322.

121 Sangharakshita describes his purchase of his first copy of the *Dhammapada* in *The Rainbow Road from Tooting Broadway to Kalimpong*, *Complete Works*, vol. 20, p. 115.

122 André Gide's *L'Immoraliste* was published in France in 1902. An English translation with the title *The Immoralist* was brought out in 1930.

123 André Gide's *Les nourritures terrestres* is a prose poem. It was published in France in 1897. *Les nouvelles nourritures* was published in 1935. They were both translated into English by Dorothy Bussy and published under the title *Fruits of the Earth, including Later Fruits of the Earth* (1949).

124 Madras was officially renamed Chennai in 1996. Calcutta was officially renamed Kolkata in 2001.

125 Immediately after his 'Going Forth' in August 1947 Sangharakshita (or Dharmapriya as he then called himself) and his friend, Satyapriya, took a train from New Delhi to Madras where they visited Adyar, the headquarters of the Theosophical Society, and stayed at the Ramakrishna Math or monastery where the *Vedanta Kesari* was produced, a magazine that published a number of articles by Sangharakshita (collected in *Early Writings 1944–1954*, Ibis Publications, Ledbury 2014, *Complete Works*, vol. 7). The journey to Madras and Sangharakshita's time there is described in *The Rainbow Road from Tooting Broadway to Kalimpong*, *Complete Works*, vol. 20, pp. 227–8.

126 This first meeting between Sangharakshita and Dhardo Rimpoche is recounted in

Facing Mount Kanchenjunga, *Complete Works*, vol. 21, pp. 451–3.

127 The stay in Bangalore in 1949, during which Sangharakshita and his friend were invited to an evening of Ouija Board Spiritualism, and their visit to Yalahankar Swami, the one-eyed guru, is described in *The Rainbow Road from Tooting Broadway to Kalimpong*, *Complete Works*, vol. 20, chapter 40.

128 The Flora Fountain situated in the Fort district of southern Mumbai depicts the Roman goddess Flora. It was built in 1864 during the British Raj.

129 Annie Besant (1847–1933) was throughout her life an influential figure and a powerful orator, known first as a socialist, active in England, who was prosecuted for promoting birth control and was involved in the strike of match girls in 1888. After meeting Madame Blavatsky she became interested in theosophy and in association with Charles Leadbeater went on to lead a branch of the Theosophical Society from Adyar, India. She and Leadbeater were responsible for bringing up Jiddu Krishnamurti to be the world messiah (a role he rejected). She went on to be involved in politics, campaigning for Indian Home Rule and in 1917 became the first woman president of the Indian National Congress.

130 D. T. Suzuki (1870–1966) was a Japanese translator and prolific author of books on Japanese Buddhism, especially Zen.

E. J. Thomas (1869–1958) was an English classicist and Pāli scholar who wrote books on Buddhism and is known especially for his *Jātaka Tales* (with H. T. Francis), (1916); and *The Life of Buddha as Legend and History* (1927).

131 Mme Wadia was born in 1901 in Colombia. Her name before marriage was Sophia Comacho.

132 A reference to Edward Conze (ed.), *Buddhist Texts Through the Ages*, which was published the same year (1954) by Bruno Cassirer, Oxford.

133 Let observation with extensive view,
Survey mankind, from China to Peru;
Remark each anxious toil, each eager strife,
And watch the busy scenes of crowded life…

These are the opening lines of Samuel Johnson's poem 'The Vanity of Human Wishes: The Tenth Satire of Juvenal Imitated' (1748).

134 'Taking Refuge in the Buddha' in *Complete Poems 1941–1994*, Windhorse Publications, Birmingham 1995, pp. 161–2 (*Complete Works*, vol. 25). Sangharakshita describes how he came to write the poem at a time of difficulty and

disappointment when he felt he had 'no earthly refuge'. See *Facing Mount Kanchenjunga*, *Complete Works*, vol. 21, p. 429.

135 The Lal Bagh or Red Garden is an extensive botanical garden in Bangalore (Bengaluru). It was commissioned by the Mughal ruler Hyder Ali in 1760 and completed by his son to became one of the great features of the city.

136 Narada Thera, known for his ultra-formalism, appears several times in *Facing Mount Kanchenjunga*, *Complete Works*, vol. 21. His view on the imperative for monks as regards not appreciating beauty can be found on p. 397.

137 Swami Vivekananda's assertion that Hinduism had killed Buddhism with a loving embrace was often repeated in Sangharakshita's hearing by Hindus whom he met. It is possible he came across the remark in one of Vivekananda's writings, all of which he had read.

138 The stay of Sangharakshita (then Dharmapriya) and his friend, Satyapriya, at the ashram in Muvattupuzha is related in *The Rainbow Road from Tooting Broadway to Kalimpong*, *Complete Works*, vol. 20, chapters 30–6.

139 The meeting with Nataraja Guru is recounted in *The Rainbow Road from Tooting Broadway to Kalimpong*, *Complete Works*, vol. 20, p. 295.

140 UP stands for Uttar Pradesh, the state in northern India from which the Brahmin hailed.

141 A. R. Kulkarni, 'Bhikshu Sangharakshita's Lecture Tour in Nagpur', in *Maha Bodhi*, vol. 62, no. 11 (November 1954), p. 446.

142 Ibid., p. 446.

143 Ibid., pp. 446–7.

144 M. K. Gandhi's *Hind Swaraj* was written in 1909 and advocated Indian independence which he said could be achieved through passive resistance. It was written in Gandhi's native Gujarati but banned in India by the British rulers. It was translated into English by Gandhi himself and published in 1910 under the title *Hind Swaraj or India Home Rule.* The English edition circulated widely.

145 A. R. Kulkarni, 'Bhikshu Sangharakshita's Lecture Tour in Nagpur' *Maha Bodhi*, vol. 62, no. 11 (November 1954), p. 447.

146 Ibid.

147 Ibid.

148 Ibid., pp. 447–8.

149 Ibid., p. 448.

150 André Gide's *Si le grain meurt* (*If It Die…*) is firstly an autobiography recounting his early years as a child in Paris up to his engagement to his cousin in 1895. In the second part of the book he writes

about his discovery of his homosexuality during a trip to Algeria, partly in the company of Oscar Wilde. *Si le grain meurt* was published in French in 1924. It was translated into English by Dorothy Bussy and published under the title *If It Die ... An Autobiography* in 1935. The title is a reference to a passage from the Gospel of St John: 'Unless a kernel of wheat falls to the ground and dies, it remains only a single seed. But if it dies, it produces many seeds.' (*The Bible*, John 12:24.)

151 'Pronunciation of Pali: A Suggestion for the Sixth Buddhist Council' by Himavantavasi in *Maha Bodhi*, vol. 61, no. 9 (September 1953); and *Anagarika Dharmapala: a Biographical Sketch, and other Maha Bodhi Writings*, Ibis Publications, Ledbury 2014, pp. 97–8 (*Complete Works*, vol. 8).

152 'Vaiśākha Dāna' in *Maha Bodhi* vol. 62, no. 4, April 1954, pp. 122–5; and *Beating the Drum*, Ibis Publications, Ledbury 2012, pp. 106–9 (*Complete Works*, vol. 8).

153 1. Himavantavasi, 'In the Light of the Dhamma: From a Sincere European Buddhist' in *Maha Bodhi*, vol. 62, no. 2 (February 1954), pp. 53–4; and *Anagarika Dharmapala: a Biographical Sketch, and other Maha Bodhi Writings*, Ibis Publications, Ledbury 2014, pp. 108–9 (*Complete Works*, vol. 8).
2. Himavantavasi, 'In the Light of the Dhamma: A Strange Experience' in *Maha Bodhi* vol. 62, no. 4 (April 1954), pp. 120–1; and *Anagarika Dharmapala: a Biographical Sketch, and other Maha Bodhi Writings*, Ibis Publications, Ledbury 2014, pp. 112–3 (*Complete Works*, vol. 8).

154 'Controversy' in *Maha Bodhi*, vol. 62, no. 3 (March 1954), pp. 90–4; and *Beating the Drum*, Ibis Publications, Ledbury 2012, pp. 100–4 (*Complete Works*, vol. 8).

155 'Controversy' in *Maha Bodhi*, vol. 62, no. 3 (March 1954), pp. 92–3; and *Beating the Drum*, Ibis Publications, Ledbury 2012, pp. 102–3.

156 'Welcome "Western Buddhist"' by Himavantavasi in *Maha Bodhi*, vol. 61, no. 11 (November 1953, (page numbers unknown); and *Anagarika Dharmapala: a Biographical Sketch, and other Maha Bodhi Writings*, Ibis Publications, Ledbury 2014, pp. 101–2 (*Complete Works*, vol. 8).

157 The saying that 'a leopard cannot change his spots' comes from the *Bible*: 'Can the Ethiopian change his skin, or the leopard his spots?' *The Bible*, Jeremiah 13:23.

158 The story, known as the *samudra manthana* or churning of the ocean, can be found in book 8 of the

Bhāgavata Purāṇa, one of the eighteen great ('*Mahā*') *Purāṇas*. It includes the story of the origin of *amṛta*, the nectar of immortality.

159 1. Sister Nivedita (1867–1911) was an Irishwoman, originally Margaret Noble, who met Swami Vivekananda in London and became his disciple, following him to India where she met and became close to Sarada Devi, the consort of Sri Ramakrishna. Sister Nivedita opened a school for girls in Calcutta, nursed the sick during a plague epidemic, travelled, and wrote books including *The Master As I Saw Him: Being pages of the life of the Swami Vivekananda* (1910).

2. Charles Andrews (1870–1940) was a Church of England priest, missionary, teacher, and advocate of Indian independence, a close friend of M. K. Gandhi whom he is credited with persuading to leave South Africa and return to India.

3. Mirabehn (1892–1982), originally Madeleine Slade, came from the British aristocracy. She had a great love of Beethoven and promoted his music in Britain. She went to India in 1925 as a disciple of Gandhi, accompanying him to the Round Table Conference in London in 1931. She met with some of the great statesmen of the time to plead the cause of India's independence; and also spent time under arrest in Pune. She established an ashram, campaigned for the environment in Kashmir where forests were being decimated, and wrote books. For the last two decades of her long life she lived in Vienna.

4. Sri Krishna Prem (1898–1965), originally Ronald Nixon, after life-changing experiences in the First World War, taught at the University of Lucknow where he met Sri Yashoda Mai (Monica Devi Chakravarti, wife of the vice-chancellor of the university) who followed a Gaudiya Vaishnavite spiritual tradition. She became his spiritual teacher and together they founded an ashram near Almora of which, after her death in 1944, he became the head. He wrote a number of books which brought Vaishnavite Hinduism to the notice of the West.

5. Verrier Elwin (1902–1964) was an anthropologist whose first contact with India was as a Christian missionary but who, after staying in a Gandhian ashram, converted to Hinduism. He became an expert on the tribal peoples of central and north-eastern India, and was at different times married to two tribal women. He became an advisor to the Indian government under Nehru on tribal affairs.

160 'The Veil of Stars' was published in *The Enchanted Heart*, Ola Leaves, London 1980. This quotation is on p. 163. See also *Complete Poems 1941–1994*, Windhorse Publications, Birmingham 1995, p. 495 (*Complete Works*, vol. 25).

161 Lama Govinda is quoting from Novalis' *Fragmente über Poesie* (1798). 'Dichter und Priester waren im Anfang eins, und nur spätere Zeiten haben sie getrennt....' Novalis was the pen name of Philipp Freiherr von Hardenberg (1772–1801), born in one of the small German states near the Harz mountains. He studied law and then geology but read widely in literature and philosophy whilst also pursuing a keen interest in science and industry, specifically the salt mine. He came to know Schiller, Goethe, Herder, Tieck, Schelling, and other notable literary and philosophic figures of the age. He died of tuberculosis before he was thirty and left an extraordinary legacy of writing that combines the literary, poetical, philosophical-scientific and 'mystical'.

162 'The Religion of Art' is the second of four essays in *The Religion of Art*, Windhorse Publications, Cambridge 2010 (*Complete Works*, vol. 26).

> Beauty is truth, truth beauty,
> – that is all
> Ye know on earth, and all ye
> need to know.

are the final lines of John Keats' *Ode on a Grecian Urn* written in 1819.

163 Sangharakshita wrote the poem 'Messengers from Tibet' in a mood of 'unusually intense inspiration': *Facing Mount Kanchenjunga*, *Complete Works*, vol. 21, p. 62. The poem is included in *Complete Poems 1941–1994*, Windhorse Publications, Birmingham 1995, pp. 101–2 (*Complete Works*, vol. 25).

164 'Invocation' in ibid., p. 93.

165 I. B. Horner's review of *Messengers from Tibet and Other Poems* can be found in *Maha Bodhi*, vol. 62, no. 10, October 1954, pp. 405–6. The book of poems was published by Hind Kitabs Ltd., Bombay, on sale for Rs 1–8.

166 Clare's response to Sangharakshita's poems is described in *The Rainbow Road from Tooting Broadway to Kalimpong*, *Complete Works*, vol. 20, p. 103.

167
> If you can meet with
> Triumph and Disaster
> And treat those two
> impostors just the same ...

From Rudyard Kipling's poem 'If –' (1910).

168 *Mahāmaṅgala Sutta*, *Sutta-Nipāta* 2.4, verse 11. H. Saddhatissa (trans.), *The Sutta-Nipāta*, Curzon Press, London 1985, p. 30; and E. M.

Hare (trans.), *Woven Cadences of Early Buddhists* (*Sutta-Nipāta*), Oxford University Press, London 1945, p. 42.

169 *A Survey of Buddhism*, *Complete Works*, vol. 1, p. 15.

170 Sangharakshita's Going Forth is described in *The Rainbow Road from Tooting Broadway to Kalimpong*, *Complete Works*, vol. 20, p. 226. See also note 9.

171 From 'The Awakening of the Heart' in *The Enchanted Heart*, Ola Leaves, London 1980, pp. 131–7; and *Complete Poems 1941–1994*, Windhorse Publications, Birmingham 1995, pp. 401–14 (*Complete Works*, vol. 25).

172 The eight requisites (*aṭṭha parikkhāra*) or basic necessities are (1) an outer robe, (2) an inner robe, (3) a thick double robe for winter, (4) an alms bowl, (5) a razor, (6) a needle and thread, (7) a girdle or belt, and (8) a water strainer for removing impurities from drinking-water.

173 To the first sixty-one *arhants* the Buddha said,

> Go now and wander for the welfare and happiness of the many, out of compassion for the world ... Teach the Law [Dharma] that is good in the beginning, good in the middle, and good in the end ... Explain a Holy Life that is utterly perfect and pure.

Bhikkhu Ñāṇamoli, *The Life of the Buddha*, Buddhist Publication Society, Kandy 1978, p. 52. See also Vinaya Piṭaka i.21(*Mahāvagga* 1.11), in I. B. Horner (trans.), *The Book of the Discipline*, part 4, Pali Text Society, Oxford 1996, p. 28.

174 And sometimes he walked 'to give my spirit ease'. See 'Up and down the gravel path...' *Complete Poems 1941–1994*, Windhorse Publications, Birmingham 1995, p. 143 (*Complete Works*, vol. 25).

175 A reference to the British statesman Winston Churchill (1874–1965), famous as the prime minister who brought the United Kingdom through the Second World War (which had ended only a few years previous to the time with which this memoir is concerned).

176 Sangharakshita was introduced to Princess Pema Tsedeun or 'Coo-Coo La' by Ryan Swale. She possessed 'beauty, charm, intelligence, and vitality ...' all to a high degree, all set off by her rich, elegant Tibetan attire. 'The total effect was subtly devastating.' *Facing Mount Kanchenjunga*, *Complete Works*, vol. 21, p. 29.

177

> House-builder, (now) you are seen! Never again shall you build (me) a house. Your rafters are all broken, your ridgepole shattered. The

(conditioned) mind too has gone to destruction: one has attained to the cessation of craving.

Sangharakshita (trans.), *Dhammapada*, Windhorse Publications, Birmingham 2001, verse 154, p. 58 (*Complete Works*, vol. 15).

178 The parable of the burning house can be found in Bunnō Katō and W. E. Soothill (trans.), *The Threefold Lotus Sutra*, Kosei Publishing, Tokyo 1975, pp. 85ff. Sangharakshita's commentary on the parable can be found in *The Drama of Cosmic Enlightenment*, chapter 3, in *Complete Works*, vol. 16.

179
> Rose a nurse of ninety years,
> Set his child upon her knee –
> Like summer tempest came
> her tears –
> 'Sweet my child, I live for
> thee.'

From Alfred Lord Tennyson's poem, 'Home they Brought her Warrior Dead' from *The Princess* (1847) a serio-comic narrative poem dealing with relations between men and women on which the Gilbert and Sullivan comic opera *Princess Ida* is based.

180
> At ten o'clock one evening, having finished my meditation, I opened my eyes to find myself surrounded by seven or eight tall black figures.

The Rainbow Road from Tooting Broadway to Kalimpong, *Complete Works*, vol. 20, p. 310.

181 William Shakespeare, *The Merchant of Venice*, Act V, Scene i, lines 57–8. Lorenzo is showing his lover, Jessica, the beauties of the heavens.

182 Burma Raja's rescue of Sangharakshita from the Dharmodaya Vihara and his stay in the guest cottage is related in 'Burma Raja and the Devas', *Facing Mount Kanchenjunga*, *Complete Works*, vol. 21, chapter 7.

183 *Sic transit gloria mundi* means 'so passes worldly glory'. From 1409 to 1963 the words were part of the papal coronation service, a reminder to the popes of the ephemeral nature of earthly pomp and glory.

184 How Sangharakshita was turned back from entering Ceylon in 1947 is recounted in *The Rainbow Road from Tooting Broadway to Kalimpong*, *Complete Works*, vol. 20, pp. 229–30.

185 How Sangharakshita was refused ordination by the monks at Sarnath is described in ibid., pp. 390–1.

186 A first volume of Karl Marx's *Das Kapital* (translated as *Capital*, *Critique of Political Economy*) was published in 1867. It is described as 'a foundational text in materialist economics, philosophy and politics'.

Two further volumes were published posthumously, prepared by Friedrich Engels and based on Marx's notes.

187 St Paul, then known as Saul of Tarsus, was a Jew who had been persecuting Christians. After a vision of Christ on the road to Damascus he himself became a Christian. See *The Bible*, Acts 9:3–9. He went on to found Christian churches in Asia Minor and Europe. His letters or epistles to the new churches are included in the New Testament.

188 Vladimir Lenin's *The State and Revolution* was published in Russian in 1917. It deals with the role of the state in existing society and with the need for revolution to establish the rule of the proletariat.

189 David Guest (1911–1938) was a British mathematician and philosopher who headed a Communist 'cell' in Cambridge. He was killed in the Spanish Civil War. His *Dialectical Materialism* was published posthumously.

190 Sangharakshita first read Hegel during the Second World War when he was working for the London County Council. His thinking was at that time strongly influenced by Hegel's ideas – he described it as 'Neo-Hegelian' (See *The Rainbow Road from Tooting Broadway to Kalimpong, Complete Works*, vol. 20, pp. 81 and 83). *Selections from Hegel* was one of the very few volumes Sangharakshita selected – mainly on account of their size – to take with him when, in 1944, as a young conscript, he left England for India (ibid., p. 107).

191 *The Brothers Karamazov* (1880) was Fyodor Dostoevsky's final novel. It is set in the Russia of his time. A patricide is central to the plot. The themes explored have deep philosophical import including God, free will, faith, doubt, and reason.

192 The question, in its original German, was, 'Was will das Weib?' Freud was speaking to Princess Marie Bonaparte, a one-time patient who went on to help Freud's escape from the Nazis.

> The great question that has never been answered, and which I have not yet been able to answer, despite my thirty years of research into the feminine soul, is 'What does a woman want?'

Ernest Jones, *Sigmund Freud: Life and Work*, Hogarth Press, London 1953, vol. ii, part 3, chapter 16, p. 421.

193 *Dhammapada* 34:

> As a fish threshes from side to side when taken from one abode to another and cast on dry land, so the mind throbs and vibrates (with the strain) as it abandons the domain of Māra.

Sangharakshita (trans.), *Dhammapada*, Windhorse Publications, Birmingham 2001, p. 22 (*Complete Works*, vol. 15).

194 Sangharakshita's English translations and elucidations of the 'Salutation to the Three Jewels' (*Tiratana Vandanā*) and the *Maṅgala Sutta* are included in *Complete Works*, vol. 15. The *Maṅgala Sutta* (Auspicious Signs) and the *Ratana Sutta* (Jewel *Sutta*) can be found at *Sutta-Nipāta* (2.4 and 2.1). See H. Saddhatissa (trans.), *The Sutta-Nipāta*, Curzon Press, London 1985, pp. 24 and 29.

195 The worldly-wise Sam Weller first appears in the tenth chapter of Charles Dickens' *The Pickwick Papers* (1836). Mr Pickwick takes him on as personal servant and companion on his travels.

196 The *kuṇḍalinī* is the primal energy said to be coiled up at the base of the spine. The yogi seeks to rouse the energy and direct it through the subtle median channel up the spine to the 'thousand petalled lotus' chakra or focal energy point at the crown of the head. *Maṇipūra* (lit. jewel city) is the third primary chakra according to Vedic tradition. It is located above the navel and is associated with the element fire and with transformation.

197 All these articles can be found in *Maha Bodhi*, vol. 63, no. 5 (May 1955): (1) Edward Conze, 'Meditation on Emptiness', pp. 203–11; (2) Lama A. Govinda, 'Time and Space and the Problem of Free Will', pp. 180–6; (3) Sangharakshita, 'The Transcendental Unity of Buddhism', pp. 157–64; (4) Sangharakshita, 'The Reign of Law', pp. 231–2. 'The Reign of Law' is also included in *Beating the Drum*, Ibis Publications, Ledbury 2012, pp. 133–4 (*Complete Works*, vol. 8).

198 The *Guhyasamāja Tantra* (Tibetan *Gsang 'dus rtsa rgyud*) translates as 'Tantra of the Secret Community'. It is regarded as one of the most important of the Buddhist tantric scriptures. Its origins are obscure as it was passed on orally through different lineages but it may date back to the eighth century CE.

199 According to late Sinhalese tradition, the Vaiśākha full-moon day is the anniversary not only of the Buddha's attainment of Enlightenment but also of his birth and his *parinirvāṇa*.

200 *Dhammapada* 194. For an alternative translation see Sangharakshita (trans.), *Dhammapada*, Windhorse Publications, Birmingham 2001, p. 70 (*Complete Works*, vol. 15).

201 Sangharakshita's visit to Gangtok with the Sacred Relics is related in *Facing Mount Kanchenjunga*,

Complete Works, vol. 21, chapter 11.

202 The Inner Line Permit (ILP) was introduced by the British in 1873. The Line was then a demarcation beyond which the British government could not guarantee protection of its subjects. It related to areas in the north-east which were partly populated by tribal peoples. The requirement for an ILP continued after Indian Independence and Partition. To this day (2018) one has to apply for an ILP to cross certain frontiers. After 1947 Sikkim, which had been a princely state of British India, continued its status as a 'protectorate' with its own Maharaja. (The monarchy was deposed in 1975 and, after a referendum, Sikkim became a state of the Indian republic.)

203 The *Laṅkāvatāra Sūtra* teaches the primacy of consciousness, or mind-only, through exchanges between the Buddha and the bodhisattva Mahāmati. The scene is set in Laṅkā, the home of the king of the *rākṣasa* demons. The *sūtra* was composed in Sanskrit and translated into Chinese. The earliest extant translation dates to 443 CE. The first translation from Chinese into English was by the Zen scholar and prolific writer, D. T. Suzuki. It was published in 1932.

204 A *chuba* is a long coat, usually made of wool or of sheepskin, worn by the Himalayan peoples of Tibet and elsewhere.

205 ADC stands for *aide-de-camp* i.e. a personal assistant or secretary to the Maharaj Kumar.

206 The lectures are mentioned in *Facing Mount Kanchenjunga*, *Complete Works*, vol. 21, p. 195. As a result of the visit to Gangtok with the Sacred Relics, and the lectures mentioned here, a branch of the YMBA had been set up but, like its Darjeeling counterpart, it very soon collapsed (ibid., p. 234).

207 'Bhikshu Sangharakshita's Gangtok Lectures' in *Maha Bodhi*, vol. 63, no. 7 (July 1955), p. 312.

208 The parable of the burning house from the *White Lotus Sūtra* can be found in Bunnō Katō and W. E. Soothill (trans.), *The Threefold Lotus Sutra*, Kosei Publishing, Tokyo, 1975, pp. 85ff. Sangharakshita's commentary on the parable can be found in *The Drama of Cosmic Enlightenment*, chapter 3, in *Complete Works*, vol. 16.

209 The editor was P. V. Bapat. *2500 Years of Buddhism* was published by the Publications Division of the Ministry of Information and Broadcasting, Government of India, New Delhi, 1956. 'Cultural and Political Implications of Buddhism for the Modern World' is to be found pp. 447–78; and is included

in *Complete Works*, vol. 7. Sangharakshita reviewed the book for the *Maha Bodhi*, vol. 65, no. 9 (September 1957), pp. 376–7.

210 Sangharakshita met Jagadish Chandra Chatterjee (or Chatterji) in April 1947 at the *Dharma Parishad* or All-India Religions Conference held in Ahmedabad. They were the two Buddhist delegates – although Chatterjee was actually a Hindu (see *The Rainbow Road from Tooting Broadway to Kalimpong*, *Complete Works*, vol. 20, p. 178). Chatterjee features in several of the subsequent chapters of *The Rainbow Road* where he is referred to as 'Pandit-ji'. Finally the two young men, Dharmapriya and Satyapriya (later Sangharakshita and Buddharakshita), are confronted with the extent of his deceptions and leave him – to his outrage (ibid., p. 225). His book *Kashmir Shaivism* was published in 1914.

211 Lilian Silburn (1908–1993) was a disciple of Lakshman Joo Raina (1907–1991), a 'mystic' and teacher of the Kashmir Shaivite tradition who set up an ashram in Srinagar from where he taught disciples from different parts of the globe. In the course of her life Lilian Silburn translated from Sanskrit the core scriptures of Kashmir Shaivism. Her *Kuṇḍalinī: The Energy of the Depths, A Comprehensive Study Based on the Scriptures of Nondualistic Kaśmir Śaivism* was published in 1988.

212 (1) Grace Constant Lounsberry (1876–1974) was an author and translator who published over thirty works including *Buddhist Meditation in the Southern School: Theory and Practice for Westerners*, published in 1935, which has been through numerous editions. She also published works in a number of other genres including *Love's Testament: A Sonnet Sequence* (1906) and *Delilah: a Drama in Three Acts* (1904).
(2) Alexandra David-Néel (1868–1969) was a Belgian-French explorer and a prolific writer. She spent four years in Sikkim becoming a trusted advisor to its leader, Sidkeong, and then journeyed to Tibet where she returned some years later, incognito, managing to visit the nearby monasteries before being discovered (foreigners were not allowed to enter Tibet). On her return to Europe she wrote many books. Her *Mystiques et Magiciens du Tibet* (*Magic and Mystery in Tibet*) (1929) was one of the highly influential books of its time in opening the doors of the East to Western readers. Sangharakshita includes her as one of his *Great Buddhists of the Twentieth Century*, Windhorse Publications,

Birmingham 1996, pp. 18–21 (*Complete Works*, vol. 11).

213 'Next to our preceptor, she was for us the most important person at Kusinara.' The meeting with Mother Vipassana and the part she played in the *śāmaṇera* ordination is related in *The Rainbow Road from Tooting Broadway to Kalimpong*, *Complete Works*, vol. 20, pp. 403–11.

214 During the Second World War, V-1s were the German flying bombs or 'doodlebugs' that bombarded London and South-East England in the summer of 1944. (They were superseded by V-2s.) V-1s were being launched while Sangharakshita was attending one of the Buddhist Society meetings, but

> either out of Buddhist equanimity or British phlegm we continued to meditate, not stirring even when, a few minutes later, the windows rattled with the blast of an explosion.

In the summer of 1944 a V-1 hit the Lingwood home and totally destroyed it. By apparent coincidence no one was at home at the time. See *The Rainbow Road from Tooting Broadway to Kalimpong*, *Complete Works*, vol. 20, pp. 103–4.

215 Kenneth W. Morgan, *The Path of the Buddha: Buddhism Interpreted by Buddhists*, Ronald Press Co., New York 1956.

216 The PEN Society was founded in London in 1921; the acronym stood for 'Poets, Essayists, Novelists'. It quickly spread to many other countries. Its charter, adopted in 1948, states, among other things:

> Members of PEN should at all times use what influence they have in favour of good understanding and mutual respect between nations and people; they pledge themselves to do their utmost to dispel all hatreds and to champion the ideal of one humanity living in peace and equality in one world.

Mme Wadia was the founder of the PEN All-India Centre, and the founder and first editor of its journal, *The Indian PEN*.

217 The parable of the raft is told in the *Alagaddūpama Sutta*, *Majjhima Nikāya* 22 (i.134–5); Bhikkhu Ñāṇamoli and Bhikkhu Bodhi (trans.), *The Middle Length Discourses of the Buddha*, Wisdom Publications, Boston 1995, pp. 228–9; or I. B. Horner (trans.), *The Collection of the Middle Length Sayings*, vol. i, Pali Text Society, London 1976, pp. 173–4.

218 This person was Dinoo Dubash. Fifty-five years later work began on bringing together the collection

of letters written by Sangharakshita to Dinoo over the subsequent two decades. The earlier letters refer to many of the events and some of the characters who appear in these pages of *In the Sign of the Golden Wheel* and *Precious Teachers.* The book, with an introduction telling more of Dinoo's life and times, was published as *Dear Dinoo: Letters to a Friend* in 2011. See *Complete Works*, vol. 21.

219 Nichiren, the founder of the Japanese sect bearing his name, lived in the thirteenth century CE. He termed the mantra *namu myōhō renge kyō* ('homage to the Lotus of the Good Law') a summation of the *Lotus Sūtra*, and his followers adopted the incantation.

220 Lafcadio Hearn (1850–1904) was of Greek and Irish parentage. He worked as a journalist in the United States where he became known for his vivid reporting of macabre murder cases and for his sympathy to the causes of black Americans. In later life he went to Japan, married a Japanese woman, took a Japanese name and was naturalized. His sometimes exotic writings about his adopted country were influential in bringing Japanese culture to the attention of the West. Hearn's *Gleanings from Buddhafields: Studies of Hand and Soul in the Far East*, published in 1897, was one of the early books on Buddhism read by Sangharakshita in his teens.

221 1. Ernest Hemingway (1899–1961) was an American writer of novels and short stories. He won the 1954 Nobel Prize for Literature. *The Old Man and the Sea* (1952) was his last novel to be published in his lifetime. It tells the story of a Cuban fisherman and his battle with a fish of great size.
2. Kenneth Walker (1882–1966) was an English surgeon and author. He was concerned to explore the limitations of Darwin's theory of evolution through natural selection. His other interests included extrasensory perception and radionics. His *Venture with Ideas* (1952) was subtitled 'Meetings with Gurdjieff and Ouspensky' with both of whom he studied.
3. Axel Münthe (1857–1949) was a Swedish medical doctor and psychiatrist who spent his adult life in France and Italy. A philanthropist, he was known for treating the poor without charge, and for his concern to promote animal welfare. *The Story of San Michele* was written in English and published in London in 1929, becoming a best-seller. It is a series of memoirs taking in many aspects of his life, including his meetings with famous men, such as Louis Pasteur

and Guy de Maupassant, and the poor such as those he treated during a cholera epidemic in Naples.

4. Dinanath Gopal Tendulgar (1909–1971) was an Indian writer and documentary film maker. His *Mahatma: Life of Mohandas Karamchand Gandhi* (1951) was in eight volumes with a foreword by the then prime minister Jawaharlal Nehru.

222 1. Ralph Waldo Emerson (1803–1882) was a leading voice in the American transcendentalist movement communicating his ideas through hundreds of lectures throughout America and essays on subjects such as nature, self-reliance, and the poet. He summed up his work as being concerned with 'the infinitude of the private man'.

2. Edgar Allan Poe (1809–1849) was an American writer of short stories, detective stories, and science fiction. He is known especially for his 'Gothic' works with a twist of the macabre.

3. Walt Whitman (1819–1892) was an American poet and journalist. He developed the use of free verse. His best known work is *Leaves of Grass.* The first edition was published in 1855 with just twelve poems. He revised it many times and the last edition is a collection of over four hundred poems. His poems celebrate life, both the life of the senses and of the spirit, and the lives of the ordinary people of America.

4. Harriet Beecher Stowe (1811–1896) was an American writer and abolitionist. Her anti-slavery novel *Uncle Tom's Cabin* (1852) was one of the best-selling books of the century.

223 William Faulkner (1897–1962) is another American writer, best known for his novels and short stories with plots and characters based in the American South, and for his 'stream of consciousness' writing. In 1949 he received the Nobel Prize for Literature.

224 William Somerset Maugham (1874–1965) was a British writer of short stories, novels, and plays, and one of the most popular writers of his time. He drew on his experience as a physician, as a spy, and on his travels in Spain, India, China, and elsewhere. Among his most well known writings are *Of Human Bondage* (1915) and *The Moon and Sixpence* (1919).

225 At the outbreak of the Second World War in 1939, Burma was under British rule. Japan joined the war on the side of Nazi Germany as one of the Axis Alliance countries. Towards the end of 1941 Japan invaded and occupied Burma. In 1945 Burma became independent. During Japanese occupation it is estimated that 170,000 to 250,000 civilians died.

226 *Nakkhatta Jātaka: Jātaka* no. 49 in E. B. Cowell (ed.), *Jātaka Stories*, vol. i, Robert Chalmers (trans.), Pali Text Society, London 1973, pp. 125–6. For the original Pāli see V. Fausboll (ed.), *The Jātaka together with its commentary*, vol. i, Pali Text Society, Oxford 1990, p. 258.

227 Sangharakshita's experiences of precognition are described in *The Rainbow Road from Tooting Broadway to Kalimpong*, *Complete Works*, vol. 20, pp. 73–4.

228 This experience of clairvoyance is described in ibid., pp. 215–16.

229 *A Survey of Buddhism*, *Complete Works*, vol. 1, p. 394.

230 Sarojini Naidu (1879–1949) was a child prodigy who began writing poetry at the age of eleven. She attended Madras University at the age of twelve and then (1895–1898) King's College, London, and Girton College, Cambridge. She joined the Indian national movement, becoming, in 1925, the second woman president of the Indian National Congress. From 1915–1918 she gave lectures all over India on nationalist themes, social welfare, and women's empowerment. She played a leading role in the Civil Disobedience movement, and spent periods in prison. She was on close terms with Gandhi (whom she liked to call 'Mickey Mouse', a reference to his protruding ears). After Independence, in 1947, she became governor of United Provinces state (now Uttar Pradesh), a post she retained until her death. A collection of her poetry appeared as *The Sceptred Flute: Songs of India* (1928).

231 Sangharakshita writes about his discovery of Sarojini Naidu's poetry in *The Rainbow Road from Tooting Broadway to Kalimpong*, *Complete Works*, vol. 20, p. 113. His article, 'Krishna's Flute: the Poetry of Sarojini Naidu' is in *Early Writings 1944–1954*, Ibis Publications, Ledbury 2014 (*Complete Works*, vol. 7). 'Sometimes,' he writes 'it must be confessed, she wearied of [her] brilliant life, and the cry escaped from her lips: "O I am tired of strife and song and festivals and fame, / And long to fly where cassia-woods are breaking into flame".' See ibid., p. 60.

232 John Ruskin, *Praeterita*, para. 195. Oxford University Press, Oxford 1978, p. 159. *Praeterita* was published between 1885 and 1889 in twenty-eight parts.

233 *Puttamaṃsa* ('son's flesh') *Sutta: Nidānasaṃyutta*, *Saṃyutta Nikāya* ii.98 (12.63); see Bhikkhu Bodhi (trans.), *Connected Discourses of the Buddha*, Wisdom Publications, Boston 2000, pp. 597–9; or C. A. F. Rhys

Davids (trans.), *The Book of the Kindred Sayings*, part 2, Pali Text Society, Oxford 1997, pp. 67–70. The four kinds of nutriment about which the Buddha speaks are edible food, sense-impression or contact (through eye, ear, nose, tongue, body, and mind), volitional thought, and consciousness.

234 *Mahāsaccaka Sutta*, *Majjhima Nikāya* 36 (i.245). Bhikkhu Ñāṇamoli and Bhikkhu Bodhi (trans.), *The Middle Length Discourses of the Buddha*, Wisdom Publications, Boston 1995, p. 339; and I. B. Horner (trans.), *The Collection of the Middle Length Sayings*, vol. i, Pali Text Society, London 1976, p. 300.

235 'The Monk and the Prophet', an appendix to *Dear Dinoo: Letters to a Friend* (*Complete Works*, vol. 21, pp. 519–619), sketches an outline of Dr Mehta's very unusual life and discusses the friendship between the two men. Other members of Dr Mehta's circle are also described, including Sundri Vaswani.

236 Dr B. R. Ambedkar's *Buddha and the Future of His Religion*, was first published in the *Maha Bodhi*, April–May 1950. See also *Dr Babasaheb Ambedkar, Writings and Speeches*, vol. xvii (part 2), Education Department, Government of Maharashtra, Bombay 2003. It was through Sangharakshita writing to Dr Ambedkar to express his appreciation of the article that the two men first came into personal contact. See *Facing Mount Kanchenjunga*, *Complete Works*, vol. 21, p. 90.

237 The Siddharth College of Arts, Science and Commerce was founded in 1945 by the People's Education Society. The Society had been founded the previous year by Dr Ambedkar. Sangharakshita returned to the College in 1982 to give a talk on 'Buddhism and Education'. See *Complete Works*, vol. 9, pp. 435–48.

238 It was U Chandramani who had officiated at Sangharakshita's *śāmaṇera* ordination at Kusinara in 1949. See *The Rainbow Road from Tooting Broadway to Kalimpong*, chapter 45, in *Complete Works*, vol. 20.

239 Sangharakshita's meetings with Dr Ambedkar are also recounted in *Ambedkar and Buddhism*, chapter 2, in *Complete Works*, vol. 9.

240 See Letters 1 and 2 written to Dinoo at this time in *Dear Dinoo: Letters to a Friend* in *Complete Works*, vol. 21, pp. 493–7.

241 A *sistrum* is a kind of metal percussion instrument that was used in Ancient Egypt. It is shaken to make a sound.

242 In 'An Occidental Ear Listens to Indian Music' Sangharakshita describes his responses to his first concert of Indian music

which took place in Ceylon in 1944. See *Early Writings 1944–1954*, Ibis Publications, Ledbury 2014, pp. 95–7 (*Complete Works*, vol. 7).

243 Maharashtra state, with Bombay (later Mumbai) as its capital came into existence in 1960.

244 Letter 3 in *Dear Dinoo: Letters to a Friend* in *Complete Works*, vol. 21, pp. 499–500. The notes following the letter say more about who are the various persons mentioned here.

245 A *gaddi* is a kind of cushion, especially one used on a princely throne.

246 In the gospel of St Luke in the *Bible* it is related how Jesus came to the home of two sisters, Martha and Mary. Mary sat at Jesus' feet listening to him while Martha was hurrying about preparing and serving the food. See *The Bible*, Luke 10:42.

247

> A prophet is not without honour, but in his own country, and among his own kin, and in his own house.

The Bible, Mark 6:4, King James Version.

248 The American Christian evangelist, Frank Buchman (1878–1961), launched the Moral Re-Armament movement in 1938 at a meeting in East London attended by 3,000 people. His message was that for economic recovery there needed first to be moral recovery. The idea appealed to many at that time.

249 In *A Survey of Buddhism*, *Complete Works*, vol. 1, p. 261, Sangharakshita speaks of the bodhisattvas as

> purely transcendental personages – bright effluences of ... the Absolute – eternally existent outpourings of the compassion which is wisdom and the wisdom which is compassion.

250 Quoted in 'Buddha Jayanti and the Secular State' in *Maha Bodhi*, vol. 64, no. 7 (July 1956), p. 384; and *Beating the Drum*, Ibis Publications, Ledbury 2012, p. 164 (*Complete Works*, vol. 8).

251 For example, the *Brahmajāla Sutta*, *Dīgha Nikāya* 1 (i.10–12) gives a long list of fortunetelling 'low arts' from which the Buddha 'holds aloof'. See M. Walshe (trans.), *The Long Discourses of the Buddha*, Wisdom Publications, Boston 1995, pp. 71–3; or T. W. Rhys Davids (trans.), *Dialogues of the Buddha*, part 1, Pali Text Society, London 1973, pp. 16–26.

252 These ideas were expressed some years later in an editorial 'Stars and Stupidity' published in the *Maha Bodhi*, vol. 70, no. 2 (February 1962), pp. 68–9. See *Beating the Drum*, Ibis Publications,

Ledbury 2012, pp. 251–3 (*Complete Works*, vol. 8).

253 'The Coming Year' in *Maha Bodhi*, vol. 64, no. 1 (January 1956), p. 32; and *Beating the Drum*, Ibis Publications, Ledbury 2012, pp. 147–9 (*Complete Works*, vol. 8).

254 'The Inner Preparation' in *Maha Bodhi* vol. 64, no. 2 (February 1956), p. 72; and *Beating the Drum*, Ibis Publications, Ledbury 2012, pp. 150–1 (*Complete Works*, vol. 8).

255 'Buddhism and the Indian Languages' in *Maha Bodhi* vol. 64, no. 3 (March 1956), p. 113; and *Beating the Drum*, Ibis Publications, Ledbury 2012, pp. 152–4 (*Complete Works*, vol. 8).

256 'Buddha Jayanti Among the Birds' in *Maha Bodhi*, vol. 64, no. 4 (April 1956), p. 148; and *Beating the Drum*, Ibis Publications, Ledbury 2012, pp. 155–7 (*Complete Works*, vol. 8).

257 'Ring in the New' in *Maha Bodhi*, vol. 64, no. 5 (May 1956), p. 272; and *Beating the Drum*, Ibis Publications, Ledbury 2012, pp. 158–60 (*Complete Works*, vol. 8).

258 The story of Narada Thera and the vitamins is recounted in *Facing Mount Kanchenjunga*, *Complete Works*, vol. 21, pp. 396–7.

259 'The World Celebrates Buddha Jayanti' in *Maha Bodhi*, vol. 64, no. 7 (July 1956), p. 360.

260 *Facing Mount Kanchenjunga*, *Complete Works*, vol. 21, p. 7.

261 Sangharakshita elucidates the *trikāya* doctrine more fully in *A Survey of Buddhism*, chapter 2, section 6 in *Complete Works*, vol. 1; and *The Three Jewels*, chapter 5, in *Complete Works*, vol. 2.

262 *A Survey of Buddhism*, *Complete Works*, vol. 1.

263

> If a man does not make new acquaintance as he advances through life, he will soon find himself left alone. A man, Sir, should keep his friendship in constant repair.

According to his biographer, James Boswell, the remark was made by Dr Johnson in 1755 to the painter, Sir Joshua Reynolds. See 1755: aetat. 46 in James Boswell, *Life of Johnson*, first published in 1791.

264 'Autumn Thoughts' was first published as an editorial in the October 1951 edition of *Stepping-Stones*, the monthly journal of Himalayan religion, culture, and education, that Sangharakshita founded soon after this arrival in Kalimpong in 1950. Together with other editorials and essays it is included in *Crossing the Stream*, Windhorse Publications, Birmingham 1996, pp. 111–14 (*Complete Works*, vol. 7).

265 The North-East Frontier Agency or NEFA refers to lands in the north-east corner of

India, being a political division inaugurated under British rule that continued after Indian Independence until 1972 when the area became known as the Union Territory of Arunachal Pradesh. In 1987 Arunachal Pradesh was recognized as a state.

266 The 'First Sermon' is the 'Discourse of the Turning the Wheel of the Dharma' or *Dhammacakkappavattana Sutta*, *Saṃyutta Nikāya* 56.11 (v.421); see Bhikkhu Bodhi (trans.), *The Connected Discourses of the Buddha*, Wisdom Publications, Boston 2000, pp. 1843–6; or F. L. Woodward (trans.), *Book of the Kindred Sayings*, part 5, Pali Text Society, London 1979, pp. 356–60.

267 An account of Sangharakshita's *bhikkhu* ordination is given in *Facing Mount Kanchenjunga*, *Complete Works*, vol. 21, pp. 107–9.

268 Sangharakshita's *bhikkhu* ordination took place in November 1950. The discovery that his ordination as a *bhikkhu* was technically invalid occurred in November 1956. In 1993, he published an essay: *Forty-Three Years Ago: Reflections on my Bhikkhu Ordination*. This, together with *Was the Buddha a Bhikkhu? A Rejoinder to a Reply to Forty-Three Years Ago* (*Complete Works*, vol. 2), expresses some of the conclusions that his reflections, ignited by the 'rude shock' he had at Sarnath in November 1956, gave rise to; reflections whose ramifications for what it means to be a Buddhist are very far reaching indeed. See Nagabodhi's Foreword to *The Three Jewels I*, *Complete Works*, vol. 2.

269 It was at Kusinara that Sangharakshita's 'lower' or *śāmaṇera* ordination had taken place in May 1949. See *The Rainbow Road from Tooting Broadway to Kalimpong*, *Complete Works*, vol. 20, pp. 408–10.

270 Sangharakshita wrote a poem at the time: 'To the Recumbent Buddha'. See *Complete Poems 1941–1994*, Windhorse Publications, Birmingham 1995, pp. 72–3 (*Complete Works*, vol. 25).

271 This momentous occasion is described in vivid detail in *Ambedkar and Buddhism*, chapter 7, *Complete Works*, vol. 9. The twenty-two vows are listed in an appendix in that volume, pp. 541–2 and in volume 2, p. 656.

272 This was the Buddha's teaching to Bahiya of the Bark Garment who requested the Buddha three times – even though the Buddha was on his almsround – to give him a teaching 'for my good and happiness for a long time'. The Buddha finally told him to train himself thus: 'In the seen, only the seen....' *Udāna* 1.10. See John D. Ireland (trans.),

The Udāna and the Itivuttaka, Buddhist Publication Society, Kandy 1997, p. 21.

273 Tenzin Gyaltsen was known as Khunu Lama. He was born in 1894 in Himachal Pradesh, India, not far from the Tibetan border. He went to Sikkim to give himself a general education before going to Tibet to embark on Dharma studies. He learned from many of the foremost teachers of the time but was not interested in lineage and preferred to describe himself simply as a disciple of Nāgārjuna. He believed that rather than prestige or renown it was 'the feeling in a teacher's heart' that mattered. He chose a life of poverty and yet was renowned for his generosity – as illustrated by Sangharakshita's encounter with him. He instructed the Dalai Lama on the text by which he himself tried to live, the *Bodhicaryāvatāra* of Śāntideva. For an inspiring and moving account of his life see an article by Beth Halford based on an interview with his disciple, Baling Lama, published in the Foundation for the Preservation of the Mahayana Tradition (FPMT) magazine, *Mandala*, July–December 2015, pp. 27–31.

274 Power tends to corrupt, and absolute power corrupts absolutely. Great men are almost always bad men.

John Dahlberg-Acton (1834–1902) known as Lord Acton, historian and moralist, in a letter of 1887 to Bishop Mandell Creighton. See J. N. Figgis and R. V. Laurence (eds.), *Historical Essays and Studies*, Macmillan, London 1907.

275 Yet still one solitary tear
Would hang on the cheek of time
In the form
Of this white and gleaming Taj Mahal.

From 'Shah Jahan' by Rabindranath Tagore (1861–1941).

276 I passed the square and scripted gate
And saw the tombs with fluttering breath;
For all without was life and hate,
And all within was love and death.

See *Complete Poems 1941–1994*, Windhorse Publications, Birmingham 1995, p. 227 (*Complete Works*, vol. 25).

277 The Suez Crisis (also known as the Second Arab-Israeli War) took place in late October and early November 1956 when Israel, with help from France and Great Britain, invaded Egypt with the aim of gaining western control of the strategic Suez Canal. (The

Suez Canal was originally built 1859–1869 to connect the Mediterranean and Red Seas.) Pressure from the United Nations, the Soviet Union, and the USA led to the withdrawal of the invaders.

278 'mid this tumult Kubla heard from far
Ancestral voices prophesying war!

from 'Kubla Khan' by Samuel Taylor Coleridge written, he explained, after an opium-induced dream, in 1797.

279 'Pecksniffian' means hypocritical or affecting to have high moral principles, after Seth Pecksniff in Charles Dickens' novel, *Martin Chuzzlewit* (1842–1844).

280 Indira Gandhi (1917–1984) was Nehru's daughter. She became India's third Prime Minister, serving from 1966 to 1977 and again from 1980 until her assassination (by her own bodyguards) in 1984. Her successor as Prime Minister was her son Rajiv Gandhi, then only forty years old, who served from 1984 to 1989. At the time of Sangharakshita's meeting with Nehru, his grandsons Rajiv and Sanjay – who was to die aged thirty-three in an aircraft accident – were just twelve and ten years old.

281 Sangharakshita met Jawaharlal Nehru (1889–1964), the first Prime Minister of independent India (1947–1961), three times. He was first introduced to Nehru at the Anandamayi Ashram in Dehra Dun in 1947. (See *The Rainbow Road from Tooting Broadway to Kalimpong*, *Complete Works*, vol. 20, pp. 190–1). Their second meeting, one not recorded in Sangharakshita's memoirs, took place, probably in 1953, when Nehru visited Kalimpong, the township where Sangharakshita was resident. See *Beating the Drum*, Ibis Publications, Ledbury 2012, p. 94 (*Complete Works*, vol. 8). The third meeting was the one recounted here.

282 A *shamiana* is a kind of Indian marquee often used for weddings and other occasions.

283 A reference to D. H. Lawrence's satirical poem 'Nottingham's New University' which begins:

In Nottingham, that dismal town
where I went to school and college,
they've built a new university …
in grand and cakey style.

284 The Hindu 'Sanātana Dharma' or Eternal Law refers to religious duties incumbent on all Hindus such as generosity, good will, and forbearance. It is contrasted with *svadharma* or 'own duty' which depends on one's caste. In cases of conflict, the latter, caste duty, comes first.

285 The story of the town mouse and the country mouse is one of Aesop's fables. The country mouse, who is poor, can only offer the visiting town mouse plain food. The proud town mouse invites the country mouse for fine food in the town, but while eating they are scared off by dogs. The moral of the tale is that it is better to be safe, though poor, than live an opulent life in fear.

286 The meeting between Mañjuśrī and Vimalakīrti can be found in R. A. F. Thurman (trans.), *The Holy Teaching of Vimalakīrti*, Pennsylvania State University Press, University Park and London 1976, p. 43.

287 'The Tide Turns' in *Maha Bodhi* vol. 64, no. 10 (October 1956), pp. 466–7; and *Beating the Drum*, Ibis Publications, Ledbury 2012, pp. 169–70 (*Complete Works*, vol. 8).

288 Letter 8 in *Dear Dinoo: Letters to a Friend*, *Complete Works*, vol. 21, pp. 519–20.

289 'Buddha or Karl Marx' in *Dr Babasaheb Ambedkar, Writings and Speeches*, vol. iii, Education Department, Government of Maharashtra, Bombay 1987, pp. 441–62.

290 *The Buddha and His Dhamma* was Ambedkar's attempt to answer the need for a 'Buddhist Bible' which he had identified in 1951 in his article, 'Buddha and the Future of His Religion' (see note 236). It was published posthumously the year after his death (1957). For a concise summary of its contents and an indication of its significance see *Ambedkar and Buddhism*, chapter 8, in *Complete Works*, vol. 9.

291 There is a brief description of Sangharakshita's talks given in Nagpur in December 1957 in the 'News and Notes' section of the *Maha Bodhi*, vol. 65, no. 2 (February 1957), p. 58.

292 Letter 9 in *Dear Dinoo: Letters to a Friend, Complete Works*, vol. 21. p. 523.

293 Ibid.

294 'Is Buddhism for Monks Only?' was published as a booklet under the auspices of the Maha Bodhi Society of India with a Preface by the author dated 26 December 1956:

> Coming to Calcutta a few days ago, I was told that a person reputed to be a scholar in Buddhism had of late been exerting himself to convince people that Buddhism was a religion not for the laity, but for monks only. This dialogue, originally published in the August 1949 issue of the *Maha Bodhi* journal, is being brought out in its present form in confutation of this mischievous and quite erroneous idea. My thanks are due to an *upāsikā* of Bombay, who wishes to remain anonymous, for

having kindly met the cost of publication.

The '*upāsikā* from Bombay' was Dinoo Dubash. The dialogue, which is between two young men of Calcutta, Ram and Hari, was translated into Bengali and performed in local schools. 'Is Buddhism for Monks Only?' can be found in *Early Writings 1944–1954*, Ibis Publications, Ledbury 2014 (*Complete Works*, vol. 7).

295 'Buddhism and Art' was later published as 'The Meaning of Buddhism and Value of Art' in *The Religion of Art*, Windhorse Publications, Cambridge 2010 (*Complete Works*, vol. 26).

296 1. This was Tenzin Gyatso, (b. 1935), the Fourteenth Dalai Lama, who was enthroned as Dalai Lama in 1940, and assumed his temporal (i.e. political) duties as head of state in 1950, just as China invaded Tibet. After the 1959 uprising against China he was to flee Tibet and live in exile in India but at the time of this memoir he was still living in his native land. The title 'Dalai Lama' comes from *dalaiyin*, the Mongolian word for 'big' or 'ocean', and the Tibetan 'lama' meaning master or guru. It was first conferred on Sonam Gyatso (1543–1588) of the Gelug school of Tibet by the Mongolian leader Altan Khan (1507–1582) who adopted Buddhism as the Mongolian state religion. The 'great fifth' Dalai Lama, Ngawang Lobsang Gyatso (1617–1682), was the first Dalai Lama to have both spiritual and temporal power over all Tibet. The Dalai Lamas came to be seen as embodiments of the bodhisattva Avalokiteśvara.
2. This was the Tenth Panchen Lama, Lobsang Trinley Lhündrub Chökyi Gyaltsen (1938–1989) who assumed his title in 1949. 'Panchen' comes from the Sanskrit *paṇḍita*, (from the Indian tradition, a title awarded to scholars who had mastered the 'five sciences'), and the Tibetan *chen* meaning 'great'. The First Panchen Lama was tutor to the 'Great Fifth' Dalai Lama and there continued to be a close connection between the two, the Panchen Lama being involved in the 'recognition' of a new *tulku* as Dalai Lama. Traditionally the Panchen Lama was a *tulku* of the Gelug school, and head of the Tashilhunpo Monastery of Shigatse, with temporal power over some neighbouring districts.

297 'Dr Ambedkar' in *Maha Bodhi*, vol. 65, no. 1, January 1957, pp. 25–6. See also *Beating the Drum*, Ibis Publications, Ledbury 2012, p. 174 (*Complete Works*, vol. 8).

298 Chattrul Sangye Dorje was born in 1913 so would have

been about forty-four at this time. (He lived to be 102.)

299 Sangharakshita came to know the Tharpa Choling Gompa abbot when the latter had been elected vice-chairman and Sangharakshita general secretary of the committee that organized the reception of the Sacred Relics of Śāriputra and Maudgalyāyana in Kalimpong in 1951. Their first meeting is recounted in *Facing Mount Kanchenjunga*, *Complete Works*, vol. 21, pp. 176–8.

300 1. The *Diamond Sūtra* or *Vajracchedikā Prajñāpāramitā Sūtra* is probably one of the earliest Mahāyāna Perfection of Wisdom *sūtras*. Originally in Sanskrit, the first translation that Sangharakshita read was by William Gemmell, published by Trench Trübner, London, in 1912. He later read a translation by Max Müller published by the Oxford University Press in 1894 as part of the *Sacred Books of the East* series.

2. The *Laṅkāvatāra Sūtra* was composed in Sanskrit in the second half of the fourth century CE. D. T. Suzuki's English translation was published in 1932. Selections from the *sūtra* can be found in D. Goddard (ed.), *A Buddhist Bible*, Beacon Press, Boston 1970. Sangharakshita mentions he was reading the *sūtra* at the time he was invited to Sikkim by the Maharaj Kumar, see p. 241 above. For more on the *sūtra* see note 203.

3. *The Life of Milarepa* is *Tibet's Great Yogī Milarepa*. Sangharakshita first read it in 1946, in Singapore awaiting demobilization, in an abridged version in the 1938 edition of Dwight Goddard's *A Buddhist Bible*.

> As I read it my hair stood on end and tears came into my eyes. If I had any doubts about the nature of my vocation they were now dispelled.

See *The Rainbow Road from Tooting Broadway to Kalimpong*, *Complete Works*, vol. 20, p. 151. *Tibet's Great Yogī Milarepa* was translated from the Tibetan by Lama Kazi Dawa-Samdup and published in full in 1951 for Dr W. Y. Evans-Wentz's celebrated Oxford Tibetan Series.

4. *The Golden Rosary of the Precepts of the Gurus* by Gampopa is the first of seven treatises included in W. Y. Evans-Wentz, (ed.), *Tibetan Yoga and Secret Doctrines, Or Seven Books of Wisdom of the Great Path, According to the Late Lama Kazi Dawa-Samdup's English Rendering*, which was published in 1935. Selections from the text are included in Dwight Goddard's *A Buddhist Bible*, under the title, 'The Supreme Path'.

In later years Sangharakshita would give lectures and

seminars on all these texts. See (1) *Wisdom Beyond Words*, *Complete Works*, vol. 14 for his commentary on the *Diamond Sūtra*; (2) 'Turning About in the Deepest Seat of Consciousness', which draws on teachings from the *Laṅkāvatāra Sūtra*, in *The Meaning of Conversion in Buddhism* in *Complete Works*, vol. 2; and (3) *Milarepa and the Art of Discipleship* I *and* II, *Complete Works*, vols. 18 and 19.

301 Sangharakshita describes how he first came to read the *Diamond Sūtra* and its impact upon him in *The Rainbow Road from Tooting Broadway to Kalimpong*, *Complete Works*, vol. 20, p. 85.

302 Edward Conze, *Buddhism: Its Essence and Development*, Windhorse Publications, Birmingham 2001, p. 16.

303 Sangharakshita wrote to Dinoo on 26 February 1957 explaining the situation he was in and his vision for a new Buddhist centre or vihara and appealing for funds. She replied on 19 March with the promise of a thousand rupees and ideas for her own 'dream cottage' which could be built in the vihara grounds. See Letters 13 and 14 in *Dear Dinoo: Letters to a Friend*, *Complete Works*, vol. 21. pp. 534–41.

PRECIOUS TEACHERS

304 *Nāva Sutta, Sutta-Nipāta* 2.8, verse 1. For alternative translations see H. Saddhatissa (trans.), *The Sutta-Nipāta*, Curzon Press, London 1985, p. 35; and E. M. Hare (trans.), *Woven Cadences of Early Buddhists (Sutta-Nipāta)*, Oxford University Press, London 1945, p. 47.

305 Sangharakshita recounts these travel experiences in full in 'In the Land of the Great Disciples'. See *The Rainbow Road from Tooting Broadway to Kalimpong*, chapter 49, *Complete Works*, vol. 20.

306 As related in *In the Sign of the Golden Wheel*, p. 376 above.

307 *Crossing the Stream*, Windhorse Publications, Birmingham 1996, p. 204 (*Complete Works*, vol. 7). The essay was included in the collection *The Path of the Inner Life* first published by FWBO Publications, London 1975.

308 Thomas Merton (1915–1968) was an American Trappist monk whose interest in meditation and other faiths brought him into contact with the Dalai Lama, D. T. Suzuki, Thich Nhat Hanh, and others. His *Seeds of Contemplation* was published in 1949 in which year Sangharakshita was given a copy by a Roman Catholic priest. See *The Rainbow Road from Tooting Broadway to Kalimpong*, *Complete Works*, vol. 20, p. 463. The passage in which Merton discusses surrender of the personal will to a spiritual

superior is in the chapter on 'Freedom Under Obedience'. See Thomas Merton, *New Seeds of Contemplation* (*Seeds of Contemplation* enlarged and revised), New Directions Publishing, New York 1972, pp. 191ff.

309 China invaded Tibet in the autumn of 1950, quelling resistance, sometimes brutally, and eventually annexing the country to the People's Republic of China to which, they believed, it had belonged since the previous century. There was an uprising in 1956 in which many Tibetans died. In 1959 (two years later than the point Sangharakshita has reached in his story) the Dalai Lama fled to India.

310 The six *abhijñās* (Pāli *abhiññās*) consist of five mundane (*lokiya*) powers which are attainable through concentration (*samādhi*): the ability (1) to travel any distance or take on any form at will, (2) to see everything, (3) to hear everything, (4) to know another's thoughts, and (5) to recollect former existences. A sixth is attainable through insight (*vipassanā*): the extinction of the *āsavas*. The *abhiññās* are enumerated in many places in the Pāli canon; for example, in the *Ākankheyya Sutta*, *Majjhima Nikāya* 6 (i.34–5); see Bhikkhu Ñāṇamoli and Bhikkhu Bodhi (trans.), *The Middle Length Discourses of the Buddha*, Wisdom Publications, Boston 1995, pp. 116–7; or I. B. Horner (trans.), *The Collection of the Middle Length Sayings,* vol. i, Pali Text Society, London 1976, pp. 43–4.

311 Sangharakshita had been introduced to the Princess not long after his arrival in Kalimpong. See *Facing Mount Kanchenjunga*, *Complete Works*, vol. 21, p. 29.

312 Sangharakshita's six-month stay at the guest cottage of Prince K. M. Latthakin or 'Burma Raja' as he was known, is recounted in *Facing Mount Kanchenjunga*, chapter 7, *Complete Works*, vol. 21.

313 'Transformation of Life and World in the Sutra of Golden Light' was a series of eight lectures given in 1976. The penultimate lecture, 'Buddhist Economics', concerns the significance of the goddess Śrī who appears in the *sūtra*. These lectures formed the basis of Sangharakshita's *Transforming Self and World: Themes from the Sūtra of Golden Light* which is included in *Complete Works,* vol. 16.

314 *Dorje* is the Tibetan word for a *vajra* or diamond thunderbolt. Sangharakshita's elucidation of this rich symbol of Tantric Buddhism can be found in 'The Sacred Thunderbolt', *Creative Symbols of Tantric Buddhism*, chapter 3, *Complete Works*, vol. 13, pp. 165ff.

315 Sangharakshita's English translation and elucidation of the 'Salutation to the Three Jewels (*Tiratana Vandanā*) is included in *Complete Works*, vol. 15.

316 Lha Tsering – whom Sangharakshita's friend Marco Pallis used to refer to as 'the Long-Lived Deva' (the literal translation of his name) – was Sikkimese by birth but had spent the war years as an officer in the British Army. He was a member of the committee for the reception of the Sacred Relics of Śāriputra and Maudgalyāyana in Kalimpong in 1951. See *Facing Mount Kanchenjunga, Complete Works*, vol. 21, pp. 175 and 182–3.

317
> 'Tis good to be off with the old love
> Before you be on with the new.

From a Scotch ballad, used as the motto for *Women; or, Pour et Contre. A Tale*, (1818) by Irish protestant clergyman, novelist, and playwright, Charles Maturin.

318 Sangharakshita met Mr Tharchin through their mutual friend, Marco Pallis. 'Colourful and contradictory', he had been born in Ladakh but was somehow a Scottish Presbyterian. His anti-communist views made him popular as an editor. He was also proprietor, printer, and publisher of the *Tibet Mirror*. See *Facing Mount Kanchenjunga*, *Complete Works*, vol. 21, pp. 164–6.

319
> When shall we three meet again?
> In thunder, lightning or in rain?

are the opening lines of William Shakespeare's dramatic tragedy *Macbeth*, spoken by one of the three witches.

320 After the mass conversions to Buddhism by the followers of Dr Ambedkar in October 1956 (see above in *In the Sign of the Golden Wheel*, chapter 23, pp. 356ff.), Sangharakshita spent part of most of the years prior to leaving for England touring among the new Buddhists, continuing the work that Dr Ambedkar had set in motion before his untimely death.

321 In fact, it seems the Kazini's stories about her past were sometimes just that – stories. When I was working in 2011 on the introduction to Sangharakshita's *Dear Dinoo*, I came across postings on the internet by the Kazini's grand-daughter, Claire Jordan. Her researches into family history had led her to the conclusion that her grandmother was 'both fabulous and a fabulist'. (See also notes 323–4 and 372–5 below.)

322 Sangharakshita came across the *Diamond Sūtra* while browsing a secondhand bookshop in London in the

summer of 1943. The impact it had on him on first reading is described in *The Rainbow Road from Tooting Broadway to Kalimpong*, *Complete Works*, vol. 20, p. 85.

323 'Sahiba of Chakhung initiated into Buddhism' in the 'News and Notes' section, *Maha Bodhi*, vol. 66, no. 6 (June 1958), pp. 221–2. Given what has already been said about the Kazini's reliability, we cannot know whether all of this is true.

324 Other sources testify to the Kazini's friendship with Eric Blair (George Orwell).

325 Major Joseph E. Cann, or Upāsaka Joseph E. Cann, as he preferred to be styled, moved to Kalimpong from Lucknow to help the newly founded Young Men's Buddhist Association, arriving there in the summer 1950. He is a prominent character in *Facing Mount Kanchenjunga*, *Complete Works*, vol. 21, see especially pp. 45–8; and in *In the Sign of the Golden Wheel* (above).

326 The Gelug school was founded by Tsongkhapa (1357–1419). He was a reformist, stressing strict adherence to the Vinaya in Ganden monastery which he founded – the first of the three great scholastic monasteries of Tibet. (The other two, Sera and Drepung, were founded by his disciples.) Tsongkhapa brought together the Mind Training (*lojong*) teachings of Atiśa and others from the Kadam school, and the *lamrim* or stages of the path teachings, so the Gelug school was sometimes called the New Kadam school. His most influential work is the *Great Exposition of the Stages of the Path* (Tibetan: *Lamrim Chenmo*). The Dalai Lama is a monk from the Gelug tradition, although recognized as a spiritual leader by all Tibetans.

327 The other three main schools of Tibetan Buddhism are: (1) Nyingma, meaning 'ancient', founded in the eighth century. It is based on the first, or ancient, translations of Buddhist texts from Sanskrit to Tibetan. The founding of the school is associated with Śāntarakṣita, the abbot of the great Indian Buddhist university of Nālandā, and the historical-cum-mythical figure of Padmasambhava, who together founded Samye, the first Buddhist monastery in Tibet. Nyingma was the only form of Buddhism in Tibet for three hundred years. Its central and distinctive practice is Dzogchen (Great Perfection): seeing into the nature of mind or *rigpa*.
(2) The Kagyu school or school of the whispered transmission (i.e. oral transmission) began in Tibet with Marpa (1012–1097) who received teachings from the Indian *siddha*, Nāropa, on the doctrine and practices of Mahāmudrā ('great seal') which are concerned with the

principal stages of meditation. From Marpa the lineage continued with Milarepa and Gampopa. The Kagyu school divided into many sub- and even sub-sub-schools. (3) The Sakya tradition was founded by Drogmi (c.993–c.1077), a scholar and translator who studied under Nāropa at the Indian Buddhist university of Vikramaśīla. The central teaching of Sakya is *lamdre* (the path and its fruit) based on the *Hevajra Tantra*. The first Sakya monastery was built in 1073 near Shigatse in southern Tibet.

Sangharakshita describes the four main schools of Buddhism in Tibet in *Tibetan Buddhism*, Windhorse Publications, Birmingham 1996 (*Complete Works*, vol. 13, pp. 15–34).

328 Shortly before the tour in the spring of 1949 with his teacher Jagdish Kashyap in the 'Land of the Great Disciples' (which culminated with their arrival in Kalimpong), Sangharakshita (who was staying with Kashyap-ji in Benares) was invited by Venerable M. Sangharatana Thera of the Sarnath Maha Bodhi Society to accompany him to Bodh Gaya for a special ceremony to consecrate a wall that had been built around the Maha Bodhi's rest house. Though not very interested in the wall, Sangharakshita was very keen to visit Bodh Gaya:

> Bodh Gaya! Bodh Gaya! How many people have come to you in the course of ages!... I shall always remember how beautiful you were the first time I saw you, when my heart was young, and you made me your own!

The Rainbow Road from Tooting Broadway to Kalimpong, *Complete Works*, vol. 20, pp. 453–6.

329 This first meeting with Dhardo Rimpoche is also described in *Facing Mount Kanchenjunga*, *Complete Works*, vol. 21, pp. 451–3.

330 The tour of the Eminent Buddhists of the Border Areas and the deepening of the friendship with Dhardo Rimpoche is also described above in *In the Sign of the Golden Wheel*, chapter 22, pp. 329ff.

331 George Roerich (1902–1960) was born in Russia, the son of painter and explorer Nicholas Roerich (whose painting of Mount Kanchenjunga features on the cover of volume 21 of the *Complete Works*.) George Roerich studied in England, America, and France, his studies including Sanskrit and Pāli. He was, though, especially, a Tibetologist, known for his translation of the *Blue Annals*, the fifteenth-century history of Tibet; and for compiling a Tibetan–English dictionary. He lived in Kalimpong from about 1947 until returning to Russia

in 1957 where he continued to work in the field of Buddhist studies.

332 Ani-la first appears in the memoirs as Miss Delannoy. See *Facing Mount Kanchenjunga*, *Complete Works*, vol. 21, p. 445. She features rather more in *In the Sign of the Golden Wheel*, first as 'Anagarika Dharmarakshita' after her ordination by a Bengali monk in Calcutta; then as Thupten Chhokyi after her ordination as a *śrāmaṇerī* by Dhardo Rimpoche in the summer of 1954 – after which she was referred to as 'Ani-la' or 'Reverend Auntie', this being for Tibetans the customary way of referring to, or addressing, a female monastic.

333 In 1950s Kalimpong there lived people of many different ethnic and national backgrounds. Most numerous were the Nepalese. Of generally Buddhist background were the exiled Tibetans, the Bhutia (locally born Tibetans), Newar, Tamang, Sikkimese, and Bhutanese. The Lepchas were 'small and shy' and came from the forests of Sikkim. Other residents of the Himalayan town were Indians who had come from the plains, a few Chinese, and a few Europeans.

334 A *kukri* is a curved knife.

335

Among all branched things,
I for beauty choose
The yellowness and slimness of bamboos,
Whose bunched leaves twinkle on a gusty day
And back and forth the clattering branches sway.

The first of five verses from the poem 'Bamboos'. *Complete Poems 1941–1994*, Windhorse Publications, Birmingham 1995, p. 103 (*Complete Works*, vol. 25).

336 The attribution of these words to the Prophet of Islam appears to be apocryphal, as does the attribution of an almost identical proverb involving the hyacinth rather than the rose attributed to the Persian poet Sa'adi, while a Chinese proverb suggests selling half the loaf and buying a lily.

337

Selling wild orchids at my door one day
A man said, 'In the woods are many more...'

Complete Poems 1941–1994, Windhorse Publications, Birmingham 1995, p. 148 (*Complete Works*, vol. 25).

338 The Vinaya refers to a case when the 'sexual features of a woman appeared on a certain monk' and the 'sexual features of a man appeared on a certain nun'. For this occurrence of spontaneous sex change the Buddha responded, 'I allow the same teacher, the same ordination, the same rainy seasons together with the nuns' or, in the second case, 'with the monks'. Vinaya Piṭaka iii.34–5.

See I. B. Horner (trans.), *The Book of the Discipline*, part 1, Pali Text Society, Oxford 1996, p. 54.

There is also the case in the *Vimalakīrti-nirdeśa* , chapter 7, when a goddess changes the elder Śāriputra into her female form and herself into his male form (much to his consternation!). Her purpose, however, is metaphysical: to show that ultimately there is neither male nor female. See R. A. F. Thurman (trans.), *The Holy Teaching of Vimalakīrti*, Pennsylvania State University Press, University Park and London 1976, pp. 61–2.

339 Cyril Henry Hoskins (1910–1981) believed himself to be 'hosting' the spirit of a Tibetan lama, Tuesday Lobsang Rampa (born on a Tuesday). His *The Third Eye: the Autobiography of a Tibetan Lama* was published in England in 1956. The title refers to an operation which he claimed opened his third eye. He was unmasked by the British press in 1958 (the year Jivaka came to Kalimpong), and had gone to live in Ireland. He went on to write many other books including *Living with the Lama: 25 Years with Lobsang Rampa*, dictated to Rampa by his cat, Mrs Fifi Greywhiskers.

340 Known as a spiritual teacher or 'mystic', George Ivanovich Gurdjieff (c.1870–1949) was born in Armenia (then in the Russian empire) and grew up among people of many ethnic and religious backgrounds. After a period of wandering, he arrived in Moscow and began to teach his 'Fourth Way'. He established small communities in southern Russia, and later set up his Institute for the Harmonious Development of Man near Paris. He visited America many times and had many pupils there. His teachings concern the development of the body, the emotions, and the mind.

Pyotr Demianovich Ouspenskii (1878–1947) studied mysticism and esotericism, searching for a new wisdom. He met Gurdjieff in 1915 and became his disciple. He separated from him in 1924, but continued to teach the Gurdjieff system in England and the USA.

341 Blessed Lord, who caused all holy Scriptures to be written for our learning: Grant us so to hear them, read, mark, learn, and inwardly digest them...

This is the Collect for the Sunday closest to 16 November from the Anglican *Book of Common Prayer*. The first *Book of Common Prayer* dates back to 1549.

342 Michael Dillon/Lobzang Jivaka, *Out of the Ordinary: A Life of Gender and Spiritual Transitions*, edited and with an introduction by Jacob Lau

and Cameron Partridge, was eventually published in 2016.

343 Sramanera Jivaka, *Growing Up into Buddhism*, Maha Bodhi Society, Calcutta 1960, was, according to the author, 'intended for the "teen-ager" ... who is having a Western or Western-type education.' The first part contains a chapter on each of the stages of the Noble Eightfold Path, on the Four Noble Truths, and on the Three Refuges. The second part looks at 'Thoughts and Ideas'.

344 Lobzang Jivaka, *The Life of Milarepa, Tibet's Great Yogi*, John Murray, London 1962.

345 1. The semi-derelict bungalow was The Hermitage, where Sangharakshita lived from June 1951 until October 1954 when he moved to Craigside, but he continued to give Durga, his older cousin (Sachin), and others lessons.
2. Durga is introduced in *In the Sign of the Golden Wheel*, p. 167 above. Sangharakshita gave him lessons in history and English literature (and later on in geography, Indian administration, and civics).
3. The older cousin was Sachin (Sachindra Coomar Singh), son of the local doctor. Sangharakshita came to know him well. He accompanied Sangharakshita on journeys to Calcutta (where he had relations) and to Darjeeling. He often features in the previous two memoirs. See also note 25.

346 'Hope' in *Complete Poems 1941–1994*, Windhorse Publications, Birmingham 1995, p. 204 (*Complete Works*, vol. 25).

347 James Cousins (1873–1956) was an Irish poet and playwright, a member of the circle that included W. B. Yeats and James Joyce. He was interested in the occult and theosophy and spent the later part of his life in India, where he came to know Rabindranath Tagore, M. K. Gandhi, and Sri Aurobindo. *A Tibetan Banner* was published in 1926.

348 These editorials were published in the following issues of the *Maha Bodhi:*
1. 'The Buddhist World': vol. 67, no. 10 (October 1959), p. 303.
2. 'Spreading the Dharma': vol. 67, no. 1 (January 1959), pp. 26–7.
3. 'A Serious Matter': vol. 69, no. 8 (August 1961), p. 254.
4. 'Stop the Rot': vol. 68, no. 8 (August 1960), pp. 258–9.
5. 'A Disturbing Dispute': vol. 69, no. 3–4 (March–April 1961), pp. 82–3.
6. 'Religion vs God': vol. 68, no. 6 (June 1960), pp. 197–8.
7. 'Stars and Stupidity': vol. 70, no. 2 (February 1962), pp. 68–9.
8. 'More Vandalism': vol. 69, no. 6 (June 1961), pp. 200–1.

9. 'Rainy Season Retreat': vol. 66, no. 8 (August 1958), pp. 283–4.
10. 'Meditation on a Flame': vol. 66, no. 10 (October 1958), p. 351.

The *Maha Bodhi* editorials were later collected and published in *Beating the Drum*, Ibis Publications, Ledbury 2012 (*Complete Works*, vol. 8).

349 'Words and Meaning', *Maha Bodhi*, vol. 67, no. 9 (September 1959), p. 288. See also *Beating the Drum*, Ibis Publications, Ledbury 2012, p. 213 (*Complete Works*, vol. 8).

350 Sangharakshita's first volume of memoirs was published (minus the first ten chapters that deal with his childhood) as *The Thousand-Petalled Lotus* by Heinemann, London 1975. (The first ten chapters were published separately as *Learning to Walk* by Windhorse Publications, Glasgow 1990.) In 1997 the memoir was restored to its original dimensions and published by Windhorse Publications under the title *The Rainbow Road*, the rest of the title being subsumed to a subtitle: 'From Tooting Broadway to Kalimpong: Memoirs of an English Buddhist'. The full title as originally intended has been restored for the *Complete Works* edition. This is volume 20, *The Rainbow Road from Tooting Broadway to Kalimpong*.

351 During his time in Kalimpong Sangharakshita wrote the first thirty-two chapters, or rather, he was in the middle of chapter thirty-two when he put the manuscript aside. He did not return to it until ten years later i.e. 1972, as he explains in his 1990 Introduction to *Learning to Walk*. See *Complete Works*, vol. 20, pp. 475–8.

352 *The Three Jewels: An Introduction to Buddhism* was published by Rider and Co, London in 1967, and in an American edition in 1970 by Anchor Books. Windhorse Publications published a second and third edition in 1978 and 1991. The fourth edition, also published by Windhorse Publications, had a new Preface and a new subtitle: *The Three Jewels: the Central Ideals of Buddhism*. It is included in *Complete Works*, vol. 2, pp. 1–232.

353 *The Three Jewels* in *Complete Works*, vol. 2, p. 7.

354 *The Eternal Legacy: An Introduction to the Canonical Literature of Buddhism*, published by Tharpa Publications, London 1985. A second edition was published by Windhorse Publications in 2006 which included a new Preface (*Complete Works*, vol. 14).

355 The article commissioned by the Syndics of the Oxford

University Press was for a second edition of *The Legacy of India*. The first edition, edited by G. T. Garratt, came out in 1938 and included one chapter on Buddhism by the Belgian translator and scholar, Louis de Vallée Poussin. When, having completed his article, Sangharakshita heard nothing further from the publisher, he assumed they had decided not to use the article and so included it instead in the fifth edition (1980) of *A Survey of Buddhism* as the Introduction to that work. This Introduction was included in all subsequent editions of the *Survey* up to and including the ninth edition published by Windhorse Publications in 2001. For the *Complete Works* edition, however, which is included in volume 1, Sangharakshita's *magnum opus* is restored to its original length. The article, which was published in pamphlet form as 'A Bird's Eye View of Indian Buddhism' by Sinhanad Publications, Pune 1990, is included with other articles written in India in volume 7. See Sangharakshita's account of the article in *The History of My Going for Refuge* in *Complete Works*, vol. 2, pp. 452–3.

356 From Robert Browning's 'Abt Vogler' published in his collection *Dramatis Personae* (1864). In the poem Abt Vogler (in reality an eighteenth-century organist and composer) reflects on music and its power to raise man to the heights of divine experience.

357 A reference to the *Laṅkāvatāra Sūtra*. See notes 203 and 300.

358 Olaf Stapledon's *Star Maker* (1937) is regarded as one of the finest works of science fiction of the twentieth century. It includes descriptions of a multiplicity of universes.

359 The following brief notes give an indication of the international breadth and variety of genres that constituted Sangharakshita's reading of Western literature:
1. *Don Quixote* parts I and II (1605 and 1615), by the Spaniard Miguel de Cervantes, is one of the earliest European novels.
2. *The Faerie Queene* (1596) is an epic poem by Englishman Edmund Spenser.
3. *Poetical Works of Robert Burns* was published by Oxford University Press in 1912. Burns (1759–1796) wrote his poems in the Scots dialect.
4. *Conversations with Goethe*, vols. i–iii (1836–1848) by Johann Peter Eckermann record the conversations of German polymath, Johann Wolfgang von Goethe during the last nine years of his life when Eckermann was his secretary.
5. *Hard Times* (1854) is a novel by the English

Victorian novelist, Charles Dickens.
6. *The History of Henry Esmond* (1852) is an historical novel by William Makepeace Thackeray.
7. *Anna Karenina* (1877) is a novel by the great Russian novelist, Leo Tolstoy.

360 Sangharakshita describes the conflict between Sangharakshita I and Sangharakshita II in *The Rainbow Road from Tooting Broadway to Kalimpong*, *Complete Works*, vol. 20, pp. 451–2.

361 'The Meaning of Buddhism and the Value of Art' and 'The Religion of Art' were written probably in 1953. They are published with two other essays in *The Religion of Art*, Windhorse Publications, Cambridge 2010 (*Complete Works*, vol. 26). Around New Year 1954 Sangharakshita gave a lecture on 'The Meaning of Buddhism and the Value of Art' at the Ramakrishna Mission in Calcutta at the invitation of his friend Irene Ray (see *In the Sign of the Golden Wheel*, p. 77 above).

362 *Facing Mount Kanchenjunga*, *Complete Works*, vol. 21, p. 93.

363 The doctrine of the three bodies of the Buddha (*trikāya*) is elucidated in *A Survey of Buddhism*, chapter 2, section 6 in *Complete Works*, vol. 1, pp. 250–64; and *The Three Jewels*, chapter 5 in *Complete Works*, vol. 2, pp. 39–46.

364 See 'The Refusal to Make Obeisance upon Meeting with the King of Tibet', canto 61 in Yeshe Tsogyal, *The Life and Liberation of Padmasambhava*, *Part II: Tibet*, Dharma Publishing, California 1978, pp. 376–83.

365 Sangharakshita's elucidations of the *Hṛdaya Sūtra* and *Vajracchedikā Prajñāpāramitā Sūtra* (i.e. the *Heart Sūtra* and the *Diamond Sūtra*) can be found in *Wisdom Beyond Words*, *Complete Works*, vol. 14.

366 Rai Bahadur Densapa, also known as Berniak Kazi, appears in *In the Sign of the Golden Wheel*. For a description see p. 242 above.

367 Equivalent to 'sponsored by the Palace' i.e. by the Sikkimese royalty.

368 As well as the Going for Refuge and Prostration practice and the Vajrasattva visualization and purification practice, the *mūla yogas* include two other practices: the generation of the *bodhicitta* and the offering of the mandala. All four are practised by members of the Triratna Buddhist Order, whilst the Going for Refuge and Prostration practice may be taken up by Mitras training for ordination. See also note 370.

369 See 'The Qualities of the Lake of Dhanakośa, the Lake

of Parturition', canto 14 in *The Life and Liberation of Padmasambhava, Part I: India*, Dharma Publishing, California 1978, p. 87. In canto 17, the King Indrabhūti discovers the future Padmasambhava sitting on a lotus in the lake, already eight years old (ibid., p. 95).

370 The *Tharpe Delam* is an extract from *The Ornament of the Guru's Realisation*, a meditation manual written by the great Tibetan scholar and poet, Jamgon Kongtrul (1813–1899), based on a *terma* attributed to Padmasambhava. The *Tharpe Delam* describes three levels of practice. (1) The General Preliminaries are reflection practices to develop an intense renunciation of *saṃsāra* and a strong motivation to practise the Dharma. They include reflections on the preciousness of human life, the transitoriness of mundane existence, the law of karma, and the sufferings of the six realms. (2) The Main Preliminaries are the four *mūla yogas* (see note 368) and the *guru yoga*. The four *mūla yogas* are: the Going for Refuge and Prostration practice, the generation of the *bodhicitta*, the meditation and mantra recitation of Vajrasattva, and the offering of the mandala. (3) The Special Preliminaries are a set of further practices including an additional *guru yoga* and the practice of the purification of the six realms. The reflections of the General Preliminaries, as well as the four *mūla yogas* and the *guru yoga* (the latter usually in an adapted form known as the *kalyāṇa mitra yoga*), are regularly practised by members of the Triratna Buddhist Order based on the version given to Sangharakshita by Dhardo Rimpoche.

371 C. G. Jung, *Synchronizität als ein Prinzip akausaler Zusammenhänge* (Synchronicity – *An Acausal Connecting Principle*) (1952).

372 Claire Jordan, the Kazini's granddaughter writes:

> after discovering that [her grandmother, the Kazini] had been going around telling people that she was a Belgian aristocrat and her father was Field Marshall Mannerheim of Finland, I investigated her real origins in more depth and discovered that her true family was at least as interesting as the one she borrowed.

According to Claire's research, the Kazini's real father was George Shirran, a Scot, a soldier, and later, a Chief Inspector for the Scottish Royal Society for the Prevention of Cruelty to Children. http://members.madasafish.com/~cj_

whitehound/family/George_Shirran_b1866.htm (retrieved 15 May 2018).

373 The Kazini's first husband, according to Claire Jordan's research, was Bertram Langford Rae. He married Ethel Maud – as she then was – in 1923 when she was nineteen and they sailed for Burma the following year where Bertram became Superintendent of the District Police. The future Kazini left her husband and returned to Scotland in 1930. They were legally divorced in 1940.

374 Roderick (Rory) Langford Rae was born in 1927 in Rangoon. When his mother, the future Kazini, left his father in 1930, and returned to Scotland, she left Rory with her sister. He was sent to public school, joined the army in 1944, and then worked in Malaysia. His daughter, Claire, was born in Scotland in 1959 to Kathleen, whom Rory had met at a pub he frequented. They did not marry – 'They were divided by religious differences – Rory wanted to bring me up as a Catholic and my mother didn't.' Rory went out the same year to work on the tea plantations in Assam.

375 Rory died in 1965. The Kazini must have reported the news to Sangharakshita (who had returned to England in 1964), when he visited his friends in Kalimpong in late 1966. See *Moving Against the Stream*, Windhorse Publications, Birmingham 2003, chapter 47 (*Complete Works*, vol. 23).

376 Daniele Varè, *The Last Empress*, John Murray, London 1936.

377 The Dalai Lama fled Tibet in March 1959, arriving in Mussoorie the following month. He took up residence in Birla House, which had been requisitioned by the Indian government for the Dalai Lama and his government in exile. At this time the Dalai Lama was twenty-three years old. He stayed in the town for a year before moving to Dharamsala.

378 The Dalai Lama's reception at Everton Villa is described above in *In the Sign of the Golden Wheel*, chapter 24, pp. 368ff.

379 Milarepa's life-story is told in W. Y. Evans-Wentz (ed.), *Tibet's Great Yogi Milarepa:* published in 1928; and *The Life of Milarepa*, Lobsang P. Lhalungpa (trans.), published in 1977. Sangharakshita's elucidations of the story of Milarepa and his disciple Rechungpa based on *The Hundred Thousand Songs of Milarepa*, Garma C. C. Chang (trans.), Shambhala Publications, Boston and Shaftesbury 1962, are in vols. 18 and 19 of the *Complete Works.*

380 Lama Govinda writes of his life-changing meeting with Tomo Geshe Rimpoche in part 1 of *The Way of the White*

Clouds, first published by Hutchinson and Co., London 1966.

381 'Epilogue: Guru and Chela and the Journey into the Light', ibid., pp. 283–7.

382 John Blofeld, *The Way of Power: A Practical Guide to the Tantric Mysticism of Tibet*, Allen and Unwin, London 1970.

383 'The Bonfire Built by the King of Zahor Who Later Repented': canto 41 in Yeshe Tsogyal, *The Life and Liberation of Padmasambhava, Part I: India*, Dharma Publishing, California 1978, p. 257.

384 Trijang Rimpoche (1901–1981) was a lama of the Gelug tradition who was junior tutor to the Dalai Lama. He would go on to teach many Westerners.

385 1. Dudjom Rimpoche (1904–1987) was appointed first Supreme Head of the Nyingma tradition by the Fourteenth Dalai Lama. A great scholar and preserver of Nyingma texts, he was also a poet. He organized the building of monasteries and retreat centres in India, Nepal, and Bhutan.
2. Mindoling Doong Rimpoche, or Mindrolling Trichen Rimpoche (1930–2008), became the titular head of the Nyingma school in 2003. He was a married lama. His daughter, Khandro Rimpoche, has become well known as a teacher in the West.
3. This was the eighth Khamtrul Rimpoche, Dongyud Nyima (1931–1980), who left Tibet in 1958 and settled in Kalimpong. He later moved to Himachal Pradesh where he oversaw the rebuilding of the Khampagar monastery at a place named by the Tibetans Tashi Jong. As an accomplished artist he contributed statues and paintings. He is known as the 'root guru' of the English Buddhist nun, Tenzin Palmo.
4. Dhardo Rimpoche (1917–1990) was educated at Drepung monastery and was later appointed as abbot of the Tibetan monastery at Bodh Gaya. He founded the Indo-Tibetan Buddhist Cultural Institute in Kalimpong in 1952.
5. Tomo Geshe Rimpoche (1866–1936) was educated at Tashi Lhunpo monastery, afterwards spending twelve years meditating in mountain wildernesses. He later returned to populated places and became associated with monasteries in Ghoom, Kurseong, and Kalimpong's Tharpa Choling monastery. Lama Anagarika Govinda was his disciple (see note 380).
6. Pabongkhapa Rimpoche was presumably the successor to the famous Pabongkhapa Rimpoche of the Gelug tradition, author of *Liberation in the Palm of your Hand*, who died in 1941.

7. The second abbot to be appointed head of Tharpa Choling Gompa was known as Drepung Tsawa Khangtsen Mani Tulku.

386 *From Genesis to the Diamond Sutra*, Windhorse Publications, Birmingham 2005, p. 45. (*Complete Works*, Vol. 13, p. 560.)

387 In chapter 23 of the *Saddharma Puṇḍarīka Sūtra* (*White Lotus Sūtra*) the bodhisattva Loveliness

> wrapped himself in a celestial precious garment, bathed in perfumed oil, and by his transcendent vow, burned his own body.

Bunnō Katō and W. E. Soothill (trans.), *The Threefold Lotus Sutra*, Kosei Publishing, Tokyo, 1975, p. 305.

388 Sister Vajira, *The Sutta-Nipata, Part I: Uragavagga*, Mahabodhi Society, Saranath, 1941; and *The Sutta-Nipata, Part II: Culavagga*, Mahabodhi Society, Saranath, 1942.

389 St Paul wrote to his disciple, Timothy, 'Drink no longer water, but use a little wine for thy stomach's sake and thine often infirmities.' *The Bible*, 1 Timothy 5:23, King James Version. See also note 187 for more on St Paul.

390 Khantipālo, *Noble Friendship: Travels of a Buddhist Monk*, Windhorse Publications, Birmingham 2002. In chapter 7 Khantipālo gives an interesting, honest, and appreciative description of Sangharakshita and life in the vihara with reflections on their friendship (pp. 83–7).

391 Ibid., p. 86.

392 Phra Khantipalo, *Tolerance: A Study from Buddhist Sources*, Rider and Co., London 1964.

393 'The Nature of Buddhist Tolerance' in *Crossing the Stream*, Windhorse Publications, Birmingham 1996, pp. 165–73. (*Complete Works*, Vol. 7.) It is one of the essays from *The Path of the Inner Life*, a collection that was first published by FWBO Publications, London 1975.

394 The Buddha is shown criticizing wrong views, or showing up wrong views, numerous times in the early scriptures. The very first *sutta* of the first *Nikāya* or division of the Pāli canon, the *Brahmajāla Sutta*, is concerned with wrong views. It begins – pertinently no doubt – with a teaching on Buddhist tolerance. The Buddha tells his disciples that they should not get upset when others disparaged him (or the Dhamma or Sangha); nor elated if others praised them. Rather they should simply look to see whether what has been said is correct or incorrect and if incorrect put the correct view forward. He then looks in turn at sixty-two wrong views. See *Brahmajāla Sutta*, *Dīgha Nikāya* 1: T. W. Rhys Davids (trans.), *Dialogues of the Buddha*, part 1, Pali Text

Society, London 1973, pp. 67–90; or M. Walshe (trans.), *The Long Discourses of the Buddha*, Wisdom Publications, Boston 1995.

395 'The Nature of Buddhist Tolerance' in *Crossing the Stream*, Windhorse Publications, Birmingham 1996, pp. 172–3. Burning heretics for the good of their souls was instigated by the Roman Catholic church's Inquisition. It was branded an auto-da-fé or 'act of faith'. The first recorded example took place in Paris in 1242 but most took place two centuries later. One nineteenth-century estimate suggested that between the years 1484 and 1525, 28,540 Europeans were burnt in this manner. Modern scholars put the figure far lower, though still at several thousand.

396 Khantipālo, *Noble Friendship: Travels of a Buddhist Monk*, Windhorse Publications, Birmingham 2002, pp. 155–6.

397 Khantipālo, *Noble Friendship: Travels of a Buddhist Monk*, Windhorse Publications, Birmingham 2002, p. 138.

398 *Buddhist Meditation, Systematic and Practical. A Talk by the Buddhist Yogi C. M. Chen*, written down by B. Khantipālo, was published in Kalimpong in 1967 in an edition of 1,000 copies printed by the Mani Printing Works. Khantipālo writes about the sessions with Yogi Chen, and the teachings that were given in *Noble Friendship: Travels of a Buddhist Monk*, Windhorse Publications, Birmingham 2002, pp. 140–8.

399 The four sights are not mentioned in the Pāli canon as concrete encounters of the historical Buddha. They are presented as 'the thought occurred to me …': see *Sukhamāla Sutta, Aṅguttara Nikāya* i.144, in Bhikkhu Bodhi (trans.), *The Numerical Discourses of the Buddha*, Wisdom Publications, Boston 2012, pp. 239–42; or F. L. Woodward (trans.), *The Book of the Gradual Sayings*, vol. i, Pali Text Society, Oxford 2000, p. 128; also the *Ariyapariyesanā Sutta, Majjhima Nikāya* 26 (i.163); Bhikkhu Ñāṇamoli and Bhikkhu Bodhi (trans.), *The Middle Length Discourses of the Buddha*, Wisdom Publications, Boston 1995, p. 256; or I. B. Horner (trans.), *The Collection of the Middle Length Sayings*, vol. i, Pali Text Society, London 1976, p. 207. In early Pāli sources the legendary account of the four sights is only described in connection with the Buddha Vipassī; see the *Mahāpādana Sutta, Dīgha Nikāya* 14 (ii.22–8); M. Walshe (trans.), *The Long Discourses of the Buddha*, Wisdom Publications, Boston 1995, pp. 207–10; or T. W. Rhys Davids (trans.), *Dialogues of the Buddha*,

part 2, Pali Text Society, London 1971, pp. 18–22. In later texts, for example the *Nidāna-kathā*, *Buddhavaṃsa*, and *Lalitavistara*, the story is applied to the Buddha. The *Mahāvastu* gives a particularly graphic account of the four sights; see J. J. Jones (trans.), *Mahāvastu*, vol. ii, Pali Text Society, London 1987, pp. 145–53. See also Aśvaghoṣa, *Buddhacarita*, book 3, verses 26–62. Max Müller (ed.), *Buddhist Mahāyāna Texts*, Motilal Banarsidass, Delhi 1894, pp. 30–5; or E. H. Johnston, *The Buddhacarita*, Motilal Banarsidass, Delhi 1984, pp. 37–43.

400 Of Dhardo Rimpoche Khantipālo writes: 'one could say with confidence: Here is a true Bodhisattva'. He recounts something of Dhardo Rimpoche's life, and his own experiences of him in Kalimpong, in *Noble Friendship: Travels of a Buddhist Monk*, Windhorse Publications, Birmingham 2002, pp. 152–7.

401 One of Sangharakshita's first publications was entitled 'The Bodhisattva Ideal'. It was written before his departure for India in 1944 and published in the London Buddhist Society's magazine, *The Middle Way*, vol. 19, no. 4 (November–December 1944) under the name Dennis Lingwood. He was then eighteen. See *Early Writings 1944–1954*, Ibis Publications, Ledbury 2014, pp. 41–7 (*Complete Works*, vol. 7).

402 The *Avataṃsaka Sūtra* is one of the greatest – and longest – Mahāyāna *sūtras*. It had a profound influence especially on East Asian Buddhism. Composed originally in Sanskrit, it was translated into Chinese in the second and third centuries CE. Its themes include the mutual interpenetration of phenomena and the multiplicity of universes. 'The Vows of the Bodhisattva Samantabhadra' come from the final part of the *sūtra*, and were included in a small work, *The Two Buddhist Books in Mahāyāna*, translated and compiled by Upasika Chihmann, which Sangharakshita read in his teens soon after reading the *Diamond Sūtra* and the *Sūtra of Wei Lang*. See *The History of My Going for Refuge*, section 13, in *Complete Works*, vol. 2, p. 454.

Śāntideva's *Śikṣā-samuccaya* or 'Compendium of Instruction [for novice bodhisattvas]' is principally a collection of quotations from the Mahāyāna *sūtras*. Sangharakshita came across a copy of this work in his room at the Dharmodaya Vihara where he stayed when he first arrived in Kalimpong in the spring of 1950, and copied out several pages into his notebook. See *Facing Mount*

Kanchenjunga, *Complete Works*, vol. 21, p. 23.

403 Articles inspired by the bodhisattva ideal include 'The Bodhisattva Ideal' (1944) (see note 401) and 'A Modern Bodhisattva', an editorial written for the *Maha Bodhi*, vol. 65, no. 9 (September 1957) in which the bodhisattva qualities expressed in the life of Anagarika Dharmapala are described. See also *Beating the Drum*, Ibis Publications, Ledbury 2012, pp. 183–6 (*Complete Works*, vol. 8).

Poems inspired by the bodhisattva ideal include 'The Bodhisattva':

> Because I could not muse
> apart
> In world-oblivious ecstasy,
> But felt like fire-drops on
> my heart
> The tears of all humanity ...;

and 'The Bodhisattva's Reply':

> 'What will you say to those
> Whose lives spring
> up between
> Custom and circumstance
> As weeds between wet stones.

See *Complete Poems 1941–1994*, Windhorse Publications, Birmingham 1995, pp. 107 and 178 (*Complete Works*, vol. 25). 'The Bodhisattva' was the second of Sangharakshita's poems to be published in the *Illustrated Weekly of India*. For many years it was one of his most popular poems, being reprinted in Buddhist magazines all over the world. See *Facing Mount Kanchenjunga*, *Complete Works*, vol. 21, p. 89.

404 *The History of My Going for Refuge*, section 13 in *Complete Works*, vol. 2, p. 455.

405 For more about Dhardo Rimpoche's life and work see Suvajra, *The Wheel and the Diamond: The Life of Dhardo Tulku*, Windhorse Publications, Glasgow 1991.

406 Related in *In the Sign of the Golden Wheel*, chapter 22 above.

407 For more on the qualities of the bodhisattva and the six perfections to be practised by one dedicated to the bodhisattva ideal, see *The Bodhisattva Ideal*, *Complete Works*, vol. 4. This volume includes *The Endlessly Fascinating Cry*, Sangharakshita's exposition of Śāntideva's *Bodhicaryāvatāra* or 'Guide to a Bodhisattva's Way of Life'.

408 Khantipālo describes the ceremony in *Noble Friendship: Travels of a Buddhist Monk*, Windhorse Publications, Birmingham 2002, pp. 157–8.

409 The sixty-four precepts or *bodhisattva-saṃvara-śīla* taken by Sangharakshita are included in an appendix to *Complete Works*, vol. 2, pp. 657–9. Khantipālo reflects on the precepts and how they were passed on to

him and Sangharakshita in *Noble Friendship: Travels of a Buddhist Monk*, Windhorse Publications, Birmingham 2002, pp. 158–61.

410 Khantipālo records the day in ibid., p. 164. There is also a brief record in the News and Notes, *Maha Bodhi*, vol. 70, no. 7 (July 1962), p. 254. And Sangharakshita wrote a poem: 'Planting the Bodhi Tree'. See *Complete Poems 1941–1994*, Windhorse Publications, Birmingham 1995, p. 251 (*Complete Works*, vol. 25).

411 Sangharakshita's poem 'Tibetan Refugee' was written around this time. See *Complete Poems 1941–1994*, Windhorse Publications, Birmingham 1995, p. 245 (*Complete Works*, vol. 25).

412 The *Bhaiṣajya-guru-vaiḍūrya-prabhā-rāja Sūtra* was translated into Chinese first by Dharmagupta and a little later by Xuanzang, both in the seventh century CE. The Medicine Buddha, Bhaiṣajya-guru, became as important for some Chinese Buddhists as Śākyamuni and Amitābha.

413 Kodandera Madappa Cariappa (1899–1993) was Commander-in-Chief of the Indian army from 1949 to 1953, the first Indian to be appointed to that post.

414 Arriving in Colombo by boat, Sangharakshita (who then called himself Dharmapriya) and his friend, Satyapriya (Robin Banerjee, later Buddharakshita), were not allowed to disembark. To the immigration officer who enquired as to their nationality, they explained that having renounced the world they had none. However philosophically correct, this was 'from the official point of view entirely unsatisfactory'. They had to return to India by the next boat. *The Rainbow Road from Tooting Broadway to Kalimpong*, *Complete Works*, vol. 20, pp. 229–30.

415 A few years later Sangharakshita wrote:

> Tenderly smiling, White Tārā
> Sits on a mountain of green jade,
> Telling through the ages the mantra of Great Compassion
> On her crystal rosary of the tears of men.

'The Crystal Rosary' in *Complete Poems 1941–1994*, Windhorse Publications, Birmingham 1995, p. 258 (*Complete Works*, vol. 25).

WITH ALLEN GINSBERG IN KALIMPONG

416 *Howl*, also known as *Howl for Carl Solomon*, to whom the poem is dedicated, was written in 1954–5 and published in the 1956 collection *Howl and Other Poems.* Due to the poem's explicitly sexual references, Lawrence Felinghetti of City Lights Publishing was tried on

obscenity charges in a widely publicized court case. He was eventually acquitted, the poem being judged to be of 'redeeming social importance'.

Kaddish, also known as *Kaddish for Naomi Ginsberg (1894–1956)*, was written on the death of Ginsberg's mother and explores questions that death raises. ('Kaddish' refers to the prayer of mourning in the Jewish tradition.) It was published in 1961, the year before the meeting in Kalimpong with Sangharakshita, in *Kaddish and Other Poems*.

417 Other Beat Poets included William S. Burroughs whose novel, *Naked Lunch* (1959), narrated by fictitious heroin addict William Lee, was also the subject of an obscenity trial; and Jack Kerouac whose *On the Road* (1959) about travels across America features Ginsberg, Burroughs, and others to whom he assigns different names.

418 Gary Snyder was born in 1930, and is best known as a poet who studied and practised Zen Buddhism; and for his concern with environmental issues. He was associated early on with the Beat Generation – he was a friend of Jack Kerouac and Allen Ginsberg.

419 Sister Vajira was an English-born nun in the Theravādin tradition whom Sangharakshita came to know quite well. He found her a 'kind, generous woman'. See *Precious Teachers*, p. 519 and p. 566 above.

420 For more about Mr Chen or 'Yogi Chen' see *Precious Teachers*, chapter 13 above.

421 The famous Albert Hall poetry reading took place on 11 June 1965 when Allen and other poets read to a crowd of some 7,000 people in an auditorium 'filled with a marijuana smoke, flying paper darts and foliage'.

422 The meeting in London is recounted in *Moving Against the Stream*, Windhorse Publications, Birmingham 2003, p. 106 (*Complete Works*, vol. 23).

423 Allen Ginsberg died in 1997. This piece was included in Bill Morgan and Bob Rosenthal (eds.), *Best Minds: A Tribute to Allen Ginsberg*, Lospecchio Press, New York 1986, pp. 246–8. It was subsequently published in the collection *The Priceless Jewel*, Windhorse Publications, Glasgow 1993.

INDEX

Introductory Note

References such as '178–9' indicate (not necessarily continuous) discussion of a topic across a range of pages. Wherever possible in the case of topics with many references, these have either been divided into sub-topics or only the most significant discussions of the topic are listed. References to illustrations are in italic.

A GUIDE TO THE COMPLETE WORKS OF SANGHARAKSHITA

Gathered together in these twenty-seven volumes are talks and stories, commentaries on the Buddhist scriptures, poems, memoirs, reviews, and other writings. The genres are many, and the subject matter covered is wide, but it all has – its whole purpose is to convey – that taste of freedom which the Buddha declared to be the hallmark of his Dharma. Another traditional description of the Buddha's Dharma is that it is *ehipassiko*, 'come and see'. Sangharakshita calls to us, his readers, to come and see how the Dharma can fundamentally change the way we see things, change the way we live for the better, and change the society we belong to, wherever in the world we live.

Sangharakshita's very first published piece, *The Unity of Buddhism* (found in volume 7 of this collection), appeared in 1944 when he was eighteen years old, and it introduced themes that continued to resound throughout his work: the basis of Buddhist ethics, the compassion of the bodhisattva, and the transcendental unity of Buddhism. Over the course of the following seven decades not only did numerous other works flow from his pen; he gave hundreds of talks (some now lost). In gathering all we could find of this vast output, we have sought to arrange it in a way that brings a sense of coherence, communicating something essential about Sangharakshita, his life and teaching. Recalling the three 'baskets' among which an early tradition divided the Buddha's teachings, we have divided Sangharakshita's creative output into six 'baskets' or groups: foundation texts; works originating in India; teachings originally given in the West; commentaries on the Buddhist scriptures; personal writings; and poetry, aphorisms, and works on the arts. The 27th volume, a concordance, brings together all the terms and themes of the whole collection. If you want to find a particular story or teaching, look at a traditional term from different points of view or in different contexts, or track down one of the thousands of canonical references to be found in these volumes, the concordance will be your guide.

1. FOUNDATION

What is the foundation of a Buddhist life? How do we understand and then follow the Buddha's path of Ethics, Meditation, and Wisdom? What is really meant by 'Going for Refuge to the Three Jewels', described by Sangharakshita as the essential act of a Buddhist life? And what is the Bodhisattva ideal, which he has called 'one of the sublimest ideals mankind has ever seen'? In the 'Foundation' group you will find teachings on all these themes. It includes the author's *magnum opus, A Survey of Buddhism*, a collection of teachings on *The Purpose and Practice of Buddhist Meditation*, and the anthology, *The Essential Sangharakshita*, an eminently helpful distillation of the entire corpus.

2. INDIA

From 1950 to 1964 Sangharakshita, based in Kalimpong in the eastern Himalayas, poured his energy into trying to revive Buddhism in the land of its birth and to revitalize and bring reform to the existing Asian Buddhist world. The articles and book reviews from this period are gathered in volumes 7 and 8, as well as his biographical sketch of the great Sinhalese Dharmaduta, Anagārika Dharmapala. In 1954 Sangharakshita took on the editing of the *Maha Bodhi*, a journal for which he wrote a monthly editorial, and which, under his editorship, published the work of many of the leading Buddhist writers of the time. It was also during these years in India that a vital connection was forged with Dr B. R. Ambedkar, renowned Indian statesman and leader of the Buddhist mass conversion of 1956. Sangharakshita became closely involved with the new Buddhists and, after Dr Ambedkar's untimely death, visited them regularly on extensive teaching tours.

From 1979, when an Indian wing of the Triratna Buddhist Community was founded (then known as TBMSG), Sangharakshita returned several times to undertake further teaching tours. The talks from these tours are collected in volumes 9 and 10 along with a unique work on Ambedkar and his life which draws out the significance of his conversion to Buddhism.

3. THE WEST

Sangharakshita founded the Triratna Buddhist Community (then called the Friends of the Western Buddhist Order) on 6 April 1967. On 7 April the following year he performed the first ordinations of men and women within the Triratna Buddhist Order (then the Western Buddhist Order). At that time Buddhism was not widely known in the West and for the following two decades or so he taught intensively, finding new ways to communicate the ancient truths of Buddhism, drawing on the whole Buddhist tradition to do so, as well as making connections with what was best in existing Western culture. Sometimes his sword flashed as he critiqued ideas and views inimical to the Dharma. It is these teachings and writings that are gathered together in this third group.

4. COMMENTARY

Throughout Sangharakshita's works are threaded references to the Buddhist canon of literature – Pāli, Mahāyāna, and Vajrayāna – from which he drew his inspiration. In the early days of the new movement he often taught by means of seminars in which, prompted by the questions of his students, he sought to pass on the inspiration and wisdom of the Buddhist tradition. Each seminar was based around a different text, the seminars were recorded and transcribed, and in due course many of the transcriptions were edited and turned into books, all carefully checked by Sangharakshita. The commentaries compiled in this way constitute the fourth group. In some ways this is the heart of the collection. Sangharakshita often told the story of how it was that, reading two *sūtras* at the age of sixteen or seventeen, he realized that he was a Buddhist, and he has never tired of showing others how they too could see and realize the value of the '*sūtra*-treasure'.

5. MEMOIRS

Who is Sangharakshita? What sort of life did he live? Whom did he meet? What did he feel? Why did he found a new Buddhist movement? In these volumes of memoirs and letters Sangharakshita shares with his readers much about himself and his life as he himself has experienced it, giving us a sense of its breadth and depth, humour and pathos.

6. POETRY, APHORISMS, AND THE ARTS

Sangharakshita describes reading *Paradise Lost* at the age of twelve as one of the greatest poetic experiences of his life. His realization of the value of the higher arts to spiritual development is one of his distinctive contributions to our understanding of what Buddhist life is, and he has expressed it in a number of essays and articles. Throughout his life he has written poetry which he says can be regarded as a kind of spiritual autobiography. It is here, perhaps, that we come closest to the heart of Sangharakshita. He has also written a few short stories and composed some startling aphorisms. Through book reviews he has engaged with the experiences, ideas, and opinions of modern writers. All these are collected in this sixth group.

In the preface to *A Survey of Buddhism* (volume 1 in this collection), Sangharakshita wrote of his approach to the Buddha's teachings:

> Why did the Buddha (or Nāgārjuna, or Buddhaghosa) teach this particular doctrine? What bearing does it have on the spiritual life? How does it help the individual Buddhist actually to follow the spiritual path?… I found myself asking such questions again and again, for only in this way, I found, could I make sense – spiritual sense – of Buddhism.

Although this collection contains so many words, they are all intent, directly or indirectly, on these same questions. And all these words are not in the end about their writer, but about his great subject, the Buddha and his teaching, and about you, the reader, for whose benefit they are solely intended. These pages are full of the reverence that Sangharakshita has always felt, which is expressed in an early poem, 'Taking Refuge in the Buddha', whose refrain is 'My place is at thy feet'. He has devoted his life to communicating the Buddha's Dharma in its depth and in its breadth, to men and women from all backgrounds and walks of life, from all countries, of all races, of all ages. These collected works are the fruit of that devotion.

We are very pleased to be able to include some previously unpublished work in this collection, but most of what appears in these volumes has been published before. We have made very few changes, though we have added extra notes where we thought they would be useful. We have had the pleasure of researching the notes in the Sangharakshita Library at 'Adhisthana', Triratna's centre in Herefordshire, UK, which houses his own collection of books. It has been of great value to be able to search among the very copies of the *suttas*, *sūtras* and commentaries that have provided the basis of his teachings over the last seventy years.

The publication of these volumes owes much to the work of transcribers, editors, indexers, designers, and publishers over many years – those who brought out the original editions of many of the works included here, and those who have contributed in all sorts of ways to this *Complete Works* project, including all those who contributed to funds given in celebration of Sangharakshita's ninetieth birthday in August 2015, and to a further outpouring of generosity after Sangharakshita's death in October 2018. All these donors have made the publication of this series possible, and we are very grateful. Many thanks to everyone who has helped; may the merit gained in our acting thus go to the alleviation of the suffering of all beings.

Vidyadevi and Kalyanaprabha
Editors

THE COMPLETE WORKS OF SANGHARAKSHITA

I FOUNDATION

VOLUME 1 A SURVEY OF BUDDHISM / THE BUDDHA'S NOBLE EIGHTFOLD PATH
A Survey of Buddhism
The Buddha's Noble Eightfold Path

2 THE THREE JEWELS I
The Three Jewels
The Meaning of Conversion in Buddhism
Going for Refuge
The Ten Pillars of Buddhism
The History of My Going for Refuge
My Relation to the Order
Extending the Hand of Fellowship
Forty-Three Years Ago
Was the Buddha a Bhikkhu?

3 THE THREE JEWELS II
Who is the Buddha?
What is the Dharma?
What is the Sangha?

4 THE BODHISATTVA IDEAL
The Bodhisattva Ideal
The Endlessly Fascinating Cry (seminar)
The Bodhisattva Principle

5 THE PURPOSE AND PRACTICE OF BUDDHIST MEDITATION
The Purpose and Practice of Buddhist Meditation

6 THE ESSENTIAL SANGHARAKSHITA
The Essential Sangharakshita

II INDIA

7 CROSSING THE STREAM: INDIA WRITINGS I
Early Writings 1944–1954
Crossing the Stream
Buddhism in the Modern World: Cultural and Political Implications
The Meaning of Orthodoxy in Buddhism
Buddhism in India Today
Ordination and Initiation in the Three Yānas
A Bird's Eye View of Indian Buddhism

WINDHORSE PUBLICATIONS

Windhorse Publications is a Buddhist charitable company based in the UK. We produce books of high quality that are accessible and relevant to all those interested in Buddhism, at whatever level of interest and commitment. We are the main publisher of Sangharakshita, the founder of the Triratna Buddhist Order and Community. Our books draw on the whole range of the Buddhist tradition, including translations of traditional texts, commentaries, books that make links with contemporary culture and ways of life, biographies of Buddhists, and works on meditation.

To subscribe to the *Complete Works of Sangharakshita,* please go to: windhorsepublications.com/sangharakshita-complete-works/

THE TRIRATNA BUDDHIST COMMUNITY

Windhorse Publications is a part of the Triratna Buddhist Community, an international movement with centres in Europe, India, North and South America and Australasia. At these centres, members of the Triratna Buddhist Order offer classes in meditation and Buddhism. Activities of the Triratna Community also include retreat centres, residential spiritual communities, ethical Right Livelihood businesses, and the Karuna Trust, a UK fundraising charity that supports social welfare projects in the slums and villages of India.

Through these and other activities, Triratna is developing a unique approach to Buddhism, not simply as a philosophy and a set of techniques, but as a creatively directed way of life for all people living in the conditions of the modern world.

For more information please visit thebuddhistcentre.com